Storey's
Conveyancing

Storey's Conveyancing

Fifth Edition

Amarjit Hunjan   MA
Solicitor;
Senior Lecturer, Department of Professional Legal Studies,
De Montfort University

Sheree Peaple   MA
Solicitor;
Senior Lecturer, Department of Professional Legal Studies,
De Montfort University;
Chief External Examiner for the Law Society

Butterworths
LexisNexis™

Members of the LexisNexis Group worldwide

United Kingdom	Butterworths Tolley, a Division of Reed Elsevier (UK) Ltd, Halsbury House, 35 Chancery Lane, LONDON, WC2A 1EL, and 4 Hill Street, EDINBURGH EH2 3JZ
Argentina	Abeledo Perrot, Jurisprudencia Argentina and Depalma, BUENOS AIRES
Australia	Butterworths, a Division of Reed International Books Australia Pty Ltd, CHATSWOOD, New South Wales
Austria	ARD Betriebsdienst and Verlag Orac, VIENNA
Canada	Butterworths Canada Ltd, MARKHAM, Ontario
Chile	Publitecsa and Conosur Ltda, SANTIAGO DE CHILE
Czech Republic	Orac sro, PRAGUE
France	Editions du Juris-Classeur SA, PARIS
Hong Kong	Butterworths Asia (Hong Kong), HONG KONG
Hungary	Hvg Orac, BUDAPEST
India	Butterworths India, NEW DELHI
Ireland	Butterworths (Ireland) Ltd, DUBLIN
Italy	Giuffré, MILAN
Malaysia	Malayan Law Journal Sdn Bhd, KUALA LUMPUR
New Zealand	Butterworths of New Zealand, WELLINGTON
Poland	Wydawnictwa Prawnicze PWN, WARSAW
Singapore	Butterworths Asia, SINGAPORE
South Africa	Butterworths Publishers (Pty) Ltd, DURBAN
Switzerland	Stämpfli Verlag AG, BERNE
USA	LexisNexis, DAYTON, Ohio

© Reed Elsevier (UK) Ltd 2001

A CIP Catalogue record for this book is available from the British Library.

ISBN 0 406 93760 5

Printed and bound in Great Britain by Butler & Tanner Ltd, Frome, Somerset

Visit Butterworths LexisNexis *direct* at www.butterworths.com

This book is dedicated to David, Simon, Thomas and Edward.

PREFACE

Our aim in writing the fifth edition of this book was to provide a comprehensive but concise guide to the modern conveyancing system. We hope it will prove a useful source of information for the student, the solicitor and the licensed conveyancer.

There have been a number of important developments in conveyancing since the fourth edition was published and we anticipate many more in the near future. The Land Registry has made great strides in its aim of using electronic resources more fully, and we have recently seen the introduction of real time priority and the Land Registry's Direct Access system. The government is currently looking at the whole conveyancing process and there is a strong possibility of radical changes in the way conveyancing is carried out, in order to streamline the system and prevent gazumping. The National Land Information Service has also recently been piloted and may shortly be launched nationwide. We have attempted to provide coverage and commentary on those new developments which are actually in place; prospective developments have been mentioned where appropriate.

We would like to thank Ian Storey for providing such a sound original from which to work (and, in Sheree's case, for teaching her conveyancing in the first place!); John Thurston for his advice on the Trustee Delegation Act 1999; the staff at Butterworths for their patient support; all those students from whom we have learned so much; and finally our respective partners and families, for being there for us.

Sheree Peaple
Amarjit Hunjan
Leicester
November 2001

FOREWORD

I would like to add briefly to the preface, to thank Sheree and Amarjit for keeping alive a project which I started with the first edition of *Conveyancing*, as long ago as 1983. My other commitments since the fourth edition appeared in 1993 have meant that the fourth edition was the last in which I could be involved, so I am very grateful to Sheree and Amarjit for writing this fifth edition. The law and practice of conveyancing have changed significantly in the 18 years since the first edition, and continue to change at even greater pace. I hope that, with Sheree's and Anmarjit's input, this edition will be even more useful to those, whether students or practitioners, who are seeking an understanding of the conveyancing transaction and of its component parts.

Ian Storey
Nottingham
November 2001

Contents

TABLE OF STATUTES

References in **bold** indicate where the Act is set out in part or in full.

List of Cases

Freehold and Leasehold Conveyancing

1 INTRODUCTION

The law of conveyancing is essentially the law relating to the creation and transfer of estates and interests in land. Typically, conveyancing involves buying – or selling – residential property such as a house, or commercial property such as office premises. The tendency is to employ a lawyer (solicitor or licensed conveyancer) to do this. Why is this, when one does not normally use a solicitor on other sales or purchases; for example, when buying a book?

The first difference between the two transactions lies in the nature of what is being sold. A seller cannot 'own' land in the same way that he can 'own' a book, that is to say that he cannot own land absolutely, but only have an estate in it. Since 1925 there have been only two legal estates in land.[1] Firstly, there is the fee simple absolute in possession, which is the freehold estate and which represents the closest one can come to owning land absolutely. Secondly, there is the term of years absolute which is the legal leasehold estate. That is not all. A freehold or leasehold estate may be subject to a whole range of other interests. These include legal interests such as easements, rentcharges and mortgages, and equitable interests such as covenants. Land could also be subject to planning restrictions or a compulsory purchase order. In addition, the subject matter of the sale is normally not a vacant piece of land, but land with buildings on it. These may be in a poor state of repair or they may have been built without planning permission. We can see then, that the subject matter of the sale is quite complicated and indeed many of the buyer's solicitor's efforts will be directed towards finding out as much as possible about the property.

A second difference lies in the method of transfer of estates in land. A book is normally bought by taking possession and paying the purchase price. This is not a suitable method of transfer of land. The Law of Property Act 1925 provides, with a few exceptions, that the transfer or creation of a legal estate or interest must be by a deed.[2] A deed is a written document which will include the names of the parties to the transaction as well as a description of the property and a statement of the estate or interest being created or transferred. So, for example, a deed may transfer a freehold or leasehold estate from seller to buyer, or create a new legal easement such as a right of way, or create a new leasehold estate. The deed is signed by the parties in the presence of witnesses.[3]

A third difference between buying a book and buying land is in the proof of ownership provided. A purchaser buying a book normally neither demands nor

---

1 Law of Property Act 1925, s 1(1).
2 Ibid, s 52.
3 Law of Property (Miscellaneous Provisions) Act 1989, s 1.

receives any proof from the shop that they do own the book; he assumes that they do from their possession of it. Such an assumption would be extremely foolish in the case of land. One cannot really be in possession of land in quite the same way that one can be in possession of a book. One can be in occupation of it but that does not necessarily suggest that the occupant is the owner of a freehold or leasehold estate. He could be a mortgagee, a tenant under a weekly tenancy, a licensee, or even a mere squatter. Also, land is inevitably 'second-hand'. A buyer of land will thus demand some proof from the seller that he does own what he is selling. How can the seller provide this? Let us take as an example someone selling freehold property, such as a house and garden. As a deed is needed each time the property is transferred, a collection of deeds will have accumulated. There will be, in addition, other documents under which the property has passed. For example where the owner has died there will be a grant of probate or administration as evidence that the property has passed to his personal representatives, and there may then be an assent transferring the legal estate in the property to a beneficiary under the will or intestacy. This bundle of deeds and other documents is called collectively the title deeds to the property, or more correctly to that particular estate in the property, and is passed on to successive owners. A seller will demonstrate his ownership of the estate being sold by giving the buyer details of the more recent of the deeds and other documents and events affecting the property. The buyer will then be able to trace a chain of ownership from a chosen starting point through to the seller.

This demonstration by the seller that he does own what he is selling – or deducing title as it is called – does have disadvantages. It is repetitive, because title must be deduced each time the property is sold. More fundamentally, it provides no guarantee to a buyer that the seller does own what he is selling, for there may be some defect prior to the point at which the chain of title commences. If the system was allowed to continue, the number of title deeds would eventually become unmanageable. It was as a result of such criticisms that a process was originated whereby the ownership of a particular estate in a piece of land could be registered, with the register then becoming the proof of ownership. The pre-registration title deeds lose their importance and a transfer of ownership can be recorded by changing the name of the owner in the register. This system of registered conveyancing is governed by the Land Registration Act 1925 as amended. There have recently been a number of developments relating to the way registered title is dealt with, and these are detailed in Chapter 2.

There are, then, two systems of conveyancing in operation at present, the traditional system based on title deeds and the more modern system where ownership of the estate has been registered. The main difference lies in the way that title is deduced to the buyer.

2 Basic principles

A discussion of conveyancing must inevitably assume a certain knowledge of the theoretical land law principles upon which conveyancing is based. The purpose of this chapter is to reiterate these principles, including the law relating to registration of title.

I LAND LAW

We have already seen that there are only two legal estates in land, the freehold estate and the term of years absolute.[1] In addition there are a number of legal interests in land including easements, rentcharges and mortgages.[2] An easement is a right, such as a right of way or a right of light, which exists for the benefit of one piece of land over another piece of land. A legal easement will be for an interest equivalent to a legal freehold or leasehold estate. That is to say, a right of way for the benefit of freehold land will be a 'freehold' easement, whilst if for the benefit of leasehold land it will be a 'leasehold' easement and come to an end at the same time as the lease. A rentcharge is a periodical payment charged on a particular piece of land. Put simply, it is rather like rent, but relates to freehold land. (The Rentcharges Act 1977 provides for the eventual extinguishment of most rentcharges but one that will continue is the estate rentcharge; this may arise if, for example, a flat in a block of flats is subject to a rentcharge representing a contribution to the cost of maintaining shared facilities such as the grounds of the block of flats.) A mortgage over property is normally taken as security for a loan and it gives the lender certain rights over the property, including a power of sale.

There are also various equitable interests in land including covenants and equitable mortgages.[3] A covenant will be imposed on land for the benefit of other land. If restrictive, it will prevent some use or other activity in relation to the land affected. If positive, it will impose a positive obligation, for example to contribute to the maintenance of a road. (Strictly speaking, positive covenants are not normally interests *in land*, but they are of as much concern to the conveyancer as restrictive covenants.) There are various rules which regulate the passing of the benefit and burden of covenants when the land respectively benefited and burdened is sold.

---

1   Law of Property Act 1925, s 1(1).
2   Ibid, s 1(2).
3   Ibid, s 1(3).

An equitable mortgage is a mortgage which is prevented from being a legal mortgage due to the lack of the formality necessary to constitute a legal mortgage. For example, a legal mortgage must be by deed but an equitable mortgage could be created by a document which is not a deed. Since 27 September 1989, when the Law of Property (Miscellaneous Provisions) Act came into force, equitable mortgages can no longer be created informally and so the conveyancer is now much less likely to come across them.

The main difference between legal and equitable interests (at least with regard to land, title to which is unregistered) lies in their effect on a purchaser of the legal estate affected by the interest. The general rule is that a purchaser of a legal estate will take subject to legal interests affecting the estate quite irrespective of whether he knows about them or not, but he will only be bound by equitable interests if he has notice of them. This could be actual, constructive or imputed notice.

However, if the interest is capable of registration as a land charge under the Land Charges Act 1972, the buyer will take subject to it if it is registered but not if it is not registered, in both cases irrespective of notice.[4] One registrable legal interest is a puisne legal mortgage. This is a mortgage not protected by deposit of title deeds and in practice it will normally be a second mortgage. Examples of registrable equitable interests are restrictive covenants created after 1925 and estate contracts.

2   REGISTRATION OF TITLE

i   Introduction

As we saw in the last chapter, the main disadvantages of the traditional system of conveyancing, based on use of the title deeds, are that the investigation of the seller's title by the buyer must be repeated on every transaction and that the investigation is purely historical and not conclusive. The system of registration of title seeks to overcome these difficulties by providing a once and for all registration of the title to a particular estate in a particular piece of land, at the Land Registry. The register becomes the conclusive evidence of the estate owner's title and contains the information which would be found in the title deeds such as the estate owner's name, a description of the property and the estate held by the owner.

Before dealing with the system of registration of title in detail, it should be emphasised that the register is a register of title not of land, and that there may be two or more titles registered in respect of the same piece of land; for example a freehold estate, a headlease, and an underlease. Each estate would be registered with a separate title.

ii   Registration with separate title

Only certain estates or interests are capable of being registered with separate title, or capable of 'substantive registration' as it is called; they are the 'estates capable of subsisting as legal estates'.[5] This expression includes not only the legal freehold and leasehold estates but also the legal interests and charges under the Law of Property Act 1925, section 1(2) and so would include legal easements, rentcharges and

---

4   Land Charges Act 1972, s 4. See further in ch 11, section 1i.
5   Land Registration Act 1925, s 2(1).

mortgages.[6] However, the Land Registration Rules provide that the benefit of an easement cannot be registered separately but can only be registered as appurtenant to the dominant estate, title to which is registered.[7] Mortgages cannot be registered with separate title where there is an existing right to redeem the mortgage,[8] as there will be in the vast majority of cases, and although rentcharges are capable of registration with separate title they are only rarely encountered.

In practice, then, the only estates or interests capable of substantive registration are the freehold estate of a fee simple absolute in possession and the leasehold estate of a term of years absolute. There are two leasehold estates which *cannot* be registered with separate title:[9]

(a) a mortgage term with a subsisting right of redemption;[10]
(b) a lease with 21 years or less left to run.[11]

To the extent that interests — such as easements, covenants and leases (whether registered with separate title or not) — adversely affect a freehold or leasehold estate which is registered then, apart from mortgages, they can be classified as either overriding interests or minor interests in relation to the title affected.[12] They can, if necessary, be protected by some entry on the register of that title. Mortgages of registered titles can also be protected by an entry on the register of the title.

I First registration

We have said that registration of title to a particular estate is a once and for all process, and we have seen which estates are capable of substantive registration. We can now examine the rules which govern when title to a particular unregistered estate can, or must, be registered. This process of first registration can be either compulsory or voluntary.

2 Compulsory registration

Historically, whether substantive registration of title to a particular estate was compulsory depended on whether there was a Compulsory Registration Order (CRO) in force for the area in which the land was situated. Such orders were made by Order in Council,[13] and their existence was revealed by a search of the Public Index Map at the Land Registry.[14] However, as from 1 December 1990, the whole of England and Wales has been a compulsory registration area.[15]

For many years, the only triggering events for compulsory first registration under section 123 of the Land Registration Act 1925 were:

---

6 Land Registration Act 1925, s 3(xi).
7 Land Registration Rules 1925, r 257. Easements which adversely affect land title to which is registered are dealt with at section vi, below.
8 Land Registration Act 1925, ss 4(b), 8(1).
9 Prior to the Land Registration Act 1986, which amended s 8(2) of the Land Registration Act 1925, leases which contained an absolute prohibition against assignments inter vivos were not registrable. Section 3 of the 1986 Act now provides for registration provided that the restriction on alienation is noted on the register.
10 See fn 8, above. A mortgage term is in theory a term of years absolute, subject to cesser on redemption.
11 Land Registration Act 1925, s 8(1).
12 See below, section vi.
13 Under Land Registration Act 1925, s 120.
14 See ch 6.
15 Registration of Title Order 1989.

a) A conveyance on sale of a freehold. This included transactions for which monetary consideration was given, but not, for example, gifts or exchanges where no equality money was paid.
b) A grant of a new lease for a term of more than 21 years
c) The assignment of a lease which had more than 21 years left to run at the date of the assignment.

However, this could mean that a property could change hands several times without first registration being triggered; for example, where property passed by inheritance. In order to speed up the process of getting the whole of England and Wales registered, a number of new triggers were introduced by the Land Registration Act 1997, which inserted a new section 123 and section 123A into the Land Registration Act 1925. The effect was that, from 1 April 1998, first registration will be triggered by:

a) A qualifying conveyance of the freehold estate.[16]
b) The qualifying grant of a lease for a term of more than 21 years.[17]
c) The qualifying assignment of a lease with more than 21 years left to run at the date of the assignment.[18]
d) Any disposition of the land effected by an assent, if it is a disposition of the freehold estate or of a lease having more than 21 years left to run.[19]
e) A first legal mortgage, which is secured by deposit of title deeds, of a freehold or a lease with more than 21 years to run at the date of the mortgage.[20]

A 'qualifying' conveyance, grant or assignment is one:

i. for valuable consideration
ii. by way of gift
iii. in pursuance of a Court Order.[1]

Thus the number of triggering events has been substantially increased to include gifts, exchanges and assents and so on, which should help to ensure greater land registration over a shorter period.

The time limit for submission of the deeds to the Land Registry following such a triggering event is two months from the date of the disposition.[2]

The sanction for not applying for registration within two months is that the transaction becomes void once the two month period has expired, so far as the legal estate is concerned, until registration is effected. The legal estate thus reverts to the transferor, who holds the equitable interests in the land as a bare trustee for the transferee.[3] The two month period can be extended[4] and applications for registration outside the period will usually be allowed provided some reasonable explanation is given. Application for first registration is made to the District Land Registry for the area in which the property is situated.

A further change introduced by the 1997 Land Registration Act provides that the grant of a lease of a dwellinghouse by a local authority under the 'Right to

---

16 Land Registration Act 1925 (as amended), s 123(1)(a).
17 Ibid, s 123(1)(b).
18 Ibid, s 123(1)(c).
19 Ibid, s 123(1)(d).
20 Ibid, s 123(2).
 1 Ibid, s 123(6).
 2 Ibid, s 123A(2).
 3 Ibid, s 123A(5).
 4 Ibid, s 123A(3).

Buy' provisions of the Housing Act 1985, Part V is a triggering event, whether or not it is for more than 21 years.[5]

Once title to an estate is registered, then on any disposition of it, the legal estate only passes on registration of the disposition.[6] This is a fundamental principle of the system of registration. So if a registered title is sold, or given away, the legal estate only passes to the buyer or donee once he is registered as proprietor in place of the seller or donor. However, the word 'disposition' which we have used above, and which is used in the Land Registration Act 1925, is defined to include not only the transfer of the whole or part of a registered freehold or leasehold estate, but also the grant of a lease out of such an estate.[7] If the superior title out of which a lease is being granted is registered, then the grant of the lease is a disposition of that title and the lease must be registered or no legal estate will pass to the lessee. The lease, if capable of registration, must be so registered.[8] Thus if a lease for over 21 years[9] is granted out of a registered title then it must be registered with separate title and until it is, no legal estate will pass; there is no two month time limit. An intending lessee can discover whether the superior title is registered from his search of the Public Index Map.

3. Voluntary Registration

Historically, voluntary registration was only possible where a Compulsory Registration Order was in force. Now of course such an order applies throughout England and Wales. In order to encourage voluntary registration, the Land Registration Fees Order 1988, which came into force on 1 April 1999, provides for a 25% reduction in fees for voluntary registration.

iii   Classes of title

On applying for first registration, there are a number of alternative classes with which the applicant's title may be registered. These are:

— absolute (freehold or leasehold)
— possessory (freehold or leasehold)
— qualified (freehold or leasehold)
— good leasehold

l   Registration with absolute title

The effect of first registration with absolute title is to vest in the estate owner (or 'registered proprietor' as he becomes) the freehold or leasehold estate together with all rights appurtenant to the land[10] and subject *only* to:[11]

(a)   matters which are entered on the register of the title;[12]
(b)   overriding interests;[13]

---

5   Land Registration Act 1997, s 4.
6   Land Registration Act 1925, ss 19(1), 19(2), 22(1), 22(2).
7   Ibid, ss 18, 21.
8   Notice of the lease may also be entered on the register of the superior title; see section vi, below.
9   And therefore capable of substantive registration.
10   For example, easements existing for the benefit of the land.
11   Land Registration Act 1925, ss 5, 9.
12   For example, covenants affecting the land; see section vi, below.
13   See section vi, below.

(c) (if the proprietor is not entitled to the land for his own benefit, for example if he holds as a trustee) minor interests[14] of which he has notice; as between himself and the persons entitled to such interests, he will be bound by those interests;[15]

(d) (if the estate is leasehold) all express or implied covenants and obligations in the lease.[16]

These are the only interests that affect the registered proprietor and so first registration can have what is referred to as a 'curative' effect. For example, if the unregistered title was subject to a covenant (which is not an overriding interest) and which is by error not mentioned on the register, then the proprietor will hold the land free from it, unless the person who has the benefit of the covenant can have the register rectified.[17] Rather more importantly, there is a discretion under section 13(c) of the Land Registration Act 1925 to allow registration, even with absolute title, of a title which though technically defective is nevertheless a title under which there is no prospect of the owner's possession and enjoyment of the land being affected; in other words where the owner has a 'good holding title'.

2   Registration with other classes of title

The effect of registration with other classes of title is described in the Land Registration Act 1925 by reference to the effect of registration with absolute title. Registration with possessory title has the same effect as registration with absolute title save that the registration does not prejudice the enforcement of any right affecting the title which was in existence at the date of first registration.[18] In other words, the registered proprietor is additionally subject to all rights affecting the title in existence at the date of first registration and the 'guarantee' provided by the register does not extend to any such rights. A possessory title might be granted if the applicant had lost all his title deeds. With a qualified title, it is some specified interest which is excepted from the effect of registration and to which the guarantee of the register does not extend; specified, that is, either by date (for example all interests arising before a specified date) or by reference to a specific document (for example all the interests arising under a particular deed).[19] A qualified title is rare in practice and arises most commonly where there has been a breach of trust in the past.[20]

Much more common is a good leasehold title. Registration has the same effect as registration with absolute leasehold title save that the registration does not prejudice the enforcement of any right affecting the lessor's title to grant the lease.[1] In other words the guarantee of the register does not extend to the freehold and any superior leasehold titles and the registered proprietor is subject to any rights, such as covenants or easements, affecting these titles[2] and to any rights affecting the lessor's power to grant the lease.[3] Absolute leasehold title will only be given where all superior titles

---

14   See section vi, below.
15   For example, a trustee or personal representative is bound by the interests of the beneficiaries, even though they are not mentioned on the register and are not overriding interests.
16   Perhaps rather oddly, the lease does not form part of the register.
17   Rectification is considered at section vii, below.
18   Land Registration Act 1925, ss 6, 11.
19   Ibid, ss 7, 12.
20   A solicitor should be wary of accepting such a title and should always check with his client's lender if appropriate.
1   Land Registration Act 1925, s 10.
2   A lessee is only subject to such rights as are in existence at the time of the grant of the lease.
3   For example, a provision in a mortgage entered into by the lessor, prohibiting him from granting any leases.

can be examined by the Land Registry, either because they are already registered or because the applicant for first registration with absolute leasehold title can also deduce the superior titles. In practice many Building Societies and other mortgagees view good leasehold titles, and also any as yet unregistered leasehold title where the superior titles are not also deduced, with an understandable degree of circumspection. Indeed, a number of lenders now refuse to accept good leasehold title unless an examined epitome of the freehold title is produced and may still insist on defective title indemnity insurance. As will be seen later, unless the buyer's contract with the seller provides that he can investigate the superior titles, he will be in no position to satisfy the mortgagee's requirement.

3   Upgrading title

The Land Registration Act 1925 as amended by the Land Registration Act 1986 provides for a title to be upgraded in certain circumstances:

(a)   the Registrar, if satisfied as to the title, or if the land has been registered for at least twelve years and the Registrar is satisfied that the registered proprietor is in possession (meaning in actual occupation or in receipt of rents and profits), may and must, on application[4] by the proprietor, convert possessory freehold title to absolute freehold;[5]

(b)   the Registrar, if satisfied as above, may and must, on application[6] by the proprietor, convert possessory leasehold title to good leasehold;[7]

(c)   the Registrar, if satisfied as to the freehold and any superior leasehold title may, and on application by the proprietor must, convert good leasehold title to absolute leasehold;[8]

(d)   the Registrar, if satisfied as to the title, may, and on application by the proprietor must, convert a qualified title to absolute freehold or good leasehold as the case may be.[9]

Transitional provisions in respect of titles registered before 1 January 1987 are contained in the Land Registration Act 1986, section 1(2).

iv   Form of the register

Each title is given an individual title number. The register for each title is split into three different parts: the property register, the proprietorship register and the charges register.

I   Property Register

This describes the land, normally with a brief verbal description and a reference to an official plan called the filed plan which is based on ordnance survey maps.[10] It will state the estate held — freehold or leasehold — and if the latter, it will give brief details of the lease, including its date, parties, term, rent and any provision prohibiting

---

4   Conversion is commonly done on registration of a transfer on sale.
5   Land Registration Act 1986, s 1(2), Land Registration Act 1925, s 77(2).
6   See fn 4, above.
7   Land Registration Act 1986, s 1(2), Land Registration Act 1925, s 77(2).
8   Land Registration Act 1986, s 1(1), Land Registration Act 1925, s 77(1).
9   Land Registration Act 1986, s 1(3), Land Registration Act 1925, s 77(2).
10   Land Registration Act 1925, s 76(a).

assignment or subletting without consent. It may also include a statement of any rights which exist for the benefit of the land[11] although registration does automatically vest such appurtenant rights in the proprietor.[12]

2 Proprietorship Register

This states the class of title and the name and address of the registered proprietor. It will also contain any entries restricting the proprietor's rights of disposition, for example where the proprietor is the tenant for life of settled land, or, more commonly, where there are joint registered proprietors who hold the property as tenants in common.

When the property is transferred the name of the new proprietor will be added and the name of the previous proprietor removed.

3 Charges Register

This contains details of encumbrances adversely affecting the title, for example rights of way over the land, covenants, leases and mortgages.

Unless such third party rights are overriding interests, in general terms they will not bind the proprietor (nor any purchaser from him) unless they are mentioned on the register,[13] and the Charges Register is the appropriate place for them to be recorded. So on first registration mention must be made in the Charges Register of all such adverse interests[14] and as they arise in the future they can be similarly noted. If an interest, for example a mortgage, is discharged, the entry is removed altogether.

4 Land Certificates and Charge Certificates

The actual Land Register, that is the collection of registers of individual titles, is kept at the various District Land Registries around the country, which also deal with all registrations and other applications. On first registration the registered proprietor will be issued with a Land Certificate. This is a copy of the register of that title, including the plan, contained in an outer folder, which constitutes the actual Certificate and bears the Land Registry seal. The Certificate shows the date upon which it was last brought up to date with the entries in the register, which normally happens whenever the Certificate is produced to the Registry. If the property is subject to a mortgage or legal charge, protected by an entry in the charges register and thus called a 'registered charge', then the Land Certificate will be retained by the Registry[15] and the mortgagee will be issued with a Charge Certificate which is in similar form to the Land Certificate and has attached to it the mortgage deed. If there are further registered charges then Charge Certificates will be issued to the other mortgagees. Recently, it has become common for lenders to request the Land Registry to retain the Charge Certificate under s 63 of the Land Registration Act 1925: if this is the case, the following entry will appear on the Charges Register:

> The charge certificate relating to the charge dated [   ] in favour of [name of lender] has been retained in H M Land Registry (Section 63 of the Land Registration Act 1925.)[16]

---

11   Land Registration Rules 1925, r 254.
12   See section iii, 1 above.
13   Ibid.
14   Land Registration Rules 1925, r 40. By the Land Registration Act 1925, s 70(2), this includes easements even if they are overriding interests.
15   Land Registration Act 1925, s 65.
16   For more details, see Land Registry Practice Leaflet No 31, issued November 1999.

v   Dealings with registered titles

We have mentioned that all dispositions of land, the title to which is registered, must take effect by the appropriate alteration to the register. Thus on a straightforward sale of a registered title the buyer will apply for his name to be added to the proprietorship register and the seller's name removed; until this happens the seller retains the legal estate because he is still shown as proprietor on the register, and the register is conclusive.

The effect of a registered disposition is, as might be expected, similar to the effect of first registration in that the buyer, or donee, has vested in him the legal estate together with all appurtenant rights and subject only to entries on the register, overriding interests and, in the case of a leasehold title, all express or implied covenants and obligations in the lease.[17] If the title is possessory, qualified or good leasehold then the buyer or donee is also subject to the additional matters thereby excepted from the effect of registration. If the disposition is made without valuable consideration, for example by gift, the donee is also bound by any minor interests subject to which the donor held the property.[18]

By section 64 of the Land Registration Act 1925, the Land Certificate must be produced on an application for registration of any disposition of the title. If there is a registered charge then the Land Certificate will already be at the Land Registry but the Charge Certificate will have to be produced if the registered charge is to be discharged, unless this too is held at the Registry under section 63.

vi   Third party interests in registered land

Third party interests in land, title to which is registered, can be:

(a)   registered with separate title, for example leases capable of such registration;
(b)   overriding interests;
(c)   minor interests;
(d)   registered charges.

The first category has already been dealt with; the other categories have been mentioned in passing and must now be fully explained.

I   Overriding interests

The crucially important characteristic of overriding interests is that they are binding on the registered proprietor and anyone who deals with him (for example a buyer) irrespective of notice, and in particular, irrespective of whether they are mentioned on the register or not. As a result the majority of overriding interests will not be mentioned on the register.[19]

Overriding interests are a blot on the landscape of the system of registration of title. If the ideal is a register which shows conclusively the land and all interests affecting it, then the existence of overriding interests is far from desirable. However, they are necessary in practical terms, as it may not be possible to ascertain all the interests that do affect land at the time of first registration. The categories of overriding

---

17   Ibid, ss 20, 23.
18   See section 2 iii, above.
19   By the Land Registration Act 1925, s 70(2) easements adversely affecting land should be entered on the register on first registration even though they are overriding interests.

interests are in theory closed and they are listed in section 70(1) of the Land Registration Act 1925.[20] However, judicial decisions interpreting section 70(1) have broadened at least one of the categories.[1]

The categories of overriding interests are set out below.

Section 70(1)(a): A varied collection of rights comprising principally profits à prendre and legal easements. Certain easements such as rights of way, water and drainage are mentioned specifically. In addition, rule 258 of the Land Registration Rules 1925 provides that all rights appurtenant to land,[2] which adversely affect land the title to which is registered, are also overriding interests. The effect of this is to ensure that the rights which impliedly pass on a conveyance by virtue of the Law of Property Act 1925, section 62 are overriding interests as regards the land adversely affected.

This category of overriding interests is obviously of great practical importance.

Section 70(1)(b): Certain tenurial liabilities, now virtually obsolete.

Section 70(1)(c): The liability to repair the chancel of a church.

Section 70(1)(d): Liabilities in respect of embankments and sea and river walls.

Section 70(1)(e):[3] Payments in lieu of tithe and tithe redemption annuities, now in effect extinguished by the Finance Act 1988, section 56.

Section 70(1)(f): Rights being acquired under the Limitation Acts. If this provision were not included one could only acquire title to registered land by prescription with great difficulty; the prescriptive right in the course of acquisition would have to be protected by some entry on the register, which would clearly become impracticable.

Section 70(1)(g): The rights of every person in actual occupation of the land or in receipt of the rents and profits thereof, save where enquiry is made of such person and the rights are not disclosed. This category has potentially very far-reaching effects. The rights must be rights in land, but they need not be in any way connected with the occupation of the land and could be rights which would otherwise rank as minor interests. Moreover the occupation does not have to be reasonably discoverable; there is no exact equivalent here to the unregistered conveyancing doctrine of notice. It is sufficient that the right is an interest in land and that the owner of the right is in occupation or in receipt of rents and profits. The following are all examples of rights which have been held to be overriding interests:

(a) a lessee's right to purchase the freehold reversion, contained in his lease;[4]
(b) a seller's lien for unpaid purchase money;[5]
(c) the rights of a beneficiary under a trust for sale.[6]

However, certain rights are incapable of being overriding interests even though the owner of the right is in possession. Such rights include:

---

20   Interests in coal and coal mining are also overriding interests: Coal Industry Act 1994, s 67, Sch 9, para 1(1).

1   In particular *Williams & Glyn's Bank Ltd v Boland* [1981] AC 487, [1980] 2 All ER 408, HL, and subsequent cases; see s 70(1)(g), below.

2   Including, apparently, most equitable easements, subject to notice; *Celsteel Ltd v Alton House Holdings Ltd* [1985] 2 All ER 562, [1985] 1 WLR 204, confirmed in *Thatcher v Douglas* [1996] NLJR 282

3   See also Tithe Act 1936, s 13(11).

4   *Webb v Pollmount Ltd* [1966] Ch 584, [1966] 1 All ER 481.

5   *London and Cheshire Insurance Co Ltd v Laplagrene Property Co Ltd* [1971] Ch 499, [1971] 1 All ER 766.

6   *Williams & Glyn's Bank Ltd v Boland* [1981] AC 487, [1980] 2 All ER 408, HL; see further at ch 6, section 8 iii.

(a)   the statutory right of occupation under the Family Law Act 1996;[7]
(b)   the rights under the Leasehold Reform Act 1967;[8]
(c)   possibly, the rights of a beneficiary under a Settled Land Act 1925 settlement. Section 86(2) of the Land Registration Act 1925 provides that such rights take effect as minor interests 'and not otherwise'. It might nevertheless be argued that they could be overriding interests under section 70(1)(g).[9]

Section 70(1)(h): In the case of a possessory, qualified or good leasehold title the interests excepted from the effect of registration. This accords with the definition of the effect of such registration.

Section 70(1)(i): Rights under local land charges unless and until protected on the register.

Section 70(a)(j): Various manorial rights.

Section 70(1)(k):[10] Leases for a term of 21 years or less. Such a lease will be thus an overriding interest as against any registered superior title. This is a corollary of the rule that leases for over 21 years are capable of registration with separate title.

Section 70(1)(l): Various mineral and mining rights.

A purchaser of a registered title takes subject to overriding interests which are in existence at the date of registration of his purchase, which is generally taken as the date of his application for registration. However, the purchaser will not be subject to the interest of an occupier, under section 70(1)(g), unless the occupier was also in occupation at the time of completion of the purchase.[11] A mortgagee is in the same position as a purchaser and thus potentially subject to the interests of occupiers. Arguably the mortgagee has a greater risk, particularly in the case of a re-mortgage, where anyone with a 'right' under section 70 (1) (g) may well be in occupation both at the time of completion of the mortgage and at the date of its registration.

The conveyancing problems caused by section 70(1)(g) are discussed in later chapters.

2   Minor interests

If an interest affecting a registered title is not an overriding interest, nor a mortgage protected as a registered charge, it must be a minor interest. A buyer will take free of it, that is to say it will be overridden on a disposition for value of the registered title affected, unless it is protected in the appropriate way on the register. Minor interests include some leases, interests arising under trusts and settlements, interests arising under dispositions capable of substantive registration but not yet so registered[12] and the more familiar litany of third party interests such as estate contracts and restrictive covenants.

7   Section 31 (10) (b).
8   Section 5(5).
9   In any event, since strict settlements can no longer be created, following the implementation of the Trusts of Land and Appointment of Trustees Act 1996, the point may be purely academic.
10   As amended by Land Registration Act 1986.
11   *Abbey National Building Society v Cann* [1991] 1 AC 56, [1990] 1 All ER 1085, HL. There has been much discussion as to the meaning of 'actual occupation', but it is clear that occupation as a licensee will not suffice; *Strand Securities Ltd v Caswell* [1965] Ch 958, [1965] 1 All ER 820; an infant child occupies as a 'mere shadow' of its parents, even if it has a beneficial interest in the property by virtue of contributions; *Hypo-Mortgage Services Ltd v Robinson* [1997] 2 FCR 422, [1997] 2 FLR 71. However, occupation of part only of the premises will still constitute 'actual occupation'; *Ferrishurst v Wallcite Ltd* [1999] Ch 355, [1999] 1 All ER 977.
12   For example the interest of a buyer of a registered title who has not yet applied for registration of his purchase.

3   *Protection of minor interests by notice*

The normal method of protecting a minor interest is by entry of a notice in the Charges Register of the title affected. This method can be used to protect leases which do not take effect as overriding interests,[13] freehold restrictive covenants,[14] rights of occupation under the Family Law Act 1996, estate contracts and other specified interests.[15] The effect is that the registered proprietor is subject to the interest[16] and any disposition by him is similarly subject, but only of course so far as the interest is itself valid – if the Charges Register contains notice of a restrictive covenant, the burden must still be shown to pass under general land law principles for a purchaser to be bound by it.

The entry of a notice depends on the applicant producing the Land Certificate.[17] If this is not available because the registered proprietor will not cooperate, a caution may be the appropriate means of protection. If the property is subject to a registered charge, the Land Certificate is retained at the Registry; it is treated as being available and a notice can be entered, although for the chargee to be bound, the Charge Certificate should be produced. Exceptionally, the Land Certificate need not be produced on an application for entry of a notice to protect the Family Law Act 1996 right of occupation or in relation to an access order under the Access to Neighbouring Land Act 1992.[18] In both cases, the ability of the person wishing to register the interest to obtain the land or charge certificate is likely to be problematic, hence the reason for the exceptions.

The position of leases deserves special mention. We have seen that leases for over 21 years are capable of registration with separate title and that leases of 21 years or under are overriding interests. More fundamentally, the grant of a lease out of a registered title is a 'disposition' and the lease must be registered for the lessee to obtain a legal estate. If the lease is capable of registration with separate title then the lessee must apply for this, but in addition the lessee should apply for notice of the lease to be entered on the Charges Register of the reversionary title. This then completes the process of registration. The Land Certificate *need not* be produced, provided that the lease was granted at a rent without a fine.[19] Unfortunately, many leases in practice are granted at a fine (ie a premium), for example the long lease of a newly built dwelling house on a housing estate. In such a situation the prospective lessee ought to ensure that his contract includes a provision compelling the lessor to make his Land Certificate available if his title is registered.

Finally, it should be noted that section 70(1)(k) only covers a legal lease as opposed to an equitable lease or an agreement for a lease. The latter could be overriding interests under section 70(1)(g) but should otherwise be protected by notice, and again a prudent lessee will ensure that the written agreement provides for the superior landlord to deposit his Land or Charge certificate at the Land Registry.

4   *Protection of minor interests by caution*

The Land Registration Act 1925[20] provides that any person interested in a registered title may lodge a caution in the Proprietorship Register, the effect being that before

---

13   Land Registration Act 1925, s 48.
14   Ibid, s 50.
15   Ibid, s 49.
16   Ibid, s 52.
17   Ibid, s 64(1)(c).
18   Ibid, s 64(7).
19   Ibid, s 64(9)(c); *Strand Securities Ltd v Caswell* [1965] Ch 958, [1965] 1 All ER 820, CA.
20   Land Registration Act 1925, s 54.

any disposition of the land can be registered the cautioner is given an opportunity to establish his interest.[1] The Land Certificate does not have to be produced when lodging a caution and this is an alternative method to entry of a notice, where the Land Certificate is not available. It may well be the appropriate method of protecting an estate contract or a writ or order relating to the land. Before 1981 it was the commonly used method of protecting the (then) Matrimonial Homes Act 1967 right of occupation, but since 1981 this is to be done only by notice.[2] A registered proprietor can try and have cautions removed, if he thinks they are unjustified, by having them 'warned off', rather than waiting until there is a disposition of the property.[3]

It is also possible to register a caution against first registration where title to land is not yet registered.[4] This may be done if, for example, the title deeds have been lost and the owner wishes to be informed of any application for first registration so that he can establish his prior claim.

5   Protection of minor interests by restriction

Unless there is anything on the register to the contrary, anyone dealing with a registered proprietor can assume that his powers of disposition are unlimited. In particular, the Land Registration Act 1925 provides that no one dealing with a registered title shall be affected by notice of a trust,[5] although this is subject to the possibility of the beneficiary's interest being an overriding interest.[6] In fact, the powers of the registered proprietor may be limited; for example if the registered proprietor is a trustee, or a tenant for life of settled land or a charity. The appropriate method of recording this on the register, and protecting the minor interests involved, is by means of a restriction in the Proprietorship Register.[7] Thus where two persons who are beneficial tenants in common apply for registration, the survivor will have no power to deal with the property and the following restriction will be entered:[8]

> No disposition by a sole proprietor of the land (not being a trust corporation) under which capital money arises is to be registered except under an Order of the Registrar or the Court.

A similar restriction will be imposed on registration of the tenant for life of settled land as proprietor, preventing registration of any disposition unless it is authorised by the Settled Land Act 1925 and capital money is paid to the trustees of the settlement.[9]

It is also possible to make an independent application for the entry of a restriction. This may be appropriate in relation to partnership property. It could also arise where a matrimonial home is in the sole name of the husband, but the wife has an equitable interest. The wife may apply for the entry of the joint proprietorship restriction. The Land Certificate must normally be produced and in such a situation it may not be available. There are three other alternatives. Firstly, her interest may be an overriding

---

1   Ibid, s 55.
2   Family Law Act 1996, s11 prohibits the entry of a caution.
3   Land Registration Rules 1925, r 218. There are special rules relating the warning off of a pre-1981 registered caution relating to occupation of a matrimonial home; Land Registration (Matrimonial Homes Rights) Rules 1997.
4   Land Registration Act 1925, s 53.
5   Ibid, s 74.
6   *Williams & Glyn's Bank Ltd v Boland* [1981] AC 487, [1980] 2 All ER 408, HL.
7   Land Registration Act 1925, s 58.
8   Ibid, s 58(3); Land Registration Rules 1925, r 213 (as amended); Land Registration Rules 1989, r 6.
9   Land Registration Act 1925, s 86(3).

interest under section 70(1)(g) of the Land Registration Act 1925. Secondly, she could apply for entry of a notice on the register under section 49(1)(d) of the Act requiring payment of capital money to at least two trustees, although again this depends on production of the Land Certificate. Thirdly, she can apply to lodge a caution to protect her interest for which of course the Land Certificate need not be produced.[10]

6   Protection of minor interests by inhibition

An inhibition in the Proprietorship Register completely prohibits the registration of any dealings with the land[11] and is normally only used consequent on the registered proprietor's bankruptcy. The bankruptcy order is registered in the Land Charges Registry in the register of writs and orders and an inhibition automatically entered in the Proprietorship Register of any registered land owned by the bankrupt.[12] The bankruptcy petition will have been similarly protected by a pending action being registered in the Land Charges Registry and a creditor's notice automatically entered in the Charges Register.[13]

On a company's liquidation, the liquidator may apply for notice of his appointment to be entered on the register.[14]

7   Mortgages of registered titles

The normal method of creating a mortgage or legal charge over land, the title to which is registered, is by a registered charge, which is registered in the Charges Register of the title. The mortgagee is then issued with a Charge Certificate. A registered proprietor may mortgage his land in any way appropriate to unregistered land although until it is protected as a registered charge the mortgage only takes effect in equity and is a minor interest, requiring protection by notice or caution.[15]

It is also possible to create a lien over land, the title to which is registered, by depositing the Land Certificate with the lender.[16] The lien so created can be protected by entry of notice of deposit (or notice of intended deposit if the Land Certificate is not yet available, for example it is still at the Registry for registration of a purchase). The Land Certificate need not be produced on application for entry of a notice of deposit which, confusingly, takes effect as a caution.[17]

8   Comparison of third party interests in registered and unregistered conveyancing

In the earlier part of this chapter we dealt with the effect of third party interests on a purchaser of unregistered land. We can now see that the scheme of protection in relation to registered titles is quite different. A purchaser takes subject to overriding interests and to minor interests protected on the register but free from other interests. Although there is a superficial resemblance in the effect of legal interests in unregistered conveyancing and overriding interests in registered conveyancing, and in the effect of interests registrable under the Land Charges Act 1972 in unregistered

---

10   *Elias v Mitchell* [1972] Ch 652, [1972] 2 All ER 153; *Belcourt v Belcourt* [1989] 2 All ER 34, [1989] 1 WLR 195.
11   Land Registration Act 1925, s 57.
12   Ibid, s 61(3).
13   Ibid, s 61(1).
14   Land Registration Rules 1925, r 185(2) (as amended).
15   Land Registration Act 1925, s 106 as substituted by the Administration of Justice Act 1977, s 26.
16   Ibid, s 66.
17   Land Registration Rules 1925, r 239, substituted by SI 1995/140, r 4(1).

conveyancing and minor interests in registered conveyancing, these categories do not coincide one with the other and should be considered quite separately.

A first legal mortgage of unregistered land will be protected by deposit of the title deeds with the mortgagee, subsequent legal and equitable mortgages being registrable as land charges under the Land Charges Act 1972. As we have just seen, the normal method of mortgaging registered land, whether it be a first or subsequent mortgage, is by registered charge.

vii Rectification and indemnity

Although the main advantage of a system of registration of title is the guarantee that the register provides, there is the ever-present possibility that the register may be rectified if it contains an error.[18] However, if it is rectified then anyone suffering loss as a result may be able to claim compensation.

The grounds on which the register can be rectified are set out in section 82(1) of the Land Registration Act 1925. Rectification can be ordered by the court or, in certain circumstances, by the registrar. The court's power to rectify must be justified on one of the grounds in the Act – there is no general discretion.[19] There is a restriction on any rectification which will adversely affect the title of a registered proprietor who is in possession. Rectification in such circumstances can only be ordered[20] to give effect to an overriding interest (such as a prescriptive right); to give effect to an order of the court; if the proprietor has caused or substantially contributed to the error by fraud or lack of proper care; or if it would be unjust not to rectify.

An indemnity, ie compensation, is available if a person suffers loss by reason of rectification or by reason of an error on the register that is not rectified.[1] No indemnity is payable if the applicant (or someone through whom he claims otherwise than for value) caused or substantially contributed to the loss by fraud or lack of proper care. Neither would an indemnity be payable to a registered proprietor if the register were rectified to reflect an overriding interest; the proprietor would not be adversely affected by the rectification as he would have been bound by the overriding interest anyway. The amount of the indemnity is assessed at the time of rectification if the register is rectified, but at the time of making of the error on the register if the register is not rectified.[2]

viii Recent developments at the Land Registry

The Land Registry has made strenuous efforts in recent years to become more IT friendly, and has pioneered a number of initiatives in e-conveyancing. Many of these are set out at appropriate points in other chapters, but a summary of the main initiatives and changes is provided below:

1) *Land Registry Direct* – is a recently introduced electronic service whereby solicitors can obtain instant access to over 18 million registers of title[3] using their own PCs and normal Web browser software. This enables solicitors to view

18 See, for example, *Argyle Building Society v Hammond* (1984) 49 P & CR 148, CA.
19 *Norwich and Peterborough Building Society v Steed* [1993] Ch 116, [1993] 1 All ER 330, CA.
20 Land Registration Act 1925, s 82(3).
1   Ibid, s 83. An indemnity is also payable if loss is suffered by reason of an error in an official search certificate, or by the Registry losing or destroying documents.
2   Land Registration Act 1925, s 83(6).
3   As at March 2001.

computerised registers (using the postcode where the title number is not known), obtain details of any pending applications or searches with priority, send correspondence to the registry, and perhaps most importantly, apply for office copies, Index Map searches, official searches[4] and land charges searches.

2) *Computerisation of the Index Map* – the Registry is in the process of converting all its paper based maps into electronic format, and this will contribute to the Registry's aim of open access to land information.

3) *Real Time Priority* – this was extended on 28 May 2001 to all substantive applications and official searches. This is designed to provide a more precise priority system, in order to ensure accuracy and certainty in land registration and to facilitate e-conveyancing. All applications and searches will now have both the date and time they were lodged entered on the database of pending applications, and this will determine their priority.[5] In addition, all copy registers and search results will now quote a time as well as a date.

4) *Outline applications* – Linked to the Real Time Priority initiative is the new outline application service.[6] An outline application can be lodged under rule 83A of the Land Registration Rules 1925, to reserve periods of priority, before submitting the paper application, for interests which cannot be protected by official searches (for example, assents, matrimonial homes rights, cautions and inhibitions). The system can only be used to give priority to applications relating to the whole of the property, not part, and cannot be used in respect of first registration applications. In addition, the interest to be protected must exist at the time the outline application is lodged. The outline application must be made by telephone, Land Registry Direct, or in person. The applicant will be given details of the priority time and also when it expires. The supporting papers must then be lodged, and the outline application reference number must be quoted. Guidance on how to lodge an outline application is available in Land Registry Leaflet CDA2.

5) *Dematerialisation of charge certificates* – This scheme is designed to cut down on the amount of paperwork involved in the conveyancing process, and was developed in conjunction with the Nationwide Building Society. The aim is for the Land Registry to retain the charge certificate and mortgage deed; the lender is not issued with a copy. Where the system is in operation, solicitors will not receive a charge certificate on completion of a transaction, but will simply be sent copies of the register. The procedure is set out in more detail in Chapter 15.

6) *ENDS* – this is a new system for discharging mortgages relating to registered titles. Instead of using paper forms, an electronic message is sent to the Registry by the lender to confirm that the mortgage is discharged. The procedure is described in more detail in Chapter 15.

Many of the Land Registry's publications can be viewed on-line at *www.landreg.gov.uk*.

In addition to the above Land Registry initiatives, there have of recent years been moves by the government to try to expedite the conveyancing procedure and to exploit the use of technology.

One recent development is the National Land Information Service (NLIS). The service aims to speed up conveyancing and so cut down on gazumping by providing all necessary information about a piece of land at the touch of a button. The Service was nationally launched on 19 July 2000, following a pilot which was carried out in

---

4   See ch 11.
5   See ch 11.
6   Introduced by the Land Registration (No 3) Rules 2000.

Bristol. The Bristol pilot provided electronic access to information provided by a wide range of bodies, including local, water and coal authorities, the Land Registry, Highways Agency, Ordnance survey and many others, and the aim is to extend this service countrywide so that conveyancers will be able electronically to obtain information on a property quickly and efficiently. It remains to be seen how successful the scheme will be in practice. More detail can be obtained from the NLIS website at www.nlis.org.uk.

3 OUTLINE OF A TYPICAL TRANSACTION

For the rest of the first part of this book we will be looking chronologically at the various stages of a conveyancing transaction. It is important to have an initial overall view of the typical transaction in order to put into context its constituent parts. The normal conveyancing transaction, loosely called buying and selling, will fall into one of three categories: the sale of a freehold, the assignment on sale of an already existing lease, and the grant of a new lease out of a freehold or leasehold. A lease granted out of the freehold is normally called a headlease and a lease granted out of another lease is called an underlease. For example if a builder is selling an estate of new houses or the units in a commercial development, he may, if he owns the freehold, sell the freehold of the individual houses or units or grant long leases of them. If he only has a leasehold interest he can either assign the lease in respect of each house or unit or, as is perhaps more likely, he could grant underleases. If leases or underleases are granted, then when the original buyers of the houses or units in their turn sell, they will in effect be assigning the lease or underlease.

The outline that follows is applicable to all three types of transactions and when we deal with the transaction in detail in the following chapters we shall examine the various possibilities. The assignment of a lease, in particular, is very similar to the sale of a freehold and both are examined fully in the following chapters. The grant of a lease stands to some extent on its own, involving, as it does, the creation of a new legal estate rather than the transfer of an existing one, although the conveyancing procedure is essentially similar. Thus, whilst the following chapters do make reference to the grant of a lease, this transaction and, in particular, the contents of the lease are examined further in Chapter 17, which also reiterates the differences dealt with in the earlier chapters, between the assignment of a lease and a freehold sale.

The transaction is usually divided into two distinct stages – the stage leading up to the formation of a binding contract for the sale of the property, and the stage following that which culminates in the legal estate vesting in the buyer. The legal estate does not pass to the buyer on the formation of the contract of sale; the parties merely become contractually bound to buy and sell on the terms contained in the contract. The second stage can be seen as the performance of these contractual obligations.

THE LAW SOCIETY'S NATIONAL CONVEYANCING PROTOCOL

In March 1990, the Law Society first introduced a national conveyancing protocol for domestic conveyancing, marketed under the name TransAction. Adoption of the protocol is voluntary and in practice is used in most conveyancing transactions. Essentially, it is an agreed procedure for a residential conveyancing transaction, and it is intended to streamline the conveyancing process. It is possible to vary the terms of the protocol, and this should be done by agreement with the other side and in writing. The Fourth edition of the Protocol was introduced on the 1 May 2001 and called transaction 2001. It takes into account the requirements of rules 6(3) and 15 of the Solicitor's Practice Rules and the Council of Mortgage Lender's handbook.[1] The procedure under the protocol will be dealt with wherever appropriate in the following chapters. A copy of Transaction 2001 and associated forms are set out in full in the Appendix.

On the assumption that Protocol has been adopted the outline of a typical transaction is as follows:

(1) The seller must first of all find a buyer, either himself or by using an estate agent. Both seller and buyer's solicitors should check their respective client's identities if they are not known to them, and comply with rule 15 of the Solicitor's Practice Rules. They should, if acting for the lender on a mortgage, comply with the CML handbook. This will require the solicitor to see and keep a copy of the client's passport or other ID as specified. In addition, each solicitor must verify that the other firm is genuine. They should also explain the Protocol procedure to their respective clients and get their authority to disclose relevant information about the transaction to the other side. This may be a problem for the buyer who may not wish the seller to know that he is for example having difficulty in securing a mortgage offer in case the seller decides to sell to another party. This does not constitute a variation of the Protocol, and obviously without the client's permission, the duty of confidentiality would prohibit such disclosure to the seller's solicitor.

(2) A buyer having been found, the seller's solicitor will need to assemble the draft contract documentation, which will be sent to the buyer's solicitor. He must first of all be satisfied that the seller can sell what he wants to and he will therefore examine the seller's title, in much the same way as the buyer's solicitor will eventually do. He will need the title deeds, or if title to the property is registered he will want the Land Certificate, or Charge Certificate if there is a registered charge. If the title is registered he will apply to the District Land Registry for a set of official photocopies of the entries on the register (called 'office copies'), which will be more up-to-date than the copy entries in the Certificate. If the Certificate has been retained by the Registry under section 63 of the Land Registration Act 1925 he will only receive office copies. If the title is unregistered the seller's solicitor prepares and sends to the buyer's solicitor details of the recent deeds and other events under which the property has passed. This can be in the form of an abbreviated précis called an 'Abstract of Title' or in the form of a list of the deeds and other documents together with photocopies, called an 'Epitome of Title'. He will also make the land charges searches against the names of the seller and other estate owners, and make a search of the public index map.

In addition he will prepare the Seller's Property Information Form which gives details of the property and the Fixtures Fittings and Contents Form. This pre contract package can then be sent to the buyer's solicitor along with the draft contract in duplicate.

(3) The draft contract which the seller's solicitor prepares must incorporate the Standard Conditions of Sale and will describe the property (both physically and by stating the estate being sold) normally by reference to the deeds, or to the register if

1   Law Society Gazette, 24th May 2001.

title is registered. The contract will mention any matters subject to which the property is held and similarly any matters of which the property has the benefit. For example, the property may be subject to, or have the benefit of, easements or covenants. The draft contract will also include the terms upon which the property is sold, including of course the price.

(4) The draft contract is normally prepared in duplicate and both copies sent to the buyer's solicitor for approval. At this time the parties are under no obligation whatsoever[2] and the draft contract is merely a basis for negotiating the terms, which will be included in the actual contract.

(5) The buyer's solicitor will examine the draft contract to ensure that it is acceptable and accords with the buyer's requirements and, if the buyer is taking out a mortgage to provide part of the purchase price, that it will accord with the mortgagee's requirements as well.

(6) The buyer may have a survey done. Unless the seller built the property, it is sold as it stands and it is up to the buyer to satisfy himself as to its physical condition.

(7) The buyer's solicitor makes a number of searches and enquiries, with the object of finding out all he can about the property. These include enquiries of the seller through his solicitor, a local land charges search and additional enquiries of the Local Authority, an inspection of the property and perhaps other searches and enquiries in particular cases. Transaction 2001 recommends that the buyer should be provided with a contract report once the results of searches and enquiries have been received and analysed.

(8) If the buyer is taking out a mortgage to provide part of the purchase price, he must satisfy himself that the mortgage money will be available when needed on completion; in domestic (residential) conveyancing, he will ensure that a mortgage offer has been made and that the money will be available when he needs it.

(9) There is inevitably a delay between a buyer seeing a property he wishes to purchase and exchange of contracts. This is caused by the necessity to make searches and enquiries, agree on the contract and arrange finance. In the domestic conveyancing context, the buyer may also have a property to sell and wish to synchronise the two transactions. As the parties are not under any binding obligation during this pre-contract period, there is the possibility of 'gazumping'.[3] This is where the seller, having received a better offer, threatens to sell elsewhere unless the buyer agrees to increase the purchase price. In a slow-moving market the buyer could threaten to withdraw and buy another property unless the purchase price were reduced. There may of course be genuine reasons why the buyer does want the purchase price reduced; he may have discovered on his survey that the property is in a poor state of repair and needs money spent on it.

(10) The buyer's solicitor examines the title to ensure that the seller can comply with the contract and convey what he has contracted to. If he cannot, then prima facie he is in breach of contract; for example if the property is subject to a restrictive covenant which was not revealed in the contract. If the buyer's solicitor wants clarification of any point he will raise an enquiry called a Requisition on Title, pointing out the defect and requiring the seller to remedy it.

---

2   Except in the rare case where the parties have already entered into an informal binding contract.
3   The Government has attempted to address the problem of gazumping and how to streamline the process of buying and selling in England and Wales in a consultation paper: 'The key to Easier Home Buying and selling' DETR Publications 1999, ISBN 1 85112 134. The Homes Bill 2000 was introduced, containing a number of measures designed to streamline conveyancing, but this was not enacted due to lack of parliamentary time and it has not yet been re-introduced.

(11) If the buyer is taking out a mortgage, the title will also have to be investigated by the solicitor for the mortgagee. A mortgage is in effect just another sort of conveyancing transaction, like a sale or a lease. The buyer, having purchased the property, immediately mortgages it by a mortgage deed to the mortgagee, as security for a loan from the mortgagee, which is used in order to help pay the purchase price of the property. The mortgagee will be just as concerned as the buyer that the title to the property is good and will wish to examine the title before making the mortgage advance. Duplication in the examination of title is often avoided particularly in domestic conveyancing by the solicitor for the buyer also acting for the mortgagee, so that he only investigates the title once, for both his clients. He must, of course, ensure he acts in accordance with his instructions and the CML handbook if applicable.

(12) Assuming both parties still want to proceed, and are agreed on the terms, they can now enter into the formal contract. Each party signs one copy of identical contracts. Normally the draft contract as amended is used although if there have been substantial amendments it may be re-typed. These two parts are then physically exchanged either at the office of one of the solicitors or through the post, and only when the exchange is complete is the contract formed. If contracts are exchanged by telephone, the Law Society's formulae for exchange should be used. Similarly if exchange is effected by post the procedure laid out under the Law Society's code for postal exchange should be followed. The contract usually provides for a deposit to be paid on exchange, normally 10% of the purchase price. As a result of the exchange each party has a contract signed by the other party.

(13) The next stage in the process of investigation of title is for the buyer's solicitor to make certain searches, with the object of discovering whether there are any third party interests of which he is not aware, which are going to be binding on the buyer. These searches will differ according to whether the title is registered or not. If the title is registered, the main search will be at the District Land Registry; if not, it will be a search of the Land Charges Register under the Land Charges Act 1972. If a third party interest, such as a restrictive covenant, is revealed, then the seller will again be prima facie in breach of contract unless the covenant was revealed in the contract. Similar searches will also be done on behalf of a mortgagee.

(14) The buyer's solicitor will now prepare the purchase deed. In unregistered conveyancing the deed will be a conveyance (of freehold land) or an assignment (of an existing lease). In registered transactions it will be a 'transfer' of registered freehold or leasehold land. The deed will describe the land, in a similar way to the contract, and name the parties to the transaction. The deed is submitted to the seller's solicitor for approval and return along with the Completion Information and Requisitions on Title Form. Once the deed has been approved it is then engrossed, ie the final copy is typed. The buyer has to execute the deed and then the deed is then sent to the seller's solicitor for execution by the seller.

One procedural difference on the grant of a lease is that the draft lease is normally prepared by the seller's (lessor's) solicitor at the same time as the draft contract, with the contract providing for the eventual lease to be in the form of the draft annexed. The lease itself – the deed – may then be prepared by the buyer's or seller's solicitor, after exchange of contracts.

The word 'conveyance' is often used to mean not just the unregistered freehold deed but in a wider sense to mean any purchase deed including an assignment and transfer and also a lease, mortgage or assent. In particular, this is the meaning of the word in the Law of Property Act 1925[4] and the word will normally be used in its

---

4 Section 205(1)(ii).

wider sense in this book, unless the context shows otherwise.

(15) The mortgagee's solicitor (who may also be the buyer's solicitor) will prepare the mortgage deed if the buyer is taking out a mortgage. This must be executed by the buyer and the mortgage advance obtained from the mortgagee in readiness for completion.

(16) The final stage in the transaction is called 'completion'. The date for completion is normally agreed in the contract. The buyer's solicitor hands over the balance of the purchase price and the seller's solicitor hands over the executed purchase deed, all the other old deeds and the Land Certificate or Charge Certificate if the title is registered. If the buyer is entering into a mortgage, the mortgagee receives all these documents of title and the executed mortgage deed, in return for the mortgage advance. If the property was mortgaged, as is likely, the seller's solicitor will pay off the mortgage(s) out of the proceeds of sale, and the mortgage(s) will be discharged.

(17) After completion the deed must be produced to the Inland Revenue and probably stamp duty paid. If the title is registered the buyer's solicitor will have to apply for the disposition to be registered at the appropriate District Land Registry. The buyer will not get the legal estate until this is done, whereas on an unregistered transaction the legal estate passes to the buyer on completion. However, if title is unregistered, it will normally be subject to compulsory first registration, and the buyer's solicitor will have to apply for first registration of title. In both cases application will also be made to register the buyer's new mortgage as a registered charge.

(18) In domestic conveyancing, it often happens that a person is both selling one house and buying another, and normally exchange of contracts and completion must be co-ordinated to avoid leaving, or risking leaving, that person with two houses or no house at all. If the person to whom a buyer is selling his own house is himself selling, one has the beginnings of a chain, which can make co-ordination of the transaction a major administrative problem for the solicitors involved.

If protocol is not adopted the procedure is usually as above, except that title does not have to be deduced until after exchange of contracts has taken place. Requisitions on title will also therefore take place after exchange subject to the time limits imposed by the Standard Conditions for Sale. The other main differences are that in a non protocol transaction the seller's solicitor is not obliged to provide any searches (although they may do so if they have them in their possession), and that the use of the various forms specified above is not required.

4 FORMATION OF THE CONTRACT

I INTRODUCTION

We have seen from the preceding chapter that the parties to a conveyancing transaction will normally enter into a contract which binds them to buy and sell; this contract is then performed, culminating in completion when the deed necessary to transfer the legal estate is handed over. There is nothing to prevent the parties proceeding straight to the completion stage, without entering into either a formal or informal contract. This might be thought to be a method of reducing the length of time taken by a conveyancing transaction but its main disadvantage is that a party can never be sure that the other party will complete until the very last minute.

If we assume that the parties do follow the conventional procedure of first entering into a contract, there is a specific requirement which this contract must satisfy. In respect of contracts created before 27 September 1989, this requirement is to be found in section 40 of the Law of Property Act 1925. However, section 40 has now been repealed by the Law of Property (Miscellaneous Provisions) Act 1989, and contracts created after 27 September 1989 must comply instead with section 2 of the 1989 Act.

i Law of Property (Miscellaneous Provisions) Act 1989, section 2

Under section 2, the contract must be in writing. There is no scope, as there was under section 40 of the Law of Property Act 1925, for an oral contract to be evidenced in writing. There are two other major differences between section 40 and section 2. Firstly, the written contract under section 2 must be signed by both parties. Secondly, non-compliance with section 2 leads to there being no contract at all; section 2 lays down requirements for the validity of the contract whereas section 40 was only concerned with the contract's enforceability.

Section 2 reads as follows:

(1) A contract for the sale or other disposition of an interest in land can only be made in writing and only by incorporating all the terms which the parties have expressly agreed in one document or, where contracts are exchanged, in each.

(2) The terms may be incorporated in a document either by being set out in it or by reference to some other document.

(3) The document incorporating the terms or, where contracts are exchanged, one of the documents incorporating them (but not necessarily the same one) must

be signed by or on behalf of each party to the contract.

(4) Where a contract for the sale or other disposition of an interest in land satisfies the conditions of this section by reason only of the rectification of one or more documents in pursuance of an order of a court, the contract shall come into being, or be deemed to have come into being, at such time as may be specified in the order.

(5) This section does not apply in relation to—

(a) a contract to grant such a lease as is mentioned in section 54(2) of the Law of Property Act 1925 (short leases);

(b) a contract made in the course of a public auction; or

(c) a contract regulated under the Financial Services Act 1986;

and nothing in this section affects the creation or operation of resulting, implied or constructive trusts.

(6) In this section—

'disposition' has the same meaning as in the Law of Property Act 1925;

'interest in land' means any estate, interest or charge in or over land or in or over the proceeds of sale of land.

(7) Nothing in this section shall apply in relation to contracts made before this section comes into force.

(8) Section 40 of the Law of Property Act 1925 (which is superseded by this section) shall cease to have effect.

ii Scope of section 2

Section 2 applies to any contract for the sale or other disposition[1] of an 'interest in land'.[2] An interest in land is specifically defined in subsection 6 as meaning not only any estate, interest or charge in or over land but also any estate, interest or charge in or over the proceeds of sale of land. Thus section 2 will apply to a contract for the disposition of such an equitable interest in land.

By virtue of subsection 5, section 2 does not apply to a contract to grant a lease for a term not exceeding three years, to which section 54(2) of the Law of Property Act 1925 applies; nor to a contract made in the course of a public auction; nor to a contract regulated under the Financial Services Act 1986. As section 40 of the Law of Property Act 1925 has been repealed, there is now no requirement of writing whatsoever for a contract for the sale of land made at a public auction. Subsection 5 also provides that section 2 does not affect the creation or operation of resulting implied or constructive trusts

iii Requirements of section 2

A contract within the scope of section 2 must be in writing and signed by or on behalf of both parties. The written document must incorporate all the terms which the parties have expressly agreed. This may be achieved either by the terms being set out in the document or by there being reference in the document to 'some other document' or documents; section 2(2).

All terms which have been agreed by the parties must be included in the written contract, either by setting them out or by reference to some other document or

---

1   'Disposition' is defined in the Law of Property Act 1925, s 205(1)(ii).
2   'Land' presumably has the same meaning as in the Law of Property Act 1925, s 205(1)(ix).

documents. Thus if on the sale of residential or office accommodation the price is to include furniture or carpets, this term should be included in the formal contract. If it is not, the whole contract for the sale of the property becomes invalid, [3] although it may be possible to argue that there is a collateral contract for the sale of the chattels – furniture and carpets – and that this can be severed from the main contract thereby saving the validity of the main contract. This was indeed the approach of the court in *Record v Bell*.[4]

The basic provision in section 2 is therefore for one written document, incorporating all the terms, and signed by all the parties. There is however a saving provision for exchange of contracts. Normal conveyancing procedure is for two identical contracts to be prepared, one signed by the seller and one signed by the buyer, and the two are then exchanged to achieve the formation of the contract. This procedure will satisfy section 2 provided that each part of the contract does incorporate all the terms agreed. There is nothing in section 2 requiring the two parts of the contract to be identical but as we shall see later[5] if they are not identical there will be no valid exchange.

Non-compliance with the requirements of section 2 means that there is no binding contract in existence, and that the equitable doctrine of part performance is no longer available to documents that fail to meet the requirements of section 2. Instead the innocent party may use the equitable doctrine of proprietary estoppel. This should be distinguished from non-compliance with section 40, which led to a valid but unenforceable contract.

If a concluded contract is varied after exchange, the procedure used to achieve the variation must produce a document which satisfies section 2 in relation to the varied contract. It would be dangerous simply to deal with a variation in correspondence; it would be better to have a separate exchange of signed documents referring to the main contract and then to the variation.[6]

One further effect of section 2 is that solicitors can probably if they wish cease to use the expression 'subject to contract' on their pre-contract correspondence. This has been done in the past to avoid the inadvertent creation of a section 40 memorandum of any existing oral contract, but given the repeal of section 40 this is obviously no longer necessary. The use of the 'subject to contract' expression also prevents the creation of a contract, by correspondence between the solicitors, but as we have already seen solicitors do not in any event have implied authority to sign such a contract. 'Subject to contract' should still be used if there is a document which prima facie does satisfy section 2 but which the parties do not intend to be a binding contract. This is considered further in Chapter 8, section 2i.

There are other implications of section 2 outside the normal conveyancing transaction. It has in the past been possible to create an equitable mortgage by deposit of title deeds. This took effect as a contract to create a legal mortgage and despite the lack of any section 40 memorandum could be enforced by part performance. Now, unless section 2 is satisfied, which it clearly is not in the absence of any written document, there can be no binding contract and part performance is not available. As a consequence mortgagees will insist on a legal charge, to protect their interests. There are also difficulties in relation to the grant and exercise of options. An option exists when the owner of property, the grantor of the option, gives the grantee a right

---

3   *Wright v Robert Leonard (Development) Ltd* [1994] NPC 49, CA.
4   [1991] 4 All ER 471, [1991] 1 WLR 853.
5   See ch 8, section 2ii.
6   *McCausland v Duncan Lawrie Ltd* [1996] 4 All ER 995, [1993] 1 WLR 38.

to buy the property provided that he indicates he does wish to buy within a certain period of time. The grantee would normally pay a sum of money for this right to buy the property exercisable for a certain period. Options are often used in a commercial context where a developer is assembling a site from various different sellers and does not wish to be committed to buy any of the various parts of the site until he is sure he can buy them all. He will take options on them and if and when he has been able to assemble the whole site, he will exercise the options. There has been some doubt over the correct legal analysis of an option. The predominant view was that it is an irrevocable offer to sell,[7] but there was another view that it is a conditional contract,[8] in which case section 2 would merely need to be satisfied at the time the option is granted. If an option is an irrevocable offer to sell, there must presumably be a contract at the stage of the granting of the option whereby the grantor agrees not to withdraw the offer, which must satisfy the requirements of section 2. When the option is exercised, a contract for sale is created, and this contract must satisfy section 2 also. There is clearly a danger that a letter or notice from the buyer exercising the option, simply signed by the buyer, will not satisfy the requirements of section 2, at least unless the signature of the seller on the original option agreement could be taken as the seller's signature on the contract for sale itself. However, comfort is to be derived from the decision in *Spiro v Glencrown Properties Ltd.*[9] It was held that an option is neither a conditional contract nor an irrevocable offer, but *sui generis*; nevertheless, the grant of an option was within the scope of section 2, and the requirements of section 2 only had to be satisfied on the grant, rather than on the exercise, of the option.

iv   Position on non-compliance with section 2

If section 2 has not been complied with, part performance is not available; there is no contract to part perform. If a term has been missed out of the written contract it may be possible to argue the existence of a collateral contract which is severable from the main contract.

---

7   See eg *Helby v Matthews* [1895] AC 471, HL.
8   See eg *Griffith v Pelton* [1958] Ch 205, [1957] 3 All ER 75, CA.
9   [1991] Ch 537, [1991] 1 All ER 600.

5 DRAFTING THE CONTRACT

I   INTRODUCTION

Because of the requirements of section 2 of the Law of Property Act (Miscellaneous Provisions) 1989, the procedure is for a written contract to be prepared. Such a formal contract will consist very broadly of two parts: the particulars, which describe the subject matter of the sale, and the conditions, which state the terms on which it is being sold. This chapter deals with the preparation of such a formal contract.

A solicitor will in fact probably base the contract on a standard form, supplied by law stationers or available on a word-processor. This will include a comprehensive set of general conditions. There used to be two main sets of general conditions: the Law Society Conditions and the National Conditions. These were amalgamated in 1990 to form the Standard Conditions, which were then revised in 1992 and again in 1995 when a third edition[1] was published. These Standard Conditions can then be amended or added to as the particular transaction demands, although the TransAction 2001 for residential conveyancing suggests amendments are kept to a minimum.

When a contract contains no conditions to cover a particular situation, the contract is said to be 'open' on that point and the rights of the parties are normally prescribed by common law or statute. A completely open contract would contain no conditions whatsoever.

2   PREPARATION FOR DRAFTING

It is the seller's solicitor's job to draft the contract. In order to do this he must firstly establish in consultation with the seller exactly what the seller proposes to sell, and on what conditions, and secondly ensure that the seller can do so by examining the seller's title. He must therefore obtain the title deeds or, if the title is registered, details of the register entries. The seller himself may have the deeds or the Land Certificate, or they may already be in the possession of the seller's solicitor, if he acted on the purchase. They might be held by the seller's previous solicitor, who will probably require a written authority from the seller before releasing them. If the seller's property is in mortgage, the deeds or (first) Charge Certificate will be with the first mortgagee, or held at the Land Registry under section 63 of the Land Registration Act 1925 (see Chapter 2). The solicitor will have to ask the mortgagee whether the

---

1   Reproduced in the Appendix.

deeds or Certificate can be released to him on his undertaking to return them on demand, or else to repay the amount owing under the mortgage. A mortgagee will normally release the deeds against such an undertaking, particularly if the solicitor is on the panel of the solicitors whom the mortgagee is willing to instruct to act for it on repayment of the mortgage. If not, the seller's solicitor will have to be content at this stage with an abstract or epitome prepared and supplied by the mortgagee' solicitor. If the title is registered, the seller's solicitor can always apply for office copies of the register entries and will normally do so even if the Land or Charge Certificate is immediately available. They give the up-to-date state of the register and will be needed to amplify the description of the property in the contract and to deduce title.

A further possibility is that the deeds or Land Certificate may be with a bank. If the bank is merely holding them for safe keeping, they will be released on the seller's authority. If on the other hand they are security for a loan or overdraft, the solicitor may have to give some undertaking in respect of the proceeds of sale; perhaps to pay the net proceeds to the credit of the seller's account at the bank. As with all undertakings, the solicitor should ensure that he gets his client's instructions before giving the undertaking and that he will be able to comply with its terms.

The seller's solicitor will then examine the seller's title to ensure that the seller can convey what he proposes to. If there are any defects in the title,[2] the solicitor can then draft the appropriate condition in the contract to cover the situation. The examination of title will involve not only an inspection of the deeds (or abstract or epitome) or register entries, but also the appropriate searches; in fact the seller's solicitor is following the same procedure as will be followed by the buyer's solicitor in due course, and detailed consideration of this will be left until we deal with that stage of the transaction.

3   THE PARTICULARS

The particulars will include both a 'physical' and a 'legal' description of the property to be sold. For unregistered land[3] there will normally be an existing physical description in the deeds, or more particularly in the most recent conveyance of freehold property or in the lease in respect of leasehold property. The seller's solicitor must consider whether this is accurate and adequate and, if it refers to a plan, whether the plan is accurate and up to date. If so, the existing description can be utilised in the particulars in the contract, either by reproducing it, or by making reference to the deed containing it, in which case a copy will have to be provided with the draft contract – and as the deed containing the description will presumably form part of the abstract or epitome with the draft contract; this is a very common practice, and is a requirement of the TransAction 2001 for residential conveyancing. If the existing description or plan is insufficient, then a fresh description must be inserted in the contract and/or a new plan prepared. If a new plan is prepared, the seller's solicitor may wish to negotiate with the buyer's solicitor as to the sharing of the cost of the plan. An appropriate condition – for example that the cost be shared equally – can then be inserted in the contract.

For land the title to which is registered, the seller's solicitor will normally rely on the description in the Property Register (which includes a reference to the filed plan)

---

2   Defects in title are explained at sections 4i and 4ii, below.
3   The shortened terms 'registered land' and 'unregistered land' will be used to indicate that the relevant title to the land is registered or unregistered, respectively.

and state in the particulars that the property is that which is comprised under the particular title number. He would then have to send with the draft contract at least a copy of the entries in the property register and the filed plan, and more probably a full set of office copies of all the entries in the register, as the conditions in the contract will no doubt refer to the entries in the Charges Register, and copies of the register entries will have to be provided in due course to deduce title. Again, this is standard practice, and a requirement of the Protocol. If the Standard Conditions of Sale are in use, Standard Condition 4.2.1 provides that proof of title must be by office copies.

If the sale is of only part of the property comprised in the deeds or the register then a fresh description will be essential and probably also a plan. If the title is registered the filed plan could be used, suitably adapted.

The 'legal' description will normally be a statement that the property is freehold, or leasehold held for the remainder of the term granted by the lease. If the latter, the contract should state whether it is a headlease or an under-lease.[4] The lease will probably have been referred to in the particulars as containing the physical description and will be referred to again in the conditions, so a copy or abstract will accompany the draft contract. Again, this is no hardship as the lease will have to be sent as part of the abstract of title anyway.

On the grant of a lease, the full description and plan will be inserted in the draft lease, which will normally be sent with the draft contract, which will then simply refer to the draft lease for the description.

If there is no statement as to the estate being sold it is implied that it is freehold, unless the purchaser knows that it is not.[5] If the title to the land is registered, the description 'registered land' implies that the title is absolute freehold.[6] The class of the title should therefore always be stated.

4   THE CONDITIONS

The conditions contain the terms upon which the property is sold. There will be general conditions, which will be applicable to most contracts – the Standard Conditions will normally be used – and there will be conditions which will vary from contract to contract, being peculiar to a particular contract, which are often called special conditions. Before looking at both of these we must examine the rule which lays down what matters, despite anything else, must be included in the conditions; that is the rule prescribing the seller's duty of disclosure.

i   The vendor's duty of disclosure

The seller is under no general duty of disclosure. This is the reason that a buyer has to make the various searches and enquiries considered in the next chapter. (Under the TransAction 2001, the seller voluntarily supplies certain information about the property, which he would otherwise be under no obligation to provide, on a standard property information form; the seller also initiates the pre-contract searches and enquiries and supplies them to the buyer with the draft contract. However, it is still for the buyer to satisfy himself that the results of the searches and enquiries are satisfactory and if necessary to make further searches and enquiries.)

4   *Re Russ and Brown's Contract* [1934] Ch 34, CA.
5   *Timmins v Moreland Street Property Co Ltd* [1958] Ch 110, [1957] 3 All ER 265, CA.
6   *Re Brine and Davies' Contract* [1935] Ch 388.

The protocol aside, the duty of any seller under an open contract is simply to disclose latent defects in title, that is to say defects in title that are not apparent on inspection. Examples of these defects in title, sometimes called incumbrances, are easements over the property, covenants affecting the property, tenancies of the property, and agreements, for example for the maintenance of a party wall or a shared passageway. In short, anything which detracts from the full unencumbered ownership of the property.

Given that the open contract duty of disclosure only extends to latent defects of title, it is vital that the property is inspected by or on behalf of the buyer as he will be taken to be aware of patent defects, that is defects apparent upon inspection. It has to be said that not many defects of title will be patent, but one example might be a right of way across the property.

Despite the duty of disclosure being limited to latent defects in title, the safest course for a seller is to disclose any defect of title in the contract and not to rely on the fact that it may be apparent on inspection.

Under an open contract, a buyer cannot complain about the non-disclosure of a matter which he knew about at the date of the contract,[7] although there is an exception in the case of a mortgage which is a removable defect of title in the sense that the seller can remove it by paying it off and having it discharged, and the buyer is entitled to assume that this will be done. Again, the seller's solicitor would not rely on the buyer's knowledge of a defect of title, which may be difficult to prove, but would disclose the defect in the contract.

The seller's duty of disclosure is limited to defects of title and does not extend to physical defects and defects in the quality of the land unless they are also defects in title. The buyer, '…if he does not protect himself by an express warranty [must] satisfy himself that the premises are fit for the purposes for which he wants to use them, whether that fitness depends on the state of their structure or the state of the law or any other relevant circumstances'.[8] A similar rule applies to planning matters, so that unless the seller makes some positive statement that the present or intended use is authorised under the planning legislation the buyer has no claim against the seller should this not turn out to be the case.[9] The seller's duty of disclosure is also limited to matters which will bind the buyer. If in unregistered conveyancing there is a restrictive covenant created after 1925 which has become unenforceable due to non-registration as a land charge, or if a pre-1925 restrictive covenant has become unenforceable following a bona fide purchase without notice of it, then the seller need not disclose the covenant.

The provisions in the Standard Conditions make some change to the seller's duty of disclosure.

Under 3.1.1, the seller is selling the property free from incumbrances other than those mentioned in 3.1.2. Standard Condition 3.1.1 therefore contains a duty to disclose incumbrances other than those mentioned in 3.1.2. The buyer needs to be alive to the fact that he is buying the property subject to the incumbrances set out in 3.1.2. There are five categories of incumbrance included in 3.1.2. Firstly, and most obviously, there are incumbrances mentioned in the agreement itself. The seller will perform the duty of disclosure inherent in 3.1.1 by disclosing incumbrances in the agreement, and the buyer then obviously buys the property subject to these.

---

7   *Timmins v Moreland Street Property Ltd* [1958] Ch 110, [1957] 3 All ER 265, CA.
8   Per Devlin J in *Edler v Auerbach* [1950] 1 KB 359 at 374, approved in *Hill v Harris* [1965] 2 QB 601, [1965] 2 All ER 358, CA. Of course on the sale of freehold land, the seller's solicitor would have to disclose the existence of a restrictive covenant, as a defect in title.
9   See ch 7.

The second category of incumbrance mentioned in 3.1.2 is an incumbrance discoverable by inspection of the property before exchange of contracts. This is a clear echo of the open contract duty of disclosure which, remember, is only to disclose latent as opposed to patent defects in title. However, it is not terribly clear what level of inspection is being assumed in 3.1.2. Must, for example, the incumbrance be discoverable upon reasonable inspection? It would be unwise to rely on this element of 3.1.2 and best practice from the seller's point of view would be for the incumbrance to be disclosed in the contract.

The third category of incumbrances in 3.1.2 are incumbrances which the seller does not and could not know about. This is a useful provision from the seller's point of view, clearly placing the risk of any hidden incumbrances on the buyer; if there are incumbrances which the seller does not and could not know about, the effect of 3.1.2 is that the buyer must take subject to these and cannot complain. Again, the wording of this provision is not particularly clear when it refers to incumbrances which the seller 'could not know about'. This is presumably a reference to constructive knowledge on the part of the seller, perhaps to matters which were discovered when the seller bought the property but which the seller has actually forgotten about; if so, reference to the file containing details of the earlier transaction will be necessary. It is probably also a reference to constructive knowledge to be derived from the registration of interests, for example in the Land Charges Register in respect of unregistered title. Again, it would be advisable to do a search of the register in order actually to find out about those interests. The seller's solicitor may be persuaded that it is advantageous to amend this element of 3.1.2 so that it simply refers to matters of which the seller has no actual notice, but the buyer's solicitor may be less than willing to accept this restriction on the seller's duty of disclosure.

The fourth category in 3.1.2 is entries made before the date of exchange of contracts in any public register save the registers maintained by the Land Registry, the Land Charges Department or the Companies Register. The effect is that there is still a clear duty to disclose matters mentioned in those three registers but, those registers apart, the buyer needs to satisfy himself about entries in any other public register because he is, by definition, buying the property subject to them. The most obvious example of such a register would be the Register of Local Land Charges, discussed in Chapter 6.

The fifth and final category of incumbrance mentioned in 3.1.2 is 'public requirements'. These are defined in Standard Condition 1.1.1(j) as 'any notice, order or proposal given or made (whether before or after the date of the contract) by a body acting on statutory authority.' The most common examples will be notices issued by a local authority or a local planning authority, such as enforcement notices. These are discussed in more detail in Chapter 8. The inclusion of public requirements in a list of 'incumbrances' may possibly present difficulties. Such matters may well not normally be within the open contract common law duty of disclosure. The fact that public requirements are clearly envisaged as 'incumbrances' might be taken as an indication of the extent of incumbrances under 3.1.1 and therefore as an extent of the duty of disclosure inherent in 3.1.1. Although under 3.1.2 the buyer is purchasing subject to public requirements, other similar matters which do not amount to public requirements, as defined, might conceivably be within the duty of disclosure under 3.1.1. If this is thought to be a problem, one solution from the seller's point of view might be to expand the definition of public requirements, subject to which the property is being sold, as widely as possible.

In condition 3.1.1 there is no provision, which was commonly found in previous sets of provisions including the first edition of the Standard Conditions, stating that the buyer is purchasing the property subject to anything which would have been revealed by the searches, enquiries and inspections which a prudent buyer would make before exchange of contracts (as to which see Chapter 6). A provision along these lines might be a useful addition from the seller's point of view although it may well not absolve the seller from his underlying duty of disclosure; if the seller is aware of an incumbrance then he should disclose it.[10]

Despite the literal wording of conditions 3.1.1 and 3.1.2, which suggest that the seller is under no duty to disclose incumbrances included in the list under 3.1.2 and that the buyer is buying subject to those incumbrances, it may be unwise for the seller to rely too heavily on the list in 3.1.2 and not disclose incumbrances of which he is aware and which fall within the categories in 3.1.2. In *Rignall Developments Ltd v Halil*[11] the contract contained a condition that the buyer would be deemed to have made a local land charges search and to have knowledge of all matters that would be disclosed thereby and that the buyer would purchase subject to such matters. The buyer did not in fact do a search of the local land charges register. There was an entry of which the seller had notice but which the seller, in reliance on the condition in the contract, had failed to disclose. The court found that in the absence of disclosure by the seller of the incumbrance of which the seller had notice, the seller could not rely on the condition in the contract.

It can be seen that conditions 3.1.1 and 3.1.2 do make some amendment to the open contract duty of disclosure discussed earlier. Nevertheless in practice the most prudent course for a seller is to disclose all matters of title, which adversely affect the property. There is space for this on the standard form of agreement, which incorporates the Standard Conditions, on the front page under the heading 'incumbrances'. The advantage of this is that by Special Condition 2 on the rear of the contract form, the buyer is unable to question and raise requisitions after exchange about any matter disclosed as a burden on the property.

Under Standard Condition 3.1.3, there is a continuing duty of disclosure, or at least a duty to pass on information, after exchange of contracts. 3.1.3 provides that after exchange of contracts, the seller is to give the buyer written details without delay of any new public requirement (as defined in 1.1.1(j)) and of anything in writing which the seller learns about concerning any incumbrances subject to which the property is sold. These incumbrances subject to which the property is sold are the five categories of incumbrance set out in 3.1.2. Whilst it is clearly sensible that the buyer be informed of any developments subsequent to exchange of contracts, 3.1.3 does seem to impose on the seller a duty to disclose matters after exchange of contracts which, had they existed before exchange of contracts, would on the face of it have been outside the seller's duty of disclosure; remember that the literal effect of 3.1.1 and 3.1.2 is that the buyer is buying a property subject to incumbrances listed in 3.1.2 which in turn means that, on the face of it, the seller does not need to disclose them.[12]

Standard Condition 3.1.4 further provides that the buyer is to bear the cost of complying with any outstanding public requirement and is to indemnify the seller against any liability resulting from a public requirement.

In the Standard Conditions there are also provisions in respect of disclosure of the contents of the lease in respect of leasehold property[13] and of details of existing tenancies of the property.[14]

---

10   *Nottingham Patent Brick and Tile Co v Butler* (1885) 15 QBD 261.
11   [1988] Ch 190, [1987] 3 All ER 170; see also *Nottingham Patent Brick and Tile Co v Butler*, above; *William Sindall plc v Cambridgeshire County Council* [1994] 3 All ER 932, [1994] 1 WLR 1016, CA.
12   But see fns 10 and 11, above.
13   See the next section, ii.
14   See section xvi.

It is important that the seller's solicitor does investigate the seller's title before drafting the contract, so as to enable him to disclose in the contract any defects in the title discovered; the danger is that he assumes the title is in order without making a full investigation. The buyer's remedies should the seller fail to discharge his duty of disclosure are dealt with in Chapter 16.

We can now consider the conditions, which may be included in the contract, commencing with a statement of the defects in the title.

ii   Disclosure of defects in title

As indicated in the previous section, consequent on the seller's duty of disclosure there will be a statement in the contract of the interests subject to which the property is being sold. What then are these defects of title, which the seller must disclose? They fall broadly into two categories. Firstly, there are defects, which relate to the title to the property. These include the matters mentioned in the previous section, such as covenants affecting the land and easements over the land. They will be noted on a proper examination of title from the deeds or the register and from the appropriate searches. As with the physical description, they may be reproduced in the conditions in the contract or merely referred to in the conditions as being contained in a particular deed, an abstract or copy of which is then attached to the contract. For registered land, reference to the Charges Register may be appropriate, with office copies accompanying the draft contract, although the solicitor must not ignore the possibility of there being overriding interests. The Charges Register will also include details of any existing mortgage over the property and as the sale is presumably not subject to this, it should be excluded from the reference in the conditions to the Charges Register. If there are matters such as restrictive covenants affecting the property, but for some reason no details of them were available at the time of first registration, then the Charges Register will say so. A defect such as this should be drawn specifically to the attention of the buyer in the contract.[15]

If the property is leasehold it is likely that the lease, which is being assigned, will contain a large number of covenants and other provisions. If so, reference to the lease in the conditions, with a copy sent with the contract, is the only practicable way of disclosing them. The seller's duty under an open contract is to disclose any onerous or unusual covenants in the lease[16] but normally all will be disclosed in the manner mentioned. The Standard Conditions provide that full details of the lease should be supplied to the buyer who is then deemed to purchase with full notice of the lease terms.[17]

The seller's duty under an open contract, and under Standard Condition 3.1.1 as amplified by 3.1.2, is to convey free from encumbrances. This first category of defects of title constitute what can loosely be called encumbrances over the property and this is why the seller must disclose them.[18]

The second category of defects of title affect the seller's right to convey the property rather than the property itself. An example would be where there has been in the past

---

15   *Faruqi v English Real Estates Ltd* [1979] 1 WLR 963.
16   *Re White and Smith's Contract* [1896] 1 Ch 637; see also *Aslan v Berkeley House Properties Ltd* [1990] 2 EGLR 202, CA (disclosure of likelihood of exercise of break-clause by lessor).
17   SC 8.1.2.
18   It may be that these encumbrances are not in the nature of easements and covenants which will be acceptable to a buyer, but are matters which make it extremely unlikely that anyone will purchase the property, such as options or rights of pre-emption. The seller would have to disclose them, and may thereby be unable in practice to sell.

a sale by a mortgagee whose power of sale may not have arisen, or a sale of trust property to a trustee. Such situations will be more readily appreciated when we have dealt with the whole question of examining title in Chapter 10. They are clearly of great importance because they mean that the seller may not be able to convey the property at all, rather than just that the seller can only convey subject to an encumbrance. They will normally only occur in unregistered conveyancing for, as we have seen, a buyer of registered land is entitled to assume that the registered proprietor does have the power to deal with the land in the absence of any entry to the contrary on the register.[19]

How should the seller' solicitor deal with such a defect? He may provide in the contract that the buyer will 'accept such title as the seller has' or 'will make no objection to the seller's title'. In order to rely on such a condition the seller must have disclosed any defects of title of which he knew. Additionally, even though the seller may be able to rely on such a condition, he will be refused specific performance if he can only show a thoroughly bad title, although he would still be allowed to forfeit the buyer's deposit if the buyer refused to complete.[20]

Similarly the seller cannot conceal a defect in title by stipulating that the title to be deduced to the buyer shall commence after the defect. In *Becker v Partridge*[1] a contract for sale of property held under an underlease did not disclose that there were breaches of a covenant in a superior lease, giving rise to the possibility of forfeiture, and of which the seller knew or ought to have known.[2] The superior lease was not to be included in the title to be abstracted to the buyer but he found out about the breaches of covenant and was entitled to rescind the contract.

The correct procedure, then, is for the contract to include a full disclosure of the position in the conditions and *then* to provide that the buyer buys with full notice of the defect and shall raise no objection on account of it. The buyer can then evaluate the risk (and if necessary try and arrange insurance cover in respect of it) before deciding whether to proceed.

iii   Title Guarantee

The Law of Property (Miscellaneous Provisions) Act 1994 changed the law relating to the seller's capacity. Before the act came into force on the first July 1995, the contract conditions would often contain a statement of the seller's capacity. There were a number of alternatives which included:

(a)   beneficial owner – where the seller owned the whole legal estate and equitable interest in the property, eg a sole owner;
(b)   trustee – for example trustees of land or a tenant for life of settled land;
(c)   personal representative;
(d)   mortgagee;
(e)   settlor;
(f)   under an order of the court.

The importance of these expressions was that the capacity in which the seller conveys and was expressed to convey in the deed dictated the covenants for title which the seller

---

19   Subject to overriding interests.
20   *Re Scott and Alvarez's Contract* [1895] 2 Ch 603, CA. The title in that case rested on a forged deed. There is now discretion to order payment of the deposit under s 49(2) of the Law of Property Act 1925.
 1   [1966] 2 QB 155, [1966] 2 All ER 266, CA.
 2   See also *Aslan v Berkeley House Properties Ltd* [1990] 2 EGLR 202, [1990] 37 EG 81, CA.

impliedly gave to the buyer in the deed. This has now been replaced by title guarantees: the seller can give a full title guarantee, a limited title guarantee or no title guarantee at all. In giving a full title guarantee the seller is covenanting that he (a) can transfer the property to the buyer or grant him a lease as appropriate; (b) will at his own cost do all that he reasonably can to pass the title to the buyer; and (c) is transferring the property free from all encumbrances, rights exercisable by third parties and encumbrances and rights that he does not and could not reasonably be expected to know about.

If the property is leasehold a further covenant that the lease is subsisting and there has been no breach of covenant that could lead to forfeiture is given. Absolute owners of both the legal and equitable estate usually give full title guarantee. Limited title guarantee repeats the first two covenants given in full title guarantee along with the covenant given in respect of leasehold property, but the covenant relating to encumbrances and third party rights is restricted. The covenant given states that the seller has not since the last disposition for value, charged or encumbered the property by creating a subsisting charge or right over the property enforceable by a third party, nor has he suffered the property to be charged or encumbered in this manner and knows of no one else who has created such charges or encumbrances. Personal representatives or trustees who have limited knowledge of the history of the property may give this title guarantee. Finally the seller may vary the guarantee or may decide to give no title guarantee but the latter will probably make the property very difficult to sell. If limited or no title guarantee is offered, and the buyer is buying with the aid of a mortgage, it is vital to ensure that the mortgagee's instructions are taken as to whether the situation is acceptable. This will be dealt with in more detail in Chapter 16, but the expressions which when used in the deed give rise to implied covenants for title are those listed above.

iv   Rights appurtenant to the property sold

We have dealt with the need for disclosure of existing covenants, easements and other interests affecting the property. There may of course be easements existing for the benefit of the property, for example a right of way over adjoining property or up a shared passageway. There may be covenants of which the property enjoys the benefit, for example that the adjoining property must only be used as a private dwelling house. These should also be mentioned in the contract, either in the conditions or the particulars. If the title is unregistered then, as before, the simplest way will be by reference to the deed or deeds containing the details. If the title is registered, and if they are mentioned in the Property Register, they may be incorporated in the particulars by a reference to the Property Register. On the grant of a lease, they would normally be included in the draft lease which would be referred to in the contract.

v   Sale of part

In addition to disclosing *existing* easements affecting property, when the seller is selling or leasing only part of the property he owns and is retaining property adjoining or nearby, he may wish to impose new easements over the property he is selling for the benefit of the property he is keeping. He must also consider what, if any, easements the sold property is to have over the retained property.

To take the latter point first, the seller's solicitor in drafting the contract must be aware of the effects of the rule in *Wheeldon v Burrows*.[3] This states that on a 'grant'

---

3   (1879) 12 Ch D 31, CA.

(which includes a contract for sale or lease) by an owner of part of his property, he will impliedly grant to the buyer all quasi-easements which are:

(a) continuous and apparent;
(b) necessary to the reasonable enjoyment of the property sold; and
(c) used prior to and at the time of the sale by the owner for the benefit of the part sold.

One must talk in terms of quasi-easements as one cannot have an easement over one's own land. However, if there are rights which satisfy the above three conditions, then the contract impliedly includes them and the buyer is entitled to have them in the deed. To take an example, if the owner of a house and large garden is selling the house but keeping part of the garden on which to build himself a bungalow, and if the owner was in the habit of crossing the part of the garden he is keeping to gain access to the house, he may find that he has impliedly contracted to grant this right of way to the buyer of the house. The seller's solicitor may wish to negate the effect of *Wheeldon v Burrows* and this he can do by an appropriate condition in the contract. The Standard Conditions contain a condition providing that the buyer shall not be entitled to any right of light or air over any retained land.[4] Retained land is defined in Standard Condition 3.4.1 as simply being land 'near' the sold property; it would be better for the retained land to be specifically described in the contract (and the deed).

The rule in *Wheeldon v Burrows* is only a rule of implied grant and does not operate to imply reservations, that is easements reserved by the seller over the property he is selling. In the above example, if the seller were keeping the house and selling part of the garden there would be no implied reservation of the right of way over the part sold off. If the seller does wish to reserve easements over the property he is selling or leasing there must be some specific provision in the contract. The Standard Conditions contain a condition to cover this situation; it states that the seller and buyer each have easements over each other's land as would have been implied had the retained land also been sold simultaneously to another buyer.[5] In that case, the rule in *Wheeldon v Burrows* would apply to both sales and what would be grants of easements in favour of one part would be reservations of easements over the other part.[6] The effect is that *Wheeldon v Burrows* is made to operate 'in reverse' to reserve easements over the land sold, as well as grant them for the benefit of the land sold over the land retained.

Some doubt will always remain as to whether existing quasi-easements do meet the conditions set out in *Wheeldon v Burrows* or not, so the best course for the seller's solicitor is to exclude in the special conditions the effect of *Wheeldon v Burrows*, and maybe also the Standard Condition, and then to state specifically in the special conditions what easements are to be granted and reserved.

vi   Imposition of new covenants

We have dealt with existing easements and new easements, both over the property and for its benefit, and we have also similarly dealt with existing covenants. When the seller is selling part of his land he may wish to impose *new* covenants over the

---

4   SC 3.4.2.
5   Ibid.
6   *Hansford v Jago* [1921] 1 Ch 322.

part being sold for the benefit of the land he is keeping, or vice versa. He can thereby retain some control over the use to which the land he is selling is put. In particular if the seller is a builder developing a new housing estate, he may wish to impose covenants on the sale of the individual plots in order to preserve the character of the development.

Assuming that a covenant is to be given by the buyer, a special condition must be inserted in the contract stating that the buyer will in the deed enter into the covenant, the full wording of which is then given. The wording of the covenant will be important as the seller's solicitor will wish to ensure both that the burden of the covenant will run with the land if possible and also that the benefit of the covenant will run with the seller's land. To take first of all the position on the sale of part of the freehold (or of an existing leasehold), the benefit of the covenant will run with the seller's land in most circumstances if the covenant touches and concerns that land and either the benefit is assigned to the seller's successor in title or the benefit has become annexed to the seller's land. Annexation may be deduced from surrounding circumstances or may be achieved by the language used in the original covenant; for the latter the covenant should actually state that it is for the benefit of the whole *or any part or parts* of the seller's retained land.[7] The retained land itself should be adequately identified.

The burden of a covenant imposed on the sale of part of a freehold or part of an existing leasehold does not run with the land at law, but the burden of a restrictive covenant will run in equity if either it was made for the benefit of the seller's retained land[8] or there is a Building Scheme as defined in *Elliston v Reacher*.[9] This is where buyers of individual plots on a building estate have all given restrictive covenants on the basis that they are to be enforceable by all the other buyers, the intention being that the covenants will be for the benefit of all the plots sold. If there is a Building Scheme then the covenants are mutually enforceable between the various buyers and their successors in title. If the builder is selling the freehold of the individual plots his solicitor should ensure that the estate does qualify as a Building Scheme.[10]

The alternative would be for the builder to grant leases of the individual plots which will then avoid the problems of the covenants running with the land, because the *benefit and burden* of both *restrictive and positive* covenants *in leases* will normally pass to the assignees.[11] If there is a Letting Scheme – requirements similar to a Building Scheme – the covenants in the lease will also be mutually enforceable between the various lessees and their assignees.

The position regarding positive covenants in relation to freehold land or imposed on the sale of part of an existing lease is acute; the burden does not run with the land at law or in equity. On the development of a freehold housing estate, positive covenants can be made to run with each individual plot by imposing a rentcharge,[12] either for a purely nominal amount to serve as a 'peg' on which to hang positive

---

7   *Marquess of Zetland v Driver* [1939] Ch 1, [1938] 2 All ER 158, CA, cf *Re Ballard's Conveyance* [1937] Ch 473, [1937] 2 All ER 691. See also *Federated Homes Ltd v Mill Lodge Properties Ltd* [1980] 1 All ER 371, [1980] 1 WLR 594, CA (cf *J Sainsbury plc v Enfield London Borough Council* [1989] 2 All ER 817, [1989] 1 WLR 590 re pre-1925 covenants) and *Roake v Chadha* [1983] 3 All ER 503, [1984] 1 WLR 40. The law is somewhat uncertain, and to be on the safe side the formula suggested in the text should be included to ensure annexation.

8   *Tulk v Moxhay* (1848) 2 Ph 774; this requirement will normally be satisfied on a sale of part.

9   [1908] 2 Ch 665, CA. See also *Emile Elias & Co Ltd v Pine Groves Ltd* [1993] 1 WLR 305, PC.

10   Other conditions are laid down in *Elliston v Reacher* (above), apart from that mentioned.

11   The running of covenants in leases is dealt with in more detail in ch 17, below.

12   A rentcharge is a legal interest, which is thus binding on buyers irrespective of notice. Covenants imposed in support of the rentcharge can thus effectively run with the land.

covenants[13] or, if the covenant is for payment of a sum of money – perhaps a contribution to the maintenance of some common area – the rentcharge can be for that variable sum.[14] However, since the Rent Charges Act 1977 no new rent charges can be created, apart from certain 'estate' rent charges and one or two other fairly obscure types. Apart from this a positive covenant may be enforced on the basis that if the property has the benefit of a right of way with a positive covenant to contribute to its maintenance, the owner will not be allowed to take the benefit – the right of way – without also submitting to the burden – paying the contribution.[15] Otherwise enforcement of a positive covenant may depend on the existence of a chain of indemnity covenants, which are considered below. Again, if a housing estate is developed by granting leases (or sub-leases if the builder only has a leasehold interest) of the individual plots, these problems can be avoided.

We have discussed the imposition of new covenants for the benefit of the seller's land but it is quite possible, particularly on the development, say, of a block of flats, that the seller will enter into covenants with the buyer for the benefit of the buyer's property. Thus, the seller might covenant to maintain the common parts and the buyers of the individual flats would covenant to each pay a proportionate amount of the cost.

vii   Indemnity covenants

If a covenant is so expressed that the original covenantor will remain liable even after he has parted with the property – for example a covenant to erect 'and ever thereafter maintain' a fence – then he ought to take an indemnity, in the form of an indemnity covenant, from the person to whom he disposes of the property. He will remain liable for any breach of the covenant and ought to be indemnified against the consequences of any future breach. The person to whom the covenantor disposes of the property, having given an indemnity covenant, will then take a similar covenant when he in turn disposes of the property, and so on. A chain of indemnity covenants is thus built up and if the original covenant is a positive covenant, on a sale of freehold it may still be possible for the covenantee to enforce the covenant against the present owner of the property 'down the chain'. This method of enforcement is not ideal as the intervening owners may have disappeared or failed to take an indemnity covenant and thus broken the chain. It is, though, better than nothing and if the covenantee desires to take advantage of it then the original covenant should be appropriately worded so as to ensure the covenantor's continuing liability.

For leases created before 1st January 1996,[16] on an assignment for value of leasehold land title to which is not registered, there will be implied in the deed of assignment a covenant for indemnity by the buyer in respect of the covenants in the lease.[17] The seller need not stipulate for such a covenant in the contract. In the case of leasehold land the title to which is registered, the indemnity covenant is implied whether the assignment is for value or not.[18] In the case of 'new leases'[19] the Landlord and Tenant (Covenants) Act 1995 has repealed Law of Property Act 1925 section 77 and the Land Registration Act 1925 section 24 which inserted an implied indemnity

---

13   Rentcharges Act 1977, s 2(4)(a).
14   Ibid, s 2(4)(b).
15   *Halsall v Brizell* [1957] Ch 169, [1957] 1 All ER 371.
16   Landlord and Tenant (Covenants) Act 1995, s 1.
17   Law of Property Act 1925, s 77(1)(c). Also there may be an implied right to indemnity under *Moule v Garrett* (1872) LR 7 Exch 101.
18   Land Registration Act 1925, s 24(1)(b).
19   Landlord and Tenant (Covenants) Act 1995, s 1.

covenant into an assignment of a lease. However, an assignee may still find himself liable under the terms of an Authorised Guarantee Agreement (see Chapter 17) and should therefore include an express indemnity clause. If the property is freehold there is some authority for saying that under an open contract the seller can require the buyer in the purchase deed to indemnify him against any continuing liability.[20] The safest course is to insert a condition in the contract to provide that the buyer will in the deed give an express indemnity covenant. The Standard Conditions provide[1] that if the seller will remain bound by any obligation affecting the property, the buyer is to enter into an indemnity covenant. On the grant of a lease, as on the sale of freehold, no indemnity covenant will be implied and so if an indemnity covenant is appropriate – eg on the grant of a lease out of a freehold subject to a covenant – the appropriate condition should be inserted in the contract and an indemnity covenant included in the lease.

viii   Licence to assign

If the property being sold is leasehold, or in other words there is to be an assignment of the lease, then it may be that the lease contains a provision that there be no assignment without the consent or licence of the lessor.[2] If so, then under an open contract, the seller is under a duty to use his best endeavours to obtain the licence.[3] If it is not forthcoming by the time for completion then the buyer can – and presumably will – rescind the contract, recovering his deposit and interest and also the costs of investigating the title.[4] The rule in *Bain v Fothergill*[5] has in the past prevented him from obtaining full damages unless the seller has not used his best endeavours to obtain the licence, for example if he has induced the lessor to withhold the licence,[6] but the rule in *Bain v Fothergill* has now been abolished by section 3 of the Law of Property (Miscellaneous Provisions) Act 1989.

The contract may well include a condition to cover the point. The Standard Conditions provide that if consent to assign (or sub-let) is required, the seller is to apply for the consent at his expense and use all reasonable efforts to obtain it, and the buyer is to provide all information and references reasonably required.[7] If, three working days before the contractual completion date, either the consent has not been given or has been given subject to a condition to which the buyer reasonably objects, either party may rescind the contract by notice to the other party.[8] On such rescission,[9] the seller must repay the deposit to the buyer with accrued interest.[10] However, if a party is in breach of his obligations under the condition (as we have just seen, the seller is obliged to apply for consent and the buyer is obliged to provide information and references), he loses his right to rescind if the licence is not given; in practice however the other party probably would rescind. Condition 8.3 is fairly brief and some additions to it may be considered. As we will see in Chapter 17, there is a statutory

---

20   See for example *Moxhay v Inderwick* (1847) 1 De G & Sm 708.
1   SC 4.5.4. Note that no covenant is implied in the deed; it must be express.
2   See further ch 17.
3   *Day v Singleton* [1899] 2 Ch 320, CA.
4   *Re Marshall and Salt's Contract* [1900] 2 Ch 202.
5   (1874) LR 7 HL 158.
6   *Day v Singleton*, above.
7   SC 8.3.2.
8   SC 8.3.4. Notice is governed by SC 1.3.
9   SC 7.2.
10   Defined at SC 1.1.1(a).

restriction on the lessor unreasonably refusing consent; the question arises under 8.3 of whether a seller would have to apply to the court for a declaration that the lessor's refusal was unreasonable,[11] although in practice the time limit under the condition may be too short to entertain such an application. Some elaboration on the meaning of 'all reasonable efforts' in the condition might be helpful. A seller might also wish to impose some time scale on the provision of information and references by the buyer and also insert a provision obliging the buyer to enter into a counterpart licence under which he may covenant with the lessor to perform the obligations in the lease, although this may be implicit in the wording of 8.3.4(b) under which the buyer can only object to a condition subject to which the licence is given if it is reasonable to so object. Another amendment could provide for the seller to be able to rescind if the landlord wished to impose unreasonable conditions on the seller.

Although the time limit under 8.3.4 is three working days before the contractual completion date, there is much to be said for delaying exchange of contracts until the licence to assign is forthcoming, particularly when the client is both buying and selling as is likely in residential conveyancing. If contracts are exchanged and the licence is not forthcoming then, although as we have seen there will be a right to rescind the contract, the client will remain bound on his other contract to buy or sell, and this will be, to say the least, inconvenient. In a commercial transaction it may be more appropriate to tie in the contractual completion date to the date of the giving of the licence, by providing that the parties should complete within say five working days of the seller giving notice to the buyer that licence had been granted, perhaps with a long stop date of say four months after which either party could rescind if licence was not forthcoming by that date. The Commercial Property Standard Conditions of Sale have adopted these provisions and also added another option, which is that there is no court declaration that the consent has been unreasonably withheld.

ix   Deposit

Under an open contract no deposit is payable. Normally the seller will require a deposit to be paid on exchange of contracts, both as part-payment of the purchase price and as some sort of guarantee that the buyer will complete; for if the buyer unjustifiably refuses to complete, the seller can forfeit the deposit even though he has suffered no loss.[12] If the deposit is paid to the seller's solicitor then he will hold it, in the absence of any provision to the contrary in the contract, as agent for the seller.[13] This means that the buyer loses control of the deposit and it can be paid over to the seller. An alternative capacity in which the seller's solicitor – or any other deposit holder – may take the deposit is as stake-holder. The position regarding any interest on a deposit held as stake-holder is dealt with by the special conditions.[14]

A stake-holder cannot pay the money to either party unless and until that party has become lawfully entitled to it,[15] as for example the seller would be, following completion. Obviously the buyer would prefer the deposit to be held by a stake-holder, for if he becomes entitled to rescind and have the deposit returned, it is ready and

---

11   See *Bickel v Courtenay Investments (Nominees) Ltd* [1984] 1 All ER 657, [1984] 1 WLR 795, a case on a corresponding provision in the National Conditions.
12   See further ch 16, below.
13   *Ellis v Goulton* [1893] 1 QB 350, CA.
14   SC 2.2 provides for accrued interest to be paid to the seller on completion.
15   See *Hastingwood Property Ltd v Saunders Bearman Anselm* [1991] Ch 114, [1990] 3 All ER 107.

waiting for him; if held by a solicitor it will not have been paid into the seller's client account. If on the other hand the deposit has been held by the seller's solicitor as the seller's agent, it may have been paid to the seller and the buyer will merely have a right of action against the seller for that sum, although the buyer would also have a lien over the property he had contracted to buy, to the extent of the deposit.[16] The seller may have a very good reason for wanting the deposit to be paid to his solicitor as agent; he may wish to use it straightaway, either to ease his cash flow position in a commercial transaction or, in residential cases, to put towards the deposit on a property he is buying. The capacity in which the seller's solicitor holds the deposit is therefore a matter for negotiation between the parties.

If the buyer becomes entitled to the return of the deposit on rescission, he may find that the person holding the deposit has gone bankrupt or is otherwise unable to pay. After the formation of a binding contract, the position is clear; whether the deposit is held by a stake-holder or by an agent, the loss must be borne by the seller and he would have to reimburse the buyer.[17] The position where there is not yet a binding contract – for example as a result of the common practice of paying a small deposit to an estate agent when the parties agree to proceed 'subject to contract' – is less clear. It would seem following *Sorrell v Finch*[18] that because a buyer is entitled to demand repayment and is under no obligation to pay any deposit, the risk should be borne by the buyer. The Estate Agents Act 1979 provides that deposits are to be held on trust for the person entitled to them,[19] which on the above principles would presumably mean the buyer before exchange of contracts.

A seller's solicitor holding a deposit as stake-holder acquires no interest in the deposit, and must transfer it to another stake-holder if both parties so request; *Rockeagle Ltd v Alsop Wilkinson*.[20]

If a contract provides for payment of a deposit, which is then not paid, it could either be said that payment was a condition precedent to the formation of the contract or that payment was a term of the contract, the breach of which entitles the seller to rescind.[1] The practical effect will be the same whichever interpretation is preferred; the seller will be able to re-sell. However, if the latter interpretation is adopted, the seller does have the option of affirming the contract and in due course suing for the deposit if necessary. Subsequent cases have favoured this latter interpretation. In *Millichamp v Jones*,[2] it was held that the seller could rescind the contract for non-payment (*and* sue for damages for breach of contract). This was also the approach in *Damon Cia Naviera SA v Hapag-Lloyd International SA, The Blankenstein*,[3] a shipping case. Non-payment of the deposit will most often arise when a deposit is paid by cheque which is subsequently dishonoured. Solicitors should be wary of the form in which the deposit is paid and in particular should be most hesitant about accepting the buyer's personal cheque – or if they do they should delay exchange until the cheque has been presented and cleared to avoid being in breach of the Solicitors Accounts Rules 1998.

16   See ch 16, below.
17   *Rowe v May* (1854) 18 Beav 613; *Ellis v Goulton*, above. If the deposit-holder was the seller's solicitor, the buyer may be able to make a claim on the Law Society Compensation Fund.
18   [1977] AC 728, [1976] 2 All ER 371, HL.
19   Section 13. By s 14 the estate agent must pay the deposit into a client account and by s 16 must arrange insurance in respect of it.
20   [1992] Ch 47, [1991] 4 All ER 659, CA.
 1   *Myton Ltd v Schwab-Morris* [1974] 1 All ER 326, [1974] 1 WLR 331. The case does not decide which.
 2   [1983] 1 All ER 267, [1982] 1 WLR 1422.
 3   [1985] 1 All ER 475, [1985] 1 WLR 435, CA.

The Standard Conditions contain provisions relating to the deposit in condition 2.2. A deposit of 10% of the purchase price is payable and unless the sale is by auction, payment is to be made by a banker's draft or a solicitor's cheque drawn in either case, on a clearing bank as defined in condition 1.1.1(d). Although the conditions do not define the expression 'purchase price' the implication from the front page of the contract form is that in calculating a 10% deposit, any additional amount payable for chattels or other items is ignored. The basic position is that the deposit is paid to the seller's solicitor as stake-holder on terms that on completion it is to be paid to the seller with accrued interest.[4] Accrued interest is defined as the interest actually earned if the deposit money has been placed on deposit or in a Building Society share account or otherwise the notional interest which would reasonably have been earned by the deposit money in an account with a clearing bank on seven days' notice of withdrawal; in either case the seller's solicitor can deduct any proper charges for handling the money.[5]

However the Standard Conditions do allow the seller to use all or part of the deposit as a deposit on a purchase by the seller of another property in England and Wales for his residence; indeed the deposit money may be passed even further up the chain by the seller's own seller. The position, contained in condition 2.2.2, is that the seller can use all or part of the deposit in this way provided that it is held on terms equivalent to the Standard Conditions terms as to the deposit;[6] this means that ultimately the deposit must be held by a solicitor as a stake-holder. A solicitor for a buyer must decide whether he is prepared to contract on the Standard Conditions unamended and therefore allow the seller to use the deposit in this way. If he is not prepared to do this, the condition will clearly need to be amended. Even if the buyer's solicitor is prepared to allow the seller's solicitor to use the deposit, he may well wish to take further steps for the buyer's protection such as to enquire about the ultimate destination of the deposit money. There may be problems if the purchase by the seller was completed before the buyer's own contract because on such completion the deposit would presumably be released to the seller further up the chain.

Furthermore, the buyer would actually want to know whether his deposit was being used by the seller or not; under the conditions as they stand the seller can simply use all or part of the deposit without notifying the buyer that this has been done. If the seller has used the deposit, it has presumably been held by the seller's solicitor as agent rather than stake-holder and, as we have seen, the buyer has a lien over the property in respect of it. If the buyer is not aware that the money has been used by the seller he will not be aware of having the lien and the consequent opportunity to register it to protect it.

It may be that in a chain of residential conveyancing transactions, with each seller using the deposit received on his sale to go towards the deposit on his own purchase, the end of the chain – the seller who is not also purchasing a property – is a builder selling a newly built or newly converted property. It may also be that the builder would wish its solicitor to hold the deposit as agent rather than stake-holder so that the money can be released to the builder immediately on exchange. This will necessitate an amendment to the Standard Conditions because under Standard Condition 2.2.3 the deposit is to be held by the seller's solicitor as stake-holder. However, such a situation will also necessitate amendments to all the other

---

4   SC 2.2.3.
5   SC 1.1.1(a).
6   Ie SC 2.2.2 and 2.2.3.

contracts in the chain, because under all those other contracts the sellers will only be allowed to use the deposit on their own purchases if it is held on terms equivalent to conditions 2.2.2 and 2.2.3, that is to say if it is ultimately held by a stake-holder. Condition 2.2.2 would therefore need to be amended in all the contracts in the chain.[7]

More generally, the buyer's solicitor needs to consider whether it is appropriate for the seller to receive interest on the deposit. This may seem particularly inequitable to a buyer who has had to borrow money for the deposit and who is therefore paying interest on the loan. In which circumstances might a buyer need to borrow money to raise the deposit? In a residential transaction, this would be a short-term loan repayable on completion rather than a long-term method of funding the purchase. If, for example, the buyer is a first time buyer obtaining a mortgage of 95% of the purchase price, this means that the buyer is only finding 5% of the purchase price from his own resources, but the 95% is not available until completion; a mortgagee will not normally release any part of the mortgage advance before completion. If the buyer has to pay a 10% deposit, he will need to borrow a further 5% on exchange, which he can then repay out of the mortgage advance on completion. Similarly if the buyer is selling his own property but for some reason the deposit he is receiving on the sale had to be held as stake-holder; he could not use it to put towards the deposit payable on his purchase and may have to borrow to raise the deposit, paying off the loan out of the proceeds of sale on completion.

It may be in such situations that the seller will agree to accept a deposit of less than 10%. If so the seller will want to be sure of recovering the full 10% if he is ever in a position to forfeit the deposit. This is achieved by Standard Condition 6.8.4 whereby if the seller serves a notice to complete[8] on the buyer, the buyer is forthwith to pay a further deposit equal to the balance of a 10% deposit. From the seller's point of view, it might be useful if this condition were amended to provide for interest to be payable if the buyer did not pay the sum due. From the buyer's point of view, he may wish to fix the deposit at, say, 5% and so amend Standard Condition 2.2.1 to show 5%, and delete Standard Condition 6.8.4.

Turning now to the consequences of non-payment of the deposit, Standard Condition 2.2.4 provides that if any cheque in payment of all or part of the deposit is dishonoured on first presentation, the seller may within seven working days of being notified that the cheque has been dishonoured, give notice to the buyer that the contract is discharged by the buyer's breach. The seller would presumably then have a right to damages for breach of contract.

It would be negligent not to advise the seller of the benefits of taking a deposit.[9] In residential conveyancing, as an alternative to actually paying a deposit, particularly for a buyer who is not readily able to pay on exchange the deposit required by the seller and who would therefore otherwise have to borrow the money on a bridging loan, there are deposit guarantee schemes available. On payment of a premium by the buyer, the insurer agrees to pay the specified deposit to the seller should the buyer fail to complete; the seller will naturally wish to ensure that in that situation the insurer will pay the deposit quickly. If the insurer does have to pay the deposit, he can recover it from the buyer. However, the deposit guarantee schemes are not generally available to first time buyers and in any case, are not frequently used in practice.

---

7 This is not the view put forward by the author of the article 'Your Questions Answered' in the TransAction bulletin produced in 1990.
8 Notices to complete are discussed in ch 16.
9 *Morris v Duke-Cohan & Co* (1975) 119 Sol Jo 826.

x   Exchange of contracts

If the contract is to be brought into existence by the conventional method of exchange, it is important to establish the precise moment at which such exchange takes place. If it occurs by personal exchange of contracts between the two solicitors there is no problem but there may be difficulties if as is common the exchange takes place through the post. Normally the buyer's part, plus deposit, is posted to the seller's solicitor who will in return post the seller's part back to the buyer's solicitor. In *Eccles v Bryant and Pollock*[10] it was held that exchange takes place not before the second part is posted. This is fairly obvious, but it was specifically not decided whether the exchange would be complete at the time of posting the second part or only on its receipt. The former would be the case if the normal contractual postal rule applied,[11] but this is unclear[12] and there are grounds for arguing that the contract should not come into existence until the second part is received by the buyer. If the contract came into existence at the time of posting of the second part and the buyer never in fact received it, he might find proof of compliance with section 2 of the Law of Property (Miscellaneous Provisions) Act 1989 awkward if he tried to enforce the contract against the seller. He would also be without an important document of title should he wish to sub-sell. However, the Standard Conditions provide that the contract shall be made when the last part is posted if exchange is by post, and when the last post is deposited at a document exchange if exchange of contracts is via a document exchange.[13]

As an alternative to the conventional method of exchange, the parties may agree over the telephone that the contract shall become immediately effective and that if the solicitors still hold the part of the contract signed by their own client, then this shall be held irrevocably to the order of the other party.[14] Exchange by telephone has become by far the most popular method over the past few years. The Standard Conditions contain provisions for such a procedure[15] but it will be dealt with in more detail when we look at the process of exchange of contracts in Chapter 8.

xi   Vacant possession

In the absence of any provision to the contrary – ie under an open contract – the seller is bound to give vacant possession on completion.[16] This presumption is probably rebuttable by for example the property not being vacant when inspected by the buyer, but the seller's solicitor ought to state quite clearly in the contract that vacant possession is not to be given if that is indeed the case. The Standard Conditions are silent on the question of vacant possession; the pre-printed Special Conditions on the contract form provide two alternatives,[17] for vacant possession or for a sale subject to tenancies, details of which are then given. Obviously one of the alternatives is deleted. It is not only tenancies which will amount to breaches of a term for vacant possession. In *Wroth v Tyler*[18] the

---

10   [1948] Ch 93, [1947] 2 All ER 865, CA.
11   See, for example, *Household Fire and Carriage Accident Insurance Co Ltd v Grant* (1879) 4 Ex D 216, CA.
12   See, for example, *Holwell Securities Ltd v Hughes* [1974] 1 All ER 161, [1974] 1 WLR 155, CA.
13   SC 2.1.1.
14   *Domb v Isoz* [1980] Ch 548, [1980] 1 All ER 942, CA. The Law Society has established formulae for solicitors intending to exchange in this way; see ch 8.
15   SC 2.1.2.
16   *Cook v Taylor* [1942] Ch 349, [1942] 2 All ER 85.
17   Special Condition 5.
18   [1974] Ch 30, [1973] 1 All ER 897.

breach was a class F land charge registered against the seller in respect of the statutory right of occupation of the seller's spouse.[19] In *Cumberland Consolidated Holdings Ltd v Ireland*[20] it was a large quantity of solidified cement in the basement of a warehouse, which formed a substantial interference with the enjoyment of a substantial part of the property. In *Topfell Ltd v Galley Properties Ltd*[1] there was held to be a breach when the seller of a two-storey property, the top floor of which was tenanted but the lower sold with vacant possession, did not disclose an order made by the Local Authority to the effect that the building could only be used to house one household. There already was one household on the top floor, meaning that the seller could not give vacant possession of the lower floor.

xii   State and condition of the property

We have already seen that the seller is under no duty to disclose physical defects in the property. The common law rule applicable to an open contract is 'caveat emptor'.[2] This is confirmed by the Standard Conditions, which provide that the buyer accepts the property in the physical state it is in on exchange of contracts save where it is constructed or converted by the seller.[3] In that case there may be liability under the Defective Premises Act 1972 and/or the National House Building Council Scheme,[4] or some other insurance scheme or indeed in negligence, the latter possibly even where the seller has himself made improvements and alterations and provided that the buyer shall buy with full notice of the actual state and condition of the property.[5] A Local Authority which negligently approves defective work will probably not be liable.[6]

The buyer would be well advised to have a professional survey made as part of his pre-contract enquiries.

If however the seller has deliberately concealed a physical defect, this may amount to a fraudulent misrepresentation that the property is not defective in that respect, and the seller may thus be liable. In *Gordon v Selico Co Ltd*,[7] the seller had covered up dry rot in the property, and was held liable to the buyer (in fact, an intending lessee).

xiii   Auction sales

At an auction the contract is made by the acceptance of the final bid. Nevertheless, despite the exception to section 2 of the Law of Property (Miscellaneous Provisions) Act 1989,[8] a written contract is normally prepared by the seller's solicitor in consultation with the auctioneer, and this is made available for inspection by a prospective buyer for some time before the actual auction – normally at least a week. It is then this contract that the

---

19 Family Law Act 1996.
20 [1946] KB 264, [1946] 1 All ER 284, CA. Compare *Hynes v Vaughan* (1985) 50 P & CR 444, where there were piles of rubbish on the property, but not enough to mean that the seller could not give vacant possession.
1 [1979] 2 All ER 388, [1979] 1 WLR 446.
2 See for example *Terrene Ltd v Nelson* [1937] 3 All ER 739.
3 SC 3.2.1.
4 See section xxi, below.
5 *Hone v Benson* (1978) 248 Estates Gazette 1013 but see *D & F Estates Ltd v Church Comrs for England* [1989] AC 177, [1988] 2 All ER 992, HL and *Murphy v Brentwood District Council* below.
6 See *Murphy v Brentwood District Council* [1991] 1 AC 398, [1990] 2 All ER 908, HL.
7 [1986] 1 EGLR 71.
8 See ch 4.

prospective buyers are offering to enter into by means of their bids. The contract is normally exchanged immediately after the auction. An auctioneer will hold a deposit as stake-holder in the absence of any agreement to the contrary.

The Sale of Land by Auction Act 1867 provides that the contract must:

(a)   state whether the property is sold without reserve or subject to any reserve price.[9] A reserve price is a price below which the property will not be sold (ie if the bidding does not reach the reserve price the seller can withdraw the property). The reserve price itself does not have to be disclosed;
(b)   state whether any right to bid is reserved. If so, then assuming the sale is subject to a reserve price the seller or any one other person may bid.[10]

The Standard Conditions provide that:[11]

(a)   the property is subject to a reserve price;
(b)   the seller reserves the right to bid up to the reserve price;
(c)   the auctioneer can refuse to accept a bid;
(d)   the auctioneer can resolve any dispute, or put the property up again at the last undisputed bid.[12]

A solicitor may have to advise the seller whether to sell by auction or in the more normal manner which is called a sale 'by private treaty'. At an auction the seller can be sure of obtaining the best price from those present, but if, as in domestic conveyancing, the seller is also buying a property there may be serious problems of synchronisation if he sells at auction and he may also be limiting the number of potential buyers, as not everyone will be in a position to attend an auction and enter a contract immediately. As a prospective buyer's solicitor will warn his client, there may be similar problems of synchronisation for the buyer if he is also selling a property. As the buyer at an auction is committing himself to pay the deposit immediately and the balance of the purchase price on the completion date, his financial arrangements including any mortgage must be finalised before the auction, and this may not be possible for some prospective buyers.

Auctions are more commonly used in commercial transactions or, in residential conveyancing, by persons other than the ordinary domestic house-owner, who may be under some sort of duty to obtain the best price available, for example a mortgagee exercising a power of sale or personal representatives selling property which forms part of the deceased's estate.

xiv   Fixtures, fittings and chattels

If an item is a fixture, then it will pass with the land without any express mention of it in the contract – for example, plants in the garden of a house. If the seller wishes to keep for himself any fixtures, some specific condition should be inserted in the contract excluding them from the sale. It is sometimes difficult to decide whether a particular item is a fixture or not – for example in a house, fitted cupboards, or the various fittings in a shop – and in such cases it is safer to put a special condition in the contract. The difficulties are illustrated by the case of

---

9   Sale of Land by Auction Act 1867, s 5.
10   Ibid, ss 5, 6.
11   SC 2.3.
12   The efficacy of such a term was confirmed in *Richards v Phillips* [1969] 1 Ch 39, [1968] 2 All ER 859, CA.

Hamp v Bygrave,[13] in which some garden ornaments were held to be chattels, but because the seller regarded them as included in the sale they were to be treated as fixtures – they were not mentioned in the contract.

Similarly if the seller is also selling chattels, such as curtains or carpets, or in a shop, the moveable display cabinets or even the till, which will not pass with the land automatically, the buyer will want these to be specifically mentioned in the conditions, and may also want the price to be apportioned between the property and the chattels to achieve a possible saving of stamp duty.[14] In *Dean v Andrews*,[15] a prefabricated greenhouse, bolted to a concrete plinth which then rested on its own weight, was held to be a chattel and the buyer who had refused to surrender it had to compensate the seller.

The Standard Conditions provide that, so far as chattels sold are concerned, the contract takes effect as a contract for the sale of goods whether or not a separate price is payable for the chattels.[16] This means that there will be an implied warranty by the seller that the chattels are his to sell.[17] There is also a provision that the buyer will only become owner of the chattels on actual completion, thus ensuring that he does not acquire the chattels before he acquires the property.[18] As a result the chattels are at the seller's risk until completion.

xv   Identity and boundaries

Conditions can be put in the contract covering the identity of the property and its boundaries. The Standard Conditions state that the seller shall not be required to prove the exact boundaries and that the seller is not bound to prove the ownership of boundary fences, hedges or walls nor to identify part of the property held under different titles further than he can do so from information in his possession.[19] However, the buyer may, if it is reasonable, require the seller to make or obtain a statutory declaration about these matters.[20]

Whilst it might be difficult to establish the exact boundaries and their ownership, the seller should be encouraged to make every effort to do so.[1] Many disputes between neighbours arise as a result of imprecise boundaries and uncertainty as to their ownership. Nevertheless the seller may wish to exclude the buyer's right to demand a statutory declaration under the Standard Conditions, which would mean that the buyer would have to address this issue before exchange of contracts.

xvi   Evidence of tenancies

In pursuance of the seller's duty of disclosure and the implication that vacant possession will be given, the contract may not only disclose the existence of any

---

13   (1982) 266 Estates Gazette 720.
14   Such an apportionment must be genuine, and not amount to a fraud on the Inland Revenue, otherwise the whole contract could be void for illegality: *Saunders v Edwards* [1987] 2 All ER 651, [1987] 1 WLR 1116, CA. In addition, the solicitor must take care not to be deemed a party to such fraud.
15   (1985) 135 NLJ 728.
16   SC 9.2.
17   Sale of Goods Act 1979.
18   SC 9.3.
19   SC 4.3.1.
20   SC 4.3.2.
 1   See *Scarfe v Adams* [1981] 1 All ER 843, CA.

tenancies of the property, but also stipulate the evidence of them which the buyer will receive. It is probably more likely that a commercial property will be sold subject to existing tenancies rather than a residential property.

Under Standard Condition 3.3.2 the seller has to provide the buyer with full details of each tenancy, or copies of the documents embodying the terms of the tenancy. Condition 3.3.2 contains a number of other provisions. The seller is to inform the buyer without delay if the lease ends, or if the seller learns of any application by the tenant in connection with the lease. The seller is then to act as the buyer reasonably directs with the buyer indemnifying the seller against all consequence, loss and expense.[2] The reference to any application by the tenant in connection with the lease will include in a commercial context an application by a tenant for a new lease under the provisions of the Landlord and Tenant Act 1954, Part II (dealt with in Chapter 20). However, if such an application is anticipated or ongoing, more detailed provisions may be needed in the contract to cover the situation.

Under 3.3.2 the seller is not to agree to any proposal to change the lease terms without the consent of the buyer, and is to inform the buyer without delay of any change which may be proposed or agreed. It is not clear whether this provision would cover a review of the rent under the terms of a rent review in the lease, but it certainly would not cover determination of the rent review by an arbitrator or an independent expert; this is not a situation where the seller will 'agree' the rent. Again if there is an anticipated or ongoing rent review under the lease subject to which the property is being sold, a more detailed special condition may be necessary.

Condition 3.3.2 also provides that the buyer is to indemnify the seller against all claims arising from the lease after actual completion. If this is to be interpreted as referring only to claims made after completion where the cause of action arose after completion, a seller may wish to amend by special condition to provide for an indemnity whenever the cause of action arose.

In appropriate circumstances further provisions will need to be made in the contract for the sale of tenanted property, over and above those in Standard Condition 3.3.2. Thus the question of arrears of rent at completion may need to be specifically addressed as, in the absence of any provision to the contrary, the right to sue for arrears will probably pass to the buyer on completion. If the seller as landlord is providing certain services to the tenant and is able to recover the cost of these under a service charge, there may need to be a condition in the contract whereby the seller agrees to provide the necessary documentation to substantiate the cost of services provided prior to completion but to be accounted for to the tenant after completion. (Service charges are explained in more detail in Chapter 17.)

xvii   Title

The question of the title which will be deduced to the buyer following exchange of contracts is of fundamental importance. We must deal in turn with freehold and leasehold property, both unregistered and registered.

I   *Sale of freehold, the title to which is not registered*

We have seen in Chapters 1 and 3 that title is deduced by providing the buyer with an abstract or epitome of recent dealings under which the property has changed hands: a history of the property, including not only sales but also, for example, the

---

2   SC 3.3.2(b).

death of a joint tenant or the grant of probate to the estate of a deceased owner. How far back should this history go, or in other words what is to be the length of the title? With what sort of deed or other document must it start? Statute provides a partial answer, and the open contract rule. The Law of Property Act 1925, section 44(1) as amended by the Law of Property Act 1969 provides that the buyer can require the title to be deduced for at least the last 15 years; thus the instrument with which the abstract starts, or the root of title as it is called, must be *at least 15 years old at the date of the contract*. Under an open contract the root must also be a 'good root'; there is no statutory definition of this but the common law definition[3] is an instrument which:

(a) deals with or shows title to the whole legal and equitable interest contracted to be sold (although the equitable interests need not be dealt with if they are over-reached, eg on a sale by trustees of land);
(b) contains an adequate description of the property (in theory, the description should probably not refer to a description or plan in an earlier deed, but in practice such roots are often accepted and the earlier deed also abstracted);
(c) contains nothing to cast any doubt on the title.

Adopting this definition, the best root will be a conveyance on sale and this is certainly the most common root in practice. However, a voluntary conveyance (ie deed of gift) can also be a good root as can an assent by personal representatives, and it seems to be accepted in practice that a post-1925 mortgage can be a good root even though in theory it should not be, not dealing with the whole of the legal estate. A post-1925 will, on the other hand, cannot be a good root.

After the root, all dealings and other events affecting the property must be deduced and an unbroken chain of ownership shown, culminating in the seller.[4]

The root is normally specified in the conditions;[5] if not, the open contract rules apply and a good root at least 15 years old must be shown. The Standard Conditions do not contain any alteration of the open contract position.[6]

There is nothing to prevent the parties agreeing in the conditions on a root less than the statutory 15 years old, although in *Re Marsh and Earl Granville*[7] it was held that the nature of the root must then be clearly stated. In that case, it was not made sufficiently clear in the contract that the root was a voluntary conveyance and the court refused to award the seller a decree of specific performance. There are serious disadvantages for the buyer in accepting a title of less than the statutory 15 years, for the buyer will be taken to have constructive notice of all equitable interests of which he would have had notice had he insisted on a full statutory title.[8] This can best be illustrated by reference to an example:

1920 – Conveyance on sale A to B imposing restrictive covenants
1950 – Conveyance on sale B to C stated to be subject to the restrictive covenants
1984 – Conveyance on sale C to D but with no mention of the restrictive covenants (the conveyance would of course have mentioned the covenants if it had been properly drafted)
2001 – Contract on sale D to E specifying the 1984 conveyance as the root of title and again not mentioning the restrictive covenants

3   Taken from *Williams on Vendor and Purchaser* (4th edn) p 124.
4   Or someone whom the seller can compel to convey — see ch 9, section 1, below.
5   There is provision for this on the front page of the Standard Contract form.
6   SC 4.2.1.
7   (1882) 24 Ch D 11.
8   *Re Nisbet and Pott's Contract* [1906] 1 Ch 386, CA.

The root satisfies the statutory 15 year rule; it is over 15 years old at the date of contract. The enforceability of covenants created before 1926 depends on the equitable doctrine of notice. E will not, it would appear, have notice of the covenants if they have not been disclosed in the contract as they will not be discovered on an examination of the title starting with the root in 1984. The covenants will not be enforceable against E.[9]

If in the above example the conveyance from C to D had been in 1990 rather than 1984, but still specified in the contract as the root, then it would not satisfy the statutory requirement being only eleven years old at the date of the contract. Again E will not have actual notice of the covenants, but had he insisted on a statutory title, the root would have been the 1950 conveyance – the most recent conveyance over 15 years old at the date of the contract – and he would have had notice of the covenants as they are mentioned in the 1950 conveyance. In accepting the short title, he is taken to have constructive notice of the covenants and they will be enforceable against him.

A similar rule applies to interests which depend for their enforceability on registration as land charges, for example post-1925 restrictive covenants. If in the example above the conveyance creating the restrictive covenants had been in 1930 rather than 1920, we would have:

1930 –   Conveyance A to B imposing restrictive covenants, which are then protected by registration against B's name
1950 –   Conveyance B to C stated to be subject to the covenants
1984 –   Conveyance C to D with no mention of the covenants
2001 –   Contract D to E specifying the 1984 conveyance as the root and again not mentioning the covenants

Again, the root satisfies the statutory 15 year requirement. E will have no actual knowledge of the covenants[10] and will not discover their existence when he does a land charges search before completion. He will not search against B's name, against which the covenants are registered, because the title deduced to him does not include B's name. He will none the less be bound by the covenants because they are registered. He will be entitled to receive compensation under the Law of Property Act 1969, section 25.[11] If in the example we again assume that the conveyance from C to D was in 1990 rather than 1984, and specified as the root, then as before if E had insisted on his statutory entitlement, the root would have been the 1950 conveyance. In that case E would have discovered the existence of the covenants, both because the 1950 conveyance mentions them and because B's name is now included in the title, and a land charges search could be made against him which will reveal the registration of the covenants. E will therefore not be entitled to compensation under section 25.

2   Grant of a lease out of an unregistered title[12]

The open contract position can be summarised as follows:

(a)   On the grant of a headlease (ie a lease granted out of the freehold) the lessee is not entitled to have the freehold title deduced at all.

---

9   Or his successors in title, *Wilkes v Spooner* [1911] 2 KB 473, CA.
10   The covenants should have been disclosed by the seller as they will be binding on the buyer in any event.
11   See ch 16, below; he may also have a claim against the seller for breach of the duty of disclosure. Land charges searches are considered in detail in ch 11, below.
12   See further in ch 17, below.

(b) On the grant of an underlease (ie granted not out of the freehold but out of another (superior) leasehold), the underlessee is entitled to have deduced the lease out of which his underlease is being granted (ie the underlessor's lease) and also an abstract or epitome of title to that lease going back at least 15 years (but not going back before the date it was granted).[13] In other words, the abstract will start with the lease out of which the underlease is being granted and will then show a chain of ownership of that leasehold estate – the series of assignments of the lease, grants of probate, assents etc – culminating in the present under lessor, but with the proviso that because of the operation of the 15 year rule, if the under lessor's lease was granted more than 15 years before the date of the contract, there may be a gap in the abstract between that lease and the most recent disposition that is at least 15 years old at the date of the contract. The 15 year rule is really the same rule that applies on the sale of a freehold.

The underlessee does not get any other superior title deduced; for example the freehold title is not deduced.

It is in the interests of a lessee to be able to investigate all the superior titles and in particular the freehold title. This may have been subject to some adverse interest such as an easement or covenant to which the lessee will also be subject, although he will not be able to discover its existence.[14] If the adverse interest is registered as a land charge, then neither will the lessee be able to claim compensation under the Law of Property Act 1969, section 25, because the section does not apply to this situation.

Similarly if he cannot examine the superior title, the lessee cannot discover whether any superior leases and in particular the headlease were validly granted or not (for example, the requisite consent of a mortgagee to the grant of a lease may not have been obtained). Further, on first registration, only good leasehold title would be registered rather than absolute leasehold.

Whether the lessee will attempt to have a condition inserted in the contract to the effect that the freehold and other superior titles should be deduced probably depends on the nature and length of the lease. If a buyer/lessee is buying a new house on a building estate, or a flat in a newly built or converted block, the developer may as we have already seen grant a long lease of the individual flat or house rather than sell the freehold. The transaction will proceed on normal conveyancing lines with a contract followed by the grant of the lease, and the purchase price (which is in effect a premium on the grant of the lease) will be more or less the same as would be paid were the freehold being sold. The buyer/lessee would be unwise to part with his money without being satisfied that the developer had a good title. If the buyer were financing his transaction by means of a mortgage, then a Building Society or a bank would be unlikely to lend unless the freehold title and any superior leasehold title were deduced, so that they could ensure that the property was good security for the loan.

The Standard Conditions do amend the open contract position. Condition 8.2.4 provides that the seller is to deduce a title, on the grant of a headlease or an underlease for a term in excess of 21 years, which will enable the buyer to register the lease at the Land Registry with absolute leasehold title. As we have already seen in Chapter 2, for the buyer to obtain an absolute leasehold title for his new lease, he must be able to deduce the freehold and any superior leasehold titles. Thus the Standard Conditions

13 Law of Property Act 1925, s 44(1), (2), (4).
14 See for example *White v Bijou Mansions Ltd* [1937] Ch 610, [1937] 3 All ER 269.

oblige a lessor to deduce the freehold and any superior leasehold title where the new lease will be for a term in excess of 21 years. If the seller/lessor is unable or unwilling to do this, condition 8.2.4 will need to be amended. This does represent a major change to the open contract rule.

3   Assignment on sale of a lease, the title to which is not registered

The open contract rule is really the same as that applicable on the grant of an underlease – rule (b) above. The buyer (assignee) is entitled to have deduced the lease that he is buying together with an abstract or epitome of title to it going back at least 15 years (but again not going back before the date of grant of the lease).[15] This rule applies whether the lease is a headlease or an underlease, but the buyer cannot investigate the superior title, leasehold or freehold, and therefore is faced with the same problem as has been outlined in the previous section.

Let us look at some examples of the operation of the statutory open contract rules contained in this and the previous section.

1951 – 99 year headlease granted out of the freehold by F to L
1961 – Assignment on sale of the headlease by L to A
1971 – Underlease granted by A to B
1981 – Assignment on sale of the underlease by B to C
1991 – Sub-underlease granted by C to D
2001 – Assignment on sale of the sub-underlease by D to E

To represent this diagrammatically:

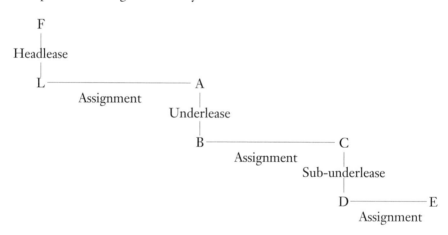

Under an open contract the various buyers would have been entitled as follows:

L in 1951 – Nothing
A in 1961 – Headlease F to L
B in 1971 – Headlease F to L, assignment L to A
C in 1981 – Underlease A to B
D in 1991 – Underlease A to B, assignment B to C
E in 2001 – Sub-underlease C to D

To give a further example of the rule applying to an assignment, or to the grant of an underlease:

15   Law of Property Act 1925, s 44(1), (3).

1940 – 99 year headlease granted out of the freehold by F to L
1950 – Assignment on sale L to A
1960 – Assignment on sale A to B
1970 – Assignment on sale B to C
1980 – Assignment on sale C to D
1990 – Assignment on sale D to E
2001 – Underlease E to G

Diagrammatically:

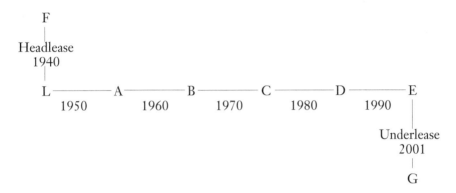

Title deduced under an open contract[16] to:

L in 1940 – Nothing
A in 1950 – Headlease F to L
B in 1960 – Headlease F to L, assignment L to A
C in 1970 – Headlease F to L, assignments L to A, A to B
D in 1980 – Headlease F to L, assignments A to B, B to C
E in 1990 – Headlease F to L, assignments B to C, C to D
G in 2001 – Headlease F to L, assignments C to D, D to E

An assignment of a lease will be a fairly common transaction in domestic conveyancing field – once there has been a long lease of a house or flat of the kind mentioned in the previous section, every sale of it will of course be an assignment of the lease. Similarly, a lease of commercial premises may also be sold and assigned. In such circumstances a buyer/assignee will want to examine the freehold and any superior leasehold titles (for exactly the same reason that we have seen that a lessee will want to examine the freehold and superior titles), which as we have seen he is not entitled to do under the open contract rule. However, the Standard Conditions make no amendment to the open contract provision although the first edition of the Standard Conditions and the Law Society Conditions which they replaced did improve the position from the buyer's point of view. The buyer's solicitor, and the buyer's mortgagee's solicitor, will have to consider whether the position is acceptable to the buyer. Particularly if the lease was granted a relatively short time ago, the buyer should be advised to insist on the seller deducing the freehold and other superior leasehold titles. A seller will be unable to comply if he does not himself have the necessary evidence of the freehold or superior leasehold title. The seller will in practice only

16 Assuming for the sake of the illustration that the current rules had been in operation since 1925.

have evidence of the freehold title if on the grant of the lease, the freehold title was deduced and an abstract or epitome of the freehold title supplied to the original lessee. This abstract or epitome would then be handed on to successive buyers of the leasehold interest.

Even if a seller does have evidence of the freehold or superior leasehold title, he may not be in a position to deal with any requisitions on the title. The contract might therefore provide that the abstract or epitome of the freehold and/or superior leasehold, accompanying the draft contract, would be supplied to the buyer, but that the buyer should accept it and not have any right to object or raise requisitions on it.

4   Sale of freehold, the title to which is registered

The Land Registration Act 1925, section 110 provides the open contract rule, that on a sale or other disposition to a buyer of registered land (not including a lease or a mortgage or charge but including for example a sale of part):

(a)   Under section 110(1), the seller shall provide the buyer with copies of the subsisting register entries and filed plan and copies of any documents noted on the register as affecting the land (for example a deed containing a schedule of restrictive covenants).[17] The seller cannot contract out of this obligation and must bear the cost unless the purchase price is £1,000 or under in which case the cost is borne by the buyer in the absence of anything to the contrary in the contract.

The Standard Conditions are a little more generous to the buyer, providing that all copies shall be office copies.[18]

(b)   Under section 110(2), the seller shall at his own expense supply the buyer with the necessary evidence of rights and interests as to which the register is not conclusive[19] and of any other matters excepted from the effect of registration,[20] to the extent that the buyer would have been entitled were title to the property not registered. This obligation is reiterated in SC 4.2.1 but could be amended by special condition.

5   The grant of a lease out of a registered title

If the lease to be granted is a headlease, ie is to be granted out of a registered freehold, the Land Registration Act 1925 does not affect the general principle that the lessee is not entitled to examine the lessor's title under an open contract. The position is the same as under section 2 above; the lessee gets nothing and section 110 of the Land Registration Act 1925 expressly does not apply. If the lessee does want to examine the lessor's title and to be provided with office copies of the register entries then he must negotiate for the inclusion of a condition to this effect in the contract.

If the lease to be granted is an underlease, ie to be granted out of a lease the title to which is registered, then the position is not so straightforward. We have seen that

---

17   Until December 1990 the register was private and s 110 therefore also provides that an authority to inspect the register, which the buyer will need for his pre-completion search, is to be supplied. However, since December 1990 the register has been open to public inspection and no authority to inspect is necessary.

18   SC 4.2.1. This type of condition will not fall foul of s 110(3) which provides that 'it shall not be necessary for the vendor to furnish ... any ... other ... evidence of title ...'; *Wood v Berkeley Homes (Sussex) Ltd* (1992) 64 P & CR 311, CA.

19   Including rights existing for the benefit of the land as well as adverse rights such as overriding interests.

20   For example under a qualified or possessory title.

in relation to unregistered land, the under lessee is entitled to examine the under lessor's title, commencing with the under lessor's own lease. So it might be expected that in respect of registered land, the under lessee would be entitled under section 110 to details of the underlessor's title and if so, the position would be similar to that prevailing on the assignment of a registered lease discussed in the next section. However, section 110 itself states that it does not apply to a 'lessee' and in the Act 'lease' is defined to include 'underlease',[1] so section 110 may not apply. On the other hand section 110 does apply to a 'disposition', an expression which would otherwise include an underlease.[2] On the basis that section 110 on the above analysis is somewhat ambiguous, the conveyancer would be well advised to include a condition in the contract stating exactly what title is to be deduced.

Even if a lessee or under lessee cannot investigate the superior title or titles, if the latter are registered he may still be granted an absolute leasehold title as the superior titles may be examined internally by the Registry.

Standard Condition 8.2.4, which we considered in section 2, is also applicable to the grant of a lease out of a registered title. As we saw in section 2, under 8.2.4 if the term of the new lease exceeds 21 years the seller/lessor must deduce a title which will enable the buyer/lessee to register the lease at the Land Registry with absolute title. If the seller's title is registered with absolute title, freehold or leasehold, then 8.2.4 presents no real problem and the seller will simply deduce his title in the normal way under section 110 of the Land Registration Act 1925. If, however, the seller has a title less than absolute, or a good leasehold title, then on the face of it he cannot comply with 8.2.4 and a special condition would have to be inserted in the contract to amend 8.2.4.

6   Assignment on sale of a lease the title to which is registered

This is a disposition to which the Land Registration Act 1925, section 110 does apply and therefore the position is the same as for a registered freehold title discussed under heading 4 above, with the difference that the vendor must also supply, as in unregistered conveyancing, a copy or abstract of the lease being sold; the lease does not form part of the register. The Act makes no difference to the position regarding the superior title; in other words under an open contract the buyer is not entitled to examine it. For the reasons already mentioned above, the buyer's solicitor may wish to insert a condition in the contract providing for the superior title to be deduced, although if the leasehold interest being sold is registered with absolute leasehold title there is no need for this. However, if the buyer is buying a good leasehold title then he is subject to the same uncertainties concerning the validity of the grant of the lease and the existence of adverse interests affecting the superior title as have already been mentioned in relation to unregistered leases, and the buyer (and his mortgagee) would want the freehold and any superior leasehold title to be deduced. As with an unregistered title the seller may be in no position to comply.

7   Production of Land Certificate

Difficulties can arise on the grant of a lease out of a registered title because unless the lease is granted at a rent without a fine, the Land Certificate must accompany the application for registration of the lease.[3] The lessor is apparently under no obligation

---

1   Land Registration Act 1925, s 3(x).
2   Ibid, s 21(5).
3   Land Registration Act 1925, s 64; *Strand Securities Ltd v Caswell* [1965] Ch 958, [1965] 1 All ER 820, CA.

to make the Land Certificate available and in such a situation the solicitor for the buyer/lessee should negotiate for the inclusion in the contract of a condition providing that the seller/lessor will make the Certificate available for production.

xviii   Lost deeds

Where title deeds to unregistered land have been lost, the open contract rule is that the seller must produce secondary evidence – by means of statutory declarations, copies, drafts etc – of the contents and execution of the lost deeds and the circumstances surrounding their loss.[4] In such a situation the seller's solicitor will normally insert a special condition in the contract stating exactly what proof of title will be provided. If all the deeds have been lost, the seller's solicitor may state in the contract that a statutory declaration of undisturbed possession for a particular period of time will be supplied, showing what is in effect a possessory title.[5]

Standard Condition 4.2.3 provides that where title is unregistered, the seller must produce either the original of every relevant document or an abstract, epitome or copy marked as examined either against the original or against an examined abstract or copy.[6] If the seller is unable to do this, either because some deeds have been lost or because abstracts, epitomes or copies do not bear the appropriate marking, a special condition will be needed to amend 4.2.3.

xix   Completion

Under an open contract, completion must take place within a reasonable time.[7] Standard Condition 6.1.1 provides that the completion date is 20 working days after the date of the contract. By condition 6.2, completion is to take place in England and Wales, either at the seller's solicitor's office or at some other place which the seller reasonably specifies. The time of day before which completion must take place is also stated. Condition 6.1.2 provides that if the money due on completion is received after 2pm, completion is to be treated as taking place on the next working day for purposes of calculating any apportionments of income and outgoings payable on the property and rather more importantly for the purpose of calculating compensation for late completion under condition 7.3.[8] The corresponding obligation on the seller under condition 6.1.3 is to vacate the property by 2 pm; if the seller does not do so, condition 6.1.2 does not apply and completion is not deemed to have taken place on the next working day. The reason for a time for completion being stated is primarily to allow the seller's solicitor to bank the completion money before the banks shut. If a client is both buying and selling, as in many domestic conveyancing transactions, it may be prudent to bring the time for completion in the sale contract forward so as to ensure that the sale proceeds are received in time for them to be used on completion of the purchase.

The Standard Conditions also contain provision for the means of payment of the money on completion. The open contract rule is probably that payment must be made by legal tender, although the conventional procedure is for payment to be made by a banker's draft. Under Standard Condition 6.7, payment must be made by either:

---

4   *Re Halifax Commercial Banking Co Ltd and Wood* (1898) 79 LT 536, CA.
5   See for example *George Wimpey & Co Ltd v Sohn* [1967] Ch 487, [1966] 1 All ER 232, CA.
6   The marking of documents as examined against originals is considered in ch 14, section 3ii.
7   *Johnson v Humphrey* [1946] 1 All ER 460; see also *Dean v Upton* [1990] EGCS 61, CA.
8   Compensation for late completion is dealt with in ch 16.

(a) legal tender;
(b) by a banker's draft drawn on a clearing bank, which is defined as a bank which is a member of the Clearing House Automated Payments System;[9]
(c) a direct credit to a bank account nominated by the seller's solicitor – this would cover the conventional method of paying the purchase price, apart from by a banker's draft, which is for the buyer's solicitor's bank to transfer the money directly into the client account of the seller's solicitor's bank;[10]
(d) an unconditional release of a stake-holder deposit.

The completion date will in fact normally be specified in a special condition,[11] thus overriding the general condition, and may only be fixed immediately before exchange. If the completion date is written in after exchange, then the alteration ought to be initialled by the parties, which would be inconvenient. There is some authority for saying that insertion of a completion date is merely an administrative matter and will not affect the validity of the contract.[12]

If a client is both selling and purchasing, then unless he is not dependent on the sale proceeds to provide part of the purchase money, or can lodge elsewhere and store his furniture, the two transactions will have to be completed on the same day.

The date for completion will not normally be taken as being of the essence of the contract, unless the property is of a particular character such as the sale of a public house as a going concern.[13] In the normal domestic conveyancing transaction it would be intolerable for time to be of the essence of completion[14] as there are a number of reasons why completion may be delayed for a day or two or even longer, particularly where completion of a purchase is dependent on the sale of another property. The contract will however provide for the rights of the parties when there is delay in completion and for service of a notice to complete to make time of the essence.[15]

On the purchase of a new property which is in the course of being built, it is unlikely that the seller/builder will agree to a specific completion date being inserted in the contract, as there are a number of factors which could delay the building of the property which would be outside the immediate control of the builder. In such a contract there will normally be a condition that the builder will finish the property with reasonable expedition and that the buyer will then complete within a particular period, say one or two weeks, of being notified that the property is finished. This period will allow both the buyer and his prospective mortgagee to inspect the property and make arrangements for completion.

---

9   SC 1.1.1(b).
10   The payment of the purchase money on completion is considered further in ch 14.
11   There is space for the insertion of a completion date on the front page of the Standard Contract form.
12   *Smith v Mansi* [1962] 3 All ER 857 at 865, CA per Russell LJ; approved by Lord Denning MR in *Storer v Manchester City Council* [1974] 1 WLR 1403 at 1408, CA; the repeal of s 40 of the Law of Property Act 1925 and its substitution by s 2 of the Law of Property (Miscellaneous Provisions) Act 1989 may have affected the position. Neither will a special condition for completion, included in the contract form and neither deleted nor completed on exchange, but left blank, override the general condition so as to leave either an open or even an unconcluded contract (ibid). In *Walters v Roberts* (1980) 258 Estates Gazette 965 the parties left the completion date to be agreed in the future; it was held that in the absence of such agreement, there was an implied term that completion would take place as under an open contract, within a reasonable time.
13   *Lock v Bell* [1931] 1 Ch 35.
14   SC 6.1 provides that time is not of the essence.
15   See ch 16, below.

xx   Other common general conditions

There are a number of other matters commonly dealt with by conditions, and on which the Standard Conditions do make provision. These include insurance and the risk of damage to the property; the time for delivery of the abstract and requisitions; additional rights of rescission and restrictions on other remedies such as those for misdescription and misrepresentation; the position where the buyer is given possession before completion; the content of the purchase deed; the apportionment of outgoings; and the rights of the parties if completion is delayed including the payment of interest. These matters will be dealt with at the appropriate stage of the examination of the conveyancing transaction in subsequent chapters.

The seller's solicitor should not lose sight of the need to amend or delete general conditions, as the occasion demands. This has already been mentioned in relation to areas such as the grant and reservation of easements on a sale of part, the seller's capacity and the completion date. The seller's solicitor should consider whether other amendments are necessary; achieved by an appropriately worded special condition as discussed in section xxi.

Finally, it is worth noting the comment on general conditions in *Lyme Valley Squash Club Ltd v Newcastle under Lyme Borough Council*[16] that where a general condition was included (dealing with the grant of easements on the sale of part; an old Law Society Condition) and 'no one gave it a thought', then it was right to go behind the condition; indeed the outcome of the case was that the plaintiffs did have a right to light which would have been expressly excluded had the condition been allowed to operate. This attitude does seem to undermine some of the purpose of having an all-embracing set of general conditions, but the implication, that the solicitor should be aware of the effect of the general conditions in a particular case, is clear.

xxi   Other special conditions

No discussion of special conditions can be exhaustive as by definition they are peculiar to a particular transaction. For example, in a mining area there may be a condition that the seller will assign to the buyer the benefit of any right to claim compensation for damage caused by subsidence. It is part of the seller's solicitor's job to advise his client on appropriate conditions, both in the sense of matters to be included in the deed such as the imposition of new easements and covenants, and conditions regulating the conduct of the sale. By way of an example we will look briefly at one quite common transaction, the sale by a builder of a new house on an estate, or flat in a new block of flats.

If the seller owns the freehold, the initial decision must be whether he will be selling the freehold of the individual units or granting long leases. If the seller himself owns a leasehold interest he could assign the lease in respect of each unit but it would be far simpler to grant underleases. In addition to advantages in respect of the enforceability of covenants, a leasehold scheme does bring in some income to the seller in the form of rent.[17]

The contract for sale will have to contain a fresh description of the property, probably by reference to an estate plan. The latter can also be deposited with the Local Authority and the District Land Registry if title is registered, to simplify the task of making searches. There will be provision for the grant and reservation of easements

---

16   [1985] 2 All ER 405 at 411, 412.
17   See further in ch 17. A mortgagee may be reluctant to lend on the security of a freehold, as opposed to leasehold, flat.

including rights of drainage, passage of cables and common rights of way such as shared pathways. There may be a quite lengthy list of covenants with the object of preserving the character of the development, and in the case of flats there will be some provision for the maintenance of any common parts such as stairs and gardens, and for payment of a service charge to meet the cost of such maintenance. Rather than include all these provisions separately in the contract it may be easier to draft a model form of conveyance (or transfer or lease) and provide in the contract that the deed shall be in that form. If the title is registered, the model can be submitted to the Registry in advance for approval. Instead of a filed plan, which may be large, the seller may instead supply a Form 102 which certifies that the buyer's plot is comprised in the seller's title.

If the house or flat has not yet been built, there will be a condition in the contract – or a separate contract – regulating this. The builder may agree to erect the property 'in a workmanlike manner'[18] according to a specification. The property will also normally have the benefit of the NHBC (National Housing Building Council) scheme; it is highly unlikely that a mortgagee will lend money on the security of a new property which does not have the benefit of the NHBC scheme.[19] Briefly, the builder – who must be registered with the NHBC under the NHBC scheme – agrees to build the property in a workmanlike manner in accordance with the NHBC standards, and remedy defects appearing within two years. There is also a standard insurance policy under which the NHBC protects the buyer against the builder's bankruptcy or other breach by the builder of his obligations to remedy defects, and also provides a ten-year guarantee in respect of major structural defects. There are some exclusions and limitations but in practice the scheme costs the buyer nothing.[20] The main documents involved are an offer of cover; an acceptance form which should be signed by the buyer and returned to NHBC immediately after exchange; a notice of cover; and the booklet explaining the extent of the cover. In recent years, some insurance companies have started to offer policies providing similar benefits to those under the NHBC scheme. If offered such a policy as an alternative to NHBC cover, the conveyancer should check its terms carefully and take instructions from the buyer's mortgagee where appropriate.

The contract must make quite clear what is included in respect of decoration, fitted units, paths, boundary walls and similar matters. The time for completion will probably be fixed by reference to the finishing of the work rather than any specific date.

The builder's solicitor must also consider whether he should ask the buyer to make 'stage' payments at various times before the property is actually finished. This will benefit the builder's cash flow position although the buyer may find it financially awkward, even with a co-operative mortgagee.

The purpose of a special condition may be to override one of the general conditions such as the Standard Conditions. Care must be taken to ensure that any special condition inserted in the contract does not raise doubts about the construction of the contract due to some inconsistency between the special condition and the general condition. In *Balabel v Mehmet*[1] a contract subject to National Conditions of Sale incorporated a special condition allowing the purchaser into occupation before completion on certain terms. The position of a purchaser in occupation before completion was also covered in the National Conditions and the inconsistency between the relevant National

---

18 This will be implied; *Hancock v B W Brazier (Anerley) Ltd* [1966] 2 All ER 901, [1966] 1 WLR 1317, CA.
19 The NHBC scheme was re-launched in 1988 under the name 'Buildmark'. There is also a similar scheme called 'Foundation 15'. The pre-1988 NHBC scheme involved slightly different documentation to the Buildmark scheme.
20 The NHBC produces literature on the scheme both for solicitors and buyers.
 1 [1990] 1 EGLR 220, CA.

Condition and the special condition created major problems of construction. For example, one of the questions which the Court of Appeal had to decide was whether the provision for termination of the purchaser's licence to occupy, by the purchaser being given a certain number of days' notice by the vendor, a provision contained in the National Conditions, was applicable to the purchaser's occupation under the special condition, which on the face of it required the purchaser vacate on the expiry of a stipulated period of time from exchange of contracts.

Similarly in *Newberry v Turngiant Ltd*[2] the contract was subject to Law Society Conditions of Sale so far as 'not inconsistent' with the actual terms of contract. Law Society Condition 22 provided for the payment of compensation for late completion; compensation was payable by the party in default in certain circumstances. Compensation could be calculated at interest on the purchase money for the period of delay. Clause 8 of the actual contract provided that if completion did not take place on the contractual completion date the purchaser should pay interest. There was thus some inconsistency between the circumstances in which interest was payable under Law Society Condition 22 and the circumstances in which interest was payable under clause 8 of the contract. The purchaser was actually claiming that the delay was the vendor's fault and the purchaser was claiming compensation under Law Society Condition 22. However, the Court of Appeal decided that the purchaser's claim failed; Condition 22 was inconsistent with clause 8 and was therefore not incorporated into the contract, meaning of course that the purchaser could not claim compensation under it.

xxii   Void conditions

In dealing with the contents of a contract, it should be mentioned that there are some conditions considered so unfair to a buyer that even if the seller includes them in the draft contract and they are not removed at the buyer's request, they will be void. The most important are:

(a)   a condition precluding the buyer from objecting to the lack of or insufficient stamping on a document forming part of the title, or providing that the buyer is to pay for the proper stamping of such a document;[3]
(b)   a condition precluding the buyer from examining a power of attorney under which a document of title has been executed;[4]
(c)   a condition restricting the buyer in his choice of solicitor or providing that the conveyance will be prepared by the seller's solicitor at the buyer's expense;[5]
(d)   a condition that the buyer shall accept title made by the concurrence of the persons entitled to equitable interests, if title can be made discharged from those interests by them being over-reached, for example on a trust of land, trust for sale or Settled Land Act 1925 settlement.[6]

5   COMMUNICATION WITH THE SELLER

It will be obvious that the seller's solicitor will need a good deal of information from his client in the early stages of the transaction. Matters such as the whereabouts of

2   (1991) 63 P & CR 458, CA.
3   Stamp Act 1891, s 117.
4   Law of Property Act 1925, s 125(2).
5   Ibid, s 48.
6   Ibid, s 42(1).

the deeds and, if the property is mortgaged, the mortgagee's reference number so that the deeds can be requested; the easements to be granted and reserved on a sale of part; the name of the seller's estate agent; details of the buyer and the price agreed; any fixtures to be retained or chattels to be sold; the anticipated completion date; these are just some of the matters dealt with in this chapter.

In addition the solicitor should confirm with the seller the financial basis of the transaction. If the property is in mortgage, he will need to know the amount owing on the mortgage and indeed on any second mortgages; this information can be obtained from the mortgagees if necessary. The existence of second mortgages will be revealed on a proper investigation of title, even if the seller omits to mention them. In unregistered conveyancing they will be protected as land charges and in registered conveyancing there will be some mention of them on the register.

The solicitor will need to know whether the seller plans to purchase another property and if so whether the two transactions must be co-ordinated. He will also have to advise the seller on any liability to capital gains tax or any other relevant tax. In practice capital gains tax is rarely payable in domestic conveyancing because of the exemption which applies to the sale of a dwelling house which is the seller's main or only residence. If the seller owns more than one house, he can elect which is his main residence. The exemption covers the grounds of the dwelling house up to half a hectare and also a separate disposal of part of the grounds provided it takes place prior to the sale of the dwelling house.[7] The exemption still applies for up to three years after the seller has ceased to reside in the property. If part of the property has been used exclusively for business, the exemption will not apply to part of the gain.

Although most of these matters can be covered in the initial interview between the solicitor and his client, the solicitor should never lose sight of his fundamental obligation to keep his client fully informed at all times.

6   PROCEDURE

The contract will be drafted in duplicate and both copies sent to the buyer's solicitor for approval. The draft forms a basis for negotiation between the parties. The particulars or conditions may make reference to earlier deeds or in the case of a registered title to the register entries. For that reason it is very common for the whole of the abstract or epitome, or office copy entries, to be sent to the buyer's solicitor with the draft contract. If the buyer's solicitor does not investigate the title at this stage, he should make quite clear that he has only looked at the documents provided for the purpose of enlarging on the references made in the contract.

In view of the inevitable delay before contracts are exchanged and the ever-present possibility that a prospective buyer may withdraw, a seller may wish to send out draft contracts to more than one prospective buyer, so that he can exchange contracts with the first buyer who is in a position to do so. The Law Society has issued rules for a seller's solicitor involved in such a 'contract race'. The seller's solicitor must disclose in writing to each prospective buyer's solicitor (or the buyer himself if he is unrepresented) that they are involved in the contract race or, if the seller refuses to authorise such disclosure, the solicitor must cease to act for him.[8] The seller's solicitor should, however, avoid creating a binding contract obliging the seller to exchange contracts with the first buyer in a position to do so.[9]

---

7   Taxation of Chargeable Gains Act 1992, ss 222, 223 and 287.
8   Rule 6A, Solicitors Practice Rules 1990.
9   See *Daulia Ltd v Four Millbank Nominees Ltd* [1978] Ch 231, [1978] 2 All ER 557, CA.

6 THE BUYER'S PRE-CONTRACT SEARCHES AND ENQUIRIES

It will be apparent from the seller's limited duty of disclosure that the buyer's solicitor will have to instigate a number of searches and enquiries, with the object of collecting information about the property which the seller is not under a duty to disclose but which may influence the buyer in his decision whether or not to proceed with his purchase and exchange of contracts. Some searches and enquiries are done in all cases and others only where circumstances demand.

I LOCAL LAND CHARGES SEARCH

This search should be made on the purchase of both unregistered and registered land (local land charges are overriding interests in relation to registered land[1]). The matters that are protected as local land charges are as the name implies essentially local in nature and are set out in the Local Land Charges Act 1975. They include planning matters such as enforcement notices and conditional planning permissions; tree preservation orders; certain compulsory purchase orders; the listing of buildings as being of special historical or architectural interest; various financial charges for expenses incurred by the Local Authority; and others. A register of local land charges is kept by District Councils and London Borough Councils. The register is in twelve parts, all of which should be searched. The Standard Conditions provide[2] that the property is sold subject to matters disclosed by the searches and enquiries which a prudent buyer would have made before entering into the contract, which would include the register of local land charges, but a seller should still disclose local land charges of which he is aware.[3]

The search

The search can be done personally or by applying for an official certificate of search on a standard form. In both cases a fee is payable. A personal search is quicker, but there are advantages in the official search certificate, including for the solicitor the protection given by the Local Land Charges Act 1975, section 13, which provides

---

1   Land Registration Act 1925, s 70(1)(i).
2   SC 3.1.2(d).
3   *Rignall Developments Ltd v Halil* [1988] Ch 190, [1987] 3 All ER 170, see ch 5, section 4i.

that a solicitor is not answerable for any loss caused by reliance on an erroneous official certificate. Another disadvantage of a personal search, whether by the buyer's solicitor or by an agency specialising in such searches, is that it might not be very easy for the buyer to establish liability against the person making the search who has apparently made an error. It is important, therefore, if contemplating a personal search, to ensure that the search agency involved is both reputable and backed by appropriate indemnity insurance. In addition, if the buyer is purchasing the property with the aid of a mortgage, and the solicitor is acting for both buyer and lender, it is important to establish in advance whether or not a personal search will be acceptable to the lender. It is also prudent to explain to the buyer the reason for choosing this method and to obtain the buyer's written instructions.

As registration is by reference to the land affected, a description of the land, preferably with a plan, must be submitted with the application for an official search. The official certificate of search is not conclusive. An interest registrable as a local land charge is binding whether or not it is revealed on a search and indeed whether or not it is even registered. There is provision for compensation for persons acquiring an interest for valuable consideration in the land searched against; this would cover a lessee and a mortgagee as well as a buyer. Compensation is payable if an interest registrable as a local land charge is not revealed on a personal search because it was not registered, or is not revealed on an official certificate of search either because it was not registered or because of an error in the preparation of the certificate.[4] To obtain compensation, the search must have been made before 'the relevant time' which is the date of the contract for sale, unless either the contract is in some way conditional on the outcome of the search or there is no contract, in which case the relevant time is the date of the conveyance. For the purpose of obtaining compensation, a buyer can take the benefit of a search requisitioned by someone else, for example the seller or an earlier abortive buyer, provided he knew of the contents of the search before the relevant time.[5] The amount of the compensation will be the loss suffered by reason of the interest not being registered or revealed. If the property is mortgaged, the compensation can be claimed by the mortgagee, who would apply it in reduction of the amount owing under the mortgage.[6]

The search is essentially an information-gathering exercise and gives no protection against the future creation of local land charges. It would be negligent for a solicitor not to effect such a search for a buyer and there are clearly dangers in relying on an out-of-date search. There is no official expiry date on a local search but three months is generally considered an appropriate 'shelf-life'.

2   ADDITIONAL ENQUIRIES OF THE LOCAL AUTHORITY

Many matters affecting the property which are of a local nature are not registrable as local land charges. With the local land charges search is inevitably sent a list of additional enquiries of the appropriate council (district, borough, London borough, or Unitary authority). Again, a fee is payable. There is a standard form of enquiries agreed between the Law Society and the Local Authority associations. Some of the questions are quite detailed and it may be fair to say that even some practising solicitors are unaware of their precise nature; it is only when a question to which one

---

4   Local Land Charges Act 1975, s 10.
5   Ibid, s 10(3).
6   Ibid, s 11.

would have expected a negative answer receives a positive answer, or vice versa, that the alarm bells ring.[7] There follows a brief summary of the questions on the current form.

i   The enquiries

(1)   This question deals with planning provision and asks whether there are any structure, local, development, unitary or non-statutory plans and if so what the plan indicates as the use of the area in which the property is situated. The response will be important both in giving an overview of the planning proposals for the area and in ensuring that the designated use and the proposed use of the particular property which the buyer is interested in are the same – if the property is designated as 'residential' for example, the buyer may find difficulty in getting planning permission for a commercial use.

(2) This question concerns drainage from the property. It asks whether the property drains into a public sewer for both foul drainage and surface water. When a new sewer is built, then by a scheme similar to that applicable when a new road is made up, the developer will enter into an agreement (with supporting bond) under section 104 of the Water Industry Act 1991. The question asks whether the Council is aware of such a scheme but the buyer may also need to check with the appropriate water authority; recently, some councils have refused to answer this question, indicating that the solicitor should enquire directly of the water authority. This enquiry is especially relevant where the property is newly constructed, as it is unlikely in such a situation that the sewers will be adopted. The buyer's solicitor needs to ensure that the agreement and bond are in place (copies will usually be provided by the seller's solicitor) and that the amount and provider of the bond is acceptable to any lender. If the property does not drain into a public sewer, the question asks whether there is a public sewer within 100 feet of the property. If the property drains into a private sewer, the buyer's solicitor should check both the existence of an easement, and maintenance costs.

(3) This question asks whether the roads and paths, being the postal address or additionally specified on the form, are maintainable at the public expense. This would normally be the case as they will have been adopted by the local authority. If not, for example with a newly built property, the buyer will wish to enquire of the seller both to confirm the rights of way that do exist over the roads and paths and to establish who is responsible for their maintenance. If the roads and paths are not maintained at public expense, the problem for the buyer lies not only in probably being liable for a contribution to their maintenance, but also the risk that the local authority may by resolution decide to make up the roads in which case the buyer would be liable for a proportion of the cost thereof, calculated by reference to the length of the frontage of the property on to the road. The question on the form also asks whether any such resolution has been made.

When a new estate is built the roads will often not be made up by the builder until some or all of the properties have been sold. The buyer of a new property on an estate should thus ensure that in the conveyance from the builder, the latter covenants to make up the roads and paths on the estate. However, this is not really sufficient for

---

7   In *JGF Properties Ltd v Lambeth London Borough* [1986] 1 EGLR 179, it was suggested that the questions and answers are unintelligible to the layman. The case also illustrates the dangers of relying on a telephone enquiry of the Local Authority, not least being the difficulty of proof.

the buyer as if the builder should go into liquidation or for some other reason fail to make up the roads, they may be made up by the local authority and the buyer charged a proportion of the cost. To guard against this possibility, the buyer should ensure that the builder has entered into an agreement with the local authority under section 38 of the Highways Act 1980, agreeing to make up the estate roads and paths. This agreement should be supported by a financial bond of a sufficient amount to cover the cost of the work should the builder default. The question on the form does ask whether there is any such agreement and bond in existence. Although the buyer's prime concern will be that the agreement and bond relates to the road in front of the property being bought, the buyer should also ensure that the agreement and bond covers the other estate roads; it would be most inconvenient for the buyer if he had to drive across muddy unmade roads to reach his property and it would certainly decrease the value of the property until the roads were made up. Again, the lender should also be consulted as to the acceptability of any agreement and bond, and copies should be obtained from the seller's solicitor.

(4) This asks whether the Council has been notified by the Secretary of State of any proposed new trunk road or motorway or of construction of a subway, flyover, footbridge, underpass, elevated road or dual carriageway, in either case within 200 metres of the property. There are further questions about the existence of any proposals for highway construction.

(5) This question asks whether there are any outstanding statutory or informal notices issued by the Council under the Public Health Acts, Housing Acts, or Highways Acts.

(6) This question asks whether there are any proceedings in respect of infringement of Building Regulations. The buyer's solicitor should pay particular attention to the reply to this question if there has been any recent building activity at the property.

(7) The Council keeps a register of planning applications and the result of each application. This question asks for details of any entries relating to the property in that register and where it can be inspected.

(8) This question also concerns planning. It asks for details of entries in the register of enforcement notices and stop notices and where the register can be inspected. It also asks for details of any proposed enforcement or stop notice or any other notice or proceedings relating to a contravention of planning control. Both questions 7 and 8 will be relevant, again, where there has been recent building activity, for example where the property has been recently built or extended.

(9) This asks whether the Council has resolved to make a direction under Article 4 of the Town and Country Planning General Development Order restricting permitted development, except where this is shown in the official Certificate of Search.

(10) This asks whether the Council has made any orders revoking or modifying planning permission, or discontinuing an existing planning use or any tree preservation orders.

(11) This asks whether the Council has paid any compensation where the Secretary of State has refused to grant permission for development. This will affect the compensation paid on any subsequent compulsory acquisition of the property.

(12) This question asks whether the property is within a conservation area, except as shown in the official Certificate of Search. This will apply to property so designated before 1974, or very recently where no entry has yet been made on the official certificate. This is important as alterations or improvements to property in a conservation area may be subject to greater control and the buyer needs to be aware of this fact.

(13) This question asks whether the Council has made any compulsory purchase orders except those shown in the official Certificate of Search.

(14) This question asks whether the property is included in a programme of slum clearance or in a general improvement area, renewal area, or housing action area. Since the 1960s there has been a continuous drive to clear slum dwellings from inner cities and it will be rare nowadays that the buyer's solicitor will receive an affirmative response on this front.

(15) This question asks whether the property is in an area subject to a smoke control order except where this is shown in the official Certificate of Search. This will restrict the buyer's choice of fuel to smokeless if such an order is in force, and he should be made aware of this, preferably in writing. Breach of the order could result in a fairly hefty fine.

(16) This question asks whether there have been any proposals for the construction of a railway within 200 metres of the property. The reason for this question is fairly obvious, and again an affirmative response should be investigated further and reported to the buyer.

There are a further 17 optional enquiries, which will only be answered if a specific request to do so is made and at an additional fee over and above the fee for the standard enquiries. These are questions which will only be relevant to particular types of property. For example, questions ask whether the property is an enterprise zone, an urban development area or a simplified planning zone, and other questions deal with hazardous substance consents, the proximity of pipelines and whether the property is in a National Park or Area of Outstanding Natural Beauty. The buyer's solicitor should consider whether in a particular case any of these additional enquiries, and indeed any other enquiries not covered by the standard form, should be made of the Local Authority.

ii   Replies to the enquiries

When the replies to the enquiries are received they should be scrutinised carefully to see whether any of the information disclosed is prejudicial to the buyer and whether any further enquiries need to be made of the local authority, the seller or both. The majority of enquiries are so drafted that the buyer's solicitor will be hoping for a negative answer. Should anything untoward be revealed then the buyer's solicitor should inform the buyer and lender if appropriate as soon as possible and obtain instructions.

The form contains a statement that the Local Authority and its officers will only be liable for an error in answering the enquiries if there has been negligence. It would seem that there could be not only tortious liability in negligence but also liability in contract, as a fee paid for the answers to the enquiries.[8]

This 'exclusion clause' might then possibly have to be read subject to the reasonableness test in the Unfair Contract Terms Act 1977. As with the local land charges search, it is not necessary that the buyer made the enquiries, for the buyer can take the benefit of replies to enquiries requisitioned by some other person provided he was aware of their contents before the relevant time.

These enquiries should be made in respect of every purchase of land, registered or unregistered. Of course, the replies to the enquiries give no guarantee that the

---

8   *Coats Patons (Retail) Ltd v Birmingham Corpn* (1971) 69 LGR 356; see also *Johnson v Bournemouth Borough Council* [1992] EGCS 73, CA.

situation covered by the question will not change at some time in the future, so again there is a danger in relying on out-of-date replies.

3   INFORMATION FROM THE SELLER

i   Enquiries

The need for enquiries directed at the seller through his solicitor is a very obvious consequence of the seller's limited duty of disclosure. The buyer's solicitor will probably again use a standard form as the basis for his enquiries, such as those produced by the various stationers.[9] This will commonly include enquiries on matters such as the ownership of boundary walls and fences; the existence of any disputes relating to the property, for example about the exact position of a boundary; whether the property has the benefit of the NHBC scheme; the existence of any guarantees in relation to the property, e.g. for wood that has been treated for rot or insect attack; the route of services to the property such as gas, electricity and drainage;[10] the arrangements for shared drives and any other easements; whether all covenants affecting the property have been observed; planning matters, including whether there has been any recent development which would have required planning permission; the fixtures and fittings that are to pass with the property, including oil remaining in the storage tank where the property has oil-fired heating; the exact scope of the seller's liability for paths, drives and laying out the garden on the purchase of a newly constructed house; and details of any service charge payable.

The enquiries on any standard form are not intended to be exhaustive and the buyer's solicitor's duty is to raise all appropriate enquiries; if the standard form is used then such further enquiries must be added as may be appropriate in each particular case. Similarly, inappropriate enquiries should be deleted. So if the property is subject to a tenancy, be it residential, business or agricultural, the buyer may require further information. Equally, the buyer may wish to enquire about the state of repair and maintenance of the heating system. If vacant land is being sold for building or other purposes, the buyer may wish to know if the land is subject to flooding, and of course it will be vital to make appropriate enquiries regarding contaminated land (see section 10 below). The enquiries can also be used to clarify a provision in the draft contract, although negotiation as to the terms of the contract may be dealt with more conveniently in correspondence.

The usefulness of the enquiries depends on the attitude of the seller and his solicitor. The seller is under no obligation to answer any enquiries, although he will normally do so. The replies given may be so equivocal as to be virtually useless to the buyer. For example, if the buyer raises enquiries about the physical state of repair of the property, and the heating system, he may be told simply to rely on his own inspection and survey. Other replies may only be answered 'so far as the seller is aware'. The reason for such vague replies is that a reply may amount to a representation and if false involve the seller in liability for misrepresentation although a statement that the seller 'is not aware' involves an implied representation that the seller has taken reasonable steps to find out.[11] The standard form of enquiries may contain a disclaimer stating that the accuracy of replies is not guaranteed and that other

---

  9   For example, the forms produced by Oyez.
 10   See *Strover v Harrington* [1988] Ch 390, [1988] 1 All ER 769.
 11   *See William Sindall plc v Cambridgeshire County Council* [1994] 3 All ER 932, [1994] 1 WLR 1016, CA.

appropriate searches and enquiries and inspections should be made, but this is of little effect and will not prevent answers being representations of fact.[12] The Standard Conditions also purport to restrict the seller's liability for misrepresentation; see Chapter 16. In addition to the seller's potential liability, the disclaimer on the standard form may also exclude liability in negligence on the part of the seller's solicitor to the buyer, but the case of *Gran Gelato Ltd v Richcliffe (Group) Ltd*[13] indicates that the seller's solicitor owes no duty of care to the buyer. In any event, the seller's solicitor may be liable in negligence to the seller himself, if the solicitor has been negligent in the answering of enquiries! In practice, the seller's solicitor should at the very least take detailed instructions from the seller and try to be as informative as possible in the replies to enquiries. The buyer's solicitor can then examine the replies given and, if dissatisfied with any reply, can take the point up again with the seller's solicitor.

ii   The National Conveyancing Protocol

Where the Law Society's National Conveyancing Protocol is in use, the information the buyer needs will be provided in the shape of the Seller's Property Information Form or Seller's Leasehold Information Form. The latest version of the Protocol is TransAction 2001, launched on 1 May 2001. This provides for prescribed forms of seller's enquiries before contract to be used – the Seller's Property Information Form (SPIF) for freeholds, and the Seller's Leasehold Information Form (SLIF) for leasehold properties. These are standard forms which the seller's solicitor will hand to his client when initially instructed. At the same time he will hand his client a standard Fixtures, Fittings and Contents form. This allows the seller to specify in some detail not just which fixtures will be left or removed but also which chattels, including such mundane but vital items as toilet roll holders! The seller is also asked to confirm that all items included in the estate agents' particulars (if any) are included in the sale, and that all items remaining in the property belong to the seller outright. It also reminds the seller to make good any damage caused by the removal of fixtures, and to remove all his property on completion. The fixtures, fittings and contents form can in due course be attached to and form part of the contract. The seller completes these forms to the best of his knowledge and returns them to his solicitor. The seller's solicitor then considers the replies which the seller has given and completes Part II of the form on the basis of those answers, combined with the information he can gather from the deeds in his possession. He is required to confirm on his part of the form that he has checked the information provided by the sellers against the deeds in his possession, so of course it is vital that the solicitor does do such a check. Failure to do so would amount to failure to act in the best interests of the client, and would be a potential breach of rule 1 of the Solicitors Practice Rules 1990, and could also amount to negligence.

The latest version of the SPIF includes more detailed questions than before on planning and building control, and also contains a reminder that any changes to the property could result in its banding being changed after completion. The new form also contains more questions than previously on the mechanics of the sale, to ensure all parties are fully informed about matters such as proposed completion dates and amounts of deposit available.

---

12   *Walker v Boyle* [1982] 1 All ER 634, [1982] 1 WLR 495. See also *Cremdean Properties Ltd v Nash* (1977) 244 Estates Gazette 547, CA.
13   [1992] Ch 560, [1992] 1 All ER 865.

The SLIF is very similar to the SPIF, but provides additional information; for example, details of service charge, landlord's notices and so on.

Solicitors are permitted to reproduce the SPIF and SLIF forms themselves under TransAction 2001, provided they follow the Law Society's requirements of copying onto good paper and stating that the form is part of the TransAction scheme.

The completed forms are then sent to the buyer's solicitor as part of the initial package, together with other relevant information such as guarantees, copies of planning permissions and building regulations consent, and highways and water agreements and bonds. At present, the package does not have to include the local search or a survey or report on the condition of the property, but these might be required if and when the Homes Bill 2000 is re-introduced.

One criticism of the conveyancing process before the introduction of the TransAction Protocol was the tendency of solicitors, keen to ensure they had covered all possible problems, to produce their own 'standard' forms of enquiry with copious questions covering the most abstruse queries, with some additional questions thrown in for good measure! Unsurprisingly, sellers' solicitors became tired of answering these (sometimes irrelevant) queries and one of the aims of the Protocol was to limit the number of enquiries to keep them to a manageable number whilst still covering all the essentials. For this reason, solicitors are discouraged from adding extra enquiries to the Seller's Property Information Form.

4   SEARCH OF THE INDEX MAP

This search is made at the District Land Registry. It will reveal whether title to the freehold or leasehold estate in all or any part of the land is already registered, and whether there are any cautions against first registration. The search ought to be made in all cases where title to the land sold is unregistered.[14] There is a prescribed form of search,[15] which should be accompanied by a plan. Searches can be made by post or in person, or by Land Registry Direct if the solicitor subscribes to this scheme.[16]

This search is supplied by the seller under the Protocol.

5   COMMON REGISTRATION SEARCH

A search in the register kept under the Commons Registration Act 1965 will reveal whether all or any part of the land is registered as a common, or town or village green. This would mean that certain local rights existed over the land which would almost certainly adversely influence the buyer's decision to buy. A search should be made if the land has never been built on or if it has ever belonged to the Local Lord of the Manor, unless the buyer's solicitor is acquainted with the land and knows that it is not affected.[17] Where the property concerned is new or recently built, the buyer's solicitor will often find that the seller's solicitor will provide a copy of the results of this search as part of the pre-contract package. There is a standard form of search (CR1) which is sent to the appropriate County Council or London Borough Council or Unitary Authority, with a plan and a fee. The search should be made whether the land is

---

14   On the grant of a lease, the search should be made against the reversionary title.
15   Form 96. See Land Registration Rules 1990, Land Registration (Open Register) Rules 1991.
16   See ch 2, 2viii.
17   *G & K Ladenbau (UK) Ltd v Crawley and de Reya (a firm)* [1978] 1 All ER 682, [1978] 1 WLR 266.

unregistered or registered as rights of common are overriding interests in respect of registered land.[18] The seller could also be asked about the recent use of the land.

This search would be made by the seller's solicitor under the Protocol.

6   COAL AUTHORITY SEARCH

If the land is in an area of past, present or potential future mining, the buyer's solicitor will need to make a Coal Authority search. The Law Society publishes a directory to enable solicitors to ascertain whether the property is in an area where a search is necessary. There is a standard form search Con29M, which should be accompanied by a plan although this is not obligatory. A fee is payable. The search is sent to the appropriate office of the Coal Authority, ascertainable from the directory. The aim of the search is to discover the position with regard to mining underneath the property. Although compensation is payable in respect of subsidence damage caused by mining, the buyer may possibly wish to withdraw in the light of the result of the search and may also wish to check that the property is adequately constructed to minimise subsidence damage.

As well as making the search, the buyer's solicitor should also ask the seller, through his solicitor, whether the property has sustained subsidence damage, whether any claim has been made in respect of the damage and how the claim was resolved (ie by repair being effected or by compensation being paid). If compensation has been paid, obviously no further compensation will be paid in respect of the same damage; it is therefore important for a buyer to establish whether or not compensation has already been paid.

In addition, the buyer should take careful note of the views of his surveyor and should ensure that this point is specifically covered in any case where the property is in danger of mining subsidence being a problem.

Under the Protocol, this search is made by the buyer.

7   SEARCH IN THE CENTRAL LAND CHARGES REGISTRY

The Law of Property Act 1925, section 198 provides that registration of a land charge in the Central Land Charges Registry is notice to all persons for all purposes. The Law of Property Act 1969, section 24 makes it clear that this provision does not apply to a buyer before exchange of contracts. If section 198 had been applicable, a seller would have been able to argue that since a buyer had notice of the land charge by virtue of its registration, the seller would be under no duty to disclose it, as his duty of disclosure, at least under an open contract, does not extend to defects of title of which the buyer is aware. Section 24 makes it clear that the seller remains under a duty to disclose a land charge and therefore in theory at least there is no need for the buyer's solicitor to make a search of the Land Charges Registry at this stage.[19]

If there is a land charge registered which the seller has failed to disclose and the buyer discovered it after exchange of contracts, then the buyer would normally have an action for damages for breach of contract or possibly rescission. This will inevitably involve the buyer in some inconvenience and delay, particularly where the buyer is himself selling a property. It may be in the buyer's interest to actually

---

18   Land Registration Act 1925, s 70(1)(a).
19   See also SC 3.1.2(d) which excepts entries in the Land Charges Register from the encumbrances subject to which the property is sold.

find out whether there are any charges in existence *before* exchange of contracts. If there are, he can then refuse to proceed and exchange contracts unless and until the matter is satisfactorily resolved. This could be particularly appropriate if there was a Class F land charge registered, which protects a non-owning spouse's statutory right of occupation of the matrimonial home.[20] This could arise if the seller was a spouse who was the sole owner of the legal estate in the matrimonial home being sold; the other spouse may have registered a Class F. Although the seller would be under a duty to procure the cancellation of the registration[1] or else be in breach of contract and have to pay damages,[2] the buyer may prefer to find out by a search of the Land Charges Registry before exchange of contracts whether there is any such charge registered and then simply not proceed and look for another property to buy if there is a registration of which the seller is unable to arrange for cancellation. The buyer may have wasted some money in abortive conveyancing costs but this may be preferable to a lengthy action for damages for breach of contract. The ways by which the buyer can be satisfied that the Class F will be cancelled are dealt with in Chapter 8. However, even if a clear search is obtained before exchange of contracts there is always the possibility of a registration being made before completion. Some protection against this eventuality may be obtained by the buyer's solicitor, once he is aware of the existence of the spouse, insisting on the insertion of a special condition in the contract providing for the spouse to sign to confirm that she has no beneficial interest in the property, and will not enter a class F land charge between exchange of contracts and completion. This is not foolproof – if she does breach her agreement and enter a charge, the buyer will have the delay and expense of procuring its removal.

The search, if done, need normally only be made in respect of unregistered land. In respect of a registered title, the Family Law Act 1996 charge is protected by notice, the existence of which would be apparent from the register. Assuming the buyer is sent a full set of up-to-date office copy entries of the register, there will be no need to make any search.

Under the Protocol, the seller's solicitor would make a land charges search against the seller and any other appropriate names and provide it with the package of information sent to the buyer.

8   INSPECTION OF THE PROPERTY

There are a number of reasons why it is important for the property to be inspected before exchange of contracts.

i   Physical defects

The seller is under no duty to disclose any defects in, and makes no warranty about, the state and condition of the property being sold.[3] The rule caveat emptor (buyer beware) applies to the sale of land. The buyer must satisfy himself about this and would be well advised to employ a professional surveyor to prepare a report.[4] The

---

20 Family Law Act 1996.
1 Ibid, Sch 4, para 4.
2 *Wroth v Tyler* [1974] Ch 30, [1973] 1 All ER 897.
3 See, however, *Gordon v Selico Co Ltd*, ch 5, section 4xii, above.
4 In *Low v RJ Haddock Ltd* [1985] 2 EGLR 247, it was even held, surprisingly, that the buyer suing in respect of damage caused by spreading tree roots might be contributorily negligent if he had not arranged a survey at the time of purchase.

scope of such a survey would be agreed in advance but would usually cover the structure of the property, the incidence of dry and wet rot and insect attack, the electrical wiring, the plumbing system and other similar matters.[5] The surveyor could be liable in negligence for any errors in his report, subject to any exclusion clause and to the effects of the Unfair Contract Terms Act 1977. It is a good idea for the buyer's solicitor to go through the survey report with his client before proceeding to exchange contracts – of course, the solicitor is not a surveyor and cannot be expected to comment on the technical aspects of the report, but it is submitted that he does have a duty to ensure that his client understands the report and knows how to proceed with any further action which might be needed.

If the buyer is taking out a mortgage to provide part of the purchase price, he may be unwilling to go to the expense of a surveyor's report when he knows that the mortgagees will themselves have had a surveyor's report on the property, and indeed the buyer will have paid for this. There are a number of reasons why the buyer may be better advised not to rely on this survey but to have one done for himself. The scope of the mortgagee's survey may be quite limited, in that the mortgagee is only interested in ensuring that the property is adequate security for the amount of the loan, which may be substantially less than the purchase price. Thus, the lower the amount of the mortgage in relation to the amount of the loan, the less careful the survey may need to be. Past practice has been for some mortgagees not to allow the buyer to even see their survey report. Most mortgagees have now changed this practice and are willing to allow the buyer to see the report, although its scope may still be quite limited. Moreover it does appear that a surveyor who negligently prepares a report for a mortgagee may be liable not only to the mortgagee but also to the buyer.[6] As a result, many mortgagees have introduced a clause in the mortgage application form, excluding liability for (negligent) surveys. However, in *Smith v Eric S Bush*[7] it was held that such clauses were ineffective, not passing the 'fair and reasonable' test in the Unfair Contract Terms Act 1977 in relation to run-of-the-mill residential properties although different considerations will apply to commercial premises.

If a buyer does want his own survey, which given the limited scope of the mortgagee's survey[8] is advisable, some saving in cost could be achieved by using the same surveyor who is preparing the mortgagee's report; most mortgagees will ask the buyer what level of survey he requires. On the purchase of a new house with the benefit of the NHBC scheme it will not normally be necessary for the buyer to have his own survey done, but the mortgagee will still normally arrange for a surveyor to inspect the property once it is finished. Some buyers will want to commission a surveyor to look not so much at the property itself but more on the surrounding land, to advise on matters such as potential flooding and environmental concerns.

---

5   The RICS provide a standardised survey and valuation report which falls short of a structural survey but which is sufficient for most properties. This is usually referred to as a 'Home Buyers Report'.

6   *Yianni v Edwin Evans & Sons* [1982] QB 438, [1981] 3 All ER 592; *Smith v Eric S Bush* [1990] 1 AC 831, [1989] 2 All ER 514, HL. Liability will be limited to damages, based on the difference in value between what the buyer was expecting to get and what he actually got: there is not element of damages for inconvenience, distress etc; *Watts v Morrow* [1991] 4 All ER 937, [1991] 1 WLR 1421 confirmed in *Patel v Hooper and Jackson* [1999] 1 All ER 992, [1999] 1 WLR 1792. Where a surveyor employed by a building society negligently prepares a report for the lender (whether a basic valuation or house buyer's report) the borrower is entitled to complain to the building society's ombudsman under Sch 12 of the Building Societies Act 1986, as the valuer is effectively treated as the lender's agent: *Halifax Building Society v Edell* [1992] Ch 436, [1992] 3 All ER 389.

7   *Smith v Eric S Bush*, above.

8   See *Roberts v J Hampson & Co* [1989] 2 All ER 504 at 510.

It is unlikely that, simply by making a mortgage advance for the purchase of the property, a mortgagee would be liable on any implied warranty or representation that the purchase price was reasonable. However, under a code of practice adopted by the Building Societies Association, in relation to Building Society mortgages, the borrower will be informed in writing by the Building Society whether or not, and if so to what extent, the society gives any assurance that the price agreed to be paid for the property on which the advance is to be secured is reasonable. In normal circumstances the Building Society will indicate that 'the society does not warrant by the making of any advance the price agreed to be paid for the property is reasonable' or 'the society gives no assurance by the making of an advance that the price agreed to be paid for the property is reasonable'. (Section 30 of the Building Societies Act 1962 did provide that the making of an advance by a Building Society implied a warranty that the purchase price was reasonable; in practice section 30 was invariably excluded and it has now been repealed by the Building Societies Act 1986.)

There is another compelling reason why the property should be inspected before exchange of contracts. This is to check that the property as described in the contract accords with the property as enclosed by the physical boundaries on site. If a boundary wall has been erected in the wrong place, this may mean that a neighbour has acquired title by adverse possession to land to which the seller has the paper title and which is being transferred to the buyer.

ii   Other defects in title

The seller is not under a duty to disclose defects in title if they are patent, that is to say if they are apparent on reasonable inspection. The property should be inspected to ascertain whether there are any such defects, for example rights of way. If this inspection is carried out by the buyer rather than his solicitor, then the solicitor must ensure that the buyer knows what he is looking for. Under Standard Condition 3.1.2(b), the property is sold subject to incumbrances discoverable by inspection, thus underlining the need to make such an inspection.

There may be other defects in title which are not patent (and which the seller must therefore disclose), but which may in fact be discoverable by the buyer by investigation of the occupier of the property. For unregistered land, there is a rule that as between the buyer and an occupier who has some interest in the property, the buyer has constructive notice of interests reasonably discoverable from enquiry of the occupier.[9] This will mean that the interests will be binding on the buyer. For example, if the occupier is a tenant, the buyer may have constructive notice of the existence and terms of the tenancy agreement. However, as between the seller and the buyer such a defect in title may not be patent and the seller would have to disclose it under an open contract or else be in breach of contract.[10] In the case of registered land, under the Land Registration Act 1925, section 70(1)(g), the rights of persons in possession (including both occupation and receipt of rents and profits) are overriding interests and will be binding on a buyer unless enquiry is made of such person and the rights are not disclosed. Again as between seller and buyer some such rights may well not constitute patent defects in title. The seller may also be in breach of contract if the contract specifically provides for vacant possession.

---

9   *Hunt v Luck* [1902] 1 Ch 428; Law of Property Act 1925, s 199(1)(ii)(a).
10   *Caballero v Henty* (1874) 9 Ch App 447, CA. The effect of SC 3.1.2(b) is unclear; conceivably it means that the buyer is purchasing subject to the occupier's interest.

As we have already seen in connection with the central land charges search, a buyer may prefer to try and obtain actual knowledge of an interest by which he will be bound, so that he can decide on that basis whether to proceed to exchange, rather than relying on being able to sue the seller if he fails to comply with his duty to disclose the interest. On this basis it may be advisable to make enquiries of occupiers at this stage.

There are differences in the rules applying to registered and unregistered land. The Land Registration Act 1925, section 70(1)(g) covers the rights of persons not only in occupation of the property but also in receipt of rents and profits and would therefore include the rights of a lessor of the property. The rule in *Hunt v Luck* for unregistered land does not extend so far. Also the enquiries necessary in respect of unregistered land are limited by section 199[11] of the Law of Property Act 1925, which provides that a buyer shall not be fixed with constructive notice of any matter unless it would have come to his knowledge if such enquiries and inspections had been made as ought reasonably to have been made. There is no such limitation on the operation of section 70(1)(g); the occupation need not be discovered from reasonable enquiry and inspection. Further, for registered land, the time at which one looks to see who is in occupation for the purpose of section 70(1)(g) is quite specific. For registered land, it is those persons who are in occupation at the date of completion of the purchase who may have overriding interests binding on the purchaser.[12] All the buyer and his solicitor can do at this stage is find out who is in occupation now and take precautions in case those people are still in occupation on completion.

The first task for the buyer and his solicitor is to find out who is in occupation.[13] The registered land position is illustrated by the case of *Williams & Glyn's Bank Ltd v Boland*[14] which decided that a wife's equitable interest in a matrimonial home which was in her husband' sole name could be an overriding interest under section 70(1)(g) if she was in occupation. Furthermore, she would still be in occupation for the purposes of section 70(1)(g) even though her husband was also in occupation. In these circumstances her equitable interest, acquired for example by some financial contribution and giving a right to possession of the property, would be an overriding interest and be binding on a buyer or, in the actual case, a mortgagee. This principle is not confined to spouses but will extend to anyone with an equitable interest, for example an aged relative who has contributed to the cost of building a granny flat, or the occupier of commercial premises. The task of discovering whether anyone of this nature is in occupation is difficult if not impossible. Consider the position, in domestic conveyancing, if the spouse or cohabitee or granny or whoever has an equitable interest is out shopping or at work when the buyer calls to look at the property. Or if he or she is away on holiday or has been driven from the property by the violence of someone else in the property. The person with the equitable interest may still be in occupation for the purposes of section 70(1)(g) and the equitable interest will still be an overriding interest, but it will be extraordinarily difficult for the buyer or his solicitor to find out about the occupier. The position as relates to unregistered land is slightly better from the buyer's point of view in that as we have seen, for the buyer to have constructive notice of the equitable interest and therefore be bound by it, the interest must be discoverable from reasonable enquiries. However, there will still be problems. The effect of section 199 was considered in *Kingsnorth*

---

11   Section 199(1)(ii)(a).
12   *Abbey National Building Society v Cann* [1991] 1 AC 56, [1990] 1 All ER 1085, HL.
13   For a discussion of what is meant by 'occupation', see ch 2, section 2vi.
14   [1981] AC 487, [1980] 2 All ER 408, HL.

Trust Ltd v Tizard[15] where it was held that an inspection at a time pre-arranged with the seller was not sufficient. The case also confirms that the necessary presence for occupation is not negatived by regular and repeated absence. The case actually concerned the position of a mortgagee (and is considered further in chapter 13) but is presumably equally applicable to a buyer; the task of the buyer and his solicitor, in relation to both registered and unregistered title, is difficult and, as the law stands, unrealistic.

There may be a question on a standard form of enquiries of the seller which asks for details of anyone in occupation and any rights they may have in the property. There is also a statement about occupiers on the property information form. This is not that much use for the buyer, save for probably making the seller liable for misrepresentation should he provide incorrect information. In particular under section 70(1)(g) the enquiry must be addressed to the occupier for the buyer to be able to take free of the interest if it is not revealed. The buyer cannot rely on the seller's word. This, then, is the second task for the buyer and his solicitor: having discovered who is in occupation, to ascertain what if any rights the occupier may have. Although we have said that under section 70(1)(g) if the rights are not revealed on enquiry of the occupier they are not overriding interests and will not be binding on the buyer, in practice it may well be that the spouse or cohabitee is quite unaware of the equitable interest which he or she has. Indeed the occupier may refer the enquiry to the seller's solicitor, who is then placed in an awkward position. Looking at matters *purely* from the point of view of the seller, he would rather the rights were not disclosed to the buyer because there would then be less danger of the buyer being bound by them. There would be a conflict of interest between the seller and the occupier and it might not be appropriate for the seller's solicitor to advise the occupier as well.

What if the inspection does reveal an occupier with an interest in the property? The buyer's solicitor will need to take steps to ensure that the purchaser is not bound by the interest. The ways in which this could be done in respect of an occupier's equitable interest are discussed in Chapter 8, section 1 iv below. For registered land, if the occupier leaves when the seller leaves and is not in possession on completion, then the whole problem disappears, because the occupier's rights will not be binding on the buyer. Unfortunately the buyer cannot see into the future and must still be protected against the occupier's interest.

The equitable interest of a spouse, which has been discussed above, must be distinguished from a spouse's statutory right of occupation of the matrimonial home,[16] which must be protected as a Class F land charge, or a notice if the title is registered. Although the search for and enquiry of occupiers should be pursued in every case, perhaps the most common situation in which there may be problems along these lines in domestic conveyancing is where the seller is a sole spouse, the other spouse having an equitable interest. This will then also raise the problem of a registration of the other spouse's statutory right of occupation.

9   OTHER SEARCHES AND ENQUIRIES

The list of enquiries cannot be exhaustive. The buyer's solicitor should make all the searches and enquiries appropriate to the particular case. For example, if the property abuts a river or canal, enquiries may need to be made of the National Rivers Authority

---

15   [1986] 2 All ER 54, [1986] 1 WLR 783.
16   Under Matrimonial Homes Act 1983.

or British Waterways Board respectively. If the property is close to a railway, a search can be made of Railtrack, to discover matters such as routes of track, responsibility for maintenance and so on.

10   ENVIRONMENTAL ISSUES

There has been a great deal of concern in recent years over land which may have been contaminated by pollutants, particularly as development sites become scarce and more and more 'brownfield' sites are being used. This concern is exacerbated by the fact that liability for contaminated land can lie with the owner or occupier for the time being.[17] The owner or occupier will also be liable for migrating contaminants; ie any which spread to neighbouring land. The local authority is responsible for identifying contaminated land and, once identified, the owner/occupier will be responsible, possibly jointly with the original contaminator, for cleaning up the land. Originally, when the legislation was introduced, many conveyancers felt that it would only be necessary to make searches and enquiries regarding contaminated land for commercial property, but it is becoming more common for these to be done in a domestic setting. Some firms will carry out environmental checks on residential property as a matter of course, while others do so only if there is an apparent risk that contamination has occurred.

If acting for a buyer, particularly of a new property, the solicitor should undertake or arrange the following:

a)   The usual pre-contract searches and enquiries, being sure to include the additional questions regarding contaminated land on the local authority enquiries.
b)   Enquiries of the seller, including, for example, previous and present use of the site, any known environmental pollution, any disputes relating to environmental matters etc.
c)   Enquiries of other bodies, such as the Coal Authority, Environment Agency, Health and Safety Executive etc.
d)   In some cases, environmental investigation; this will be done by an independent environmental specialist and may be either a paper based investigation or may include site visits, soil sampling etc. depending on the perceived degree of risk of contamination.

Once such investigations have been completed, the solicitor, in consultation with his client and the client's lender (if any), will need to decide whether to proceed with the purchase. Warranties and indemnities may be sought from the seller in appropriate cases, for example, where the seller is a developer who bought the brownfield site and was responsible for the clean up operation. Insurance might also be possible.

11   COMMUNICATION WITH THE BUYER

It is of the utmost importance that the buyer's solicitor informs the buyer immediately of any matter revealed by the various searches and enquiries which could affect the buyer's decision to proceed. If this is done in a meeting or over the phone, any possibly controversial points should always be subsequently confirmed in writing. On

---

17   Environmental Protection Act 1990, Part IIA and Environment Act 1995.

occasion, the buyer may need to be advised that it is unwise to proceed with a purchase because of adverse matters discovered on the search results; in such a case, the buyer's solicitor should always obtain a disclaimer from his client confirming that he has been advised not to proceed but wishes to do so notwithstanding. In addition, the buyer's solicitor must remember he is also acting for the lender and the lender's view specific instructions must also be obtained. TransAction 2001 recommends that a written contract report should be provided in all cases.

7 PLANNING LAW IN CONVEYANCING

I INTRODUCTION

In broad terms there are three controls over the erection and alteration of buildings and the use to which land and buildings can be put. These are:

(a) any provisions such as easements and more particularly covenants subject to which the property is held;
(b) the Town and Country Planning legislation and the need for planning permission;
(c) Building Regulation consent.

The buyer will be concerned on two counts. Firstly, he will want to establish that what he is buying is in no way in breach of the foregoing, or in other words that the seller has complied with any restrictions and obtained all necessary consents. The buyer's enquiries before the contract are aimed at establishing this. The seller may be asked in preliminary enquiries to state the present use of the property; there is no statement of use in the property information form. The seller should also be asked to state whether there has been any work done at the property which might have required planning permission; this is covered by the property information form. The seller should also be asked to supply copies of planning permissions and building regulation consents; these should accompany the property information form. If the property is subject to restrictive covenants, the seller should be asked to confirm that they have been complied with and to produce any necessary consents or approvals. The property information form also deals with consents under covenants. The local land charges search and additional enquiries of the Local Authority are also directed in part at establishing whether there has been any breach of planning control.[1] The new edition of the Seller's Property Information Form (SPIF) was introduced on 1 May 2001 and contains two new questions relating to 'Changes to the Property' and 'Planning and Building Control', again with the intention of informing the buyer of any potential breaches of planning control.[2]

The buyer's second consideration will be to establish whether his proposals for the property will fall foul of the controls mentioned. If he wants to extend a dwelling house, will this be in breach of any restrictive covenants? Will he require planning

---

1 Question 8 on the current [1994] form. Question 6 enquiries about breaches of building regulations.
2 See Appendix.

permission or building regulation consent? What if he wants to alter commercial premises to suit his business, or run a different type of business and so change the use of the premises? This is really part of a more general question of whether the property is suitable for the buyer's purposes, which both the buyer and his solicitor will have to consider before exchange of contracts.

If on the sale of freehold land there is a restrictive covenant affecting the property then as we have seen the seller is under a duty to disclose this.[3] It may be a covenant restricting the type of building which can be erected on the land, or its size, or the number of buildings. It may provide that no building can take place without the prior approval of plans by the covenantee. It may restrict the use to which the land or any buildings are put. The existence of an easement may also restrict development of the property; it is inadvisable to build over a right of way unless it can be re-routed to the satisfaction of parties concerned. Again, we have seen that the seller is under a duty to disclose such easements unless they are apparent on inspection. However, apart from the above, the seller gives no general implied warranty that the use of the property is authorised, either as regards his own use or the buyer's intended use.[4]

Building regulations are made under the Public Health Acts. They deal with the way in which new buildings and alterations are constructed. They regulate such matters as the preparation of the site, the materials to be used, ventilation and the structural stability of the building. Put simply, whereas planning permission covers what is to be built, building regulations cover how it is to be built. Building regulation consent is sometimes called byelaw approval, because building control is administered by the local authority, but under the Building Act 1984, a private 'approved inspector' can be engaged to supervise building control, rather than the local authority. One such approved inspector is a subsidiary of NHBC. The approved inspector will be appointed by a notice which suspends the local authority powers. The inspector ultimately issues a 'final certificate' of compliance with building regulations.

Planning permission cannot be dealt with quite so briefly.

2   PLANNING CONTROL

i   Background

The policy of the planning authorities will be reflected in a development plan. This consists of two elements, the structure plan and the local plan. The structure plan is prepared by the County Council and contains the Council's detailed policy for the area. Local plans cover a much smaller area and are prepared by District Councils. They will go into more detail than the structure plan and will deal with the policy for individual pieces of land. In Greater London and the Metropolitan and Unitary authorities, structure and local plans are replaced by unitary development plans, prepared by the London Borough Councils and the Metropolitan/Unitary authorities.

---

3   Also, where the property sold is leasehold, any onerous or unusual covenants in the lease should be disclosed, see ch 5, above; the seller's solicitor will of course examine the whole of the contents of the lease.

4   In *Hill v Harris* [1965] 2 QB 601, [1965] 2 All ER 358, CA, an under lessee was permitted by his lease to use the premises for certain purposes. This use was in fact prohibited by the headlease but the under lessee had no claim against the under lessor. (An under lessee's solicitor should examine the contents of the headlease; he has the contractual right to do so under an open contract, though this could be excluded by special condition.)

The Standard form of additional enquiries of the Local Authority does include a question about the existence and contents of the various plans.[5]

ii   When is planning permission needed?

The general principle is that planning permission is needed for 'development'. This is defined as:

(a) the carrying out of building, engineering, mining or other operations in, on, over or under land, or
(b) the making of any material change in the use of any buildings or other land.[6]

It is specifically provided that the change of the use of a dwelling house to use as two or more dwelling houses is a material change of use and thus development. However, certain matters are specified as not constituting development and therefore not needing permission. These include works of alteration, improvement or maintenance which do not materially affect the external appearance of a building;[7] the use (not construction) of any buildings or other land within the curtilage[8] of a dwelling house for any purpose incidental to the enjoyment of the dwelling house as such;[9] the use of land for agriculture and forestry;[10] and in the case of buildings or other land used for a purpose contained in a class specified in an order made by the Secretary of State, the use thereof for any other purpose contained in the same class.[11] That order is presently the Town and Country Planning (Use Classes) Order 1987 as amended. This contains 16 detailed classes, and the change of use from a use within one class to another within the same class will not constitute development and not require permission. Class A1 comprises use as a shop, with certain exceptions including shops for the sale of hot food. Thus a grocer's shop can become a butcher's shop without the need for planning permission. Class A2 comprises use for financial, professional or other services appropriate to a shopping area. Class A3 includes use for the sale of food or drink for consumption on the premises and use for the sale of hot food for consumption on or off the premises. Class B1 comprises office use not within Class A2 and use as a light industrial building; Class B2 covers use as a general industrial building. The other classes are very specific in their content.

As well as the matters which the legislation provides do not constitute development, there are certain other matters which may constitute development but in respect of which permission is not required.[12] An example would be the resumption of the use of land for a previously authorised use following service of an enforcement notice.[13]

iii   General Permitted Development Order

Permission is needed for development, with the exceptions just mentioned. There may be no need to actually apply for planning permission, because permission may

---

5   Question 1 on the current [1994] form.
6   Town and Country Planning Act 1990, s 55(1).
7   Ibid, s 55(2)(a).
8   This means the area surrounding the house which is regarded as part of the house. For a normal dwelling house, it includes the garden.
9   Town and Country Planning Act 1990, s 55(2)(d).
10 Ibid, s 55(2)(e).
11 Ibid, s 55(2)(f).
12 Ibid, s 57.
13 Ibid.

be granted for certain sorts of development by a General Permitted Development Order. The current Order is the General Permitted Development Order 1995. The Order contains a number of classes of 'permitted' development in respect of which the General Permitted Development Order itself grants planning permission and there is no need for a separate application for permission. (The development may of course require building regulation consent.) Part 1 Class A of the Order relates to the enlargement, improvement or alteration of a dwelling house, provided that a number of conditions are met, including a limitation on the size of the development. Part 1 also includes porches subject to size limits and hard standing for vehicles in Classes D and F. Part 1 Class E covers the provision or alteration of any building, within the curtilage, required for a purpose incidental to the enjoyment of the dwelling house, again subject to certain conditions.

Part 2 Class A covers the erection of fences and walls with certain height limits. Part 3 covers certain changes of use, for example from use class A3 to A1 or A2, and B2 to B1. There are many other classes in the Order covering fairly specialised areas.

Under Article 4 of the Order of the Secretary of State or the Local Planning Authority (subject normally to confirmation by the Secretary of State) may make a direction that particular types of development are to be excluded from the classes of development permitted by the Order. The existence of such a direction will be revealed by the additional enquiries of the Local Authority.[14]

iv Application for planning permission

Unless permission is not needed or is granted by the General Permitted Development Order, it will be necessary to apply for planning permission. If there is some doubt as to whether express permission is needed or not, an application can be made to the Local Planning Authority for a Certificate of Lawful Use which is on the lawfulness of an existing use, or a proposed use[15]

Application for permission is made to the Local Planning Authority, that is the District Council or London Borough Council. The application is made on a form supplied by the Local Planning Authority and it is accompanied by a plan identifying the land concerned and describing the development, giving the reasons for determining the use to be lawful, specifying the date of the certificate and the appropriate fee. It must also be accompanied by a certificate stating that the applicant is either the sole owner of the land or that he has duly notified other owners of the application.[16] 'Owner' in this context includes the freehold owner and any person holding a leasehold interest with at least seven years still to run. Anyone who genuinely hopes to acquire an interest in land may apply for planning permission in respect of it.

It is possible to apply merely for 'outline' planning permission. This is an application for approval in principle of the erection of a building subject to the subsequent approval by the Local Planning Authority of detailed matters such as the design of the building, external appearance, access, drainage and other similar provisions. The outline permission if granted will be subject to these 'reserved matters' which will be specified in the permission. Providing that application for approval of the reserved matters is made within three years of the outline permission,[17] the Local Planning Authority cannot go back on its original decision of principle.

14   Question 9 on the current [1994] form.
15   Town and Country Planning Act 1990, s 191 and s 192.
16   Ibid, s 65 and Art 6 General Development Procedure Order.
17   Town and Country Planning Act 1990, s 92.

The Local Planning Authority must decide whether to grant or refuse the application and give the applicant notice of the decision within eight weeks of the application. This period can be extended by agreement. If no such notification is made then the applicant is entitled to deem the application refused and pursue an appeal. The grant of permission may be made subject to conditions.[18] but these must fairly and reasonably relate to the development. The Local Planning Authority keeps a register of applications and the decisions made on them.[19] Details of entries in this register are revealed by the additional enquiries of the Local Authority.[20] Conditions imposed on permissions granted after 1 August 1977 are registrable as local land charges.[1]

There is appeal to the Secretary of State against a refusal of permission (including a deemed refusal) and against conditions subject to which approval is given.[2] Notice of appeal must be given within six months of the decision. The Secretary of State may allow or dismiss the appeal and can deal with the applications as if it had been made to him in the first instance; so conditions could be added which were not imposed by the Local Planning Authority.

v   Effect of permission

The permission attaches not to the applicant personally, but to the land.[3] Permissions are subject to an implied condition that development must commence within five years from the date of the grant of permission.[4] In the case of an outline permission, development must commence within five years of the grant of the outline permission or two years of approval of the reserved matters, whichever is the later.[5]

Additionally, if development has not been completed within the above periods, then the Local Planning Authority can serve a completion notice, stating that the planning permission will cease to have effect on a specified date, being not earlier than twelve months from the date of the notice.[6] The notice must be confirmed by the Secretary of State.

vi   Enforcement

A breach of planning control occurs if development is carried out in respect of which the necessary permission has not been obtained or if conditions subject to which permission has been granted are not complied with. To enforce planning control, the Local Planning Authority may serve an enforcement notice. This must be served on the owner and occupier of the land affected.[7] If the breach of planning control consists of:

(a) the carrying out of building or other operations (ie the first limb of development as defined in section ii, above) either without permission or in breach of the conditions attached to a permission, or
(b) changing the use of any building to use as a single dwelling house,

18   Ibid, s 70.
19   Ibid, s 69.
20   Question 7 on the current [1994] form.
 1   Local Land Charges Act 1975, s 2(1).
 2   Town and Country Planning Act 1990, s 78.
 3   Ibid, s 75.
 4   Ibid, s 91.
 5   Ibid, s 92.
 6   Ibid, s 94.
 7   Town and Country Planning Act 1990, s 172.

then an enforcement notice can only be served within four years of the breach. Otherwise – that is to say for all other changes of use – the time limit is ten years.[8] The notice must state the alleged breach of planning control, the steps required to remedy the breach, the date on which the notice becomes effective (being not less than 28 days from the date of service) and the date by which the required steps must be taken, that is the compliance period.

Before the notice takes effect an appeal can be made to the Secretary of State and the notice will not then take effect until after the termination of the appeal. The grounds of appeal are specified in the Town and Country Planning Act 1990, section 174 and include the ground that planning permission ought to be granted for the development which constitutes breach of planning control; that the compliance period is too short; and that the notice was served out of time. Non-compliance with an effective enforcement notice is subject to a summary conviction of up to £20,000 or an unlimited amount on indictment.[9]

The Local Planning Authority may wish to stop the breach of planning control before the enforcement notice takes effect, particularly if there is an appeal pending to the Secretary of State. The Local Planning Authority can, at any time after service of an enforcement notice but before it has become effective, serve a stop notice.[10] This will state the activity which is to be stopped, being some or all of the activities alleged by the enforcement notice to be a breach of planning control. Non-compliance with a stop notice is dealt with in the same way as for breach of enforcement notices. If the enforcement notice is eventually quashed on appeal, any person who suffers loss as a result of a stop notice can claim compensation from the Local Planning Authority.[11] The existence of an enforcement notice or a stop notice is revealed by the local land charges search and the additional enquiries of the Local Authority.[12]

As a consequence of the time limit on enforcement action, it is possible to apply for a certificate of lawfulness of existing use or development,[13] where there is no express permission, but the time limit for enforcement action has expired. A buyer requiring reassurance that the use of land is authorised might ask the seller to obtain such a certificate.

---

8   Ibid, s 171B.
9   Town and Country Planning Act 1990, s 179.
10 Ibid, s 183.
11 Ibid, s 186.
12 Question 8 on the current [1994] form.
13 Planning and Compensation Act 1991, s 10.

8 EXCHANGE OF CONTRACTS

I ARE THE PARTIES READY?

i Approval of the draft contract

Having found out as much as possible about the property, the buyer's solicitor must consider the proposed contract and decide whether it is acceptable or whether he should try to negotiate some change. This is a two-fold process – making sure that both the property and the terms on which it is to be sold are satisfactory both from the buyer's point of view and from the buyer's solicitor's professional point of view. If there is negotiation about the terms then the seller's solicitor will be bearing similar matters in mind in acting for his client, as indeed will have been the case when the contract was drafted in the first place. The buyer's solicitor will examine terms such as the length of title offered, the amount of deposit required and the rights of the parties should completion be delayed in order to ensure that these are acceptable to the buyer or at least the best terms available. As regards the property, the solicitor must consider whether in the light of his enquiries and the description of the property and interests affecting it in the contract, the property is suited to the requirements of the buyer. By way of illustration, if the buyer is a developer buying land on which to build a housing estate, the land would be of no use if there were no comprehensive right of access to a public road, or no right of drainage, or if there were a restrictive covenant preventing building (unless suitable indemnity insurance were available or some other sensible solution presented itself). Similarly when a buyer buys a new house on such an estate he will require a right of way over the estate roads until they become public roads, rights of passage of drains, pipes and cables and a scheme of restrictive covenants to preserve the character of the development. He may want a right to enter onto neighbouring property to repair drains. If he has a shared drive he will want a right of way over his neighbour's half and a provision made for maintenance. On the same lines, if the buyer is buying a house which has been built right up to the boundary of one side of a plot, without leaving a strip of land between the house wall and the boundary, the buyer's solicitor should ensure that the property has the benefit of a right of entry onto the neighbouring property for the purpose of effecting repairs to the house.[1]

If there should be a restrictive covenant affecting the property which will be enforceable against the buyer and which will render it unsuitable for the buyer's purposes, then instead of withdrawing, the buyer could attempt to have the covenant

---

1   If there is no such right, the Access to Neighbouring Land Act 1992 may provide a solution.

discharged or take out insurance against it ever being enforced. The Lands Tribunal has power to discharge or modify any restrictive covenant affecting freehold land if:

(a) the restriction is obsolete due to changes in the character of the property or neighbourhood or other circumstances, or

(b) the restriction impedes some reasonable use of the land *and* either the persons entitled to the benefit of the covenant get no practical benefit from it or the restriction is contrary to public interest *and* in either case money will be an adequate compensation to the persons entitled to the benefit if the covenant is discharged or modified, or

(c) all persons of full age and capacity entitled to the benefit of the covenant have expressly or impliedly consented to the discharge, or

(d) the discharge will not adversely affect the persons entitled to the benefit of the covenant.[2]

The Tribunal can also award compensation for loss resulting from the modification or discharge. In practice, because of the cost and time factor, an application to the Tribunal may not be a realistic possibility for a potential buyer.

It may be possible to arrange insurance against the covenant ever being enforced. Full disclosure would have to be made to the insurers who would for a single premium issue a policy for indemnity up to a specified amount. If a policy is already in existence the solicitor for the buyer should ensure that the benefit will be assigned to the buyer and that the amount of the indemnity is satisfactory; if it is too low, perhaps representing the value of the property when the policy was taken out, it may be possible to increase it by paying an additional premium.

Once the buyer has given instructions to proceed, one part of the contract, which will have been sent to the buyer's solicitor in duplicate, will be returned to the seller's solicitor approved (as amended if necessary) in readiness for exchange. If the contract has been amended substantially then it may be re-typed. If it has been amended then it is crucially important that both parts are similarly amended.[3] It is vital that the two parts are identical to comply with the Law of Property (Miscellaneous Provisions) Act 1989, section 2.

ii Financial arrangements

The seller's solicitor will need to ensure that the proceeds of sale will be sufficient to pay off all mortgages over the property and in addition meet any other expenses such as estate agent's fees and the seller's solicitor's own costs. If capital gains tax is payable then provision should be made for this also. The solicitor will probably have discovered at an early stage what mortgages there are over the property and what amounts are owing. He will have had to approach the first mortgagee to obtain the deeds or Charge Certificate (unless the Charge Certificate is held at the Land Registry,[4] in which case he will obtain details from the lender to enable him to obtain office copies of the entries on the register (if he wishes to obtain the certificate he

---

2 Law of Property Act 1925, s 84. This provision also applies to covenants in certain leases.
3 See for example *Harrison v Battye* [1974] 3 All ER 830, [1975] 1 WLR 58, CA. Since the Law of Property (Miscellaneous Provisions) Act 1989, there can be no question of a contract arising through exchange of correspondence: *Commission for the New Towns v Cooper (GB) Ltd* [1995] Ch 259, [1995] 2 All ER 929.
4 Land Registration Act 1925, s 63; see ch 2, section 2 iv; and section 3, for more details on electronic and 'paper free' conveyancing generally.

will need the lender's written authority, though) and he could if necessary request at that stage a statement of the amount owing. The investigation of title he does before drafting the contract will probably include, for unregistered land, a land charges search against the seller. This will have been provided by the seller's solicitor if the TransAction 2001 Protocol is in use. This will reveal any further mortgages, which the seller may have forgotten to mention; for a registered title, they will be apparent from the office copies. Again there is no harm in approaching the second mortgagees at this stage to check the amount owing under their respective mortgages.

The buyer's solicitor should ensure that on the completion date the buyer will be in a position to hand over the required money. If in a residential transaction some of this is being generated by the contemporaneous sale of the buyer's existing house, this will lead to problems of synchronisation, dealt with below. In calculating the amount needed by the buyer, his solicitor should bear in mind his own costs and disbursements in acting on the purchase as well as the costs of the mortgagee's solicitors, if the buyer is buying with the aid of a mortgage. These costs will be payable by the buyer. (The buyer's solicitors may also be acting for the mortgagee but there will still be additional costs for so doing.)

As many domestic conveyancing clients will be both buying and selling property with the same solicitor acting on both transactions, the solicitor will have to consider both the proceeds of sale and also the amount required to complete the purchase, the balance of the former probably making up part of the latter.

A typical buyer will require financial assistance with the purchase from some outside source and the buyer's solicitor may be asked to advise on various sources of finance. On a house purchase there are two common types of mortgage, the repayment mortgage and the endowment mortgage, though pension and interest only mortgages are also occasionally encountered. A mortgage of commercial premises may simply provide for interest to be paid during the term of the mortgage, with the principal repayable at the end of the term. The fixed charge (mortgage) over the specific property may be accompanied by a floating charge over the whole of the mortgagor company's assets, to allow the mortgagee to appoint an administrative receiver.[5]

1   Repayment mortgage

The essence of a mortgage is that a sum called the principal is advanced by the mortgagee on terms for repayment of the principal and payment of interest. These terms will be contained in the mortgage deed which will also mortgage (or charge) the property to the mortgagee. This gives the mortgagee certain rights, the most fundamental of which is a power of sale in certain circumstances. Under a repayment mortgage the term over which it is anticipated that the principal will be paid is fixed, although the mortgagor can pay off the mortgage at any time. With a fixed term, of say 15, 20 or 25 years, it is possible to calculate a monthly instalment which, if paid for the whole of the term, and assuming a constant rate of interest, will pay off both principal and all interest accruing by the end of the term. The mortgage deed will doubtless provide for variation of the interest rate and thus the monthly instalment necessary to pay off the mortgage over the agreed term will fluctuate. Individual instalments can be apportioned as between payment of interest and repayment of principal. It may be that the instalments paid over the first few years of the term are mainly interest and the amount attributable to repayment of principal increases throughout the term but alternatively it may be that the payment of interest and repayment of principal is spread equally over the term and that each instalment represents a similar

---

5   Insolvency Act 1986, s 29(2); this will allow the mortgagee to block the appointment of an administrator.

amount of interest and principal. The proportion of each payment attributable to interest or principal used to be important when tax relief was available on the payment of interest on a mortgage but since Mortgage Interest Relief at Source (MIRAS) was abolished in 2000, this distinction is less relevant. However, it will still be important should the borrower become unemployed or get into financial difficulties, where state benefits may be available to assist with the interest element (but not the principal repayment) of any mortgage.

Repayment mortgages are obtainable from a variety of sources including building societies and banks. It may be necessary to advise the buyer on the relative merits of loans from different mortgagees. In particular the solicitor can compare the possible fluctuations of bank and building society interest rates. Some mortgagees will charge differing rates of interest according to the size of the loan. Some solicitors are wary of giving any financial advice on mortgages for fear of falling foul of the Financial Services Act 1986,[7] but of course only the giving of investment advice is regulated by this Act; mortgage advice is not investment advice, as a mortgage is a debt, not an investment.

To protect the mortgagor from the effect of fluctuating interest rates, many mortgagees will offer 'fixed rate' mortgages, where the interest rate – and thus the repayment – is fixed for an initial period which may vary from one to perhaps five or more years. Sometimes these deals have strings attached; the most common being penalties for redemption within the fixed rate period, or a tie-in after the fixed rate period has finished. A one-off fee may also be payable.

All mortgagees will limit the amount of the loan by reference to the income of the mortgagor or mortgagors and the value of the property to be mortgaged; applicants for a mortgage will have to pay for a valuation for that purpose. If the loan is to be in excess of a certain proportion of the value of the property – say 80% – then some mortgagees will take out a single premium guarantee policy. This is to insure against the mortgagee being unable to recover the whole amount owed on a sale of the property, because the mortgage debt is greater than the market value of the property. This became a major issue in the early to mid 1990s, with the fall in property prices leading to this 'negative equity' situation – the 'equity' being the market value less the outstanding mortgage debt, and negative equity occurring where the debt is greater than the market value.[6] In recent years, however, perhaps because of the adverse publicity generated, these schemes have become less popular and many lenders now only charge a premium where the loan to value ratio is high – say 95%, whilst others have dropped them altogether. The premium for this policy is payable, needless to say, by the mortgagor.

The older the applicant the shorter the term of mortgage which is likely to be on offer. In certain circumstances, for example if the applicant's income might fluctuate, the mortgagee might require a guarantor (perhaps one of the applicant's parents if the applicant is particularly young, or conversely the applicant's child if the applicant is nearing or past retirement age) to join in the mortgage deed to guarantee that repayments will be made.

2   Endowment mortgage

The difference between an endowment mortgage and an ordinary repayment mortgage is that as well as the mortgagor mortgaging the property, he – or they – will also assign to or deposit with the mortgagee a life insurance policy on his – or

6   See further in ch 10, section 6.
7   Soon to be replaced by the Financial Services and Markets Act 2000, which is likely to come into force in late 2001.

their – life or lives. The policy is calculated to produce a sum equivalent to the principal advanced under the mortgage at the end of the term and the term of the policy will be the same as the term of the mortgage. The mortgage instalment repayments are made up wholly of payments of interest, the principal being repaid at the end of the term (assuming the mortgage is not paid off earlier) with the sum produced by the life insurance policy. The mortgagor must also pay the premiums on this policy; policies taken out before March 1984 qualified for tax relief at 15% but policies taken out after that date do not qualify for tax relief. An advantage of this scheme is that the death of a mortgagor whose life is insured will automatically generate the funds to pay off the mortgage. Such a benefit is also available under an ordinary repayment mortgage by means of a special insurance policy called a mortgage protection policy which guarantees, on death, repayment of the sum then outstanding on the mortgage. There has been some criticism in recent years of endowment policies; poor performances in the money markets have on occasion resulted in the final sum payable under the policy being substantially less than is needed to pay off the mortgage. The popularity of endowment type mortgages has, perhaps not surprisingly, waned somewhat in the last few years.

A solicitor should give careful thought before he recommends either a repayment or a particular endowment mortgage to a client particularly in the light of the Financial Services Act 1986 and the Solicitor's Investment Business Rules 1990. If he is to give specific investment advice (for example, as to the merits of different insurance companies' policies) he must be licensed and regulated under the Act, though he can give generic advice (for example, whether an endowment or repayment type mortgage would be better for his client) without the need for regulation. If giving advice on a particular policy, he should consider the ultimate sums to be realised by it, and whether these are guaranteed or merely estimated. He should consider the position if the house has to be sold after only a short while – the surrender value of the policy in the first few years – and how easy it will be to use the same policy on the purchase and mortgage of another property when the house is sold. It also tends to be the case that as interest rates rise, endowment mortgages become less favourable than repayment mortgages. There is also less room for temporarily decreasing the mortgage repayments to offset high interest rates or a period of unemployment.

If any commission is payable to the solicitor in respect of a policy the solicitor should account to the client for it, under rule 10 of the Solicitors Practice Rules 1990, if it is over £20, unless the client agrees it can be retained.

There are also other types of mortgage such as mortgages linked to personal equity plans and to personal pension schemes, which may have tax advantages for certain borrowers, and also 'interest only' mortgages.

3   Mortgage offer

Before the buyer commits himself by exchange of contracts to paying the purchase price (less deposit) on completion, he must be sure that he will be in funds to complete on the contractual completion date. In a residential transaction, it is vital that the buyer receives before exchange of contracts a mortgage offer, intimating that the advance will be available by completion. He otherwise runs the risk that the advance is not available on completion and that unless he can find the money from elsewhere, he may eventually lose his deposit and even have to pay damages to the seller.

The buyer's solicitor must ensure that any conditions attached to the mortgage offer can be met. In certain circumstances there may be a provision that the mortgagee will retain some of the advance pending some specified condition. If on a newly built housing estate the roads are not yet adopted nor is there a Highways Act Agreement and Bond, the mortgagee may make a retention in case the builder defaults in making up the roads, in which case the cost of so doing is borne proportionately by the properties abutting the road making such properties worth that much less. This is also a valid reason for the buyer in these circumstances making a retention from the balance of the purchase price payable on completion and indeed the buyer's solicitor should try and agree before exchange of contracts that in such circumstances a retention, commonly of the amount retained by the mortgagee, can be made on completion. The money can be released when the roads are adopted or a Highways Act Agreement and Bond comes into existence, whichever is the earlier.

The mortgagee may also make a retention in respect of repairs which have to be done to the property. As it is unlikely that these will be done before completion, the buyer's solicitor should check that the buyer does not need the retained money in order to pay over the balance of the purchase price on completion and that the buyer can afford the repairs; a builder's estimate will be needed.

Another condition of the mortgage offer may refer to payment of the single premium of the guarantee policy if the advance is in excess of a certain percentage of the mortgagee's valuation of the property. Some mortgagees will add the premium on to the advance.

On a mortgage of leasehold property, the mortgagee may require the freehold and any superior titles to be deduced, unless the lease is registered with absolute title. The buyer's solicitor should ensure that the contract with the seller contains an equivalent provision. On a mortgage of a recently built property, the mortgagee will want the property to have the benefit of the NHBC scheme or equivalent.[8]

4   Deposit

As well as ensuring that sufficient money will be available to complete the purchase, the buyer's solicitor must ensure that there will be sufficient money available on exchange of contracts to pay the deposit, normally fixed by the contract at 10% of the purchase price. If the buyer is selling a property at the same time, as is commonly the case in a residential transaction, he may wish to use the deposit he receives on his sale to put towards the deposit he must pay on his purchase. This can be done under Standard Condition 2.2.2. Even if this money can be used, there will probably be a balance to make up, if the price which the buyer is paying on his purchase is greater than that for which he is selling his present property. If the buyer is a first time buyer then he will have to find all of the deposit. The excess of the purchase deposit over a sale deposit, or the whole of the deposit in the case of the first time buyer, will normally come from the buyer's savings. If the buyer is obtaining a mortgage in excess of 90% of the purchase price – say 95% – he will not wish to pay a 10% deposit. The mortgage is providing 95% of the purchase price and the buyer is therefore only finding, from other sources, 5%. The mortgage is only available on completion and the buyer will therefore wish to pay a deposit of only 5%. His solicitor should negotiate for the inclusion of such a term in the contract. The alternative is a bridging loan. Similarly, if the buyer cannot use the deposit on his sale because it is held as stake-holder, he may conceivably have to take out a bridging loan in order to help him pay the deposit on his purchase. This can then be repaid on completion (of the sale) when the money does become available but it does involve the buyer in paying interest on the loan. Assuming the loan is from the buyer's bank, the buyer's solicitor would have to give an undertaking to the bank that the net proceeds of sale (after payment of outstanding mortgages, the amount needed to finance completion of the purchase, solicitor's costs etc.) would be paid to the credit of the buyer's account at the bank; the bank would then need to be satisfied about the

---

8   See ch 13 for more detail on recent developments regarding mortgages.

likely amount of these net proceeds. A bank may have a standard form of undertaking which the buyer's solicitor would be asked to sign, but he must first check that the terms of such an undertaking are satisfactory. In particular the undertaking should be limited to money which is actually received by the buyer's solicitor and which will be available for repayment of the bridging loan. An easier and more common solution to the problem of a shortfall between the deposit on the client's sale and that on his purchase is to negotiate a reduced deposit on the purchase.

The buyer's solicitor will need to ascertain whether any preliminary deposit has been paid, for example to the seller's estate agent, as this will count towards the contractual deposit. On exchange, the deposit will normally be paid by means of the buyer's solicitor's cheque. If some of the money is coming from the buyer in the form of a cheque, the buyer's solicitor should make sure he receives this well in advance of exchange so that it can be cleared before being drawn against.

iii   Sale of part of mortgaged property

If the seller is selling part of the property the whole of which is subject to a mortgage, he can either pay off the whole mortgage in the usual way using the proceeds of sale, or, particularly if the proceeds will be quite small, he may approach the mortgagee to see if the mortgagee will agree to release from the mortgage the part being sold. The mortgagee may do this, particularly if all or part of the proceeds of sale are paid in reduction of the amount owing under the mortgage. The seller's solicitor should ensure that the mortgagee's approval is obtained before exchange because if the approval is not forthcoming, the seller will have to pay off the whole of the mortgage in order to be able to convey the property to the buyer free of it.[9]

iv   Sale by a sole spouse

1   Family Law Act 1996

If the matrimonial home is in the sole name of one spouse then the other non-owning spouse can register a statutory right of occupation as a Class F land charge in respect of unregistered land or a notice in respect of registered land. Unless the seller can procure the cancellation of the charge, he will be in breach of contract with the buyer and liable to pay damages.[10] If the charge or notice is already registered before exchange of contracts then the seller's solicitor should advise the seller not to proceed until he is sure that the charge can be cancelled on or before completion. This could mean reaching some sort of agreement with the seller's spouse or more probably the spouse's solicitors, perhaps involving some share of the proceeds of sale, although it must be said that the charge protects a right of occupation, not an interest in the proceeds of sale.[11] If the buyer's solicitor has discovered that there is a charge registered, he will advise the buyer not to exchange contracts until he is satisfied that the charge will be cancelled. He may require the other spouse to join in the contract or sign some separate declaration not to enforce the charge against the buyer. He will require an undertaking from the seller's solicitors to hand over on completion

9   See eg *Re Daniel* [1917] 2 Ch 405.
10   See eg *Wroth v Tyler*, mentioned in ch 5, section xi above. However, the buyer may in some circumstances succeed in having the charge vacated, and so take the property free from it: *Kaur v Gill* [1988] Fam 110, [1988] 2 All ER 288, CA.
11   *Barnett v Hassett* [1982] 1 All ER 80, [1981] 1 WLR 1385.

an application for cancellation of registration of the charge signed by the seller's spouse; ideally the signed application could be handed over on or before exchange of contracts. All this will only be possible if the seller has managed to reach some agreement with the spouse. The case of *Holmes v H Kennard & Son*[12] illustrates the pitfalls. A buyer's solicitor was held negligent for accepting an application to cancel a *caution* signed by the seller's wife's solicitors rather than an application to cancel a *notice* signed by the wife personally; the notice was therefore not cancelled after completion and in the meantime the wife had changed her mind.

Even if there is no charge registered before exchange of contracts, the seller is still taking some risk in proceeding because if a charge should be registered after exchange of contracts but before the buyer's solicitor has obtained his pre-completion search then the seller will still be in the position of having to procure the cancellation of the charge or else of being in breach of contract. Where the seller and spouse are living together quite happily there will be no problem but if the parties should be separated or separating, it might in some cases be advisable for the seller's solicitor to suggest that the other spouse be approached before exchange of contracts rather than risk the possibility of a charge being registered after exchange

2   Occupier's equitable interest

Even though the matrimonial home may be in the sole name of one spouse, the other spouse may have an equitable interest, for example by having made a contribution to the purchase price. We have already seen that, in broad terms, if a spouse with an equitable interest is in occupation of the property being sold then that interest may be binding on the buyer.[13] If the buyer or his solicitor has discovered that the other spouse is in occupation before exchange of contracts, and has or may have an equitable interest, then again the buyer should be advised not to proceed unless satisfied that he will take the property free from the equitable interest. The buyer may require the other spouse to join in the contract to confirm that the interest (and also any Family Law Act charge) will not be enforced against the buyer,[14] and join in the conveyance. The spouse could also be asked to confirm, by joining in the contract, that she will not register any new Family Law Act charge. Alternatively the buyer should obtain a form of consent to the sale, signed by the other spouse. Finally, there is the option of appointing a second trustee and thereby overreaching the interest on the sale to the buyer, although this will not remove the problem of a Family Law Act registration, nor will it solve the practical problem how to physically remove the reluctant spouse!

The foregoing applies not only to a sale by a spouse where the other spouse has an equitable interest and is in occupation but to any other sale where there is an occupier with an equitable interest, for example some other relative or a cohabitee.

v   Co-ordination of two transactions

If a client is dependent on the sale of one property for the purchase of another, as is often the case in domestic conveyancing, the two must proceed side by side. Exchange

---

12   (1984) 49 P & CR 202, CA.
13   See ch 6, section 8 ii, above.
14   This would be ineffective if the spouse (or other occupier) had a protected tenancy: *Appleton v Aspin* [1988] 1 All ER 904, [1988] 1 WLR 410, CA: See also *Woolwich Building Society v Dickman* [1996] 3 All ER 204, where it was held that even a tenant's written consent to a mortgage will not subordinate the tenant's rights under a protected tenancy to those of the lender, resulting in the tenant having an overriding interest under s 70(1)(g) Land Registration Act 1925.

of contracts must be contemporaneous and the completion date in both contracts must be the same. To avoid losing a property he wishes to buy, the client may wish to exchange contracts on a purchase before exchanging contracts on his sale; and vice versa. The dangers are obvious; if on the other transaction contracts never are exchanged – which is perfectly possible – then the client is left with either two properties or no property at all. He would then need, respectively, a bridging loan to fund his purchase; or somewhere to live and store his furniture! If a client insists on pursuing this risky strategy, written instructions must, of course, be obtained.

vi   Completion date

Before, and normally just before, exchange the parties must agree on a completion date and insert it in both parts of the contract. If the transaction is one of a chain of house sales and purchases all of which must be completed on the same date, it could take some time and negotiation before arrangements are made which are satisfactory to all concerned. If the standard form of contract is used there is provision for the insertion of the completion date on the front page. If this is not done Standard Condition 6.1.1 will apply.

vii   Sale by auction

If the buyer is intending to buy a property at an auction, all the steps which are normally taken before exchange of contracts must be taken before the auction. This includes all the pre-contract searches and enquiries and making financial arrangements for payment of the deposit and the balance of the purchase price on completion. Bearing in mind that the contract for sale at an auction will be binding on the fall of the auctioneer's hammer, it may be difficult if not impossible to co-ordinate two transactions one of which is proceeding by way of an auction.

2   EXCHANGE OF CONTRACTS

i   Conditional contracts

The parties may wish to make the contract dependent on the satisfaction of some external condition. An obvious example would be on the purchase of land for building, where the buyer would only want to buy if planning permission was available and the contract could thus be made conditional on planning permission being granted. If the parties propose entering a conditional contract, the condition must be sufficiently precisely stated otherwise the contract may be void for uncertainty. A contract which is 'subject to the purchaser obtaining a satisfactory mortgage' will be void for uncertainty[15] although if surrounded by more precise stipulations it could be valid.[16] It would seem that a contract conditional on the buyer securing a mortgage offer for a specified sum and on terms which would be acceptable to a reasonable borrower can be valid, as it imports a degree of objectivity. A contract 'subject to preliminary enquiries and searches' might be void for uncertainty or might be a valid contract conditional on the buyer's solicitor being satisfied as to these matters.[17]

---

15 *Lee-Parker v Izzet (No 2)* [1972] 2 All ER 800, [1972] 1 WLR 775.
16 *Janmohamed v Hassam* [1977] 1 EGLR 142.
17 *Smith and Olley v Townsend* (1949) 1 P & CR 28, cf *Ganton House Investments Ltd v Corbin* [1988] 2 EGLR 69.

For the contract to actually take effect, the condition must be satisfied:

(a) by the date so specified, or if no date is specified
(b) by the date specified in the contract for completion, or if there is no such date
(c) within a reasonable time.[18]

For the first two time limits, (a) and (b), time is of the essence. Unless the condition is satisfied within the appropriate time limit, the contract fails and either party can treat it as discharged. This will be the case where within the time limit the condition positively failed (eg planning permission being refused) or there is no resolution of the condition one way or the other (eg no decision having yet been given on an application for planning permission). Unless the condition has positively failed, the parties are bound and cannot withdraw from the contract until the time limit has passed, but must wait and see whether the contract is to become effective or not. As might be expected, the Standard Conditions are not in the form of a conditional contract.

If the condition of a conditional contract is entirely for the benefit of one party (eg a planning permission condition for the buyer's benefit) apparently that party can waive the condition and enforce the contract.[19]

In *Millers Wharf Partnership Ltd v Corinthian Column Ltd,*[20] a contract was expressed to be 'conditional' on certain permissions and consents being obtained, with a provision that if they were not obtained by a specific date, either party could 'at any time thereafter' rescind the contract by written notice. As it turned out the condition was not satisfied by the specific date. At that point neither party rescinded; the court had to consider whether, if the condition was subsequently satisfied, the purchaser could thereafter rescind. The court decided that the proper interpretation of the contract, and in particular the reference to rescission 'at any time thereafter', was that the purchaser could rescind even after the condition had been satisfied.

The conditional contract could contain a term which imposes an obligation on one or other of the parties, such as obtaining the landlord's consent to the assignment of a lease.[21] A conditional contract should be distinguished from an agreement which is 'subject to contract'[1] or 'subject to the preparation and approval of a formal contract'[2] the effect of which is that there is no concluded binding contract between the parties at that stage. The 'subject to contract' qualification is often inserted by solicitors in their pre-exchange of contract letters so as to avoid creating a contract by the correspondence. The 'subject to contract' qualification can be removed if the parties subsequently expressly or impliedly so agree.[3] There may,

18 *Aberfoyle Plantations Ltd v Cheng* [1960] AC 115, [1959] 3 All ER 910, PC.
19 *Heron Garage Properties Ltd v Moss* [1974] 1 All ER 421, [1974] 1 WLR 148.
20 (1990) 61 P & CR 461, [1991] 1 EGLR 192.
21 See eg *Property and Bloodstock Ltd v Emerton* [1968] Ch 94, [1967] 3 All ER 321, CA.
 1 *Spottiswoode, Ballantyne & Co Ltd v Doreen Appliances Ltd* [1942] 2 KB 32, [1942] 2 All ER 65, CA.
 2 *Winn v Bull* (1877) 7 Ch D 29.
 3 In *Griffiths v Young* [1970] Ch 675, [1970] 3 All ER 601, CA, a 'subject to contract' qualification was held to have been waived by a subsequent telephone conversation. In *Sherbrooke v Dipple* (1980) 41 P & CR 173, CA, it was held that once negotiations are made 'subject to contract' then any agreement reached as a result of those negotiations will be subject to contract unless either expressly made otherwise or the circumstances are so exceptional as to lead to the implication that the subject to contract qualification has been abandoned. In that case, the agreement was reached after an interruption in negotiations of over twelve months but it was still governed by the subject to contract qualification originally imposed. See also *Henderson Group plc v Superabbey Ltd* [1988] 2 EGLR 155. The replacement of s 40 of the Law of Property Act 1925 by s 2 of the Law of Property (Miscellaneous Provisions) Act 1989 has arguably removed the need for the qualification.

however, be exceptional circumstances in which an agreement expressed to be subject to contract is nevertheless held to constitute a binding contract. *Alpenstow Ltd v Regalian Properties plc*[4] was such a case, where a 'subject to contract' agreement provided a detailed timetable for submission and approval of a draft contract, and exchange of contracts; the normal meaning of 'subject to contract' was held to be incompatible with the nature and terms of the agreement. (There has also been a suggestion that a defendant could be estopped from pleading that an agreement was 'subject to contract' if in the circumstances it would be inequitable to do so.[5]) The effect of a contract made 'subject to survey' or 'subject to a surveyor's report' was thought to be the same as a subject to contract stipulation, indicating that there was no concluded contract between the parties.[6] However, the more recent case of *Ee v Kakar*[7] suggests that there could be a valid conditional contract made subject to survey.

In dealing with contracts created informally, for example by correspondence, there is one further possibility, which is that despite some qualifying words there is a provisional yet binding contract which it is intended will be replaced eventually by a formal contract. Thus in *Branca v Cobarro*[8] there was a 'provisional agreement until a fully legalised agreement' was drawn up and signed. Nowadays, though, this would be less likely to be the case as informal contracts will be subject to the provisions of the Law of Property (Miscellaneous Provisions) Act 1989.

ii   Exchange of contracts

Before the two parts of the contract are exchanged they must be signed by the seller and buyer respectively. The solicitor will normally take this opportunity of explaining to his client the contents of the contract and the result of the pre-contract searches and enquiries.[9] TransAction 2001 recommends that the buyer should always be provided with a written contract report.

Signature will normally be by the client personally; the solicitor has no implied authority to sign the contract on his client's behalf but this can of course be given expressly.[10] Where the client is buying with the aid of a mortgage, the lender will have laid down conditions, which the solicitor is obliged to comply with, regarding the verification of the identity of his client.[11] In addition, so far as identification is concerned, regard must be had to the Money Laundering Regulations 1993 (although appropriate identification on both these fronts should have taken place at the start of the transaction). Finally, the Law Society's 'Green Card' warning on property fraud should be kept in mind, and watch be kept for fraudulent or fictitious buyers, sellers or even solicitors, as well as for any unusual instructions.

---

4   [1985] 2 All ER 545, [1985] 1 WLR 721.
5   *Salvation Army Trustee Co Ltd v West Yorkshire Metropolitan County Council* (1980) 41 P & CR 179, cf *A-G of Hong Kong v Humphreys Estate Ltd* [1987] AC 114, [1987] 2 All ER 387, PC.
6   *Marks v Board* (1930) 46 TLR 424.
7   (1979) 40 P & CR 223.
8   [1947] KB 854, [1947] 2 All ER 101, CA.
9   On the extent of such explanation see *Booth v Davey* [1988] NLJR 104, CA.
10   A solicitor signing on behalf of a client should ensure that he is given express authority by all the clients on whose behalf he is signing, for example, by both of two joint owners, otherwise he may be liable for breach of warranty of authority: *Suleman v Shahsavari* [1989] 2 All ER 460, [1988] 1 WLR 1181. See also *Penn v Bristol and West Building Society* [1997] 3 All ER 470, [1997] 1 WLR 1356, where instructions were taken from only one of two co-owners, the solicitor involved mistakenly believing that the other was in agreement.
11   See ch 13.

An auctioneer does have implied authority to sign for both parties. One other matter to be checked on or before exchange is that the two parts of the contract are identical. In *Harrison v Battye*[12] one part was amended to show an agreed reduced deposit but the other part was not so amended. Exchange of these two would not effect a contract, subject to the equitable remedy of rectification.

Exchange of two identical parts of the contract is the normal method adopted by the parties of bringing the contract into existence and the method contemplated by the Standard Conditions. However, there is more than one way in which the exchange can be effected.

1   Exchange by personal attendance

The two parts of the contract can be exchanged in the office of one or other of the solicitors or in any other convenient place. This may happen if the two solicitors' offices are close to each other. The buyer's solicitor hands over the buyer's part and the deposit and in return the seller's solicitor hands over the seller's part. Of course, the difficulty with personal exchange is that of synchronisation where the client is selling and buying.

2   Exchange by post

This is a more common method of exchange than personal exchange. We have already mentioned the difficulty of knowing at what precise moment the contract does come into existence, a difficulty remedied by provision in the Standard Conditions stating that it is on the posting of the second part.[13] Normally the buyer's solicitor will post the buyer's part and the deposit; when the seller's solicitor receives this he will post the seller's part. Of course even at this late stage there is no obligation on the seller to send his part. He could if he wished instruct his solicitor to return the buyer's deposit and call the whole deal off.

Mistakes happen even in the best run offices and it may be that the seller's solicitor by mistake sends to the buyer's solicitor not the seller's part of the contract but the buyer's part which has just been sent to him. There is a suggestion in *Harrison v Battye*[14] that this error would be overlooked and that the part retained by the seller's solicitor would be appropriated to the buyer by virtue of the covering letter sent to the buyer's solicitor purporting to enclose it. This suggestion perhaps gains some support from the reasoning in *Domb v Isoz*,[15] below.

The Standard Conditions also refer to exchange via a document exchange, and provide that the contract is made when the second part of the contract is deposited at the document exchange.[16]

Postal exchange is only infrequently used; the problem again, is one of synchronisation where there is a chain of transactions.

3   Exchange by telephone

The practice of exchanging contracts by telephone has been given the blessing of the Court of Appeal. Each solicitor may still hold the part of the contract signed by his own client and the process of exchange may not yet have begun. It may be important

---

12   [1974] 3 All ER 830, [1975] 1 WLR 58, CA.
13   SC 2.1.1.
14   Above.
15   [1980] Ch 548, [1980] 1 All ER 942, CA.
16   SC 2.1.1.

that the parties enter into the contract at short notice, but exchange of contracts by personal attendance may be out of the question. It is possible for the two solicitors to agree over the telephone that the contracts be treated as exchanged, each part then being appropriated to the other party. This is seen as effecting an exchange of the two parts rather than as a separate oral contract for sale.[17] The Law Society has issued a variety of formulae for exchange of contracts by telephone. These each involve the solicitor giving undertakings, and therefore it is advisable that the firm considers its policy as to who is allowed to conduct telephone exchanges.

The formulae are as follows:

Formula A

Formula A applies where one solicitor holds both (signed) parts of the contract. This may occur where, for example, the solicitor acting for the first time buyer at the bottom of the chain sends his client's part of the contract, together with the deposit cheque, to the seller's solicitor. The solicitor holding both parts of the contract then telephones the other party's solicitor and:

i)   they check and agree that both parts are identical. If any last minute alterations are needed, it is vital that the wording on each contract is identical, and although such alterations can be agreed on the telephone (subject to having received the client's authority to make the amendment and to sign it on the client's behalf), it is preferable that exchange is delayed until the amendment has been faxed to the other solicitor and formally agreed;

ii) the solicitor holding both parts confirms that he has them, and the deposit cheque;

iii) they agree the completion date to be entered into the contract;

iv) they discuss and agree any changes to the formula (for example, if the deposit cheque is to be sent to someone other than the seller's solicitor);

v)   they agree that exchange shall be deemed to have taken place, and agree the time of exchange; and

vi) the solicitor holding both parts confirms that he will send his client's part (with deposit if appropriate) to the other solicitor by first class post or document exchange the same day.

The solicitor holding both parts then completes each with the date of exchange, and the date of completion, before sending his client's part off. Each solicitor makes an attendance note covering:

a)   the date of exchange;

b)   the time of exchange;

c)   the agreed deposit;

d)   the agreed completion date;

e)   the identity of the person at the other firm with whom the exchange took place (not just the firm's name); and

f)   any agreed variations to the contract or the formula for exchange.

Formula B

Formula B is similar to Formula A but applies where each solicitor holds his client's signed part of the contract. The procedure is very similar to Formula A and works as follows:

---

17   *Domb v Isoz* [1980] Ch 548, [1980] 1 All ER 942, CA.

i)   each solicitor checks and agrees that both parts of the contract are identical.
ii) each confirms that he holds his client's part and the buyer's solicitor confirms he holds the deposit cheque;
iii) they agree the completion date to be entered into the contract;
iv) they discuss and agree any changes to the formula;
v)   they agree that exchange shall be deemed to have taken place, and agree the time of exchange; and
vi) they each confirm that they will send their client's part (with deposit if appropriate) to the other solicitor by first class post or document exchange the same day.

They then each complete their part of the contract with the date of exchange, and the date of completion, before sending it off to the other solicitor. Each solicitor makes an attendance note covering:

a)   the date of exchange;
b)   the time of exchange;
c)   the agreed deposit;
d)   the agreed completion date;
e)   the identity of the person at the other firm with whom the exchange took place; and
f)   any agreed variations to the contract or the formula for exchange.

It seems that this method of exchange is within a solicitor's implied authority from his client and so no express authority would be required. This method of exchange is also contemplated by the Standard Conditions.[18] Efficacious though it is, there do seem to be some risks attached to the procedure.[19] The two parts of the contract might by oversight not be identical, a particular risk under Formula B. The buyer's solicitor might send no deposit or send it late.[20] It may be that by oversight one of the parts of the contract, at the time of the telephone exchange, is not signed. The biggest problem is that of synchronisation, dealt with below.

Careful checking should, however, eliminate most of these risks and exchange by telephone is by far the most popular and efficacious method.

iii   Payment of the deposit

The deposit will normally be paid by the buyer's solicitor's cheque and the Standard Conditions make specific provision for this as an alternative to a banker's draft.[1]

If the deposit is paid by the buyer's personal cheque, the seller's solicitor must delay exchange until the cheque has been cleared, as it could amount to a breach of the Solicitors Accounts Rules 1998 if the client's cheque is subsequently dishonoured. The consequences of non-payment of the deposit, ie a deposit cheque being dishonoured, have been considered in Chapter 5.

iv   Synchronisation

If a domestic conveyancing client is selling one property and buying another, a solicitor may have to synchronise exchange on both contracts. If exchange in both

---

18   SC 2.1.2.
19   See [1987] Law Soc Gaz 3313.
20   Although this would presumably amount to professional misconduct. It has been held that the late payment of the deposit under Formula B does not entitle the seller to treat the contract as discharged by breach: *Khan v Hamilton* [1989] EGCS 128.
 1   SC 2.2.1.

cases is to be effected personally, the solicitor could collect the buyer's part of the contract and deposit on his client's sale, then exchange contracts on his client's purchase and finally return to hand over his client's part of the contract on his sale and so effect that exchange. The only area of risk is that after exchanging on his client's purchase and before concluding the exchange on his client's sale, the latter could 'go off' and his client's buyer's solicitor could demand return of his part of the contract and the deposit. It is more likely that the exchanges will be effected by post. If the solicitor receives the contract from the buyer on his client's sale, then exchanges contracts on his client's purchase and finally concludes the exchange on his client's sale by sending off his client's part of the contract, then the period during which there is some risk will be between the posting of the seller's part on his client's purchase and its receipt; on receipt the solicitor can immediately post his client's part of the contract on his sale thus concluding that exchange. This period of risk can be minimised if he asks the seller's solicitor, on his client's purchase, to telephone him as soon as the seller's part of the contract has been posted so that he can then immediately post his client's part on his client's sale. This of course assumes that the effective date of exchange is the date of posting of the second part of the contract.

There is an alternative method which avoids the solicitor having to 'sit on' the buyer's part of the contract which has been sent to him on his client's sale whilst he exchanges on his clients' purchase. In advance of exchange, the solicitor sends off his client's part of the purchase contract to the seller's solicitors, to be held by them to his order. When he receives the buyer's part of the contract on his client's sale, he can by a telephone call release his client's part of the purchase contract and again ask to be informed by telephone when the seller's part is posted, whereupon he can then conclude the exchange on his client's sale. However, he might not be able to send off the deposit in advance of exchange. On the whole, though, it is extremely rare to find postal exchange used where synchronisation is needed.

It is relatively straightforward to synchronise a telephone exchange and a postal exchange if the telephone exchange is on the client's purchase; the solicitor receives the buyer's part contract on his client's sale, exchanges by telephone on the client's purchase, then immediately posts the client's part contract on the sale. It is not so easy to synchronise if the telephone exchange is on the sale, and in the case of two telephone exchanges, on the face of it one must precede the other unless the solicitor can speak into two telephones simultaneously. To solve this problem, the Law Society have produced a third formula, Formula C, to be used in a chain of transactions when contracts are to be exchanged over the telephone and exchange is to be synchronised.[2] Formula C or a variation of it is the most popular form of exchange.

Formula C can be used either where one solicitor holds both parts of the contract or where each solicitor holds their client's own part. For the purpose of the following example, we will assume that each solicitor holds his own client's part. Under Formula C the exchanges take place in two stages:

Stage One

i)   Each solicitor confirms he holds his client's duly signed part of the contract (and deposit, if appropriate). As with Formulae A and B, they need to check and confirm that both parts are identical.

---

2   Formula C is set out in the Appendix. See further [1989] Law Soc Gaz 26, 15 March explaining Formula C, and [1991] Law Soc Gaz 45, 11 December, dealing with an amendment to Formula C to include the possibility of communications under Formula C by fax.

ii) Each solicitor agrees that he will exchange contracts by an agreed time later that day if requested.
iii) They agree the amount of deposit which will be available, and the completion date which will apply when they exchange.
iv) They agree any amendments to the contract or the formula.
v) Each solicitor makes an attendance note of the conversation.

The seller's solicitor is then free to exchange contracts on his client's own purchase, using Formula A or B as appropriate. He then telephones the buyer's solicitor again (obviously, before the agreed time) and proceeds to stage two of the procedure.

Stage Two

i) The parties agree that exchange shall be deemed to have taken place, and agree and note the time.
ii) Each agrees to send his client's part to the other the same day by first class post or document exchange, with deposit cheque if appropriate.

As mentioned, attendance notes will need to be kept of both stages. That for stage one will note:

a) the agreed latest time for exchange;
b) the agreed deposit;
c) the agreed completion date;
d) the identity of the person at the other firm; and
e) any agreed variations to the contract or the formula.

The stage two attendance note will include:

a) the date of exchange;
b) the time of exchange; and
c) the name of the person at the other firm.

A Formula C exchange is probably not within the normal solicitor/client relationship and therefore written irrevocable authority from the client should be obtained. A standard form of authority is included in the formula.

Formula C is not without its difficulties. Firstly, a solicitor will want a gap between the latest time that he can be telephoned back by the seller's solicitor on his client's purchase, and the latest time for him to telephone the buyer's solicitor on his client's sale. If that gap is to be as much as a half hour, the chain does not have to be very long before it becomes impracticable to achieve everything on the same day. Furthermore, in order for the second part of the formula which achieves the actual exchange of contracts to be effective, the buyer's solicitor has to undertake as part of the formula that either he or some other named person in his office will be available up to the final time for exchange to receive the telephone call from the seller's solicitors. This is an undertaking like any other, and should not be given lightly. Despite these drawbacks, Formula C is based on solicitors' undertakings and is therefore probably preferable to the rather vague notion of 'releasing the buyer's part of the contract up the chain' which some solicitors operated before the Law Society produced Formula C in 1989, and which some still do operate.

Under the Protocol, exchange over the telephone must be by Formula A, B or C.

In a chain of transactions, there may be problems over payment of the deposit. If a buyer is using part or all of the deposit which he is receiving on his related sale to go towards the deposit on his purchase, his solicitor may need to send the deposit off on the purchase before he has received the deposit coming in on the sale. For example, under Formula C, the buyer's solicitor on exchange has to undertake, as

under Formula A or B, to send off the deposit by first class post or through
ient exchange. He will not at that stage have received the deposit on his
sale, ... will not receive that until the next day at the earliest. This is a problem
which could be avoided by payment of the deposit via a bank telegraphic transfer
rather than through the post or document exchange, but a more convenient method
of solving the problem may be to have the deposit paid from one end of the chain
direct to the other end of the chain rather than it passing through everyone's hands
up the chain. At its simplest, this would involve a deposit of the same size in each
transaction, otherwise there may be 'topping up' amounts to be paid up the chain.
Thus Formula C refers to the buyer's solicitor undertaking to dispatch 'or to arrange
for the dispatch' of the deposit. Again, this is an undertaking which should not be
given lightly.[3] It should nevertheless be made clear to a client in the middle of a
chain that although he may not be actually physically paying a deposit, because the
money is travelling direct from one end of the chain to the other, he has nevertheless
paid a deposit and the deposit is subject to forfeiture exactly as any other deposit.
It is also unclear what happens if the deposit, paid from one end of the chain to the
other, is not actually paid; presumably all the contracts in the chain can be treated
as discharged by the various sellers. If it is agreed that the deposit is to be passed up
the chain in this way, this will constitute a variation to the formula and should be
noted as such.

v   Other methods of creating the contract

Exchange of a formal contract in two identical parts is only one way of bringing the
contract into existence, although it is by far the most common way. It might be, for
example, that there is to be only one contractual document, to be signed by both
parties.[4] The main advantage of the conventional method of exchange is that it is the
two parts of a formal contract which also satisfy the requirements of the Law of
Property (Miscellaneous Provisions) Act 1989, section 2, and that as a result of the
exchange each party has in his control the document necessary to satisfy section 2
should he wish to enforce the contract.

vi   Timescale

It may be that a solicitor finds himself in the position of trying to urge the other party
into an early exchange of contracts. The dangers are illustrated by the case of *Goff v
Gauthier*.[5] Here, the vendor's solicitor told the purchaser's solicitor that unless
contracts were exchanged, the contract would be withdrawn and a draft contract would
be sent to another purchaser. The vendor's solicitor made this statement in good
faith based on his client's instructions, but the court found that as a matter of fact the
vendor did not intend to withdraw the contract and send out a draft contract to another
purchaser. The vendor's solicitor's statement had therefore been a misstatement of
fact, and amounted to an actionable misrepresentation.

If a party is wishing to buy time in negotiations, it is possible to enter into a valid
'lock-out' agreement whereby a vendor agrees not to negotiate with any other potential

---

3   The Law Society and the Conveyancing Standing Committee of the Law Commission have
     approved such a 'leapfrogging deposit' in the appendix to a joint report 'Deposits – No Time
     for Change!', July 1989.
4   See eg *Smith v Mansi* [1962] 3 All ER 857, [1963] 1 WLR 26, CA.
5   (1991) 62 P & CR 388. See further in ch 16, section 1 i.

purchasers. However, to satisfy the requirement of certainty, the agreement should stipulate the time for which the vendor cannot enter negotiations with other purchasers.[6]

3 THE POSITION AFTER EXCHANGE

i Dating the contract

Once the solicitor receives the other party's part of the contract it should be dated with the date of exchange, ie the date of posting of the second (seller's) part or the date of the telephone exchange.[7] This is important because some time limits under the Standard Conditions are calculated by reference to the date of the contract. The agreed completion date should have been entered in the contract before exchange.[8]

ii Protecting the contract

The contract is an 'estate contract' and can be protected by entry of a Civ land charge (unregistered land) or a notice or caution (registered land). If the property is subsequently sold to another buyer, then even if he has notice of the first contract he will not be bound by it unless it is so protected before completion of his purchase, or more accurately before his solicitor obtains his pre-completion search. If the contract is not protected and the seller does sell the property to another buyer, then although the first buyer will be able to recover damages from the seller he will not be able to enforce the contract against the second buyer and have the property conveyed to him. If his contract had been registered then it could be enforced against the second buyer who in practice would then never have bought the property. The practice is not to register the contract in every case but only when there are particular circumstances which make it advisable, such as a long period of time between exchange of contracts and completion, or a suspicion of the seller's intentions. For a registered title, a notice can only be entered if the Land Certificate is available, otherwise a caution is the appropriate method of protection. For unregistered land, the registration – like any other land charges registration – to be effective must be made against the name of the estate owner at the time of registration.[9] This will normally be the seller. There is a presumption that the correct name of the estate owner is the name appearing in the deeds. If a registration is made against a name which is in fact not the estate owner's correct name then this will give no protection against another buyer who searches against the correct name. The problem is more acute if the buyer is a sub-purchaser, that is if the seller has himself entered into a contract to purchase the property, and that contract has not yet been completed (the usual course is that the conveyance is made directly to the sub-purchaser). At the time of registration of the sub-purchase contract the owner of the legal estate is not the seller, but the person from whom the seller has contracted to buy, and it is against his name that the sub-purchase contract must be registered, even though he is not directly affected by it.[10] The sub-purchaser

---

6 *Walford v Miles* [1992] 2 AC 128, [1992] 1 All ER 453, HL; see also *Pitts v PHH Asset Management Ltd* [1993] 4 All ER 961, [1994] 1 WLR 327. Note, however, that the courts will not grant an injunction to enforce a lock-out agreement, but will only order damages: *Tye v House* (1997) 76 P & CR 188, [1997] 2 EGLR 171.

7 SC 2.1.1, 2.1.2.

8 See ch 5, section xix.

9 Land Charges Act 1972, s 3(1).

10 *Barrett v Hilton Developments Ltd* [1975] Ch 237, [1974] 3 All ER 944, CA.

may not know his name or even be aware that his purchase is a sub-purchase until he receives the abstract or epitome, which may sometimes be after exchange.

iii   Insurance

On the sale of land under an open contract, the risk passes at the time of the contract rather than completion and the buyer should make arrangements for insurance of the property to take effect from exchange of contracts. The seller will normally not cancel his insurance but maintain his policy until completion in case the buyer does not complete and the seller is left with the property. If the buyer is buying with the aid of a mortgage it is common for the mortgagee, particularly in domestic conveyancing, to arrange the insurance of the property, charging the premiums to the buyer. This insurance cover might only commence on completion, as it is only at that stage that the mortgagee is subject to any risk, but if requested the mortgagee will arrange for the insurance cover to commence on exchange of contracts. If the property is leasehold and particularly if it is a flat, there may be some provision in the lease requiring the insurers to be approved by the lessor, or even specifying a particular insurance company. The mortgagee's approval would then have to be obtained to this arrangement. In this case it may be simpler for the buyer to take over the seller's existing policy rather than for him to take out a completely fresh policy.

If the buyer does not take out insurance then in certain circumstances he can take the benefit of the seller's policy if that is still in existence. The Law of Property Act 1925, section 47 states that money payable under the policy to the seller after the date of the contract in respect of damage to the property shall be paid over to the buyer on completion or when received if later, provided that there is no stipulation to the contrary in the contract, that the insurers give their consent and that the buyer pays a proportionate part of the premium. Insurance companies commonly give their consent but as we shall see, the Standard Conditions exclude section 47. There is also an old statutory provision in the Fires Prevention (Metropolis) Act 1774 under which certain persons can compel an insurance company to spend the insurance money on reinstating the property, but the application of this Act to a buyer is somewhat doubtful.

It is therefore imperative for the buyer under an open contract to arrange for insurance cover from exchange of contracts. If he does not do so then, unless he can claim under either of the statutory provisions referred to above, or unless the damage is due to the seller's lack of care, he must complete and pay the full purchase price, and will have no claim on any insurance money paid to the seller.[11] If the seller does receive the full purchase price he will have suffered no loss and will have to repay any insurance money he has received.[12]

As we have seen, the Standard Conditions exclude section 47.[13] However, the major, indeed radical, change introduced by the Standard Conditions is the replacement of the open contract rule with a provision that risk does not pass on exchange; the seller retains the risk until completion. The seller is under a contractual obligation to transfer the property in the same physical state as it was at the date of the contract (fair wear and tear excepted).[14] This means that the buyer will be able to claim damages from the

---

11   *Rayner v Preston* (1881) 18 Ch D 1, CA.
12   *Castellain v Preston* (1883) 11 QBD 380, CA considered in *Lord Napier and Ettrick v Hunter* [1993] AC 713, [1993] 1 All ER 385.
13   SC 5.1.4.
14   SC 5.1.1.

seller if the seller is unable to transfer the property in the state it was in on exchange, even though the damage to the property was entirely accidental. The seller must therefore clearly maintain insurance on the property in order to be able to claim on his insurance policy to fund the damages which may be payable to the buyer. However the seller is under no actual obligation to the buyer to insure the property.[15]

If the damage to the property has been severe, the buyer may be able to rescind the contract. Standard Condition 5.1.2 provides that if at any time before completion the physical state of the property makes it unusable for its purpose at the date of the contract (whatever that might mean!), the buyer may rescind the contract, and the seller may rescind the contract if the damage to the property is damage against which the seller could not reasonably have insured or which it is not legally possible for the seller to make good (for example because he cannot get planning permission). 5.1.2 will probably apply where the damage to the property has been particularly severe, or of a particular type which means that the property is unusable for its purpose, perhaps involving the interruption of essential services such as water or electricity.

The position under the Standard Conditions may be thought to be not entirely satisfactory. From the point of view of the seller, even if the seller is to retain the risk until completion, the seller may wish to delete the buyer's right of rescission under 5.1.2. If 5.1.2 is retained, the wording may need to be amended. As it stands the buyer may rescind if 'at any time before completion' the physical state of the property makes it unusable for its purpose. On a literal reading, the buyer could rescind even though the physical state could be remedied by the contractual completion date; it might be better if 5.1.2 referred to the physical state at completion.

If 5.1.1 is to stand, the seller will want to maintain insurance on the property because if the property is damaged the seller will be in breach of contract and have to pay damages to the buyer under 5.1.1. That claim for damages may be met by the proceeds of the insurance. However, many insurance policies contain exclusions and limitations. For example, damage to the boundary walls or fences may not be within the scope of the policy unless it is accompanied by damage to the main building. Thus if a boundary wall collapses, the seller could find that he is obliged to compensate the buyer under 5.1.1 even though he has no claim on his own insurance policy. 5.1.1 is thus unattractive to a seller.

From the point of view of the buyer, the provisions of 5.1.1. and 5.1.2, representing an improvement on the open contract position, are on the face of it attractive to the buyer. Because the seller is retaining the risk, the buyer will have an action for damages against the seller if the property should be damaged between exchange of contracts and completion. However, the seller is under no duty to insure. This may not be acceptable to the buyer. A buyer will want more than a bare claim in damages against the seller. He will want to ensure that the claim can be met; he will want to know that the seller has insured the property and has insured it to its full reinstatement value. Thus from the buyer's point of view 5.1.3 could be amended to provide that the seller should insure the property to full reinstatement value and to provide for the buyer to be able to inspect the policy and the receipt for the most recent premium.

Even this may not satisfy a buyer. Assuming that the damage is not sufficient to bring into play 5.1.2, the buyer must still complete and his remedy is in damages under 5.1.1. A buyer may prefer to insure himself and therefore be dealing direct with the insurance company rather than making a claim for breach of contract against the seller, who then attempts to recover under his own policy. In other words it may make sound practical sense for the buyer to insure in any event. Indeed, as mentioned

---

15   SC 5.1.3.

earlier, in residential conveyancing transactions the buyer's mortgagee may have the property on insurance cover from exchange of contracts. If there is insurance for both buyer and seller, the contract should contain a condition covering this double insurance, to the effect that, if the proceeds of any insurance policy effected by one party are reduced by reason of the existence of any policy effected by the other party, the purchase price should be adjusted. This is necessary because insurance companies will not pay out twice for the same damage even though there are two policies, and if both seller and buyer have taken out insurance, they may each only receive a part of the total claim. Thus if 5.1.1 does not apply, the condition should provide that the purchase price is abated by the amount of the reduction of the purchaser's claim.

There are two further points. Firstly, the wording of 5.1.1 and 5.1.2 raises the question of damage to the property occurring shortly prior to exchange of contracts, unbeknown to the buyer and possibly even unbeknown to the seller. The seller's duty under 5.1.1 is to transfer the property in the same physical state as it was at the date of the contract. It seems that if the property is damaged shortly prior to exchange, on the face of it the seller is not in breach of 5.1.1. Similarly, 5.1.2 makes reference to the purpose of the property at the date of the contract. There would seem to be some advantage in the buyer inspecting the property shortly prior to exchange.

Secondly, if the property is damaged and therefore compensation is payable under 5.1.1, there is no indication in the Standard Conditions as to whether the buyer can demand that the purchase price be reduced to reflect this compensation, or whether the buyer would have to pay over the full purchase price on completion and then seek to recover damages from the seller.[16] If a special condition is inserted to provide that the compensation can be taken into account on completion, some method would have to be devised to resolve any dispute about the amount of compensation.

There are therefore a number of possible amendments to the Standard Conditions, including reinstating the open contract rule with risk passing on exchange; inserting a provision for double insurance; keeping 5.1.1 but excluding 5.1.2 and the possibility of rescission; keeping 5.1.1 and 5.1.2 but requiring the seller to insure the property and produce evidence of this; and clarifying the time for payment of compensation under 5.1.1.

4   THE EFFECT OF A BINDING CONTRACT

i   Position of the seller

The seller remains the owner of the legal estate until this passes to the buyer as a result of the conveyance or transfer. Nevertheless the buyer does have an equitable interest by virtue of the contract, and the seller is in a position similar to that of a trustee. He has a duty of care towards the property, to exercise reasonable care to keep the property in a condition in which it was at the date of the contract.[17] This duty lasts until completion, whether the seller remains in actual occupation or not (unless the buyer takes up occupation). The seller must not damage the property himself[18] nor allow others to damage it.[19] He must do ordinary repairs necessary to

---

16   Compare amounts payable under SC 6.3 and SC 7.3, which can be taken into account on completion; SC 6.4.
17   *Clarke v Ramuz* [1891] 2 QB 456, CA of course under SC 5.1.1, this duty is extended to all damage to the property however caused, save only fair wear and tear.
18   *Phillips v Lamdin* [1949] 2 KB 33, [1949] 1 All ER 770.
19   *Clarke v Ramuz*, above.

maintain the property, at his own expense. He should not let the property – for example if a subsisting tenancy is terminated – without consulting the buyer, although there is a difficulty here. The seller does retain a personal interest in the property as he will be left with it if the buyer does not complete, so the buyer's wishes cannot be paramount. However, if the buyer also offers an indemnity against loss then probably the seller would have to follow his wishes. The Standard Conditions contain a specific condition dealing with the position after exchange of contracts on the sale of a tenanted property. The seller is to inform the buyer without delay if the tenancy ends; the seller is then to act as the buyer reasonably directs provided that the buyer agrees to indemnify him against all consequent loss and expense. The seller is to inform the buyer without delay of any proposed change in the tenancy terms and is not to agree to any change without the buyer's consent.[20]

The seller's position also differs from that of a trustee in that he can retain the property until completion. He can also keep the income (eg rents) of the property until at least the date fixed for completion in the contract although he must also pay the outgoings (eg rates and any ground rent if the property sold is leasehold).[1]

ii   Position of the buyer

As risk passes on exchange of contracts, under an open contract the buyer must bear any losses occurring after that date and is also entitled to any gains which are of a capital nature. The seller is entitled to retain the income and must bear the outgoings. The buyer's liability for losses is amply illustrated by his liability for any damage to the property, under an open contract, not caused by a breach of the seller's duty of care. Similarly if the property is made subject to a compulsory purchase order after exchange, the buyer must still complete.[2] The buyer's entitlement to gains in the property of a capital nature is illustrated by his taking the benefit of any increase in the value of the property, the price having been fixed by the contract. This is shown by *Lake v Bayliss*[3] where the seller, having contracted to sell the property to a buyer, re-sold it to a second buyer at a higher price. The first buyer had not protected his contract and thus could not enforce it against the second buyer. He could, provided he acted promptly, take the proceeds of the second sale in lieu of the property.

We have seen that prima facie the buyer is not entitled to any insurance money paid out to the seller in respect of damage to the property. Similarly where the seller contracts to sell a tenanted property free of the tenancy, and the tenant on leaving the property before completion pays a sum ('dilapidations') to the seller in respect of damage or disrepair to the property for which the tenant is liable under his repair covenant, the seller does not have to hand this over to the buyer.[4] This seems sensible as the agreed price for the sale would presumably reflect vacant possession and the current state of the property. The property is being sold with vacant possession, and not subject to but with the benefit of the tenancy. On the same lines where property subject to a requisitioning order was sold free of the order, the compensation payable on derequisitioning could be kept by the seller;[5] he is selling the property with vacant possession, not subject to but with the benefit of the requisitioning order.

---

20   SC 3.3.2(b); see also *Earl of Egmont v Smith* (1877) 6 Ch D 469; *Abdulla v Shah* [1959] AC 124, [1959] 2 WLR 12, PC. See further in ch 5, section 4 xvi.
1   See further at ch 14, section 2, below.
2   *Hillingdon Estates Co v Stonefield Estates Ltd* [1952] Ch 627, [1952] 1 All ER 853.
3   [1974] 2 All ER 1114, [1974] 1 WLR 1073.
4   *Re Lyne-Stephens and Scott-Miller's Contract* [1920] 1 Ch 472, CA.
5   *Re Hamilton-Snowball's Conveyance* [1959] Ch 308, [1958] 2 All ER 319.

The Standard Conditions provide that the buyer is to bear the cost of complying with any outstanding public requirement and is to indemnify the seller against any liability resulting from a public requirement.[6] On the sale of a tenanted property, the buyer is to indemnify the seller against all claims arising under any tenancy after actual completion, even if void against a buyer for want of registration.[7]

iii   The buyer in possession before completion

If the seller allows the buyer access to an empty property so that he can start cleaning and decorating, there may be some slight risk to the seller but this is perhaps off-set by the beneficial effect on the property. However, if the buyer takes actual possession, the danger for the seller is that the buyer may become a tenant and therefore difficult to remove, and will in any event lose the spur to complete on time, leaving the seller in the meantime with neither the property nor his money. The danger for the buyer is that he is taken to have waived his right to raise requisitions and to have accepted the seller's title however defective it may be.

The open contract position is that the buyer must pay interest on the outstanding balance of the purchase money from the time he goes into possession and the seller's liability to maintain the property ceases. The Standard Conditions provide that in such circumstances the buyer is a licensee and not a tenant; the terms of the licence are set out in Standard Condition 5.2.2, including a provision for payment of a fee to the seller calculated at interest on the outstanding purchase price for the period of the licence, and an obligation on the buyer to keep the property in as good a state of repair as it was when he went into occupation (fair wear and tear excepted).

Other terms of the licence are set out in 5.2.2. The buyer is liable for outgoings but is entitled to keep any rent from any part of the property which he does not occupy. The buyer may permit 'members of his household' to occupy the property, the Standard Conditions betraying something of a domestic conveyancing bias here. The buyer is to insure the property in a sum not less than the purchase price against all risks in respect of which comparable premises are normally insured and under 5.2.3, Condition 5.1 ceases to apply and the buyer assumes risk until completion (presumably even if the buyer withdraws again from occupation prior to completion). The buyer is not to alter the property. It may be appropriate in some circumstances to add to these provisions by imposing further restrictions on the buyer, perhaps to comply with the covenants in a lease of a leasehold property. On occasions, the reason for the buyer wishing to take up occupation is so that he can make alterations or improvements, and in this case the contract will have to be amended accordingly. The insurance obligation might also be more closely defined, perhaps specifying some particular insurance company.

Condition 5.2.5 provides that the licence ends on the earliest of completion date, rescission of the contract, or five working days' notice given by one party to the other. The reference to the completion date is presumably to the contractual completion date as defined in 1.1.1(e). As the obligation to pay interest only subsists for the period of the licence, if a buyer is allowed into occupation before completion and completion is delayed beyond the contractual completion date, the licence has ended on the contractual completion date. The obligation to pay interest therefore also ceases on the contractual completion date. In these circumstances the seller would presumably wish to be in a position to obtain not only compensation (perhaps by way of interest)

---

6   SC 3.1.4.
7   SC 3.3.2(d); see ch 5, section 4 xvi.

under Condition 7.3 for late completion, but also interest under 5.2 in respect of the buyer's continued occupation. In this situation Condition 5.2.6 comes into play, providing that if the buyer is in occupation after the licence has come to an end, and the contract is subsequently completed, the buyer must pay compensation for the continued occupation at the same rate as the licence fee. However, this does not cover the situation where the contract is never completed. Perhaps this problem could be avoided if Standard Condition 5.2 were amended to provide for the buyer to pay interest in respect of the period of occupation rather than the period of the licence.

By virtue of Condition 5.2.4, the buyer is not in occupation for the purposes of 5.2 and therefore not liable to pay a fee under the terms of the licence if he is merely exercising rights of access given solely to do work agreed by the seller. This would presumably cover repair, cleaning or decoration but it is important that the work is agreed with the seller and that the buyer does not go beyond the scope of this agreement. In addition, the parties should incorporate provisions into the contract as to what is to happen if the transaction is not completed – for example, is the buyer entitled to compensation, or is he obliged to put the property back to the state it was in before he started the work?

Finally, by Condition 5.2.7, the buyer's right to raise requisitions is unaffected by his occupation of the property.

iv Death of one of the parties after exchange of contracts

The death of one of the parties between exchange of contracts and completion does not affect the contractual obligations.[8] If the seller is a sole beneficial owner, his personal representatives are bound by the contract. If the deceased is one of a number of joint owners of the legal estate, for example as trustees or personal representatives, the survivors are still bound by the contract. If the seller's death leaves a sole surviving trustee, another trustee may have to be appointed. If a buyer dies, his personal representatives are bound to proceed with the purchase although if he was buying with the aid of a mortgage, there could be difficulties in finding the money (though if he was buying with the aid of an endowment mortgage, his life policy should have been put into force on exchange of contracts and the proceeds from this should supply the necessary funds). It is the person entitled to the property under the deceased's will or intestacy who is ultimately responsible for providing the purchase money.[9]

The position on the bankruptcy of either party is considered in Chapter 10.

---

8   The Law Commission has produced proposals relating to the service of notices following the death of a party to the contract.
9   See Administration of Estates Act 1925, s 35.

9 DEDUCING TITLE

I SELLER'S OBLIGATIONS

The seller, must demonstrate that he does own and thus can sell exactly what he has contracted to sell. In other words he deduces title to the buyer. He must either show that *he* owns and can convey the property or that someone else, whom he can compel to convey, owns it. The former is most common, but an example of the latter would be where the director of a company personally contracted to sell property which was in fact owned by the company. If he had a controlling interest in the company and could thus compel it to convey, the buyer could not object to the title offered.[1] In *Re Bryant and Barningham's Contract*[2] trustees of settled land with no power of sale contracted to sell trust property. The tenant for life, who did have a power of sale, offered to convey to the buyer but the court upheld the buyer's refusal to accept this, as the trustees could not compel the tenant for life to convey. The trustees were thus in breach of their contract with the buyer. In the rather similar case of *Re Baker and Selmon's Contract*,[3] beneficiaries requested a trustee to sell. The trustee had no power of sale but because title could be made with the concurrence of the beneficiaries, and the trustee would compel them to co-operate as they had requested the sale, the buyer had to accept the title offered. The same principle applies if the contract is a sub-sale, that is where a seller contracts to sell to a buyer and before completion, the buyer contracts to sell to a sub-purchaser. (The deed would normally be direct from seller to sub-purchaser.) Having had title deduced to him, the buyer can in turn deduce title to the sub-purchaser. He can show that the legal estate is in the seller and that by his contract with the seller he can compel the seller to convey to the sub-purchaser. The contract thus forms part of the title he is deducing. He must ensure that his contract with the seller contains nothing prohibiting this arrangement; the Standard Conditions only contain a restriction on sub sales in relation to contracts for leasehold property.[4] The buyer would also want to ensure that the completion dates and contract rates in the two contracts coincided. He would also need to check that there were no

---

1 *Elliott and H Elliott (Builders) Ltd v Pierson* [1948] Ch 452, [1948] 1 All ER 939.
2 [1890] 44 Ch D 218, CA.
3 [1907] 1 Ch 238. However, the Law of Property Act 1925, s 42(1) now provides that a stipulation in the contract that the buyer shall accept a title made with the concurrence of beneficiaries is void if the equitable interests of the beneficiaries could be overreached under the Law of Property Act 1925 or the Settled Land Act 1925 (or any other statute).
4 S.C. 8.2.5 and 8.3.3.

special conditions in the first contract restricting sub sales. Once the sub sale contracts have been exchanged it would be prudent for the sub purchaser to protect his interest by registering a caution if the land is registered or a C(iv) land charge against the name of the landowner in the case of unregistered land.

The title to be deduced to the buyer, and the manner of deducing it, will be covered by the conditions in the contract or failing that by the appropriate open contract rule. The contract can affect the deducing of title in two ways. Firstly, it can reveal defects in the title to which the buyer will not be able to object on examination of the title deduced to him. If the seller fails to disclose a defect this does not mean that the buyer can automatically reject the title and rescind the contract, for the defect may not be such as to involve the buyer in an appreciable risk of his title being affected. In *MEPC Ltd v Christian-Edwards*[5] there was evidence of a contract to purchase the property in 1912, which was referred to as still in existence in 1930. The House of Lords held that at the time of the contract with the buyer in 1973, it was beyond reasonable doubt that the buyer was not at risk from the defect and that the seller had shown a good title. Secondly, the contract can control the manner in which title is deduced, for example the length of title offered in the case of unregistered land; the root of title as we have seen is normally stated in the contract. In fact the seller is not strictly bound to deduce title in the manner stated in the contract, for if he can correct some post-root defect by showing adverse possession the buyer may be forced to accept this. A period of 12 years adverse possession is sufficient to defeat most claims. In *Re Atkinson and Horsell's Contract*[6] the contract provided for title to commence in 1842. In 1874 there was a serious defect – the wrong person took under a will – and therefore the title from that point on was wholly bad. However, the seller could show adverse possession by himself and his predecessors in title from 1874 to the time of the contract and the buyer was forced to accept this title. This should be distinguished from the situation in *George Wimpey & Co Ltd v Sohn*[7] where the contract stipulated that title to a particular piece of land was to be a statutory declaration of 20 years adverse possession. The seller was only able to give a declaration of 12 years adverse possession and the buyer was not forced to accept this.

How then is title deduced to the buyer? We must deal separately with unregistered and registered land.

2   UNREGISTERED LAND

Title in unregistered land is evidenced by the title deeds, and title is deduced by letting the buyer have details of the more recent of the title deeds, starting with the root of title and tracing a chain of ownership through the seller (or someone he can compel to convey). We have already seen in Chapter 5 how far back the title must go, and therefore how old the root of title must be, under open contract rules and Standard Conditions for sales of both freehold and leasehold land. On a sale of freehold land for example, the open contract rule preserved by the Standard Conditions is that title must commence with a good root of title which is at least 15 years old at the date of the contract. The other requirements for a good root and the consequences of accepting a short root of title are discussed in detail in Chapter 5.

---

5   [1981] AC 205, [1979] 3 All ER 752, HL.
6   [1912] 2 Ch 1, CA; in practice, if the seller relies on a possessory title then this will normally be made clear in the contract.
7   [1967] Ch 487, [1966] 1 All ER 232, CA.

i Abstract or epitome

The seller's solicitor will be unwilling to hand the title deeds over to the buyer's solicitor at this stage for examination; if not for fear that they might not be returned, at least because they might be lost. The traditional method of deducing title is to prepare a painstaking summary or précis of the various deeds and other documents, at the same time transposing them into the past tense. The document so prepared is called an abstract of title. The abstract effectively tells the buyer what was included in all the deeds and other documents which have been abstracted. Abbreviations are used whenever possible and sometimes whole clauses in a deed, if in a standard form, can be abbreviated. The result is pretty incomprehensible to the layman and to the non-conveyancing lawyer too. Preparation of an abstract is very time-consuming; as it is almost impossible to dictate, it must be written out and then typed up. It is far quicker and indeed more accurate simply to photocopy the deeds and other documents and to attach to a bundle of photocopies an index or epitome which details each document. This method of deducing title, the epitome plus photocopies, is the modern method and one cannot imagine that many abstracts are prepared nowadays. The copy documents should be numbered to correspond with each entry on the epitome and the copies must be legible and complete. Particular attention should be paid to ensuring that matters such as stamps or memoranda endorsed on the back of a deed are included in the photocopy. Any plans which are copied must be coloured to correspond with any colouring on the original. The copies must be durable.

The seller's solicitor will probably not have to start from scratch in preparing the abstract or epitome because he will normally have the abstract or epitome which was supplied to the seller when he bought. He can simply pass this on to the buyer – having checked its accuracy – together with a supplemental epitome (or abstract) bringing the title up to date. In a typical case the supplemental epitome would contain details of the conveyance to the seller and the seller's mortgage(s). Although abstracts may not be prepared very often nowadays, a solicitor must still be adept at handling them as old abstracts may still be used to deduce title for years to come.

The abstract or epitome is prepared at the seller's expense. The Standard Conditions reiterate the seller's duty to provide an abstract or epitome.[8]

ii Contents of the abstract or epitome

The word abstract is commonly used to denote either an abstract or an epitome and, to avoid repetition, this practice will be followed here. The abstract starts with the root of title and then traces in chronological order a chain of ownership through to the seller or someone whom he can compel to convey. In theory title should be shown to both the legal estate and equitable interests and the chain of both should be traced, but as machinery exists for the over-reaching of equitable interests, for example by trustees for sale, it will in practice only be necessary to deduce title to the equitable interests in the rare case when they are not over-reached (for example, where the survivor of two co-owners who hold on a beneficial tenancy in common sells as beneficial owner by deducing title to the deceased's equitable interest, which has been left by will to the survivor and vested in him by an assent). All deeds,

---

8   SC 4.2.2.

documents and other events affecting title to the property must be included in the abstract.[9] This will include the following:

(a) Conveyances, or for leasehold property, assignments – the legal estate passes under a conveyance and conveyances (or assignments) will predominate in most abstracts. Of course both conveyances on sale and voluntary conveyances (deeds of gift) must be abstracted.

(b) Discharged mortgages – the buyer's solicitor will want to satisfy himself that the mortgage has been properly discharged. The mortgage and the receipt (which operates as a discharge) would both be abstracted. In general terms this rule also applies to second (puisne) legal mortgages, that is legal mortgages not protected by deposit of title deeds, which will be with the first mortgagee; and also to equitable mortgages. However, it is conceivable that exceptions could be found. A puisne legal mortgage is registrable as a Ci land charge. If that registration has been cancelled on the discharge, as it ought to have been, the mortgage could no longer bind a buyer[10] and it is arguable that it need not be included in the abstract. It seems that the same argument could be applicable to discharged equitable mortgages which are registrable as Civ (or possibly Ciii) land charges.

(c) Subsisting mortgages – although these are presumably to be discharged on completion out of the proceeds of sale, they must be included in the abstract. The buyer will not be unduly concerned, for mortgages are an example of removable defects in title, which the buyer is entitled to assume will be removed by the seller; in the case of a mortgage, by discharge. Again, both second legal mortgages and equitable mortgages should also be abstracted. Practice is sometimes not to abstract equitable mortgages, but if they are protected by registration they will show up when the buyer's solicitor does his pre-completion search. If the abstract does not provide details of the mortgage, the buyer's solicitor will raise a requisition.

On a sale by a mortgagee exercising his power of sale, the buyer takes free of mortgages over which the seller mortgagee has priority.[11] So on a sale by first legal mortgagee, the buyer will take free of any second legal or equitable mortgages whether they are registered or not, and they need not be included in the abstract.

(d) Leases – subsisting leases or tenancies of the property must be included in the abstract. The Standard Conditions provide for details of leases and tenancies to be provided to the buyer before exchange.[12] Leases which have expired by effluxion of time need not be abstracted, but leases which have terminated by surrender should still be included in the abstract.

(e) Grants of probate or administration – but the will of a deceased estate owner need not be abstracted. The legal estate in the property of the deceased passes to his personal representatives and the evidence of this is the grant of probate or administration. The grant forms a link in the chain and should thus be abstracted where the estate owner has died.

---

9 If the seller has lost some or all of the deeds, this would normally be disclosed in the contract. Even if this were not done, the buyer would have to accept the situation if the seller could produce satisfactory secondary evidence of contents and execution of the missing documents, such as copies, drafts and statutory declarations; *Re Halifax Commercial Banking Co Ltd and Wood* (1898) 79 LT 536.

10 Land Charges Act 1972, s 4(5).

11 Law of Property Act 1925, s 104(1).

12 SC 3.3.2.

(f) Assents by personal representatives – a deceased estate owner's personal representatives will either sell the property or else vest the legal estate in a beneficiary under the terms of the will or intestacy. The document used to transfer the legal estate to a person entitled under the will or intestacy, as opposed to a buyer, is normally an assent; as such it should be included in the abstract.

(g) Deaths – when the estate owner has died, then although the death may be mentioned in the abstract, the point is effectively covered by the grant of probate or administration. However, if one of two or more joint tenants holding the legal estate dies – meaning that the survivor(s)acquire the legal estate by survivorship – it is the mere fact of the death that is important. The death would be mentioned in the abstract as it is an event under which the legal estate passes. The seller would have the original death certificate available and, if preparing an epitome, would include this (a certified copy is no longer sufficient)[13]. Theoretically the seller can just supply the buyer with the date of the death and leave it to the buyer to obtain the death certificate, but the seller usually has the certificate available. If a new trustee is appointed, the deed of appointment would be abstracted.

(h) Contract – if the seller is sub-selling, his own contract to purchase would be included as the final link in the chain of title.

We have already mentioned that it is not normally necessary to deduce the title to equitable interests. For example, on the sale of settled land by a tenant for life there is normally no need for the buyer to see the trust instrument, and indeed he is not entitled to see it, but merely the vesting deeds or assents which trace the passage of the legal estate from one tenant for life to the next.[14] The equitable interests will be overreached.

Land charges search certificates, obtained on past purchases of the property, are included in the abstract if protocol is adopted. If protocol is not adopted there is no obligation on the seller to do this but it can save the buyer money if he can rely on the old searches instead of repeating them, and they can also be useful in discovering whether a land charge such as a Dii restrictive covenant has become void for non-registration.

Although the root of title under an open contract need only be 15 years old, if any of the documents in the abstract do refer back to pre-root deeds then the seller must provide the necessary information.[15] If a deed in the abstract describes the property by reference to a plan contained in a pre-root deed then a copy must be provided. If an abstracted deed refers to covenants in an earlier pre-root deed then that deed must be abstracted. This means that the buyer's solicitor might be confronted by fairly elderly abstracts of these deeds, prepared some time ago and possibly even handwritten.

3   REGISTERED LAND

Deducing title to land the title to which is registered is, as we have seen in chapter 5, covered by the Land Registration Act 1925, section 110, as amended where permissible by conditions in the contract. Briefly, the buyer normally gets office copy entries of the register and filed plan. If appropriate, he will also get an abstract or epitome, as for unregistered land, of any matters on which the register is not conclusive

---

13   [2001] Law Soc Gaz, 8 March.
14   See ch 10, section 2 iii.
15   Law of Property Act 1925, s 45(1).

or any matters excepted from the effect of registration. Provision of office copy entries is a far simpler process than provision of an abstract or epitome. In addition there is no need to supply details of the seller's existing mortgage which will be discharged on completion, even though this will appear on the charges register of the title.

On a sub-sale, it is not possible to comply fully with the statutory requirements as the register will not show the (sub)-seller as registered proprietor. The sub-purchaser will receive office copies of the proprietor's title and a copy of the contract between the proprietor and the sub-seller. A client, having recently bought a registered title, may wish to sell it before the Land Registry has dealt with the application to register his purchase. This is not really a sub-sale, as the client has already completed his purchase, and applied for registration. He will wish to provide in the contract that the buyer will accept a transfer from him, although at that stage he will not yet be the registered proprietor. However, section 110(5) of the Land Registration Act 1925 poses a problem; it provides that a purchaser of registered title can always require the seller to become registered, and it applies despite any agreement to the contrary in the contract. There are a number of ways around this: the initial contract could be completed before the sub sale. However the disadvantage of this method is that both purchase deeds would probably attract stamp duty. Alternatively the seller could act as a nominee of the sub purchaser, assign the benefit of the original contract to the sub purchaser and complete the original sale as nominee of the sub purchaser. The advantage of this method is that the second purchase deed would not attract stamp duty.

Section 110(5) does not apply to a pending first registration of title; that is, where a client has bought an unregistered title, subject to compulsory first registration, and now wishes to re-sell it before the Land Registry has dealt with his application for first registration and registered him as proprietor. He can do so by providing in the contract with the buyer that the buyer will accept a transfer from him, having investigated the unregistered title and having seen a certified copy of the application for first registration.[16]

Since the advent of real time priority at the Land Registry (see Chapter 2), office copies will now show the time created as well as the date.

4   DELIVERY OF THE ABSTRACT

For ease of reference, in this section the word abstract will be used to connote either an abstract, an epitome or the details supplied under the Land Registration Act 1925, section 110.

The open contract rule is that the abstract must be delivered within a reasonable time. Conditions in the contract should amplify this to provide a definite time limit. The Standard Conditions state that the abstract must be delivered immediately after exchange of contracts.[17] Time is not of the essence of this requirement and any delay by the seller would be reflected merely in the general provisions for delay in completion considered in Chapter 16.[18] Common practice is for the abstract to be delivered before exchange of contracts. The draft contract may refer to a deed in the

---

16   The seller will face problems if he has not applied for first registration within the appropriate period, ie within two months from completion; *Pinekerry Ltd v Needs (Kenneth) (Contractors) Ltd* (1992) 64 P & CR 245, CA. For the searches to be made by the buyer, see ch 11 section 2.
17   SC 4.1.1.
18   However, time could be made of the essence by service of notice by the buyer, *Behzadi v Shaftesbury Hotels Ltd* [1992] Ch 1, [1991] 2 All ER 477, CA.

abstract or epitome or to the contents of the register in the case of registered land, for both a description of the property and for details of easements and covenants. This would be much less cumbersome than repeating a long description or list of covenants verbatim in the contract, but it does mean that the buyer will want to see a copy of the deed or the register so that he can fully appreciate the provisions of the contract. Even if the abstract is not needed by the buyer for this purpose, it may be sent with the draft contract simply for administrative convenience; this is now almost universal practice. Under the TransAction 2001, the abstract (including in the case of an unregistered title land charges searches against the seller and other estate owners) must be delivered to the buyer as part of the package of information which the buyer receives at the outset.

10 INVESTIGATING TITLE

I   INTRODUCTION

The purpose of the buyer, by his solicitor, investigating title is simply to check that the seller has deduced title properly, that is to ensure that the seller can convey what he has contracted to convey.[1] The buyer's solicitor will be on the lookout for the types of defect in title which were mentioned in Chapter 5. These are defects such as restrictive covenants or easements which relate to the property; if they have not been disclosed by the seller, this means that although the seller can convey property, he cannot convey the property that he has contracted to convey. The second sort of defect of title affects the seller's ownership of the property and means that the seller cannot really convey anything at all, at least not a good title. An example would be where the seller is purporting to exercise his power of sale as a mortgagee, but that power of sale has not arisen. Because of the nature of registration of title, the second type of defect is mainly confined to unregistered conveyancing. If the seller's solicitor has done his job property in preparing the draft contract, then the investigation of title should not reveal any defects in title which have not already been disclosed by the contract.

Investigation of title is a process made up of a number of stages. In investigating an unregistered title, the buyer's solicitor must examine the abstract, on the assumption that it has been correctly prepared. He will then check that assumption by verifying the abstract against the original deeds, and also make certain searches, principally a search in the central land charges register and an inspection of the property. For a registered title, the buyer's solicitor will examine the register entries, but if the contract describes the property and matters affecting it by reference to the register entries, there will be no surprises. He must then bring up to date the copy entries from which he has been working, by means of a search at the district Land Registry, and also check for any over-riding interests and other matters on which the register is not conclusive. This will also entail an inspection of the property.[2]

We can now look at a number of problems which can occur, principally where the powers of an estate owner are limited in some way, whether the estate owner is the present seller or, in the case of an unregistered title, he was one of the seller's predecessors in title. We shall be concerned principally with unregistered titles but

---

1   In fact in the vast majority of cases title will be investigated before exchange of contracts; see further under section 23, ii, below.
2   Because of Land Registration Act 1925, s 70(1).

we shall also see how the problem is resolved in the context of a registered title. Before drafting the contract, the seller's solicitor should examine the title in order to discover any defects and then disclose them in the contract. We shall therefore examine not only provisions that exist for the protection of a buyer in particular cases, but also pay regard to the approach of the seller's solicitor to see how he deals with a particular problem.

2   DISPOSITIONS OF SETTLED LAND

i   Basic framework

Generally speaking, since the Trusts of Land and Appointment of Trustees Act came into force on 1 January 1997, it has not been possible to create new strict settlements.[3] The strict settlement should therefore soon be an extinct animal, but clearly the practitioner may still come across strict settlements created before the new Act and should know how to deal with title issues where settlements exist. The definition of settled land in the Settled Land Act 1925 includes, inter alia, land limited to persons in succession (for example, where property is left by will to A for life, remainder to B absolutely).[4] The legal estate in settled land will be vested in a tenant for life. There will be a trust instrument which will contain the terms of the settlement, including the names of the beneficiaries and the trustees and any extension of the tenant for life's statutory powers. An example of a trust instrument would be a will creating a settlement. There will also be a vesting instrument, vesting the legal estate in the tenant for life. When the tenant for life dies, the trustees will become his special personal representatives by virtue of a special grant of probate or administration limited to the settled land. They will then execute another vesting instrument vesting the land in the person next entitled as tenant for life, and so on. The vesting instrument can be an assent if by personal representatives but otherwise must be a deed. A vesting instrument must contain the 'statutory particulars'[5] that is:

(a) a description of the land;
(b) a statement that it is vested in the tenant for life on the trusts;
(c) a statement of any extension of the tenant for life's powers;
(d) the names of the trustees;
(e) the name of anyone empowered to appoint new trustees.

If there is no tenant for life – for example where the tenant for life would be a minor – the legal estate is vested in the 'statutory owners' who are normally the trustees.[6] They have the powers of the tenant for life.[7]

The land may cease to be settled land on the death of the tenant for life, for example if the end of the 'chain' of beneficiaries is reached. If land is settled on A for life remainder to B then on A's death B becomes absolutely entitled. The land will then devolve on the deceased tenant for life's ordinary personal representatives who will vest the property in the person entitled to it – B in the above example – by an ordinary assent or deed. When the settlement is at an end the trustees can be called upon to

---

3   Trusts of Land and Appointment of Trustees Act 1996, s 2(1).
4   Settled Land Act 1925, s 1(1)(i).
5   Ibid, s 5(1).
6   Ibid, s 117(1)(xxvi).
7   Ibid, s 23.

execute a deed of discharge,[8] but there would be no need for this in the above situation as it would be clear that the land was no longer subject to the settlement and indeed a buyer must assume that this is the case.[9]

ii   Powers of tenant for life

By section 13 of the Settled Land Act 1925, where a tenant for life has become entitled to have a vesting instrument executed in his favour then until such instrument has been executed, no purported disposition by any person[10] can pass a legal estate. There is protection for a bona fide purchaser without notice of the tenant for life's entitlement, but the solicitor acting on a sale of settled land will ensure that the seller *is* tenant for life and has a vesting instrument in his favour.

I   Authorised dispositions

By section 18 of the Settled Land Act 1925 any disposition by the tenant for life (or statutory owners) must be authorised either by the Act or by an extension of the tenant for life's powers (which would be mentioned in the vesting instrument). Otherwise the disposition will be void. Where the tenant for life is disposing of the land, his solicitor must therefore ensure that the disposition is authorised. Provision for the protection of purchasers is dealt with in section iii 3, below.

2   Power of sale or exchange

By section 38 of the Settled Land Act 1925 the tenant for life has a power to sell or exchange the land. By sections 39 and 40 the sale or exchange must be for the best consideration that can reasonably be obtained. This is of particular importance to the solicitor for a tenant for life who is selling.[11]

3   Power of leasing

The tenant for life does have a power to grant leases of the settled land. These must be at the best rent reasonably obtainable. There are fairly detailed rules in the Act concerning the length and type of such leases.[12]

4   Other powers

The Act lists other miscellaneous powers of the tenant for life including a power to mortgage the land for certain purposes.[13]

iii   Provisions affecting purchasers[14]

I   Purchasers cannot see the trust instrument

The buyer is not entitled to see the trust instrument and if the last vesting instrument contains the statutory particulars, he must assume that the vesting instrument was

---

8   Ibid, s 17.
9   Ibid,, s 110(5).
10   Other than a personal representative.
11   See section iii 3 below for protection of buyers.
12   Settled Land Act 1925, ss 41–48.
13   Ibid, ss 49–71.
14   A purchaser in this context means a purchaser in good faith for value including a lessee and mortgagee; ibid, s 117(1)(xxi).

made to the correct person, that the persons named as trustees are the property constituted trustees of the settlement, that the statutory particulars are correct and that the statements contained in any deed of discharge are correct.[15] This rule prevents the buyer going 'behind the curtain' and concerning himself with the actual trust. (There are exceptions to the rule in certain relatively rare circumstances.) The buyer can of course see from the vesting instrument that the land is settled, who the trustees are, and whether the tenant for life's statutory powers have been extended. The last point in particular may need to be checked if the tenant for life is granting a lease to the buyer. If new trustees have been appointed, a buyer will need to see a deed of declaration, declaring who the trustees are; the buyer does not see the actual deed of appointment. The deed of declaration is in effect a supplement to the last vesting instrument, which will have contained the names of the then trustees as part of the statutory particulars.

2   Over-reaching the interests under the settlement

A conveyance or other disposition by the tenant for life will over-reach all the provisions of the settlement and all interests arising under it including annuities, limited owners charges and general equitable charges even if registered as land charges.[16] However, by section 18 of the Settled Land Act 1925 the buyer must pay any capital money, for example the purchase price, or the premium on a grant of a lease, to the trustees of the settlement being at least two in number (or being a trust corporation). The vesting instrument will reveal who the trustees are.

3   Compliance with the requirements of the Act

We have seen that a sale or exchange must be for the best consideration reasonably attainable. Section 110(1) of the Settled Land Act 1925 provides that on a disposition by the tenant for life or statutory owners, a purchaser in good faith shall be conclusively taken to have given the best consideration reasonably attainable, as against all other persons entitled under the settlement. However, it may be that this provision does not protect the buyer who does not realise he is dealing with a tenant for life, the latter having suppressed the settlement.[17]

iv   Registered titles

The registered conveyancing approach to settled land is relatively simple. The registered proprietor will be the tenant for life (or statutory owners). Because of the limitation on powers of disposition, a restriction is entered in the proprietorship register.[18] Typically this will say:[19]

> No disposition by the proprietor of the land under which capital money arises is to be registered unless the money is paid to A and B (the trustees of a settlement of whom there must be not less than two nor more than four unless a trust corporation is a trustee) or into Court. Except under an order of the Registrar no disposition by the proprietor of the land is to be registered unless authorised by the Settled Land Act 1925.

15   Settled Land Act 1925, s 110(2).
16   Settled Land Act 1925, s 72.
17   *Weston v Henshaw* [1950] Ch 510, but this is inconsistent with *Re Morgan's Lease* [1972] Ch 1, [1971] 2 All ER 235.
18   Land Registration Act 1925, s 58.
19   Ibid, form 9; there is a similar form where the statutory owners are the registered proprietors.

On the death of the tenant for life, his special personal representatives will execute a vesting assent in favour of the next tenant for life who will then apply for registration as proprietor.

3   DISPOSITION BY TRUSTEES

i   **Basic framework**

The concept of the trust of land was introduced by the Trusts of Land and Appointment of Trustees Act 1996 (TLATA). Prior to this, in most cases where land was statutorily required to be held by trustees (for example, where land was beneficially owned by two or more people concurrently), this was deemed to be on trust for sale, with a duty to sell but a power to postpone. TLATA was introduced in order to recognise the reality of land ownership in the twentieth century – that land was primarily purchased as a home, not as an investment, and for this reason the Act abolished the doctrine of conversion. The Act was retrospective in effect, so now all former trusts for sale are simply trusts of land, as are all new trusts of real property. A trust of land may be created expressly or may be implied by statute in the following circumstances.

(a)   Personal representatives hold the land of an intestate on trust, with power to sell.[20]
(b)   Where land is held jointly, it is held on a trust of land.[1] The legal estate must be held on a joint tenancy since a tenancy in common cannot exist at law; the equitable interests may be held on a joint tenancy or a tenancy in common. For example, if land is conveyed to A and B as beneficial joint tenants then A and B hold the legal estate as joint tenants on trust for themselves as joint tenants. If land is conveyed to A and B as tenants in common, they hold the legal estate as joint tenants on trust for themselves as tenants in common. If land is conveyed to A and B jointly for life with remainder to C, TLATA will impose a trust of land (as strict settlements were abolished by the Act).
(c)   Where trustees have lent money and have taken a mortgage over land as security, then if the mortgagor's right of redemption should be extinguished, the trustees hold the property on trust.[2] This is rare in practice.

There can be no more than four trustees of land so if land is conveyed to A, B, C, D and E jointly, the effect is that A, B, C and D – the first four named in the deed – hold the legal estate on trust for all five. The most common trust of land encountered in practice in domestic conveyancing is that which arises when property is held jointly by a husband and wife or cohabiting couple.

The essence of a trust of land is that the trustees hold the legal estate on trust for the beneficiaries – who may of course be, and often are, the same people as the trustees.

Prior to the introduction of TLATA, the trustees' primary duty was to sell the property (with power to postpone the sale) and pay the proceeds to the beneficiaries. There was much judicial argument as to whether this gave the beneficiary a right in land, and as to whether the beneficiary had a right to occupy the property. Under the new Act, the beneficiary's right to occupy is underlined,[3] and it is made plain that

---

20   Administration of Estates Act 1925, s 33.
1   Law of Property Act 1925, ss 34–36.
2   Ibid, s 31.
3   Trusts of Land and Appointment of Trustees Act 1996, s 12.

beneficiaries have a right in land, not in personalty.[4] If the trustees decide to sell the property, the consent of all of them is required. If there is a difference of opinion between them, or if any beneficiary wants (or does not want) a sale to take place, there is a provision in the Act for an application to be made to the Court, who will decide the issue.[5] Such an application might not be appropriate in the case of a husband and wife, being better made in matrimonial property proceedings.[6]

ii   Powers of trustees

The solicitor acting for sellers who are trustees of land may in appropriate circumstances first have to check that the trust is still subsisting and that the correct persons have been appointed trustees although this would not be necessary in the case of a straightforward husband and wife joint tenancy. Trustees of land have by TLATA all the powers of an absolute owner, which includes the power to sell, charge or lease the land, and the power to purchase land for any purpose.[7] Prior to the introduction of the Act, trustees' powers were statutorily quite limited, and it was common for trustees' powers to be extended by the document creating the trust, often to include the powers of an absolute owner. It may be that the consent of some person or persons is necessary before the trustees can exercise their powers, although this would not be relevant to the ordinary husband and wife situation. The provision for consent may be made expressly in an express trust. Where the consent of more than two persons is required, the consent of any two of them is sufficient for a purchaser.[8] The trustees must so far as practicable consult all beneficiaries of full age and give effect to their wishes, so far as this is consistent with the general purposes of the trust.[9] In the typical husband and wife case, where the beneficiaries are the same persons as the trustees, this is clearly unnecessary.

iii   Provisions affecting purchasers[10] from trustees

1   Appointment of trustees

A purchaser is not concerned to establish that the proper persons have been appointed trustees.[11]

2   Consents to the disposition

If the consent of more than two persons is required then the consent of any two will in favour of a buyer be deemed sufficient.[12] In addition the buyer is not concerned with the consent of someone who is not of full age.[13] However, these provisions are

---

4   Ibid, s 3.
5   Ibid, s 14.
6   *Williams v Williams* [1976] Ch 278, [1977] 1 All ER 28, CA, cf *Re Holliday* [1981] Ch 405, [1980] 3 All ER 385, CA and *Re Evers's Trust* [1980] 3 All ER 399, [1980] 1 WLR 1327, CA.
7   Trusts of Land and Appointment of Trustees Act 1996, s 6.
8   Ibid, s 10.
9   Ibid, s 11.
10   A purchaser in this context means a purchaser in good faith for valuable consideration, including a lessee and a mortgagee; Law of Property Act 1925, s 205(1)(xxi).
11   Law of Property Act 1925 s 24(1) as amended by the Trusts of Land and Appointment of Trustees Act 1996.
12   Ibid, s 26(1).
13   Trusts of Land and Appointment of Trustees Act 1996, s 10.

only for the benefit of the buyer and the seller/trustees would still have to meet their obligations vis-à-vis the beneficiaries by getting all necessary consents including the consent of the parent or guardian of a minor.

3   Over-reaching the equitable interest

A purchaser is not concerned with the trusts affecting the proceeds of sale.[14] The equitable interests under the trust will be over-reached by a conveyance to a buyer provided that he pays his purchase money to the trustees who must be at least two in number or a trust corporation.[15] Although a sole trustee could pass a good title in a transaction where no capital money arises, such as a lease without a premium,[16] on a sale it is vital that there be at least two trustees to whom the buyer can pay the purchase money. If the buyer completes with a sole trustee, the equitable interests under the trust are not over-reached and the buyer takes subject to them. If one of two tenants in common dies, the legal estate, which must be held on a joint tenancy, vests in the survivor but the deceased's equitable interest passes under his will or intestacy. The trust thus continues with the survivor as sole trustee holding on trust for himself and whoever is entitled to the deceased's share. To deal with the property another trustee must be appointed. The power of appointment, if not specified when the trust was created, can be exercised by the remaining trustee.[17] The appointment should be made by deed.[18] If coincidentally the person entitled to the deceased's share is the survivor, then he has an alternative to appointing a new trustee and selling as trustees. He is now solely beneficially entitled to the property. He has the legal estate by survivorship and once the deceased's equitable share has been vested in him by an assent from the deceased's personal representatives, he has the whole of the equitable interest too. Deducing title this way is rather clumsy though, involving as it does deducing title to the equitable interest. Any stipulation in the contract that title will be made by the beneficiaries of a trust joining in the deed is void if title could be made by the trustees over-reaching the equitable interests of the beneficiaries.[19]

If one of two beneficial joint tenants dies, the survivor takes the whole legal and equitable interest and becomes a sole beneficial owner.

The requirement of payment of capital money to at least two trustees does not affect the right of a sole personal representative to give a valid receipt.[20]

iv   Registered titles

In principle this is similar to the settled land position. The trustees, being the owners of the legal estate, will be the registered proprietors and there will be a restriction in the proprietorship register, typically:

> No disposition by a sole proprietor of the land (not being a trust corporation) under which capital money arises is to be registered except under an order of the Registrar or of the Court.

14   Ibid, s 27(1), as amended by the Trusts of Land and Appointment of Trustees Act 1996, s 25(1).
15   Law of Property Act 1925, ss 2(1)(ii), 2(2), 27(2) as amended. It is clear that ther doctrine of over-reaching still applies even after the new Act: *Birmingham Midshires Mortgage Services Ltd v Sabherwal* (1999) 80 P & CR 256.
16   Subject to the lease being within the trustee's powers.
17   Trustee Act 1925, s 36(1).
18   This will have the effect of vesting the legal estate in the (surviving and) new trustee(s), without the need for any separate conveyance of the legal estate.
19   Law of Property Act 1925, s 42(1) as amended.
20   Ibid, s 27(2).

However, if the trustees are beneficial joint tenants, there is no need for this restriction, as the survivor will be a sole beneficial owner and can deal with the property as he wishes.

4 SALE BY SOLE SURVIVING BENEFICIAL JOINT TENANT

i The problem

As mentioned in the previous section, the last surviving beneficial joint tenant becomes absolutely entitled as sole beneficial owner. The legal estate and the equitable interests are held as joint tenants and so the survivor takes the whole legal and equitable interest. The Law of Property (Amendment) Act 1926 confirmed that the survivor could deal with the land as if it were not held on trust. The difficulty for a buyer from the survivor, and subsequent buyers, was in knowing whether the survivor was what he claimed to be; whether he was a survivor of beneficial joint tenants or of beneficial tenants in common. If the latter, then although he would have the legal estate, the trust would continue and unless he could show that he had become entitled to the whole equitable interest as well, he would be a sole trustee and the equitable interest would not be over-reached on a sale to the buyer. A problem arises because a beneficial joint tenancy can be severed quite simply and thereby converted to a beneficial tenancy in common. This is done by one joint tenant serving a written notice of severance on the other joint tenants[1] and it also occurs automatically on the bankruptcy of a joint tenant. A mortgage by a joint tenant of his interest will also sever the joint tenancy. How can a buyer from someone who claims to be the survivor of joint tenants, or indeed a subsequent buyer, be sure that the tenancy had not been severed? The answer is that the buyer is given a measure of statutory protection.

ii Protection of purchaser

The protection is contained in the Law of Property (Joint Tenants) Act 1964, which is deemed to take effect at the same time as the 1925 property legislation (ie 1 January 1926). Where there has been a sale by a sole surviving joint tenant since 1925 then a purchaser can rely on the protection of the Act. The Act states that in favour of a purchaser, the survivor of two or more joint tenants shall be deemed to be such and to be solely beneficially entitled to the property, provided that:

(a) the conveyance by him states that he is solely and beneficially interested – such a statement would commonly be made in the recitals in the conveyance (before the Law of Property (Miscellaneous Provisions) Act 1994 came into force on 1 July 1995, the seller would have stated that he was selling as 'beneficial owner'); and

(b) no memorandum of severance of the joint tenancy has been endorsed on or annexed to the conveyance to the joint tenants – such a memorandum must be signed by at least one of the joint tenants and must record severance of the equitable interest on a specified date;[2] and

(c) no bankruptcy petition or bankruptcy order has been registered as a land charge against any of the joint tenants at the time of the conveyance by the survivor.

---

1 Law of Property Act 1925, s 36(2).
2 Law of Property (Joint Tenants) Act 1964, s 1(1)(a).

The Act only applies where the original conveyance was to joint tenants not tenants in common. To ensure that the protection of the Act is available the solicitor for a buyer from a survivor of beneficial joint tenants, or a subsequent buyer, should check the following:

(a) That the original conveyance was to joint tenants; this should be apparent from the abstract or epitome.

(b) That the conveyance by the survivor contains or will contain the necessary statement that the survivor is solely entitled, or (before July 1995) the survivor conveyed as beneficial owner. If the conveyance is by the personal representative of a survivor of joint tenants who has then died, the Act still applies and the personal representative would make a statement in the conveyance that the survivor at his death was solely and beneficially entitled.[3] If a buyer is faced in the abstract with a conveyance made by a survivor of beneficial joint tenants before 1964 which therefore does not contain the necessary statement, then a statement made subsequently by the survivor or his personal representative is to be treated as if it had been included in the conveyance.[4]

(c) That there is no memorandum of severance endorsed on or annexed to the conveyance to the joint tenants. This should be apparent from the abstract and it can be confirmed when the abstract is verified against the original deeds.

(d) That there are no bankruptcy proceedings registered under the Land Charges Act 1972 against any joint tenants. A land charges search can be made, and indeed would be made in any event against the joint tenants, and any bankruptcy proceedings would be revealed by this search. A subsequent buyer could normally rely on the search made at the time of the purchase from the survivor.

If all these conditions are satisfied the survivor is deemed to be a sole beneficial owner even if in reality he is not, because for example there has been a severance of which there is no memorandum on the conveyance to the joint tenants. The protection applies to a purchaser, who is defined in the Law of Property Act 1925 as a purchaser in good faith, including a lessee and a mortgagee.[5] Presumably if a buyer was *aware* that there had been severance then even though there was no memorandum of it endorsed on the conveyance, the buyer would not be in good faith and could not claim the protection of the Act. If there should be any doubt, the simplest course is for the survivor to appoint another trustee when selling, to over-reach the equitable interests.

The Act does not protect a seller and if there has been severance then he should appoint another trustee. Even if he does not, he would still hold the proceeds of sale on trust for those entitled to them.

iii   Registered titles

The 1964 Act does not apply to registered land.[6] The position is adequately dealt with by the restriction in the Proprietorship Register. If the proprietors are beneficial tenants in common then there will be such a restriction. If they are beneficial joint tenants there will not, and any buyer can rightly assume that the survivor can deal with the land; on proof of the death of one of two or more joint proprietors, his name

3   Law of Property (Joint Tenants) Act 1964, s 1(2).
4   Ibid, s 2.
5   Law of Property Act 1925, s 205(1)(xxi).
6   Law of Property (Joint Tenants) Act 1964, s 3.

will be removed from the register. Land Registry transfer forms TR1 and TP1 ask buyers to state whether they will hold as joint tenants or tenants in common. This will establish whether the restriction is necessary.

If a joint tenancy is severed then the proprietors can have a restriction entered.[7]

5   DISPOSITIONS BY PERSONAL REPRESENTATIVES

i   Basic framework

The deceased is replaced as estate owner by his personal representatives. If he left a will, the legal estate in his property passes to his executors on his death and they will apply for a grant of probate. If he died intestate, the legal estate passes to his administrators on the grant of administration. An executor could validly contract to sell property comprised in the deceased's estate before obtaining a grant of probate but a buyer could not be compelled to complete until probate had been granted and it would be prudent for the executor to make the contract conditional on obtaining the grant. The term 'personal representatives' covers both executors and administrators. Their authority is joint as regards freehold or leasehold land and all personal representatives if there are more than one must sign any contract for the sale of land[8] or execute a conveyance.[9] However, one personal representative, if there is only one, can give a valid receipt and over-reach the beneficial interests under the will or intestacy.[10]

ii   Powers of personal representatives

Personal representatives have the same powers of disposition as trustees of land.[11] This includes a power of sale. In simple terms there are two alternative courses of action for personal representatives to take in relation to land comprised in the deceased's estate. It can either be sold and the proceeds distributed in accordance with the will or intestacy or it can be vested in a beneficiary under the terms of the will or intestacy. There are two documents which a personal representative can use to transfer the property – an ordinary conveyance or assignment or transfer, or a document called an assent. To pass a legal estate, an assent must be in writing, although before 1926 it could be inferred from conduct. It must be signed by all the personal representatives but it need not be a deed (although it could be) and is thus an exception to the general rule that a legal estate can only be transferred by means of a deed. It must also name the person(s) in whose favour it is made.[12] An assent is capable of being a good root of title provided it satisfies the standard requirements of a good root. Personal representatives can use an assent to vest property in a beneficiary but will use an ordinary conveyance, transfer or assignment if selling property. If a personal representative is himself entitled to the property in some other capacity, for example because it has been left to him in the deceased's will, there must still be an assent to vest the property in him in that capacity.[13] This

---

7   Or a caution; see ch 2, section 2 vi 4.
8   Law of Property (Miscellaneous Provisions) Act 1994, ss 16(1), 21(2), Sch 2.
9   Administration of Estates Act 1925, s 2(2).
10   Law of Property Act 1925, s 27(2).
11   Administration of Estates Act 1925, s 39(1) as amended by the Trusts of Land and Appointment of Trustees Act 1996 and Trustee Act 2000.
12   Ibid, s 36(4).

even applies where there is a sole personal representative. If he has been left property in the will he must still sign an assent in his own favour, from himself as personal representative.

Personal representatives can only use an assent where the property has devolved on them.[14] In *Re Stirrup's Contract*[15] a beneficiary under a will died before an assent was made in his favour; an assent was made in favour of his personal representatives who then themselves made an assent in dealing with the property. Technically the second assent should have been a conveyance because the property did not devolve on the personal representatives. However, the court held that this did not amount to a defect in title although it should be noted that the assent in that case was executed as a deed and not just signed.

When a sole or sole surviving executor dies, his executors become the executors of the original testator and providing this chain is unbroken, the last executor in the chain is the executor of every preceding testator. The chain is broken by an intestacy or a will not appointing an executor.[16] When the chain is broken there must be a grant de bonis non in respect of the part of the previous estate not dealt with.

iii   Protection of purchasers

There are two major problems for buyers who are either buying from personal representatives or who are buying property which is shown by the abstract to have been disposed of by personal representatives in the past. The first problem is that the personal representatives might by mistake or worse have already disposed of the property to someone else before selling it to the buyer. The second problem is that personal representatives may in the past have made an assent in favour of the wrong person. In both these cases the buyer is given some statutory protection.

I   Administration of Estates Act 1925, section 36(6)

Section 36(6) of the Administration of Estates Act 1925 provides as follows:

> A statement in writing made by a personal representative that he has not given or made an assent or conveyance in respect of a legal estate shall in favour of a purchaser, but without prejudice to any previous dispositions made in favour of another purchaser deriving title mediately or immediately under the personal representative, be sufficient evidence that any assent or conveyance has not been given or made in respect of the legal estate to which the statement relates, unless notice of a previous assent or conveyance affecting that estate has been placed on or annexed to the probate or administration.
>
> A conveyance by a personal representative of a legal estate to a purchaser accepted on the faith of such a statement shall (without prejudice as aforesaid and unless notice of a previous assent or conveyance affecting that estate has been placed on or annexed to the probate or administration) operate to transfer or create the legal estate expressed to be conveyed in like manner as if no previous assent or conveyance had been made by the personal representative.

What does this mean? To take advantage of the protection, the purchaser from the personal representatives must obtain a statement in writing from them, that they have

13   *Re King's Will Trusts* [1964] Ch 542, [1964] 1 All ER 833.
14   Administration of Estates Act 1925, s 36(1).
15   [1961] 1 All ER 805, [1961] 1 WLR 449.
16   Administration of Estates Act 1925, s 7.

not made any previous assent or conveyance in respect of the legal estate in the property being sold. This statement is normally made in the recitals of the conveyance to the purchaser. If the original personal representatives have died, the statement can be made by their successors (either their executors or administrators de bonis non) and the statement will also protect the purchaser[17] in respect of dispositions by the original personal representatives. From the personal representatives' point of view, the statement will presumably only be made if it is true. However, so far as the purchaser is concerned the statement is sufficient evidence of its own truth (as to which see section 2, below) and the purchaser will still get the legal estate even if the statement is false and the personal representatives have previously disposed of the property to someone else, unless:

(a)   there is a memorandum of the previous assent or conveyance endorsed on the grant of probate or administration – the buyer's solicitor should check that there is no such memorandum; or

(b)   there has been a previous disposition (for valuable consideration) to another purchaser.[18] This could be an 'immediate' disposition if the personal representatives have previously conveyed the property to another purchaser, or a 'mediate' disposition if the personal representatives have vested the property in a beneficiary by an assent and the beneficiary has then sold the property to a purchaser before the present purported sale by the personal representatives. In both these cases the first purchaser does not lose the legal estate and the statutory provisions do not assist the present buyer from the personal representatives.

It follows that someone to whom an assent is made must protect the assent by having a memorandum of it endorsed on the grant of probate or administration or else run the risk that if the personal representatives later sell the property then the buyer will acquire the legal estate and the assentee will lose it. The Administration of Estates Act 1925, section 36(5) provides that any person in whose favour an assent or conveyance of a legal estate is made by personal representatives can require that a memorandum of it be endorsed on the grant at the cost of the estate. It is not essential that a memorandum of a conveyance to a *buyer* be so endorsed since, as we have seen, a buyer is in no danger of losing the legal estate should the personal representatives subsequently sell the same property to another buyer. However, it would cause inconvenience, and solicitors for personal representatives should automatically endorse a memorandum of any disposition, be it assent or conveyance, on the grant. Where land is subject to first registration, no memorandum is necessary.

Where the abstract reveals a conveyance by personal representatives in the past, the solicitor for the present buyer will want to check that the necessary statement had been made by the personal representatives and that there was no memorandum to the grant, relating to the property sold, at the time of the conveyance by the personal representatives. This can be checked from the abstract and if necessary by raising a requisition. It is unlikely that the seller will possess the original grant; the personal representatives would normally keep this although the seller would have a right to production. The seller will have an abstract or epitome of the grant which will have been checked against the original at the time of the purchase from the personal representatives. This is probably sufficient for the subsequent buyer's purposes as he is only interested in the state of the grant at that time.[19]

---

17   A purchaser here includes a lessee and a mortgagee.
18   A purchaser here includes a lessee and a mortgagee.
19   Although consider the advisability of relying on examined abstracts generally, discussed in section 20, below.

The effect of section 36(6) can be summarised by four examples.

Example A

(1) Personal representatives make assent in favour of A. Memorandum of assent is endorsed on grant.
(2) Personal representatives sell same property to buyer, giving section 36(6) statement.

Result

Buyer does not get legal estate, A retains it.

Example B

(1) Personal representatives make assent in favour of A. Memorandum of assent is not endorsed on grant.
(2) Personal representatives sell same property to buyer, giving section 36(6) statement.

Result

Buyer gets legal estate, A loses it.

Example C

(1) Personal representatives sell property to buyer B.
(2) Personal representatives sell the same property to buyer C, giving section 36(6) statement.

Result

C does not get legal estate, B retains it irrespective of whether a memorandum of conveyance to B is endorsed on the grant.

Example D

(1) Personal representatives make assent in favour of A. Memorandum of assent is not endorsed on grant.
(2) A sells to buyer B.
(3) Personal representatives sell the same property to buyer C, giving section 36(6) statement.

Result

C does not get legal estate, B retains it.

2   Administration of Estates Act 1925, section 36(7)

Where a buyer's solicitor sees from the abstract that there has in the past been an *assent* by personal representatives, his initial reaction would be to check that the beneficiary was under the terms of the will or intestacy the correct person to have the property. He might do this, for example, by looking at the will. However, as we saw in the last chapter, the will is normally kept off the title and would not be deduced. Instead a purchaser is given statutory protection. Section 36(7) provides that an assent or conveyance by personal representatives in respect of a legal estate shall in favour of a purchaser be sufficient evidence that the person in whose favour the assent or conveyance is made is the person entitled to have the legal estate, unless there is a memorandum of a previous assent or conveyance relating to that property endorsed on the grant or probate or administration. In the last section we were dealing with a sale by personal representatives, to which section 36(6) applies; we are now dealing with the effect on a subsequent buyer of an assent by personal representatives. The buyer's solicitor should check that there is no memorandum of any *previous* assent or conveyance on the grant. If there is not, the buyer can rely on the fact that the assent was made as sufficient evidence that it was made to the right person. This check will be made on each occasion that the title is examined in the future.

What is 'sufficient evidence'? Well, it is not conclusive evidence. If there is anything in the abstract which suggests that the assent *was* made to the wrong person then the buyer is not protected. This is illustrated by the cautionary tale of *Re Duce and Boots Cash Chemists (Southern) Ltd's Contract.*[20] The testator appointed his son as his sole personal representative and left property to his son subject to his daughter's right to live there during her lifetime. The son signed an assent in his own favour, reciting in the assent the terms of the will. The son subsequently sold the property to X who later contracted to sell to Y. On examination of title by Y, it was pointed out that the assent should have been in the daughter's favour. The will created settled land and the daughter was the tenant for life. X replied that this may be so, but that Y must rely on section 36(7). The court held that Y could not do this as there was other evidence in the abstract – in the recitals to the assent, which recited the terms of the will – from which it was quite clear that the assent had been made to the wrong person. Perhaps the moral is to avoid inserting unnecessary recitals!

3   Other provisions protecting purchaser

One of the most basic protections for a purchaser from personal representatives is that a conveyance by the personal representatives over-reaches the interests of the beneficiaries under the will or intestacy.[1] This accords with the principle that a purchaser is not concerned with the beneficial interests and the will is kept off the title. There are two further provisions protecting purchasers from personal representatives; firstly, a conveyance to a purchaser shall not be invalidated by reason only that the purchaser has notice that all debts, legacies and other expenses of the estate has been discharged[2] and secondly, a conveyance to a purchaser is also unaffected by a subsequent revocation of the personal representatives' grant.[3]

iv   Registered titles

I   Death of sole or sole surviving registered proprietor

The proprietor's personal representatives have two alternatives. They can apply for themselves to be registered as proprietors in the place of the deceased, in which case the application would be accompanied by the grant of probate or administration.[4] Otherwise they can transfer the property, either to a buyer by a deed of transfer or to a beneficiary by an assent, without themselves being registered in which case the

---

20   [1937] Ch 642, [1937] 3 All ER 788.
1   Administration of Estates Act 1925, s 39(1) as amended.
2   Ibid, s 36(8).
3   Ibid, s 37(1).
4   Land Registration Act 1925, s 41(1).

buyer or beneficiary must produce a certified copy of the grant on his application for registration.[5] Whether the personal representatives have been registered as proprietors or not, an assent by them of registered land must be in the form specified in the Land Registration Rules 1925.[6]

2 *Protection of purchaser*

Neither the Administration of Estates Act 1925, section 36(6) nor section 36(7) are relevant to registered titles, because of the conclusive nature of the register. In addition the Registrar is not concerned as to the contents of the will and will assume that the personal representatives are acting correctly.[7]

6 SALES BY MORTGAGEES

i **Power of sale**

A mortgagee has an implied statutory power of sale of the whole or part of the mortgaged property if the mortgage is made by a deed which does not exclude the power.[8] This power arises when the mortgage money becomes due. Mortgages will normally contain a provision that the mortgage must be repaid in a particular, often very short, period of time; perhaps one, three or six months. This is called the legal date for redemption of the mortgage – 'legal' because it is the date contained in the deed. In practice, of course, mortgages are not repaid on the legal date for redemption and indeed the whole idea of the mortgage is to spread repayments over a quite long period of time. The significance of the legal date for redemption is that once it has passed then the mortgagee's power of sale and other powers arise.[9] Of course even though the legal date for redemption has passed the mortgagor can still redeem (ie pay off) the mortgage in reliance on his equitable right of redemption.

So the first matter to be checked both by the solicitor for a selling mortgagee and for a buyer (either directly from the mortgagee or where the abstract shows there has been a sale by a mortgagee in the past) is that the legal date for redemption has (or had) passed and the power of sale arisen. This ought to be apparent from the mortgage deed.

A second mortgagee can only sell the property subject to prior mortgages. It is most unlikely that a buyer will be willing to buy subject to a mortgage and in practice the second mortgagee may have to sell free from the prior mortgage and redeem it on completion of the sale. This is much the same as the ordinary seller in the typical conveyancing transaction redeeming his existing mortgage on completion.

An equitable mortgagee may have a power of sale but he will not on the face of it be able to convey a legal estate to a buyer.[10] He must be empowered to pass a legal estate in some other way. He may be given a power of attorney by the mortgagor under which he could pass a legal estate. He could be given a power of attorney to execute a legal mortgage in his own favour. Alternatively the mortgagee could declare

---

5   Land Registration Act 1925, s 41(3); Land Registration Rules 1925, r. 170(1) as amended.
6   Land Registration Act 1925, s 41(4).
7   Land Registration Rules 1925, r. 170(5) as amended.
8   Law of Property Act 1925, s 101(1)(i).
9   If the amount borrowed is repayable by instalments then the mortgage money can be said to have become due, for the purposes of the power of sale arising, if one instalment has become due; *Payne v Cardiff RDC* [1932] 1 KB 241.
10   *Re Hodson and Howes' Contract* (1887) 35 Ch D 668, CA.

that the mortgagor held the property on trust for him and give him the power to remove the mortgagor and appoint new trustees. This is unlikely to be a major issue in practice, as equitable mortgages are rare.

ii   Position of the selling mortgagee

The solicitor for a selling mortgagee must ensure that the power of sale has not only arisen but has also become exercisable. The Law of Property Act 1925, section 103 states that the statutory power become exercisable:

(a)   when a notice requiring repayment of the mortgage money owing has been served on the mortgagor and has not been complied with in three months; or
(b)   when some interest is in arrear and unpaid for at least two months; or
(c)   when there has been a breach of some other express or implied provision in the mortgage. Mortgages may contain a number of provisions such as a prohibition on the mortgagor granting leases or tenancies and a provision that the power of sale shall become exercisable on the mortgagor's bankruptcy.

There are further matters to be taken into account. The mortgagee is not a trustee of his power of sale but he must take reasonable care to obtain the true market value of the property at the time he chooses to sell.[11] Prior to 1 December 1997, if the mortgagee was a building society then it had a duty under the Building Societies Act 1986, Schedule 4 to obtain the best price reasonably obtainable for the property. This provision was repealed by virtue of the Building Societies Act 1997.[12] Where the security includes a business carried on at the mortgaged property, the mortgagee has a duty to ensure that the goodwill of the business is protected so that the value of the combined asset is maximised.[13] If the mortgagee decides not to sell, but to appoint a receiver instead, the receiver's duty is more than just that of good faith; he has a duty to manage the property with due diligence, and have proper regard to its profitability.[14] A mortgagee cannot sell to himself; there is no hard and fast rule that he cannot sell to a company in which he is interested, although the sale must be in good faith and the mortgagee must have taken reasonable precautions to get the best price reasonably obtainable.[15] On the face of it a mortgagee can choose when to sell, and cannot be compelled to sell at a particular time,[16] but see the *Palk*[17] case as mentioned in section v, below.

The mortgagee will presumably wish to sell with vacant possession; assuming the mortgagor is in possession then he must be evicted. The mortgagee is prima facie entitled to possession but if he cannot get possession peaceably he must obtain a court order for possession to avoid committing an offence under the Criminal Law Act 1977. If the mortgagee *is* able to obtain possession peaceably he does not have to

11   *Cuckmere Brick Co Ltd v Mutual Finance Ltd* [1971] Ch 949, [1971] 2 All ER 633, CA. No duty is owed to someone with a beneficial interest in the property: *Parker-Tweedale v Dunbar Bank plc* [1991] Ch 12, [1990] 2 All ER 577, CA. Where the mortgagor agrees with the mortgagee that the property may be sold for less than market value, it seems the mortgagor is estopped from relying on the duty of care owed to him by the mortgagee: *Mercantile Credit Co v Clarke* (1995) P & CR 018.
12   Sections 12(1), 46(2) and Sch 9.
13   *AIB Finance Ltd v Debtors* [1998] 2 All ER 929, [1998] 1 BCLC 655.
14   *Medforth v Blake* [2000] Ch 86, [1999] 3 All ER 97.
15   *Tse Kwong Lam v Wong Chit Sen* [1983] 3 All ER 54, [1983] 1 WLR 1349, PC.
16   *China and South Sea Bank Ltd v Tan Soon Gin* [1990] 1 AC 536, [1989] 3 All ER 839, PC.
17   *Palk v Mortgage Services Funding plc* [1993] Ch 330, [1993] 2 All ER 481, CA.

bother with a court order.[18] If the property is or includes a dwelling house, the court has a discretion under the Administration of Justice Act 1970, section 36 (as amended) to adjourn the action for possession or suspend a possession order. The court can exercise this discretion if it appears that the mortgagor is likely to be able to pay the sums (ie instalments) due or otherwise remedy a breach of his obligations under the mortgage within a reasonable time.[19] The court can make the adjournment or suspension subject to conditions and it used to be common to make a possession order suspended on condition that the mortgagor pay off his arrears at a specified rate calculated to clear the arrears within one or two years. However, recent decisions suggest that the appropriate suspension, provided that there is a reasonable prospect of the mortgagor paying off the arrears, should be the whole of the remainder of the mortgage term.[20] It should be noted that the mortgagee is applying for possession (with a view to selling with vacant possession) rather than for an order for sale. The discretion is applicable to endowment as well as repayment mortgages,[21] although it did not apply for a charge to secure an overdraft, payable on demand.[22]

iii Protection of purchaser

The Law of Property Act 1925, section 104(2) provides that a purchaser is not affected by the power of sale having been 'improperly or irregularly exercised'. The solicitor for the buyer from the mortgagee, and any other subsequent buyers examining the title, must check that the power has arisen but are not concerned to see that it is exercisable. If in fact the power is not exercisable the buyer will still get a good title, although the mortgagee would be liable in damages to the aggrieved mortgagor. If the buyer from the mortgagee actually knows that the power is being improperly exercised, his title may be bad and the mortgagor may be able to recover the property. However, the buyer is under no duty to enquire about the exercise of the power and would be ill-advised to do so, unless the circumstances were such as to amount to constructive notice of the irregularity.[1]

The effect of the conveyance by the mortgagee is to pass the legal estate to the buyer subject to prior mortgages if any but free from other subsequent mortgages even if they are registered as land charges (unregistered titles) or as registered charges (registered titles). Thus in a typical situation where a first legal mortgagee is selling, the buyer takes free from any second legal or equitable mortgages. The subsequent

---

18 *Ropaigealach v Barclays Bank plc* [2000] 1 QB 263.
19 The discretion applies if the mortgagor is likely to be able to repay instalments which will fall due in the future even though there is a provision for repayment of the whole loan on default; Administration of Justice Act 1973, s 8. However, the discretion is not unlimited; see *Cheltenham and Gloucester Building Society v Ensor* (1992) unreported, CA.
20 *Cheltenham and Gloucester Building Society v Norgan* [1996] 1 All ER 449, [1996] 1 WLR 343. If there is no realistic prospect of the mortgagor being able to pay off the arrears, the court has no discretion to suspend: *First National Bank v Syed* [1991] 2 All ER 250, [1991] CCLR 37; *Bristol & West plc v Dace* [1998] unreported. Similarly, the court would normally suspend to allow the mortgagor to apply for an order for sale under s 91 of the Law of Property Act 1925; the court will not so suspend where the mortgage debt would not be fully discharged by the sale proceeds: *Cheltenham and Gloucester plc v Krausz* [1997] 1 All ER 21, [1997] 1 WLR 1558, though it does not apparently matter that the sale will not take place immediately: *National and Provincial Building Society v Lloyd* [1996] 1 All ER 630.
21 *Bank of Scotland (Governor & Co) v Grimes* [1985] QB 1179, [1985] 2 All ER 254, CA.
22 *Habib Bank Ltd v Tailor* [1982] 3 All ER 561, [1982] 1 WLR 1218, CA.
1   The protection of s 104(2) only applies to a sale under the statutory power of sale conferred by the Act, but by s 104(3) a sale is deemed to be made under the statutory power of sale unless a contrary intention appears.

mortgagees have an interest in the proceeds of sale and provided these are sufficient, they will recoup the amounts they are owed.

iv   Registered titles

The principles discussed above, including the incidence and exercise of the power of sale, apply equally to mortgages of registered land, with the necessary differences due to the particular methods of creation and protection of mortgages over registered land. By the Land Registration Act 1925, section 34(1), the proprietor of a registered charge has, subject to any entry on the register to the contrary, all the powers of a legal mortgagee.

v   Negative equity

It is appropriate here to mention the relatively recent phenomenon of 'negative equity'. This arises where the market value of the mortgaged property is less than the total amount owing on the mortgage or mortgages to which the property is subject. This could occur because the amount owed on the mortgages has been increasing because of rising arrears, although in the late 1980s and early 1990s it may have occurred because the market value of the property had fallen. The owner of the property, the mortgagor, is in difficulty if he wants to sell a property which has negative equity. As we shall see in Chapter 14, the buyer's solicitor will require an undertaking from the seller's solicitor that all existing mortgages be discharged. The normal source of funds to do this is the proceeds of sale, but in a negative equity situation these will, of course, be insufficient. Unless funds are available from elsewhere, or unless the mortgagee or mortgagees will agree to discharge the mortgages without receiving the full amount of the mortgage debt, the seller's solicitor cannot give the appropriate undertaking and this means that the property in effect cannot be sold.

Palk v Mortgage Services Funding plc[2] was a negative equity case. The market value of the property was around £283,000 and the amount owing on the mortgage was around £358,000. The mortgagee refused to agree to a sale at £283,000 and instituted possession proceedings, obtaining a suspended possession order. However, the mortgagee did not want to sell the property but to rent it out to tenants in the hope that in the meantime the market would recover and allow it to recoup the mortgage debt. This was not an attractive proposition to the mortgagor, as the likely rental income from the property was £14,000 a year whereas the interest on the outstanding mortgage debt would be accruing at around £43,000 a year. The mortgagor saw no prospect of the housing market recovering at a rate fast enough to overtake the difference between the two figures. The mortgagor therefore applied to court for an order for sale and was successful in obtaining this order. The Court of Appeal decided that it had a general discretion under section 9(2) of the Law of Property Act 1925 and that this was an appropriate case for exercise of the discretion particularly in view of the ever increasing mortgage debt, the rental income not being sufficient to keep pace with the increasing debt. Although in this case the mortgagee had commenced enforcement proceedings by obtaining a suspended possession order, and the court indicated that the mortgagee was then under a duty to act fairly to the mortgagor, it seems that the discretion under section 91(2) is not limited to such a situation. It is an overriding statutory power.

---

2   [1993] Ch 330, [1993] 2 All ER 481, CA.

Another option open to a lender, where property is co-owned and therefore subject to a trust of land, is for the lender to apply for an order for sale under section 14 of the Trusts of Land and Appointment of Trustees Act.[3]

7   DISPOSITIONS BY CHARITIES

The restrictions on dispositions of property by a charity were contained in section 29 of the Charities Act 1960. However, the relevant provisions are now to be found in the Charities Act 1993, which consolidates changes made in the Charities Act 1992. Dispositions by a charity are divided into three categories; mortgages given as security for money borrowed by the charity, leases of seven years or less, and all other dispositions.

Under section 38 of the 1993 Act a charity can enter into a mortgage as security for a loan without the need for consent from the Charity Commissioners, provided that, before executing the mortgage, the charity obtains and considers advice from a qualified financial adviser who does not have any interest in the loan being made.

Under section 36 of the 1993 Act, a charity can grant a lease for seven years or less without the need for consent from the Charity Commissioners provided that, prior to entering the agreement for the lease, the charity obtains and considers advice from a person whom the charity reasonably believes to be able to give competent advice. The charity must satisfy itself that the terms of the lease are the best which can be reasonably obtained. If the proposed tenant is a 'connected person', for example a trustee, employee or officer of the charity, the consent of the Charity Commissioners will still be needed even though the lease is to be for seven years or less.

Also under section 36, a charity can enter into any other dispositions of its land, including a sale, without the need for consent from the Charity Commissioners, provided that a number of requirements are satisfied. If any of these requirements is not satisfied, consent from the Charity Commissioners will be needed. The requirements are that the charity must obtain and consider a written report on the proposed disposition from a competent qualified surveyor; the charity must advertise the proposed disposition in accordance with the surveyor's advice; the charity must be satisfied that the terms of the proposed disposition are the best that can be reasonably obtained; and the disposition must not be made to a 'connected person'. Assuming that the requirements are satisfied, there must be a certificate to this effect in the document effecting the disposition, for example the conveyance, transfer or lease.

A transaction falling outside these provisions will require the consent of the court or the Charity Commissioners. The consent should be obtained before exchange of contracts, or the contract should be made conditional on consent being given.

In relation to a registered title, effect will be given to these limitations on a charity's powers of disposition by the entry of a restriction in the proprietorship register of title to land owned by the charity.[4]

8   DISPOSITIONS TO OR BY COMPANIES

i   Power of the company

Dispositions to or by companies incorporated under the Companies Act 1985 as amended used to be governed by the ultra vires rule. If the act of the company was

---

3   See *Bank of Baroda v Dhillon* [1998] 1 FCR 489, [1998] 1 FLR 524.
4   Land Registration (Charities) Rules 1992.

not within its objects as set out in the memorandum of association, nor incidental to those objects, then it was void. The solicitor for a seller company and indeed also a buyer company had to ensure that the company did have power to buy or sell the land.[5]

So far as a person dealing with a company is concerned, including a buyer from a company, the ultra vires rule has been very much restricted by the Companies Act 1989, section 108. This inserts new sections in the Companies Act 1985. Section 35(1) provides that:

> The validity of an act done by a company shall not be called into question on the ground of lack of capacity by reason of anything in the company's memorandum.

However, section 35(3) provides that:

> It remains the duty of the directors to observe any limitations on their powers flowing from the company's memorandum …

Section 35A(1) provides that:

> In favour of the person dealing with a company in good faith, the power of the board of directors to bind the company, or authorise others to do so, shall be deemed to be free of any limitation under the company's constitution.

Section 35A(2) further states that:

> For this purpose:
> (a) a person 'deals with' a company if he is a party to any transaction or other act to which the company is a party;
> (b) a person shall not be regarded as acting in bad faith by reason only of his knowing that an act is beyond the powers of the directors under the company's constitution; and
> (c) a person shall be presumed to have acted in good faith unless the contrary is proved.

Finally, section 35B provides that:

> … a party to a transaction with a company is not bound to enquire as to whether it is permitted by the company's memorandum or as to any limitation on the powers of the board of directors to bind the company or authorise others to do so.

ii   Registered titles

When a company applies for registration as proprietor of land, the application form requires a certificate that the company has power to hold and dispose of land. The need for a restriction in the proprietorship register may be considered if the company's powers of disposal are limited. In the absence of any such restriction a buyer can assume that the powers of disposal are not limited.

---

5   The memorandum will almost inevitably include powers to buy, sell, lease and mortgage land and see now Companies Act 1989, s 110, introducing a new s 3A to the Companies Act 1985 providing for a very wide objects clause for a general commercial company.

9   DISPOSITIONS INVOLVING MINORS

i   Capacity of minor

Before 1970 a person under 21 was a minor. From 1 January 1970 the age of majority was reduced to 18 and now a person under 18 is a minor.[6] A minor cannot hold a legal estate, although he can hold an equitable interest, in land.

ii   Dispositions to a minor

Prior to the Trusts of Land and Appointment of Trustees Act 1996, a conveyance to a minor did not transfer the legal estate but instead operated as an agreement for value to create a settlement in the proper form – by a trust instrument and vesting deed – and in the meantime to hold the land on trust for the minor.[7] If a conveyance was made jointly to a minor and an adult then the latter took the legal estate and held it on a statutory trust for sale for himself and the minor.[8] Now, as the strict settlement and trust for sale have been abolished, a conveyance to one or more infants does NOT pass the legal estate, but operates as a declaration that the land is held as a trust of land, upon trust for the minor.[9] Where property is expressed to be transferred jointly to a minor and an adult, this also takes effect as a trust of land for the benefit of the adult and minor beneficiary, with the adult or adults taking the legal estate and acting as the trustees.[10] In both cases, the rules set out above relating to trusts of land apply.[11] A minor should not be registered as the proprietor of registered land; a purported disposition of registered land to a minor does not entitle the minor to be registered until he attains majority, but in the meantime operates as a declaration that the land is to be held on trust for the minor.[12] This would be protected by a registration on the register. If a minor is by mistake registered as proprietor, the register is subject to rectification. The correct method of giving a minor an interest in land is by means of a trust of land with the legal estate vested in trustees.

   A contract for sale to a minor is binding unless repudiated during minority or within a reasonable time of attaining majority. On repudiation, the court may, if it is just and equitable, require restitution of money or property which has passed under the contract.[13]

iii   Disposition by a minor

As a minor cannot hold the legal estate he clearly cannot convey it. He can dispose of his equitable interest although this is subject to his right to repudiate the transaction during minority or within reasonable time of attaining majority. On a mortgage by a minor, the mortgagee would probably have a lien over land purchased with the aid of the mortgage.[14]

---

6   Family Law Reform Act 1969, s 1.
7   Law of Property Act 1925, s 19(1), Settled Land Act 1925, s 27(1).(both now repealed by the Trusts of Land and Appointment of Trustees Act 1996).
8   Law of Property Act 1925, s 19(2)(now repealed).
9   Trusts of Land and Appointment of Trustees Act 1996, Sch 1, para 1(1).
10   Ibid, Sch 1, para 1(2).
11   See section 3.
12   Land Registration Act 1925, s 111(1).
13   Minors' Contracts Act 1987, s 3.
14   *Nottingham Permanent Benefit Building Society v Thurstan* [1903] AC 6, HL.

iv Presumption of full age

By the Law of Property Act 1925, section 15, the parties to a conveyance (including a lease and a mortgage) are presumed to be of full age at the date thereof unless the contrary is proved. A buyer will rely on this presumption but where there is some suspicion that, for example, the seller may be a minor then perhaps the buyer's solicitor should ask to see the seller's birth certificate to confirm. Mortgagees will be particularly concerned to ensure that the borrower is not a minor.

10 MENTALLY DISORDERED PERSONS

i Before the appointment of a receiver

A contract for sale by a person suffering from mental disorder will be valid unless it can be shown that the buyer knew of the incapacity in which case it will be voidable at the instance of the patient (or his receiver or personal representatives).[15] A similar rule applies to a conveyance for valuable consideration by the patient, and to a purchase. However, a gift, ie a voluntary conveyance by the patient, is void.[16]

ii After the appointment of a receiver

A receiver may be appointed under the Mental Health Act 1983, section 99. Thereafter any disposition by the patient is void, as the effect of an order under section 99 is that the patient's property passes out of his control and into the control of the receiver subject to the court's supervision.

iii Registered titles

If the patient is a registered proprietor then on appointment of a receiver no restriction is normally entered as the receiver will have control of the land certificate. On a dealing, the Land Registry would require evidence of the receiver's power to act for the patient, ie a copy of the order. If the receiver *is* registered as proprietor there will be a restriction on the Proprietorship Register, that no disposition by the proprietor registered unless made pursuant to an order of the court.

11 DISPOSITION BY AN ATTORNEY

i Basic framework

To understand the way the law relating to powers of attorney has developed, it is important to understand the background to this area. Powers of attorney have been used for a long time to enable one individual to undertake tasks which the donor would normally be able to perform for himself, but is unable to do due to temporary illness, or being out of the country, for example. Powers could be general, allowing the attorney to do anything which the donor could himself do, or specific, relating to only certain property or actions. There were particular rules where trustees were involved.

---

15 *Broughton v Snook* [1938] Ch 505, [1938] 1 All ER 411.
16 *Elliot v Ince* (1857) 7 De G M & G 475.

Prior to 1985, there was a difficulty relating to people, particularly the elderly, who developed mental incapacity. An elderly person, perhaps becoming physically and mentally frail, might ask a trusted relative or friend to take care of their day to day affairs and grant them a general power of attorney to enable them to sign documents, cheques etc. However, if the donor then became mentally incapable, the power was automatically revoked. This resulted in an unsatisfactory state of affairs, as all the donor's assets would be frozen at a time when money might be urgently needed for the donor's care. To resolve this problem, the Enduring Powers of Attorney Act 1985 was introduced. Powers made in the prescribed form under this Act are not revoked by the donor's mental incapacity, but can continue in full force once registered with the Court of Protection. A more detailed explanation of the way the Act operates may be found in section vii below.

For the purpose of conveyancing, a power of attorney must be executed as a deed by the donor of the power,[17] and will authorise the donee of the power – the attorney – to act on the donor's behalf in dealing with his property. The power of attorney might, as mentioned above, be specific, stating what powers the attorney is to have, for example to do all things necessary to sell a particular named property, or merely to execute a particular deed. There is provision in section 10(1)[18] of the Powers of Attorney Act 1971 for a general form of power of attorney which operates to confer on the attorney authority to do on behalf of the donor anything which can lawfully be done by an attorney. The donor can choose to appoint a sole attorney, or more than one, to act jointly or jointly and severally. The attorney might be the donor's solicitor, or a relative or friend. To cover the situation where the donor is physically incapable, the power may be executed by the direction of and in the presence of the donor in which case two witnesses must be present and attest the execution.[19]

The wording of the general power is as follows:

I appoint AB of (*or* AB of .... and CD of .... jointly *or* jointly and severally) to be my attorney(s) in accordance with section 10 of the Powers of Attorney Act 1971.

The situation relating to the exercise of trustee functions used to pose some difficulty. Many properties nowadays are held by couples; a trust of land is imposed by the Trusts of Land and Appointment of Trustees Act 1996, and they hold the legal estate as trustees for themselves and the equitable interests as joint beneficiaries. What happens when one of these two is not available to execute documents in a conveyancing transaction? Prior to the Trustee Delegation Act 1999, it was not possible to use a general power of attorney to delegate a trustee function.[20] Instead, section 25 of the Trustee Act 1925 allowed a trustee to appoint an attorney, but only for twelve months. It was not possible for the donor to appoint his sole co-trustee. Section 3(3) of the Enduring Powers of Attorney Act 1985 permitted attorneys to exercise all the functions vested in the donor as trustee, which meant that an Enduring Power could also be used to allow a trustee to delegate his trustee functions, seemingly even to a sole co-trustee. The Trusts of Land and Appointment of Trustees Act 1996, section 9 introduced a limited power for trustees to delegate to a beneficiary, for any period, but not by the use of an enduring power, This power could be revoked by any trustee and in the situation where the beneficiary ceased to be beneficially entitled to an

---

17   Powers of Attorney Act 1971, s 1(1).
18   And Sch 1.
19   Law of Property (Miscellaneous Provisions) Act 1989, s 1(3)(a).
20   This position was confirmed in *Walia v Michael Naughton Ltd* [1985] 3 All ER 673, [1985] 1 WLR 1115.

interest in possession in the land. Section 25 of the Trustee Act and section 3(3) of the Enduring Powers of Attorney Act still applied and there was thus scope for considerable confusion. This was resolved by the Trustee Delegation Act 1999, which came into force on 1 March 2000.

Under the new Act, trustees have the power to delegate to an attorney if they have a beneficial interest in the land concerned.[1] The power is subject to any contrary intention expressed in the trust instrument or the power itself, and it applies to both ordinary and enduring powers. Section 3(3) of the Enduring Powers of Attorney Act 1985 is repealed in so far as powers created after 1 March 2000 are concerned. The Trustee Delegation Act does not apply to powers granted before the Act came into force. The Act also inserts a new section 25 into the Trustee Act 1925.[2] This permits a trustee to delegate all functions, but only for twelve months. Written notice, containing certain prescribed information, must be given to the other trustees, and anyone who has power to appoint a new trustee, within seven days of the power. There is a prescribed form for the power.[3]

In the common situation discussed above, where a property is owned by a couple, there is in theory nothing to prevent them delegating to one another under section 5. However, two trustees are still required to give a valid receipt for capital monies[4] - one trustee cannot therefore appoint his sole co-trustee as attorney as that would leave only one person to give the receipt.

The Trustee Delegation Act did not repeal section 9 of the Trusts of Land and Appointment of Trustees Act, so it is still possible for a trustee to delegate to a beneficiary. However, this may of limited practical use.

ii   Revocation

A power of attorney once given can be revoked. There can be express revocation by the donor and revocation will occur automatically on the donor's death, incapacity or bankruptcy. The Powers of Attorney Act 1971 has introduced a special rule in relation to what are called powers given by way of security. Security is used here in the sense of security for a loan. An example would be a power of attorney given in connection with an equitable mortgage to enable the mortgagee to pass a legal estate on exercising his power of sale as mortgagee. The Powers of Attorney Act 1971, section 4 provides that if such a power is expressed to be irrevocable (which it normally would be, there being little point if the mortgagor can revoke it at will) then so long as the interest of the attorney – the equitable mortgage in the above example – exists, the power is not revoked by the donor/mortgagor's death, incapacity or bankruptcy but can only be revoked by the donor *with the consent of* the attorney/mortgagee.

iii   Purchase from the attorney

As a first step a buyer or other person dealing with the attorney should ensure that the power does cover the transaction which the attorney is to undertake. This applies equally to a subsequent buyer where the abstract reveals a disposition by an attorney. The buyer's solicitor will wish to examine the wording of the power of attorney and to this end a buyer is always entitled to see free of charge any power of attorney which affects his title,

1   Trustee Delegation Act 1999, s 1.
2   Ibid, s 5.
3   Ibid, s 5(6).
4   Ibid, s 7.

or a copy thereof.[5] This provision applies notwithstanding any stipulation to the contrary in the contract. The copy should be a photocopy certified by the donor or a solicitor[6] to be a true copy of the original. The buyer's solicitor would also check the execution of the power (in common with all other deeds abstracted). The buyer is still entitled to see a power of attorney or a copy even if the power dates from a period before the root of title, notwithstanding the normal rule that no requisition can be raised on pre-root matters.[7]

The main problem for the purchaser buying from an attorney is that the power may have been revoked before completion. This will be difficult for a buyer to ascertain and so he is now protected by the Powers of Attorney Act 1971, section 5(2), which states that when a power of attorney has been revoked and a person without knowledge of the revocation deals with the attorney, the transaction between them shall in favour of such a person be as valid as if the power had then been in existence. Section 5(5) provides that knowledge of an event giving rise to revocation amounts to knowledge of the revocation itself. In the case of an ordinary power, the relevant knowledge is of express revocation or of the donor's death, incapacity or bankruptcy. If the buyer does not have this knowledge, he will get good title even if the power has been revoked. In the case of a power given by way of security the only relevant knowledge is of revocation by the donor with the consent of the attorney since, as we saw in the previous section, it is only in this way that the power can be revoked.[8] The Powers of Attorney Act 1971, section 5 also gives protection to the attorney in similar circumstances. If he has no knowledge that the power has been revoked then he will not be under any liability if he acts in pursuance of the power.[9]

iv   Subsequent purchasers

We can now consider the position of a buyer from the person who acquired the property from the attorney, and subsequent buyers. The title depends on whether the person who dealt with the attorney had knowledge of revocation at that time. On the face of it subsequent buyers would have to try and find this out, but again this would be most difficult in practice and the Powers of Attorney Act 1971 gives protection. This protection applies to a purchaser in good faith for valuable consideration (including a mortgagee and lessee).[10] The relevant provision is contained in section 5(4) of the Act. When the interest of a purchaser depends on whether the transaction between the attorney and the person dealing with him is valid, it is in two situations conclusively presumed in favour of the purchaser that the person who dealt with the attorney did *not* know of revocation at the relevant time. The first of the circumstances giving rise to the conclusive presumption is when the transaction between the attorney and the person who dealt with him was completed within twelve months of the date the power came into operation. If this is inapplicable, because the power was not exercised within twelve months, the purchaser must turn to the other circumstances giving rise to the conclusive presumption. This is where the person who dealt with the attorney makes a statutory declaration that he did not know of revocation at the material time. The declaration must be made before or within three months after completion of *the subsequent purchase*, ie the sale (or mortgage or lease), by the person making the declaration, the person who dealt with the attorney. Although the Act permits the declaration to be made up to three months after completion, the purchaser

5   Law of Property Act 1925, s 125(2); see also ibid, s 45(1).
6   Or a notary public or stockbroker; Powers of Attorney Act 1971, s 3(1).
7   Law of Property Act 1925, s 45(1).
8   Section 5(3).
9   Section 5(1).
10 Powers of Attorney Act 1971, s 5(6).

will doubtless require it before completion. In fact, it would be good practice for the person who dealt with the attorney to make the declaration immediately rather than waiting until he subsequently sells the property; indeed, in practice this may be inevitable. If a buyer purchases from an attorney with the aid of a mortgage, the mortgagee is a 'purchaser' within section 5(4); the interest of the mortgagee depends on the validity of the purchase by the buyer from the attorney and the buyer will have to make the statutory declaration at the time of or within three months after the mortgage.

The solicitor for the buyer from the person who dealt with the attorney must be satisfied that the buyer can rely on one of these presumptions and if necessary obtain the statutory declaration. The solicitors for subsequent buyers will also check that a presumption is applicable either by virtue of the date of the transaction with the attorney or the existence of the statutory declaration.

v   Dispositions before 1971

The Powers of Attorney Act only came into force on 1 October 1971. Briefly, the position before that date was as follows. A statutory declaration *by the attorney* as to *his* lack of knowledge of revocation had to be obtained.[11] This would be made within three months after the disposition *by the attorney*, and would be conclusive proof of non-revocation in favour of a purchaser in good faith.

vi   Registered titles

The position is governed by the Land Registration (Powers of Attorney) Rules 1986. When an application for registration is made as a result of an instrument executed under a power of attorney, the applicant must also send the original or a certified copy of the power. If the transaction was not completed within twelve months of the coming into operation of the power, the applicant must also send the statutory declaration necessary to give rise to the appropriate conclusive presumption; however, a Practice Direction dated 26 April 1991 provides that a certificate signed by a solicitor or licensed conveyancer, as to a person's lack of knowledge of revocation or a revoking event, can replace the person's statutory declaration.

vii   Enduring powers of attorney

As we have already seen, an ordinary power of attorney is automatically revoked by the donor's mental incapacity. To overcome the problems caused by this rule, the Enduring Powers of Attorney Act 1985 provides for a so-called enduring power of attorney; this is not revoked by the donor's subsequent incapacity,[12] and indeed the point of giving such a power might be specifically to allow the donor's property to be dealt with subsequent to his incapacity. The enduring power must be in a specified form executed by donor and attorney[13] and containing prescribed information explaining the effect of the power.[14] Like an ordinary power, the enduring power can be general or specific in its scope.[15] As we saw in section I above, an enduring power

---

11   Law of Property Act 1925, s 124(2).
12   Enduring Powers of Attorney Act 1985, s 1(1)(a).
13   Ibid, s 2(1).
14   Ibid, s 2(2); Enduring Powers of Attorney (Prescribed Form) Regulations 1990.
15   Ibid, s 3(1). The scope of a general power is defined in s 3(2).

of attorney cannot now be used for the exercise of trustee powers. The Act contains specific provisions about the scope of the authority of the attorney under a power, including for example the power to make gifts in certain circumstances.[16]

Prior to the donor's incapacity the power will take effect in a similar fashion to an ordinary power. On incapacity occurring, the attorney ceases to have authority under the power[17] and there must be an application for registration of the power with the Court of Protection.[18] Pending such registration, the attorney has authority, but limited to maintaining the donor and preventing loss to the donor's estate.[19] Before applying for registration, the attorney must give notice to the donor and to at least three of the donor's relatives.[20] The Act contains a list of categories of relatives in order of priority, starting with the donor's spouse and including the donor's children, parents, brothers and sisters, grandchildren etc.[1] Commencing at the head of the list, at least three relatives must be informed (or all the members of a particular class if there are more than three). Following notification, the donor or relatives have four weeks in which to object to registration. The grounds of objection, set out in the Act, include the invalidity of the power, the fact that the application is premature (ie the donor is not mentally incapable), and the unsuitability of the attorney.[2] Assuming that any objection is not upheld by the Court of Protection, the power will be registered and the attorney resumes his full authority under the power. Once registered, the power cannot be revoked by the donor without the consent of the Court.[3]

The position of persons dealing with the attorney and subsequent purchasers is similar to the position under the Powers of Attorney Act 1971 mentioned above. Prior to the donor's incapacity, and after incapacity but before registration, section 5 of the 1971 Act applies and the position is as for an ordinary power.[4] ie dependent on the lack of knowledge, by the person dealing with the attorney, of revocation or incapacity. Section 5, it will be remembered, also protects subsequent purchasers. Between application and registration, an act outside the limited scope of authority of the attorney will be valid so far as a person dealing with the attorney is concerned if that person did not know that the attorney was acting outside his authority.[5]

If a power is registered, which later turns out not to have been a valid power (eg where the donor was already mentally incapable when giving the power,[6] any transaction by the attorney will still be valid provided that the person dealing with the attorney did not know that there was no valid enduring power, and did not know of any event which would have revoked the power had it been a valid enduring power.[7] Similarly where there is a valid power of attorney, which is for some reason not a valid *enduring* power, any transaction by the attorney will be valid unless the person dealing with the attorney knows that there is no valid enduring power or that the donor has become mentally incapable.[8] In respect of these two situations, the 1985 Act contains provisions protecting subsequent purchasers similar to the

---

16 Ibid, s 3(4), (5).
17 Enduring Powers of Attorney Act 1985, s 1(1)(b).
18 Ibid, s 4(2).
19 Ibid, s 1(2).
20 Ibid, s 4(3).
 1 Ibid, Sch 1.
 2 Ibid, s 6(5).
 3 Ibid, s 7(1)(a).
 4 Ibid, s 1(1)(c).
 5 Ibid, s 1(3).
 6 For the capacity necessary to give the power, see *Re K; Re F* [1988] Ch 310, [1988] 1 All ER 358.
 7 Enduring Powers of Attorney Act 1985, s 9(2), (3).
 8 Ibid, s 9(6) and Sch 2.

provisions in section 5 of the 1971 Act[9] with the consequent need for a statutory declaration that the person dealing with the attorney does not know of revocation of the power, any revoking event, or that the power was not a valid enduring power and had been revoked by the donor's mental incapacity.

Section 5 of the 1971 Act will continue to apply to revocation by the donor's death or bankruptcy, or express revocation, but in respect of the latter, it is knowledge of the court's confirmation of revocation of a registered power, rather than the express revocation, that is relevant.[10]

The provisions of the Land Registration (Powers of Attorney) Rules 1986 also cover enduring powers with the need for statutory declarations, or similar certificates, to be provided.

12   VOLUNTARY DISPOSITIONS

A voluntary disposition, that is to say a deed of gift (be it a conveyance of freehold land or an assignment of leasehold land) can of course form a perfectly adequate link in the chain of unregistered title. However, there are certain circumstances in which a voluntary disposition of a registered or unregistered title can be set aside and the solicitor for the buyer – and seller – must check that the title is not so affected.

i   Subsequent bankruptcy

The Insolvency Act 1986, sections 339–342, as amended by the Insolvency (No 2) Act 1994, deal with the position of a buyer where there has been a transaction at an undervalue in the past. A transaction at an undervalue includes a deed of gift, a transaction (including conveyance) in consideration of marriage and a transaction (including conveyance) in which the transferor receives a consideration which is significantly less than the value of the consideration he provides. Clearly, it is important that those in financial difficulties should not be able to avoid their debts by simply giving away their assets, but at the same time it is also important that land should be freely saleable, and the question therefore is the extent to which a subsequent purchaser in good faith should be at risk of losing his property because of such a transaction. The law is basically as follows:

If more than five years has elapsed since the gift/transaction at an undervalue, a purchaser is at no risk – transactions may not be set aside after five years have elapsed. Arguably, a prudent solicitor will want to do a bankruptcy search to ensure there were no bankruptcy entries made during the five year period,

If less than two years has elapsed since the transaction, the buyer should not proceed; if the donor becomes bankrupt at any time before two years have elapsed, the transaction can be set aside on application to the Court by the trustee in bankruptcy.

If between two and five years have elapsed since the relevant transaction, the prospective buyer is in a difficult situation. A buyer from a donee will be protected if he acquires the property in good faith and for value. Lack of good faith will be presumed if:

---

9   Ibid, s 9(4).
10 Enduring Powers of Attorney Act 1985, s 9(5). There is one area of doubt under the 1985 Act, which is the extent to which knowledge of an application for registration, of registration itself, and of revocation of registration is to be implied; it is possible to make a search at the Court of Protection on payment of a fee, and a person dealing with an attorney should presumably make such a search, although it does not confer any priority period within which completion could take place in reliance on the search.

1) when he acquires the property, he has notice both of bankruptcy proceedings against the donor and of the fact that the transaction by the donor was at an undervalue or
2) he is an 'associate' of the donor or donee[11]

It may well be hard to avoid the notices mentioned in 1) above: any bankruptcy entries in the Land Charges Department will be notice of bankruptcy, whether a search is actually done or not; and a gift will be evident from the deeds (though an undervalue transaction may be harder to spot). If a search is done and reveals bankruptcy entries, the buyer should not proceed as he will be presumed to be in bad faith and so will lose the protection of the Act. Even if no entries are revealed, he arguably should still not proceed – if the donor is made bankrupt after the buyer completes but within five years, the property will be difficult to resell.

Many solicitors insist on a declaration of solvency from the donor in any event, as well as doing a bankruptcy search and obtaining insurance.

ii   Dispositions by Companies

There are broadly similar provisions in the Insolvency Act 1986 relating to dispositions by companies;

1) Disposition within the past two years – the transaction can be set aside at the instance of the liquidator if it was made to a person connected with the company.[12] If the donee was not connected, the transaction can only be set aside if the donee had notice both of the fact that the transaction was at an undervalue, and of the insolvency.

2) Disposition more than two years ago – the transaction can only be set aside if the company went into liquidation within two years of the transaction. This should be easy to check by doing a company search.

iii   Dispositions to defraud creditors

The Insolvency Act 1986, section 423 states that transactions at an undervalue made with intent to put assets beyond the reach of creditors shall be voidable at the instance of the persons prejudiced. Section 425 excepts from the operation of this rule a conveyance made (not by the debtor) for value to a purchaser in good faith with no notice of the relevant circumstances. This protection extends to subsequent purchasers without notice. So far as a buyer is concerned, if he is buying in good faith without notice of relevant circumstances, he need not be concerned further.

iv   Dispositions to avoid spouse's claims

The Matrimonial Causes Act 1973, section 37(4) provides that any disposition made by a spouse with the intention of defeating the other spouse's claim for financial relief under the Act may be set aside, unless made for a valuable consideration to a purchaser in good faith without notice of such intention.[13]

If a spouse has made a claim for a property adjustment order in matrimonial proceedings, the pending action and eventual order should be protected by

---

11   Defined in s 435 of the Insolvency Act 1986; includes certain close relatives, and employees.
12   Defined in ss 249 and 435 of the Insolvency Act 1986.
13   See *Kemmis v Kemmis* [1988] 1 WLR 1307, [1998] 2 FLR 223, CA.

registration under the Land Charges Act 1972 for unregistered land or by entry of a caution for registered land.

13   DISCHARGED MORTGAGES

i   Manner of effecting discharge

It is not sufficient merely to pay all the sums due under a mortgage. The mortgage must also be discharged. The basic method of discharge as provided by the Law of Property Act 1925, section 115, is by receipt. This must be endorsed on, written at the foot of, or annexed to the mortgage. It must also state the name of the person paying off the mortgage and must be executed by the mortgagee. It operates to discharge the mortgage and no further reconveyance, surrender or release is necessary. The form of the receipt is set out in the third schedule of the Act and is as follows:

> I .... hereby acknowledge that I have this (date) received the sum of ....
> representing the balance remaining owing in respect of the principal money secured
> by the within written mortgage together with all interest and costs, the payment
> having been made by ....
>   As witness ....

The receipt should be executed in the same way as a deed; see chapter 14, section 1 iii.

Many mortgages in domestic conveyancing are to building societies, although as more and more building societies convert to banks this becomes less the case. A building society receipt under section 115 should be sealed by the society and counter-signed by any person acting under the authority of the Board of Directors. There is also a special form of receipt which can be used by a building society and which the building society is more likely to use than a section 115 receipt. This is a receipt under the Building Societies Act 1986, (as amended by the Building Societies Act 1997), Schedule 2A. It must be endorsed on or annexed to the mortgage and it too must be sealed by the Society and counter-signed by any person acting under the authority of the Board of Directors. The chief difference from the section 115 receipt is that the Schedule 4 receipt does not name the person making payment. The form prescribed[14] under Schedule 2A of the 1986 Act is as follows:

> The .... (Note 1) Building Society hereby acknowledge to have received
> all monies intended to be secured by the .... (Note 2) deed.
>
> > ....(Note 3).
> > .... (Note 4).

> Note 1: Insert remainder of name.
> Note 2: Insert 'above written', 'within written' or 'annexed'.
> Note 3: Insert words or attestation.
> Note 4: Seal is to be affixed and counter-signed.

The receipt should follow the wording of the scheduled form exactly.

A discharge need not necessarily be in the form of a receipt and could be in the form of a deed of release. This might be appropriate if a small part of the mortgaged property was being sold off, with the mortgagee agreeing to release the part sold from the mortgage, perhaps on terms as to the purchase price being paid towards the

---

14   Building Societies (Prescribed Form of Receipt) Rules 1997.

mortgage debt. A receipt would not be appropriate and the mortgagee would either execute a separate deed of release or would join in the conveyance to the buyer to release the part sold from the mortgage.

ii   Position of buyer

Apart from the seller's mortgage or mortgages, which will be discharged on completion, the buyer's solicitor will check that all mortgages revealed by the abstract have been properly discharged. He will examine the receipts to ensure that they comply with the appropriate statutory requirements. There is one particular difficulty which may arise if the receipt is made under the Law of Property Act 1925, section 115. Section 115(2) provides that if it appears from the receipt that the money was paid by someone who was not the person immediately entitled to redeem the mortgage, then in the absence of any provision to the contrary the receipt does not operate to discharge the mortgage but as a transfer of the mortgage to the person making the payment. The effect of this transfer is that the person making payment 'steps into the shoes' of the mortgagee and the mortgage continues to subsist. If the buyer's solicitor sees from examining the abstract that a mortgage has only been transferred and not discharged because of the effect of section 115(2), he should in theory require that the mortgage be properly discharged. However, the case of *Cumberland Court (Brighton) Ltd v Taylor*[15] shows that a buyer may not in fact be adversely affected by this apparent defect in title. A sold property to B, B mortgaged it to M and B later sold it to S, the seller. The discharge of the mortgage from B to M was dated two days after the conveyance from B to S. The effect of the conveyance was to convey the property to S subject to the mortgage. After the conveyance the person immediately entitled to redeem the mortgage was S. But of course the mortgage was paid off by B. Under section 115(2) the receipt did not operate as a discharge but as a transfer of the mortgage to B. However, in the conveyance to S, B had included the standard recital that he owned the property free from incumbrances. He was thereby estopped from setting up the mortgage against S and his successors in title and the buyer, whose solicitor pointed out the defect, still got a good title from S.

There are also three statutory exceptions to the effects of section 115(2). A receipt will not impliedly operate as a transfer even though the person named as making payment is not the person immediately entitled to redeem the mortgage if:

(a)   it is expressly provided that the receipt shall not operate as a transfer,[16] or
(b)   the payment is by a trustee or personal representative out of money applicable for the redemption of the mortgage,[17] or
(c)   the payment is made by the mortgagor even though there are subsequent mortgages.[18]

iii   Registered titles

A registered charge when discharged will be deleted from the Charges Register. The Law of Property Act 1925, section 115 is inapplicable[19] and the charge is discharged

---

15   [1964] Ch 29, [1963] 2 All ER 536.
16   Law of Property Act 1925, s 115(2)(a).
17   Ibid, s 115(2)(b).
18   Ibid, s 115(3).
19   Section 115(10).

by presenting an application for its removal from the register. There is a prescribed form of application for this, which is form DS1 (or DS3 for a sale of part) in the Schedule to the Land Registration Rules 1925.[20] The form must be executed by the mortgagee and then sent to the District Land Registry along with the Charge Certificate and the appropriate application form. The wording of form DS1 is as follows:

> Title Number(s) of the Property ....
> Property ....
> Date ....
> Date of charge..............
> Lender ....
> The Lender acknowledges that the property is no longer charged as security for the payment of sums due under the charge.
> Date of Land Registry facility letter (if any)
> [To be executed as a deed by the lender or in accordance with the above facility letter.]

Alternatively, if the mortgagee is acting under the Land Registry's scheme for Electronic Notification of Discharge of mortgages (END), no paper form will be involved.[1]

14   BANKRUPTS

i   Basic framework

Bankruptcy proceedings are commenced by a bankruptcy petition. This is essentially based on the inability of the potential bankrupt to pay his debts. The petition could be presented by a creditor or by the debtor himself. If the petition is successful a bankruptcy order is made and the Official Receiver takes control of the bankrupt's property. A trustee in bankruptcy is then appointed and the bankrupt's property vests in him. A bankruptcy petition is registrable under the Land Charges Act 1972 in the register of pending actions and a bankruptcy order is registrable in the register of writs and orders. The petition and bankruptcy order are automatically so registered. As soon as practicable after the registration of the petition or bankruptcy order a creditor's notice (in respect of a petition) or a bankruptcy inhibition (in respect of a bankruptcy order) will be entered automatically in the register of title of any registered land that appears to be affected, ie that the (potential) bankrupt appears to own.[2]

ii   Bankruptcy of seller

The Insolvency Act 1986, section 284, provides that any disposition of property made after the presentation of a petition, which does lead to a bankruptcy order, is void unless made with the consent of the court. However, there is protection for a purchaser; any person dealing with the (potential) bankrupt during the period between presentation of the petition and the making of the bankruptcy

---

20   Land Registration Rules 1925, r 151.
1   See ch 2 for a fuller explanation of the Land Registry's electronic conveyancing initiatives.
2   Land Registration Act 1925, s 61.

order will still acquire good title if he acts in good faith for value and without notice of the presentation of the petition. Any person who subsequently acquires property from such a person is also protected. The petition will normally, of course, be registered. To take unregistered title first, registration of the petition in the register of pending actions will amount to notice of the petition. However, a petition which is not registered will not bind a purchaser of a legal estate in good faith for money or money's worth.[3] The registration of a petition or bankruptcy order lasts for five years and must then be renewed.[4] Additionally, the title of the trustee in bankruptcy is void against a purchaser of a legal estate in good faith for money or money's worth unless the bankruptcy order is registered,[5] and if a petition is registered the title of the trustee in bankruptcy is void against a purchaser in good faith of a legal estate for money or money's worth claiming under a conveyance made after the date of registration unless at the time of the conveyance either the registration of the petition was still in force or the bankruptcy order is registered.[6]

What this means for a purchaser[7] of a legal estate for money or money's worth in good faith is that if neither a petition nor a bankruptcy order are registered he can proceed. He will need to check for such registrations by doing a land charges search before completion. It may be sensible, if he is at all suspicious, to search before exchange of contracts. If he discovers before exchange of contracts that the seller is being made bankrupt he will not exchange contracts but either discontinue his interest in the property or await the outcome of the petition and if need be deal with the trustee in bankruptcy, or get the consent of the court. If the buyer discovers the impending bankruptcy after the exchange of contracts but before completion, for example, from his search, he will either rescind the contract[8] or wait and deal with the trustee in bankruptcy, assuming the petition is successful.

The position in relation to registered titles is similar. We have seen that the creditor's notice and bankruptcy inhibition take the place of registration under the Land Charges Act 1972. Registration under the Land Charges Act 1972 does not constitute notice in connection with registered titles and so no land charges search need be done. The Land Registration Act 1925, section 61 contains protection for a purchaser which is the broad equivalent of the protection given under the Land Charges Act 1972 in relation to an unregistered title. It provides that where a purchaser is registered as proprietor following a disposition in good faith for money or money's worth, the title of the trustee in bankruptcy will be void against such a purchaser unless a creditor's notice or bankruptcy inhibition was registered at the date of the disposition.[9] Prior to completion, the buyer's solicitor will check that there is no creditor's notice or bankruptcy inhibition on the register as indeed he will check that no other adverse entry has been made on the register since the date of the office copy entries with which he has been provided.

---

3 Land Charges Act 1972, s 5(8).
4 Ibid, s 8.
5 Ibid, s 6(5).
6 Ibid, s 6(6).
7 Including a mortgagee or lessee; ibid, s 17.
8 *Powell v Marshall, Parkes & Co* [1899] 1 QB 710, CA; time was of the essence, so it may be necessary to serve a notice to complete where (as is usual) time is not of the essence.
9 Land Registration Act 1925, s 61(6); however, a buyer who has notice of the petition or adjudication will not be in good faith.

iii Dealing with the trustee in bankruptcy

In theory, the buyer cannot compel the seller's trustee to complete because the trustee has a power to disclaim unprofitable contracts.[10] However, disclaimer by the trustee is extremely unlikely. If a buyer is dealing with the seller's trustee he will wish to see as part of the abstract of title proof of the trustee's power to act, that is to say the adjudication and the certificate of appointment of the trustee. In the case of registered titles the trustee can be registered as proprietor on production of such documents. Otherwise the buyer must produce them on his application for registration.

iv Bankruptcy of buyer

Section 284 of the Insolvency Act 1986 applies to the seller on the bankruptcy of the buyer; it is applicable to payment of money as well as to dispositions of property. Thus, if the seller has notice of a petition against the buyer he should not complete – nor indeed exchange – with the buyer as he may be liable to refund the purchase money to the buyer's trustee in bankruptcy. If he does exchange contracts and then discovers that a petition has been presented he will either serve a notice to complete[11] or wait and complete with the trustee in bankruptcy. If the seller does have to deal with the buyer's trustee he may fall foul of the latter's right to disclaim. The seller can serve a notice requiring the trustee to decide whether he will disclaim within 28 days. If he does disclaim, the seller can forfeit the deposit and prove in the bankruptcy for any further loss.

15 TRANSACTIONS INVOLVING PERSONS IN A FIDUCIARY RELATIONSHIP

There are a number of situations in which a transaction may be voidable because it involves someone in a fiduciary position, and there is a risk that he may have unfairly exploited that position. A prime example is the sale by trustees or personal representatives of the trust (or estate) property to one or more of their own number. Prima facie, the transaction is voidable at the instance of the beneficiaries. There are circumstances in which the transaction will be perfectly valid, for example if the sale was expressly authorised by the trust instrument (eg will[12]); if the consent of the court was obtained; if all the beneficiaries consented; or in the case of a personal representative if he was acquiring the property under a contract made with the deceased before he died.

A similar rule applies to parties who are in a fiduciary relationship. For example, a solicitor and his client are in a fiduciary relationship. A presumption of undue influence arises and unless the solicitor can prove that the client was fully informed, understood the nature of the transaction and that the transaction was fair, the client may be able to have the disposition between them set aside. In such circumstances, a client should always be asked to obtain independent legal advice and a prudent solicitor might well ask (with the client's agreement) for a letter from the adviser confirming the advice given.

---

10   Insolvency Act 1986, s 315.
11   See ch 16, section 2 ii.
12   See *Sargeant v National Westminster Bank plc* [1990] EGCS 62, CA.

These are matters to which a seller's solicitor must be alive, for example if he is asked to act for trustees selling trust property to one of their number. What, though, of subsequent buyers following a disposition which may be voidable? A subsequent purchaser for value without notice of the position will take free of the equitable right to have the disposition set aside and will get a good title.[13] However, if the buyer is aware of the circumstances surrounding the disposition – for example if these are apparent from the abstract – he should object to the title. The defect can often be remedied by a conveyance confirming the voidable conveyance, in which all interested parties could join, having had the benefit of independent advice.

16   MARRIAGES AND DEATHS

i   Marriages

It may be that the marriage of a person forms part of the chain of title and so is abstracted. This would happen if for example a couple bought a house before they were married, and later sold it. The woman's name in the purchase deed would not correspond with that on the sale deed, assuming she had taken her husband's name on marriage. In the case of a registered title, the register may still show the wife's unmarried name, if the couple bought before they married. The marriage is proved by the certificate obtained from the appropriate registrar. As this is a document of public record, the seller is not obliged to provide a copy of the certificate itself, but must provide details of the date and place of marriage so that the buyer may obtain his own certificate.

ii   Deaths

If the estate owner dies then, as we have already seen, the grant of probate or administration will be abstracted followed by the assent or conveyance by the personal representatives. If the abstract has to show just the death, as would be the case if one of a number of joint tenants had died, this is proved by a certificate from the appropriate registrar. Again, the certificate is a document of public record and the seller can expect the buyer to obtain his own copy, but the seller's solicitor will usually provide a copy out of courtesy if he has access to one.

A death or marriage could also be proved by a recital in a deed over 20 years old.[14]

17   STAMP DUTY

Many of the deeds and other documents in the abstract or epitome of an unregistered title will bear stamp duty. When stamp duty is paid, stamps showing the amount of duty are impressed on the deed. The abstract or epitome should indicate this. Stamping is dealt with in detail in chapter 15. Suffice to say here that the buyer's solicitor must check that all documents in the abstract which attract stamp duty are properly stamped.

---

13   If the title is registered, the register may be rectified if the disposition is set aside, subject to the limits on rectification against a registered proprietor in possession.
14   See ch 12, section 2 iii, below.

This will require a knowledge of the various rates of stamp duty in the past, which can be obtained from sets of stamp duty tables. The consequence of a document which attracts stamp duty not being stamped or being insufficiently stamped is that it is inadmissible in evidence and thus inadmissible to prove the title; it will be rejected by the Land Registry on an application for first registration of title. The buyer should require the seller to correct any deficiency by applying for late stamping. Any condition in the contract which purports to preclude the buyer from objecting to the absence or insufficiency of stamps, or to throw the cost of late stamping on the buyer, is void.[15]

Even if a deed does not attract stamp duty, particulars of it may have to be delivered to the Inland Revenue.[16] A stamp called a 'P.D.' (particulars delivered) stamp is impressed on the deed when this is done. The penalties for non-compliance are the same as for not stamping with stamp duty and so this too must be checked by the buyer's solicitor. Against this is dealt with in detail in Chapter 15.

The seller's solicitor ought to note any deficiencies in stamping when he examines the title prior to drafting the contract and deal with them immediately.

18   EXECUTION

The buyer's solicitor – and of course the seller's solicitor too – will want to check that all the deeds and other documents have been property executed. The requirements of execution are dealt with in detail in Chapter 14.

19   STATUTORY PRESUMPTIONS IN RESPECT OF LEASEHOLD LAND

Finally in this category of potentially problematical areas we should mention some matters about which the buyer may be precluded from enquiring. We have seen that in the case of leasehold land the buyer's right to examine the superior title is limited under an open contract. Hand in hand with this restriction are certain statutory presumptions. The Law of Property Act 1925, section 45(2) and (3) provide that on the assignment on sale of leasehold land, a buyer must assume unless the contrary appears that the lease and any superior leases were duty granted. On production of the receipt for the last payment of rent due before completion, a buyer must assume, again unless the contrary appears, that all the covenants and other provisions in the lease and any superior leases have been performed and observed. Of course if the buyer has been able to examine the superior title under a condition in the contract, this will be done. Even if he has not, if he discovers from some other source that the superior title is defective then he may still be able to object to the title unless the defect was disclosed by the proper condition in the contract.[17] The buyer may also wish to raise pre-contract enquiries to confirm that the covenants in the lease have been performed.

The Standard Conditions provide that the buyer shall assume that the last receipt for rent was given by the person then entitled to receive rent.[18]

The buyer is also given some protection by the Law of Property Act 1925, section 44(5), which states that where a purchaser is precluded by the Act from examining

---

15   Stamp Act 1891, s 117.
16   Finance Act 1931, s 28.
17   *Becker v Partridge* [1966] 2 QB 155, [1966] 2 All ER 266, CA; see section 22 i, below.
18   SC 6.6.

the superior title, he is not deemed to have notice of matters of which he would have had notice had he contracted to examine the title. However, this is subject to section 198 of the Act, so if something affecting the superior title is registered as a land charge, the buyer is bound by it (and cannot claim compensation under the Law of Property Act 1969, section 25).

20　INVESTIGATING TITLE – UNREGISTERED LAND

i　Examination of the abstract[19]

The first stage in the buyer's solicitor's investigation of an unregistered title is the examination of the abstract or epitome. In so doing the solicitor will be ensuring that there is an unbroken chain of ownership of the estate being sold, from the root of title right up to the present day. There must be no breaks in the chain whereby it is impossible to trace the passage of the legal estate from one owner to another; a break would occur for example if a conveyance on sale, or the death of one or two joint tenants, was not abstracted. Even a change in the spelling of the name of an estate owner from the deed whereby he bought to the deed whereby he sold may be sufficient to raise a doubt in the mind of the buyer's solicitor as to whether the person who sold was indeed the same person who had previously bought the property. There should be no defects in the abstract of the kind already mentioned in this chapter.

If the title is in order then the seller has, on the face of it, shown that he does own what he is selling. However, in examining the abstract, the buyer's solicitor will also be on the lookout for mention of adverse interests such as covenants and easements, which the seller has not disclosed in the contract; the first sort of defect in title mentioned at the beginning of this chapter. If such a defect is revealed by the abstract then unless the buyer was aware of it on exchange of contracts (under an open contract), or it was apparent on inspection,[20] the seller will be in breach of contract in that he will not be able to convey what he has contracted to convey. The buyer's solicitor will also be checking the abstract for the easements and covenants that are disclosed in the contract, to ensure for example that the wording of a covenant disclosed in the contract is correct. He will also check the description of the property.

If any point does arise on examination of the title, it is taken up with the seller's solicitor by means of a requisition. The manner in which this is done will be dealt with later in section 23. However, there is a general rule that not only is the buyer not entitled to see the title prior to the root, but neither can requisitions be raised on matters prior to the root.[1] There are three exceptions to this general rule:

(a) The buyer is entitled to have abstracted the power of attorney under which an abstracted document has been executed, even if the power was given prior to the date of the root of title.

(b) The buyer is entitled to have abstracted 'any document creating or disposing of an interest power or obligation which is not shown to have ceased or expired and subject to which any part of the property is disposed of by an abstracted document'. Under this provision the buyer could require pre-root leases to be abstracted if the property is sold subject to them. Similarly if an abstracted

---

19　If the title is leasehold, then the buyer's solicitor may also be examining the superior title(s) which may be registered or unregistered.

20　See ch 5, section 4 i; see also SC 3.1.2.

　1　Law of Property Act 1925, s 45(1).

document refers to restrictive covenants still affecting the property, which are contained in an earlier deed; the buyer would still be entitled to have the covenants abstracted even if the deed containing them was dated prior to the root of title. Likewise, if an abstracted document describes the property by reference to a plan on an earlier deed; the buyer would still be entitled to a copy even if the deed were dated prior to the root.

(c)   The buyer is entitled to have abstracted any document creating any limitation or trust, by reference to which any part of the property is disposed of by an abstracted document. This does not extend to any trust that will be over-reached.

Even though the buyer cannot normally raise requisitions on matters prior to the root of title, the seller cannot conceal a defective title by specifying a later deed as the root of title, and the buyer can still rescind if he does discover that the title is defective even though the defect is prior to the root.

If the seller refuses to answer a properly raised requisition, on the face of it this will entitle the buyer to rescind.

ii   Searches

Before completion the buyer's solicitor will do a number of searches, principally searches in the Central Land Charges Registry and an inspection of the property. These are dealt with in detail in the next chapter.

iii   Verification of the abstract

The buyer's solicitor has examined the abstract or epitome on the basis that it is a full and accurate representation of the original deeds and other documents. He must at some stage verify this assumption by checking the abstract or epitome against the original deeds. He will be particularly alert to the existence of any memoranda, such as a memorandum on a grant of probate or administration or a memorandum of severance on a conveyance to joint tenants. He may also pay particular attention to the description of the property and the wording of the covenants which may have been abbreviated in the abstract and to the execution, and stamping. Of course, if, as will probably be the case, he was provided with an epitome rather than a true abstract then the process of verification is rather easier, but it must still be done. It is easy for the back page of a conveyance containing a memorandum to escape being copied when the epitome is prepared.

Although the seller bears the expense, if any, of producing the deeds for preparation of the abstract and for handing over on completion, the buyer under an open contract bears the expense of producing the deeds for verification of the abstract, unless they are in the possession of the seller or his mortgagee or trustee,[2] although this will normally be the case. It is common practice to leave verification until completion. Whilst this can be seen as convenient in that the buyer's solicitor or his agent need only make one visit to the seller's solicitors – on completion – instead of having also to make another earlier visit for verification, it would be most inconvenient if some defect should be revealed on verification. There would inevitably be a delay on completion, which would probably have been avoided had verification taken place earlier. Similarly, on a postal completion, where verification

_____
2   Law of Property Act 1925, s 45(4).

should be handled by the seller's solicitor as agent for the buyer's solicitor.[3] The objection to the title will clearly be outside the time limit for raising requisitions, but as the defect is presumably not discoverable from the abstract or epitome alone, this will not prejudice the buyer.[4] Under Standard Condition 4.2.3 the seller is to produce to the buyer, at the seller's cost, the original of every document of title, or an abstract, or epitome or copy marked by a solicitor as examined[5] against the original or an examined abstract or examined copy. The condition does not say at what point the documents must be produced.

It is doubly important to verify the abstract against the originals if the seller is retaining some or all of the original deeds, because he is only selling part of the property to which they relate. This would probably happen, for example, on the sale of a new house on a building estate, or one unit on an industrial estate. As we shall see,[6] the buyer will have a right to production of the original deeds but the only actual evidence of his title which he will have in his possession will be the verified abstract or epitome, together of course with the conveyance to him. In such a situation the buyer's solicitor will on verification mark the abstract or epitome to the effect that he has examined it against the original deeds. The Land Registry will normally require a marked abstract or epitome on first registration.

What if there has been a sale of part in the past, and therefore the seller does not have the original deeds from prior to that point? One might think that the buyer's solicitor ought to demand that the original deeds be produced so that he can check them, although this would be at the expense of the buyer. Common practice seems to be not to do this and to rely on the accuracy of the marked abstract and this is reflected in Standard Condition 4.2.3. One wonders whether this practice would protect a solicitor from an action for negligence, if he relied on a marked abstract which was in fact incorrect. Indeed one also wonders whether a solicitor who marks an abstract or epitome negligently, failing to spot some discrepancy with the original deeds, would be liable to future buyers who relied on it. If not, the future buyer should not rely on it!

2 I   INVESTIGATING TITLE – REGISTERED LAND

i   Examination of office copy entries

As we have already seen, title to land which is registered is deduced by supplying the buyer's solicitor with copies of the register entries, normally in the form of office copy entries,[7] but possibly photocopies of the entries in the seller's Land or Charge Certificate. It is these which the buyer's solicitor must examine against the contract to ensure that the seller does own, and can convey, that which he has contracted to transfer. If, as is common, the contract refers to the Property Register and the Charges Register in the particulars and conditions of the contract then there will clearly be no difficulty and indeed the office copies will have been sent with the draft contract. However, even in this situation the buyer's solicitor must be on the lookout, for example, for restrictions in the Proprietorship Register which restrict the seller's powers of disposal.

---

3   See ch 14, section 3 iv.
4   See section 22 ii, below.
5   See next paragraph. The seller's solicitor should check that if he does not have originals, he does have properly marked documents so he can comply with 4.2.3.
6   See ch 12, section 2 xvi.
7   SC 4.2.1.

There is really no equivalent, in respect of registered land, to the process of verification as both the office copy entries and the Land Certificate are admissible evidence of the state of the register at the appropriate time.[8] However, if mere photocopies of the entries in the certificate are provided they would have to be checked against the originals.

Even though title to the land is registered, an abstract or epitome would still be provided in respect of matters upon which the register was not conclusive, if any. The requirements would be just the same as if the land were unregistered. Overriding interests would fall into this category. Furthermore, if the buyer is purchasing leasehold land then he will also want a copy of the lease as this does not form part of the register.[9]

ii   Searches

The investigation of title is continued by pre-completion searches, principally a search at the Land Registry and an inspection of the property. The object of the Land Registry search is to bring up to date the information on the state of the register which the buyer has acquired from the office copy entries (or photocopies of the seller's Land or Charge Certificate). There is no need to make a search at the Central Land Charges Registry except in relation to matters on which the register is not conclusive. For example, if the buyer were buying a property held on a good leasehold title, then if the freehold title was unregistered and the buyer was entitled by virtue of the contract to examine it, he would be provided with an abstract and would wish to do a land charges search in connection with the examination of the unregistered freehold title.

Searches are considered in more detail in the next chapter.

22   FORGERY AND IMPERSONATION

A number of cases during the 1980s and 1990s highlighted the need for the solicitor for both seller and buyer to be on guard against forgery and impersonation.

In *Ahmed v Kendrick and Ahmed*[10] a husband and wife purchased property, mortgaged it and later sold it. Throughout, the wife's signature was forged by the husband. The main part of the judgment deals with the effect of the forged sale deed. It need not concern us here save to the extent that the buyer, Mr Kendrick, only received in effect half the property and therefore had to pay again to become the full owner of the whole property. There is a passage in the judgment in which Mr Kendrick is advised to 'take legal advice as to whether or not he has any remedy against the solicitors acting for him on his original purchase'. It is however difficult to see what steps a buyer's solicitor can take to attempt to detect forgery.

In *Umeweni v J B Wheatley & Co*[11] a firm of solicitors, acting on the purchase and mortgage of a flat and a subsequent second mortgage, thought they were dealing with U. In fact they were dealing with A. who was impersonating U. At first instance the solicitors were held to be negligent on two grounds. First, they had on file two genuine letters from U which bore a totally different signature to the signature proffered by A, and whose contents demonstrated the separate identity of U and A. Secondly, the solicitors were negligent for not meeting their client to establish his

---

8   Land Registration Act 1925, ss 68, 113.
9   The buyer's solicitor may also be examining the superior title(s).
10   [1988] 2 FLR 22, [1988] Fam Law 201, CA.
11   [1989] EGCS 150; on appeal [1990] EGCS 57, CA.

identity. On appeal the finding of negligence was quashed, because the Court of Appeal accepted that the two letters relied on at first instance were not genuine. The inference from the remaining evidence was that U had authorised A to act for him. The suggestion nevertheless remains that there might be some duty on a solicitor to establish the identity of a client who is not already known to him.

A number of mortgage frauds have been based on the applicant for the mortgage either being entirely fictional or else impersonating some real person who has no knowledge of the application. The Law Society has produced a 'Green Card' warning on property fraud[12] to help prevent solicitors being unwittingly involved in a fraud. The warning advises solicitors to be on their guard against a number of suspicious circumstances including money paid direct, changes in the purchase price, unusual instructions (such as (when instructed by the seller) being asked to remit the balance of sale proceeds to someone other than the seller), and unusual transactions, for example the client having mortgages on more than one property, using aliases, or reselling properties at a profit. Again, if there are any suspicions about the transaction, solicitors are advised to consider whether signatures on all documents connected with the transaction should be examined and compared with the signatures on any other available documentation. This has echoes of the *Umeweni* case. Solicitors should also watch out for changes in the purchase price such as allowances against the purchase price, and are reminded that, when acting for the mortgagee, they should report all allowances and incentives to the mortgagee.[13]

If acting for the buyer, the solicitor should also have regard to the Council for Mortgage Lender's Handbook, if the lender subscribes to this, and to rule 6(3) of the Solicitors' Practice Rules 1990.[14] There are detailed rules in the handbook with regard to the verification of identity of the client; if the client is not previously known to the solicitor, he must obtain, copy and keep on file evidence of the client's signature from a specified list in the handbook. The solicitor must also check the credentials of any other firm of solicitors or licensed conveyancers involved in the transaction if the firm is not known to him.

23 REQUISITIONS ON TITLE

i Raising requisitions

We have already seen that if there is any aspect of the title which is unsatisfactory to the buyer's solicitor he can raise it with the seller's solicitor by means of a requisition. A requisition is so called because the buyer is pointing out the defect and 'requiring' the seller to remedy it. This right to raise requisitions is subject to the restriction on pre-root requisitions in respect of unregistered land, and to any provision in the contract. If a defect in the title is properly disclosed in the contract then the buyer cannot object to it at this stage and raise a requisition about it. If the seller has provided that the buyer accept the title offered and raise no requisitions, this will not prevent the buyer raising a requisition and objecting to a defect if the seller did not make full disclosure of the defects of which he knew. In *Becker v Partridge*[15] the seller provided

---

12 This is set out in The Guide to the Professional Conduct of Solicitors published by the Law Society (8th edn 1999, pp 501–502).
13 Ibid. Guidance on mortgage fraud – variation in purchase price, p 500.
14 A new r 6(3) dealing with the relationship between solicitors and lenders came into force on 1 October 1999. For more detail, see ch 13.
15 [1966] 2 QB 155, [1966] 2 All ER 266, CA.

in a contract for the assignment on sale of an *underlease* that the buyer should raise no requisitions on his title. The buyer discovered that there were breaches of covenant which gave grounds for forfeiture of the *headlease*. The seller had constructive notice of these defects but did not disclose them and the buyer was entitled to rescind. Similarly, although the buyer cannot raise requisitions on matters prior to the root of title, he can object if he becomes aware that there is a pre-root defect in title.

When submitting requisitions the buyer's solicitor will normally use a standard form. This may seem surprising as by definition requisitions will be peculiar to a particular title and it would not seem possible to standardise such a form. In fact most if not all of the questions on the standard form are of a procedural nature rather than being requisitions on title. In any event, with the common practice of investigating title before exchange of contracts, the standard form of requisitions is commonly now used simply to confirm information that the seller has already provided, and to confirm completion arrangements. If, however, requisitions are being raised after exchange of contracts the standard from can be used, with any requisitions arising out of the particular title added at the end of the form. The following are examples of the sort of questions which may be found on a standard form of requisitions:

(a) A request for completion statement showing the amount due on completion, including any apportionment, eg of rates or rent.
(b) Confirmation as to how and where completion is to take place and how the money is to be paid.
(c) Confirmation that in the case of leasehold property the last receipt for rent will be produced for inspection on completion, along with the receipts for outgoings in respect of which the seller is claiming an apportionment.
(d) Confirmation that existing mortgages will be discharged on or before completion. This is not really a requisition on title as the buyer is entitled to assume that existing mortgages will be paid off unless the sale has been made subject to them.
(e) If the receipted mortgage deed, or form DS1 in the case of registered land, will not be handed over on completion, an enquiry as to the form of undertaking which will be given to pay off the mortgage and forward the receipted deed or form DS1.
(f) In respect of unregistered land, an enquiry whether any abstracted documents will not be handed over on completion and confirmation that an acknowledgment and undertaking will be given in respect of any original documents retained.
(g) In respect of registered land, if the buyer has merely been provided with photocopies of the seller's Land or Charge Certificate, an enquiry as to when the Certificate was last examined with the register. This information will be needed for the pre-completion search at the Land Registry.
(h) On a sale of part of registered land, an enquiry whether the seller's Land Certificate is on deposit with the Land Registry and if so, the deposit number.[16]
(i) Again in respect of registered land, where the buyer is purchasing a new property on an estate, an enquiry whether there is an estate layout plan approved by the Land Registry so that on the buyer's pre-completion search at the Land Registry the property can be identified by reference to its plot number.
(j) Confirmation of the arrangements for delivery of keys to the buyer and/or an authority to tenants to pay their rent to the buyer in the future.
(k) The form may include a question asking whether, if the preliminary enquiries of the seller were repeated, the same replies would be given.

16 See ch 14, section 1vi.

ii   Time for investigating title and raising requisitions

Where the contract bars raising requisitions after exchange of contracts, of course all requisitions must be raised before exchange and the time limits discussed below will be irrelevant. If title is to be investigated after exchange, under an open contract requisitions must be raised within a reasonable time of delivery of the abstract. The TransAction Protocol provides that requisitions must be raised as soon as possible after exchange and in any case within the time limits contained in the contract. Standard Condition 4.1.1 lays down a timetable for investigating title. The buyer may raise requisitions within six working days after the date of the contract or the date of delivery of the seller's evidence of title, whichever is the later. The seller is to reply in writing to any requisitions raised within four working days after receiving the requisitions. The buyer may then make written observations on the seller's replies within three working days after receiving the replies. The buyer's right to raise requisitions or make observations on the seller's replies is lost after the expiration of the relevant time limit. This means that time is of the essence for these two steps and that if a buyer's solicitor fails to raise requisitions in time or fails to object to any inadequate reply to requisitions in time, the buyer loses his right to object to the title. However, this rule is subject to exceptions. Firstly, the buyer can probably still object to a fundamental defect in title, even after the time for raising requisitions has expired. This occurred in *Re Cox and Neve's Contract*[17] where the defect was an undisclosed restrictive covenant and in *Re Brine and Davies' Contract*[18] where under an open contract for sale of registered land the seller had not got absolute title. Secondly, the buyer is not subject to the time limit in respect of defects which are not discoverable from the abstract, for example defects which only show up on pre-completion searches or on verification of the abstract or epitome.

   If part of the abstract is delivered late, Standard Condition 4.1 provides that the buyer must still raise requisitions in accordance with the timetable in 4.1.1 on the evidence of title which is supplied; the buyer then has a further six working days from the delivery of the late part of the abstract to raise supplementary requisitions resulting from it. However, the buyer's solicitor would be well advised to raise as a requisition within the initial six working day limit under 4.1.1, the fact that the evidence of title is incomplete.

   Time is not of the essence for the seller to reply to requisitions but if the seller's solicitor is late in doing this, it may lead to compensation being payable for late completion under Standard Condition 7.3.[19]

   The timetable in Standard Condition 4.1.1 is based on a completion date which is no earlier than fifteen working days after the date of the contract. If the completion date is later than that, Standard Condition 4.1.4 provides that the time limits in Condition 4.1.1 are to be reduced by the same proportion as the actual completion period bears to the period of fifteen working days. Fractions of a working day are to be rounded down except that any time limit of less than one day is to be rounded up! By way of example, if completion is ten working days after exchange the time limits in 4.1.1 of respectively, six, four and three working days are reduced by the proportion of ten to fifteen, ie a factor of two-thirds. Thus six working days becomes four working days, four working days becomes two working days (the fraction is rounded down) and three working days also becomes two working days. It is important for solicitors

---

17   [1891] 2 Ch 109.
18   [1935] Ch 388.
19   See ch 14, section 2(i).

to bear in mind the effect of 4.1.4, given the importance of the time limits and the frequency of short completions. The interaction of 4.1.1 and 4.1.4, and the deemed delivery times in 1.3.6, may mean that time limits become very tight, and there would certainly be problems if second-class post was used.

iii   Modern practice

As mentioned above, it is quite common for title to be investigated *before* exchange of contracts. The seller may insist on a condition in the contract, stating that the buyer has inspected the title and will raise no requisitions on it, which would force pre-exchange investigation of title. The advantage is that both seller and buyer will know that there can be no title problems arising after exchange of contracts which may delay or even prevent completion. The possible disadvantage from the buyer's point of view is that his solicitor is doing yet more work prior to exchange of contracts, with, of course, the ever-present possibility that contracts never will be exchanged and the work will be wasted.

iv   Seller's duty

Assuming title is being investigated after exchange, the seller is bound to answer all specific questions related to the title. If the seller does not answer a proper requisition then the buyer can rescind, or compel the seller to answer by issuing a vendor and purchaser summons. If the seller's solicitor does answer requisitions which are raised out of time, he may wish to make it clear (if such be the case) that he is only answering as a matter of courtesy and is not waiving the contractual time limit.

v   The seller's contractual right to rescind

The first edition of the Standard Conditions contained a provision permitting the seller to rescind if the buyer would not withdraw a requisition.[20] This may seem surprising in view of the statement in the previous paragraph that the seller must reply to proper requisitions. At first sight it seems to offer the seller a wide escape route where, for example, he has not complied with his duty of disclosure in the contract. However, the courts interpret these provisions very restrictively. A seller will only be allowed to take advantage of such a condition and rescind if all the following requirements are met:[1]

(a) The seller must have at least some title to the property sold.
(b) The seller must not have known about the defect at the date of the contract and that lack of knowledge must not be due to the seller's recklessness.[2]
(c) The defect must be irremovable, or only removable at disproportionate expense to the seller.[3]
(d) The seller must rely on the contractual condition within a reasonable time.

---

20 SC 4.5.2 (first edition).
1 *Selkirk v Romar Investments Ltd* [1963] 3 All ER 994, [1963] 1 WLR 1415, PC.
2 *Baines v Tweddle* [1959] Ch 679, [1959] 2 All ER 724, CA.
3 In *Leominster Properties Ltd v Broadway Finance Ltd* (1981) 42 P & CR 372, a seller, who was a mortgagee exercising a power of sale, was held to be unable to rely on an equivalent National Condition in respect of a prior mortgage which the seller thought had priority.

There is no equivalent condition in the third edition of the Standard Conditions. Neither is there any similar open contract rule, as a result of section 3 of the Law of Property (Miscellaneous Provisions) Act 1989.[4]

vi   Waiver of right to raise requisitions

It is possible that submission of the draft conveyance or transfer to the seller's solicitor for approval might constitute an acceptance of the seller's title, defects and all, and a waiver of any outstanding requisitions. The Standard Conditions specifically provide that this shall not be the case.[5] Similarly, a buyer who takes possession before completion may, in some circumstances, be deemed to have waived any objection to defects in the title. The Standard Conditions again state that this shall not be the case.[6]

---

4   See ch 16, section 2 iii.
5   SC 4.5.1.
6   SC 5.2.7.

11 PRE-COMPLETION SEARCHES

I UNREGISTERED LAND

i Search in Central Land Charges Register

It may be convenient here to dispel any confusion about the various charges registers and registries that are encountered in conveyancing. Firstly, there is the Local Land Charges Register kept under the Local Land Charges Act 1975 by the Local Authority. This contains details of purely local matters and was described in Chapter 6. It is searched in respect of both registered and unregistered land before exchange of contracts. Secondly, there is the Central Land Charges Register which is only relevant to unregistered land and which is described in detail below. The system of registration *of title* is overseen by the Land Registry and there are District Land Registries for each area of the country. When title to land is registered, the register of that title is split into three parts, namely the Property Register, the Proprietorship Register and the Charges Register. The latter should not be confused with either the Central or Local Land Charges Register. Finally, the word 'charge' is often used in the sense of a legal charge or mortgage, for example in the case of a mortgage of registered land which is known as a registered charge and is protected by an entry in the Charges Register of the title.

Returning to the Central Land Charges Register, there are in fact five registers. We shall be concerned principally with the register of land charges, the register of pending actions and the register of writs and orders but there are also registers of deeds of arrangement and of annuities.

1 Land Charges Register

There are a number of classes of land charge, as follows.

Class A[1]   This is a financial charge arising out of some statutory provision which only comes into existence following an application by some person. An example would be a charge under the Landlord and Tenant Act 1927 in respect of compensation paid by the landlord to the tenant for improvements to business premises. Class A land charges are not very common in practice.

Class B[2]   This is a financial charge arising out of some statutory provision, but different from a Class A charge in that it is actually created by the statute and

---

1   Land Charges Act 1972, s 2(2).
2   Ibid, s 2(3).

does not depend on an application by some person. An example would be the Legal Aid Board's charge over property preserved or recovered under a Legal Aid Certificate.[3]

Class Ci[4]   A puisne mortgage, that is a legal mortgage not protected by deposit of title deeds with the mortgagee. This would normally be a second legal mortgage, the title deeds being held by the first legal mortgagee.

Class Cii[5]   A limited owners charge. This is an equitable charge obtained by a tenant for life or statutory owner of settled land by virtue of having paid inheritance tax on the land.

Class Ciii[6]   A general equitable charge. This is something of a mixed bag but specifically *excluded* are:

(a)   an equitable charge protected by deposit of title deeds;
(b)   a charge included in any other class;
(c)   a charge arising under a trust for sale or settlement.

A common example of a Ciii charge would be the seller's lien for unpaid purchase money or the buyer's lien for his deposit, or possibly an equitable mortgage.

Class Civ[7]   An estate contract. This is defined as a contract by an estate owner, or someone entitled to have the legal estate conveyed to him, to convey or create a legal estate. This class of charge is very common in practice. It includes the everyday contract between the seller and buyer for the sale of land and it also includes an option to purchase, a right of pre-emption,[8] an option to renew a lease, an agreement for a lease and also, strictly, an equitable mortgage which constitutes an agreement to create a legal mortgage.

Class Di[9]   A charge for unpaid inheritance tax registered by the Inland Revenue Commissioners. Again this is rare in practice.

Class Dii[10]   A restrictive covenant created after 1925, but not including a restrictive covenant contained in a lease. The latter are not registrable nor are restrictive covenants affecting freehold land created before 1926. Dii registrations are probably the most common in practice.

Class Diii[11]   An equitable easement arising after 1925. An example would be a right of way for life. This category does not include legal easements which are binding on a buyer quite irrespective of notice.

Class E[12]   An annuity created before 1926 and not registered in the then existing register of annuities. This class will become obsolete and registrations are rare in practice.

Class F[13]   This is a spouse's statutory right of occupation under Part IV of the Family Law Act 1996. By virtue of that Act a spouse who has no legal estate in the matrimonial home, or in other words who is not the sole or a joint legal owner has a registrable statutory right of occupation. Registrations are not uncommon.

---

3   Legal Aid Act 1988, s 16(6).
4   Land Charges Act 1972, s 2(4)(i).
5   Ibid, s 2(4)(ii).
6   Ibid, s 2(4)(iii).
7   Ibid, s 2(4)(iv).
8   Subject to the dicta in *Pritchard v Briggs* [1980] Ch 338, [1980] 1 All ER 294, CA; and see also *London and Blenheim Estates Ltd v Ladbrooke Retail Parks Ltd* [1993] 4 All ER 157, [1993] 1 WLR 31.
9   Land Charges Act 1972, s 2(5)(i).
10   Ibid, s 2(5)(ii).
11   Ibid, s 2(5)(iii).
12   Ibid, s 2(6).
13   Ibid, s 2(7).

2   Register of Pending Actions[14]

A pending action is defined as any action or proceedings pending in court relating to land or any interest in or charge over land.[15] An obvious example would be a dispute about the ownership of a piece of land. Also included would be a spouse's claim in divorce proceedings for a transfer of property order. Most importantly, a bankruptcy petition is also registrable as a pending action. Registration of a pending action is only valid for five years and must then be renewed.[16]

3   Register of Writs and Orders[17]

This includes not only writs and orders affecting land made by a court for the purpose of enforcing a judgment, but also bankruptcy orders. Again registration is only effective for five years unless renewed.

4   Register of Deeds of Arrangement[18]

A deed of arrangement is a document whereby a debtor agrees to hand over control of his property to his creditors in an attempt to avoid bankruptcy proceedings. Again registration is only effective for five years unless renewed.

5   Register of Annuities[19]

This is a Register of Annuities created before 1926 and registered in the then existing Register of Annuities. There can be no new registrations and the Register will in due course become obsolete. Registrations are rare in practice.

6   Effect of registration and non-registration

Registration in any of the registers constitutes actual notice of the matter registered to all persons, for all purposes connected with the land affected.[20] This is of course the reason why a search of the registers is necessary. The effect of non-registration of an interest which should be registered varies according to the register. Land charges of Classes A, B, Ci, Cii, Ciii and F are void as against a purchaser (including a lessee and a mortgagee) for valuable consideration of the land or any interest in it unless registered before completion of the purchase.[1] Land charges of classes Civ and D are void against a purchaser *of a legal estate* in the land for money or money's worth unless registered before completion.[2] A buyer's actual knowledge of an interest which is registrable but which is not in fact registered is immaterial.[3] As we shall see, an official Certificate of Search is conclusive in favour of a buyer.

---

14   Land Charges Act 1972, s 5.
15   The exact scope of a pending land action is difficult to define; see *Selim Ltd v Bickenhall Engineering Ltd* [1981] 3 All ER 210, [1981] 1 WLR 1318; *Regan & Blackburn Ltd v Rogers* [1985] 2 All ER 180, [1985] 1 WLR 870.
16   Land Charges Act 1972, s 8.
17   Ibid, s 6.
18   Ibid, s 7.
19   Ibid, s 1(4), Sch 1.
20   Law of Property Act 1925, s 198(1).
 1   Land Charges Act 1972, s 4(2), (5).
 2   Ibid, s 4(6).
 3   *Midland Bank Trust Co Ltd v Green* [1981] AC 513, [1981] 1 All ER 153, HL. Also see *Lloyds Bank v Carrick* [1996] 4 All ER 630, where an unregistered estate contract was void against a mortgagee.

Once an interest which should have been protected by registration as a land charge has become void for non-registration, it cannot normally be revived against a future buyer by later registration. To allow this would be to devalue the property in the hands of the buyer against whom the interest is void. However, a land charge such as a restrictive covenant might revive against successors in title such as squatters. By examining the date of registration of the charge and the dates of previous purchases, a buyer's solicitor will be able to ascertain whether a land charge has become void for non-registration. He may be able to see this quite easily by examining old search certificates.

As regards the other registers, a pending action will not bind a purchaser for valuable consideration without express notice of it unless it is registered.[4] As we have seen earlier, a bankruptcy petition will not bind a purchaser of a legal estate in good faith for money or money's worth unless it is registered. A writ or order will be void against a purchaser for valuable consideration unless it is registered.[5] Again, as we have seen earlier, there is a special rule for a bankruptcy order which is similar to the rule relating to the bankruptcy petition; that is, the title of the trustee in bankruptcy will be void against a purchaser of a legal estate in good faith for money or money's worth unless the bankruptcy order is registered.[6] A deed of arrangement will be void against a purchaser for valuable consideration of any land affected by it unless it is registered.[7]

7   Manner of registration

It would be difficult to deal with searches for existing registrations without first examining how those registrations are made. A registration to be valid must be made against the name of the owner, at the time of registration, of the legal estate affected.[8] We have already noticed the complications caused on a sub-sale, where the sub-seller does not have the legal estate at the time of the registration of the sub-sale contract by the sub-buyer; registration must be against the name of the seller.

There will sometimes be problems over the correct version of a person's name. In *Diligent Finance Co Ltd v Alleyne*[9] it was held that in the absence of evidence to the contrary, the correct name of the estate owner will be the name appearing in the conveyance to him. In that case a wife had registered a Class F charge against her husband in the name of Erskine Alleyne, which she believed to be his name. However, his full name, which appeared in the deeds, was Erskine Owen Alleyne. The Class F charge was therefore void against a later mortgagee who had searched against the name of Erskine Owen Alleyne,[10] because the registration had not been made against the correct name. Difficulties of this sort are inevitable in a system which relies on registration against name rather than against the land affected.

8   Against which names should a search be made?

As registrations are possible against the names of estate owners for the time being, the search ought to be against the names of all the owners of the legal estate since 1925 (the date when the register in its present form was brought into existence) in

---

4   Land Charges Act 1972, s 5(7).
5   Ibid, s 6(4).
6   Ibid, s 6(5).
7   Ibid, s 7(2).
8   Ibid, s 3(1).
9   (1972) 23 P & CR 346.
10   And therefore not discovered the Class F registration.

respect of the period of ownership of each estate owner. If there is more than one estate owner at any one time, for example where there are joint tenants, a search should be made against each name. Registrations are not 'updated' to the name of the current estate owner; if a registration is made against the name of estate owner A in say 1930, the registration stays against A's name and is not transferred into B's name when A eventually sells to B. Ideally therefore the buyer will want to know the names of all estate owners since 1925.

How does the buyer discover the names of the estate owners? The answer of course is from the abstract or epitome of title. This illustrates another of the disadvantages of a system of registration by name. It is possible, indeed very probable, that the abstract will not go back as far as 1925, or in other words that the root of title will be dated some time after 1925. The buyer will be unable to discover the names of the estate owners since 1925 but prior to the date of the root and thus will not be able to search against those names and discover any registrations made against them. Yet if there are such registrations, the buyer will be bound by them, because they are registered as land charges. In these circumstances the buyer, if adversely affected by a registration which he could not discover, may be entitled to compensation.[11] Unfortunately this provision for compensation does not extend to the buyer of leasehold land where there are undiscoverable land charges, such as restrictive covenants, registered against the superior freehold or leasehold title which the buyer is precluded – by statute – from investigating. In any event, the buyer may feel that no amount of compensation is sufficient compared to the loss, distress and disruption he has been caused.

The buyer's solicitor may be faced with problems concerning the correct name of an estate owner. If the name appears in different forms in the abstract then the buyer's solicitor can raise a requisition asking which is the correct version but it would be safer to search against all versions of the name. Even if a registration is in a slightly incorrect version of the name of the estate owner it may still be effective against someone who searches against the wrong name. This is illustrated by the case of *Oak Co-operative Building Society v Blackburn*.[12] A buyer registered a Civ estate contract against his seller in the name of Frank David Blackburn. The seller's correct name was Francis David Blackburn. Blackburn was also in the process of mortgaging the property to a Building Society who made a search against the name of Francis Davis Blackburn which revealed no entries. At first instance it was held that the search was ineffective as it was in the wrong name but that in any event the registration was also ineffective as it was in the wrong name too. The result was that the estate contract was void against the Building Society and indeed it would presumably not have mattered if the Building Society had not made a search at all. This decision was reversed in the Court of Appeal, which held that registration against a 'version' of the correct name will be effective against someone who searches against the wrong name. The Building Society were therefore bound by the estate contract because the estate contract had been registered against a version of the estate owner's correct name and the Building Society had not searched against the correct name. Exactly how close a name must be to the correct name to amount to such a version is unclear. Of course if the Building Society had searched against the correct name they would not have been bound by the estate contract.

The register is computerised. The computer will only do what it is told. The importance of giving the correct names on registration and searching cannot be

---

11   See further in ch 16, below.
12   [1968] Ch 730, [1968] 2 All ER 117, CA.

overemphasised. On searching, the computer is programmed to reveal entries against the precise name searched against and some, but not many, variations of it. For example a search against Arthur William Lee will reveal registrations against Arthur William Lee and also against A W Lee, but will not reveal registrations against Arthur Lee or Arthur W Lee or A William Lee. However, certain groups of words are treated by the computer as being the same. These include '&' and 'and'; Ltd, Limited, public limited company, plc and their Welsh equivalents; Co, Company and Companies; and Brother, Brothers and Bros. A search therefore against Arthur Lee & Co plc will also reveal registrations against Arthur Lee and Company Limited. The Companies Act 1980 caused some complications as certain companies had to change their names to a name ending in plc or public limited company or their Welsh equivalents. On the face of it this will cause no problems because of the interchangeability of Ltd, Limited, plc and public limited company as far as the computer is concerned. However, on the change of name a company might also have dropped the word company or any abbreviation of it, or the Welsh version or abbreviation, from its old name. Thus Arthur Lee and Company Limited may become Arthur Lee plc. A search against Arthur Lee plc, although it will reveal registrations against Arthur Lee Limited, will not reveal registrations against Arthur Lee and Company Limited. Thus where the buyer's solicitor sees that one of the previous estate owners is a company which has changed its name in this way he should make sure a search is made against both the old name and the new name. Quite apart from the provisions of the Companies Act 1980, if a company does change its name then a search must be made against both names for the respective periods of ownership, unless the changes are within the categories treated as equivalent by the computer.

9   Mechanics of searching

The normal method of searching is by a written application for an official search certificate. There is a standard form of application, called a Form K15. This provides a 'full' search of all parts of the register, including bankruptcy. If only bankruptcy details are required, a 'bankruptcy only' search can be performed, using Form K16. The form contains space for up to six names to be searched against. The buyer's solicitor will need a further form if he wishes to search against more than six names. We have already seen the importance of giving the correct names. On the form, there is a separate line for the surname and forename. If there should be any doubt as to whether a middle name is a second forename or part of a hyphenated surname then a search should be made against both versions.

The buyer's solicitor must also state on the form the appropriate period of ownership of the legal estate in respect of each name, in terms of years, eg 1967–1975. This is a means of excluding irrelevant registrations as a registration against the name supplied, made outside the period of ownership of the land being purchased, must have been made in respect of some other land which a person with that name owned at the time; if made in relation to the land being bought, it is clearly ineffective, as registration must be against the name of the estate owner at the time of registration.

Another means of filtering out irrelevant registrations is by requiring, on registration and searching, a statement of the county in which the land affected is situated. Thus a registration of a land charge in 1975 against a particular name in respect of land in Leicestershire will not be revealed on a search against the same name for the same year in respect of Nottinghamshire. On searching, care must be taken to state the county correctly. County boundaries were altered by the Local Government Act 1972, the changes taking place as from 1 April 1974, and there have been other changes since then. It may therefore be necessary to supply the name of any former county, either if the present county simply did not exist before 1974 (eg Avon, Tyne and Wear, South Yorkshire); or if the pre-1974 county has ceased to exist, meaning that the land is now in another county (eg Huntingdonshire); or if because of a boundary change the land has moved from one county into another. The Land Registry has issued a list of former county names (Land Charges Department Practice Leaflet 3).

Space is also given on the form for a brief description of the land. Unlike the period of ownership and the county and former county, it is not essential that this information be supplied. It will act as a further filtering device, meaning that registrations obviously affecting land other than that which the buyer is buying can be kept off the search certificate. However, if a description is given it must be correct and any former description must also be given. It will then be used when a large number of entries are disclosed against a particular name for a particular county and period of ownership. The certificate will state that entries that are clearly irrelevant have been excluded and will also include the description supplied on the application for the search and by reference to which the exclusion was made. It is not normal practice to give a description unless it is anticipated that there may be a large number of entries against a particular name as there may be, for example, against a firm of builders or a Local Authority.

An application for a land charges search can be made by post or by fax, or by Land Registry Direct. It is also possible to request the search by telephone, without using the written form of application, at an increased cost. The necessary information, that is the name, county and period of ownership, is given to the Land Charges Department over the telephone and if there are fewer than five entries for a particular name, county and period of ownership these will be read out. In any event the search certificate is then posted to confirm the result of the search. Fees are payable on all searches; firms of solicitors will usually have a credit account.

10   Official search certificate

The official search certificate will show the entries revealed by the search. It is conclusive in favour of a purchaser.[13] However, as well as informing a buyer of the existing registrations it also confers some degree of protection on a buyer. Any entry on the register made after the date of the search certificate will not bind the buyer provided that completion of the purchase takes place within 15 working days of the date of the certificate. This period of 15 working days is called the priority period because if entries are made during it, but the buyer completes before the end of it, the buyer has priority over those entries and is not bound by them.[14] Of course the buyer only gets the benefit of the protection if he has searched against the correct name. The priority period is extremely convenient in practice as if it were not available, a buyer would have to delay his search until immediately before completion. The availability of the priority period means that the search can be done say a week before the contractual completion date, to allow time for the certificate to be posted back, and completion can then take place in reliance on the search. Even if completion is delayed by a week or so the buyer will still be able to complete within the priority period. If he cannot, then a new search must be done which will of course provide a new period of priority. The date of the expiry of the priority period is given on the search certificate although strictly it should be checked by the buyer's solicitor.

---

13   Land Charges Act 1972, s 10(4). 'Purchaser' includes a mortgagee and lessee.
14   Ibid, s 11(5).

The search certificate will give brief details of all entries against the specified name in respect of land in the specified county registered during the specified period of ownership. For each land charge entry the certificate will show the type of registration, ie the class of land charge, the district and county in which the land affected is situated often including a brief description of the land such as a postal address, and the date of registration and the registration number. If a description of the land affected has been provided on the application for the search then as already mentioned the list of entries may be edited to exclude those that are obviously irrelevant.

If an entry is revealed, the buyer's solicitor may wish to obtain further details of it, either to find out what it is or to confirm that it is what he thinks it is. He can apply for an office copy of the registration which will give more details than those which appear on the certificate. This office copy should not be confused with the office copies of the register entries in respect of registered land.

The search, although commonly called a land charges search, is in fact a search of all five registers. Entries in the registers of writs and orders, pending actions and deeds of arrangement against the name specified will be revealed on the search certificate quite irrespective of the county or period of ownership specified in the search. This is to the buyer's advantage as there may be occasions particularly in relation to bankruptcy when an entry, even though made outside the period of ownership of the legal estate, has important consequences for the buyer. An example would be under the Insolvency Act 1986, section 339 where the estate owner has given the property away and then become bankrupt.

An official certificate of search protects the buyer's solicitor in that the Land Charges Act 1972 provides that he shall not be answerable for any loss arising out of an error on it nor an error on an office copy.[15]

11   Priority notice

Under section 11 of the Land Charges Act 1972, it is possible to give advance 'priority' notice of a land charge to be created in the future, so that it is treated as registered as soon as created, and is thus binding on any purchaser, however immediate.

With the advent of universal compulsory registration of title this is unnecessary,[16] but it may still be appropriate if a land charge is created by a transaction which does not lead to compulsory registration.

12   Reliance on old searches

The buyer's solicitor's duty is to search against all known owners of the legal estate since 1925. However, if the solicitors for the various previous owners have acted properly on their respective purchases there should be with the deeds the searches which were made when the previous owners bought. Although the seller is under no duty to include these old searches in the epitome, he will normally do so. There is no reason why the buyer's solicitor should repeat a search which has been made properly in the past. For example if when A bought property in 1981, a search was made against the seller for his period of ownership of 1974 to 1981, there is no point in a buyer from A in 1993 repeating that search. When the buyer's solicitor does wish to rely on an old search in this way he should check that it was made against the correct name

---

15   Land Charges Act 1972, s 12.
16   Ibid, s 14(3).

for the correct period of ownership and did specify the correct county. He should also check the date of the subsequent conveyance in order to confirm that completion did take place within the priority period of the search.

If the buyer is buying property from someone who acquired it not by purchase but by gift, it may be necessary to make a search against the donor even if such a search was made at the time of the gift. A donee is given no protection by an official search certificate and the buyer would also be concerned about the effect of the Insolvency Act 1986, sections 339-342.

Old search certificates are useful in that as well as saving the buyer money in search fees, they may already reveal whether any interests have become void for non-registration. This information could also be obtained by checking the date of registration of the interest to see whether there had been a disposition to a buyer before the interest was registered.

13   *Procedure if an entry is revealed*

The purpose of the search is to discover whether there are any matters which the buyer does not already know about but which will be binding on him. There may be some entries which come as no surprise to the buyer, for example a Dii registration in respect of a restrictive covenant which was disclosed in the contract and which is apparent from the abstract. Similarly the buyer himself may have protected his own contract by registering a Civ land charge. On the other hand if an entry is revealed which cannot be explained in this way the buyer's solicitor will immediately raise a requisition to find out what the entry relates to and how the seller proposes to deal with it. He can also obtain an office copy of the entry. For example, the seller's solicitor may have forgotten to abstract a second legal mortgage which will show up on a search certificate as it will have been registered as a Ci land charge. The seller's solicitor will then abstract the second mortgage and the buyer's solicitor can ensure that it is discharged on or before completion. If a restrictive covenant is revealed as being registered as a Dii land charge then if this has not been disclosed in the contract, prima facie the seller will be in breach of contract as he will be unable to convey what he has contracted to; he can only convey the property subject to the restrictive covenant. If a Civ entry is revealed then again the buyer's solicitor will want an explanation. The entry may simply relate to the seller's contract when he bought, in which case it can be and indeed should have been cancelled. If a Class F land charge is revealed, the buyer's solicitor will insist that it is cancelled before completion or possibly that a form of application for cancellation signed by the spouse who registered the charge is handed over on completion. If the seller's solicitor is properly prepared then he will have anticipated the problem. Otherwise, if the charge cannot be cancelled, the seller will be in breach of contract. If a bankruptcy petition or order against the seller is revealed, the buyer cannot complete but must wait and if needs be complete with the trustee in bankruptcy.

Of course it may be that there is a quite innocent explanation for some of the entries on the search certificate. They may relate to someone else with the same name or they may relate to land other than that which the buyer is purchasing.

ii   **Search in the Companies Register**

1   *Need for the search*

Prior to 1 January 1970 if a company created a land charge for securing money (potentially registrable as a class Ci land charge) this could be protected by registration in the Companies Register under the Companies Act 1948, section 95.[17] Since 1 January 1970 registration in the Companies Register on its own is insufficient to bind a purchaser for value and there must be registration in the Land Charges Register. This means that in respect of a company which owned the land being sold before 1970, it is not sufficient to make a search in the Land Charges Register but a search must also be done in the Companies Register. If a financial charge is revealed as affecting the property being sold then the same considerations apply as to any other mortgage or charge; the buyer will want it to be discharged on or before completion or else the property to be released from the charge.

A floating charge, whenever created, is not registrable as a land charge but must be registered in the Companies Register. This, then, is a second reason for making a search of the Companies Register; not only to reveal pre-1970 charges but also to reveal floating charges, whenever created. If a floating charge is revealed, the buyer will require some assurance, in the form of a letter or certificate from the chargee – often a bank – to the effect that the charge had not crystallised at the date of completion. If it has crystallised it has become a fixed charge and will be treated by the buyer like any other charge or mortgage. There are further matters about which the buyer may be concerned. He may wish to ascertain that the company was incorporated at the date of the conveyance of the property to it. He may wish to confirm that the company has not been struck off the register, or that no winding-up proceedings have started in respect of the company; if a winding up has commenced, any disposition by the company is void unless the court orders otherwise.[18]

2 Mechanics of search

There is no provision for an official search of the Companies Register, which can be searched either in London or Cardiff. The buyer's solicitor will normally instruct a firm of agents, who advertise in the legal press, to do a search and report the result. A letter of instruction to the agents should cover all points on which the solicitor wants information. The agents will charge a fee. As there is no official search so there is no protection for a buyer. The search should therefore be timed to be as close as possible to completion; the search can even be made on the day of the completion and the result telephoned by the agents.

3 Reliance on old searches

For the reasons mentioned in section 1, above, it may be necessary to make this search not only when the seller is a company but also if a company appears on the title as an owner of the property in the past. If a search was made when the company disposed of the property and this is made available to the buyer's solicitor by the seller then there may be no need to make a further search if the old search appears adequate and there are no other reasons why a fresh search should be made.

iii Inspection of the property

We have already seen how occupation of the property can fix the buyer with constructive notice of an occupier's rights.[19] A typical situation is where a spouse or

---

17 Land Charges Act 1972, s 3(7).
18 Insolvency Act 1986, s 127.
19 See ch 6, section 8 iii.

some other person has an equitable interest in the property (but does not hold the legal estate); his or her occupation gives notice of the equitable interest to the buyer. The buyer's solicitor should thus arrange for an inspection after exchange of contracts (he should already have inspected before exchange) , to see if there are any such interests discoverable by reasonable enquiries. This is rather more easily said than done. An appropriate question could be added to the requisitions although this will not prevent the occupier's rights being binding on the buyer if they are not revealed by the seller.

What though if an equitable interest *is* known to the buyer, either as a result of inspection or otherwise? If the person with the equitable interest is willing to co-operate, he or she could sign some form of consent or join in the conveyance, to release or convey his or her rights to the buyer. In this situation the person with the equitable interest should receive independent advice before signing the form.[20] Another way of dealing with the problem would be for the seller to appoint someone (who may or may not be the owner of the equitable interest) to be a second trustee and thereby overreach the interest,[1] although this leaves the trustees with the problem of disposal of the proceeds of sale. The onus is on the seller to devise a way in which the property can be conveyed to the buyer free of the equitable interest as otherwise the seller will almost certainly be in breach of contract; he will be unable to give vacant possession, and he may also be in breach of the covenants for title implied into the purchase deed after completion. However, this will be of little consolation to the buyer, who wants the property rather than an action against the seller. From the buyer's point of view it is preferable to investigate this situation, so far as possible, before exchange of contracts, to prevent the problem ever arising.

Despite the foregoing, there might be some comfort for the buyer in the cases of *Bristol and West Building Society v Henning*,[2] *Paddington Building Society v Mendelsohn*,[3] and *Abbey National Building Society v Cann*[4] which concern the position of a mortgagee who may be bound by interest of someone in the property when it is mortgaged, and which are discussed in that context in Chapter 13. Applying the cases by analogy to the seller/buyer situation, they suggest that if the occupier knows of and supports the seller's sale, he might be unable to enforce the interest against the buyer.

iv Further search of the Local Land Charges Register and enquiries of the Local Authority

It might in certain circumstances be necessary to do these searches again, particularly if a relatively long time has elapsed since such searches were made before exchange of contracts. However, they are rarely done again in practice and the registration of a local land charge or the advent of some new local authority proposals affecting the property would not normally affect the relationship between the seller and the buyer, the risk thereof being assumed by the buyer on exchange of contracts.

20 This point is discussed further in ch 13 in relation to a prospective mortgagee requiring a consent form from a prospective occupier with an equitable interest (eg the buyer's spouse).
1 Law of Property Act 1925, s 27(1).
2 [1985] 2 All ER 606, [1986] 1 WLR 778, CA.
3 (1985) 50 P & CR 244, [1987] Fam Law 121, CA.
4 [1991] 1 AC 56, [1990] 1 All ER 1085, HL.

2   REGISTERED LAND

i   **Search of the register**

1   Purpose of the search

This is the main search which needs to be done on a purchaser of registered land. Its purpose is to bring up to date the buyer's information concerning the state of the entries in the register which will have been derived from the office copy entries by means of which title was deduced. The buyer must have this up-to-date information as not only does the register describe what he is buying but he will also be affected by any entries such as notices or cautions appearing on the register. As certain entries can be made on the register without the production of the land or charge certificate, (for example, a notice registered pursuant to a spouse's Family Law Act 1996 right of occupation) entries may appear which are news even to the seller! The search (provided it is done 'with priority' will also give the buyer (and his lender) priority over any other applications which may be received, for the priority period specified on the search result.

2   Mechanics of search

There are standard forms of application for a search of the register, relating to the whole of the property for use by prospective buyers, lessees and mortgagees. These are Form 94A (for a search with priority) or Form 94C (for a search without priority)under the Land Registration (Official Searches) Rules 1993. Form 94A is sent to the District Land Registry for the area in which the land is situated. It can also be sent by fax, or requested by telephone, or delivered in person, and the Land Registry is keen to make electronic searching (via its Land Registry Direct scheme), more widespread. On the 94A form the buyer or his solicitor must certify that the buyer intends to purchase (or lease or lend money on a mortgage of) the land. The form also asks the searcher to specify the date from which details of any changes in the register are required. By virtue of the Land Registration (Official Searches) Rules 1993, this should be a date not more than twelve months previously, and so the buyer's solicitor should ensure, when he receives the Office Copies from the seller's solicitor, that these are not more than twelve months old. The date when the land or charge certificate was last examined at the registry must not be used. In certain cases, under the new electronic conveyancing systems being pioneered by the Land Registry, no office copies will have been issued – in such a case, the date to search from should be the date shown on the entries as transmitted by the registrar's computer system not more than twelve months previously.

Where the search is done by post or DX, the result will be issued the same way. Where the request is faxed, results will NOT be returned by fax but will be sent by post. If the official search is requested by phone, the registry can give a guaranteed reply over the phone provided there have been no subsisting entries since the 'search from date', and no application for first registration has been received, and no other priority period is still in existence. If any of these does apply, the registry cannot give a guaranteed result but will give details over the telephone, effectively for information only. The solicitor will then have to wait for the paper result by post for confirmation of the entries, and details of the priority period. Under the Registry's Real Time Priority system (launched on 28 May 2001),[5] an application will be given priority

---

5   Land Registration (No 3) Rules 2000.

from the date and time that its details are entered on the Land Registry's database of pending applications (the day list, a computerised record of pending first registration applications, and pending dealing applications, and record of official searches[6]). Previously, real time priority had applied to telephone and Land Registry Direct / Direct Access searches, but from 28 May 2001 this system will apply to postal and faxed search applications, as well as all applications for substantive registration. All search results will from now on have both a date and time inserted, although the time does not have to be quoted when making a search application.

3   Search of part

If the buyer is only buying part of the land comprised in the seller's title then he will only wish to know the up-to-date state of the register as it affects the part which he is buying. There is a standard form of application 94B to be used by such a buyer. This is similar to the Form 94A but must contain a reference to the part which the buyer is buying and in respect of which the search is to be done. A plan would have to be sent, showing this part, unless either it can be clearly identified by reference to the filed plan or it is a numbered plot on a new building estate of which the estate layout plan has already been deposited with the Registry. In the latter case the date of approval of the plan must be given on the form. It is important to note that searches of part can, at present, only be made by post, DX or fax – they cannot be made in person, by phone or by Land Registry Direct.

4   Official search certificate

The certificate despatched as a result of the application for a search shows all entries made since the date specified in the application. A paper certificate will be despatched whatever the method of search used. It is not conclusive but if the buyer suffers loss as a result of an error in the certificate he will be entitled to an indemnity under the Land Registration Act 1925, section 83(3). In the first part of this chapter we saw that an official land charges search certificate gave the buyer of unregistered land some protection in that if he completed within a certain period of the date of the search he was not bound by entries made in the meantime. The same principle applies to the search of the register in respect of registered land. The buyer will obtain priority over any entry made on the register between the date of the search and the date the buyer applies for registration of his purchase, but only if the buyer's application for registration is in order and is deemed to have been delivered to the District Land Registry before midnight on the thirtieth working day after the application for the search is deemed to have been delivered.[7] The date of expiry of the priority period is shown on the search certificate but this should be checked by the buyer's solicitor. If the solicitor is acting for both buyer and mortgagee, it is normal to do the search on behalf of the mortgagee: the search result will protect both the lender and the buyer, as the registration of the legal charge is dependent on the registration of the transfer.[8]

In effect, then, the period is 30 working days from the date of the search but within this period the buyer must not only complete but also *apply for registration of his purchase*. The buyer's solicitor will send off the application for the search shortly before completion is due so as to receive the search certificate before completion but also to allow sufficient time to complete and apply for registration within the

---

6   Kept under Land Registration Rules 1925, r 7A.
7   From 28 May 2001: Land Registration (No 3) Rules 2000, r 3(1), Sch 3.
8   Land Registration (Official Searches) Rules 1993, r 6.

priority period even if completion is delayed. If completion cannot take place within the priority period then a new search must be done; this will give a new period of priority and not an extension of the priority period under the original search. There is a danger that an application for registration of an interest (for example, a notice under the Family Law Act 1996) could be received between the end of priority on one search and the start of priority on the second, but this should show up on the second search result. An adverse interest such as this is not too much of a problem if completion has not taken place, as completion can be postponed whilst the problem is sorted out, or the contract could even be rescinded if the problem is incapable of solution. The problem comes where completion has taken place but there has been a delay in effecting registration; for this reason, it is very important to ensure that registration is dealt with expeditiously, and appropriate systems should be in place in the solicitor's office to ensure this.

5   Procedure if an entry is revealed

If the buyer's information about the register is obtained from recently obtained office copies then it is unlikely that any new entry will be revealed by the search. However, if some adverse entry is disclosed then the comments made in section 13 above in relation to land charges apply with equal force. For example a registered charge may be revealed which the buyer will want to see discharged. A notice in respect of a spouse's statutory right of occupation under the Family Law Act 1996 may have been entered, or an outline application received, and in this case the buyer will insist that it is removed before proceeding. A creditor's notice in respect of a bankruptcy petition or a bankruptcy inhibition following a bankruptcy order may have been entered. If the seller is selling part of a larger piece of land, he might have recently sold another part and granted an easement over the part which the present buyer is buying; this will be revealed by the search as having been noted on the register (although it is otherwise an overriding interest) and the seller will be in breach of contract unless he disclosed it in the contract.

6   Sub-sales and re-sales

On a sub-sale, the position is that the seller (S) has contracted to sell to the buyer (B1) who has in turn contracted to sell to the sub-buyer (B2) before completion of his own purchase. Completion of the two transactions will normally be co-ordinated so that there will be just the one transfer deed direct from S to B2. B1 will only be able to supply B2 with office copies showing S as the registered proprietor. B2 can still make a search based on these office copies, (and he will need to give S as the registered proprietor) but the contract between S and B1 would also have to be abstracted.

A solicitor may be acting for a client who has recently bought property and now wishes to resell it, but the Land Registry may be still dealing with this application for registration. This situation should be distinguished from a sub-sale, because completion of the client's purchase has already taken place; he now wishes to sell the property of which he is not yet shown as the registered proprietor. As we saw in Chapter 9, section 3, section 110(5) of the Land Registration Act 1925 does pose problems if the client bought a registered title; those problems aside, the buyer's solicitor can make an official search. The procedure for searching in sub-sales and re-sales is set out clearly in Land Registry Practice Advice Leaflet 5. The position is slightly more complicated in relation to a client who had bought an unregistered title in respect of which an application has been made for first registration. Although as we again saw in Chapter 9, section 3, section 110(5)does not pose problems, there is no register against which a buyer can make an official search. Unregistered title would be deduced to the buyer, together with a copy of the application for first registration.[9] The buyer's solicitor would then do a 94A search in the normal way, but would specify on the form that there is a first registration pending. The result will then disclose whether any applications have been received at the Registry other than that for first registration. The search result will afford a priority period in the usual way. Again, the procedure is described in more detail in Practice Advice Leaflet 5.

ii   Search in the Companies Register

In accordance with the basic principles of registration of title, charges created by a company for securing money would have to be noted in some way on the register of title if a purchaser for value is to be bound. There is no need therefore to search the Companies Register to discover pre-1970 charges or floating charges, as there is in the case of unregistered land. Similarly there would seem to be no other need for a search of the Companies Register as the buyer will be able to rely on the guaranteed accuracy of the register of title showing a company as registered proprietor. However, the register may be subject to rectification, and so it may be thought advisable to do a search to discover, for example, the existence of winding-up proceedings or whether the company has been struck off the Companies Register.

iii   Inspection of the property

This is of obvious importance in relation to registered land. A buyer takes subject to overriding interests whether he knows of them or not and one category of overriding interest is the rights of a person in possession or in receipt of rents or profits. We have already seen the consequence of this, particularly in the case of a spouse or other occupier with an equitable interest in the property.[10] The buyer would take subject to the spouse's equitable interest which would constitute not only a financial burden on the property but also give the spouse a right to possession. As in the case of unregistered land, the buyer's solicitor should arrange for an inspection of the property. There is no requirement that the occupation must be discoverable on reasonable inspection and we have already considered the real difficulties involved in making such an inspection. The buyer cannot rely on the seller's reply to a requisition asking whether there is anyone in occupation and if so what their rights are, because if the seller fails to disclose the information the buyer will still be bound. The time at which one must assess whether a person with an interest in the property is in possession and therefore has an overriding interest which will bind the buyer, is effectively the time of completion.[11]

If an investigation should reveal someone who may have an equitable interest, then if enquiry is made of that person and the interest is not revealed, there will be no overriding interest. Otherwise, the buyer's course of action will be the same as if the land were unregistered, discussed at section 1 iii above. It is possible to overreach the interest on a sale by trustees, even though it is an overriding interest;[12] even where

---

9   It is important that the seller has applied for first registration within the two-month time limit; *Pinekerry Ltd v Kenneth Needs (Contractors) Ltd* (1992) 64 P & CR 245, CA.
10   See ch 6, section 8 iii.
11   *Abbey National Building Society v Cann* [1991] 1 AC 56, [1990] 1 All ER 1085, HL.
12   *City of London Building Society v Flegg* [1988] AC 54, [1987] 3 All ER 435, HL.

there is no capital money to be paid over; for example in the case of a mortgage where the land is used as security for business debts, overreaching can still occur.[13]

iv   Search in the Local Land Charges Register

The comments made above in section 1 iv apply equally here.

v   Search in the Central Land Charges Register

If the buyer is buying an absolute freehold or an absolute leasehold registered title then there will be no need to do a search in the Central Land Charges Register. If the title he is buying is less than absolute then he may need to do a search in respect of that part of the title on which the register is not conclusive. For example, if the buyer is buying a good leasehold title, the superior freehold title being unregistered, then if the freehold title is deduced to him he will wish to do land charges searches in respect of it as part of the process of investigating that freehold title. For the same reason there may be a need to do a search at the Companies Register if the freehold title reveals that the freehold has been owned by a company.

Whether the freehold title is deduced depends on whether the buyer has been able to negotiate for the inclusion of an appropriate condition in the contract.[14]

3   SEARCHES MADE BY THE SOLICITOR FOR A PROSPECTIVE MORTGAGEE

Searches made by the solicitor for a prospective mortgagee are discussed in Chapter 13.

13   *State Bank of India v Sood* [1997] Ch 276, [1997] 1 All ER 169.
14   See ch 5, section 4 xvii.

12 DRAFTING THE DEED

I INTRODUCTION

It is the buyer's solicitor's task to draft the purchase deed. With a few exceptions, a deed is needed to transfer a legal estate[1] – the exceptions are an assent by personal representatives, grants of short term leases not exceed in three years and vesting orders made by the court. We shall consider in this chapter three basic forms of deed: the conveyance, used for unregistered freehold land; the assignment, used for unregistered leasehold land, and the transfer, used for registered land, leasehold or freehold. We shall not discuss here the form and contents of a lease or underlease; a discussion of the contents of a lease or underlease raises substantive questions of law, concerning the respective obligations of the parties, which are rather different to those questions raised by the contents of a conveyance, assignment or transfer. The contents of a lease or underlease will therefore be discussed in a subsequent chapter, which will also reiterate the conveyancing procedure as it applies to the grant of a lease or underlease.[2]

The buyer's solicitor has already examined the title and satisfied himself that the seller can convey the property and on that basis exchanged contracts. This means that the investigation of title, including the searches, has not revealed any defect in title that presumably has not been satisfactorily resolved. The contents of the deed will thus reflect the contract, and those matters, if any, which did not need to be disclosed in the contract.[3] If on the other hand some undisclosed defect of title is revealed after exchange of contracts, the buyer has certain remedies against the seller. If the buyer does not rescind but completion does eventually take place, the deed will necessarily refer to the covenant as clearly the seller can only convey the property subject to it.

The deed, particularly in the case of unregistered land, could be fairly lengthy as the land must be fully described and the interests such as easements and covenants of which it either has the benefit or subject to which it is held must also be mentioned. A transfer of registered land can be much shorter as it can refer quite simply to the entries in the register; it is only the property comprised in the register that the seller can sell. There may be a temptation for the buyer's solicitor when drafting a conveyance or assignment merely to repeat the contents of the most recent conveyance or assignment in the title, changing matters such as the names of the parties and the

---

1 Law of Property Act 1925, s 52(1).
2 See ch 17, below.
3 Remember that under an open contract the seller need not disclose patent defects in title or defects in title of which the buyer is aware; see ch 5, above.

consideration. This temptation is to be resisted. The previous deed may have been incorrectly drafted, as the solicitor may have discovered on his investigation of title. Also the contract may impose new obligations on the parties which must be incorporated in the conveyance or assignment. Ideally the buyer's solicitor should work from the contract when drafting the deed but of course he may then find that reference is made in the contract to earlier deeds for the exact wording of the description of the land and covenants and easements affecting it. Indeed, the new conveyance or assignment itself may follow this same practice; it will certainly shorten the deed although it may not be appropriate in every case. The buyer's solicitor will often also use a standard precedent, either of his own or obtained from a book of precedents, or available on his word-processor, to guide him on the form and wording of the deed. There are a number of different forms the deed could take, but the overriding consideration is that the deed should be precise and accurate in all respects. It is important to note that property subject to first registration may be dealt with by way of a transfer under rule 72 of the Land Registration Rules (see section 5 i), and thus the use of the conveyance is declining.

2   THE CONVEYANCE

i   Commencement

The opening words are traditionally 'This Conveyance is made the .... day of .... 20... between ....' followed by the names of the parties. The date would not of course be inserted at this stage; this is normally done on completion. In fact the effective date of a deed is the date it is delivered, which as we shall see could be before the date of completion. However, the date stated in the deed is presumed to be correct unless the contrary is shown.

ii   Parties

Who will the parties to the deed be? Obviously the seller and the buyer. If the sellers are trustees of land or personal representatives then they must all be parties to the deed. If the purchase money is to be paid to someone other than the seller, that person should join in the deed in order to give a receipt for the purchase money. The obvious example is on a sale by the tenant for life of settled land where all the trustees (being at least two in number) would join in the deed to give a receipt and thereby over-reach the equitable interests under the settlement. Another example is where the seller is a company which is in liquidation. The company will convey the property but the liquidator will join in as a party to give a receipt for the purchase money. If an order has been made under the Insolvency Act 1986, section 145, the property vests in the liquidator who would also convey the property and the company need not be a party to the deed. If a seller has become bankrupt, his trustee in bankruptcy will convey and again the seller will not be made a party.

There will be other situations in which another party joins in the deed, to release the property from some interest or to vest some interest in the buyer. So where property is held under a mortgage and part of it is to be sold, the mortgage may not be discharged but instead the mortgagee may agree to join in the deed to release the property sold from the mortgage. Similarly, on a divorce or separation property previously held in the spouses' joint names may be conveyed into one spouse's sole name; if the property is mortgaged, the mortgagee may join in to release the conveying party from his or her obligations under the mortgage. A person with an equitable interest in the property being sold may join in to convey his interest to the buyer, although normally this would not happen because a sale by the trustees would overreach the equitable interest.

On a sub-sale, where the seller has sold to the buyer (B) who has resold to a sub-purchaser (P), the deed may be directly from the seller to P. However, there are a number of reasons why B might also join in the deed. Firstly, if the resale was at a higher price than the initial sale he would join in to give a receipt for the balance paid to him. Secondly, the effect of him joining in the deed would be to convey his equitable interest to P, although this would not seem to be necessary. Thirdly, he can give a title guarantee to P.[4] Remember that the Standard Conditions contain restrictions on the power of the buyer to sub-sell for leasehold property.[5]

The buyer's solicitor should also check with his client who is to take the conveyance, ie who the buyer(s) is to be. It may be that all the solicitor's instructions have come from one spouse and the contract is in the name of that spouse but that the property is in fact to be conveyed to the spouses jointly. If so, the solicitor will also need to know whether the property is to be held by them as beneficial joint tenants or beneficial tenants in common. If on the other hand one spouse wants the property to be conveyed into his or her sole name, the solicitor should perhaps warn him or her that this does not mean that he or she can do as he or she pleases with the property; the other spouse would have a statutory right of occupation under the Family Law Act 1996[6] and may well have an equitable interest in the property as a result of contributing to the purchase price.

As well as the names of the parties, their addresses must also be given to further identify them. In days gone by their occupations were also given but there would now seem little point in this unless there are two people with the same name living at the same address. The addresses given are those at the time of execution of the deed and so the seller's address will commonly be the address of the property, unless the buyers have taken possession before completion. For a company, the address of its registered office would be given.

By way of illustration, a traditional conveyance between two sellers as joint owners and a buyer might read as follows: 'Between David Roberts and Angela Roberts both of 5 Meadow Lane Derby Derbyshire (hereinafter called the sellers) of the one part and John French of 10 Arkwright Street Worksop Nottinghamshire (hereinafter called the buyer) of the other part'. This could be shortened to '(1) David Roberts and Angela Roberts both of 5 Meadow Lane Derby Derbyshire (Sellers) and (2) John French of 10 Arkwright Street Worksop Nottinghamshire (Buyer)'.

If there were another party to the deed, for example a mortgagee joining in to release property from a mortgage, the parties would be the seller of the first part; the mortgagee of the second part and the buyer of the third part.

Traditionally punctuation is not used in deeds. The theory is that if punctuation was used it would be simple to alter it fraudulently and thereby change the meaning of the deed. The sense of the deed must be made clear without the use of punctuation. Unfortunately practice does not always accord with theory and one can encounter very long and apparently incomprehensible sentences. It may therefore be more appropriate in some circumstances to punctuate the deed.

---

4   The conveyance may state that the seller conveys to P by the direction of B. If B gives a title guarantee he then gives the appropriate covenants for title to P.
5   On the grant of a lease under SC 8.2.5 and on the assignment of a lease or the grant of a sub-lease, where the landlord's consent is required, under SC 8.3.3.
6   If it is to be the matrimonial home.

iii   Recitals

The recitals are the introductory part of the conveyance which precedes the main operative part. As such, they are normally not essential and in more modern and shorter forms of conveyance they may be left out altogether. If they are used then they have three main consequences. Firstly, a recital in a deed 20 years old is sufficient evidence of the truth of what is recited.[7] So if the death of a joint tenant is recited in a conveyance over 20 years old which is included in an abstract of title, this is sufficient proof of the death for the buyer in the absence of any evidence to the contrary. Secondly, a party to a conveyance may be estopped from denying the accuracy of a statement in the recitals. An illustration of this is provided by the case of *Cumberland Court (Brighton) Ltd v Taylor*[8] where there was a recital that the seller owned the property free from encumbrances; he was thereby estopped from setting up a mortgage which had not in fact been discharged but had been transferred to him because it was paid off after the date of the conveyance. The estoppel operates against the party making the statement and his successors in title in favour of the other party and his successors in title. Thirdly, a clear unambiguous recital may be used to assist in the interpretation of an ambiguity in the actual operative part of the deed. However, even if recitals are used, it is unlikely nowadays that they would contain anything which could be of such assistance.

The function of recitals is really twofold: to explain how the seller came to own the property sold and to state that he does indeed own it, and to explain the reason for this particular conveyance. The first sort of recital in its simplest traditional form would read:

> The seller is seised of the property hereinafter described for an estate in fee simple in possession free from encumbrances save as hereinafter mentioned.

It is largely a matter of the buyer's solicitor's personal preference as to how much detail is included. If the sale is by the survivor of two joint tenants there could be a recital of the conveyance to the joint tenants followed by a recital of the death of one of them. If the sale is by a personal representative then there may be a recital that the deceased was seised of the property at the date of his death, a recital of the death and the grant of probate to the seller. If one of two beneficial tenants in common has died, a subsequent conveyance might recite the conveyance to the tenants in common, the death, and the appointment of another trustee. None of this is essential but it does explain the background to the conveyance. As to the second sort of recital, explaining the reason for the conveyance, this will normally be because the seller has just agreed to sell the property to the buyer. A standard recital would read:

> The seller has agreed with the buyer for the sale to him of [the property] at the price of ....

If there was some other party joining in the deed, for example a mortgagee releasing the property from a mortgage of that and other property, this could also be explained in the recitals. It may be that the conveyance is resulting not from a contract for sale but from a compulsory purchase order or from an agreement to exchange land in order to settle a boundary dispute between neighbours. Again this can be explained in a recital.

---

7   Law of Property Act 1925, s 45(6).
8   [1964] Ch 29, [1963] 2 All ER 536.

The one potential disadvantage of a recital is that it will give a future buyer notice of what is recited if the conveyance forms part of a future abstract of title. This can have inconvenient results as is shown by the cases of *Re Duce and Boots Cash Chemists (Southern) Ltd's Contract*[9] and *MEPC Ltd v Christian-Edwards*.[10] There are however two situations in which a recital will normally be essential. On the sale by the survivor of beneficial joint tenants we have already seen that for the protection of the buyer the seller should make a statement that he is solely and beneficially entitled, or sells as beneficial owner.[11] Similarly on a sale by personal representatives, they should make a statement that they have not made any previous assent or conveyance in respect of the property now sold.[12] These statements are normally made in the recitals to the conveyance. If there are no recitals as such the statements will still have to be included in the conveyance.

After the recitals, the operative part to the deed is traditionally introduced by the testatum.

iv   Testatum

This traditionally says 'Now this deed witnesses as follows'. In a modern form of deed where there are no recitals the testatum can be dispensed with.

v   Consideration and receipt clause

The operative part of a conveyance contains a statement of the consideration and the seller's receipt of it. In the traditional conveyance this is the beginning of a long first clause which will go on to deal with the conveyance of the property and its description. Typically this would read 'In consideration of the sum of .... thousand pounds (£........) paid by the buyers (the receipt whereof the seller acknowledges) the seller conveys ....'. In a more modern form of conveyance the consideration and receipt clause can be separated from this long first clause; the more the deed can be broken up in this way the easier it is to read.

The Stamp Act 1891, section 5 provides that any consideration must be stated. On the other hand the receipt clause is not essential but there are three reasons why it is invariably included. Firstly, by the Law of Property Act 1925, section 67, it is a sufficient discharge to the buyer and no further receipt is necessary. This is quite important if the money is paid to trustees for sale or the trustees of a Settled Land Act settlement because it is only if the money is paid to the trustees that the equitable interests are over-reached. In the latter case the receipt clause would state that the money had been paid to the trustees rather than the seller tenant for life. Secondly, by the Law of Property Act 1925, section 68, the receipt will be sufficient evidence of payment in favour of a subsequent buyer without notice that payment was not in fact made. Thirdly, by the Law of Property Act 1925, section 69, the inclusion of the receipt clause in the conveyance is a sufficient authority to the buyer to pay the money to the seller's solicitor rather than to the seller personally.

---

9   [1937] Ch 642, [1937] 3 All ER 788; see ch 10, section 5 iii 2.
10   [1981] AC 205, [1979] 3 All ER 752, HL; see ch 9, section 1.
11   Law of Property (Joint Tenants) Act 1964.
12   Administration of Estates Act 1925, s 36(6).

vi   The operative words and statement of the seller's capacity

I   Operative words

The crucial part of the conveyance is the phrase that states that the legal estate in the property is passing from the seller to the buyer. In the traditional form of conveyance this will follow the consideration and receipt in the first clause. In a more modern conveyance it will be included in a separate clause. The usual wording is 'the seller conveys' but any words showing the seller's intention to pass the legal estate to the buyer will suffice.

2   Statement of the seller's capacity

We saw in Chapter 5 that the seller conveying and giving a title guarantee will mean that certain covenants for title by the seller will be implied into the conveyance. The nature and extent of these covenants are dealt with in Chapter 16. So if the seller was giving full title guarantee, the clause would read 'the seller with full title guarantee conveys ....'.

vii   Parcels clause

I   Introduction

Having stated that the seller is conveying, the conveyance must next state *what* the seller is conveying, by describing the property. This part of the conveyance is often called the parcels clause and in a traditional conveyance it will follow immediately after the operative words; alternatively the description could be given in a schedule at the end of the deed, referred to in the body of the deed.

2   Physical description

The parcels clause is a physical description of the property sold. It must be clear, complete and accurate. Assuming that the investigation of title has not revealed anything untoward, the description in the particulars in the contract will be the basis of the description in the conveyance. Indeed the buyer must accept the description in the contract for inclusion in the conveyance unless it is in some way inadequate. The description in the contract may well be identical with the description in the previous conveyances of the property and may or may not refer to a plan. What though, if the description in the contract is inadequate and does not accurately identify the property sold? The buyer is entitled to a fresh description which does correctly describe the property. But is the buyer entitled to have not only a verbal description but also a plan? The case law is somewhat contradictory but it seems that if a purely verbal description will afford a sufficient description the buyer cannot insist on a plan;[13] otherwise he can.[14]

3   Plan

If a plan is used it should be referred to in the verbal description. The property will normally be referred to as being either 'more particularly delineated' on the

13   *Re Sharman and Meade's Contract* [1936] Ch 755, [1936] 2 All ER 1547.
14   *Re Sansom and Narbeth's Contract* [1910] 1 Ch 741.

plan or else 'shown by way of identification only' on it. If the former words are used then, as the words suggest, if there should be any discrepancy between the plan and the verbal description the plan will prevail.[15] It is therefore important to check that the plan does accurately reflect the boundaries on site, which the buyer will have seen. Conversely if the plan is referred to as being for identification only, the verbal description will prevail. To use both formulae – to say that the property is more particularly delineated for the purpose of identification only on the plan – is meaningless,[16] but it is an expression sometimes found in conveyances. Even if a plan is expressed to be for identification only, it can still be of use; although it cannot prevail over a clear contrary verbal description it can be used to settle points which are not resolved by the verbal description because the latter is either ambiguous or totally silent on the particular point.[17] Even if the plan is, by mistake, not referred to at all in the conveyance it could still be consulted if the verbal description was unclear provided that it was either drawn on or bound up with the conveyance.[18] A plan is normally taken as showing the boundaries at ground level only.[19]

The description of the property, and in particular the use of plans, is an area where conveyancers in the past have occasionally been somewhat remiss. It is all too easy to keep repeating a description and a reference to a plan contained in a conveyance of some years ago, even though it no longer in fact represents the current position. There is for example little point in repeating in 1993 that the property sold is bounded on the East by property that in 1954 was in the possession of various named individuals, and that it is shown for identification on a fairly rough and ready sketch plan on a 1954 conveyance. Caution in abandoning old descriptions is understandable, but it does lead ultimately to sloppy and inaccurate conveyancing. It is surely far better to introduce an up-to-date plan whenever necessary. This was underlined in the case of *Scarfe v Adams*.[20] It will be vitally important, on a sale of part only of the land comprised in the conveyance to the seller, to have an accurate description and plan of the part which is being sold off. In *Scarfe v Adams*, the Court of Appeal made it clear that on a sale of part it was essential that the description was such that there was no room for doubt about the boundaries, and that the plan should be sufficiently large scale to do this. In *Jackson v Bishop*,[1] the Court of Appeal decided that a seller/developer owed a duty of care to buyers to prepare a site plan that was not misleading.

---

15 See *A J Dunning & Sons (Shopfitters) Ltd v Sykes & Son (Poole) Ltd* [1987] Ch 287, [1987] 1 All ER 700, CA; see also *Seabreeze Properties Ltd v Haw* [1990] EGCS 114.
16 *Neilson v Poole* (1969) 20 P & CR 909.
17 *Wigginton & Milner Ltd v Winster Engineering Ltd* [1978] 3 All ER 436, [1978] 1 WLR 1462, CA. *Hatfield v Moss* [1988] 2 EGLR 58, CA, illustrates the low priority given by the courts to an 'identification only' plan. The verbal description was little more than 'Number 6 flat', but the court took evidence as to what this meant, and this overrode a clear indication of the boundary of the flat on an 'identification only' plan. See also *Scott v Martin* [1987] 2 All ER 813, [1987] 1 WLR 841, CA.
18 *Leachman v L & K Richardson Ltd* [1969] 3 All ER 20, [1969] 1 WLR 1129.
19 In *Truckell v Stock* [1957] 1 All ER 74, [1957] 1 WLR 161, CA, the footings of the property projected beyond the boundary shown on the plan and although in the case of conflict between the verbal description and the plan, the plan would have prevailed, the Court of Appeal held that there was no conflict as the plan merely showed the boundaries at ground level and the verbal description including the footings which were of course below ground level.
20 [1981] 1 All ER 843, CA; see also *Spall v Owen* (1982) 44 P & CR 36; and *Toplis v Green* [1992] EGCS 20, CA.
 1 (1979) 48 P & CR 57, CA.

4   *Rules of construction*

There are a number of rules of construction which should be borne in mind when drafting the parcels clause. Firstly, if a boundary is formed by a ditch and a bank there is a presumption that the boundary runs along the side of the ditch which is further from the bank. The reasoning is apparently that the person who dug the ditch would have dug it on the extremity of his own land and thrown the earth back on to his own land to form the bank. A similar rule applies to a ditch and hedge. Secondly, where land adjoins a road there is a presumption that the adjoining landowner owns the land up to the mid-point of the road. The same presumption applies to a non-tidal river. Finally an obvious inaccuracy will not vitiate the description. If land in Nottinghamshire is referred to by mistake as being in Derbyshire the mistake will be ignored.

viii   Rights for the benefit of the property

After the physical description, there will be a statement of the rights that will exist for the benefit of the buyer, such as easements or the benefit of covenants. This will normally be introduced by the words 'together with'. There will be already existing rights which will normally have been mentioned in the contract, and new rights which the seller is granting to the buyer, for example on a sale of part of the seller's land. The latter will depend for their inclusion on some corresponding provision in the contract; the buyer cannot have a right of way granted to him in a conveyance unless the contract gives him that right. However, the buyer's solicitor should bear in mind that the rule of implied grant on a sale of part contained in *Wheeldon v Burrows*[2] does apply to a contract so if the contract is silent, the buyer may be entitled to the grant of rights in the conveyance under *Wheeldon v Burrows*. The rule also applies to a conveyance so if the conveyance in its turn is silent it will impliedly grant rights under *Wheeldon v Burrows* to the buyer. If under the contract the rule of implied grant has been expressly excluded or restricted,[3] the conveyance should give effect to this by containing a clause also expressly excluding or restricting the implied grant. As regards any new easements which the contract expressly provides should be granted to the buyer, the contract should have provided for the precise scope of the easement, the land affected by the easement and the persons to have the benefit of the easement. The conveyance must do likewise to ensure that the easement is validly granted. Note the cautionary tale of *IDC Group Ltd v Clark*,[4] where a right to use a fire-escape was described as a 'licence' and was thus held not to be an easement and so not to bind the successors in title of the land across which it passed.

There is a further manner in which the conveyance can impliedly pass rights to the buyer. The Law of Property Act 1925, section 62(1) states that:

> ... a conveyance of land shall be deemed to include and shall by virtue of this Act operate to convey with the land all buildings, erections, fixtures, commons, hedges, ditches, fences, ways, waters, watercourses, liberties, privileges, easements, rights and advantages, whatsoever, appertaining or reputed to appertain to the land or any part thereof, or, at the time of conveyance, demised, occupied, or enjoyed with, or reputed or known as part or parcel of or appurtenant to the land or any part thereof.

2   (1879) 12 Ch D 31, CA.
3   As under SC 3.3.2.
4   (1992) 65 P & CR 179, CA.

A fairly comprehensive list, which is wider than the *Wheeldon v Burrows* category of implied rights and is applicable to all conveyances and not just sales of part. However, on a sale of part a buyer may acquire, under section 62, rights over the retained land if it has been in separate occupation. The implication only arises in the absence of any express stipulation to the contrary. If the buyer under the terms of the contract is not entitled to all the rights which would impliedly pass to him under section 62 the conveyance should contain a clause excluding or restricting the effect of section 62. For the avoidance of doubt, and to prevent the buyer getting more than the seller intended, the contract on a sale of part should stipulate what rights are (and are not) to be granted to the buyer; the conveyance will then expressly deal with such rights and if necessary a clause excluding or restricting the effect of section 62 and *Wheeldon v Burrows*.

ix   Exceptions and reservations

An exception is a right adversely affecting the property which is already in existence and subject to which the property is sold to the buyer. A straightforward example would be a right of way over the property for the benefit of adjoining property, created at some time in the past. A reservation on the other hand is some new right to be created by the conveyance in favour of the seller and subject to which the buyer will take the property. An example would be the reservation, on a sale of part, of a right of way over the land sold for the benefit of the land retained by the seller. Both exceptions and reservations must be disclosed by the seller in the contract. Exceptions are incumbrances which the seller must disclose under SC 3.1.1. Equally, the seller cannot in the conveyance reserve a new right unless he has provided for it in the contract. As we have seen when drafting the contract, this is of relevance on the sale of part because although there may be implied grants of easements there will be no implied reservations. As with the express grant of an easement, care must be taken that when an easement is expressly reserved it is validly created with the scope of the easement and the dominant and servient lands being identified. Again, as with the grant of an easement, the contract should have given the full wording, to be incorporated in the conveyance.

In a traditional conveyance, the exceptions and reservations are usually stated after the parcels clause and the easements existing for the benefit of the property. The conveyance should make clear that the exceptions are already existing rights; merely repeating the wording used when the right was originally reserved may give rise to the misunderstanding that the conveyance is reserving a new right rather than simply stating that the property is subject to an already existing one. To avoid any confusion there is merit in separating the exceptions and reservations and dealing with new reservations in a separate clause from the statement of existing exceptions; this would usually be the case in a more modern form of conveyance.

x   Habendum

This is the clause which follows the parcels clause in a traditional conveyance and describes the estate which is conveyed to the buyer, which in the case of a conveyance is the freehold. The traditional wording is 'to hold unto the buyer in fee simple'. In fact, the inclusion of such words is not essential in a conveyance of the freehold. The Law of Property Act 1925, section 60 states that a conveyance of freehold land without words of limitation shall pass a fee simple or other interest of the seller or donor which he has power to convey unless a contrary intention appears from the conveyance.

A more modern form of conveyance will omit a habendum in the form suggested above, but there will be an indication, in the parcels clause, that freehold land is being conveyed.

xi   Statement of existing encumbrances

As well as the exceptions, there will also be mention of other existing encumbrances and adverse interests subject to which the property is conveyed. These will have been disclosed in the contract. Existing covenants will be mentioned here. If there has in the past been a declaration in a conveyance that the common walls with neighbouring property are party walls and jointly maintained, then this too will be mentioned here. The statement of these encumbrances is often introduced by the words 'subject to'.

xii   Reference to earlier conveyances

There are a number of areas where the buyer's solicitor, in drafting the conveyance, may wish to make some reference to the contents of an earlier conveyance. The description, both in the contract and in the proposed parcels clause, may be by reference to a more lengthy description in an earlier conveyance or to a plan attached to an earlier conveyance. The statement of existing covenants, exceptions, declarations and other encumbrances is almost bound to refer back to the conveyances which created those encumbrances. The reason is that if the buyer's solicitor is to reproduce in full the wording of the description or the easement or covenant or whatever, then although this will have the advantage that earlier conveyances need not be referred to and the conveyance will be complete in itself, it will make the conveyance extremely long. If the buyer's solicitor merely makes brief mention of the description or covenant or easement and then refers to the earlier conveyance as containing the full details, this will result in the present conveyance being much shorter but of course there is the disadvantage that the earlier conveyance must be read with the present conveyance in order for the latter to make any sense. However, given the need for first registration of title following the conveyance, after which the register replaces the deeds as evidence of title, this is not really a problem.

xiii   Conveyance to co-owners

1   Statement of beneficial interest

If the conveyance is to co-owners, for example a husband and wife, the buyer's solicitor in drafting the conveyance will want to know whether they wish to take the property as beneficial joint tenants or beneficial tenants in common. The legal estate must be held by them as joint tenants. The buyer's solicitor will have to explain to them the differences between the two capacities and the effect of those differences. He will explain that the survivor of beneficial joint tenants takes the whole of the property whereas on the death of a beneficial tenant in common his equitable share passes under his will or intestacy. He may also mention that it is always possible to sever a beneficial joint tenancy to form a beneficial tenancy in common. Normally spouses and co-habitees take as beneficial joint tenants, but if, for example, the property is being purchased by a couple who intend to get married some time after the conveyance, they may wish to hold the property initially, whilst they are still unmarried, as beneficial tenants in common.

The briefest way of stating the beneficial interests in a traditional conveyance is as part of the habendum, which would then read 'to hold unto the buyers as beneficial joint tenants' or '............. as beneficial tenants in common in equal shares'; in a more modern conveyance with no habendum, a clause may read 'the sellers convey [the property] to the buyers as beneficial joint tenants', or there may simply be a separate clause: 'the buyers hold the property as beneficial joint tenants'. There will then be an implied statutory trust of land[5] The alternative is to include a clause declaring an express trust of land. This could be in the form:

> The buyers shall hold the property hereby conveyed upon trust and shall hold the net proceeds of sale and the net rents and profits until sale upon trust for themselves as joint tenants (or … as tenants in common in equal shares).

There seems to be little advantage in including an express declaration, rather than relying on the implied trusts.

The need for the conveyance to state where the equitable interests do lie has been stressed in cases such as *Bernard v Josephs*,[6] *Walker v Hall*[7] and *Rhoden v Joseph*.[8] This is particularly important where the co-owners are not a married couple and there is therefore no power for the court to make an order transferring property on divorce.[9] The court can simply declare what the existing interests are: if the conveyance deals expressly with them this will be conclusive, but otherwise there may need to be a lengthy and expensive action to establish the interests.[10]

If co-owners expressly hold as beneficial joint tenants, this is similarly conclusive of their entitlement on severance as tenants in common in equal shares, whatever their actual contributions to the purchase price.[11]

The buyer's solicitor must carefully advise his clients on co-ownership; failure to do this may amount to negligence. Some firms prudently advise their clients in writing and ask for written confirmation that they have understood the advice.

2   Extension of the powers of the trustees of land

Extension of the powers of the trustees of land is no longer necessary as the Trusts of Land and Powers of Trustees Act 1996, section 6(1) gives trustees of land all the powers of an absolute owner. If desired these powers may be restricted expressly. However for pre-1997 conveyances it was usual to extend trustees powers.

xiv   Imposition of new covenants

Particularly on the sale of part of land the seller owns, the conveyance may contain new covenants entered into by the buyer and possibly by the seller. Again these will have been provided for in the contract where the full wording of the proposed covenants should appear. In Chapter 5 the rules governing the enforceability of covenants and the running of the benefit and the burden were considered; these will

---

5   Law of Property Act 1925,(as amended) ss 34–36.
6   [1982] Ch 391, [1982] 3 All ER 162, CA.
7   [1984] FLR 126, [1984] Fam Law 21, CA.
8   [1990] EGCS 115.
9   It is also important for a married couple; see *Taylor v Warners* [1988] Law Soc Gaz 26, 29 June.
10   See for example *Grant v Edwards* [1986] Ch 638, [1986] 2 All ER 426, CA.
11   *Goodman v Gallant* [1986] Fam 106, [1986] 1 All ER 311, CA; *Turton v Turton* [1988] Ch 542, [1987] 2 All ER 641, CA.

influence the language of the covenant. The proper place for consideration of this is at the time of drafting and approving the contract, when the wording of the covenant is settled. In particular, care should be taken over the wording of the covenant in relation to the annexation of the benefit of the covenant to the whole of the land retained by the seller, and to the continuing liability of the covenantor even after he has disposed of the land affected by the covenant if there is to be a chain of indemnity covenants in the future. The land benefited and burdened by the covenant should be accurately identified.

One situation in which there will inevitably be a large number of new covenants will be on the sale of a new house on a building estate. They may well be separated off into a schedule at the end of the conveyance. In drafting these covenants consideration should have been given to the contract stage to the special position of a building estate under *Elliston v Reacher*[12] and the potential mutual enforceability of the covenants.

xv   Indemnity covenants

We have already seen, in Chapter 5, section 4 vii, that an express indemnity covenant will be necessary if the seller is the original covenanter and on the wording of the original covenant he remains liable, or if the seller gave an indemnity covenant when he bought.

A typical indemnity covenant would read as follows:

> With the object of affording the seller a full and sufficient indemnity in respect of the said covenants but not further or otherwise, the buyer covenants with the seller that he will at all times hereafter perform and observe the said covenants and keep the seller indemnified against all actions, claims, demands and liability in respect thereof so far as the same affect the property hereby conveyed and are still subsisting and capable of being enforced.

As we saw in Chapter 5, section 4 vii, the Standard Conditions[13] specifically provide for the buyer to give an indemnity covenant if appropriate, and for the buyer to covenant with the seller to perform the original covenant. If there are joint buyers the indemnity covenant will be given by them jointly and severally.[14]

If the original covenant does not impose liability on the covenantor after he has disposed of the property, but limits his liability to his period of ownership, there is no need for any indemnity covenant.

xvi   Acknowledgment and undertaking

I   *Terms of acknowledgment and undertaking*

On completion the buyer may not be receiving the title deeds, or at least not all of them. The most likely reason for this is that the deeds relate to other land which the seller is retaining.

The Law of Property Act 1925, section 45(9) provides that the seller is entitled to keep documents of title which relate to any part of land which the seller is retaining, or

---

12   [1908] 2 Ch 665, CA; see ch 5, section 4 vi.
13   SC 4.5.4.
14   SC 1.2.

which are subsisting trust instruments, or which relate to the appointment or discharge of trustees of an existing trust. Thus a personal representative will retain the grant of probate or administration, which will be needed for other purposes in the future. It has been held that a seller is entitled to keep a deed which shows the extinguishment of a right of way over land retained by him,[15] but not a mortgage of both the land sold and a life policy, as the latter is not 'land' within the meaning of section 45(9).[16]

A buyer, though, may need to be able to produce the original deeds in the future. All that he will have in his actual possession will be the abstract or epitome of title which was examined against the originals when it was verified. Although the conveyance to the buyer will lead to first registration, and the Registry will be happy with the epitome and not demand the originals, there may be circumstances where, despite registration of title, reference to the original deed is called for; perhaps to resolve the precise position of a boundary. The buyer will therefore want, in the conveyance, an acknowledgment of his right to the production of the originals. The effect of such an acknowledgment is set out in the Law of Property Act 1925, section 64(4). It gives the buyer a right to production of the documents of title for inspection and for the purpose of any court hearing, and the right to delivery of copies of them. Any costs involved are to be paid by the person requiring production, that is by the buyer. It will be seen that the terms of the acknowledgment do not strictly give the buyer the right to make copies of the documents himself, merely to have copies made and delivered by the person with possession, that is the seller. In addition and complementary to this acknowledgment, the buyer may want an undertaking that the retained documents of title will be kept safe. The terms of such an undertaking are contained in the Law of Property Act 1925, section 64(9) and (10). The person with custody of the documents must keep them 'safe, whole, uncancelled and undefaced unless prevented from so doing by fire or other inevitable accident'. If the deeds are lost or damaged, the buyer will be entitled to damages from the person with custody of them for a breach of the undertaking.

2   The buyer's entitlement

The buyer will want an acknowledgment and undertaking in every case where deeds are retained. Will he get this? Under an open contract, the buyer is entitled to the statutory acknowledgment and undertaking in respect of documents he is not to receive. This will extend not only to previous conveyances, mortgages etc. but also to grants of probate and administration, although not to such documents as old search certificates since these are not documents of title. Nor apparently will it extend to pre-root documents of title even though in normal circumstances the seller would be under a duty to hand them over on completion.

There are further complications for the buyer. Firstly, the statutory acknowledgment (and undertaking) must be given 'to another'. Where a personal representative assents to the vesting of property in himself, he cannot give an acknowledgment in the assent. A subsequent buyer from him should try and obtain an acknowledgment in the conveyance. Secondly, the acknowledgment (and undertaking) must be given by the person with possession of the documents. If the seller's property is in mortgage, and the mortgage is not being discharged but the property sold, being part of the mortgaged property, is being released from the mortgage, the person with possession of the documents is the mortgagee. He is

---

15   *Re Lehmann and Walker's Contract* [1906] 2 Ch 640.
16   *Re Williams and Duchess of Newcastle's Contract* [1897] 2 Ch 144.

therefore the proper person to give the acknowledgment. However, the buyer is not necessarily prejudiced if he fails to obtain an acknowledgment as it appears that a person does have an equitable right to production of the documents necessary to prove his title. A third complication for the buyer is that it is usual for fiduciary owners (that is, mortgagees, personal representatives and trustees) to give only the acknowledgment for production and not the undertaking for safe custody. There seems little authority for this rule but in practice it is well established.

The Standard Conditions provide that the seller is to arrange, at his expense, that in relation to every document of title which the buyer does not receive on completion, the buyer is to have the benefit of (a) a written acknowledgment of his right to its production, and (b) a written undertaking for its safe custody (except while it is held by a mortgagee or by someone in fiduciary capacity).[17] The generality of this provision could cause a couple of problems. Firstly, it is possible to construe the condition as obliging the seller to arrange for an acknowledgment (and, if appropriate, undertaking) not only in relation to documents of title which he is retaining, but also documents of title which have been retained in the past. Thus if there has been a sale of part in the past, and the necessary acknowledgment (and undertaking) was not obtained at that time, the Standard Conditions may oblige the seller now to obtain the acknowledgment (and undertaking). A seller might find it difficult to do this, and a seller's solicitor ought to check the title before drafting the contract to ensure that all necessary acknowledgments and undertakings have been given; if they have not, the seller may wish to clarify his obligation under the Standard Conditions by means of a special condition in the contract.

The other problem arises on a sale of a mortgaged property, where the mortgage is not being discharged. We mentioned earlier that the mortgagee is the appropriate person to give the acknowledgment. A buyer would also want an undertaking but, as we have seen, mortgagees do not give undertakings. Although the seller's obligation under the Standard Conditions to 'arrange' that the buyer is to have the benefit of undertaking may cover the position, the buyer may prefer to have a specific covenant in the conveyance rather than just a contractual condition.

3   Running of the benefit and the burden of the acknowledgment and undertaking

This runs with the land and the acknowledgment and undertaking are enforceable by a buyer and his successors in title (excluding lessees), whether they hold the whole or part of the land. The burden runs with the deeds and thus the person with the custody of the deeds for the time being is bound.

4   Form

The normal wording of the acknowledgment and undertaking is as follows:

> The seller acknowledges the right of the buyer to production of the documents specified in the schedule (the possession of which is retained by the seller) and to delivery of copies of them and undertakes with the buyer for the safe custody of them.

xvii   Certificate of value

Conveyances on sale bear ad valorem stamp duty. This will be examined in more detail in Chapter 15, but it means that the duty payable is proportionate to the value

---

17   SC 4.5.5.

of the property, which in the case of a sale is the purchase price. The basic rate of duty is 1% but there is exemption if the consideration does not exceed £60,000 and if a certificate of value is included in the conveyance. It is the last clause in the conveyance and will normally read as follows:

> It is hereby certified that the transaction hereby effected does not form part of a larger transaction or of a series of transactions in which the amount or value or the aggregate amount or value of the consideration exceeds £60,000.

If the consideration exceeds £60,000 then ad valorem stamp duty is payable on a sliding scale according to the amount of consideration. If the consideration is over £60,000 but does not exceed £500,000 a certificate of value should be included to explain that stamp duty is payable but not at the full rate. If the consideration exceeds £500,000 no certificate of value is required.

Stamp duty is not payable on chattels. Any chattels which are sold with the property should not be made the subject of the conveyance but should be allowed to pass in the normal way by delivery. The consideration stated in the conveyance should be the consideration for the property alone without the chattels. This may result in some saving of stamp duty, particularly if the aggregate price of the property and the chattels is just above the £60,000 limit, and the price of the property alone just below the limit. Any such apportionment of the price between the property and the chattels should be stated in the contract and should be genuine otherwise it would amount to a fraud on the Inland Revenue to whom stamp duty is payable.[18]

xviii   Testimonium

This is the clause which introduces the execution by the parties. For a deed to be executed by individuals, the clause has traditionally read:

> In witness whereof the parties hereto have set their hands to this deed the day and year first before written.

If one of the parties is executing the conveyance under a power of attorney then mention of this will be incorporated into the testimonium. If the conveyance is to be executed by a corporation, the testimonium has traditionally referred to the corporation having 'caused its common seal to be hereto affixed'.

In a shorter more modern form of conveyance the testimonium will probably be omitted altogether.

xix   Schedules

If there are to be any schedules to the conveyance, referred to in the body of the conveyance, these are incorporated after the testimonium but before the execution and attestation. Matters commonly included in schedules are a description of the property, rights of which it has the benefit and to which it is subject, covenants, and lists of documents in respect of which an acknowledgment and undertaking have been given.

---

18   See *Saunders v Edwards* [1987] 2 All ER 651, [1987] 1 WLR 1116, CA.

xx   Execution and attestation

The last part of the deed will be the execution by the parties. An individual must sign in the presence of a witness, who then adds his own signature. Following section 1 of the Law of Property (Miscellaneous Provisions) Act 1989, sealing is no longer necessary. However, the section does provide that for a document to be a deed it must be made clear on its face that the parties intend it to be a deed; the most convenient place to do this is in the execution and attestation clause. In practice the execution and attestation may appear as follows:

Signed and delivered as a deed by   (Signature of party)

in the presence of:–

(signature and address of

witness)

There will be a similar clause for each executing party. If a party is executing under a power of attorney this may be referred to in the attestation clause. A corporation has in the past executed a deed by having its common seal affixed, attested by the signatures of a director and secretary. Following section 130 of the Companies Act 1989, the common seal of a company is not necessary, but the requirement that a document, to be a deed, needs to make it clear on its face that it is intended to be a deed also applies. The actual manner of execution, both by an individual and by a corporation, will be dealt with in detail in Chapter 14.

xxi   The conveyance and the contract

It will be obvious that there are many similarities between the contents of the contract and the conveyance. Indeed, this is to be expected as the contract contains the agreement to buy and sell the property on certain conditions and the conveyance puts this into effect, actually transferring the property. So whereas in the contract there is a description in the particulars, there is a parcels clause in the conveyance. Both will contain details of existing easements and covenants both for the benefit of the property and subject to which it is held. The contract will also contain details of any new easements and covenants to be incorporated in the conveyance.

3   ASSIGNMENT OF LEASE

In the case of unregistered leasehold it is permissible to use either a rule 72 transfer or an assignment, although an assignment is usually used for complex transactions. The form and much of the contents of the assignment of a lease are the same as in the conveyance of the freehold dealt with in the previous section. The differences between the two are mentioned below.

i   Commencement

Obviously the traditional opening words will be 'The assignment is made ....'.

ii   Parties

See section 2 ii, above.

iii Recitals

The function and effect of recitals have been discussed at section 2 iii, above. In respect of the brief statement of the seller's title there will be a difference from the conveyance. There would normally be a recital dealing with the grant of the lease and, as this is the first time that the lease will have been mentioned in the assignment, this will include the date of the lease, the parties, the term, the rent and a description of the property comprised in the lease, the latter probably by reference either to the lease or to a schedule. The recitals will then show how the present seller came to own the leasehold estate. If he is the assignee from the original lessee then that assignment can be recited. If not, then a traditional recital would read:

> By virtue of divers assignments acts and events and ultimately by [the assignment to the seller can then be recited] the said property became and is now vested in the seller for all the unexpired residue of the said term subject to the rent reserved by and the performance and observance of the covenants on the part of the lessee and the conditions contained in the lease but otherwise free from encumbrances.

The initial phrase of this clause is rather over-blown and could be omitted. If the assignment is of an underlease then the grant of the headlease (if known) could be recited as well as the grant of the underlease and the assignment of the underlease to the seller. None of these recitals is of course essential and they will probably be omitted in a modern, short deed. Other recitals, for example on a sale by personal representatives, would be included as mentioned in section 2 iii above. If a licence to assign in respect of the present assignment was necessary then this also can be recited.

iv Testatum

See section 2 iv, above.

v Consideration and receipt clause

See section 2 v, above.

vi Operative words and title guarantee

The operative words of an assignment are 'the seller assigns'. Title guarantee covenants are implied by the use of the various expressions mentioned at section 2 vi, above. As will be seen in Chapter 16, additional covenants for title are implied on a sale of leasehold land, in addition to those implied on a sale of freehold land.[19]

vii Parcels clause

In a way, the question of a description of the property which is being sold is less of a problem in an assignment than in a conveyance. This is because the property that the seller owns is that comprised in the lease and the property will of course be described

---

19   It may be necessary to modify the implied covenants for title to ensure that the seller is not impliedly covenanting that the property is in a good state of repair – see ch 16, section 4 i.

in the lease. Usually all that is necessary is either reference to the description in the lease or to a schedule to the assignment where that description can be reproduced. There may of course have been changes since the grant of the lease – for example if the lease is of a plot of land on which a house has now been built – and the description will then need to be brought up to date.

If the assignment is of only part of the property comprised in the lease, the comments made at section 2 vii, above, apply equally here and a plan will almost certainly be necessary.

viii   Rights for the benefit of the property

The lease will normally have included the grant of rights for the benefit of the property. Again, reference can be made to the lease or to a schedule to the assignment setting out these rights. If the property being sold is only part of the property comprised in the lease, ie there has been an assignment in part *in the past*, then there may be further rights granted in the assignment by which the part was sold off. If, on the other hand, the seller is *now* assigning part of the property comprised in the lease, the question of new rights to be granted in favour of the part sold off will have been considered at the contract stage and the wording of the assignment will follow that of the appropriate contractual provision. The rule in *Wheeldon v Burrows*[20] applies to a contract for sale of leasehold property and an assignment in the same way that it applies to freehold land; similarly section 62 of the Law of Property Act 1925 also applies to the assignment of a lease.

ix   Exceptions and reservations

The rights adversely affecting the property will again be found in the lease or in an assignment of part if this has occurred. If the present assignment is an assignment of part then any new reservations will be dealt with in the contract and will then be incorporated in the assignment.

x   Habendum

As the estate being sold is leasehold, a traditional habendum will read 'to hold unto the buyer for all the residue now unexpired of the term created by the lease'. Even the shortest assignment will make it clear that the property is leasehold, and will give details of the lease, in particular the term of the lease.

xi   Statement of existing encumbrances

The lease will impose an obligation to pay rent, to perform covenants and possibly to comply with other conditions. There will be a statement in the assignment that the property is subject to the rent payable under the lease and to the covenants and other conditions contained in the lease. If there has been an assignment in the past of part on which fresh covenants have been imposed then these too will be mentioned.

20   (1879) 12 Ch D 31, CA.

xii   Assignment to co-owners

See section 2 xiii, above.

xiii   Imposition of new covenants

On an assignment of part of the property comprised in the lease the seller may wish to impose new covenants, in just the same way as he may wish to do so on a sale of part of freehold land. There should be a provision in the contract stating what new covenants will be imposed. Not being covenants between lessor and lessee, there will be the usual problem over the enforceability of positive covenants; it is perhaps more likely that sub-leases of part are granted (under which the burden of positive covenants will run) than assignments of part.

xiv   Indemnity covenants

Leases created before 1 January 1996

The Law of Property Act 1925, section 77(1)(c) provides that on an assignment for valuable consideration of a lease, the assignee (buyer) impliedly covenants that in the future he will pay the rent and perform and observe all the covenants (positive or restrictive) and other conditions in the lease. He also covenants to indemnify the seller in respect of non-payment of rent or breach of any of the covenants or conditions. This is different from the position under a conveyance of the freehold where although the right to an indemnity covenant may be implied in the contract an express covenant must still be inserted in the conveyance. Section 77(1)(d) of the Act contains a similar provision in relation to the assignment for value of part of the property comprised in the lease.[1] The assignee impliedly covenants to pay an apportioned rent and to observe and perform the covenants in the lease so far as they affect his part; he also gives a covenant for indemnity. The seller, who is retaining part, also gives an implied covenant to pay the balance of the rent, to observe and perform the covenants and conditions and for indemnity.

The assignee may of course be directly liable to the lessor for breach of covenant. Provided the covenants touch and concern the land the burden of them will run with the leasehold interest under the doctrine of privity of estate. The assignee might also have been required to enter a direct deed of covenant with the lessor, to perform the covenants in the lease.

Leases created on or after 1 January 1996

The Landlord and Tenant (Covenants) Act 1995 abolished the section 77 indemnity and instead on a lawful assignment the assignor is fully released from his obligations under the lease (section 14 of the Landlord and Tenant (Covenants) Act 1995), and would therefore not require an indemnity provision. He may however be required under certain circumstances outlined in section 16 of the 1995 Act to enter into an Authorised Guarantee Agreement for the performance of the covenants by the assignee, and may require an indemnity for this.

---

1   This applies when the lessor's consent has not been obtained to the apportionment of the rent. If it has, there is an implied covenant under s 77(1)(c) relating to the part assigned.

xv **Acknowledgment and undertaking, certificate of value, testimonium, schedules, execution and attestation**

See sections 2 xvi–xx, above.

4 TRANSFER OF REGISTERED LAND

The deed necessary on the sale of land title to which is registered, freehold or leasehold, is called a transfer. Its form is prescribed by the Land Registration Rules 1925 as amended; it is form TR1 for a transfer of the whole of the land comprised in a title and form TP1 for a transfer of part.

i Stamp duty

If stamp duty is payable the Inland Revenue Stamp Office will impress the appropriate stamps in this box following completion. If no stamp duty is payable or it is payable at less than the full rate of 3.5% then one of the two certificates will need to be completed.

ii The title number

The title number of the property should be inserted in this box if the land is already registered, if not it should be left blank.

iii The property description

The property description should contain the full address of the property. If the property is leasehold, the clause may continue 'for the residue of the term granted by the registered lease'. That is all that is needed. There is no need to mention existing easements either benefiting the property nor subject to which the property is held, or existing covenants. If it is a sale of part then reference should be made to a plan with the property 'more particularly delineated' on the plan edged in red, and also refer to the retained land which is usually edged in blue.

iv Date

This should be left blank until completion.

v Transferor

The seller's full name should be filled in.

vi & vii Transferee's name and address

There is a space for the insertion of the buyer's name(s) and address. It is vital that the accurate name(s) and address is given as any error may be reproduced in the Proprietorship Register causing difficulties in the future. The address should be that at which the buyer can be contacted following completion of his purchase; this will normally be the address of the property he is buying.

viii   Consideration and receipt clause

The amount of the consideration (excluding any amount paid for chattels) should be filled in, in figures and words. This clause is sufficient to comply with the requirements of the Stamp Act 1891 discussed above.

ix   Title Guarantee

Under the Law of Property (Miscellaneous Provisions) Act 1994 the seller needs to give a title guarantee. The wording for this should be taken from the contract.

x   Declaration of Trust

If the transfer is to joint proprietors, for example a husband and wife, then the comments made in section 2 xiii above are equally applicable. There must at least be a statement of the beneficial interest. The Land Registry are really only interested in whether the survivor of joint proprietors can give a valid receipt for capital money. If the proprietors are beneficial joint tenants then the survivor can give a valid receipt and there is no need for a restriction on the register. If they are beneficial tenants in common then the survivor cannot give a valid receipt, as a sole trustee, and a restriction will be entered in the Proprietorship Register preventing the survivor from dealing with the property; he would have to appoint another trustee.[2]

xi   Additional provisions

This box gives space for definitions not covered elsewhere, eg retained land, new covenants, easements, and agreements and declarations. Again the wording of these clauses should be taken from the contract. On a sale of part, the seller may be granting or reserving easements or imposing new covenants for exactly the same reasons as on a conveyance or assignment of unregistered land. Form CS can be used as a continuation sheet if required, and attached to the transfer.

The same considerations apply as have been mentioned already in relation to unregistered land. For example, the rule in *Wheeldon v Burrows*[3] and the Law of Property Act 1925, section 62 are applicable, as is the problem of enforceability of positive covenants. New restrictive covenants will be protected by the entry of a notice in the Charges Register of the title to the part affected.

xii   Indemnity covenants

The position on the sale of freehold registered land where the seller will remain liable on covenants is similar to the position on the sale of freehold unregistered land. The seller will want an indemnity covenant in the transfer and as we have

2   *Huntingford v Hobbs* [1993] 1 FCR 45, [1993] 1 FLR 736, CA.
3   (1879) 12 Ch D 31, CA.

seen the Standard Conditions give him this right. The complicating factor in the case of registered land is that the covenant is contained in the transfer which is sent to the District Land Registry on registration but which as we have mentioned does not form part of the register. The indemnity covenant is by its very nature a positive covenant and as a rule positive covenants are not noted on the register. There is a danger that the registered proprietor who gave an indemnity covenant when he purchased may forget that he has done so and his solicitor may then fail to require an indemnity covenant when the registered proprietor himself eventually sells the property. The problem does not arise in the case of an indemnity covenant given on a conveyance giving rise to first registration, because it is perfectly possible for the solicitor to look back at the pre-registration deeds when the first registered proprietor comes to sell, to see that an indemnity covenant was given. In this situation there will be no mention of the covenant in the register; the solicitor for a first registered proprietor who is selling should remember to check whether an indemnity covenant is needed.

In respect of a transfer of leasehold land, ie the assignment of a registered leasehold title, there is an implied covenant by the transferee to perform the covenants in the lease and indemnify the transferor.[4] On the sale of part of the land comprised in the lease then both the transferee and the transferor give a similar implied covenant, in relation to their respective parts.[5] The covenants by the transferor are implied whether or not the transfer is for valuable consideration and whether or not he transfers with full title guarantee.

xiii   Acknowledgment and undertaking

Because the register is the evidence of title there is normally no need to include an acknowledgment or undertaking in respect of previous documents, certainly if the title is absolute. However, an acknowledgment (and undertaking) may be desirable in some circumstances, for example on the transfer of part of leasehold property, in respect of the lease; on the transfer of part of a possessory title, in respect of any retained pre-registration documents of title; and possibly even on a transfer by personal representatives who have been registered as registered proprietors in the place of the deceased, in respect of the grant of probate or administration.[6]

xiv   Testimonium

The prescribed forms of transfer contain no testimonium.

xv   Execution and attestation

Execution of a transfer is essentially the same as execution of a conveyance or an assignment. The position is governed by the Land Registration (Execution) Rules 1990, considered in Chapter 14. In addition, if the transfer incorporates a plan, then the plan must be signed by the transferor personally and also by the transferee or his solicitor on his behalf.

---

4   Land Registration Act 1925, s 24(1)(b).
5   Ibid, s 24(2).
6   It will need to be produced on the application for registration, although the Registry will accept a certified photocopy.

5   OTHER DEEDS

i   Transfer under rule 72

Rule 72 of the Land Registration Rules 1925 provides that a person having the right to apply for registration as first proprietor, but who is not already registered as proprietor, may deal with a title as if he were the registered proprietor, eg may use a form of transfer rather than conveyance or assignment. As all sales of freehold, and assignments on sale of leaseholds with over 21 years left to run, will give rise to first registration, the deed can be in the form of a transfer rather than a conveyance or assignment.

ii   Deed of gift

If the property is being given away rather than sold, the appropriate deed will still be a conveyance, assignment or transfer, which will be in the same form as on a sale.

iii   Assent

An assent is the document which a personal representative will normally use to vest the property in the beneficiary entitled to it under the will or intestacy. In the case of unregistered land, the assent will have the same broad structure as the conveyance or assignment; for registered land, the form of assent is prescribed by the Land Registration Rules 1997 form AS1. The operative word is of course 'assent'. An assent need not be a deed unless it contains covenants or an agreement or declaration. Recitals are not normally included but there would usually be an acknowledgment of the right of the assentee to production of the grant of probate or administration unless the personal representative is assenting to the vesting of the property in himself.

iv Mortgages

We mentioned in the earlier part of this chapter that on a conveyance or assignment of part of mortgaged property, if the mortgage is not being discharged, the mortgagee may join in the deed to release the part sold from the mortgage. This procedure is inappropriate on a transfer of part of mortgaged registered land. The correct procedure is for the mortgagee to provide a form of discharge, Form DS3, which relates just to the part to be released from the mortgage.[7]

6   PROCEDURE

Although it is the task of the buyer's solicitor to draft the deed, the contract might make quite specific provision about the form and contents of the deed. This will often happen on the sale of a house on a new building estate where there may be a standard form of conveyance, assignment or transfer, containing details of new easements and covenants, which is referred to in the contract. The appropriate time for agreeing alterations to this form is therefore before exchange of contracts.

---

7   See further in ch 13, below.

Having drafted the deed, the buyer's solicitor sends it, normally in duplicate, to the seller's solicitor for approval. Once approved, the deed, as amended if necessary, will be 'engrossed' by the buyer's solicitor, that is to say a final copy of it is prepared normally on thick, good quality paper (the paper quality must be at least 100gsm as required by the Land Registry). Any new plan will be bound up with the deed. Standard Condition 4.1.2 provides a timetable for the preparation of the deed. The buyer is to send the seller a draft deed at least twelve working days before the completion date. The seller is then to approve or revise the draft deed and either return it within four working days after the delivery of the draft or retain it for use as the actual deed. If the draft is returned, the buyer is to send an engrossment to the seller at least five working days before the completion date. Like the equivalent timetable in condition 4.1.1 for investigating title, the time limits are based on a completion date no earlier than fifteen working days after exchange of contracts. For an earlier completion date, the time limits are reduced pro rata under condition 4.1.4 in the same way as the time limits for investigating title are reduced; see Chapter 10, section 23 ii. As with the time limits for investigating title, there may be difficulties reconciling this timetable with the deemed delivery times in Standard Condition 1.3.6. The Standard Conditions specifically provide that the buyer shall not be deemed to have waived his right to raise or maintain requisitions by delivering the draft or engrossment.[8]

Under the TransAction the buyer's solicitor sends the draft deed to the seller's solicitor as soon as possible after exchange and in any case within the time limits under the Standard Conditions. The seller's solicitor returns the draft deed approved as soon as possible after receipt (and again within the Standard Conditions time limit) and the buyer's solicitor engrosses the approved draft and sends it to the seller's solicitor within the Standard Conditions time limit and in time to enable the seller to sign it before completion without suffering inconvenience.

8   SC 4.5.1.

13 Mortgages

1   REDEMPTION OF THE SELLER'S MORTGAGE(S)

If the property which the seller is selling is subject to a mortgage or mortgages then it will not be sold subject to the mortgages but they will be redeemed on or before completion of the sale. In practice, the proceeds of sale will be used to pay off the mortgages; the money will be paid to the mortgagees immediately after completion and the buyer will be given, on completion, an undertaking by the seller's solicitor that the mortgages will be so redeemed. This procedure is discussed in more detail in the next chapter. In many cases the first mortgagee, often a building society or a bank, will already have provided the seller's solicitor with the deeds, or Charge Certificate in respect of registered land, on an undertaking given by the seller's solicitors. The mortgage can then be redeemed after the completion by remitting the sum due on the mortgage to the mortgagee who will return the receipted mortgage deed (or Form DS1 or notification of END for registered land),[1] which can then be forwarded to the buyer's solicitor. The buyer's solicitor will already have been given the deeds (or Charge Certificate) on completion. The same procedure is adopted in relation to any second mortgages; the money due being sent off and the receipted deed (or in the case of registered land Form DS1 or notification of END and the further Charge Certificate if not already to hand) will be returned and then forwarded to the buyer's solicitor. If the first mortgagee has *not* released the deeds (or Charge Certificate) to the seller's solicitor then as the buyer's solicitors will want to receive the deeds (or Charge Certificate) on completion, it may be necessary to complete at the office of the solicitor for the first mortgagee. Again, this procedure will be discussed in more detail in the next chapter.

The reason that not only first mortgages but also any second mortgages must be paid off and discharged is because, assuming they are protected in the appropriate way, they will otherwise be binding on the buyer. In addition in the case of unregistered land the first mortgagee might otherwise be failing in its duty if it released the deeds to the mortgagor (the seller), who of course hands them on to the buyers; if there are any second mortgages in existence then the deeds ought to be handed to the second mortgagee or if there are more than one, the one with best claim to priority.[2] In fact the first mortgagee is only obliged to hand the deeds to the second mortgagee in

---

1   See ch 10, section 13 above.
2   Priority of second mortgages is in order of registration as a land charge. See further in section 4 ii, below.

these circumstances if it has actual notice of the existence of the second mortgage. In practice the seller's solicitors, who are acting as the mortgagee's solicitors, will have made enquiries of the seller at the start of the transaction and might do a land charge search against the seller to discover whether any second mortgages have been registered as land charges. This search may be done before exchange of contracts to check that the seller has not forgotten to tell his solicitor about any second mortgages and as part of the general investigation of title. Failing that, then assuming that the buyer's solicitor does a land charges search against the seller, as he should, this will reveal the existence of any second mortgages registered as land charges and the seller's solicitor will very soon be made aware of their existence.

2   THE BUYER'S NEW MORTGAGE

There is a general rule that a solicitor cannot normally act for both parties in a conveyancing transaction.[3] The reason is obvious: the likelihood of a conflict of interest between the parties. Nevertheless, it is quite normal in domestic conveyancing for the solicitor for the buyer also to act for the buyer's mortgagee, normally a building society or a bank, on the mortgage being entered into by the buyer to raise finance for the purchase. To understand why this is so, the nature of a mortgage must first be appreciated.

When property is mortgaged, it is really very similar to the property being sold. On a sale, the seller sells the property to the buyer. The buyer acquires the property and in return gives the seller the purchase price. The buyer is obviously concerned to find out as much as he can about the property and to establish that title to the property is good, as otherwise it would not be worth what he is paying. On the mortgage, the mortgagor mortgages the property to the mortgagee. The mortgagee thus acquires not the property but a mortgage over it, including a number of rights perhaps the most important of which is a power of sale of the property. The mortgagor receives not the sale price but the mortgage advance. The advance is in due course paid off and the mortgage discharged. However, the mortgagee is concerned to find out as much as possible about the property and to establish that the title to the property is good, because it represents the security for the loan and if the title is defective, the property may not be worth the amount lent; if the mortgagor defaults in paying off the mortgage and the property is sold, the amount recovered may not be sufficient to pay off the debt. There is therefore an identity of interest between the buyer buying the property and the mortgagee to whom the buyer is mortgaging the property. Both are concerned to establish exactly what the property is and that the seller's title to it is a good one. This is why there is nothing untoward in the buyer's solicitor acting for the building society or bank to whom the property is being mortgaged, as well as for the buyer. In fact, the solicitor will commonly have three roles. He will be acting for the buyer on the purchase, for the buyer on the mortgage and also for the building society or bank on the mortgage.

Over the past few years, however, the demands mortgagees have made on solicitors acting for both them and the lenders have become more stringent, partly because of the volume of mortgage fraud in the 1980s and 1990s, often involving dishonest conveyancers. Since then, lender's instructions as to matters such as confirmation of identity, variations in the purchase price and so on have become very precise,

---

3   Solicitors Practice Rules 1990, r 6.

culminating in the recent introduction of the Council for Mortgage Lender's Handbook.[4] This handbook, endorsed by many of the major lenders, sets out standard mortgage instructions.

The CML handbook was designed to tie in with the introduction, on 1 October 1999, of a new rule 6(3) of the Solicitors' Practice Rules 1990. The new rule sets out in detail the circumstances in which the solicitor can act for both lender and borrower. Under the rule, joint representation is only permitted if the mortgage is a 'standard' mortgage (defined in note (1) to the rule as a mortgage on standard terms, provided by an institutional lender in the normal course of its activities), and there is no conflict of interest between the parties, and the lender's mortgage instructions i) do not extend beyond those matters set out in paragraph 6(3)(c) and (e) of the rule and ii) do not require a different certificate of title to that provided for in paragraph (3)(d). The requirements which the lender can impose under paragraph 6(3)(c) are fairly extensive, and include; checking the identity of the borrower (including keeping copies of identity documents),[5] ensuring that the seller's solicitors are bona fide, giving details of the purchase price and how it is to be funded, asking the borrower to check and confirm details relating to other occupiers of the property and obtaining consents, as specified by the lender, and retaining the file on the matter for at least six years.[6]

Nevertheless it will not be in every case that the buyer's solicitor also acts for the mortgagee. Certain mortgagees will want their own solicitors to act. This does mean that there will be a certain amount of duplication of work. The mortgagee's solicitor will want to investigate the property in the same manner as the buyer's solicitor. The buyer's solicitor will therefore have to supply the mortgagee's solicitor with copies of the buyer's pre-contract searches and enquiries, the abstract or epitome of title or office copies, copies of the buyer's requisitions and the seller's replies to them, copies of the pre-completion searches made for the buyer and any other relevant information. It is clearly more convenient and more cost-effective for the buyer's solicitor to do the work for two clients, the buyer and the mortgagee. In the rest of this chapter we shall assume that this is indeed the position. However, the buyer's solicitor must not lose sight of the fact that he is acting for two clients and that he must take instructions from them both. For example, if the buyer is buying a leasehold property the mortgagee may insist that the superior title is also deduced, whereas the buyer might be resigned to not seeing any of the superior title. Similarly if the property is shown to be affected by restrictive covenants but their exact nature is unknown, the buyer may be quite happy to accept the risk whereas the mortgagee may insist at least on some sort of insurance and might even refuse to go ahead with making the advance. If a conflict of interest should arise between the buyer and the mortgagee, the solicitor will have to cease to act for one or both.[7]

The various types of mortgage and the institutions which offer them have been discussed in Chapter 8. In domestic conveyancing, the mortgagee will commonly be either a building society or a bank. The buyer will have had to pay an inspection fee on submitting his application for the mortgage in order for the mortgagee to have the property surveyed and valued. If his application is successful, the buyer will

---

4   Available free of charge on the Internet; www.cml.org.uk.
5   It is vital that the solicitor ensures he has the authority of all his clients; *Penn v Bristol and West Building Society* [1997] 3 All ER 470, [1997] 1 WLR 1356; and informs the lender of any unusual circumstances: *Bristol and West Building Society v Fancy and Jackson (a firm)* [1997] 4 All ER 582.
6   For a detailed discussion on the rule, see Law Society's Gazette, 98/21 24 May 2001.
7   Ibid, r 1.

in due course receive a formal written offer of mortgage. Before exchange of contracts, the buyer's solicitor should ensure not only that the mortgage offer has been accepted and that the advance will be available by the completion date but that the buyer will be able to comply with any conditions subject to which the offer of mortgage is made. If the buyer wants to exchange contracts on his purchase before an offer of mortgage has been received, he is running the risk of not having the funds available when he needs them on completion. In such circumstances, if the buyer insists on proceeding, he should be advised to exchange contracts conditional on receipt of a mortgage offer for an amount satisfactory to him and with conditions acceptable to him. Of course, the seller may not be willing to accept such an uncertain commitment!

i   Mortgage offer

There are a number of matters which may be the subject of conditions in the mortgage offer. Further details are given in Chapter 8.

1   Mortgage guarantee premium

If the amount being lent is not much less than the value of the property, the mortgagee will be concerned lest the value of the property should fall below the amount owing. If that happened and the mortgagee sold the property under its power of sale, it would not recover the amount owing and would be left with an unsecured debt for the balance. To avoid this difficulty mortgagees will insure the excess of the loan above a certain percentage of the value of the property. There is a single premium payable for this insurance policy. It is payable by the borrower (the buyer) and is sometimes added on to the amount of the loan to avoid the borrowing having to find it from his own savings. Such policies have been the subject of controversy in recent years as they are clearly of no benefit to the borrower but must be paid for by him. In addition, some lenders have attempted to take action against the borrower for any shortfall between the amount paid out by the insurance company and the amount owed to the lender. For these reasons, mortgage guarantee policies are no longer required by some lenders.

2   Endowment policy

If the mortgage is an endowment mortgage, that is a mortgage linked to a life assurance policy, it will be a condition of the mortgage offer that a policy in the appropriate form is issued and assigned to the mortgagee. Endowment mortgages have become less popular in recent years, as end of term sum paid is not always as high as the borrower would wish, and may even be insufficient to pay off the mortgage.

One advantage of an endowment mortgage is that funds are generated to pay off the mortgage on the death of the person whose life is insured. In the case of a married couple with young children where only one spouse is earning, the other spouse would not be left saddled with the mortgage debt on the death of the earning spouse if that spouse's life was insured. Normally both lives would be insured. This effect can also be achieved in relation to a straightforward repayment mortgage by a mortgage protection policy. For a relatively modest premium, the insurance company will pay off the outstanding balance of the mortgage at the time of death of the life insured. The premium is modest because although the chance of death increases with age, the amount owing on the mortgage is at the same time decreasing.

3   *Retentions*

The circumstances in which the mortgagee may wish to make a retention from the advance, and the effect on the buyer, are discussed in Chapter 8, section 1 iii, above.

ii   Instructions to solicitors

Once the mortgage offer has been accepted by the buyer, the solicitor will receive a set of instructions from the mortgagee, normally in a standard form. These should be perused carefully; they may contain, for example, an instruction that a leasehold title must either be absolute (if registered) or accompanied by an abstract or epitome of the superior title.

iii   Investigation of title

The examination of the evidence of title, be it an abstract, an epitome or office copy entries, is being done both for the buyer and the mortgagee. Instructions on any defect in title should therefore be obtained from both clients.

1   *Particular problems*

As the buyer can only mortgage what he has, the mortgagee will be particularly concerned to establish what if any rights affecting the property are being created as a result of the purchase. The most obvious examples of this are new easements and covenants created in the purchase deed when the seller is selling part of what he owns.

If the property mortgaged is leasehold, and the lease contains a forfeiture clause, this may be of concern to the mortgagee. The position is discussed in Chapter 17 where the lessor's remedy of forfeiture is considered.

2   *Searches*

The part of the process of investigation of title that involves searches is again being done for both the buyer and the mortgagee. In the case of unregistered land the mortgagee will have the benefit of the land charges searches obtained for the buyer. An additional search must be made for the mortgagee; as on completion the buyer is becoming owner of the legal estate and immediately mortgaging it, the mortgagee will require a land charges search against the buyer. In particular this will reveal any bankruptcy entries against the buyer; if the buyer were shown to be bankrupt then the mortgagee would not want to proceed with the mortgage. This, then, is a search which the solicitor is doing for his mortgagee client rather than for the buyer.

In the case of registered land, the normal search effected for the buyer is the official search at the District Land Registry which updates the office copy entries with any subsequent entries made on the register. If this search is done for the buyer then the mortgagee gets no protection from it. If on the other hand the search is done for the mortgagee, the search certificate also protects the buyer. If the same solicitor is acting for both the buyer and the mortgagee only one search need be done, but the application form should state that it is being done for the mortgagee.

Registrations in the Land Charges Registry are normally irrelevant when dealing with registered land as we have already seen in Chapter 11. However, most mortgagees adopt the practice of asking the solicitor to obtain for them a bankruptcy only search against the buyer in the Land Charges Register even though the title being mortgaged is registered. This is a search not in the register of land charges classes A–F but in the register of pending actions and writs and orders. It will thus reveal bankruptcy petitions and orders. The search can be made by post or fax on an official form, or by telephone or Land Registry Direct. As mentioned above, the mortgagee will not wish to proceed with a mortgage to someone who is bankrupt.

In practice it makes a lot of sense to do a bankruptcy search, or land charges search against a purchaser, before exchange of contracts. If an entry is revealed, the transaction clearly cannot proceed as planned.

The mortgagee will also be interested in the results of the pre-exchange searches such as the enquiries of the seller (or under the TransAction Protocol, the seller's property information form) and the local search and enquiries of the Local Authority. To take an example, if the property is to lose some of a garden for a road widening scheme then not only might this affect the buyer's decision to buy but it will also affect the mortgagee's decision about the size of the loan or indeed even whether any loan will be made at all. If a long time has passed since the local search and local authority enquiries were made before exchange of contracts, it might be necessary to repeat them for the mortgagee.

iv Mortgage deed

The deed by which the property is mortgaged will normally be in a standard form supplied by the mortgagee. The buyer has little choice but to agree to the terms of the deed if he wants a mortgage. Nevertheless it is important that the terms be explained to the buyer. The following is a summary of the terms most likely to be found in a standard mortgage deed.

I Nature of the deed

The structure of a mortgage is rather complex and indeed artificial, due largely to the historical evolution of mortgages. Originally, the loan would have to be repaid on the date stated in the mortgage deed, a date thus called 'the legal date for redemption' of the mortgage. If payment was not made on that day, the mortgagee could foreclose, that is he could keep the property which was mortgaged. In the case of payment being only slightly late, this was clearly inequitable, particularly where the property was worth considerably more than the amount of the loan. Equity thus stepped in to alleviate the legal position and provided that after the legal date for redemption there would still be an (equitable) right to redeem the mortgage. This is still the position. The mortgage deed will name a legal date for redemption commonly only a month or so after the date of the mortgage. The significance of this date is that once it has passed many of the mortgagee's powers arise, including the power of sale. In practice of course the mortgage will be intended to run over a period of 15, 20 or 25 years, certainly in domestic conveyancing. Assuming a constant rate of interest over that time, a monthly repayment figure can be inserted in the deed which, if paid over that period, will repay both the principal and interest over that period. In the case of an endowment mortgage when only payments of interest are made, the principal being repaid by the amount generated by a life insurance policy, the payment figure in the deed may nevertheless normally still be the figure which would be inserted in the normal repayment mortgage (including repayments of the principal) rather than a lower figure based purely on payment of interest. This protects the mortgagee against the life policy lapsing for non-payment of the premiums. The mortgagee will of course agree to accept the lower figure so long as premium payments on the policy are kept up.

In practice most domestic mortgages do not run for the full term of years; the property is sold and the mortgage redeemed out of the proceeds of sale. This could happen at any time but some mortgages might require the buyer to give a certain period of notice of redemption or to pay monthly repayments in lieu of such notice. Borrowers should be particularly careful of special deals providing for a fixed or discounted rate of interest for all or part of the mortgage term, where they may be severe penalties for repaying the mortgage within the fixed or discounted period of for a specified period thereafter.

2   Interest rate

The initial interest rate will be stated in the deed although it will normally be variable. The repayments necessary to repay the mortgage over the initially agreed term are therefore also variable.

3   Exercise of mortgagee's powers

The main power of the mortgagee is its power of sale of the mortgaged property. A statutory power of sale arises on the legal date for redemption but only becomes exercisable as against the mortgagor on default by the mortgagor. The circumstances in which the statutory power becomes exercisable are set out in the Law of Property Act 1925, section 103.[8] The mortgage deed may add to the circumstances in which the power becomes exercisable; for example many mortgage deeds make the power exercisable in the event of the mortgagor's bankruptcy or other types of insolvency.

4   Rights to grant tenancies

The mortgagor has a statutory power to grant certain leases of the mortgaged property.[9] The mortgagee when exercising its power of sale may have great difficulty in finding a buyer for tenanted property and so most mortgage deeds will exclude the mortgagor's power of leasing and provide that no leases or tenancies of the property are to be granted by the mortgagor without the mortgagee's consent.

5   Insurance

It is clearly in the interests of the mortgagee to see that the property which is security for the loan is adequately insured. To this end the mortgage deed may provide that the mortgagee has power to effect insurance with the premiums being recoverable from the mortgagor. A mortgagee does have a statutory power to insure but this is limited and the premium is only recoverable from the mortgagor in the sense that it is added to the amount owing on the loan.[10]   In practice, the mortgagor will normally be happy for the borrower to make his own arrangements for insurance provided that the lender has sight of the policy and can have its own interest noted on the policy if required.

v   Endowment mortgage – life policy

An endowment mortgage involves the assignment of a life insurance policy to the mortgagee. There will often be a deed of assignment of the policy although the policy

---

8   See further ch 10, section 6.
9   Law of Property Act 1925, s 99.
10   Law of Property Act 1925, s 101(1)(ii).

may simply be deposited with the mortgagee. The provisions of the deed may tie it in to the mortgage deed, for example allowing the mortgagee to surrender the policy should its power of sale be exercised in respect of the mortgaged property. The solicitor in his role of acting for the mortgagee should examine the title to the policy although in fact a new policy is normally issued. Depending on who is making the arrangements for the policy, the solicitor may need to enquire whether the policy is yet in force as completion approaches, and may need to advise the buyer of his position if he completes without the policy, even if the mortgagee is unconcerned. However, it appears that the solicitor is probably not liable if he fails to ensure that the policy is in force and the buyer/borrower then dies uninsured, as the borrower will have suffered no loss.[11]

If the policy is already in existence, the solicitor would need to enquire of the insurance company to check that they had not been given notice of any prior assignment of the policy, which would then mean that the policy could not be assigned to the mortgagee.

vi   Report on title

Before completion the solicitor will report anything untoward in the title to the mortgagee and will otherwise state that the title is in order. This is commonly done on a standard form report on title supplied by the mortgagee which may incorporate a request for the cheque for the mortgage advance in readiness for completion. Under rule 6(3) of the Solicitors Practice Rules there is a compulsory report on title form for all standard mortgages of residential property. Solicitors are permitted to use a 'short form' report which incorporates the full form by reference. Even where a short form is used, there are certain details which must still be included, in a specified order.[12]

There is one particular point on the title which may concern the solicitor. Dealing firstly with registered land, it has already been pointed out that the rights of an occupier of the land are overriding interests.[13] The difficulties caused to the buyer have already been examined in Chapter 11. The typical problem would be where the property is in the sole name of the seller, whose spouse is in occupation and has an equitable interest. If the spouse does not vacate the property, the buyer is bound by the equitable interest. On the same theme, there are potential difficulties for the buyer's mortgagee. There is a danger that, if there is someone in occupation of the property with an equitable interest at the time of the mortgage, the mortgagee may be bound by the equitable interest and thus be unable to sell the property free from it should it wish to exercise a power of sale. Will someone who moves in on completion with the buyer/mortgagor have an overriding interest against the mortgagee? The position is illustrated by two House of Lords cases. In *Lloyds Bank plc v Rosset*[14] a married couple bought a house which needed substantial building work doing on it. The house was to be in the husband's sole name. The wife was not making a direct financial contribution to the purchase price; money given to the husband by the trustees of a family trust was used in the purchase, although it was the common intention of husband and wife that the renovation of the house would be a

11 *Lynne v Gordon Doctors and Walton* (1991) 135 Sol Jo LB 29, not following *McLellan v Fletcher* [1987] NLJ Rep 593.
12 See note iii to r 6(3), set out in The Guide to the Professional Conduct of Solicitors 1999.
13 Land Registration Act 1925, s 70(1)(g).
14 [1991] 1 AC 107, [1990] 1 All ER 1111, HL.

joint venture after which it was to be the family home. The sellers, unusually, allowed the buyers access to the property prior to completion. Builders started work on the property and the wife was present at the property nearly every day, supervising the work and doing some redecorating. The husband, unknown to his wife, took out a loan from Lloyds Bank in order to finance the purchase and renovation work; that loan was protected by mortgage in the normal way on completion of the purchase. Soon after completion, the marriage broke down, the husband defaulted on the mortgage repayments and the bank sought possession. The wife claimed to have an equitable interest in the property and claimed to have been in occupation within the scope of section 70(1)(g) prior to and at the time of completion of the mortgage (which was completed in the normal way at the same time as completion of the purchase). However, the wife was unsuccessful, principally since the House of Lords decided that on the facts she did not have any equitable interest in the property at the time of completion. Any question of whether she had an overriding interest under section 70(1)(g) therefore did not arise.

The second case concerned a mother and son rather than husband and wife. In *Abbey National Building Society v Cann,*[15] a house was bought and registered in the name of the son with the aid of a mortgage from the Building Society. It was accepted that the mother had an equitable interest in the property by virtue of what was in effect a financial contribution. In this case then, it having been accepted that the mother did have an equitable interest, it was crucially important to decide whether the mother was in occupation within the scope of section 70(1)(g). If she was, then she would have an overriding interest which would be binding on the Building Society. We have already seen in Chapter 11, section 2 iii, that the traditional view was always that the effective date when someone must be in occupation to have an overriding interest is the date of completion. Was the mother in occupation at the date of completion of the mortgage, which had been completed in the usual way on the same date as completion of the purchase? The evidence was that, although she did not move into the property straight away, her furniture started being moved into the property about half an hour prior to the actual completion on the completion day. However, the House of Lords decided that she did not have an overriding interest. Although her furniture was being moved into the property half an hour before actual completion, a person who is in the course of moving furniture into a property is not yet in occupation for the purposes of section 70(1)(g). It seems that even if she had been present herself she would not have had an overriding interest against the Building Society. Where a purchase is being financed by a mortgage and completion of purchase and mortgage take place on the same day, as is normal practice, completion of the mortgage and purchase will be regarded as simultaneous. The mother's equitable interest in *Cann* could not come into existence until completion of the purchase, whereby the son acquired a legal estate, and therefore at the time of completion of the mortgage, simultaneous with the purchase, the mother would not have had an equitable interest and therefore clearly could not have an overriding interest. This case had the interesting effect of limiting greatly the number of people who could claim to have a right under section 70(1)(g), and in particular to exclude situations where a property was purchased rather than re-mortgaged, as a claimant would never be in occupation when completion took place – at the point when the purchase money is handed over, the claimant will probably still be helping to load the removal van!

15   [1991] 1 AC 56, [1990] 1 All ER 1085, HL.

Despite the *Cann* decision, a mortgagee will probably act cautiously. The buyer will probably be asked whether anyone will be in possession of the property after completion apart from the buyer or buyers themselves. Anyone – including not only spouses or other relatives but co-habitees and others – who may have an interest in the property can then be approached and asked to postpone their interest to the mortgage, signing a declaration or consent form confirming this or even joining in the mortgage deed. This practice does have its problems. One is relying on the buyer to be straightforward in disclosing who will be in occupation of the property. Even if the buyer does disclose the existence of such persons, it may place the solicitor in an awkward position. He is acting for the mortgagee and the buyer, and he must now obtain a declaration from, say, the buyer's wife postponing her interest to that of the mortgagee. On the face of it, this is a step which is detrimental to the interests of the wife, although if she refused to postpone her interest this would also be detrimental in that the mortgage (to her husband) might fall through. There is clearly a possible conflict of interest between the buyer and the mortgagee on the one hand and the buyer's wife on the other hand and it would seem that it is preferable to the buyer's wife to have separate advice.[16]

Broadly speaking the same difficulties apply to unregistered land, with the one difference, already commented upon in Chapter 11, that the rationale by which the mortgagee is bound by the equitable interest is the doctrine of constructive notice. In the normal situation where someone who may have an equitable interest moves in with the buyer on completion, there would seem little chance of the mortgagee being

16   The validity of these types of arrangements have been discussed in a number of cases including *Kingsnorth Trust Ltd v Bell* [1986] 1 All ER 423, [1986] 1 WLR 119, CA; *National Westminster Bank Ltd v Morgan* [1985] AC 686, [1985] 1 All ER 821, HL; *Coldunell Ltd v Gallon* [1986] QB 1184, [1986] 1 All ER 429, CA; *Barclays Bank plc v Kennedy* [1989] 1 FLR 356, [1989] Fam Law 143, CA; *Bank of Baroda v Shah* [1988] 3 All ER 24, CA; *Bank of Credit and Commerce International SA v Aboody* [1990] 1 QB 923, CA; *Barclays Bank plc v Khaira* [1992] 1 WLR 623, [1993] 1 FLR 343; and most significantly in *Barclays Bank plc v O'Brien* [1993] QB 109, CA. These are cases where an occupier with some interest in the property has been asked to sign the appropriate declaration, or join in the mortgage deed, or as in *O'Brien* where the property (and mortgage) are in joint names but the loan is for the benefit of just one party. Briefly, if undue influence or misrepresentation has been used (usually by the mortgagor) in order to obtain the signature, and the mortgagee has knowledge of this, the security will be unenforceable against the signatory. Similarly, if the mortgagor in obtaining the signature through undue influence or misrepresentation was doing so as the agent of the mortgagee. In other cases, the security will remain enforceable against the signatory despite the signature having been obtained by undue influence or misrepresentation. However, there is a special class of signatory who will be specially protected, and wives fall into this class because of 'the likelihood of influence by a husband over his wife'. In such situations in order to be able to enforce the security against the signatory, the mortgagee must take reasonable steps to try and ensure that the signatory had an adequate understanding of the nature and effect of the transaction; this will normally mean independent advice. However, this *Barclays Bank v O'Brien* dictum was held in *CIBC Mortgages plc v Pitt* (1993) 66 P & CR 179, CA to only apply to a transaction favouring a husband at the expense of his wife. The duty to ensure that the wife understood the transaction would apply where there was a loan to husband and wife as joint owners of the property and joint mortgagees and where the mortgagee was aware that the purpose of the loan was to pay the husband's debts (as was in effect the case in *Barclays Bank v O'Brien*); however, where there was nothing to put the mortgagee on notice that the transaction was anything other than a routine transaction for the joint benefit of husband and wife, there was no such duty. Subsequent cases include *Steeples v Lea* (1998) 76 P & CR 157, [1998] 1 FLR 138; and *Banco Exterior Internacional v Thomas* [1997] 1 All ER 46, [1997] 1 WLR 221, and recent cases make it clear that the lender's duty is not just to advise the wife to get independent legal advice but to ensure she does in fact receive such advice, though arguably the lender cannot be responsible for the quality of advice given.

affected by constructive notice of the interest. Nevertheless, in practice, mortgagees will probably take the same precautions as have just been discussed in relation to registered land.

If no consent form is signed, the equitable interest will not necessarily be binding on the mortgagee. The cases of *Bristol and West Building Society v Henning*[17] and *Paddington Building Society v Mendelsohn*[18] suggest that if the occupier knows of and supports the mortgage, his or her equitable interest may be subject to the mortgage anyway. This was confirmed in *Abbey National Building Society v Cann*, where the house of Lords decided that the mother's knowledge that her son would need to raise part of the purchase price from somewhere was enough to postpone her rights to those of the mortgagee lending the money. The principle was extended in *Equity & Law Home Loans Ltd v Prestridge*.[19] The occupier was aware of one mortgage but not of a remortgage for a higher figure, as a result of which the original mortgage was discharged. Nevertheless the occupier's knowledge of, and by implication consent to, the first mortgage was sufficient to enable the further mortgage to be enforced against her, at least to the extent of the amount of the loan under the first mortgage. *Woolwich Building Society v Dickman*[20] suggested that such a consent, in a registered land situation, would need to be entered on the register for the mortgagee or buyer to rely on it. However, this is clearly impractical in the context of an informal family arrangement and some doubt has been cast on this decision.

There is a particular need for care where the charge concerned is designed to secure one of a couple's business debts on the matrimonial home, and detailed guidance for solicitors was laid down by the Court of Appeal in *Royal Bank of Scotland v Etridge*.[1] The main issues are the possibility of undue influence by one spouse on the other, and the importance of ensuring that the spouse who is being asked to sign the charge, guarantee or waiver understands the implications of doing so, particularly where an 'all monies' charge is envisaged.

If the mortgage is by (at least two) trustees for sale, it will overreach the equitable interest which will then not be binding on the mortgagee.[2]

vii   Completion

Completion of the mortgage, which will take place at the same time as completion of the purchase, is discussed in the next chapter. The mortgage advance will have been received before completion, normally in the form of a cheque or electronic funds transfer from the mortgagee. This will be paid into client account before completion. The mortgagee may well be charging interest under the new mortgage from the time the cheque is presented or money transfer received or even earlier. In some circumstances it might be better to leave the cheque on the file and only present it shortly before completion. If the delay is lengthy, it may be necessary to return the mortgage advance to the mortgagee. It is clearly important to read the mortgagee's instructions and follow their prescribed procedures carefully to avoid causing the client unnecessary cost.

---

17   [1985] 2 All ER 606, [1985] 1 WLR 778, CA.
18   (1987) 50 P & CR 244, CA.
19   [1992] 1 All ER 909, [1992] 1 WLR 137, CA.
20   [1996] 3 All ER 204.
  1   [1998] 48 LSG 30.
  2   *City of London Building Society v Flegg* [1988] AC 54, [1987] 3 All ER 435, HL.

viii After completion

There are certain steps necessary to perfect the buyer's title such as stamping the purchase deed, applying for registration of title or applying for registration on a transfer of registered land. These will be discussed in Chapter 15 but as the mortgagee's title is derived from the buyer, the solicitor also has a duty to his mortgagee client to carry out these steps. Additionally there are certain steps after completion which are necessary purely from the mortgagee's point of view. It is not necessary to stamp the mortgage deed but it will be necessary to protect the mortgage as a registered charge, registered in the Charges Register of the title. In his capacity as solicitor for the mortgagee, the solicitor will apply for registration of the registered charge at the same time as applying for registration of the purchase. A Charge Certificate (unless the Charge Certificate is held in the registry – see Chapter 15) 'will be issued by the Land Registry rather than the Land Certificate, and this must be sent to the mortgagee once it has been checked. Sometimes the old pre-registration title deeds are also sent to the mortgagee; they have lost their significance as proof of the title but are not totally redundant.

ix Mortgages not contemporaneous with a purchase

It may be that a solicitor is acting on a mortgage which is not contemporaneous with a purchase, but where the mortgagor is already the owner of the property (eg a re-mortgage or second mortgage). The task of the solicitor is to find out information about the property which will concern the mortgagee and to check that the mortgagor's title is good. He will thus make the usual searches made for a buyer before exchange of contracts, will investigate title in the normal way and will make the appropriate pre-completion searches; see also section 4 ii, below. The problem of occupiers with equitable interests will be particularly acute where the mortgagor is already established in the property, and indeed most of the cases mentioned in the previous section involve non-contemporaneous mortgages. The equitable interest, if present at all, and the occupation will already be established, and it is highly likely that a second (ie non-contemporaneous) mortgagee will take subject to the interests (if any) of an occupier unless steps are taken to obtain the occupier's consent to the postponement of his or her interest to the mortgage or to overreach the interest.[3]

Additionally, the case of *Kingsnorth Trust Ltd v Tizard*,[4] considered above in Chapter 6 section 8, demonstrates the difficulty of inspecting the property in the case of unregistered title in order to satisfy section 199 of the Law of Property Act 1925. In that case, a wife was only sleeping intermittently in the property although she would return each morning. She was held to be in occupation and the mortgagee had not done enough in arranging a time with the husband to inspect the property, when of course her occupation was not discovered. The mortgagee was therefore unable to recover possession against her, but the particular facts of that case seem to have had some bearing on the level of inspection necessary.

3 REMEDIES OF MORTGAGEE

i Power of sale

This is dealt with at Chapter 10, section 6, above.

---

3   For example, see *Skipton Building Society v Clayton* (1993) 66 P & CR 223, CA.
4   [1986] 2 All ER 54, [1986] 1 WLR 783.

ii   Proceeds of sale

Most sales in practice will be by the first mortgagee. If a sale is by a second mortgagee, the sale will not normally have been made subject to the prior mortgage(s) and the first step must therefore be to discharge the prior mortgage(s) out of the proceeds of sale in accordance with the undertaking which the selling/mortgagee's solicitor will have had to give to the buyer on completion. The procedure is the same as if the mortgagor were selling and redeeming a mortgage out of the proceeds of sale.

Apart from this, the proceeds of sale are held by the mortgagee on trust and the order of application of the proceeds, after discharge of any prior mortgages, is as follows:[5]

(a)   payments of costs and expenses incidental to the sale, for example solicitor's costs and estate agent's and auctioneer's fees;
(b)   payment of principal, interest and any other costs due under the mortgage.

The mortgagee having taken what he is owed any residue must be paid to the 'person next entitled to the mortgaged property'. If there are any subsequent mortgages, this means the mortgagee with best claim to priority amongst them.

That person then holds the balance of the proceeds on a similar trust. His mortgage will have been 'over-reached' by the sale and he will pay himself the amount owed under his mortgage and hand any residue on to the person next entitled, as above. Ultimately, after the proceeds have passed through the hands of all the subsequent mortgagees (if any), the mortgagor will receive the residue.

In order for the mortgagee's solicitor to ensure that he is handing on the balance of the proceeds to the correct person, a search should be made of the Land Charges Register for unregistered land and at the Land Registry for registered land, to ascertain if there are any subsequent mortgages and if so who has the best claim to priority.

When a mortgagee exercises his power of sale the mortgage is 'discharged' by the sale and there is no need for a receipt on the mortgage.

iii   Other remedies

Particularly under a mortgage of commercial property, the mortgagee may wish to take advantage of other remedies apart from the power of sale. There may be provisions in the mortgage deed dealing with the mortgagee's power to appoint a receiver, and stipulating the powers which the receiver may have and how those powers may be exercised; for example, the receiver may be given a power of sale, which is not included in the statutory powers of a receiver as set out in the Law of Property Act, section 109.

If the mortgagor is a company, the mortgagee, as well as having a fixed charge over a specific property, may wish to take out a floating charge over the whole of the company's assets. This will enable the mortgagee to appoint an administrative receiver, which can in turn block the appointment of an administrator to the company, under the Insolvency Act 1986. The appointment of an administrator would be unwelcome to the mortgagee because it would limit the exercise of the mortgagee's powers.[6]

5   Law of Property Act 1925, s 105.
6   See Insolvency Act 1986, ss 10, 11, 29.

4   FURTHER ADVANCES AND FURTHER CHARGES

Further advances and further charges are alike in that neither normally takes place when the property is bought but at some later date when the mortgagor already owns the property and for some reason wants to increase the amount borrowed.

i   Further advances

A further advance is made when a mortgagor wishes to borrow more money from an existing mortgagee, to be added to the existing debt. Many standard mortgage deeds are expressed to be security not only for the original loan but also for any further advances made in the future. This means that no further deed is necessary when the further advance is made, merely a receipt for the additional loan. In domestic conveyancing, a mortgagor might want a further advance to assist the building of an extension onto the mortgaged property or to install central heating. The mortgagor will make an application to the mortgagee and the money will be released after the appropriate work has been done or possibly merely on an undertaking by the mortgagor to have the work done within a specified time. A further inspection fee may be payable. A further advance will result in a revised repayment figure for the monthly instalments, calculated to pay off the whole sum borrowed, with interest, over instalments, calculated to pay off the whole sum borrowed, with interest, over the original term of the mortgage. In the case of an endowment mortgage it may be necessary to increase the premiums on the life policy so that the sum payable at the end of the term of the policy will be the whole sum now borrowed.

ii   Further charges

A further charge can be a second legal mortgage or possibly an equitable mortgage. It will arise in practice when the mortgagor needs to borrow more money, perhaps for a relatively short period of time as compared to the term of the first legal mortgage. When acting for a prospective second mortgagee, a solicitor should do everything he would normally do for a first mortgagee.[7] An additional element will be a consideration of the first (and any other prior) mortgages. The first mortgage may restrict the power of the mortgagor to enter into any subsequent mortgages. Also, the amount owing under prior mortgages is highly relevant. If property is worth £95,000 and there is a first mortgage with £90,000 owing, a second mortgagee would be extremely foolish to lend a sum approaching or exceeding the balance or 'equity' as it is called of £5,000 in the property. Thirdly, the prospective second mortgagee will be concerned about any right to 'tack' which the prior mortgagee may have. Tacking occurs when a mortgagee who makes a further advance can treat the further advance as having been made at the same time as the original mortgage for the purpose of priority of repayment; the further advance is tacked to the original advance and jumps the queue over any subsequent mortgagees. Tacking can only take place if made either with the consent of the intervening mortgagees (which would be unlikely); or without notice of the existence of intervening mortgagees; or under a binding obligation in the original mortgage deed.[8] The solicitor for the second mortgagee

---

7   See section 2 ix, above.
8   Law of Property Act 1925, s 94(1).

will therefore be careful to give notice to prior mortgagees of the new mortgage, as notice by registration is technically insufficient.[9] This will normally be enough to prevent tacking. Finally, the second mortgagee may be affected by a prior mortgagee having in his mortgage deed excluded the Law of Property Act 1925, section 93 and thereby reserved a right of consolidation. The prior mortgage deed(s) should be abstracted to enable the second mortgagee's solicitor to check these points.

In practice, the real security of a second mortgage lies in the second mortgagee's interest in the proceeds of sale, after that of prior mortgagees. A disadvantage is that the second mortgagee has no control over the exercise of the first mortgagee's power of sale. The second mortgagee will normally also have a power of sale although he can only sell subject to prior mortgages and in practice would have to sell free from them and discharge them out of the proceeds of sale.[10]

The priority of further charges will be in their registration, either as land charges for unregistered land (Ci, Ciii or Civ) or as registered charges for registered land.

---

9 Ibid, s 94(2).
10 See section 3 ii, above.

14 COMPLETION

I PREPARATION FOR COMPLETION

i Title investigated

It goes without saying that before completion both solicitors should ensure that all necessary steps in deducing and investigating title have been carried out. It is not unknown for the buyer's solicitor to discover a day or so before the contractual completion date that he has forgotten to do his searches. As we have seen it is possible to request a search by telephone, by fax, and by Land Registry Direct.

ii Conditional contracts

If the contract has been made conditional on the occurrence of some external event, such as the granting of planning permission, then again it hardly needs saying that before completing the contract the parties should see whether the condition is satisfied so as to establish whether there is indeed a contract and contractual duty to complete. Under the rule in *Aberfoyle Plantations Ltd v Cheng*[1] the date for satisfaction of the condition may be the contractual completion date. In addition, although there may not be a conditional contract, the buyer may be able to rescind if certain 'conditions' are not fulfilled. An example would be if the requisite licence to assign leasehold property had not been obtained from the landlord.

iii Execution

1 Who executes?

The deed must be executed by the parties in readiness for completion when it is handed over to the buyer's solicitor. The seller – or all of them if they are joint tenants – must always execute the deed, but the buyer will only need to execute it if he is actually 'doing something' in it, for example entering into a covenant or declaring how the beneficial interest is held. If the buyer's execution is necessary, this should be done before the deed is sent to the seller's solicitor for the seller's execution in readiness for completion. The reason for this is that once the seller has executed the

---

1 [1960] AC 115, [1959] 3 All ER 910, PC.

deed, the seller's solicitor will be unwilling to let the deed go back to the buyer for him to add his execution. Nevertheless, the buyer's execution might be quite important to the seller; if the buyer is entering into an indemnity covenant or a new restrictive covenant then the seller will not want to complete before the buyer has executed the deed. The buyer's solicitor should not offer and the seller's solicitor should not accept an undertaking given on completion by the buyer's solicitor that he will have the deed executed by the buyer as soon as possible. This is quite outside the buyer's solicitor's control and should not be the subject of an undertaking.

In addition to the seller, it may be necessary for some other party to the deed to execute it. For example on the sale by a tenant for life of settled land the trustees will join in the deed to give a receipt; on the sale of part of property comprised in an unregistered title, subject to a mortgage, the mortgagee may join in to release the part sold from the mortgage.

Plans should also be signed – in the case of unregistered land to show that the signatories intend the plan to form part of the deed itself, and in the case of registered land to comply with Land Registration Rules 1925.

2   Execution by an individual

The requirements for valid execution changed on 31 July 1990. In respect of deeds executed before that date, a deed had to be signed, sealed and delivered. Firstly, then, the party had to sign or, if he could not write, place his mark on the deed.[2] Secondly, the deed had to be sealed. In times gone by this would be achieved with the aid of molten sealing wax. Latterly a small circular piece of red self-adhesive paper or 'wafer' was used. The executing party would not normally affix this himself but just sign opposite a previously affixed seal. The justification for this procedure can be found in *Stromdale and Ball Ltd v Burden*,[3] where it was said that 'if a party signs a document bearing wax or wafer or other indication of a seal, with the intention of executing the document as a deed, that is sufficient adoption or recognition of the seal to amount to due execution as a deed'.[4] Some standard form deeds such as mortgages contained the letters L.S. inside a circle opposite the space for signature. This is an abbreviation for the Latin 'locus sigilli' and indicates the place where the seal should be stuck. In a case where no seal was in fact affixed but the party did sign (across the circle) the deed was held still to have been duly executed.[5] Signing after a testimonium and attestation clause referring to sealing could also raise an estoppel as to sealing.[6]

The requirement of sealing has been abolished in relation to deeds executed after 31 July 1990 by section 1 of the Law of Property (Miscellaneous Provisions) Act 1989. After that date, a deed is validly executed by an individual if it is just signed and delivered. However, the 1989 Act introduced a number of requirements. Firstly, there is a general requirement which applies to any deed, whether executed by an individual or corporation. Section 1(2) provides that an instrument shall not be a deed unless it makes clear on its face that it is intended to be a deed by the parties to it (whether by describing itself as a deed or expressing itself to be executed or signed

---

2   Law of Property Act 1925, s 73.
3   [1952] Ch 223, [1952] 1 All ER 59.
4   Ibid at 230.
5   *First National Securities Ltd v Jones* [1978] Ch 109, [1978] 2 All ER 221, CA.
6   Confirmed in *TCB Ltd v Gray* [1986] Ch 621, [1986] 1 All ER 587, where it was held that a party executing a deed after the normal clause referring to signing, sealing and delivery was estopped from denying it was sealed when another person relied on the deed to his detriment.

as a deed or otherwise). Thus the attested clause introducing the execution may read 'signed as a deed and delivered by .... in the presence of ....'. Section 1(2) additionally provides that an instrument cannot be a deed unless it is validly executed. As we have seen, the requirement for valid execution by an individual after 31 July 1990 is signing and delivery. However, section 1(3) of the 1989 Act introduced a further requirement: the signature by the party to the deed must be in the presence of a witness who then attests the signature by adding his own signature and name and address. (Although this attestation by a witness was not an absolute requirement for execution by an individual prior to 31 July 1990, a party's signature to a deed was in practice always witnessed.)

Section 1(3) also provides that a deed may be signed not by the party to it but by someone else at his direction and in his presence, but in such a situation there must be attestation by two witnesses present at the time of the signature. This provision would be useful if the party to the deed was physically incapable of signing.

In relation to execution both before and after 31 July 1990, delivery is an essential part of an individual's execution of a deed. Delivery is a rather strange concept. It does not simply mean handing over the deed to the other party, for example handing over to the buyer on completion, although this would certainly amount to delivery. In *Vincent v Premo Enterprises (Voucher Sales) Ltd*[7] it was said that 'delivery ... means an act done so as to evince an intention to be bound. Even though the deed remains in the possession of the maker, or of his solicitor, he is bound by it if he has done some act evincing an intention to be bound.'[8] Probably signing a deed whose attestation clause referred to the deed as being delivered would be enough. Otherwise, delivery may be achieved by the client handing the signed and witnessed deed to his own solicitor in readiness for completion.[9] Delivery is the final formality of execution and the deed once delivered becomes fully effective; indeed the date of the deed is the date of delivery, the date on which the deed becomes effective. However, it will be ridiculous if the deed becomes effective, and the buyer thus acquires the legal estate, when the seller hands the signed deed to his own solicitor, before completion and before the buyer has paid the purchase price. The answer is that the delivery can be absolute or conditional. A deed delivered conditionally is called an escrow. The most common condition of a delivery by the seller will be payment of the purchase price by the buyer. This condition will normally be implied even if the deed is not delivered with this express condition. So if the seller signs the deed and hands it to his solicitor sometime before completion, the deed may be delivered but conditionally on the buyer paying the purchase price. The condition is satisfied on completion and the deed then becomes effective to pass the legal estate to the buyer.

Even though delivery may be only conditional, it does have consequences for the seller. The delivery is irrevocable. The seller, having delivered the deed conditionally in the manner described above, cannot change his mind and tear the deed up. He has committed himself to wait and see whether the condition of the delivery is satisfied. If it is, the deed becomes effective and there is nothing the seller can do about it. This is illustrated by the case of *Beesly v Hallwood Estates Ltd*.[10] A lease contained an option for the lessee to renew. The lessee exercised the option and the lessor executed a new lease. This was delivered by the lessor, conditionally on the lessee executing a counterpart lease. The lessee did so. The lessor then discovered that the option was

---

7   [1969] 2 QB 609, [1969] 2 All ER 941, CA.
8   Ibid at 619.
9   See, for example, *Venetian Glass Gallery Ltd v Next Properties Ltd* [1989] 2 EGLR 42.
10 [1961] Ch 105, [1961] 1 All ER 90, CA.

unenforceable against him. The lessor refused to carry on with the transaction, but to no avail; the condition of the conditional delivery had been satisfied and the new lease had become effective. Even if the condition had not been satisfied at the time the lessor wanted to withdraw, he would not have been able to do so; he would have had to wait and see whether the condition was satisfied.

The concept of delivery was discussed in the case of *Longman v Viscount Chelsea*,[11] albeit in the context of the grant of a lease. The *Beesly* case was described as turning on its own facts and in *Longman* the Court of Appeal decided that where, following a subject to contract agreement, the landlord had executed the lease but then withdrawn from the transaction, the lease had not been delivered at all. In the normal conveyancing transaction, the seller will execute the deed following the creation of a binding contract rather than subject to contract agreement, but if the reasoning in *Longman* is extended it would cast some doubt on the conventional view, that a deed signed by the seller and handed to his own solicitor in readiness for completion is conditionally delivered.

There appears to be no particular time limit for the satisfaction of the condition of delivery although clearly there must come a time when the seller will be entitled to withdraw if the condition has not been satisfied.

Once the condition has been satisfied, the deed is treated as having been delivered on the date of the conditional delivery.[12] The correct date of the deed is therefore the date of the conditional delivery and not the date that the condition is satisfied. That is rather odd and presumably means that most purchase deeds, being dated as they are with the date of completion, are wrongly dated.

The buyer's solicitor will not need to concern himself as to whether the seller's solicitor does have authority to deliver the deed, because section 1(5) of the 1989 Act provides that in favour of a purchaser, where a solicitor (or licensed conveyancer or agent or employee of a solicitor or licensed conveyancer) purports to deliver a deed on behalf of a party to it in the course of a transaction involving the disposition or creation of an interest in land, it is conclusively presumed that he is authorised to deliver the deed.

3 Execution by corporations

A corporation – such as a limited company – clearly cannot sign the deed. The Law of Property Act 1925, section 74 provides that in favour of a purchaser, a deed is presumed to have been duly executed by a corporation aggregate if its seal is affixed in the presence of and attested by its secretary or clerk or other permanent officer or his deputy, and also by a member of the Board of Directors or other governing body. When a seal purporting to be the corporation's seal has been affixed, attested by persons purporting to be the requisite officers, the deed shall be deemed to have been executed in accordance with section 74 and thus duly executed. The rule applies to companies, Local Authorities, Building Societies and other corporations. The requirement of sealing from the *corporation's* point of view may be contained in a company's articles of association, or the equivalent for other corporate bodies. If section 74 is not complied with, a buyer's solicitor would have to check that the deed had been properly executed by investigating such rules. Section 74 does not mention delivery but it is nevertheless necessary (though presumed from sealing); and a corporation can therefore deliver conditionally in the same way as an individual.

---

11 (1989) 58 P & CR 189, CA.
12 *Alan Estates Ltd v W G Stores Ltd* [1982] Ch 511, [1981] 3 All ER 481, CA.

In relation to companies, the position has been changed by section 130 of the Companies Act 1989, which came into force on 31 July 1990 and which inserts a new section 36A into the Companies Act 1985. Section 36A provides that a company need not have a common seal. Whether it does or not, a document signed by a director and the secretary of a company, or by two directors, and expressed to be executed by the company, has the same effect as if executed under a common seal. Thus a company can dispense with its seal and simply execute a deed by the two signatures, which do not have to be witnessed.

The question of delivery is specifically dealt with in section 36A(5), which applies whether the company executes under section 36A or the old procedure using a seal. Section 36A(5) provides that a document executed by a company which makes it clear on its face that it is intended to be a deed has effect on delivery as a deed, and it is presumed unless a contrary intention is proved to be delivered upon being executed. This will have implications for the wording of the attestation clause by a company. Under section 36A where a seal is not used, the attestation clause may read 'signed as a deed and delivered by X Ltd acting by AB (Director) and CD (Secretary)'. However, even if the words 'and delivered' were excluded, there would be a presumption of delivery under section 36A(5), although the delivery could presumably be conditional. If the company did not want to deliver the deed, there must be some evidence of non-delivery to rebut the presumption, such as a covering letter from the company, or a provision in the deed that delivery is on the date inserted in the deed on completion. This would seem to be the appropriate course of action if the deed is to be delivered by the seller's solicitor on completion rather than at the time of the signing or sealing of the deed.

Section 36A(6) provides that in favour of a purchaser, a document shall be deemed to have been duly executed by a company if it purports to be signed by a director and the secretary or by two directors and, where it makes it clear on its face that it is intended by the person making it to be a deed, to have been delivered upon its being executed. This, then, is a provision in favour of a purchaser of due execution and delivery. The presumption of delivery upon execution is, unlike section 36A(5), not subject to contrary intention being proved. Quite apart from the provisions in section 36A(5) and (6), which depend on the deed making it clear on its face that it is intended to be a deed, it should be noted that the provision in section 1(2) of the Law of Property (Miscellaneous Provisions) Act 1989, providing that a document shall not be a deed unless it makes it clear on its face that it is intended to be a deed, is of general application to all deeds whether executed by individuals, companies or other corporations.

4 Execution by attorneys

An individual who is the attorney for one of the executing parties can sign the deed in one of two ways. The attestation clause will contain some reference to the power of attorney. The attorney can either sign in his own name, adding underneath 'as attorney for …', or he can sign in the name of the donor of the power of attorney and add 'by … his attorney'.

5 Registered land

There are particular requirements in relation to the execution of a transfer of registered land. Even prior to 31 July 1990, the signature of an individual had to be witnessed. If the transfer is accompanied by a plan, the plan must be signed by the seller and by or on behalf of the purchaser. There are prescribed forms of wording for the execution of a transfer.[13] For an individual, they are 'signed as a deed by .... in the presence of ....' or 'signed and delivered by .... in the presence of ....'. For a company using a common seal, the wording is 'the common seal of .... was affixed in the presence of (director and secretary)'; for a company not using a seal it is either 'signed as a deed by .... acting by (director and secretary or two directors)' or 'signed and delivered by .... acting by (director and secretary or two directors)'. The 'signed as a deed' option would be chosen rather than the 'signed and delivered' option where delivery was delegated to the solicitor on completion.

6   Other deeds

Other deeds must be executed in readiness for completion. If the buyer is buying with the aid of a mortgage, he will have to execute the mortgage deed and perhaps a deed of assignment of the life policy. These mortgage deeds are not normally executed by the mortgagee.

7   Procedure

The purchase deed, in draft and final form, passes between the parties a number of times. As we have seen it is drafted by the buyer's solicitor and sent to the seller's solicitor for approval. It will be returned approved and possibly amended. It is then engrossed by the buyer's solicitor, executed by the buyer if this is necessary and sent to the seller's solicitor for execution by the seller in readiness for completion, when it will be handed over to the buyer's solicitor. This procedure is even longer if there is another party who must approve the draft and execute the deed, for example on a transfer of the former matrimonial home following a divorce or separation, from the joint names of the spouses into one spouse's sole name; if, as is likely, the property is subject to a mortgage then the mortgagee will be made a party to release the other spouse from his or her obligations under the mortgage.

iv   Finance

1   Redemption of seller's mortgage

If the property the seller is selling is subject to a mortgage, this will ordinarily be redeemed using the proceeds of the sale. Before completion the seller's solicitor must contact the mortgagee and ask for a redemption figure, being the amount required to redeem the mortgage on the completion date. The mortgagee would normally also give an additional daily rate to be added to the figure so that if completion and thus redemption is delayed by a few days the solicitor can still calculate the amount required to redeem the mortgage. The solicitor ought to have already checked that the proceeds will be sufficient both to redeem the mortgage and pay his own costs and any other disbursements. If the proceeds are not sufficient to redeem the mortgage, the seller's solicitor will be unable to give the buyer on completion the usual undertaking to redeem the mortgage; in the absence of this the buyer will refuse to complete and the seller will be in breach of contract.

    If the seller has any second mortgages then redemption figures should be obtained for these also, as they will need to be redeemed out of the proceeds of sale.

---

13   Land Registration (Execution of Deeds) Rules 1990.

The seller's solicitor will normally be able to rely on a redemption statement even though it has been incorrectly calculated, where this is clearly due to an error by the mortgagee. The mortgagee should still provide the receipted mortgage deed or form DS1.

2 Amount required to complete

The buyer's solicitor will want to know the precise amount required on completion. The standard Completion Information and Requisitions on Title form will contain a request for a completion statement giving this information see question 5. The bulk of the sum will be the sale price less the deposit already paid. There are two other items which may be reflected in the completion statement: apportionment and interest.

There are certain sums which may be payable in respect of the property, either in advance or in arrear. For a leasehold property the seller may have paid the rent in advance and wish to recoup a proportion of this from the buyer. If the rent is paid in arrear, the buyer will wish to deduct from the purchase price the proportion which will be paid by him in respect of the time during which the property has been in the seller's ownership. The date at which the apportionment of these outgoings is made is normally the contractual completion date; as was mentioned in Chapter 8, the seller is responsible for outgoings up to that date and the buyer afterwards. This is the open contract rule, which may be altered in the contractual conditions. In particular, if completion is delayed then apportionment may be made at the date of actual completion rather than the contractual completion date. Standard Condition 6.3.2 provides that if the property is sold with vacant possession (or the buyer is already a tenant of the property, completion is delayed, and the seller has given notice to the buyer under condition 7.3.4) apportionment is made with effect from the date of actual completion; otherwise, it is made from the contractual completion date. For the purpose of apportionments, it is to be assumed that income and outgoings accrue at an equal daily rate throughout the year.[14] If the sums to be apportioned are not known or easily ascertainable, a provisional apportionment may be made according to the best estimate available.[15] When the actual amount is known after completion, a final apportionment is to be made and notified to the other party with any resulting balance being paid no more than ten working days later. The Standard Conditions also provide that if the buyer has been given possession before completion, he is responsible for outgoings and entitled to rents (in respect of any part which he does not occupy)[16] for the period of his licence to occupy.

The second adjustment which may have to be made on the completion statement is the payment of interest. In certain circumstances, if completion is delayed or if the buyer has been given possession before completion, the buyer (and under Standard Conditions the seller) may have to pay interest on the purchase money. This is discussed in detail later in this chapter in section 2 i.

Under Standard Condition 6.4 the amount payable on completion can be adjusted to take account of apportionments under 6.3 and also compensation for late completion under 7.3, but there is no mention of the effect of damage to the property in breach of 5.1.1.

Having ascertained the amount payable on completion and checked the completion statement, the buyer's solicitor must take steps to ensure that this sum is

---

14   SC 6.3.4.
15   SC 6.3.5.
16   SC 5.2.2.

available. If it is not, and the buyer's solicitor, rather ill-advisedly, uses his own money to complete the purchase, he will have the benefit of what would otherwise be the seller's lien over the property for unpaid purchase money; *Boodle Hatfield & Co v British Films Ltd*,[17] where the buyer's solicitors completed on the strength of a cheque from the buyer which was not cleared before completion and was subsequently dishonoured.

3   Mortgage advance

If part of the purchase money is being provided by a mortgage advance, this must of course be to hand by completion. The buyer's solicitor must send off the report on title and request for the advance. Rule 6 (3) of the Solicitor's Practice Rule as amended came into force on 1 October 1999 (see Chapter 13). It introduced a common-form report on title, which could be used by all solicitors acting for both the buyer and an institutional lender in a transaction of property to be used as a private residence. The approved form of certificate or the short form certificate can be used, see Appendices.

The buyer's solicitor must read through the mortgage conditions and terms carefully before giving the report on title. If he is unable to comply with any of the conditions or the results of the title investigations and searches has revealed anything that may affect the lender's security, these must be pointed out to the lender.

If there is to be any retention, this will not be included in the sum sent to the buyer's solicitor. If for some reason the mortgage advance is not available on the completion date, the buyer may have to arrange a bridging loan until the advance does become available. This might arise if the buyer has unwisely exchanged contracts without waiting for a mortgage offer.

On an endowment mortgage, the solicitor for the mortgagee and buyer may need to make enquiries about the life policy.[18]

4   Synchronisation

Part of the purchase money may be provided from the proceeds of a contemporaneous sale. If completion of that sale is delayed or for some other reason cannot take place until after the completion of the purchase, the buyer must either delay completion of the purchase, or again, arrange a bridging loan until the sale is completed.

5   Bridging loan

Two examples in which the need for a bridging loan may arise have been mentioned above. Provided that in the first case a mortgage offer has been made and that in the second case contracts on the sale have been exchanged, the buyer should not find it too difficult to arrange a bridging loan from a bank. As the loan is only required until either in the one case the mortgage advance or in the other case the sale money comes to hand, the period of the loan will be a finite term and the bank will be virtually certain that there will be no problem over the repayment of the loan. On the other hand if in the first case no mortgage offer has yet been received or in the second case if contracts on the sale have not yet been exchanged, the bridging loan is an open ended commitment and the bank might be less likely to grant the loan.

17   (1985) 2 BCC 99, 221.
18   See ch 13, section 2 v.

A bank making a bridging loan will require an undertaking from the buyer's solicitor to pay in the first case the mortgage advance, or in the second case the net proceeds of sale, to the credit of the loan account. The buyer's solicitor should not undertake to actually repay the loan in case the mortgage advance or the net proceeds are not sufficient for that purpose. However, the bank will want some assurance as to the likely amount of the net proceeds, and also as to the deductions which will be made by the solicitor, such as the solicitor's own costs. In practice the bank may have its own standard form of undertaking; if so the buyer's solicitor should ensure that he only undertakes to do what he can in fact do and limits the scope of the undertaking to money actually received by him and available for repayment of the loan. As with all undertakings he must obtain his client's written and irrevocable agreement to the undertaking.

6   Payment of purchase price

The buyer's solicitor must make preparations to pay the purchase price on completion. Depending on how and when completion is to take place, there are in practice two methods of payment. The first is by banker's draft. This is rather like a cheque drawn on a bank, rather than on a particular account at the bank, and is thus virtually as good as cash. It will be made out in favour of the seller's solicitor. A banker's draft will be used if completion is by the buyer's solicitor personally attending at the seller's solicitor's office. It may also be used if completion is by the buyer's solicitor's agent attending at the seller's solicitor's office, if the latter is some distance from the buyer's solicitor's office. It could also be used if completion takes place not by personal attendance but through the post. The disadvantage of using a banker's draft in a postal completion is that the draft must be obtained a day or two before completion so that it can be posted; this will not normally be possible, at least in domestic conveyancing, as the necessary money will not be available if money is being provided by a contemporaneous sale.

If completion is taking place not at the seller's solicitor's office but at the office of the solicitor for the seller's mortgagee, because the seller's mortgagee will not release the deeds or the Charge Certificate to the seller's solicitor, then two banker's drafts may be needed, one payable to the seller's solicitor and the other payable to the solicitor for the seller's mortgagee. The latter would represent the redemption figure on the seller's mortgage and the former the remaining balance of the purchase monies owed to the seller. The mechanics of such a completion will be discussed in more detail later in this chapter.

Although it is clearly safer for a seller's solicitor to insist on a banker's draft, he might in some situations be willing to accept the buyer's solicitor's client account cheque, particularly if accompanied by an undertaking that it will be honoured on first presentation.

The other method of payment is by bank telegraphic transfer, or credit transfer as it is sometimes called. This can be used to transmit the completion money to the seller's solicitor if completion is by post. The seller's solicitor will provide the buyer's solicitor, before completion, with the name and address of his bank and the number of the client account. The buyer's solicitor asks his own bank to transfer the completion money from his client account to the seller's solicitor's client account. This can normally be done very quickly. The receiving bank can be asked to notify the seller's solicitor as soon as the funds are received. The credit transfer procedure is particularly useful on a contemporaneous sale and purchase where speed of the transfer of funds is very important.

The method of payment on completion may be prescribed by the conditions in the contract – see Chapter 5, section 4 xix.

v   Placing Land Certificate on deposit

If the seller is only selling part of the land comprised in his registered title, he will not wish to hand over his Land Certificate to the buyer as it relates to land that he is keeping. However, the general rule is that on an application for registration the Certificate must be produced.[19] The problem is solved by a compromise. The seller's solicitor will send the Land Certificate directly to the District Land Registry, where it is then available when the buyer's application for registration is dealt with. Afterwards, it will be returned to the seller, suitably amended to reflect the up-to-date position of the register, with the part of the land sold having been removed from the title. The land the buyer has bought will be registered under a new title number.

When the Land Certificate is sent to the Registry by the seller's solicitor, he will be given a deposit number. This can be communicated to the buyer's solicitor on or before completion and can then be quoted on the buyer's application for registration.

If the seller's property is in mortgage the Land Certificate is held at the Registry anyway. If the mortgage is only being discharged as to the part sold, a similar procedure is adopted in respect of the Charge Certificate; it is sent by the seller's mortgagee's solicitor to the Registry to await the buyer's application for registration, which will include an application for discharge of the mortgage in relation to the part sold on which application of course the Charge Certificate is needed.

It is the seller's duty to ensure that the Certificate is deposited at the Registry for use on the buyer's application for registration.[20]

2   DELAYED COMPLETION

i   Delayed completion

As time is not normally of the essence of completion, if one party does not complete on the contractual date for completion the other party cannot treat the contract as discharged by the breach but must give the first party time in which to complete.[1] However, the delay may result in some adjustment of the purchase price. The open contract approach is to treat the parties as if they had completed on the contractual completion date. The buyer therefore becomes entitled to any income received after the contractual completion date and must also bear the outgoings.[2] If the seller has remained in occupation, he must pay a fair occupation rent to the buyer for the period between the contractual completion date and the actual completion date, unless the delay is due to the buyer's default.[3] Under an open contract, the seller is entitled to receive interest on the balance of the purchase money for the period of the delay. Again this accords with the principle of treating the parties as if they had completed on the contractual completion date. If the delay is due to the wilful default of the seller, and if the interest payable to the seller would exceed the net income (if any) of the property for the period of the delay, the buyer can keep the interest and the seller can keep the income, as otherwise the seller would be profiting

---

19   Land Registration Act 1925, s 64(1).
20   Land Registration Act 1925, s 110(6).
 1   Long delay may entitle a party to withdraw without serving a notice to complete, but this is very risky: see *Graham v Pitkin* [1992] 1 WLR 403, PC.
 2   See section 1 iv 2, above.
 3   *Metropolitan Rly Co v Defries* (1877) 2 QBD 387, CA.

from his default.[4] Additionally, if the buyer is liable to pay any interest, he can put the balance of the purchase money on deposit and the seller will then only be entitled to the interest actually accruing.[5] In practice the buyer will probably not have the balance of the purchase money available to put on deposit, as some of it may be coming by way of mortgage advance which will not be available until completion. In domestic conveyancing, some of it may be coming from the proceeds of sale of the buyer's present property, completion of which may also be delayed to coincide with completion of the purchase.

As well as these adjustments to the purchase price, the innocent party may be entitled to some compensation for loss caused by the delay. Although time is not of the essence and a failure to complete on the contractual completion date does not entitle the other party immediately to withdraw, it is nevertheless a breach of contract giving rise to a liability to pay damages. This was confirmed in *Raineri v Miles*,[6] where a buyer claimed the cost of temporary accommodation necessary as a result of a delay in completion. The normal contractual rules of the measure and remoteness of damages will apply.[7]

This, then, is the open contract position, but what of contracts which are subject to the Standard Conditions? The question of apportionment of income and outgoings has already been dealt with in section 1 iv 2 above, but what of the payment of interest and compensation for late completion? The open contract interest rate used to be 4% although it is now acknowledged that it would be increased.[8] In practice the interest rate will normally be specified on the front page of the contract. Failing this, Standard Condition 1.1.1(g) provides that the contract rate of interest is the Law Society's interest rate from time to time, published in the *Law Society's Gazette*. The Standard Conditions approach the issues of compensation for delay and interest in a rather different way than the open contract rules; they in effect combine the two issues.

The general principle stated in Standard Conditions 7.3.1, is that if a party is in default in performing his obligations under the contract and completion is delayed, he must pay compensation to the other party. The principle also applies where both parties are in default; the party whose total period of default is the greater is to pay compensation to the other party. Compensation is then calculated under condition 7.3.2 at interest on the purchase price (or, where the buyer is paying interest, the outstanding purchase price). The interest is payable for the shorter of two periods: the period of delay in completion or the period of default in performing the obligation under the contract. In the latter case if both parties are in default, it will be the period by which the default of the party paying interest exceeded that of the party receiving the interest.

The provision applies in two different types of case. Firstly, it applies where the parties have complied with their obligations under the contract up to the time fixed for completion but then one party or the other has been unable to complete on the contractual completion date. Interest would be payable for the period of delay in completion. However, the provision also applies where one or other of the parties (or both) have been in default at some earlier stage; for example, if the seller has been late in replying to requisitions under the timetable contained in 4.1.1, or the buyer has been late sending a draft transfer under the timetable contained in 4.1.2. Where

---

4   *North v Percival* [1898] 2 Ch 128.
5   See, for example, *Bennett v Stone* [1903] 1 Ch 509, CA.
6   [1981] AC 1050, [1980] 2 All ER 145, HL.
7   See ch 16, section 3.
8   See *Wallersteiner v Moir (No 2)* [1975] QB 373, [1975] 1 All ER 849, CA: *Bartlett v Barclays Bank Trust Co Ltd (No 2)* [1980] Ch 515, [1980] 2 All ER 92, CA.

there has been such default and completion is delayed, interest is payable for the lesser of the two periods, of the lateness in complying with the contractual obligation and of the delay in completion.

Interest is payable for the period of default or delay without reference to any definition of working days to which some of the contractual time limits refer.[9] Weekends are not working days for the purpose of completing the transaction, so if completion is delayed from a Friday to the following Monday, this may entail payment of three days' interest.

A party who suffers loss as a result of delayed completion which is not fully compensated by payment of interest under condition 7.3 may still claim damages, but they would be reduced by the interest paid under condition 7.3.

Under 7.3.4, where the buyer is a tenant of the property, the seller can give notice before actual completion that he intends to take the net income from the property until actual completion, thus overriding the normal rule for apportionment in Standard Condition 6.3.2. If the seller does so, 7.3.4 provides that he cannot claim compensation under 7.3 for delay as well; thus if the seller does wish to be able to claim both the net income and compensation for delay this will necessitate an amendment of 7.3.4 by special condition.

On the sale of a tenanted property where the tenant is not the buyer, the Standard Conditions contain no option for the seller to take the net income until actual completion. If the seller wishes to do this, an amendment will be needed to 6.3.2 dealing with the apportionment of income and outgoings, and the amendment, by special condition, should make it clear that the seller can also claim compensation for the delay under 7.3 if that is what the seller desires.

ii   Forcing a party to complete

The preceding section has examined the compensation payable, and other financial consequences of late completion. This assumes of course that completion does eventually take place. How can a party compel the other party to complete? He has two alternatives: he can either apply for a decree of specific performance or he can make time of the essence of completion by serving a notice to complete. The latter will not in itself force the other party to complete but will make the consequences of non-completion more serious; if a party does not complete within the period of a notice to complete which has made time of the essence, then the other party is entitled to withdraw and sue for damages for breach of contract. Specific performance, notices to complete and damages for breach of contract are all considered in more detail in Chapter 16.

iii   Practical consequences of delay

If a domestic conveyancing client is both buying and selling, and one of these transactions is delayed, he faces the prospect of either delaying the other transaction (and making himself liable for interest – and/or compensation – if he does so) or completing the other transaction, which would doubtless cause inconvenience. If he completed his sale before his purchase he would need somewhere to live and to store his furniture; if he completed his purchase before his sale, he would need a bridging

---

9   Working days are defined in SC 1.1.1(n).

loan until the proceeds of sale became available. Assuming that the delay was not caused by his default, he could attempt to recover his loss from the party who caused the delay.[10]

If completion of a purchase is delayed and the buyer's solicitor is also acting for the mortgagee from whom the buyer is receiving a loan, the mortgagee client should be informed of the delay and it may be necessary to return the advance to the mortgagee pending a resolution of the delay.

3   COMPLETION

i   Method of completion

There are two principal ways in which a transaction can be completed: by personal attendance or through the post. Attendance could be by the party's solicitor or the solicitor may appoint an agent. The venue for a completion by personal attendance will normally be the seller's solicitor's office. If the seller's solicitor is not acting for the seller's mortgagee, and thus has not got the deeds or Charge Certificate, completion may take place at the offices of the solicitor for the seller's mortgagee. We shall deal firstly with a completion where the seller's solicitors do act for the seller's mortgagee (if any), which does take place at the seller's solicitor's office and where the buyer's solicitor also acts for the buyer's new mortgagee (if any). We shall then deal with the other possibilities including completing through the post.

ii   Procedure on a typical completion

1   Verification

This has been discussed already in Chapter 10, when it was noted that although there are advantages in verifying the abstract or epitome on a sale of unregistered land before completion, common practice is to leave verification until completion. The seller is then under a duty to produce the documents of title which are to be handed over and the abstract or epitome can be verified as the first step on completion. Verification is doubly important if the sale is a sale of part, because the seller will be retaining the original deeds (although the buyer will be receiving an acknowledgment and possibly an undertaking in respect of them). The buyer's solicitor will mark on his abstract that he has verified it against the originals and give the date and name of his firm. This marked abstract is the only evidence of title (apart from the purchase deed) which the buyer will have for presentation on first registration.

Again as we saw in Chapter 10, problems can occur if the property sold is property which was the subject of a sale of part sometime in the past. The seller will not have the original deeds but only the marked abstract that was obtained when the sale of part took place. The buyer's solicitor will probably rely on this marked abstract when verifying his own abstract, and not insist on production of the originals; the buyer under an open contract would have to bear the expense of the production of the originals under the Law of Property Act 1925, section 45(4). However, under Standard Condition 4.2.3 the seller's obligation is to produce, at his expense, either the original of a document of title or a marked abstract, epitome or copy. Reliance on a marked abstract is a potentially risky practice, convenient though it is, and the

---

10   See ch 16, section 3.

buyer's solicitor should at the very least check the date of examination of the marked abstract when checking for the existence of memoranda etc. If the abstract was marked against the originals *before* completion of the sale off, then it clearly offers no sort of evidence that such memoranda were not endorsed on the originals at the time of the sale off. Whilst the Standard Condition relieves the buyer of his obligation under the Law of Property Act 1925, section 45(4) to pay for production of documents not in the seller's possession (or the possession of the seller's mortgagee or trustee), it raises the question of whether the buyer *ought* to be satisfied with seeing marked abstracts.

If an original document should be lost or destroyed, the seller can comply with his obligation of production by providing secondary evidence of the contents of the document, including execution;[11] this might include a draft of the document and/or a statutory declaration as to its contents.

2   Seller's solicitor

There are a number of documents and items which the seller's solicitor will need on completion, either for handing over to the buyer's solicitor or for examination by him.

(a) The seller's solicitor will hand over all the deeds and other documents of title except where they relate to land which the seller is retaining. A seller must bear the expense of obtaining these documents for the purpose of handing over on completion.[12] In addition to the original deeds, the seller's solicitor will be handing over any other documents relating to the property, including abstracts and epitomes prepared in the past, old search certificates, and other documents which are not documents of title at all, such as planning consents and NHBC documentation.

If the land being sold is registered land not subject to a registered charge, the seller's solicitor will hand over the Land Certificate. If the property *is* subject to a registered charge, the seller's solicitor will hand over the Charge Certificate, the Land Certificate having been retained at the Land Registry. On a sale of part of registered land the Certificate will not be handed over but instead put on deposit at the Land Registry as described earlier in this chapter. Even though title to the land is registered there will still be the old pre-registration title deeds which will also be handed over on completion.

(b) In certain circumstances the buyer may require a memorandum of his conveyance or assignment to be endorsed on a document of title that the seller is retaining. This would happen if the seller of unregistered land was only selling part of the land comprised in the deeds in which case the buyer would want a memorandum of the sale off to be endorsed on the conveyance or assignment to the seller. Similarly if the seller was a personal representative and thus retaining the grant of probate or administration, the buyer would want a memorandum of the sale to be endorsed on the grant. The Standard Conditions contain no relevant provision; a special condition could spell out the buyer's right to a memorandum on a specified document (normally the conveyance or assignment to the seller) and to a copy of the memorandum on completion. The normal procedure is that the seller's solicitor will write or type an undated memorandum on the appropriate document of title in readiness for completion and then on completion he will date it and hand the buyer's solicitor a copy which can be kept with the buyer's deeds.

11   *Re Halifax Commercial Banking Co Ltd and Wood* (1898) 79 LT 536. Proof of loss must also be given although due stamping will be presumed.
12   Cf Law of Property Act 1925, s 45(4).

In neither of these circumstances is a memorandum essential; the object is to warn any future buyer of the land that part of it has already been sold off. However, if the seller does sell the same land again to another buyer, that buyer cannot acquire a legal estate because the seller no longer has a legal estate to sell; in the case of a sale by a personal representative, the first buyer is protected by the provisions of the Administration of Estates Act 1925, section 36(6). Nevertheless, some inconvenience would occur if the seller did either mistakenly or fraudulently purport to sell the same property again and the effect of the memorandum is to ensure that this will not happen. If the land is subject to first registration, a memorandum will not be necessary.

(c) The purchase deed itself will be handed over on completion. The buyer's solicitor will check that it has been duly executed by the seller. The deed will be dated with the date of completion and will therefore only be dated actually on completion. Apparently insertion of the date after execution by the parties does not invalidate the deed. A solicitor may be tempted to back-date the deed, that is to date it with a date before the actual completion date; if the priority period of a search has expired at the time of completion, the deed might be back-dated to within the priority period in order to try and obtain the priority conferred by the search. Such back-dating is totally ineffective. In the case of a land charges search, the purchase must be *completed* within the period of the search to take priority. For registered land, to gain priority the buyer must not only complete but must also apply for registration within the priority period and the latter obviously cannot be back-dated. The proper course for the buyer's solicitor in such a position is to do another search and to delay completion until the result is received. As we have seen, searches can be effected quite quickly by telephone, fax or Land Registry Direct.

(d) The buyer's solicitor will wish to inspect the most recent receipt for water rates (and rates on a commercial property) to ensure that they have been paid if part of this payment has been apportioned to the buyer in the completion statement.

(e) If the property sold is leasehold, the seller's solicitor will produce for inspection the most recent receipt for ground rent. The Law of Property Act 1925, section 45(2) provides that on the sale of leasehold land a buyer shall assume unless the contrary appears firstly, that the lease was duly granted and secondly, on production of the last receipt for rent due, that the covenants and other provisions of the lease have been performed and observed. Section 45(3) contains a similar rule in relation to superior leases on the sale of an underlease. The rule is the corollary of the open contract rules in the Law of Property Act 1925 which restrict a buyer's right to investigate title. Despite these statutory assumptions, a buyer will if possible wish to investigate the freehold (and superior leasehold) title to check that the lease was properly granted, and to raise pre-contract enquiries about possible breaches of covenant.

The receipt also, of course, provides evidence that the rent has been paid up to date. Similarly, if a leasehold property is subject to a service charge which is being apportioned, the buyer's solicitor will wish to see evidence of the charge having been paid.

On the sale of leasehold property any requisite licence to assign would also be handed over, unless already supplied.

(f) On a sale of part, the title of which is registered, the seller will wish to keep some record both of precisely what land has been sold off and of any covenants or easements imposed. The seller's solicitor will therefore keep a copy of the purchase deed which can be placed with the seller's deeds. On a transfer of part of registered land, the land sold off will be removed from the register of the seller's title and any easements or covenants in the transfer will be mentioned in the register of the seller's title if appropriate.

(g) As on completion the buyer becomes entitled to possession of the property, keys may be handed over. If the keys are held by an estate agent then he should be authorised to hand them over to the buyer. On the other hand the keys may be handed over by the parties as they move out and in respectively. The danger of this is that the actual removal out of and into the property becomes divorced from legal completion. It would not be impossible for the seller to move out and the buyer to move in only to discover that the seller, or some other person, was refusing to move out. At the very least, the seller should be asked not to hand over the keys to the buyer until his solicitor has confirmed that completion has taken place. A further refinement would be for completion to take place at the property itself. This happens very rarely, if ever, in practice but it would also have the advantage of avoiding to some extent the problem of there being occupiers of the property whose interests might, by virtue of their occupation, be binding on the buyer.[13] It might be extremely inconvenient to have both solicitors present at the property, but they could then ensure that it was vacant.

(h) What if the property is subject to a mortgage? To deal firstly with unregistered land, if the seller's solicitor also acts for the mortgagee, he will have the deeds and can hand them over to the buyer on completion. How is the buyer to see that the mortgage has been discharged? A mortgage is discharged by receipt under either the Law of Property Act 1925, section 115 or the Building Societies Act 1986, Schedule 4. This is normally endorsed on the mortgage. The buyer's solicitor will wish to see the mortgage discharged before he parts with the purchase money. However, if the funds to pay off the mortgage are being provided by the purchase money then obviously the mortgage cannot be paid off before completion! If the seller has, on completion, the receipted mortgage deed in relation to not only the first mortgage but any other second mortgages, he will be able to hand these over on completion and there is no problem. This depends on the mortgagee(s) being willing to receipt the mortgage deed *before* the money necessary to redeem the mortgage is paid, on the understanding that when the solicitor hands the receipted deed over on completion he will immediately send off the redemption figure due on the mortgage. Not many mortgagees are willing to do this, although some will receipt the mortgage deed in escrow, which means that the receipted deed can then be handed over on completion. It is likely, though, that the mortgagee will not receipt the deed until after completion when it receives the money required to pay off the mortgage. The problem of how the buyer's solicitor is then to be satisfied that the mortgage(s) will indeed be discharged is solved by the use of a solicitor's undertaking. The seller's solicitor will provide the buyer's solicitor on completion with a written undertaking to send off the redemption money to the mortgagee and to forward the receipted mortgage deed to the buyer's solicitor as soon as it is received from the mortgagee. In practice the buyer's solicitor will normally be satisfied with this sort of undertaking, provided of course that it relates to all outstanding mortgages.[14] The Law Society has issued the following recommended form of undertaking that should only be given by solicitors or licensed conveyancers:

> In consideration of you today completing the purchase of (add full address) we hereby undertake to pay over to (add mortgagee's details) the money required to discharge

---

13   See ch 11, section 1 iii and 2 iii, above.
14   From the seller's point of view the undertaking should be limited to the discharge of specific named mortgages. An undertaking by a solicitor to 'discharge all subsisting charges' is inadvisable, as it will extend to all charges, whether the solicitor is aware of them or not; see *Bray v Stuart A West & Co* [1989] NLJR 753. See also [1991] Law Soc Gaz 37 at p 15.

the legal charge dated (add date of legal charge) and to forward the receipted legal charge Form DS1 to you as soon as it is received by us from (add mortgagee's name).

It should be noted that the seller's solicitor is only undertaking to do that which is actually within his control, that is to send off the money (which he knows he will be receiving on completion) and to forward the receipted mortgage deed when it is received. He is not undertaking actually to obtain the receipted deed and if there is some hold-up on the part of the mortgagee this would not amount to a breach of the undertaking. If the mortgagee is a Building Society or a bank, the buyer's solicitor will usually be happy to take this very slight risk, knowing that he can rely on the Building Society or bank to perform its functions properly. If on the other hand the mortgagee is a private individual or company, the buyer's solicitor may not be happy with an undertaking and may insist that completion take place at the mortgagee's solicitor's offices so that the receipted mortgage deed can be actually handed over on completion.[15] The receipt should be dated at the latest with the completion date, to avoid the receipt impliedly operating a transfer.[16]

In theory the seller's solicitors, in their role of acting for the mortgagee on discharge of the mortgage, should hand the deeds over to any subsequent mortgagee of whom the first mortgagee has notice. In practice any second mortgages will also be discharged out of the proceeds of sale in the same way and so the deeds can be handed on to the buyer's solicitors.

In the case of registered land, the basic problem is the same. Assuming that the mortgage is protected as a registered charge, it is discharged by the mortgagee executing a DS1 form application for discharge of the registered charge; this is then sent to the District Land Registry along with the Charge Certificate, or by Electronic Notification of Discharge via the Land Registry's Direct access Service by computer. If the seller's solicitor has on completion the Charge Certificate and DS1 form in relation to the first and any other mortgages, he can hand them over and there is no problem. Again, this is unlikely and an undertaking will be offered to the buyer's solicitor, to pay off the mortgage and forward the DS1 form(s) when received. Remember that there will be a separate Charge Certificate for each mortgage, if there is more than one; Charge Certificates for second mortgages should either be handed over on completion if available, or included in the undertaking with the DS1 form(s).

If the seller is a company and the investigation of title has revealed a floating charge over its assets including the property being sold, the buyer's solicitor will require a letter of non-crystallisation from the chargee confirming that at the date of completion the floating charge had not crystallised.

(i) The seller's solicitor may prepare a schedule of the deeds and other documents of title which he is handing over, which the buyer's solicitor will sign on completion; this avoids any argument later about any missing deeds or documents.

(j) If in order to save stamp duty, the consideration in the purchase deed only reflects the amount paid for the property and not any additional sum for chattels, the buyer's solicitor may require a further receipt in respect of the amount paid for the chattels.

3   Buyer's solicitor

As well as examining and receiving the various documents already referred to in the previous section, the buyer's solicitor will have other matters to attend to on completion.

---

15   See section v, below.
16   See Law of Property Act 1925, s 115(2) and *Cumberland Court (Brighton) Ltd v Taylor* [1964] Ch 29, [1963] 2 All ER 536.

(a) Payment of the purchase price: this will normally be by means of a telegraphic transfer or banker's draft if completion is taking place by the buyer's solicitor attending at the seller's solicitor's office.

(b) Land charges searches: as a precise description of the property need not be given on the application for the land charges search in respect of unregistered land, the search certificate may reveal certain entries which do not in fact relate to the property sold. The buyer's solicitor may ask the seller's solicitor to certify on the search certificate that the entries do not affect the property. In fact, rather better practice would be for the buyer's solicitor to obtain office copy entries of the registrations to check for himself that they do not affect the land which the buyer is buying.

(c) Authority to release the deposit: if a deposit is held by a stakeholder, he cannot release it unless one party becomes entitled to it under the terms of the contract. Obviously on completion the seller does become entitled to keep the deposit and indeed it forms part of the purchase money. If it is held by the seller's solicitor, it can be released to the seller. However, a preliminary deposit may be held by an estate agent and before releasing the money to the seller, the estate agent might require some proof that completion has taken place and that the seller has become entitled to the money. On completion, the buyer's solicitor may have to provide a brief written authorisation to the estate agent acknowledging the seller's right to the deposit.

iii   Agency completion

If the buyer's solicitor does not wish to attend on completion because the seller's solicitor's office is too far away, he can appoint a local solicitor as his agent to attend on completion. The agent should be given full instructions in line with the matters considered in this chapter, not forgetting verification for which the agent will need the abstract or epitome. The agent will charge for his services, but this may be very much cheaper than the buyer's solicitor travelling to attend on completion personally.

The agent may be sent a banker's draft for the completion money with his other instructions through the post, but this depends on the finance being available a day or two before completion. Alternatively the money could be telegraphed to him and he could then obtain a banker's draft from his own bank. The buyer's solicitor may even telegraph the money direct to the seller's solicitor on the latter's undertaking not to release the money to his client until completion and to return the money if completion does not take place, although this does involve some slight element of risk and it might be safer to send the money to the agent.

iv   Postal completion

On a postal completion instead of the two solicitors being present and exchanging inter alia the purchase deed and other documents of title, and the money, the exchange is made through the post and the money normally sent by telegraphic transfer. The buyer's solicitor sends the purchase money and the seller's solicitor in return sends the purchase deed, other title deeds, Land Certificate or Charge Certificate etc. Whilst this arrangement has the advantage of convenience, it has the disadvantage that no one appears to be looking after the buyer's interests on completion. Who will check that the purchase deed is properly executed? Who will verify and mark the abstract? The answer is that if completion is to take place by post, the seller's solicitor must be instructed to act as agent for the buyer's solicitor, to attend to these matters. It might be thought that there would necessarily be a conflict of interest in the same solicitor acting for both seller and buyer on completion. However, it is the Law Society's view that this is not necessarily so. Postal completions are indeed very common in practice with the great majority of transactions being completed in this way.

The potential problems were highlighted by the case of *Edward Wong Finance Co Ltd v Johnson, Stokes and Masters*.[17] In that case, a firm of solicitors in Hong Kong acting for a buyer had sent the purchase money, including the mortgage advance, to the seller's solicitor on the basis of the seller's solicitor undertaking to forward the documents of title including the discharge of the seller's mortgage. However, the seller's solicitor absconded with the purchase money and the Privy Council held that the loss had to be borne by the buyer's solicitors for failing to take appropriate steps to protect their client's interests. The case caused some concern in this country as the procedure resembled that followed on postal completions. As a result, the Law Society in 1984 first issued a code for completion by post.[18] The 1998 version of the code is set out in the Appendix. Adoption of the code must be specifically agreed by the solicitors concerned; it is a feature of the TransAction 2001. The code provides that the seller's solicitor will act as agent on completion for the buyer's solicitor without any fee. The seller's solicitor undertakes that on completion he will have the seller's authority to receive the purchase money and that he will be the duly authorised agent of any existing mortgagee to receive the part of the money paid to him which is needed to discharge such mortgage. It is not yet universal for a mortgagee automatically to appoint the seller's solicitors as such agent when sending him the title documents prior to the sale. The seller's solicitor (and the buyer's solicitor too) should therefore confirm that such agency does exist.

The code further provides that the buyer's solicitor will send the seller's solicitor instructions as to what to do on completion, including verification and marking of documents, memoranda to be endorsed on deeds, the position in relation to keys, etc. In the absence of such instructions the seller's solicitor is not under any duty to examine, mark or endorse any documents. Completion is actually effected by the buyer's solicitor sending (normally by telegraphic transfer) the balance due to the seller's solicitor. The seller's solicitor will ask his bank to let him know when the funds are received and the seller's solicitor holds the funds to the buyer's solicitor's order pending completion taking place. The seller's solicitor will then complete in accordance with the agreed instructions and thereafter he holds all title documents and other items to be sent to the buyer's solicitor as agent for the buyer's solicitor. He should immediately confirm to the buyer's solicitor that he has completed and send confirmation together with the title documents and any other items to the buyer's solicitor.

The code has met with some criticism; it has been claimed that its provisions do not go far enough and that it does not meet the problem actually posed by the *Wong* decision. In particular, it has been suggested that the buyer's solicitor should seek confirmation from the seller's mortgagee (rather than just the seller's solicitor) that the seller's solicitor has the authority to receive the money to discharge the mortgage.[19] There is no obligation on the seller to agree to adopt the code and to act as the buyer's solicitor's agent on completion except under the TransAction 2001, which provides that the code will apply unless otherwise agreed. If the seller's solicitor does not co-operate then completion would have to take place by personal attendance

---

17   [1984] AC 296, [1984] 2 WLR 1, PC.
18   [1984] LS Gaz 858.
19   See [1984] Conv 158.

or attendance by an agent. Clearly the seller's solicitor would not agree to adopt the code if he thought there was any chance of a conflict of interest. If the code does apply, the specific instructions given by the buyer's solicitor should include some agreement about the time of completion. This could be important in domestic conveyancing from the point of view of synchronising two transactions.

There is one amendment to the code which the seller's solicitor may wish to negotiate. Under paragraph 3 of the code the seller's solicitor undertakes that he will be authorised by the proprietor of *any* charge on the property to receive the money needed to discharge that charge. The seller's solicitor may wish this undertaking to extend only to charges of which he is aware and for the avoidance of doubt, those charges may need to be specifically referred to in correspondence between the solicitors.

v   Completion at the office of the solicitor for the seller's mortgagee

It may be that the seller's solicitor is not also acting for the seller's mortgagee. If the seller's mortgagee is a Building Society, the seller's solicitor may not be on the Building Society's panel of approved solicitors. In this case the seller's solicitor will not have received the original deeds or Charge Certificate from the Building Society but merely, in the case of unregistered land, an abstract or epitome prepared by the Building Society's solicitor. Nevertheless on completion the buyer's solicitor will wish to examine and take away the original deeds, or the Charge Certificate in the case of registered land. The seller's solicitor will not have them. Unless the mortgagee is prepared to release them to the seller's solicitor, the answer is to complete at the office of the mortgagee or more likely its solicitor. This situation often seems to occur when the mortgagee is a Local Authority.

It is common for the buyer to pay the purchase money by means of two banker's drafts or telegraphic transfers. One will represent the amount outstanding on the seller's mortgage. This will be made payable to the mortgagee's solicitor. The other will be for the remainder of the balance of the purchase money, made payable to the seller's solicitor. On completion the first amount is paid direct to the mortgagee's solicitor who will then release the receipted mortgage deed (or DS1 form) along with the rest of the deeds (or Charge Certificate) to the seller's solicitor who can then pass them on to the buyer's solicitor. The mortgagee will normally receipt the mortgage deed or seal the DS1 form in readiness for completion, but if this is not done the buyer's solicitor might accept an undertaking, which could be given by the mortgagee's solicitor instead of the seller's solicitor.

If there are second mortgages, the seller's solicitor may give an undertaking to discharge them in the normal way. An undertaking might also be given to the first mortgagee's solicitor because unless the second mortgages are discharged, the first mortgagee's solicitor ought to hand the deeds not to mortgagor/seller but to the second mortgagee with best claim to priority.

vi   Completion of the buyer's new mortgage

The mortgage is completed at the same time as the purchase; it cannot be completed before, because it is only when the buyer has the legal estate that he can mortgage it. In practice if the same solicitor is acting for both buyer and mortgagee it is difficult actually to detect completion taking place, but one *can* say that after completion, the documents of title are held by the solicitor on behalf of the mortgagee and not the buyer. The mortgage advance would of course have been used to pay the purchase price. The mortgage deed itself would have been executed before completion and be already in the solicitor's possession.

If the buyer's solicitor does not act for the buyer's mortgagee, completion of the mortgage will be more apparent. The mortgagee's solicitor may attend on completion as well, to hand over the mortgage advance and to take away the documents of title including the new mortgage deed.

vii   Synchronisation

A domestic conveyancing client will very commonly be buying one property and selling another and we have already discussed the need to ensure synchronisation of completion by having the same completion date in both contracts. As the proceeds of sale will be required to make up the purchase price, completion of the sale should take place before the completion of the purchase and it may be necessary to specify an early time for completion by amendment of Standard Condition 6.1.2, to ensure that completion of the sale does take place sufficiently early to allow time for completion of the purchase the same day. The solicitor should wait until he has actually received the proceeds of sale before drawing against those proceeds by sending off the purchase money; otherwise he will be breaching the Solicitors' Accounts Rules 1998. The problem in practice is that the telegraphic transfer to him of the balance of the money on his client's sale may take some time and he will therefore be under pressure to send off the balance of purchase money on his client's purchase, perhaps before he has received the sale proceeds, on the assumption that they will be received.

The problem may be solved by the purchase money being telegraphed directly to a seller's solicitor further up the chain, missing out some 'links' in the chain.

15 Post-completion

i Report to the client

Immediately after completion the seller's solicitor should report to the seller that completion has taken place.

ii Compliance with undertaking to discharge seller's mortgage

The seller's solicitor must attend to this immediately. On the day of completion, he must send to the mortgagee(s) the amount required to redeem the mortgage. The mortgagee will then return the receipted mortgage deed or in the case of registered land, form DS1 (DS3 for discharges of part).

Alternatively, under a relatively new scheme piloted by the Land Registry and two building societies, (the Electronic Notification of Discharge scheme or ENDs) notification of the discharge of a mortgage can be given by the lender electronically, directly to the Registry. This system is designed to do away with paper forms and to speed up the discharge process. Once the electronic message has been sent, the lender sends written confirmation to the person redeeming the mortgage that the END has been sent. The END does not have the effect of cancelling the charge; a formal application for this on form AP1 must still be made (see iv below.) The END cannot be used to discharge part of the land; form DS3 must be used for this. The procedure which the seller must use to discharge a charge where ENDs is in use is as follows: the seller's solicitor completes form END1 which he sends to the lender with the redemption monies. The lender will then transmit the END to the registry, and will send the seller's solicitor written confirmation that this has been done. The time limit for transmitting the END to the Registry (or notifying the borrower's solicitor of any problem) is 21 days. It is possible to check with the Registry, by phone or Land Registry Direct / Direct Access, whether an END has been sent.

In the case of unregistered land, if the mortgage deed was sent to the seller's solicitor with the rest of the title deeds then it must of course be returned with the redemption money for it to be receipted. Having received the receipted mortgage or form DS1, the seller's solicitor should check it and then promptly forward it to the buyer's solicitor in accordance with the undertaking.

iii   Protection by registration

The sale of unregistered title may have created an interest which requires protection. A common example is a new restrictive covenant on a sale of part. However, as the unregistered title is subject to compulsory registration, the covenant will be noted in the usual way on the charges register of the title following first registration.

If new interests are created on a transfer of part of registered land, they will again normally be protected automatically on the buyer's application for registration. For example although a new covenant on a transfer of part of registered land is a minor interest and requires protection on the register, this will be effected when the buyer applies for registration.

iv   Cancellation of registration

The seller's solicitor will also attend to the cancellation of land charges registrations. So for example if the seller had a second legal mortgage which was protected as a Ci land charge, on redeeming the mortgage the seller's solicitor will also request the second mortgagee to cancel the registration. If the seller's spouse had registered a class F land charge (under the Family Law Act) then the buyer would have only completed on provision of a form of application for cancellation signed by the spouse who registered it. If this is handed over on completion, the buyer's solicitor will effect the cancellation by sending it off. It is an implied term of the contract that if there is a Family Law Act 1996 registration, the seller must procure its cancellation.[1]

In a registered land context, the cancellation of entries relating to registered charges such as second mortgages, and Family Law Act notices, will be dealt with on the buyer's application for registration.

v   Account to client for proceeds

As soon as possible after completion, the seller's solicitor should account to the seller for any balance of the proceeds of sale. The seller should be sent a statement showing amounts received, payments, and a balance due to (or from) the seller. This raises a number of subsidiary points.

1   Estate agent's fee

If the seller has used an estate agent, the latter will often send his account to the seller's solicitor in the expectation that it will be paid out of the balance of the proceeds of sale. Before he pays it, the seller's solicitor should check with the seller that this is what the seller intends and also check the amount of the account. If the estate agent holds a preliminary deposit from the buyer, he might retain this on account of the fee.

2   Solicitor's costs

The seller's solicitor will wish to submit and agree a figure for his own costs and disbursements so that he can deduct these from the net proceeds. The solicitor's costs may be based on a 'time costing' element calculated by multiplying the hours spent on the transaction by the hourly charging rate of the solicitor, but will more commonly be

---

1   Family Law Act 1996, Sch 4, Pt 3.

a 'flat fee'. With increased competition for conveyancing work, the solicitor will usually have been asked for a preliminary estimate of the costs or a firm quotation; and the solicitor should ensure he keeps an accurate note of this on file to avoid disputes later.

3   Capital gains tax

Although capital gains tax is payable on the gain accruing from the disposal of a property, there is an exemption which will cover the vast majority of domestic conveyancing transactions. The gain is exempt from capital gains tax if it arises on the sale of a dwelling house – including grounds up to half a hectare – which has been occupied by the seller as his only or main residence during his period of ownership.[2] There are detailed provisions to cover specific situations. For example, it is not necessary for the seller to have been in occupation for the last three years before the sale, to cover the situation of a seller who moves out of his house some time before he sells it. If the seller has more than one house, he can elect which is to be his main residence and thereby qualify for the exemption. If the tax is payable, the seller's solicitor should at the very least advise the seller of this, and at an early stage in the transaction. It may be that the seller's solicitor will also be instructed to deal with the assessment of the tax and payment out of the proceeds. There are indexation allowances and an annual CGT exemption which may reduce the amount payable.

4   Investment of proceeds

If the proceeds are substantial, and particularly if the seller is selling one property but not buying another, the solicitor may be asked to advise and deal with the investment of the proceeds. The solicitor should, of course, have regard to the Financial Services Act 1986 if he proposes to give such advice. Any discrete investment business must be conducted within the scope of the Act, and solicitors are subject to the Solicitors' Investment Business Rules 1995. Because of these controls, many solicitors avoid giving investment advice, preferring to refer their clients to an independent financial adviser. The 1986 Act will be replaced at the end of 2001 by the Financial Services and Markets Act 2000, and the Solicitors' Investment Business Rules will be repealed as from December 2001. Under the new Act, the Law Society will no longer be able to authorise solicitors to conduct investment business, but firms may be treated as 'exempt professional firms', and carry on 'exempt regulated activities' under the supervision of the Law Society. For further details, see the Financial Services Authority website at www.fsa.gov.uk or the Law Society website at www.lawsociety.org.uk.

5   Position if seller is a mortgagee exercising a power of sale

If the seller is a mortgagee, for example a Building Society, exercising its power of sale, then it is not a simple matter of accounting to the client for the proceeds. The mortgagee is a trustee of the proceeds of sale and they must be applied in a particular order. This is considered at Chapter 13, section 3 ii, above.

6   Reassignment of life policy

If the seller's mortgage was an endowment mortgage which was formally assigned to the mortgagee, it will be necessary to reassign the life policy to the seller. Notice of the reassignment should then be given to the life company.

---

2   Taxation of Chargeable Gains Act 1992, ss 222, 223, 287.

2 BUYER'S SOLICITOR

i Report to client

Immediately after completion the buyer's solicitor should inform the buyer that completion has taken place and that the buyer is entitled to possession. If the buyer's solicitor has also acted for the buyer's mortgagee, then that client should also be informed of completion. Many mortgagees have a standard form which is completed and returned to the mortgagee after completion.

ii Protection by registration

The purchase deed may create an interest in unregistered land which requires protection by registration as a land charge and which it is in the buyer's interest to so protect. On a sale of part, the seller may have entered into a new restrictive covenant affecting the land which he is retaining which would require registration as a Dii land charge. If title to land is registered, such matters are dealt with on the buyer's application for registration.

iii Cancellation of registrations

There are two registrations which the buyer's solicitor may have made which he will wish to cancel after completion. These are registration of the buyer's contract – as a Civ land charge for unregistered land or a notice or caution for registered land – and registration of the buyer's lien for the deposit (if held by the seller's solicitor as agent for the seller) – as a Ciii land charge for unregistered land or a notice or caution for registered land.

iv Registration at the Land Registry

In almost all cases the buyer's solicitor will be obliged to register the buyer's title at the Land Registry. Firstly, if title to the land is already registered, the buyer having taken a transfer (or a lease for over 21 years) of whole or part. Secondly, if title to the land is not registered, but as a result of the transaction the buyer must now apply for first registration of title under section 123 of the Land Registration Act 1925.

l Registration of a dealing in registered land

Following completion of a purchase of registered land, unless and until the buyer applies for registration as proprietor of the land, the seller's name will remain on the register and the seller will therefore retain the legal estate. In addition, as was seen in Chapter 2, a lease also counts as such a dealing and if the lease is registrable, ie for over 21 years, it must be registered with separate title to vest the legal estate in the lessee/buyer. Registration is thus vital. Registration of a transfer will be dealt with here, and registration of a new lease will be dealt with in Chapter 17.

Application for registration must be made within the priority period of the search done before completion, which is 30 working days. If not, priority over intervening entries on the register which might affect the title is lost. Therefore the buyer's solicitor must not only complete but also apply for registration within the 30 day period. There are standard forms of application provided, which vary according to whether the application is for registration of a transfer of the whole of the land in the seller's title, or of part. If the seller had a mortgage and if the buyer has bought with the aid of a mortgage then the buyer's solicitor is in fact making three applications.

(a) He is applying for the discharge of the seller's mortgage(s). This application is supported by the form DS1 and the Charge Certificate. Where the END scheme is in use, there is no need to send DS1, but the application procedure will otherwise be the same. The buyer's solicitor will need to state on the AP1 that the mortgage has been discharged by END.

(b) He is applying for the registration of the transfer from the seller to the buyer. This application is supported by the deed of transfer and by the Land Certificate, which will already be at the Land Registry if the seller had a mortgage

(c) He is applying for the registration of the new mortgage as a registered charge in the charges register. This application is being made on behalf of the mortgagee and is supported by the new mortgage deed.

It can already be seen that the application (with cover form AP1) must be accompanied by certain documents: the form(s) DS1, the Charge Certificate(s), the transfer and the new mortgage deed. If the seller had no mortgage, then the Land Certificate must be sent with the application.[3] The Land Certificate or Charge Certificate will have been handed over on completion to the buyer's solicitor.

Where the transaction was a sale of part, the Land or Charge Certificate will not have been handed over by the seller, but his certificate will have been placed on deposit at the registry and the deposit number will have been notified to the buyer's solicitor. The buyer's solicitor will then ensure that the deposit number is quoted on the AP1. As the original of the mortgage deed will be incorporated in the new Charge Certificate, a copy certified by the buyer's solicitor as being a true copy must also be sent with the application. Should there be any delay in any document being available, the application should still be submitted within the priority period and the missing document forwarded as soon as possible. For example there might be some delay in the buyer's solicitor receiving the form DS1, or there might be some delay in the transfer being returned from the Inland Revenue where it will have been sent for stamping. If this is anticipated, the appropriate procedure would be to submit the application with the unstamped deed with a request for it to be returned so that stamping could take place

The application is sent to the appropriate District Land Registry. It must be accompanied by a fee, which is based on the purchase price.[4] There is no fee payable on applying for the registration of a new mortgage made at the same time as registration of a transfer. If there is more than one buyer, the application must state whether the survivor of them can give a valid receipt, which will only be the case if they are beneficial joint tenants rather than beneficial tenants in common. In the latter case, a restriction will be entered on the Proprietorship Register preventing a sole survivor dealing with the property. If the transfer contains new restrictive covenants, as it might well do on a sale of part, a certified copy must also be sent with the application.

In due course the Land Certificate (if there is no new mortgage) or a Charge Certificate (if there is a new mortgage which will be protected as a registered charge) will be issued to the buyer's solicitor. Following a sale of part, a new title will be opened with a new title number for the part sold off and a new Land or Charge Certificate issued; the register of the seller's title will be amended to show that part

---

3   Land Registration Act 1925, s 64(1).
4   Land Registration Fee Order 1999.

of the property has been sold off and any provisions in the transfer which affect the seller's title, for example if the seller enters into new covenants or easements, will be noted on the register of his title.

On receiving the new Certificate the buyer's solicitor should check it to ensure its accuracy. If it is a Charge Certificate it will then be sent to the mortgagee. If it is a Land Certificate the solicitor will require instructions from the buyer as to its custody.

Recently there has been a trend for lenders to request that the Registry retains their Charge Certificate under section 63 of the Land Registration Act 1925. If this is the case, the Registry will issue the buyer's solicitor a copy of the register and of the filed plan (if this has been amended in any way), whilst the original charge will be retained at the Registry in case the lender requires a Charge Certificate at a later date. Titles where the Charge Certificate has been retained at the Registry will have an entry in the Charges register confirming this. If the buyer later wishes to sell the property, he should not be disadvantaged by the lack of a Charge Certificate as he can easily obtain office copies of the register, filed plan and supporting documents, if any. More information is available in Land Registry Practice Leaflet 31.

2　First registration of title

As mentioned in Chapter 2, where the buyer is buying unregistered land, the buyer must apply for first registration of his title in certain circumstances, listed in section 2 (ii) of that chapter. Thus it is highly likely that following a purchase of unregistered land, the buyer will indeed have to apply for first registration of his title. Registration following a conveyance or assignment or other qualifying transaction will be dealt with here and registration following the grant of a lease will be dealt with in Chapter 17.

The application must be made within two months of completion or the buyer will lose the legal estate that he acquired on completion. However, late applications for registration are invariably accepted and by this means the legal estate is restored to the buyer. On the application form for registration (FR1), the buyer's solicitor must certify that the title has been properly investigated. He must also certify that all interests affecting the property are disclosed in the title documents accompanying the application, or state what other interests or incumbrances exist. The Registry will wish to examine the title themselves and to this end the application must be accompanied by all the title deeds and other documents of title including abstracts, epitomes, requisitions and replies thereto and land charges search certificates. The application is also accompanied by the purchase deed and a certified copy. If the buyer has bought with the aid of a mortgage there will also be an application on behalf of the mortgagee for registration of the mortgage as a registered charge, and the mortgage and a certified copy of it must also be sent. The original mortgage is bound up with the Charge Certificate, but the original purchase deed is returned to the buyer's solicitor after registration along with the rest of the pre-registration title deeds. There is a form of schedule (Form DL) which should be used for listing the documents sent with the application. If the applicants are joint buyers the form will need to state whether they are joint tenants or tenants in common, and if the latter, the shares in which they hold the property.[5]

The application form and accompanying documents together with the fee, which is proportionate to the sale price,[6] are sent to the District Land Registry for the area in which the land is situated. If the Land Registry have any queries on their investigation of the title they will raise a requisition of the buyer's solicitor. Assuming

---

5　See section 1, above.
6　Land Registration Fees Order 1999.

that any such requisitions are satisfactorily answered, the title will be registered and a Land or Charge Certificate returned to the buyer's solicitor along with the title deeds. Again, the Certificate (if one is issued – see above) should be checked carefully for accuracy. The title deeds will not normally be needed in the future; when the property is sold title will be deduced under the Land Registration Act 1925, section 110. However, the pre-registration deeds are not totally redundant. They may contain more precise details of the boundaries of the property than the register and the filed plan. Also, any indemnity covenant included in the conveyance giving rise to first registration will not be noted in the register and thus when the first registered proprietor sells, it will be necessary to check the conveyance to him.

3   Expedited registration

On registration of a dealing with a registered title or on a first registration, it is possible to request that the application be expedited on payment of an additional fee. This might be appropriate if the buyer wished to resell quickly.

v   Stamping

The purchase deed may require stamping. There are two forms of stamping: ad valorem stamp duty and production to the Inland Revenue for the 'particulars delivered' or P.D. stamp. A purchase deed may require one or both.

I   Stamp duty[7]

Stamps to the value of the amount of duty payable are impressed on the deed. Stamp duty may be either ad valorem or at a fixed rate, for example £5.00 payable on a counterpart lease. Ad valorem duty is proportionate to the value of the property involved. Mention is made below not only of stamping purchase deeds but also the stamping requirements for other common conveyancing documents. This is important not only from the point of view of the buyer's solicitor after completion but also from the point of view of the buyer's solicitor in examining the abstract of title of unregistered land, to ensure that the abstracted documents have all been correctly stamped. The consequences of failing to have a document adequately stamped are dealt with below and in Chapter 10, section 17.

   (a)   *Conveyance on sale; assignment on sale; transfer on sale*   Under this heading are the normal purchase deeds. They all bear ad valorem duty. The current rate is on a sliding scale depending on the value of the property transferred; under £60,000 no duty is payable; values of over £60,000 but under £250,000 attract duty at a rate of 1%; over £250,000 but under £500,000 means that duty of 3% is payable, whilst a property value over £500,000 will require duty of 4%. If the transaction value is below £60,000 or in one of the 'bands' mentioned above, it will be necessary for the transfer deed to contain an appropriate certificate of value. If there are a number of connected transactions, duty is charged on the total consideration, so it is not possible to avoid duty by selling the property in a number of parts! The figures given are the current rates at the time of writing but they are changed periodically. In order to check the duties paid on deeds in the abstract it is necessary to know the rates applicable in the past; there are tables available from which the information can be ascertained.

7   See Stamp Act 1891 as amended.
8   Finance Act 1985, s 87.

(b)   *Deed of gift, ie voluntary conveyance, assignment or transfer; or any conveyance, assignment or transfer at an undervalue*   Prior to 25 March 1985 ad valorem duty was payable on the value of the property. After that date voluntary conveyances bore only fixed duty of 50p but still had to be adjudicated by the Inland Revenue.[8] (Adjudication is not in fact confined to such cases and any person interested can have a document adjudicated, that is have the Inland Revenue decide whether it bears duty and if so how much.)

However, as from 1 May 1987, the fixed duty and adjudication requirement have been removed provided that the deed includes, or has endorsed on or attached to it, a certificate signed by the transferor or his solicitor to the effect that the document falls within category L in the schedule to the Stamp Duty (Exempt Instruments) Regulations 1987. The deed does not then have to be sent to the Inland Revenue. Since 25 March 1985 ad valorem duty is payable in respect of a conveyance at an undervalue on the actual consideration.

(c)   *Leases*   The rules regarding stamp duty are rather complicated. Briefly, ad valorem duty is payable on the premium, as if it were the consideration for a straightforward sale deed, as in paragraph (a), with the exemption if the lease contains the appropriate certificate of value (provided that the rent is within certain limits). Ad valorem duty is also payable on the amount of the rent, the rate being dependent on the length of the term of the lease. Any agreement for lease should also be produced to the Inland Revenue. Duty will be payable on the agreement for lease and any duty paid will be noted on the lease itself. A counterpart lease – that is the duplicate copy of the lease which is executed by the lessee and retained by the lessor – bears a fixed duty of £5.00.[9]

(d)   *Assents*   If an assent is not sealed but just signed, it bears no duty. An assent which is sealed bore the fixed duty of 50p prior to 25 March 1985, but now bears no duty, as it will fall within categories B,C or E of the Stamp Duty (Exempt Instruments) Regulations 1987.

(e)   *Mortgages*   Mortgages used to be liable to stamp duty but this rule was abolished as from 1 August 1971.[10] Similarly, since that date vacating receipts and deeds of discharge have not attracted duty. Building Society receipts were already exempt under the Building Societies Act 1962, section 117.

(f)   *Deeds of appointment of new trustees, powers of attorney*   These are both deeds which bore a fixed duty of 50p prior to 25 March 1985, but now bear no duty.

2   Particulars Delivered Stamp

By the Finance Act 1931, section 28 (as amended), whether or not stamp duty is payable certain documents must be produced to the Inland Revenue, together with a statement of the particulars of the document, whereupon a stamp – the P.D. stamp – will be impressed on the document. The documents which must be produced are:

(a)   conveyances on sale, and transfers of registered freehold land;
(b)   leases granted for terms of seven years or more;
(c)   assignments on sale of such leases (and transfers on sale if the title to the lease is registered).

Some documents will require a P.D. stamp but not attract stamp duty, for example a conveyance on sale for under £60,000. Some documents will require both stamp duty and a P.D. stamp, for example a conveyance on sale for over £60,000.

---

9   See further at ch 17, section 2 vii.
10   Finance Act 1971, s 64.

The statement of particulars is in a standard form, often called a P.D. form, and contains information as to the identity of the parties and the property and the amount of the consideration.

3 Procedure

The stamp duty due, if any, and the P.D. form, if necessary, must be sent to the Inland Revenue with the deed within 30 days of the date of the deed. Late stamping is possible although a penalty could be charged. Under a procedure introduced in 1986, if a transfer, conveyance or assignment needs to be produced for a P.D. stamp, but does not bear stamp duty because the consideration does not exceed £60,000 and the deed contains a certificate of value, the P.D. stamping will be done at the District Land Registry, provided that registration is necessary either because title is already registered or because of compulsory first registration.

4 Failure to stamp

The effect of failing to stamp either with the appropriate stamp duty or a P.D. stamp is that the document cannot be produced in court as evidence and thus cannot be used to prove title to the property.[11] An unstamped or insufficiently stamped document is clearly not a good link in the abstract of title to unregistered land and the importance of checking stamping on examining the abstract has already been mentioned. In the case of registered land, the Land Registry will not accept an application for registration which is supported by a document which is not duly stamped. The deed of transfer on a sale must therefore be stamped before the application for registration is made which, it should be remembered, must be within the priority period of the pre-completion search. If there is any delay the application for registration should be made without the deed, which should be forwarded as soon as possible although ideally the application should be submitted as soon as possible with the unstamped deed, which is then returned for stamping.

5 Stamp duty avoidance schemes

There was a vogue in the late 1970s and early 1980s for avoiding stamp duty on conveyances by an artificial scheme based on an agreement for a lease. Such schemes have been held to be ineffective and are now caught by the Finance Act 1984, section 11; if on examination of unregistered title it appears that such a scheme was used in the past, the buyer's solicitor should raise a requisition based on the improper stamping of the conveyance unless it bears either an adjudication stamp or ad valorem duty.

vi Custody of Land Certificate or Charge Certificate

Title will normally be registered either because the property was bought by the buyer as a registered title or as a result of first registration following a buyer's purchase. If the buyer has bought with the aid of a mortgage, following registration there will be a Charge Certificate, unless the Certificate is retained at the Registry at the lender's request under section 63 of the Land Registration Act 1925, and also the old pre-registration title deeds. The mortgagee will want custody of the Charge Certificate and possibly also the old title deeds.

---

11   Stamp Act 1891, s 14(4).

If the property is not subject to a mortgage, the buyer's solicitor will have the Land Certificate and the old pre-registration title deeds. In this case the buyer's solicitor should obtain instructions as to the custody of these documents. They might be left with the buyer's solicitor for safe keeping; they might be sent to the buyer's bank for safe keeping; the buyer might even want to keep them himself although he should be advised of their importance and the need to protect them from damage, destruction or theft.

vii   Notice of assignment of leasehold land

If a lease contains a provision making the lessor's consent necessary to any assignment, that consent will have been obtained before exchange or certainly before completion. However, the lease may merely provide that the lessor (or his solicitor) is to be given notice of any assignment, and any mortgage, or receipted mortgage, within a certain time after the event, often 28 days. There will usually also be a fee payable, and in recent years such fees have increased sharply, so that whereas ten years ago a fee of £15 would have been normal, modern leases may require the payment of £100 or more. It is important that the solicitor checks this detail well before completion so that he can warn his client of the additional cost. The notice is normally sent in duplicate with the request that one copy be returned receipted. This can then be put with the Land or Charge Certificate and is evidence that the requirement has been complied with. Even if there is no covenant requiring notice to be given, a mortgagee will want notice of the mortgage to be given to the lessor so that the mortgagee might be informed of any forfeiture proceedings.

viii   Notice of assignment of life policy

If the buyer has bought with the aid of an endowment mortgage, the life assurance policy may have been assigned to the mortgagee. In his role of acting for the mortgagee, the solicitor must give notice of this assignment to the life assurance company, otherwise the life company will be unaware of the lender's interest and, in the event of the policy holder's death, might quite innocently pay the policy proceeds to the deceased's estate rather than the lender. Mortgagees will often provide a standard form of notice to ensure that the solicitor does not forget! Again, notice is normally given in duplicate and a copy returned receipted.

The life policy itself, the deed of assignment and the receipted notice will then be sent to the mortgagee along with the Charge Certificate; the life policy is security for the loan just as the property is, and the mortgagee will want custody of the policy and the assignment of it. Some mortgagees do not require a deed of assignment, but simply have custody of the policy.

ix   Registration at Companies Registry

If the buyer is a company which has bought with the aid of a new mortgage, it will be necessary to lodge particulars of the mortgage at the Companies Registry within the prescribed period of 21 days from the date of the mortgage.[12]

---

12   Companies Act 1985, s 398, as amended by Companies Act 1989.

x   Water rates and Council Tax

It is good practice to inform the Local and Water Authorities of the change of the occupier of the property as a result of the purchase. Under the TransAction Protocol, the seller's solicitors should check that the seller is aware of the need to do this.

xi   Account to client

The same principles apply to the question of the solicitor's costs as have already been discussed in the previous section.[13] If the solicitor has been acting not only for the buyer but also the mortgagee, then he will be submitting two bills, although they may be combined. There is the bill for acting for the buyer on his purchase (and also on his mortgage) and the bill for acting for the mortgagee on the mortgage, which is payable by the buyer. In respect of the latter, there are guideline charges agreed between the Building Societies Association and the Law Society, based on the size of the mortgage advance.

3   MORTGAGEE'S SOLICITOR

In the previous section we have assumed that the buyer's solicitor is also acting for the mortgagee, and we have mentioned a number of steps which are taken after completion for the mortgagee rather than the buyer. If there is a separate solicitor acting for the mortgagee, then these steps, such as giving notice to the lessor of the mortgage if the property is leasehold, and giving notice of assignment of the life policy in the case of an endowment mortgage, may be taken by the mortgagee's solicitor. However, the mortgagee's title is naturally dependent on the buyer's title; for example, the mortgagee of a registered title will not be in a position to register the mortgage as a registered charge until the buyer has registered the transfer; similarly if the necessary stamp duty is not paid on the purchase deed, this affects the mortgagee's title too. In practice therefore, the mortgagee's solicitor may take over such steps as registration and stamping, having been provided with the appropriate documentation and fees by the buyer's solicitor.

   If the mortgage deed includes an obligation to make further advances, the mortgagee will want that obligation entered on the charges register to ensure that any further advances are protected as against a subsequent registered charge. However, the Land Registry will only do this if the mortgage deed includes the wording of Land Registry Form 113, or if this form is lodged separately.[14]

---

13   Disbursements may include stamp duty, search fees and registration fee.
14   Land Registration Rules 1925, r 139A.

16 Remedies

In the typical transaction the parties enter into a contract, which is then performed, and their remedies are largely the usual contractual remedies, set in the context of a conveyancing transaction. There are a number of different areas to consider. Firstly, there are situations in which a party is entitled to refuse to complete the transaction. Secondly, we must examine the ways by which one party can attempt to force the other party to complete if he is unwilling to do so, and the consequences of completion not taking place. Thirdly, the compensation which may be payable even though completion does take place must be considered. Fourthly, we must look at the remedies that exist after completion.

I SITUATIONS IN WHICH A PARTY CAN REFUSE TO COMPLETE THE CONTRACT

i Misrepresentation

An actionable misrepresentation is a statement of fact made by a party, which is untrue, on which the other party relies and which induces the other party to enter into the contract. One is normally dealing with misrepresentation by the seller rather than by the buyer. Misrepresentation can be categorised as fraudulent, negligent or innocent.

1 Fraudulent misrepresentation

A fraudulent misrepresentation is one made knowing it is false or reckless as to whether it is false or true. The buyer can rescind and also claim damages in the tort of deceit, where dishonesty is involved.[1]

2 Negligent misrepresentation

Negligent misrepresentation is one which is not fraudulent, but where the seller cannot prove that he had reasonable grounds for believing in the truth of the statement and did so believe right up to the time the contract was made. The buyer can rescind, and/or claim damages under the Misrepresentation Act 1967, section 2(1). However,

---

1   See for example *Derry v Peek* (1889) 14 App Cas 337, HL; and see also *Thomas Witter Ltd v TBP Industries Ltd* [1996] 2 All ER 573.

the court has a power under the Misrepresentation Act 1967, section 2(2) to refuse to award rescission and to award damages in lieu. A negligent misrepresentation might also amount to the tort of negligent misstatement under *Hedley Byrne & Co Ltd v Heller & Partners Ltd.*[2]

3 Innocent misrepresentation

An innocent misrepresentation is one which is neither fraudulent nor negligent. Again, rescission is available but there is no right to damages, although as with negligent misrepresentation the court has a power to award damages in lieu of rescission.

Rescission is an equitable remedy and thus the right to rescind can be lost even through no fault of the plaintiff.[3] This is particularly important in the case of innocent misrepresentation where the only method by which damages can be obtained is in lieu of rescission; if the right to rescind is lost then of course there can be no damages either.

The right to rescission is not lost merely because the misstatement has become a term of the contract.[4]

4 Illustrations

A number of cases illustrate the incidence of misrepresentation in a conveyancing transaction. In *Heinemann v Cooper*[5] there was correspondence between the solicitors for seller and buyer concerning the level of service charge on a flat. The amount of the service charge had not in fact been fixed at the time of the sale to the buyer. The seller's solicitor wrote to the buyer's solicitor indicating that when the seller had bought, a similar enquiry had been raised about the level of the service charge and that the then sellers 'did advise that they anticipated the service charge for the first year would not exceed £250 and that appears to be a reasonable estimate in the case of a recently refurbished building'. That statement by the seller's solicitor turned out to be false because a correct estimate would have been £625 not £250. On this basis, the buyer recovered damages for misrepresentation. *Heinemann v Cooper* illustrates the role which a seller's solicitor may play in making a misrepresentation. This was also a feature of *Cemp Properties (UK) Ltd v Dentsply Research and Development Corpn.*[6] On the sale of a leasehold property, a schedule to the lease mentioned certain other documents. Perusal of these documents revealed that there were provisions as to rights of light which affected the development potential of the site. The buyer's solicitor raised a preliminary enquiry about these documents and was told that copies of the documents were not available. This statement turned out to be untrue, because copies of the documents were handed over with the other deeds on completion. Again, the buyers were able to recover damages for misrepresentation.[7]

The role of the solicitor was again under scrutiny in *Strover v Harrington.*[8] In that case, the estate agent's particulars referred to the property as having mains drainage.

2 [1964] AC 465, [1963] 2 All ER 575, HL.
3 For example, if a third party would be prejudiced by the rescission.
4 Misrepresentation Act 1967, s 1. Neither is the right lost merely because the contract has been completed, although if a third party such as a mortgagee would be prejudiced, rescission will not be granted.
5 (1987) 19 HLR 262, CA.
6 [1989] 2 EGLR 192; see also *Gran Gelato Ltd v Richcliff (Group) Ltd and others* [1992] Ch 560, [1992] 1 All ER 865.
7 See further at [1991] 34 EG 62, CA.
8 [1988] Ch 390, [1988] 1 All ER 769.

In fact the property drained into a cesspool. The estate agents realised their error and wrote to the buyer's solicitor before exchange of contracts pointing out the position. However, the buyer's solicitor never passed this information on to the buyer, and a preliminary enquiry on the question of drainage was answered by the seller's solicitor to the effect that there was mains drainage. On the strength of this false statement, the buyer sued the seller for misrepresentation. He lost, because the court decided that as his solicitor knew the correct position, having been told by the estate agent, the information was imputed to the buyer who was therefore taken as knowing the true position; he could not therefore be said to have relied on the false statement by the seller through his solicitor in replies to preliminary enquiries. (Incidentally, the court also commented that the principal means for verifying the nature of drainage is by preliminary enquiries raised by the solicitor rather than from a surveyor's report; the surveyor for the buyer had indicated in his report that the property did have mains drainage but was held not to have been negligent.)

If a statement is true at the time it is made but becomes untrue before exchange of contracts, then it should be corrected. In *Corner v Mundy*[9] a seller stated in replies to preliminary enquiries that the central heating system was in good order. This was true, but before exchange of contracts three months later the water in the radiators had frozen, causing damage. The seller was held liable for damages for misrepresentation.

Two other examples of misrepresentation are both slightly unusual. In *Atlantic Estates plc v Ezekiel*,[10] the misrepresentation arose partly because of a photograph attached to some auction particulars which showed people apparently entering and leaving premises described as 'wine bar by day, cocktail bar by night'. The freehold of the premises was being sold subject to a lease. The court decided that the particulars represented the tenant's trade as still continuing when in fact the business had ceased because the tenant had lost his licence.

Goff v Gauthier[11] was an action for damages brought by a seller following non-completion by the buyer. The buyer's defence was that the seller's solicitor had informed the buyer's solicitor that if the buyer did not exchange contracts, the deal would be off and a draft contract would be sent to another prospective buyer at a higher price. In fact it appeared that although this statement was made by the seller's solicitor in good faith, the seller had not in fact decided that the contract would be withdrawn and sent to another buyer if the existing buyer failed to exchange contracts as demanded. The court found that an actionable misrepresentation had been made and that this gave the buyer a good defence to the seller's action for damages for non-completion.

Liability for misrepresentation is not, however, absolute. In *William Sindall plc v Cambridgeshire County Council*[12] a developer purchased land from the county council and, apparently unknown to either party, there was an underground sewer in existence which interfered with the company's development plans, but would be too expensive too move. The Court of Appeal held that the council's representation that it had no knowledge of any such incumbrance was sufficient to absolve it from responsibility, as it had made reasonable enquiries to check on the existence of such things

The damages payable to a buyer will be the difference in value between the price paid and the actual market value of the property in the light of the true state of affairs.[13] It was suggested in *Syrett v Carr and Neave (a firm)*[14] that, where the misrepresentation

9   [1987] CLY 479.
10   [1991] 2 EGLR 202, CA.
11   (1991) 62 P & CR 388.
12   [1994] 3 All ER 932, [1994] 1 WLR 1016, CA.
13   *Hussey v Eels* [1990] 2 QB 227, [1990] 1 All ER 449, CA; *Cemp Properties* (above).
14   [1990] 2 EGLR 161.

related to the physical state of the property, damages could relate to the cost of the necessary repairs, but this view was disapproved in *Watts and another v Morrow*,[15] and it is clear from *Patel v Hooper and Jackson (a firm)*[16] that the cost of repairs cannot be recovered.

5   General conditions

It is likely that the buyer's remedies for misrepresentation will be in some way curtailed in the general conditions in the contract. The Standard Conditions do contain such a provision. Standard Condition 7.1 applies 'if any plan or statement in the contract or in the negotiations leading to it is or was misleading or inaccurate due to an error or omission'. This will presumably also cover errors or omissions on the property information form under the TransAction Protocol. Standard Condition 7.1 limits the right to rescission; rescission is only available either where the error or omission results from fraud or recklessness or where a party would otherwise be obliged, to his prejudice, to transfer or to accept property differing substantially from what the error or omission had led him to expect. Condition 7.1 also limits the right to damages for misrepresentations to situations where there is a 'material difference' between the description or value of the property as represented and as it is, although this may confer a right to damages for innocent misrepresentation which does not exist under an open contract.

In addition to these conditions, a standard form of answers by the seller to preliminary enquiries, which may be thought to be a potential source of misrepresentations by the seller, may state that the answers are 'believed to be correct' but that their accuracy is not guaranteed and they do not obviate the need to make appropriate searches and enquiries.[17] The Seller's Property Information Form, which has largely replaced replies to preliminary enquiries under the TransAction Protocol, contains no such disclaimer.

The Misrepresentation Act 1967, section 3 regulates terms in contracts which restrict or exclude a party's liability for misrepresentation or the other party's remedies for misrepresentation. The Standard Condition falls into this category. The effect of section 3 is that the term is of no effect except in so far as it satisfies the test of reasonableness laid down in section 11 of the Unfair Contract Terms Act 1977, the burden of proof being on the party relying on the term, ie the seller. The test referred to is that the term must be a fair and reasonable one to be included in the contract having regard to the circumstances which were or ought to have been known by the parties at the time the contract was made. The question therefore arises whether the Standard Conditions (and the disclaimer on any form of preliminary enquiries) are going to deprive the buyer of his remedies for misrepresentation. There are cases which do give some comfort to the buyer. In *William Sindall plc v Cambridgeshire County Council*,[18] it was suggested that a disclaimer such as that on the standard form of preliminary enquiries would prevent the replies from being collateral warranties, but they would still be representations. However, in *Walker v Boyle*[19] it was held that

---

15   [1991] 4 All ER 937, [1991] 1 WLR 1421.
16   [1999] 1 All ER 992, [1999] 1 WLR 1792.
17   See for example the Oyez standard form. Such a disclaimer may also purport to exclude the liability of the seller's *solicitor* to the buyer in negligence, although no such liability appears to exist; *Gran Gelato Ltd v Richcliff (Group) Ltd* [1992] Ch 560, [1992] 1 All ER 865.
18   [1994] 3 All ER 932, [1994] 1 WLR 1016, CA, applying *Cremdean Properties Ltd v Nash* (1977) 244 Estates Gazette 547, CA.
19   [1982] 1 All ER 634, [1982] 1 WLR 495.

the disclaimer on the standard form of enquiries was totally ineffective and also that the condition under review, which was the equivalent condition in the nineteenth edition of the National Conditions of Sale, did not meet the reasonableness test. That condition differs from Standard Condition 7.1, but it is significant that the court held that the condition did fall foul of section 3 despite its apparent acceptance in practice in being incorporated into a set of widely used general conditions.

The edition of the Law Society General Conditions replaced by the Standard Conditions contained a provision whereby the buyer acknowledged that he had not relied on any statements not made or confirmed in writing. This has not been included in the Standard Conditions but a seller's solicitor may wish to add it as a special condition.[20]

ii   Breach of contract

If a breach of contract is sufficiently serious, it may entitle the other party to withdraw from the contract. This will happen in practice in two main situations. Firstly, the seller may be in default in being unable to convey that which he has contracted to convey, perhaps because he has misdescribed the property or failed to disclose a defect of title or cannot give vacant possession. Secondly, a party may be entitled to withdraw where the other party fails to complete and time is or has been made of the essence.[1]

I   Misdescription and non-disclosure

Typically a misdescription might involve a misstatement of the area of the property,[2] or a description of land as simply 'registered' when the title is not in fact absolute,[3] or the description of land as being held under a lease when it is in fact held on an underlease.[4] Non-disclosure will occur where some defect such as a restrictive covenant or a right of way is not disclosed. Under an open contract if the misdescription or non-disclosure is substantial, the seller cannot force the buyer to complete and the buyer can recover his deposit.[5] If the misdescription or non-disclosure is *not* substantial then the buyer must complete although with compensation by way of a reduction in the purchase price. Whether the misdescription or non-disclosure is substantial or not, the buyer can always insist on completing, with an appropriate reduction in the purchase price. If the misdescription operates in the buyer's favour, the seller cannot claim an increase in the purchase price and will be forced to complete unless the court refuses the buyer specific performance on the ground of hardship to the seller; the buyer could instead claim damages for breach of contract.

Standard Condition 7.1, mentioned in the previous section as relevant to misrepresentation, is wide enough to cover misdescription too, referring as it does to errors or omissions in 'any plan or statement in the contract'. Under 7.1 a seller as well as a buyer may rescind if he would otherwise be obliged to transfer property to his prejudice.[6]

---

20   It may not be effective; see *Goff v Gauthier* (1991) 62 P & CR 388.
 1   These are not the only situations in which a party can withdraw, but they are the most common in practice. So, for example, if the buyer fails to pay a deposit the seller can withdraw, always assuming there is a contract in existence.
 2   For example *Watson v Burton* [1956] 3 All ER 929, [1957] 1 WLR 19.
 3   *Re Brine and Davies' Contract* [1935] Ch 388.
 4   *Re Russ and Brown's Contract* [1934] Ch 34, CA.
 5   *Flight v Booth* (1834) 1 Bing NC 370.
 6   SC 7.1.3(b).

2 Failure by the seller to show good title

We have seen that there are in essence two sorts of defect of title.[7] If the seller cannot show good title because of the existence of some defect such as a right of way or restrictive covenant which he has failed to disclose then, as mentioned in the preceding section, if the defect does substantially affect the property the buyer will be able to withdraw from the contract and, on the face of it, sue the seller for damages for breach. If the defect is a Family Law Act 1996 registration then it becomes an implied term of the contract that the seller will procure its removal;[8] if it is not removed then again the seller is in breach of contract and the buyer can withdraw and sue for damages.[9] Likewise if the seller is unable to give vacant possession as a result of some undisclosed tenancy of the property.

The other sort of defect of title is the more 'technical' type, such as a flaw in the abstract of unregistered title. This again means that the seller cannot show a good title and that the seller is in breach of contract; the buyer can 'rescind' and sue for damages. However, the seller's duty to show good title is not an absolute duty and there are degrees of 'goodness', as is shown by the case of *MEPC Ltd v Christian-Edwards*[10] where an investigation of title in 1973 revealed a contract for sale in 1912 not shown as having been discharged; the House of Lords held that good title had nevertheless been shown. A refusal by the seller to answer a properly raised requisition will similarly entitle the buyer to 'rescind'. In *Barclays Bank plc v Weeks Legg and Dean*[11] it was confirmed that a good marketable title was not a perfect title, but one which, in the event of a sale, a reluctant purchaser would be compelled to accept.

3 Failure to complete

Time is not normally of the essence of completion of a conveyancing transaction but it can be made of the essence by service of a notice to complete. This procedure is dealt with later in this chapter. Once time has become of the essence of completion by virtue of the notice, then if a party fails to complete this will amount to a breach of the contract entitling the other party to withdraw and claim damages for breach of contract.

iii Rescission under a specific contractual right

The contract may specifically provide that a party can in certain circumstances rescind the contract. So, for example, Standard Condition 5.1.2 allows the buyer to rescind if the property becomes unfit for its purpose. The seller on such rescission repays the deposit (with accrued interest) and the buyer returns all documents that have been sent to him.[12]

iv Rescission for fraud, undue influence or mistake

Under ordinary contractual principles it may be possible to rescind in such cases.

---

7 See ch 5, section 4 ii, above.
8 Family Law Act 1996, Sch 4, para 3.
9 *Wroth v Tyler* [1974] Ch 30, [1973] 1 All ER 897.
10 [1981] AC 205, [1979] 3 All ER 752, HL.
11 [1999] QB 309, [1998] 3 All ER 213.
12 SC 7.2.

v   Damages

The word 'rescission' can bear a number of meanings. On rescission in the sense of setting the contract aside for misrepresentation or mistake, there can also be a claim for an indemnity, the object of which is to compensate a party in respect of obligations already incurred under the contract.[13] In a conveyancing context rescission by the buyer may therefore be accompanied by a claim for return of the deposit and payment of any costs so far incurred in investigating the title. Rescission, though, in the sense of one party being entitled to withdraw from the contract as a result of a breach by the other party, can be accompanied by a claim for damages.[14] This will cover the situations mentioned in section ii, above. The amount of damages is discussed below.[15]

2   FORCING COMPLETION ON AN UNWILLING PARTY

If a party is unwilling to complete, and does not fall within any of the categories which permit him to withdraw from the contract, then the other party has two main remedies: he can apply for a decree of specific performance or else he can serve a notice to complete.

i   Specific performance

This is merely an ordinary contractual remedy in a conveyancing context. It is an equitable remedy and will only be granted if damages are not an adequate remedy. On a contract for the sale of land this is almost invariably the case. Similarly it is also subject to the other equitable bars such as undue delay.[16] In the unusual case of *Patel v Ali*,[17] specific performance was refused to a buyer on the basis of hardship to the seller, who since the date of the contract had been hit by many misfortunes, including serious illness.

A party is entitled to apply for a decree of specific performance when there is reason to believe that the other party will not perform the contract and complete. Thus in *Hasham v Zenab*[18] the buyer applied for specific performance before the completion date where the seller, having signed the contract, tore it up. Normally however the application will be made after the completion date has passed or after a notice to complete has expired and completion has still not taken place. It should be emphasised that there is no need to serve a notice to complete before applying for specific performance, but a party may wish to try that remedy first and if it fails then proceed to apply for specific performance; alternatively, he could then claim damages. If a decree of specific performance is obtained but cannot be carried out then damages can be awarded for breach of contract.[19]

---

13   Such rescission essentially restores the pre-contract position. Damages may of course be payable under the Misrepresentation Act 1967; see section 1 above.
14   See *Buckland v Farmer and Moody* [1978] 3 All ER 929, [1979] 1 WLR 221, CA, confirmed in *Johnson v Agnew* [1980] AC 367, [1979] 1 All ER 883, HL.
15   See section 2 iii.
16   But see *Lazard Bros & Co Ltd v Fairfield Properties Co (Mayfair) Ltd* (1977) 121 Sol Jo 793.
17   [1984] Ch 283, [1984] 1 All ER 978.
18   [1960] AC 316, [1960] 2 WLR 374, PC.
19   Chancery Amendment Act 1858, s 2; Supreme Court Act 1981, s 50.

ii   Notice to complete

Where a party has not been willing to complete on the completion date given in the contract, the other party clearly requires some process whereby he can make time of the essence of completion, so that if completion still does not take place he can treat the contract as at an end, sue for damages and, if the seller, resell the property, or if the buyer, look for another property to buy. This procedure is the service of a notice to complete. Under an open contract the notice must specify a further period within which the other party must complete and that further period must be a reasonable period; this will obviously create some uncertainty. It used to be thought that the party serving the notice also had to wait until there had been an unreasonable delay after the contractual completion date, before serving the notice, but this view was corrected in *Behzadi v Shaftesbury Hotels Ltd*.[20] Not surprisingly the Standard Conditions contain provisions for a procedure which eliminates these difficulties. Standard Condition 6.8 provides that at any time on or after the contractual completion date, one party may give the other notice to complete. It then becomes a term of the contract that the parties are to complete within ten working days of giving the notice to complete, excluding the day on which the notice is given.[1] Time is of the essence. Under an open contract and also expressly under the Standard Conditions, the notice is only valid if the party serving it is ready, willing and able to complete.[2] The Standard Conditions specifically provide that a seller is not unable to complete merely because there is an outstanding mortgage on the property, if that mortgage could (and would) be redeemed out of the proceeds of sale on completion.[3] Otherwise, if the seller is not in a position to pass good title, he cannot serve a valid notice to complete.[4]

Once a valid notice to complete has been served, it binds both parties, so that if the party serving the notice himself defaults and does not complete in time, the consequences are just the same as if the party on whom the notice is served is in default. So in *Oakham Ltd v Bernstein & Co (a firm)*,[5] the seller was in breach when it served a notice to complete which expired on a public holiday and then refused to complete on the previous day on religious grounds. (The problem could be avoided under Standard Conditions by specifying non-working days in the contract.)

If after service of the notice time is then extended by agreement, time can again be made of the essence by a further notice. If after expiry of a notice a party still refuses to complete, the other party may further attempt to enforce the contract by applying for a decree of specific performance or may withdraw and sue for damages for breach of contract.

---

20 [1992] Ch 1, [1991] 2 All ER 477, CA.
 1 In *Dimsdale Developments (South East) Ltd v De Haan* (1983) 47 P & CR 1, it was held that a notice which did not satisfy the general conditions (because it was too short) could nevertheless still be regarded as an effective common law notice; see also *Delta Vale Properties Ltd v Mills* [1990] 2 All ER 176, [1990] 1 WLR 445, CA, where the notice was ambiguous.
 2 SC 6.8.1, 6.8.2.
 3 SC 6.8.2, this overcomes the problem in *Cole v Rose* [1978] 3 All ER 1121, which had indicated that if the parties had not agreed how the mortgage was to be discharged (the seller's solicitors were unable to give the usual undertaking), the seller might not be in a position to serve a notice.
 4 See, for example, *Tanap Investments (UK) Ltd v Tozer* [1991] EGCS 108, where the seller had not properly deduced title; however, see also *Bechal v Kitsford Holdings Ltd* [1988] 3 All ER 985, [1989] 1 WLR 105; valid notice to complete by seller despite misdescription in contract.
 5 (1984) 49 P & CR 282.

It may be possible to treat a contract as discharged by breach simply as a result of a long delay in completion without serving a notice to complete, but this would be extremely risky and the best advice must be to serve a notice to complete.[6]

Under Standard Condition 6.8.4, on receipt of a notice to complete the buyer who has paid less than a 10% deposit must forthwith pay a further deposit to make the total amount up to the 10% figure.

iii Damages if completion does not take place

We have mentioned a number of situations in which a party may rescind the contract and sue for damages, for example if the seller cannot give vacant possession in accordance with the contract or if a party fails to comply with a notice to complete. The damages are those recoverable under the ordinary contractual rule in *Hadley v Baxendale*,[7] that is, the plaintiff can recover the loss which arises in the normal course of events from the breach or which may reasonably be supposed to have been in the contemplation of the parties at the time of the contract as the probable result of the breach. The loss is normally assessed at the date of the breach. The damages payable to a seller will ordinarily be the contract price of the property (which he would have received under the contract but has not) less the current market value of the property and allowing for the additional expense if he does resell the property.[8]

Standard Condition 7.5 provides that if the buyer fails to complete in accordance with the notice to complete, the seller may forfeit and keep any deposit and accrued interest, may resell the property and may claim damages. The buyer must return the documents he has received from the seller and cancel any registration of the contract.

Both under an open contract and under Standard Condition 7.5 the seller can forfeit the deposit even if he suffers no loss,[9] although if he does claim damages he must give credit for the deposit. However, by the Law of Property Act 1925, section 49(2), the court is given a discretion to order repayment of the deposit to the buyer even where the seller would normally expect to be able to forfeit the deposit, for example, if the buyer had refused to complete. The factors relevant to the exercise of this wide discretion include the conduct of the parties, the gravity of the matters in question and the amount of the deposit.[10] Thus, if the deposit is very large, being 10% of a very large purchase price, the court may feel it is fairer to let the buyer have the deposit back, leaving the seller with a claim in damages for his actual loss (if any). This jurisdiction is not to be confused with equitable relief against penalties – the court will not regard forfeiture of a 10% deposit as a penalty. There was an

---

6   *Graham v Pitkin* [1992] 2 All ER 235, [1992] 1 WLR 403, PC.
7   (1854) 9 Exch 341.
8   The Law Society Conditions which were replaced by the Standard Conditions specifically provided for the seller to claim as liquidated damages any loss incurred on the resale of the property within a year of the contractual completion date, where the buyer had failed to comply with a notice to complete. There is no such provision in the Standard Conditions.
9   A deposit in excess of 10% of the purchase price may well be seen as a penalty, in which case the seller would not be able to forfeit it but would be limited to claiming his actual loss; *Workers Trust and Merchant Bank Ltd v Dojap Investments Ltd* [1993] AC 573, [1993] 2 All ER 370, PC.
10 *Universal Corpn v Five Ways Properties Ltd* [1979] 1 All ER 552, CA; see also *Schindler v Pigault* (1975) 30 P & CR 328; *Maktoum v South Lodge Flats Ltd* (1980) Times, 22 April; *Behzadi v Shaftesbury Hotels Ltd* [1992] Ch 1, [1991] 2 All ER 477, CA; and *Country and Metropolitan Homes (Surrey) Ltd v Topclaim Ltd* [1996] Ch 307, [1997] 1 All ER 254.

interesting application of section 49(2) in *Dimsdale Developments (South East) Ltd v De Haan*,[11] where the court ordered return of the deposit on condition that the buyer paid the seller's expenses of the sale.

The damages payable to a buyer will normally be the market value of the property at the date of the breach, less the contract price which the buyer would have paid, but there may be other elements of loss recoverable as well. For example, the buyer may have intended to redevelop the land and thereby make a profit which has now been lost. In such a case, as a result of the rule in *Hadley v Baxendale*, the buyer's prospect of recovering his loss of profit will depend largely on whether the seller was aware of the buyer's plans. In *Diamond v Campbell-Jones*[12] the seller was unaware and the buyer could not recover his loss of profit whereas in *Cottrill v Steyning and Littlehampton Building Society*[13] the seller was aware of the buyer's intention to develop and damages did include an element of loss of profit.

In *Lake v Bayliss*,[14] the seller, in breach of contract, resold the property to a second buyer. Because the first buyer had not protected his contract by registration, the sale to the second buyer went ahead and the second buyer did acquire the legal estate. However, the first buyer was able to recover from the seller the excess of the price received by the seller from the second buyer over the price agreed for the first purchase. In effect, the first buyer was being given the increase in the value of the property.

There used to be a rather archaic rule that if the seller was in breach of contract only because he could not show good title, the buyer could only recover his deposit and expenses of investigating title and not ordinary contractual damages for loss of bargain.[15] In respect of contracts made after 27 September 1989, this rule has now been abolished by section 3 of the Law of Property (Miscellaneous Provisions) Act 1989.

Standard Condition 7.6 specifically provides that if the seller fails to complete, the buyer may 'rescind' and if so, the seller is to repay the deposit with accrued interest, the buyer is to return his documents and at the seller's expense to cancel any registration of the contract, but that the buyer retains his other rights and remedies. The reference to the buyer retaining his other rights and remedies clearly preserves his right to damages.

3   DAMAGES PAYABLE EVEN THOUGH COMPLETION DOES TAKE PLACE

Firstly, there will be many situations in which completion does take place as planned but one party, particularly the buyer, may be entitled to some compensation. These have been mentioned in the first section of this chapter. For example the seller may be guilty of misrepresentation but rescission may be refused or not sought by the buyer, who may instead seek damages. A misdescription in the contract may be minor and the buyer may still be bound to complete, but with a reduction in the purchase price. Despite the existence of an undisclosed defect in title, or the seller's inability

11   (1983) 47 P & CR 1.
12   [1961] Ch 22, [1960] 1 All ER 583.
13   [1966] 2 All ER 295, [1966] 1 WLR 753.
14   [1974] 2 All ER 1114, [1974] 1 WLR 1073.
15   *Bain v Fothergill* (1874) LR 7 HL 158; see also *Day v Singleton* [1899] 2 Ch 320, CA; *Molhotra v Choudhury* [1980] Ch 52, [1979] 1 All ER 186, CA; *Wroth v Tyler* [1974] Ch 30, [1973] 1 All ER 897; *Ray v Druce* [1985] Ch 437, [1985] 2 All ER 482; *Sharneyford Supplies Ltd v Edge* [1987] Ch 305, [1987] 1 All ER 588, CA; and *Seven Seas Properties Ltd v Al-Essa* [1989] 1 All ER 164, [1988] 1 WLR 1272.

to give vacant possession, the buyer may still complete in which case again his damages will be assessed under the ordinary contractual principles. So for example in *Beard v Porter*[16] the seller could not give vacant possession in accordance with the contract. The buyer recovered the difference between the value of the property with vacant possession (ie the contract price) and the value with the sitting tenant. As he was buying the house to live in, he could also recover the costs incurred on the purchase of another house in which he could live, and the cost of his lodgings until he could move into his second house.

Another rather different situation in which compensation may be payable even though completion does take place is if completion takes place late. This is a breach of contract and the party in default is liable in damages, as was confirmed in *Raineri v Miles*.[17] (Assuming any notice to complete is complied with, it is not a breach which gives rise to a right to 'rescind' but merely damages as time is not normally of the essence in relation to the contractual completion date.) Compensation in these circumstances is discussed in Chapter 14, section 2.

If completion takes place after a specified time on the completion date, this may entitle the seller to compensation.[18]

4   OTHER POST-COMPLETION REMEDIES

Mention has already been made of some remedies which may be claimed after completion. Thus rescission for misrepresentation is still available after completion. In general, the terms of the contract merge into the deed on completion, although some do survive and can be sued on after completion, such as a term that vacant possession be given on completion.[19] Standard Condition 7.4 provides that completion does not cancel liability to perform any outstanding contractual obligation.

There are other remedies, against the seller and others, which specifically relate to the post-completion period.

i   Covenants for title

In certain situations, the seller will, in the conveyance or assignment, impliedly give certain covenants for title. The seller's implied covenants for title to some extent replace the seller's obligations under the contract, which merges into the deed, although Standard Condition 7.4 expressly states ' Completion does not cancel liability to perform any outstanding obligation under this contract'. They can be extended or modified in the deed.

Normally, the contract will specify whether the seller is giving a 'full' or 'limited' title guarantee, and the number and type of covenants for title which will be implied depend on the type of title guarantee given.[20] Such covenants will apply even where the disposition is not for value. Where the contract is silent on the type of guarantee, Standard Condition 4.5.2 provides that the seller transfers with full title guarantee. Full details of the implied covenants are set out in Chapter 5, section 4iii.

---

16   [1948] 1 KB 321, [1947] 2 All ER 407, CA.
17   [1981] AC 1050, [1980] 2 All ER 145, HL.
18   See ch 5, section 4 xix; SC 6.1.2.
19   *Hissett v Reading Roofing Co Ltd* [1970] 1 All ER 122, [1969] 1 WLR 1757.
20   Law of Property (Miscellaneous Provisions) Act 1994, s 1.

If there has been a breach of a covenant for title which the buyer becomes aware of after completion, he can take action on the covenant, but the most likely remedy will be damages.

Rule 77A of the Land Registration Rules 1925 provides in effect that nothing appearing on the register, and no overriding interest of which the buyer has notice, can amount to a breach of the implied covenants.

ii   Compensation for undiscoverable land charges

As land charges registration is only relevant to unregistered titles, so is this compensation. Land charges are registered against the name of the estate owner at the time of registration. Thus to be sure of discovering all registrations, the buyer should search against the names of all estate owners right back to 1925. It is very likely that he will not know all these names; he will only know the names of estate owners mentioned in the abstract or epitome which will probably commence after 1925. Yet by virtue of the Law of Property Act 1925, section 198, the buyer will still be deemed to have notice of the matters so protected as a result of registrations. If the registrations do only come to light after completion of his purchase, he may be somewhat aggrieved. He could have an action against the seller under the covenants for title, but rather better from his point of view is the possibility of compensation from central funds under the Law of Property Act 1969, section 25. In order to qualify for this compensation, two conditions must be met. Firstly the buyer must have had no actual knowledge of the charge at the time of completion (excluding of course notice by virtue of the Law of Property Act 1925, section 198). Secondly the charge must be registered against the name of an estate owner who was not revealed as such by the 'relevant title'. The latter phrase means the title to which the buyer would have been entitled under an open contract (for example for a freehold, at least 15 years), or any longer title to which the buyer was in fact entitled under the terms of his contract. This means that if the buyer contracts for a title shorter than the statutory period and a title of statutory length would have revealed the name of the estate owner against whom the charge was registered, the buyer will not get compensation. By section 25(9) and (10), compensation is not payable in respect of charges registered against titles which the buyer is precluded by statute from investigating on the grant or assignment of leases and underleases; the buyer will nevertheless be bound by such charges.

iii   Rectification of the register and indemnity

The remedies of rectification of the register and indemnity apply only in the case of registered land, and are discussed in Chapter 2. They are remedies against the Land Registry rather than the seller and are available to persons other than the parties to the conveyancing transaction.

iv   Liens

The seller has a lien over the property in respect of any unpaid purchase money following completion.[1] He will protect this lien by retaining the deeds (of

---

1   The lien may not protect additional sums payable under the contract: *Woolf Project Management Ltd v Woodtrek Ltd* (1987) 56 P & CR 134.

unregistered land), or registering a notice or caution (for registered land). In the latter case, the lien could be an overriding interest under the Land Registration Act 1925, section 70(1)(g) if the seller did remain in possession.[2] Once the money has been paid, the registration should be cancelled.

If the buyer has paid his deposit to the seller's solicitor as agent for the seller, he will have a lien over the property to the extent of his deposit which should be protected by the appropriate registration. This would be done after exchange of contracts.

5   SCOPE OF SOLICITOR'S DUTY

The remedy of a client in a conveyancing transaction may involve an action against the client's solicitor for breach of his duty of care. A few cases can be considered, by way of illustration.

In *McManus Developments Ltd v Barbridge Properties Ltd*[3] the issue centred around a disputed boundary. The redevelopment potential of the site hinged on the proper position of a boundary fence. Between exchange of contracts and completion, tenants of neighbouring property had moved the fence to what they claimed to be its true position. The buyer's solicitors had protested about this to the seller's solicitors; they were told that the fence had been moved back. They accepted this and did not warn their clients that there might be a problem. The Court of Appeal held that this could constitute negligence; it revealed a potential boundary dispute, even though the fence may have been restored to its original position.

Neighbour v Barker[4] concerned an elderly couple who purchased a bungalow. Their solicitors advised then to have the property surveyed but the purchasers decided against this. Answers to preliminary enquiries revealed that the property had the benefit of an NHBC certificate although this had now expired. After exchange of contracts the purchasers noticed for the first time a number of cracks and bulges in the structure. The purchasers indicated that they did not wish to complete until they had received a surveyor's report. They were told by their solicitors that if they did not complete they might lose their deposit and probably have to pay damages; the cheapest course of action would be to complete. The purchasers did complete but sued their solicitors claiming that the appropriate advice should have been to wait until the result of the survey was known. The purchasers lost the action although they did succeed in an action for misrepresentation against the seller based on replies to preliminary enquiries. The misrepresentation arose because the NHBC certificate had not in fact expired; it had been discharged because of subsidence at the property which had been compensated for under the NHBC certificate. The purchasers were arguing that with the benefit of hindsight, the advice to complete was negligent, because if the misrepresentation had been appreciated at that time, the purchasers would have been able to rescind. As it was they had paid over the purchase price and were now faced with an action against the sellers to recover damages. The court found, quite rightly, that one cannot judge compliance with the duty of care with the benefit of hindsight.

In *Worboys v Cartwrights*[5] solicitors were held to be negligent for not having advised in clear terms that there was an element of risk in a course of action whereby

---

2   *London and Cheshire Insurance Co Ltd v Laplagrene Property Co Ltd* [1971] Ch 499, [1971] 1 All ER 766; this can apply even where the seller is in occupation of part only of the property; *Wallcite v Ferrishurst Ltd* [1999] Ch 355, [1999] 1 All ER 977.
3   [1992] NPC 49, [1992] EGCS 50, CA.
4   [1992] 2 EGLR 149, CA.
5   [1992] EGCS 110.

the client's property was sold by auction before the client was in a position of being sure to obtain vacant possession of another property.

In *Atkins v Atkins*[6] a mother was buying a property with one of her sons. As a result of the mother's difficulties in meeting the repayments on a mortgage of £9,800, the property was being sold by the mother to herself and her son for the sum of £9,800, the purchase being with the aid of another mortgage. The mother and the son were to be joint mortgagors but in the event, the son arranged for a mortgage of £30,000. The mother signed the mortgage deed but was not informed of the amount of the advance. The solicitors assumed that she knew of her son's intentions and had discussed them with him; the son in fact was wanting to use the excess of the mortgage advance to buy a public house. It was held that the solicitors were negligent in that they should have explained the financial consequences of the transaction to her.

Similarly, in *Royal Bank of Scotland v Etridge (No 2)*,[7] Mrs Etridge was the legal owner of property which it was intended should be mortgaged to secure her husband's business overdraft. The lender was concerned to ensure that Mrs Etridge was fully advised of the implications of this course of action. The solicitors acting for both Mr and Mrs Etridge were also instructed by the lender, and the lender asked the solicitors to explain the effect of the charge to Mrs Etridge and to provide a certificate to the effect that they had done so. Later, Mrs Etridge claimed she had been subject to undue influence, and it then transpired that the solicitors had not in fact explained the charge to her despite their certificate. The Court of Appeal found that the lender was entitled to assume that the solicitors had carried out in full all their duties to all their clients, and so it was the solicitors who were at fault and not the lender. The Court of Appeal laid down detailed guidelines in that case on the procedure to be adopted by solicitors when asked to advise a spouse in these circumstances; to avoid a future negligence claim, the solicitor must ensure that the spouse fully understands the nature of the charge and is not subject to undue influence.

Finally, in *Cottingham v Attey Bower & Jones*,[8] it was held that a solicitor could be liable for neligence in failing to take all reasonable steps to obtain copies of building regulations consents.

---

6   [1993] EGCS 54.
7   [1998] 4 All ER 705, [1998] 3 FCR 675.
8   [2000] EGCS 48.

Landlord and Tenant

17 GRANT AND ASSIGNMENT OF LEASES

I   INTRODUCTION

The first part of this book has dealt with sales of both freehold and leasehold property. However, as indicated at the beginning of the book, in this chapter the particular features of a leasehold transaction will be reiterated. When talking of the sale of leasehold property we normally mean the assignment of a lease and, of course, this transaction has been considered in the first part of the book. However, for that lease to exist in the first place it must have been granted at some time in the past; in domestic conveyancing, normally when the house was built and the first 'buyer' was granted a lease by the builder or developer. When the first buyer (strictly the tenant) sells he assigns the lease as does that second buyer when he in turn sells, and so on.

The grant of a lease is a transaction which we have not, so far, considered in all its detail although we have mentioned in the first part of the book certain aspects of it; for example, the open contract rule as to the title deduced on the grant of a lease was considered in Chapter 5. The grant of a lease is different from both the sale of a freehold or the assignment of a lease in that a legal estate is not just being transferred but a new legal estate created.

In this chapter we shall look first of all at the grant of a lease, both where the lease is granted out of the freehold (a headlease) and where it is granted out of a leasehold interest (an underlease). We shall also look at the problems posed by particular types of lease, such as a lease of business premises at a market rent with a rent review clause, and the lease of a flat in a block of flats. We shall then reiterate those features of the typical conveyancing transaction considered in the first part of this book which are peculiar to the assignment of a lease as opposed to the sale of the freehold.

2   GRANT OF LEASE

i   Introduction

The obvious question which must first be answered is why a lease should be granted rather than the freehold being sold. In the context of domestic conveyancing, the answer may be that the builder or developer of a new estate who grants leases of the houses on the estate may not own the freehold of the land on which the houses are built, but merely a leasehold interest in it, in which case he would probably grant a lease (in fact, an underlease) of part of the property comprised in the original lease (the individual house) rather than assign part of the original lease. However, this does not explain why the builder of a new housing estate who does own the freehold should decide not to sell the freehold of the individual houses but to grant long leases of them. The reasons are probably threefold. Firstly, the builder will be able to receive some income in the form of rents, although the rents of the individual houses will not be very great. Secondly, he or his successors in title will hope in due course to be able to take over the houses again when the leases do eventually expire, although the longer the lease the less important this consideration will be and as we shall see in the next chapter, the tenant may have a right to purchase the freehold under the Leasehold Reform Act 1967. Thirdly, and most importantly, certainly to the lawyer, the creation of a landlord/tenant relationship means that there are normally no problems over the running of the benefit and burden of covenants contained in the lease, even if they are positive covenants. This contrasts with the position on the sale of freeholds where we have already seen that the burden of positive covenants does not run. Thus by granting a lease the builder or developer can keep more control over the property and can ensure that an estate development retains its character by the use of covenants. This is of even more importance when one is dealing with a block of flats. Because of their very nature, it is crucially important that the flat owners' various maintenance and repairing obligations are enforceable, as well as the restrictions on the use of the flats, and other regulations concerning activities of people living in close proximity. This may be difficult to achieve if the freehold of the individual flat is sold, so much so that many mortgagees are unwilling to lend money on the security of a freehold flat.

There are, of course, many different types of lease: formal and informal, short and long, fixed term and periodic. In the domestic conveyancing context, the lease with which we shall be dealing in this chapter will be the relatively long term - 75, 99, 200 or even 1,000 years is not unknown – lease of a house or a flat, which, as we have seen, will normally have been granted when the house or flat was built or converted. The length of the term will be such that the buyer will think of himself as a buyer and owner rather than a tenant of the lease. The term is also such that the capital sum or premium paid on the grant of the lease will be broadly equivalent to the freehold value of the property, and this will also be the case on subsequent assignments of the lease, at least until the end of the term is approached. The rent will be a very low, nominal, sum.

In this chapter we shall also be looking at a lease of commercial premises. Although the essential contents of such a lease will be broadly similar to the contents of a lease of a flat or a house, the term is likely to be much shorter; perhaps 10, 20, 25 or 30 years. The rent will be a full open market rent and it is less likely that a premium will be paid on the grant or the assignment of the lease. The lease will normally contain a rent review clause permitting the rent to be adjusted, normally upwards, to current market rent levels periodically during the term of the lease – typically every five years. Although under such a lease it will be crucial for the landlord to be able to enforce both positive and restrictive covenants against the original tenant and subsequent assignees of the lease, the landlord will presumably have deliberately decided to grant a lease rather than sell the freehold interest in order that the property attracts income in the form of rent rather than the capital gain achieved on the sale of the freehold.

ii   Contents of the lease

The lease of a house or flat will normally be drafted by the landlord's/seller's solicitor and sent with and referred to in the draft contract. There is obvious scope for negotiation over the terms of the draft lease, which the eventual contract will commit the parties to enter into, although on the development of an estate the lease will normally be in a standard form and the builder or developer may be very resistant to any amendments. In the commercial context, the lease will again be drafted by the landlord's solicitor and doubtless be the subject of negotiation between the parties. It is possible that the transaction will proceed directly to the grant of the lease (ie completion) rather than there being an initial contract or agreement for the lease.

1   Parties

The parties will be named and described as in a conveyance. The power of a party to grant a lease may vary according to the capacity in which he holds the freehold or leasehold estate out of which the lease is to be granted. Obviously the leasing powers of an absolute owner are unlimited. The powers of other estate owners can be limited. A company's powers may be regulated by its memorandum of association. A tenant for life (or statutory owner) of settled land has certain leasing powers under the Settled Land Act 1925, sections 41–48. Mortgagees and mortgagors have certain statutory powers of leasing although these are often modified or excluded in the mortgage deed in which case the consent of the mortgagee may be needed to the grant of the lease. For further details of the capacity of estate owners and the protection of purchasers, reference should be made to Chapter 10.

In a commercial lease a guarantor may join in the lease to provide a guarantee or surety for the liability of the tenant under the lease. The guarantee provision in the lease should be examined closely to see how extensive the liability of the guarantor will be. If the lease was entered into before the provisions of the Landlord and Tenant (Covenants) Act 1995 came into force on 1 January 1996, ie an old lease[1] it may only extend to the liability of the original tenant whilst he is still tenant under the lease; it may extend to the continuing liability of the original tenant even after an assignment of the lease (as to which see section iii 13, below); or it may extend to a direct guarantee of the liability of all subsequent assignees. For new leases created after the 1995 Act came into force section 24 (2) of the 1995 Act provides that where the tenant is released from future liability under the lease, the guarantor is released to the same extent as the tenant. However both the outgoing tenant and guarantor may be required to enter into Authorised Guarantee Agreements (AGA) guaranteeing the performance of the lease covenants by the incoming tenant. There may be a provision for the guarantor to take a new lease following disclaimer on the tenant's bankruptcy or liquidation.

2   Date

As with any other deed, the date of the lease is the date of delivery although the date expressed in the lease will be presumed to be the date of delivery in the absence of any evidence to the contrary. The date of the lease should be distinguished from the date of commencement of the term which will be given in the lease, and which may be different from, and is often earlier than, the date of the lease itself.

Recitals are not often included in a lease but they can be inserted if desired.

3   Consideration

It may be that there is no capital sum, or premium, changing hands on the grant of a lease and that the consideration is merely the rent and the covenants given by the tenant.

---

1   See section 12 below.

If there is a premium, it must be mentioned, not least for stamp duty purposes. There will normally be a receipt clause as well, as in a conveyance. Whether there is a premium will depend on the sort of lease being granted. On a long lease of a house granted by the developer of a new building estate then there will always be a premium which will be much the same as the price for which the developer could have sold the freehold.

4   Operative words

In a lease the landlord is normally expressed to 'demise' or 'lease' to the tenant although any words indicating the intention of the parties will be sufficient.

5   Parcels

There must be a physical description of the property comprised in the lease. All that was said about the parcels in a conveyance, and the need for precise description, is equally applicable here. This is all the more important in the case of a lease of part only of a building, for example a flat or a suite of offices.

The need for a clear definition of the demised property is important not only for the obvious reason of defining the extent of the property which the tenant will own, but also because other covenants in the lease such as a covenant to repair may be expressed by reference to the definition of the demised premises. An inaccurate plan on a lease caused real difficulties on subsequent rent review in *Kensington Pension Developments Ltd v Royal Garden Hotel (Oddenino's) Ltd.*[2]

6   Easements

On the grant of a lease, particularly a lease of part of a building or part of a plot of land owned by the landlord, consideration must be given to the easements which the tenant will require and the easements which the landlord will wish to reserve. Again all that was said in relation to a conveyance of freehold land is equally applicable, including the rules contained in *Wheeldon v Burrows*[3] and the Law of Property Act 1925, section 62.

The tenant will wish to ensure that he has the benefit of all the necessary rights for access to the property and for services to and from the property. The right to use a car park can sometimes present problems. If there is to be a right to park within a general car parking area, this is probably best expressed as an easement, but a right to park in a specific car parking space may not constitute a valid easement as it gives exclusive use of the space and may be best given effect to by including the car parking space in the demised property.[4]

Given the lack of any rule of implied reservation in favour of the landlord, the landlord will wish to reserve expressly all necessary easements over the property, for example for the passage of services through the property running to and from other parts of the development. There may also be an exclusion of the implied grant of any easement of light, and a reservation of the right to develop adjoining property, particularly in a commercial lease.

Both landlord and tenant will need to consider the arrangements for the maintenance of the media through which the easements pass, for example roads,

---

2   [1990] 2 EGLR 117.
3   (1879) 12 Ch D 31, CA; see ch 12, section 2 viii, ix.
4   See *London and Blenheim Estates Ltd v Ladbroke Retail Parks Ltd* [1993] 1 All ER 307, [1992] 1 WLR 1278.

passageways and drains. It may be that under the lease the landlord is responsible for the maintenance of the 'common parts' of the development which do not belong to any of the specific tenants, such as roads and passageways but that the landlord will recover the cost of maintaining these common parts via a service charge (see section iii 4, below).

Under the lease the tenant may be responsible for the maintenance of media such as drains passing through the demised premises but the landlord would probably wish to reserve a right to enter the premises if needs be to effect such maintenance, in which case there may be provisions in the lease regulating the exercise by the landlord of this right of access.

7   Habendum

The traditional 'habendum' in a lease will indicate the length of the term and its commencement date, assuming it is a lease for a fixed term. In the case of a lease of a house or flat the term would normally be at least 75 or 99 years, and often much longer; in a lease of a shop or office, the term may be only 20 or 10 years, or even less.

The habendum will also state the commencement date of the term. This may be the date of the lease or it could be before or after the date of the lease. However, it must not be more than 21 years after the date of the lease otherwise the lease may fall foul of the rule against perpetuities and be void.[5]

8   Reddendum

The 'reddendum' follows the habendum. It indicates that rent is payable and states the amount and how often it is to be paid. The question of payment of rent is dealt with in detail in the next section.

9   Payment of rent

The amount of rent payable will depend on the type and size of the property and the length of the lease. The rent of a new house on a building estate on a long lease will be quite low;[6] a lease of business premises may attract a full market rent, with no premium.

The amount of rent will be specifically stated. In a long lease, the parties may wish to include some provision by which the rent can be increased although this is unlikely in a long term residential lease; there might however be an increase to a predetermined level after a particular period of time, for example halfway through the term. In a lease of business premises, there will normally be a provision for 'rent review' at stipulated intervals during the term with specific machinery by which the new rent can be calculated.[7]

In the absence of any provision to the contrary, rent under a fixed term tenancy is payable at the end of each year. However, the lease will normally specify not only the periods for which rent is payable – for example quarterly or yearly – but the date on which such payments must be made. The lease will normally make rent payable in advance rather than in arrear. Typically rent under a fixed term tenancy may be made payable quarterly in advance, payment being made on stated days, perhaps on the usual quarter days. These are Lady Day (25 March), Mid-summer Day (24 June),

5   Law of Property Act 1925, s 149(3).
6   This will also avoid Housing Act 1988 protection for the tenant.
7   See further in section iv, below.

Michaelmas Day (29 September) and Christmas Day (25 December). In the case of leases created before 1 January 1996 the tenant does not lose his obligation to pay rent by assigning the lease. If a subsequent assignee does not pay the rent then the landlord may be able to recover it from the original tenant. The tenant is of course entitled to be indemnified, but that is not necessarily much consolation if the assignee has no funds.[8] In the case of all commercial leases the Landlord and Tenant (Covenants) Act 1995 introduced a provision whereby a landlord who is seeking to recover a fixed charge (ie rent, service charge payments, liquidated sums payable under the lease or interest on such sums) from a former tenant or guarantor is required to serve a default notice under section 17 of the Act, within six months of the sum becoming due, or he will lose his right to recover that sum. The landlord needs to take care when serving a default notice as a person who pays in settlement of the notice can call for an overriding lease to be granted to him under section 19 of the 1995 Act.

Occasionally in a commercial lease the rent will be linked in some way to the turnover of the tenant's business. This may particularly be the case for, say, the lease of a shop on a new out of town retail park where the potential tenants may be somewhat apprehensive about committing themselves to a lease with a full market rent at a time when they may be unsure how much business may be attracted to the development. In such a turnover rent provision there are a number of factors which need to be considered. The rent may be based completely on turnover or there may be a fixed minimum rent level with a turnover uplift. The turnover on which the rent is based must be precisely defined. There will be a percentage to be applied to the turnover to produce the turnover rent or uplift. This percentage will vary according to the type of business of the tenant; it would be a low percentage figure if the tenant's business was high turnover with low profit margins but a high percentage if the tenant's business was a low turnover business with high profit margins. Because of the significance of the tenant's business there would have to be specific provisions in the lease relating to change of the use of the premises to another business and relating to assignment of the lease. There would also need to be some provision for ascertaining the turnover figure and for arbitration in relation to any disputes.

10   Covenants

The lease will invariably contain covenants detailing the obligations of the parties in various areas. Covenants are dealt with in detail in the next section.

11   Certificate of value

This will be included in the lease for the same reasons as warrant its inclusion in a conveyance, that is to take advantage of the stamp duty exemption.

---

8   See also section iii 13, below. The liability of the original tenant following assignment will not extend into a statutory continuation of the lease under the Landlord and Tenant Act 1954, Part II unless the lease expressly so provides; however, the lease may well provide that the original tenant is liable for the 'term' of the lease; the 'term' being defined as the contractual term together with any statutory continuation; *City of London Corpn v Fell, Herbert Duncan Ltd v Cluttons* [1993] QB 589, [1993] 2 All ER 449, CA; see also *Mirror Group (Holdings) Ltd* [1993] BCLC 538, [1992] BCC 972.

iii   Covenants

I   Covenant by tenant to pay rent, rates and taxes

As well as a reservation of the rent there will also normally be an express covenant by the tenant to pay; if not it will be implied. The tenant also impliedly covenants to pay rates[9] and certain other charges and taxes imposed on the property. The lease will normally contain express provision that the tenant will pay rates and taxes. A tenant remains liable to pay rent even after the premises are destroyed, for example by fire. However, the lease may contain express provision for abatement of the rent in these circumstances.[10] If the landlord has failed to comply with his covenant for repair, the tenant can have the repairs done and deduct the cost from his rent.[11] He should not however withhold rent to try and persuade the landlord to comply with his repairing obligations.

2   Covenant by tenant not to repudiate the landlord's title

There is an implied covenant by the tenant not to do anything which could prejudice the landlord's title, such as assisting someone else to set up a title adverse to the landlord.

3   Covenant by tenant to permit the landlord to enter and view the state of repair

If the landlord is under an obligation to repair as a result of either an express covenant in the lease or a statutory obligation, the tenant impliedly covenants to allow the landlord to enter and view the state of the premises. However, as mentioned in section 10 below, the landlord is unlikely to be liable for repairs on a long term residential lease or for internal repair under a shorter term business lease. If the repairing obligation is on the tenant, the landlord will usually insist on an express right to enter the premises to check that the repairing obligation is being met. Then in the case of default by the tenant the landlord will rely on another express covenant that is commonly found in the lease allowing him to enter the demised premises and do the repair himself recovering the cost from the tenant: see *Jervis v Harris*.[12]

4   Covenant by tenant to pay a service charge

Particularly if the lease is one of a number of units, such as a flat in a block of flats, or a shop in a shopping mall, the landlord may perform certain services for the tenants, such as maintenance of 'common parts' such as stairs and lifts and probably also the structure and exterior of the building. Other services may include the upkeep of the gardens of a block of flats, or the security in a shopping mall. The landlord will covenant to perform these services and all the tenants will covenant in their leases to pay an annual service charge to reimburse the landlord. This could be expressed to be paid as additional rent in which case the landlord could forfeit for non-payment as for rent. The amount of this service charge will vary from year to year.

---

9   Rates are now inapplicable to domestic property but are still relevant for leases of commercial property.
10   See section 9, below.
11   *Lee-Parker v Izzet* [1971] 3 All ER 1099, [1971] 1 WLR 1688.
12   [1996] Ch 195, [1996] 1 All ER 303, CA.

The Landlord and Tenant Act 1985 as amended, imposes restrictions on service charges in relation to dwellings.[13] In the Act a service charge is defined as an amount payable for services, repairs, maintenance or insurance or the landlord's costs of management. The landlord can only recover the costs he incurs to the extent that they are reasonable, and if the costs are incurred on the provision of services or the carrying out of works, they can only be recovered if the services or works are of a reasonable standard. If the service charge is payable in advance of the costs being incurred then the landlord can only recover an amount that is reasonable. Where costs incurred on the carrying out of works exceed a prescribed amount the landlord must obtain at least two estimates for the works, one of them from a person wholly unconnected with the landlord, and a notice accompanied by a copy of the estimates must be given to each of the tenants, inviting observations. The landlord must then pay regard to any observations.

The tenant is also entitled to a summary of costs incurred by the landlord, certified by a qualified accountant who is not connected with the landlord.

The Housing Act 1996 contains the procedure for landlords seeking to forfeit the lease for non-payment of service charges. The landlord's section 146 notice must contain a statement confirming that section 81 of the Housing Act 1996 applies, and set out its effect, and the right of re-entry cannot be exercised until 14 days after the court order.

The provisions of the Landlord and Tenant Act 1985 do not apply to service charges payable in respect of commercial premises. The leases should therefore contain sufficient provisions to protect the interest of the landlord and the tenants, although in *Finchbourne Ltd v Rodrigues*[14] the Court of Appeal held that there was an implied provision that the landlord could only recover such sums as were fair and reasonable.

The simple objective of the landlord is to be able to recover all sums spent by way of providing services. The service charge provision in the lease will therefore include a statement of the substantive services which the landlord must or may provide and probably also a statement of the types of expenditure incurred in providing those services which the landlord can recover from the tenant. In relation to the provision of substantive services, the landlord will presumably be under an obligation to provide basic services such as repair and cleaning of the common parts. There may be a discretion for the landlord to provide other services apart from those which he is under an obligation to provide and this discretionary provision may well include a general 'sweeping up' clause to try to ensure from the landlord's point of view that if a particular item has not been expressly included in the list of services, the landlord can nevertheless recover the cost of providing it. A tenant should be wary of the landlord's discretion to provide services being drawn too widely and also should be aware that the landlord will be under no obligation to provide these discretionary services.[15]

There have been many cases where the courts have had to interpret a service charge provision which has not been drafted as well as it might have been, and where the landlord has been trying to claim under a general 'sweeping up' provision for some item of services which should perhaps properly have been listed specifically.[16]

---

13 Landlord and Tenant Act 1985, ss 18–30. The provisions apply to all dwellings, not just flats.
14 [1976] 3 All ER 581, CA.
15 See *Russell v Laimond Properties Ltd* (1983) 269 Estates Gazette 947.
16 See *Rapid Results College v Angell* [1986] 1 EGLR 53, CA; *Lloyds Bank plc v Bowker Orford* [1992] 2 EGLR 44.

The landlord will also want the list of types of expenditure incurred on providing the services which the landlord can recover to be as widely cast as possible, and certainly to include, for example, the cost of engaging employees or contractors to provide the services, the cost of managing agents and the cost of borrowing and bank charges.[17] There may also be provision for the building up of a reserve fund or a sinking fund to provide in the first case for periodic anticipated expenditure such as the external decoration of the premises every few years, or in the second case to provide for large unanticipated items of expenditure, such as the replacement of a lift, which would otherwise lead to an unusually large service charge in the year in which the expense was incurred.

The lease will contain some provision for the division of the service expenses between the various tenants, most commonly on the basis of the floor area occupied by tenants under their various leases.

Ideally a tenant would like the lease to contain an obligation on the landlord to consult with the tenants before undertaking work of a substantial nature. However, the danger for a landlord in such a provision is that the courts may construe compliance with it as a condition precedent to the landlord being able to recover the cost of the work.[18] There will be a mechanism for a regular, probably annual, service account and normally for the advance payment of an estimated service charge and an adjustment following the annual account. There may be a provision for certification of the service charge account by a specified person, perhaps a qualified accountant or surveyor. The lease may provide that the accountant or surveyor may be an employee of the landlord or the landlord's managing agent. The lease may also provide that the certificate is to be conclusive of matters of fact or even also on matters of law.[19]

5   Covenant by tenant not to assign or sub-let

The lease may include a provision against the tenant assigning the lease or granting a sub-lease or both. In a commercial lease further types of disposition may also be prohibited including charging, parting with possession, sharing possession or granting licences. The purpose is to protect the landlord's interest by ensuring that no one apart from the tenant can have an interest in the property. No such covenant is to be implied. If the covenant is absolute, that is if it is not qualified by any reference to the landlord's consent, the landlord will be perfectly entitled to refuse to give the tenant consent to assign or sub-let as the case may be. Any such assignment or sub-letting would be a breach of covenant and the lease would be liable to forfeiture. Such an absolute covenant is clearly prejudicial to the tenant particularly if the lease is for a fixed term of any length, and the tenant must seriously consider the implications before accepting such a provision in his lease. However, the covenant is not broken by an assignment by operation of law such as occurs on the death or bankruptcy of the tenant.

The covenant may not be absolute, but provide instead that there is to be no assignment (or sub-letting) without the licence or consent of the landlord. In this case it will be implied, even if the lease does not expressly so provide, that such consent must not be unreasonably withheld.[20] Nor can the landlord demand payment of a

---

17   See *Boldmark Ltd v Cohen* (1985) 19 HLR 136, CA.
18   See *Northways Flats Management Co (Camden) Ltd v Wimpey Pension Trustees Ltd* [1992] 2 EGLR 42, CA.
19   See *Nikko Hotels (UK) Ltd v MEPC plc* [1991] 2 EGLR 103.
20   Landlord and Tenant Act 1927, s 19(1)(a).

'fine' for his consent[1] although he does have the right to demand payment, of a reasonable sum for expenses incurred in connection with the consent, for example legal expenses.[2] If the lease is a building lease of over 40 years then no consent is needed to assign or underlet at any time more than seven years before the end of the term, although notice does have to be given to the landlord. A building lease is a lease made in consideration of the erection or improvement of buildings.[3]

Assuming that there is a qualified covenant, in what circumstances would the landlord's refusal be held to be reasonable? If the refusal is made on grounds that do not concern the personality of the proposed assignee or the effect of the proposed assignment then it is probable that it will be held to be unreasonable.[4] In particular, any licence will be *unlawfully* withheld in so far as it is withheld on grounds of colour, race, ethnic or national origins[5] or sex;[6] there is, though, an exception for 'small premises' where the accommodation is shared with the landlord or a near relative.[7] The express covenant in the lease may further limit the landlord's grounds for refusal, by providing for example that consent will not be refused in the case of assignment to a 'respectable responsible person'.[8]

It is unlikely that there will be an absolute or even a qualified covenant in a long term residential lease; there may, however, be a covenant to give notice of assignments (and mortgages) after the event, together with a small fee.

If in a lease of commercial premises there is, as would be usual, a qualified covenant against assigning or sub-letting, to what extent can the lease impose conditions on the landlord's consent being given, in the light of section 19(1)(a) of the Landlord and Tenant Act 1927 which, as we have seen, states that the consent must not be unreasonably withheld? In particular many leases will contain an obligation on the tenant who wishes to assign or sub-let to obtain a direct deed of covenant whereby the assignee or sub-lessee enters into a new covenant with the landlord, to perform the covenants in the lease. There is often also a provision enabling the landlord to require guarantors from the assignee or sub-lessee. There is some authority, not under section 19(1)(a) but under section 19(1)(b) relating to building leases, which suggests that such provisions may not be caught by section 19(1)(a), and may therefore not in themselves have to be reasonable, particularly if they are expressed not as conditions for the landlord giving consent but simply as obligations imposed on the tenant in the event of an assignment or sub-letting.[9]

In giving consent to an assignment, the landlord does not owe a duty to the original tenant to see that the assignee is financially sound;[10] and this may have implications for the original tenant of an lease created before the Landlord and Tenant (Covenants) Act 1995 came into force as he will remain liable under the covenants in the lease for the whole term of the lease (as to which see section iii 12 below) so that if the assignee does fail to pay rent, the landlord can turn to the original tenant and demand rent from him.

1   Law of Property Act 1925, s 144.
2   Landlord and Tenant Act 1927, s 19(1)(a).
3   Ibid, s 19(1)(b).
4   *Re Gibbs and Houlder Bros & Co Ltd's Lease* [1925] Ch 575, CA; *Tredgar v Harwood* [1929] AC 72, HL. See also *Bromley Park Garden Estates Ltd v Moss* [1982] 2 All ER 890, [1982] 1 WLR 1019, CA and *International Drilling Fluids Ltd v Louisville Investment (Uxbridge) Ltd* [1986] Ch 513, [1986] 1 All ER 321, CA.
5   Race Relations Act 1976, s 24.
6   Sex Discrimination Act 1975, s 31.
7   Race Relations Act 1976, s 22(2); Sex Discrimination Act 1975, s 32(2).
8   *Moat v Martin* [1950] 1 KB 175, [1949] 2 All ER 646, CA.
9   *Vaux Group plc v Lilley* (1990) 61 P & CR 446.
10 *Norwich Union Life Insurance Society v Low Profile Fashions Ltd* (1991) 64 P & CR 187, CA.

The 1995 Act (section 22) also introduced a new section 19A, which relates to qualified alienation covenants against assigning (it does not apply to sub-letting or charging). Essentially it allows the parties to agree the circumstances or conditions that have to be met before the landlord will give the consent. Then provided the landlord withholds his consent on the stated grounds, he will not be acting unreasonably. The conditions can either be framed in absolute terms or give the landlord the discretion to determine an issue. If the landlord is required to use his discretion that must be exercised reasonably or the tenant can insist on review of the landlord's determination by an independent third party who should be mentioned in the lease.

The Landlord and Tenant Act 1988 introduced a number of provisions to further help the tenant seeking permission to assign. The burden of proof lies with the landlord. The Act requires the landlord to respond to the tenant's request within a reasonable time, give his decision in writing together with the reasons for refusal if he intends to withhold his consent (section 1). The landlord can only rely on the reasons that are given in his written response.[11] If the tenant suffers a loss caused by the landlord's unreasonable delay he may be liable to pay damages to the tenant. The 1988 Act is discussed in more detail later in the chapter at 3ii.

6   Covenant by tenant not to make improvements or alterations

Again there is no implied covenant that the tenant is not to make improvements or alterations to the property, but there may be an express covenant which again may be either absolute or subject to the landlord's consent. The purpose is to protect the landlord both from any unwelcome changes to the property and from any potential liability to compensate the tenant for improvements at the end of the tenancy. If there is a qualified covenant, there is a statutory implication that the consent must not be unreasonably withheld, in the case of improvements.[12] Although the statutory provision refers merely to improvements, most alterations will be improvements. The statutory provision does not preclude the right of the landlord to require the payment of a reasonable sum in respect of any decrease in the value of the premises (or any adjoining premises of the landlord) and in respect of legal and other expenses incurred in connection with the consent, nor does it preclude the right to require an undertaking from the tenant to reinstate the premises to their original condition if the improvement does not add to the letting value of the premises.

7   Covenant by tenant restricting his use of the property

There are a number of reasons why the landlord should want to restrict the use to which the property can be put. Most commonly in the case of business premises such as a shop, the landlord will own other shops in the vicinity and will want to control the use of the shop so as to prevent any duplication and to enable him to plan the development and make other units attractive to potential tenants. On the lease of a new house on a building estate the landlord will wish to restrict the use of the house to residential use only. The restriction, particularly on business premises, may affect the rent which the landlord can expect to negotiate under the lease. If there is an express covenant then again it may either be absolute or qualified by reference to the landlord's consent, but in the latter case there is no implication that the consent must not be unreasonably withheld. This could of course be inserted as an express provision

11   *Footwear Corpn Ltd v v Amplight Properties Ltd* [1998] 3 All ER 52, [1999] 1 WLR 551.
12   Landlord and Tenant Act 1927, s 19(2).

in the covenant. However, the landlord cannot as a condition of giving consent demand any sum of money other than in respect of any decrease in the value of the premises (or adjoining premises of the landlord) or in respect of legal and other expenses incurred in connection with the consent.[13]

A common covenant on a similar theme is that the tenant must not do or permit or suffer to be done on the premises anything which may become a nuisance or annoyance to the landlord or neighbouring owners and occupiers.

The provisions of the Law of Property Act 1925, section 84 concerning application to the Lands Tribunal for the discharge or modification of restrictive covenants are also applicable to restrictive covenants in leases for terms of more than 40 years of which at least 25 years have expired.[14]

8   Landlord's covenant for quiet enjoyment

If there is no express covenant by the landlord for quiet enjoyment such a covenant will be implied. The covenant can be restricted in which case the landlord covenants that the tenant's possession will not be interrupted by acts of the landlord or of persons claiming lawfully through or under him. Alternatively the covenant can be absolute in which case the landlord also covenants that the tenant's possession will not be disturbed by lawful acts of anyone through whom the landlord claims title, ie the landlord's predecessors in title. An express covenant can be either absolute or restricted. In the absence of an express covenant the implied covenant will be in the restricted form.

9   Landlord's covenant not to derogate from his grant

The landlord impliedly covenants not to derogate from his grant, that is not to do anything which will interfere with the use for which the premises were let. So in *Aldin v Latimer Clark, Muirhead & Co*[15] the landlord let part of his land to the tenant for the purpose of drying timber. The landlord erected on his adjoining land a building interfering with the flow of air to the tenant's land and thus preventing timber from drying. This constituted a breach of covenant. In these circumstances a landlord would be well advised to try and include in the lease a specific provision allowing him to use his adjoining land in any way he thinks fit whether or not it prejudices the tenant's enjoyment of the property comprised in the lease. It should be noted that there is in general no implied covenant by the landlord that the property leased is suitable for the tenant's needs. There is no implied covenant even that the use specified in the lease is lawful.[16]

10   Covenant to repair

The lease may contain express provision as to the repairing obligations of either or both parties. The tenant under a long term residential lease would normally be liable for all repairs, subject to the builder's contractual liability in building the house, and the NHBC provisions.[17] However, on the lease of a flat, being part of a building, the tenant may only be responsible for internal repair with the landlord being liable for

---

13   Landlord and Tenant Act 1927, s 19(3); this provision only applies if the change of use does not involve structural alteration.
14   Law of Property Act 1925, s 84(12).
15   [1894] 2 Ch 437.
16   See for example *Hill v Harris* [1965] 2 QB 601, [1965] 2 All ER 358, CA.
17   See ch 5, section 4 xxi.

repairing the structure and exterior of the building and the common parts such as lifts and passageways; the landlord would recover the cost of performing this repair obligation under a service charge. Similarly on a lease of commercial premises; if the property is a separate building, the likelihood is that the tenant will be fully responsible for repair whereas if it is only a lease of part of a building, for example a suite of offices in an office block, the tenant may be liable only for internal repair with the landlord responsible for the exterior and structure and with the landlord again recovering the expense under a service charge provision.

As well as repair covenants there will normally be some additional express covenant to decorate both internally and externally on a cyclical basis of perhaps every three, four or five years. Again, on a lease of part of a building the landlord may be responsible for external decoration with the tenant only responsible for internal decoration.

In deciding whether work falls within the scope of a repair covenant, the court must, of course, construe the words used in the covenant in the lease. However, even with a standard covenant to 'repair' there will always be some uncertainty as to the precise scope of the covenant. For example, the normal standard of repair has been defined as 'such repair as having regard to the age, character and locality of the house would make it reasonably fit for the occupation of a reasonably minded tenant of the class who would be likely to take it'.[18] The wording of the repair covenant will be interpreted by the courts not in a vacuum but in the context of the particular building and the state which it was in at the date of the lease. 'Look at the particular building, look at the state which it is in at the date of the lease, look at the precise terms of the lease and then come to a conclusion whether on a fair interpretation of those terms in relation to that state, the requisite work can fairly be termed repair.'[19] It has been suggested that there may be three different tests to be applied separately or concurrently, and in the light of the nature and age of the premises, their condition when the tenant went into occupation and the other express terms of the tenancy. They are (1) whether the work goes to the whole or substantially the whole of the structure or only to a subsidiary part; (2) whether the effect of the work is to produce a building of a wholly different character to that which has been let; (3) the cost of the works in relation to the value of the building and their effect on the value and life span of the building.[20] A repair covenant will not normally be interpreted by the courts as requiring a tenant to totally rebuild the whole premises, although if the covenant quite clearly does extend to such rebuilding the court will give effect to it, as for example in *Norwich Union Life Assurance Society v British Railways Board*[1] where the covenant obliged the tenant 'when necessary to rebuild, reconstruct or replace [the premises]'. The repeated emphasis clearly demonstrated the meaning of the covenant. This sort of covenant is more usual in a long-term residential lease, where the term of the lease, perhaps 99 or 200 years, is so long that the tenant accepts all the responsibilities of 'ownership'.

If there is some deterioration to the premises, it may not be a successful defence for breach of the covenant for repair to show that the deterioration is due to some inherent defect in the premises whether this be a design defect or a building defect.[2] This is an issue which should be considered by the tenant of a new commercial building. If the tenant is to enter into a full repairing covenant he would ideally like

---

18   *Proudfoot v Hart* (1890) 25 QBD 42, CA.
19   *Brew Bros Ltd v Snax (Ross) Ltd* [1970] 1 QB 612, [1970] 1 All ER 587, CA.
20   *McDougall v Easington District Council* (1989) 87 LGR 527, 58 P & CR 201, CA.
 1   [1987] 2 EGLR 137.
 2   *Ravenseft Properties Ltd v Davstone (Holdings) Ltd* [1980] QB 12, [1979] 1 All ER 929.

disrepair resulting from some inherent defect to be excluded from the scope of his repair covenant. Failing this he may want some contractual arrangement whereby he could make a claim against the true instigator of the defect be it the architect or the builder, or he may be able to take advantage of some project insurance.

Similarly the tenant of an old building under a full repairing covenant must be alive to the risk of having to spend substantial sums of money on the building, even under a fairly short lease. In *Elite Investments v Bainbridge (TI) Silencers*[3] a factory built in 1940 had a corrugated iron roof which was effectively beyond repair at the end of the lease. The court held that repairing the roof was within the scope of the tenant's covenant to repair and that applying the tests mentioned earlier the tenant was not having to provide the landlord with an entirely different property to that which was comprised in the lease.

There is clearly a difficulty of drawing a precise line where the scope of a covenant to repair ends and the area beyond repair, which one could perhaps call replacement or improvement, begins. In *Roper v Prudential Assurance Co Ltd*[4] renewal of the electrical wiring in the premises was held to be within the scope of a tenant's covenant to repair. The covenant to repair clearly extended to the wiring; the tenant argued unsuccessfully that the repair covenant did not include the replacement or renewal of the wiring. In *New England Properties plc v Portsmouth News Shops Ltd*[5] the tenant was under an obligation in the lease to reimburse the cost of repairs effected by the landlord, under a service charge. The court held that the landlord's covenant to repair did extend to the replacement of a roof even though it was clear that the original design of the roof was inadequate.

A covenant either to put and keep the premises in repair or simply to keep the premises in repair may result in some immediate expense, particularly on the part of a commercial tenant, to remedy the existing disrepair at the start of the lease. In drafting the lease consideration might be given to defining the tenant's obligation as simply to maintain the state and condition of the premises in the condition in which they were at the commencement of the lease. However, some record will need to be kept of the state of the premises at the time usually by a schedule of condition prepared by a surveyor. On a lease of premises where the tenant carries the whole repairing liability, other drafting considerations will be the precise wording of the repair covenant and whether it is to go beyond repair to include rebuilding, renewal and replacement, and whether there is to be a specific covenant for the tenant to repair on being given notice of disrepair by the landlord, with provision for the landlord to effect repairs himself in default and recover the cost from the tenant; in the latter case, the landlord will also need to reserve rights of access to the premises. Where there are split repairing liabilities between landlord and tenant, with the landlord liable for external repairs and the tenant liable for internal repair, it will be important to ensure that the 'external' and 'internal' parts of the premises are clearly defined and that there is no physical part of the premises unaccounted for under the combined repairing covenants.

There are two statutory provisions which may affect the duty to repair. Firstly under the Occupiers' Liability Act 1957, section 2, where the landlord retains part of a building under his control, such as a common staircase, he owes a duty of care to the tenant and the tenant's visitors. Secondly under the Defective Premises Act 1972, section 4, where the landlord has an obligation or right to repair, then he has a duty of care to anyone who might reasonably be affected by the lack of repair.

3 [1986] 2 EGLR 43.
4 [1992] 1 EGLR 5.
5 (1993) 67 P & CR 141.

11   Covenant to insure

There will normally be an express covenant in the lease dealing with insurance. It is clearly in the interests of both landlord and tenant that the premises should be properly insured. The lease will therefore contain a covenant either by the landlord or tenant to insure. On the long lease of a house, it is most likely that the tenant would insure although the landlord may wish to exercise some control over who the property is insured with. On a lease of a flat it is perhaps more likely that the landlord will insure the whole building including all the flats; if there is damage, perhaps by fire, it is likely that more than one flat will be damaged and it will be easier to claim against one insurer rather than the various insurers of the various separate flats, as would be the position if each tenant was responsible for his own insurance. Similarly in relation to commercial premises, although here it is perhaps more likely that the landlord will insure in any event (and of course recover the cost under a service charge or by a separate payment by the tenant sometimes called an 'insurance rent').

To take as an illustration of a lease where the landlord covenants to insure, there will be a definition of the risks against which insurance should be taken out – the 'insured risks' – which will normally comprise a list of specified perils such as fire and flood together with a residual discretion for the landlord to insure against other risks. There should also be some statement of the extent of the cover which would normally include not only full rebuilding and reinstatement costs but also the associated professional fees, clearance of the site and probably also the loss of rent which the landlord will suffer whilst the property is unoccupied. The landlord will probably covenant to provide details of the policy and of its continued existence by means of the most recent receipt for the premium. The tenant would probably also enter into a number of covenants, to comply with the insurers' requirements; not to do anything which would vitiate or void the landlord's policy; and perhaps not to effect any insurance of his own. In the situation where the landlord insures and recovers the premium from the tenant there is no obligation on the landlord to find the cheapest premium - *Havenridge Ltd v Boston Dyers Ltd.*[6]

So, what if the worst happens and the premises are damaged by an insured risk, for example by fire? The lease may contain a covenant by the landlord to reinstate the premises if they are damaged by an insured risk, although very often the lease will not go quite as far as this but will simply oblige the landlord to expend the insurance money on reinstating the premises. This may then lead to difficulty if the insurance proceeds are not sufficient. Ideally the lease should address this situation and provide a solution; in the absence of any specific provision in the lease a tenant might be concerned that he may be liable for any shortfall under his repairing covenant although quite often a repairing covenant is defined to exclude damage caused by an insured risk. If it is the tenant who is insuring, there will be a provision obliging the tenant to reinstate the premises.

There will also normally be a provision in the lease suspending the tenant's rent either wholly or partly if the premises are damaged by an insured risk so as to make them uninhabitable by the tenant either in whole or in part. There is, however, normally an overall time limit placed on the suspension of rent provision in the lease, most commonly three years. What then at the end of the three years if the premises have not yet been reinstated? What indeed if during the three-year period it becomes quite obvious that the premises never will be reinstated, perhaps because planning permission is refused? Again, the lease should contain the answer. At the very least, the tenant will want a break clause enabling him to terminate the lease at the end of the three-year

6   [1994] 2 EGLR 73.

period if the premises have not been reinstated. In fact a tenant would really want to be able to break the lease earlier than the end of the three-year period as soon as it became apparent that the premises would not be reinstated by the end of that period.

Finally, what if the lease is terminated by this sort of break provision; what happens to the proceeds of the insurance claim, if this has not been expended on reinstating the property? On the face of it if the landlord has taken out the insurance the proceeds belong to the landlord. This might not be appropriate particularly if there were a number of years left to run on the lease; in terminating the lease, the tenant has lost a valuable asset. Some leases will therefore provide for apportionment of the insurance proceeds according to the value of the respective interests of the landlord and tenant.

12   Enforceability of covenants

This area of law has changed significantly with the introduction of the Landlord and Tenant (Covenants) Act 1995, and from the date the Act came into force all new tenancies were governed by the new rules on enforceability of covenants. New tenancies were those created on or after 1 January 1996 unless executed pursuant to an agreement entered into before that date, or pursuant to a court order or option made before that date. It is possible for a lease that was granted before the 1995 Act came into force, that was subsequently varied, to fall within the definition of a new lease for the purposes of the Act, if the variation amounted to a deemed surrender and re-grant.

The tenant's position on assignment is covered in section 5 which provides that if the lease does not contain any restriction on assignment, the tenant will be automatically released from any future liability under the lease on a lawful assignment ie one that does not breach the alienation covenant. If the assignment is in breach of the alienation covenant (and therefore an unlawful assignment), the tenant must wait until the next lawful assignment until he is released from further liability under the lease. If the lease contains a restriction on assignment by including an absolute or qualified alienation covenant, on a lawful assignment the tenant will be released from future liability, but will probably be required to enter into an Authorised Guarantee Agreement (AGA) under section 16 of the 1995 Act. This would mean that the tenant guarantees the performance of the covenants by the assignee until the assignee disposes of his interest in the property. The assignor can be treated as the principle debtor and in the event that the lease is disclaimed he may be required under section 16(5) to enter into a new lease with the landlord.

The landlord is not released from future liability under the lease automatically on the assignment of the reversion, but must apply to the tenant under the procedure set out in section 8 of the 1995 Act. The landlord has to apply to the tenant either before, or within four weeks of the assignment of the reversion in the prescribed form. The tenant can respond to the landlord's application by serving a prescribed notice within four weeks of the landlord's notice, stating whether or not he consents to the release. If the tenant does not object to the landlord's release from future liability under the lease or if he does nothing, the landlord is released. If the tenant does not consent to the release, the landlord can apply to the court that may order the landlord to be released if it considers it reasonable to do so.

The 1995 Act also provides in section 3 that the benefit and burden of all the landlord and tenant's covenants (other than personal covenants) shall automatically pass to their respective successors in title.

All tenancies that are not new tenancies are still governed by the old rules on privity. The Law of Property Act 1925, section 141, provided that a tenant's covenant has reference to the subject matter of the lease, and successors in title of the landlord will be able to claim its benefit. Under the rule in *Spencer's* case,[7] provided that a tenant's covenant touches and concerns the land, it will bind successors in title of the tenant, ie assignees of the lease. As with section 141, it does not matter whether the covenant is positive or restrictive. A covenant touches and concerns the land or has reference to the subject matter of the lease if it affects the landlord *qua* landlord and the tenant *qua* tenant, rather than merely personally. The covenants likely to be found in a typical lease will touch and concern the land except a covenant by the landlord giving the tenant the option to purchase the reversion.

By the Law of Property Act 1925, section 142, provided that the landlord's covenant has reference to the subject matter of the lease, it will bind successors in title to the landlord's interest, ie the reversion. It can be enforced by anyone in whom the lease is vested, ie by subsequent assignees of the lease. Again, this applies to positive and restrictive covenants.

There may be mutual enforceability restrictive of covenants between tenants if there is a letting scheme, analogous to a building scheme – see Chapter 5, section 4 vi. The original tenant will remain liable on his covenants in the lease, even though he has assigned the lease. He will therefore require an indemnity covenant from an assignee when he sells the lease, and this will normally be implied; see section 3 iii, below.

This continuing liability, for example, to pay rent, may be most unwelcome in a commercial lease, and the indemnity for the assignee to whom the original tenant sold will be useless if that assignee is now insolvent and it is a subsequent assignee who is now not paying rent, causing the landlord to seek rent from the original tenant. The original tenant might try to negotiate for a release once he had assigned the lease, or for some mechanism whereby he always had a continuing right of indemnity directly against every assignee.

13   Variations

Under section 18 of the 1995 Act and the *Friends Provident Life Office v British Railways Board* case,[8] any variation of the lease (other than an immaterial variation) that would prejudice the original tenant or guarantor, extending his obligations further than originally agreed by the parties, would operate to release him from the increased liability, unless he consented to the variation.

iv   Rent review

In a lease of commercial premises there will normally be a rent review provision whereby the rent is brought into line with current market values periodically during the term of the lease. Essentially a rent review clause consists of two elements: the mechanical part which deals with the frequency of the review and how the review is to be operated, and the substantive part which states the criteria on which the new rent is to be fixed.

1   Frequency of review

The lease may contain a list of specific review dates or the review may be stipulated to take place on periodic anniversaries of an initial date, perhaps the date of grant of

---

7   (1583) 5 Co Rep 16a.
8   [1996] 1 All ER 336.

the lease or date of commencement of the term. Typically the period of the review will be five years. There is some advantage in having a rent review falling due at the very end of the contractual term as the rent so fixed will see the landlord through any period of continuation of the term under the Landlord and Tenant Act 1954 (see Chapter 20) and will avoid the need for the landlord to apply for an interim rent under the 1954 Act; the interim rent will probably be less than the market rent fixed under a rent review clause.

The lease should state that the reviewed rent should be fixed as at the relevant review date (ie the dates on which review falls due, for example every five years), rather than being fixed as at the time the reviewed rent is determined, which may be later than the review date if there are delays in operating the rent review or delays in the determination process.[9]

2   Machinery for instigating rent review

There are a range of possibilities for the mechanics of the rent review clause. Typically in an older lease there may be a formal procedure perhaps involving the landlord serving a notice to initiate the rent review; the lease may stipulate that the landlord should suggest a new rent in this so-called 'trigger notice'. The tenant may then have to serve a counter notice if he disagrees with the suggested new rent and there will be some mechanism for the matter to be referred to the determination of an arbitrator or an expert. These various notices and counter notices may have to be served within quite tight limits. A more modern lease will contain a much less formal and more relaxed procedure, perhaps simply with an opportunity for landlord and perhaps also for tenant to initiate the determination of the new rent by having the matter referred to an arbitrator or expert. The only time limit may be that the appointment of an arbitrator or expert should not be made before the review date, or perhaps earlier than, say, three months prior to the review date.

Whenever there is a time limit it should be clear whether time is of the essence of that limit or not. If time is of the essence, then the particular step, for example service of the landlord's trigger notice, cannot be taken outside the time limit. If time is not of the essence, time can be expanded very elastically and the step may be taken well beyond the specified time limit.[10] So in drafting the rent review clause, if there are to be time limits as part of the procedural mechanism, there should be a clear statement of whether or not time is of the essence. In the absence of such a statement the court in construing the clause will have to decide whether it was intended impliedly that time should be of the essence. Although the court's initial approach will be that time will not be impliedly of the essence[11] there may nevertheless be circumstances in which the court may hold that time is impliedly of the essence.[12] Hence the need for a clear statement, to avoid this uncertainty.[13]

---

9   See *Glofield Properties v Morley (No 2)* (1989) 59 P & CR 14, [1989] 2 EGLR 118, CA and *Prudential Assurance Co Ltd v Grey* [1987] 2 EGLR 134.

10 See for example *Amherst v James Walker Goldsmith & Silversmith Ltd* [1983] Ch 305, [1983] 2 All ER 1067.

11 *United Scientific Holdings Ltd v Burnley Borough Council* [1978] AC 904, [1977] 2 All ER 62, HL.

12 See for example *Metrolands Investments v J H Dewhurst* [1986] 3 All ER 659, CA; *Henry Smiths Charity Trustees v AWADA Trading & Promotion Services Ltd* (1984) 47 P & CR 607, CA; *Mecca Leisure Ltd v Renown Investments (Holdings) Ltd* (1984) 49 P & CR 12, CA; *Mammoth Greeting Cards Ltd v Agra Ltd* [1990] 2 EGLR 124; *Kings Estate Agents Ltd v Anderson* [1992] 1 EGLR 121; *Art and Sound Ltd v West End Litho Ltd* (1991) 64 P & CR 28, [1992] 1 EGLR 138; and *Starmark Enterprises Ltd v CPL Distribution Ltd* [2000] EGCS 81.

13 See for example *Panavia Air Cargo v Southend Borough Council* (1988) 56 P & CR 365, [1988] 1 EGLR 124, CA; and *Shuwa Ashdown House Corpn v Grayrigg Properties Ltd* [1992] 2 EGLR 127.

In operating the procedure under a rent review clause care should be taken to ensure that a notice or counter notice served under the clause complies with the requirements laid down in the clause. However, it does appear that the courts may take a fairly relaxed view particularly in the case of a tenant's counter notice objecting to the new rent proposed by the landlord, where the counter notice may still be held to be valid and effective if it makes it clear that the tenant objects to the rent even though it may not satisfy other criteria laid down in the clause such as, for example, a suggestion of the new rent which the tenant would be willing to pay.[14]

3   Reference to determination by an expert arbitrator

The clause will doubtless provide that in the absence of agreement between landlord and tenant as to the new rent, the dispute is to be referred for determination by an expert or arbitrator. The lease will normally contain opportunity for landlord and tenant to agree on the expert or arbitrator or failing that for one party to apply to the Royal Institute of Chartered Surveyors for an appointment.

There are a number of differences between the roles of an arbitrator and an expert. The arbitrator is performing a quasi-judicial function and bases his decision on evidence and arguments submitted to him. The arbitrator therefore cannot decide the case without receiving evidence from the parties normally in the form of rents agreed for comparable properties. An expert on the other hand decides the case on the basis of his own expert knowledge although he may be required by the rent review clause to receive submissions from the parties. The conduct of an arbitration is governed by the Arbitration Act 1996; there is no statutory code governing the expert procedure. Significantly, there is some possibility of appealing from an arbitrator's decision on a point of law under the Arbitration Act; however, it may be exceedingly difficult or impossible to appeal even on a point of law against the decision of an expert. If under the rent review clause the parties have entrusted the expert with a final decision on matters of fact and law, the decision cannot be challenged simply on the ground that it is erroneous in law unless it can be shown that the expert has not performed the task assigned to him. If he has merely asked himself the right question but answered it wrongly, his decision will still be binding.[15]

Further, under the Arbitration Act 1996 the costs of an arbitration are at the discretion of the arbitrator. An expert only has the power to award costs if this is given to him by the rent review clause. On the other hand an arbitrator is not liable for negligence as opposed to an expert who is so liable. Expert determination is often regarded as cheaper and quicker than arbitration although this is not necessarily the case. On the whole expert determination may be more appropriate where the issues are very straightforward, perhaps where the amount of the rent is not that great, and where the decision will not form a precedent for the rest of the landlord's property portfolio. Arbitration may be more appropriate where there are difficult issues raised by interpretation of the rent review clause. A landlord may be able to have it both ways; the rent review clause may provide that the rent on each successive review should be fixed by an arbitrator or an expert, at the landlord's option.

---

14   See for example *Barrett Estate Services Ltd v David Greig (Retail)* [1991] 2 EGLR 123; *Patel v Earlspring Properties Ltd* [1991] 2 EGLR 131, CA and *Prudential Property Services Ltd v Capital Land Holdings Ltd* [1993] 1 EGLR 128. However, the court may take a stricter view if the effect of the notice is to elect for arbitration; *Horserace Totalisator Board v Reliance Mutual Insurance Society* (1982) 266 Estates Gazette 218.

15   *Nikko Hotels UK Ltd v MEPC plc* [1991] 2 EGLR 103 following the belatedly reported 1989 Court of Appeal decision in *Jones v Sherwood Computer Services Ltd* [1992] 2 All ER 170, [1992] 1 WLR 277, CA; see also *Postel Properties Ltd v Greenwell* (1992) 65 P & CR 239.

4   The hypothetical lease

Turning now to the part of the rent review clause which will set out the criteria on which the new rent will be fixed, it is important to appreciate that the surveyor (expert or arbitrator) will not be fixing the rent for the residue of the actual lease between the actual landlord and the actual tenant; instead, the rent review clause will provide that the rent is to be the open market rent which will be payable between a hypothetical willing landlord and a hypothetical willing tenant. The rent review clause will then go on to deal with the contents of this hypothetical lease and the open market scenario in which it is notionally operating. The underlying assumption will be that the hypothetical lease contains the same terms as the actual lease although as we shall see the rent review clause may stipulate otherwise. There will also be certain matters to be assumed as being the case which are not in fact the case in reality, and equally certain facets of the open market scenario will be disregarded, partly in order to redress the potentially distorting effect of the assumption of an open market letting between the hypothetical willing landlord and the hypothetical willing tenant, and partly, from the landlord's point of view, to achieve as high a rent as possible. These assumptions and disregards are considered below.

5   The premises

The premises to be comprised in the hypothetical lease will doubtless be the premises comprised in the actual lease, but equally any doubt about the extent of the premises comprised in the actual lease may therefore become an issue on rent review as was the case in *Kensington Pension Developments Ltd v Royal Garden Hotel (Oddenino's) Ltd*.[16]

In the absence of anything in the rent review clause to the contrary, the premises will be taken in their state at the rent review date rather than their original state at the commencement of the lease; *Sheerness Steel Company plc v Medway Ports Authority*.[17]

6   Assumption of fitness for occupation and use

The rent review clause may contain an assumption that the premises are fit for the immediate occupation and use of the hypothetical willing tenant and further that the premises are fully fitted out to the hypothetical willing tenant's needs. The objective of these assumptions from the landlord's point of view is to keep the rent up, by assuming that the premises are in an ideal state from the hypothetical tenant's point of view, and to prevent the rent being discounted by taking account of any notional rent free fitting out period which in the open market an incoming tenant might be able to negotiate. Whilst provisions such as these may be included in rent review clauses the courts have in recent years been interpreting them very restrictively and it should not be assumed that they will be given their literal meaning.[18]

---

16   [1990] 2 EGLR 117.
17   [1992] 1 EGLR 133, see also *Laura Investment Co Ltd v Havering London Borough Council* [1992] 1 EGLR 155.
18   See for example *Orchid Lodge (UK) Ltd v Extel Computing Ltd* [1991] 2 EGLR 116, CA; *Iceland Frozen Foods plc v Starlight Investments Ltd* [1992] 1 EGLR 126, CA; *London & Leeds Estates Ltd v Parabas Ltd* [1993] 1 EGLR 121, CA; and *Pontsarn Investments Ltd v Kansallis-Osake-Pankki* [1992] 1 EGLR 148, in which the court held that an assumption that the premises were fit for immediate occupation and use meant that they were simply ready to be fitted out by the tenant and therefore that the assumption did not prevent the tenant arguing for a discount off the rent to take account of the notional rent free fitting out period which an open market tenant would be able to negotiate.

7   User covenant

A particularly restrictive user covenant in the actual lease which is not in any way modified by the rent review provisions will have a depressing effect on the rent fixed on rent review as clearly the lease will be worth less to the incoming hypothetical tenant.[19] However, if the user covenant in the actual lease restricts use to the use of the actual original tenant, this will be taken as a covenant in the hypothetical lease to use for the business of the hypothetical tenant rather than the actual original tenant, which would be patently absurd; *Law Land Co Ltd v Consumers Association Ltd*.[20]

If during the lifetime of the lease the landlord gives consent to a change of use, consideration needs to be given either in the drafting of the original lease or the drafting of the consent to change, of the effect on subsequent rent review; is the rent to be fixed on the basis of the original user covenant or the user covenant as subsequently modified?[1] The lease, or the consent, should make specific provision.

8   Other covenants

If other covenants in the actual lease, such as repair covenants or alienation covenants, would seem unduly onerous to an incoming tenant, the landlord may attempt to rewrite these covenants to some extent so far as the covenants in the hypothetical lease are concerned, to keep the reviewed rent up. In all fairness a tenant could not really be expected to agree to such a provision in the rent review clause; if his lease contains the onerous provision then surely he should be able to argue that the rent should be discounted to reflect it.

9   Rent review in the hypothetical lease

The rent review clause should make it quite clear whether there is to be an equivalent rent review clause in the hypothetical lease, as this will affect the level of the rent. In the absence of an express provision the court will normally take it that there is to be a rent review provision in the hypothetical lease but any uncertainty is avoided by the inclusion of an express provision.[2]

10   Length of term of hypothetical lease

The length of the term of the hypothetical lease will also be a factor which will influence the rent to be fixed under the hypothetical lease. There are a number of possibilities including the residue of the actual term of the lease, the original term of the lease, or a specified fixed period of perhaps seven or ten or fifteen years. If the residue of the actual term is used, there should also be a minimum fixed term to cater for rent review close to the end of the original term. Note that wording such as 'for a term equivalent to the term hereby granted' or 'for a term of years equivalent to the said term', although at first sight a reference to the original term, will not be construed

---

19   *Plinth Properties Investments Ltd v Mott Hay & Anderson* (1978) 38 P & CR 361, CA.
20   [1980] 2 EGLR 109, CA.
1   See for example *SI Pensions Trustees Ltd v Ministerio De Marina De La Republica Peruana* [1988] 1 EGLR 119; *Post Office Counters Ltd v Harlow District Council* (1991) 63 P & CR 46 and *Lynnthorpe Enterprises Ltd v Sydney Smith (Chelsea) Ltd* [1990] 2 EGLR 131, CA.
2   See for example *National Westminster Bank plc v Arthur Young McClelland Moores & Co (No 2)* [1991] 3 All ER 21, [1991] 1 WLR 1256.

by the courts as such. The term granted by the lease is not simply a term of years but a term of years starting on the actual commencement date and the provisions quoted are therefore disguised references to the residue of the term of the actual lease.[3]

If the rent review is silent the court will normally regard the length of term of the hypothetical lease as being the residue of the term of the actual lease.[4]

I I   Assumption of vacant possession

There will normally be an assumption that the willing tenant is taking a lease of the whole of the property with vacant possession. In case the willing tenant would desire to sublet, there will be an accompanying assumption that the hypothetical willing tenant has already had the benefit of any rent free subletting period,[5] analogous to the assumption that any rent free fitting out period has already been enjoyed.

I 2   Other assumptions

As well as the assumption that any rent free periods have already been enjoyed there may well also be an assumption that the tenant and possibly also the landlord have performed the covenants under the lease, and an assumption that if the premises have been destroyed or damaged (by an insured risk) that they have been restored; thus the rent is fixed for the reinstated building. Of course the tenant may not be paying this rent as rent may be suspended whilst the premises are not capable of being occupied. There may also be an assumption that the tenant has done no work on the premises which would diminish the rental value of the premises.

I 3   Disregard of improvements

It will be rather tough on a tenant who has paid money for improvements to the property to find that these are taken into account in ascertaining the new rent which the tenant is to pay. There will therefore normally be a disregard of improvements perhaps modelled on the equivalent disregard under the Landlord and Tenant Act 1954, section 34 (see Chapter 20). The clause should specify the time when the improvements have to have been made to qualify for the disregard, perhaps up to 21 years prior to the date of rent review, and the person making the improvements to qualify for the disregard, presumably the tenant or the tenant's predecessors in title, and maybe also sub-tenants. The clause may or may not cover improvements made prior to the date of the grant of the lease.

The provision will commonly exclude from the disregard improvements made in pursuance of an obligation to the landlord; in giving consent for improvements to be made, the landlord may therefore wish the tenant to enter into a binding covenant to do the improvements. Furthermore, as the lease will probably also contain a covenant to comply with statutory obligations, improvements which are made in pursuance of statutory obligations are also made in pursuance of the covenant to the landlord, and the tenant would find that having paid for these improvements he was now paying rent for them as well. The tenant may therefore wish to negotiate an exception from the exclusion to the disregard, to cover improvements made in pursuance of statutory obligations.

---

3   *Ritz Hotel (London) v Ritz Casino* [1989] 2 EGLR 135; *Lynnthorpe Enterprises v Sydney Smith (Chelsea) Ltd* [1990] 2 EGLR 131, CA.
4   See for example *British Gas plc v Dollar Land Holdings plc* [1992] 1 EGLR 135.
5   Largely as a result of *99 Bishopsgate v Prudential Assurance Co Ltd* [1985] 1 EGLR 72.

14   Disregard of goodwill

The rent review clause will normally contain a disregard of the effect of the goodwill of the tenant, the tenant's predecessors in title and perhaps also any sub-tenants, again modelled on section 34 of the Landlord and Tenant Act 1954.

15   Disregard of occupation

Again based on section 34, the rent review clause will normally disregard the effect of the occupation of the tenant and predecessors in title and possibly also sub-tenants.

16   VAT

A landlord will have an option to impose VAT on the payments made under the lease and in particular on the rent. As the effect of the exercise of this option may be to make the premises unattractive, at least to certain types of incoming tenant (those who cannot recover VAT such as financial sector tenants), one sometimes encounters a provision in a rent review clause, to protect the landlord's position and keep the reviewed rent as high as possible, whereby it is to be assumed that the hypothetical tenant will be able to recover all VAT or perhaps whereby the effect of imposing VAT is to be disregarded.

v   Determination of the tenancy

It is convenient here to consider the ways in which a tenancy may be terminated. A fixed term tenancy may expire by effluxion of time, ie by the term running out. It may come to an end by surrender. Surrender may be express or implied. An express surrender is agreed between the parties. A surrender can also be implied for surrounding circumstances, such as the tenant accepting a new tenancy before the old one has expired or the landlord accepting possession of the premises with the intention of terminating the tenancy. A fixed term tenancy can also be determined by merger or by the operation of a break clause. Merger occurs when the same person, usually the tenant, acquires the leasehold interest and the reversion. The leasehold interest merges into the reversion. A break clause is in effect an option to determine a lease before the end of the term. It may be exercisable by the landlord or the tenant or either. Usually unless the contrary is expressed, time is of the essence in break clauses.[6] A fixed term tenancy can also be determined by forfeiture. Forfeiture is a remedy of the landlord on breach of covenant by the tenant, which involves the landlord bringing the lease to an end. The landlord's right to forfeit must be contained in an express provision in the lease and it will not be implied. A typical forfeiture clause will state that if the rent is in arrear for 21 days, whether formally demanded or not, or if the tenant is in breach of any of his covenants, then the landlord can re-enter the property and the lease is thereby determined. Sometimes the landlord will be given the right to forfeit if the tenant becomes bankrupt or, being a company, goes into liquidation.

　　If the tenant is in breach of covenant and the landlord has the right to forfeit, he must decide whether to forfeit or not. He can expressly waive his right to forfeit and it would be impliedly waived if he did something showing an intention to treat the

---

6   *United Scientific Holdings v Burnley Borough Council* [1978] AC 904, [1977] 2 All ER 62. However see *Mannai Investments Co Ltd v Eagle Star Life Assurance Co Ltd* [1997] 1 EGLR 57 and *Havant Holdings Ltd v Lionsgate H Investments Ltd* [1999] 47 LS Gaz R 34.

lease as continuing, in the knowledge of the facts giving rise to the right to forfeit. Implied waiver will most commonly occur by the landlord demanding or accepting rent. However, the waiver only relates to existing breaches of covenant and it does not extend to future breaches or continuing breaches (for example, breach of a covenant to repair or breach of a covenant relating to use of the property). The procedure on forfeiture depends on whether the landlord is forfeiting for non-payment of rent or breach of some other covenant.

1   Forfeiture for non-payment of rent

The forfeiture proviso in the lease will inevitably dispense with the requirement to make a formal demand for rent before forfeiture. Although the landlord may re-enter peaceably,[7] in practice he will probably bring an action for possession. If the tenant pays the arrears and the landlord's costs before the court hearing he will be granted relief against the forfeiture, which means that the lease is not forfeited but continues as before. The provisions for relief are in fact slightly different in the High Court and the County Court; in effect the tenant can apply for discretionary relief within six months of the landlord re-entering under a possession order, or without time limit if the landlord peaceably re-enters.

2   Forfeiture for breach of other covenants

The landlord must first of all serve a notice under the Law of Property Act 1925, section 146. This must:

(a) specify the breach of covenant;
(b) require the tenant to remedy the breach if it is capable of being remedied – some breaches, such as a breach of covenant against assignment or sub-letting, will be irremediable;
(c) require compensation if the landlord desires it.

If the breach is of a repairing covenant, then where the lease is for at least seven years of which at least three years are still to run, the section 146 notice must refer to the tenant's right under the Leasehold Property (Repairs) Act 1938 to serve a counter-notice within 28 days. If the tenant does so, the landlord needs the leave of the court to proceed with forfeiture and this leave will only be given on one of five specified grounds, for example if an immediate remedy would be cheaper compared to the expense if repair were postponed.[8] In specifying the breach of the repairing covenant in the notice, the landlord will normally prepare a schedule of dilapidations detailing the lack of repair.

After service of the notice, the landlord must allow reasonable time for the tenant to remedy the breach and to make compensation if requested, or to consider his position if the breach is irremediable.[9] Failing the tenant remedying the breach and making compensation, the landlord can proceed with forfeiture, again by peaceable re-entry or by bringing a possession action. The tenant is given the right by section 146(2) to apply to the court for relief whether the landlord re-enters peaceably or seeks a possession order. The court has a wide discretion to grant relief but application

---

7   Provided that there is no one on the premises opposed to the re-entry; Criminal Law Act 1977, s 6.
8   See *Associated British Ports v C H Bailey plc* [1990] 2 AC 703, [1990] 1 All ER 929, HL.
9   See eg *Cardigan Properties Ltd v Consolidated Property Investments Ltd* [1991] 1 EGLR 64; *Billson v Residential Apartments Ltd* [1992] 1 AC 494, CA; revsd [1992] 1 All ER 141, HL.

must be made before the landlord actually re-enters the premises under a possession order; although relief can still be granted after peaceable re-entry.[10] If the breach relates to internal decorative repairs, the tenant can apply to the court under the Law of Property Act 1925, section 147 to be relieved from liability for such repairs on the grounds that the notice is unreasonable, although this does not apply to a breach of a covenant to put the property in repair at the beginning of the tenancy.

On the grant of a new lease, it may be necessary for the tenant to be satisfied that there is no possibility of the tenant under a previous lease, terminated by forfeiture, applying successfully for relief. However, the Court of Appeal in *Fuller v Judy Properties Ltd*[11] indicated that 'if the new tenant is unaware of the old tenant's (equitable) right to apply for relief, he will take free of it'.[12] Nevertheless it is probably good practice for the landlord to inform the old tenant that the premises are to be relet, to in effect invite him to apply for relief; if the old tenant fails to do so, he will presumably not obtain relief if he applies after the reletting.

The landlord can recover the expense of preparing and serving a section 146 notice from the tenant where he does actually forfeit, where he waives forfeiture or where the tenant is granted relief. However, if the tenant complies with the notice, the landlord cannot recover the cost of it under section 146 and so an express clause is often inserted in the lease giving the landlord the right to recover the costs of the notice from the tenant in these circumstances.

3   Breach of condition against bankruptcy

The Law of Property Act 1925, section 146 does not apply to forfeiture for breach of a condition against bankruptcy in respect of certain property, including agricultural land and furnished dwelling houses. Even in respect of other leases, a section 146 notice is not needed after the first year following the tenant's bankruptcy.

4   Position of sub-tenants

If a lease is forfeited and thereby terminates, any underleases granted out of that lease must also terminate. Thus forfeiture of a lease can be disastrous for any sub-tenants. Sub-tenants have a right to apply for relief against forfeiture of the superior lease quite independently of the tenant of the lease which is liable to forfeiture.[13] This becomes of importance if the tenant himself cannot apply for relief or else fails in his application. On an application by a sub-tenant, the court has discretion to grant relief, which is effected by the court ordering a new lease between the landlord and the sub-tenant. The conditions of the lease will be such as the court thinks fit although the term cannot be longer than the unexpired term of the sub-tenant's old lease. A sub-tenant in this context includes a mortgagee of a lease.

vi   Procedure

The procedure on the grant of a long lease of a house or flat is essentially similar to the conveyancing procedure already discussed in the earlier part of this book. There

---

10   *Billson v Residential Apartments Ltd*, above.
11   (1991) 64 P & CR 176, CA.
12   But see *Bhojwani v Kingsley Investment Trust Ltd* [1992] 2 EGLR 70, in which *Fuller* was not cited and which reaches a contrary conclusion.
13   Law of Property Act 1925, s 146(4); see for example *United Dominions Trust Ltd v Shellpoint Trustees Ltd* [1993] 4 All ER 310, 67 P & CR 18, CA.

will normally be a contract in the same form as discussed in the first part of this book. The Standard Conditions of sale are applicable on the grant of a lease.[14] Rather than setting out the detailed provisions of the lease, the contract will probably provide that the lease is to be in the form of a draft supplied with the contract.[15] If a property is being newly built then there may be a separate term of the contract, or a separate contract, covering the erection of the property, as discussed in Chapter 5. The landlord/seller's solicitor will require instructions on the contents of the lease and the term, and will also have to advise on the clauses which are appropriate for inclusion, probably using a standard form precedent. He will also have to investigate title. In particular he may discover that there is a current mortgage, with the mortgagee's consent being necessary to the proposed lease. If there are covenants affecting the freehold title, the solicitor may wish to insert a condition in the contract providing for an indemnity covenant to be included in the lease.

The tenant/buyer's solicitor (for the prospective tenant of a house or flat under a long lease will regard himself as a buyer) will make all the usual searches mentioned in Chapter 6. He will also need to consider the terms of the draft contract and draft lease, and any incumbrances such as covenants affecting the freehold title which have been disclosed, in the same way as he would for a buyer of freehold land; and if necessary try and negotiate some amendment. The seller/landlord's solicitor will deduce title.[16] Under an open contract the tenant is entitled to no title at all on the grant of a headlease and only a limited title on the grant of an underlease.[17] In particular, the tenant is not entitled to examine the freehold title. However, the buyer/tenant will *want* to examine the freehold and any other superior leasehold titles. The reasons for this have already been considered at Chapter 5, section 4 xvii 2, above. It is thus essential that the buyer's solicitor negotiates for the inclusion in the contract of some provision allowing the buyer to examine title. If he does not, then not only is the buyer putting his money at some risk but he is much less likely to find a mortgagee willing to lend on the security of the property and he may find that when he comes to sell the property and assign the lease, he will have difficulty finding a buyer; if the appropriate title was not deduced to him then he cannot in turn deduce it to his buyer. Standard Condition 8.2.4 provides that if the term of the lease exceeds 21 years, the seller must deduce a title which will enable the buyer to register the lease with an absolute title. This means that the landlord/seller must deduce his own title; if that title is leasehold, and is not registered with absolute leasehold title, he must also deduce the freehold and any superior leasehold titles. If the superior leasehold and freehold titles are registered they will be deduced by use of office copy entries under the Land Registration Act 1925, section 110. If unregistered then an abstract or epitome will be used with the freehold title being deduced for the usual minimum of 15 years. The buyer's solicitor can then examine the title and make the necessary searches as discussed in the first part of this book.

vii   Completion

Both the lease and an exact copy of it, called a counterpart lease, are prepared. Standard Condition 8.2.6 provides that the seller/landlord is to engross the lease and the counterpart of it and is to send the counterpart to the buyer/tenant at least five working

---

14   SC 8.2.1. Under SC 8.2.5, the buyer cannot transfer the benefit of the contract.
15   SC 8.2.3.
16   On or before exchange, as discussed in ch 9.
17   See ch 5, section 4 xxii 2, 5.

days before the contractual completion date. The actual lease executed by the landlord will be handed over to the buyer/tenant on completion but the buyer will execute the counterpart lease, which is then retained by the landlord.[18] Execution is effected in the same way as for any other deed. The landlord will normally be executing under an implied condition as to execution of the counterpart by the tenant and payment of the premium, or will be delegating delivery to his solicitor on completion. The counterpart lease gives the landlord a record of the contents of the lease and as it is executed by the tenant, it is needed by the landlord to enforce the covenants in the lease. Obviously the buyer/tenant will not receive any actual title deeds on a lease granted out of unregistered land but if the superior leasehold and freehold titles are unregistered and have been deduced, he will want to verify his abstract or epitome against the originals if possible. The balance of the purchase price, in effect a premium on the grant of the lease, will be handed over on completion. If rent or estimated service charge is payable in advance, the buyer/tenant may have to pay an apportioned sum on completion, and for his part will wish to receive any necessary consent of the seller/landlord's mortgagee or superior landlord.

viii   Post-completion matters

1   Stamping

The stamp duty position on the grant of a lease is considered in Chapter 15 at section 2 v; if the lease contains a certificate of value, the premium does not exceed £60,000, and the rent does not exceed £600, then no stamp duty will be payable on the premium. Otherwise duty is payable on the premium and on the rent, (dependent on the amount of the rent and the length of the term of the lease). A lease for seven years or more does fall within the provisions for production in the Finance Act 1931. The counterpart lease bears a fixed duty of £5.

2   Registration under the Land Registration Act 1925

Application will have to be made for first registration of title to the lease at the appropriate District Land Registry if the lease is for a term of over 21 years, within 2 months. If the reversionary title is registered then title to the lease must be registered if the lease is for a term of over 21 years, as a disposition of the registered reversionary title, within the priority period of the pre-completion search. Whether absolute leasehold or good leasehold title is registered will depend on whether the superior title(s) can be deduced. If the reversionary title is registered the lease will in addition need to be noted on the register of the reversionary title. To this end, the contract should include a condition that the landlord's Land Certificate be put on deposit at the Land Registry and the deposit number supplied to the buyer on or before completion; this was dealt with in Chapter 2 section 2 vi 3.

3   Other matters

If the lease contains a provision requiring notice of any assignment or mortgage to be given to the landlord, and the buyer/tenant has bought with the aid of a mortgage, then notice of the mortgage will have to be given. As in any other conveyancing transaction, the buyer/tenant's solicitor would have to consider the question of custody of the deeds, which will comprise the lease and a Land

18   SC 8.2.7.

Certificate or Charge Certificate. The lease and Charge Certificate would, of course, be sent to the mortgagee if there was a mortgage.

ix   Acting for the mortgagee

In the same way that on a purchase of freehold or leasehold land a buyer's solicitor will normally also act for the buyer's mortgagee, there is normally no problem and no conflict of interest in the solicitor for the buyer/tenant of a house or flat also acting for the mortgagee who is providing the purchase price (the premium) on the grant of the lease. As in any other transaction the mortgagee will naturally be concerned about the title and the result of various searches; however, there are a number of matters of particular concern to the mortgagee on the grant of a lease which have been incorporated into the Council of Mortgage Lenders' (CML) handbook for England and Wales 1999. A mortgagee will wish to ensure that the freehold (and any other superior leasehold) titles are deduced. The mortgagee will wish to ensure that absolute as opposed to good leasehold title will be granted. For the reasons explained in section iii above the buyer will also be concerned on the same account. Secondly, the mortgagee will want to ensure that the property is accurately defined including any legally enforceable rights of access along with all requisite rights of support and shelter and easements. In addition that the assignment and repair covenants are appropriate to the type of lease being considered. Further the mortgagee will wish to be aware of any provisions in the lease concerning insurance covers of all parts of the building. Thirdly, the mortgagee will not accept as security a lease which contains a provision for forfeiture on the tenant's bankruptcy in either the lease itself or the headlease; it is in just such a situation that the mortgagee would want the loan to be secured and if the lease is forfeited the security in effect disappears. Fourthly, the mortgagee may be concerned about the unexpired term of the lease and may not agree to lend unless there is as much as 60 years unexpired residue.

Further if a management company is involved the last three years company accounts should be checked, and a company search undertaken. The borrower should execute a blank stock transfer form and become a member of the company if it is limited by guarantee. The maintenance of common parts must be enforceable at the request of the tenant and there should be a covenant by the landlord that all the leases in the block are the same, if not indemnity insurance will be required. For leases created after 1 September 2000 where the management company is responsible for carrying out repairs, if the company does not have any estate or interest in the flats the landlord must covenant to carry out the repairs or the tenants must form the management company.

The mortgagee will in addition, be concerned about the ability to assign should it repossess the property and will not accept any restriction on the right to assign or charge a long lease of residential property. It will also want to ensure that there is no possible forfeiture of the lease on other grounds, for example for non-payment of rent. We have already seen that relief will be available to the mortgagee, who will be in the position of under lessee. However, such relief may depend on the mortgagee being aware of the forfeiture proceedings in time.[19] Ideally, the mortgagee would like a covenant in the lease to the effect that the landlord should inform the mortgagee of any proposed forfeiture. However, rules of court require a landlord to give notice

---

19   See *Abbey National Building Society v Maybeech Ltd* [1985] Ch 190, [1984] 3 All ER 262 and *Smith v Metropolitan City Properties Ltd* [1986] 1 EGLR 52; and also Administration of Justice Act 1985, s 55.

of forfeiture proceedings to any mortgagee of whom he is aware, thus the mortgagee will insist that the landlord was given notice of the mortgage, whether required by the lease or not.

In the case of flying freeholds they are unlikely to be acceptable to the lender. For full details of the CML's requirements for leasehold property see the CML handbook.

x Flats

We have already considered the advantages of an estate of houses being disposed of by granting long leases rather than selling the freehold. Many of these advantages apply with all the more force when the property is a block of flats with the individual flats being sold; such matters have been considered in section 1 and in Chapter 5, section 4 xxi. There will be a much greater need to identify accurately the property being sold which will be part of a building with, therefore, no immediately obviously delineated division between the various parts. For example, are the flat owners to own the outside walls of their flat? Is a flat owner at the top of the building to own the roof above his flat? There will be a correspondingly greater need for easements to be accurately stated, both easements to be granted to flat owners and easements to be reserved. There will need to be easements relating to the route of services such as drains through the flats and through the common parts. Similarly, it is vital that the flats are properly insured; this may be achieved by the landlord insuring all the flats under a block policy or there may possibly be a separate policy for the individual flats and the common parts of the building and grounds. The effect of a flat being destroyed by fire and not having been insured would be disastrous, not only for the owner of that particular flat but for the other flat owners in the block as well.

Because of the close proximity within which the flat owners are living there will probably be quite extensive covenants covering what can and what cannot happen in the flats. There will also be provision for maintenance and repair of the various common parts, such as the staircase and lifts, the external structure of the building and the grounds. There will probably therefore be a covenant to pay a service charge in relation to the expense of such matters to the landlord who would himself covenant in the leases to be responsible for repair and maintenance of the common parts. We have already noted the restriction and control over such service charges in section ii above. However, the builder or developer of the flats may not wish to be saddled with this maintenance and repair responsibility and may wish to have no further concern with the development once leases of all the individual flats have been granted. One way of achieving this and also giving the flat owners more control over their immediate environment would be for the common parts to be vested in a management company whose members would be the various flat owners from time to time. This management company would then be responsible for the repair and maintenance of the common parts and it would be to this management company that the flat owners paid their service charges; as members of the management company they would clearly have much more control than if the landlord were still in charge. The management company could even take a transfer of the landlord's reversion, so that the tenants become their own landlord, through the medium of the management company. If there is a management company, on the sale of each flat a share in the management company would also be transferred.

xi Underleases

If the landlord only has a leasehold interest himself, the lease which he grants will be an underlease. From the sub-tenant's point of view this means that there will be a superior leasehold title as well as the freehold title. On investigating title, therefore, the sub-tenant/buyer's solicitor will wish to be able to investigate the superior leasehold title as well as the freehold title. When we considered the open contract rule in Chapter 5 section 4 xvii, we saw that in relation to unregistered title the buyer could examine the immediately superior leasehold title – out of which the underlease was being granted – but not the freehold title nor any other intermediate leasehold title. In relation to registered title, section 110 of the Land Registration Act 1925 is inapplicable. From the buyer's point of view, therefore, in both cases a special condition is needed in the contract entitling the buyer to examine the freehold and superior leasehold titles whether by means of abstract and epitome or office copy entries. Standard Condition 8.2.4 covers the point.

The buyer's solicitor will also be concerned about the contents of the superior lease(s). It may reveal that the superior landlord's consent is necessary to any underlease.[20] Additionally, the buyer/sub-tenant will normally be subject to the covenants contained in the superior lease. If there is any breach of those covenants then this could, as we have seen, lead to forfeiture of the superior lease although, again, we have seen that the sub-tenant does have the right to apply for relief against forfeiture of the superior lease. The seller/under lessor would require an indemnity in the underlease against breach of the convenants in his own (the superior) lease.

3   ASSIGNMENT OF LEASE

i   Introduction

We have now seen how a lease (or underlease) is granted. We have already dealt with the assignment of such a lease in the conveyancing section forming the first part of this book. The object of this section is to reiterate the main differences between the freehold transaction and the assignment of a lease.

ii   Drafting the contract

As part of the process of investigating title prior to the drafting of the contract the seller's solicitor may discover that the landlord's consent is necessary to the proposed assignment to the buyer. The seller's solicitor would therefore have to request such consent and there may well be conditions in the contract covering the point. Standard Condition 8.3 is discussed in Chapter 5 section 4 viii. However, in purely practical terms the buyer may wish to ensure that the landlord's consent is forthcoming before exchange of contracts as otherwise, if the consent is not forthcoming, then although the buyer will be able to rescind the contract, there would be difficulties if he has a synchronised sale proceeding at the same time. The written consent from the landlord would be handed over on completion, if not before.

We saw in section 2 iii 5 and ix earlier in this chapter that a landlord's position with regard to giving consent for assignment and the requirements under the CML handbook.[1] In all cases where consent is necessary, the tenant should apply for the consent even if he is sure that it will be refused. If it is refused then he can either go ahead and assign (or sub-let) or seek a declaration from the court that the refusal was

---

20 SC 8.3 would then be applicable; see ch 5, section 4 viii. See also the effect of the Landlord and Tenant Act 1988, section 3 ii, below.
1   See section ix above

unreasonable. The latter, although it takes time, will be preferable and indeed the proposed assignee or sub-lessee may insist on it. The danger in the former course is that the tenant and the proposed assignee or sub-lessee are gambling that if the landlord brings proceedings for breach of the covenant, probably by way of forfeiture, the court will agree that the refusal was unreasonable. There can be no guarantee of that.

When a licence or consent is given it is normally in writing and may also be recited in the assignment or sub-lease; the lease might in fact require the consent to be in writing, in which case an oral consent would be insufficient unless the landlord could be shown to have waived the requirement of writing.

When the seller's solicitor applies for consent, he may be asked by the landlord's solicitor to give an undertaking to pay the landlord's solicitor's costs involved in the consent to assign. He may even be asked to give an undertaking which would oblige him to pay the costs whether or not the consent to assign was forthcoming; even if the undertaking was silent on the point, it might be construed as obliging the seller's solicitor to pay the costs whether or not the consent was granted.[2] If a seller's solicitor is asked to give such an undertaking, he should give careful thought as to whether the undertaking should be given at all and whether it should be limited to cases where consent to assign is forthcoming. The seller's solicitor might also wish to stipulate a maximum sum payable under the undertaking, and to ensure that he had received sufficient money on account from his client to cover it.

The Landlord and Tenant Act 1988 imposes a number of obligations on the landlord who receives an application for consent to assign.[3] Once the landlord has received a written application for consent, he owes a duty to the tenant (ie the seller) to give consent within a reasonable time (except in cases where it is reasonable not to give consent).[4] Within a reasonable time he must also serve on the tenant written notice of his decision whether or not to give consent, specifying any conditions subject to which the consent is given and, if consent is withheld, the reasons for this. The landlord cannot impose unreasonable conditions. If a sub-tenant wishes to assign (or sub-let) and the head lease includes a provision that the tenant shall not give consent to the sub-tenant without the approval of his landlord, the landlord owes a duty to the sub-tenant in similar terms, ie to give approval within a reasonable time and to serve written notice of his decision. A landlord is also under a duty to pass on within a reasonable time any application received by him from the tenant for consent to anyone else whose consent the landlord believes is necessary – such as a superior landlord. Breach of any of these duties may be the subject of a claim for breach of statutory duty and in such a claim, the burden is on the landlord to prove that he is not in breach of duty.

The practical effect of the 1988 Act is to strengthen the hand of the seller's solicitor if the landlord is slow in dealing with an application for consent. It is unclear exactly how long a 'reasonable' time will be although in *Midland Bank plc v Chart Enterprises Inc*[5] a period of about 2½ months following the tenant's application for consent during which the landlord did nothing was held to amount to unreasonable delay. The 1988 Act may also assist a seller's solicitor who wishes to resist giving an

---

2   *Goldman v Abbott* [1989] 2 EGLR 78, CA.
3   The Act also applies to consent to sub-letting, charging or parting with possession, as does the Landlord and Tenant Act 1927, s 19(1) which imposes the duty not unreasonably to withhold consent.
4   The Act does not affect the criteria for a reasonable refusal, as to which see section iii 5 above; *Air India v Balabel* [1993] 2 EGLR 66, CA.
5   [1990] 2 EGLR 59.

undertaking to pay the landlord's costs in relation to the consent. The Law Society has expressed the opinion that a landlord's solicitor who refused to produce the draft documentation for a licence to assign until an undertaking was given would eventually be in breach of the duty under the 1988 Act to give consent within a reasonable time.[6]

When drafting the particulars and special conditions of the contract, the seller's solicitor will normally make reference to the provisions of the lease, both for the description of the property (assuming the description in the lease is still up-to-date), for the remaining term of the lease and for the covenants and easements which the property is subject to. If the seller is only selling part of the property comprised in the lease there may well, of course, be new covenants and easements in addition to those in the lease.

When we considered the open contract rule in relation to the title which would be deduced to the buyer in Chapter 5, section 4 xvii, we saw that the open contract rule for unregistered title did not entitle the buyer to examine the freehold (or any superior leasehold) title, but just to an abstract of the leasehold title being sold going back at least 15 years (but not before the grant of the lease). The buyer's solicitor would therefore wish to include a condition in the contract entitling the buyer to examine the freehold and any superior leasehold title. If the title to the lease is registered section 110 of the Land Registration Act 1925 applies and the seller will have to deduce title in accordance with that section providing, inter alia, copies of the register entries. If the title is absolute there will be no need to examine the superior title, but if only good leasehold, the position is as for unregistered title. The Standard Conditions do not add to the open contract entitlement, so from the buyer's point of view, a special condition will be necessary.

The buyer's solicitor will make the usual searches and enquiries. One additional point may be that the buyer's solicitor might wish to try and establish that all the covenants in the lease have been duly performed and observed; for example, if the lease contains a covenant against making any extension to the property without the landlord's consent the buyer's solicitor may want to establish where there has been any such extension and if so, whether consent has been given. As on the sale of the freehold the buyer's solicitor would have to consider whether the property is appropriate for the buyer in terms of the various covenants and easements which it is subject to, and of which it has the benefit.

The TransAction 2001 is of course applicable to the sale of a leasehold as it is to the sale of a freehold. We have already seen in Chapter 6 that the raising of preliminary enquiries of the seller concerning the property is largely replaced under the protocol by the seller providing information at the outset on a property information form. For leasehold properties there is an additional property information form dealing with additional matters of relevance to leaseholds. The form is included in the Appendix and incorporates details of any management company and any complaints about the breaches of covenants. There is also an additional property information questionnaire headed 'leasehold questionnaire', which is designed to produce the information necessary to complete the additional property information form. This, too, is included in the Appendix.

ii   The deed of assignment/transfer

If Protocol is adopted, having, investigated title, either by means of abstract or epitome for unregistered title or copy entries of the register for registered title and contracts

---

6   [1989] Law Soc Gaz 11, 7 June.

will be exchanged in the usual way. The usual searches will be made depending whether the title is registered or unregistered. The purchase deed will either be a deed of assignment if the title is unregistered or a transfer if the title is registered. The particular features of these deeds were considered in Chapter 12, sections 3 and 4. The main differences between an assignment and a conveyance are that the estate being sold will be referred to as the remainder of the term granted by the lease also Standard Conditions 3.2.2 and 3.2.3 limit the additional covenants for title that are implied on a sale of leasehold title under section 4(1)(b) of the Law of Property (Miscellaneous Provisions) Act 1994, and a statement to this effect will probably have been included in the contract and needs to be reflected in the purchase deed.

If the title is registered the deed of transfer will follow the form of a freehold transfer, save that there may again be reference to the remainder of the term of the lease being vested in the buyer. There will be a similar need to modify the implied covenants for title but an indemnity covenant on the part of the buyer will be implied whether or not value is given by the buyer, ie whether it is a sale or a gift.

iv   Completion

In preparing for completion the seller's solicitor may have to deal with apportionments of the rent and any service charge, and on completion the buyer will wish to inspect the last receipt for rent on completion for the reasons set out in Chapter 14, section 3 ii 2E.[7] The deeds handed over on completion will include the lease and if the title is unregistered the various assignments, mortgages, grants of probate and other documents under which the property has passed. There may also be a marked abstract of the freehold and any superior leasehold titles, if these are being deduced. If title is registered, then in addition to the lease there will be the Land Certificate or Charge Certificate and in the case of a good leasehold title there may again be a marked abstract of the superior leasehold and freehold title although if this were available, absolute leasehold title would presumably have already been obtained. In both cases, there would be the assignment or transfer and if the development is managed by a management company whose members are the owners for the time being of the houses or flats there will be a share certificate in that company and a transfer of that share.

v   Post-completion matters

Ad valorem stamp duty is payable on an assignment or transfer in the same way as on a conveyance of the freehold. The provisions of the Finance Act 1931 relating to production also apply to that assignment on sale of a lease granted for a term of seven years or more and thus a P.D. form will need to be filled in and sent with the assignment or transfer to the Inland Revenue or, if stamp duty is not payable, to the District Land Registry. If title to the lease is already registered, it will be necessary to apply for registration of the purchase within the priority period of the search which will have been done before completion. If title is not registered, but the lease has more than 21 years left to run, first registration is compulsory. The process of registration is considered in Chapter 15, section 2 iv and the process of stamping in Chapter 15, section 2 v.

---

7   Under the Protocol, the receipt may be supplied with the additional property information form.

If the lease contains a covenant requiring that notice be given to the landlord of any assignment or mortgage or receipt of a mortgage, then notice must be given; such notice is normally given in duplicate and the landlord is requested to return one copy of the notice receipted which is then placed with the deeds. Even if there is no such covenant a mortgagee will wish to make the landlord aware of his interest in order to be informed should the landlord commence forfeiture proceedings in respect of the lease in future.

vi   Underleases

We saw in section 2 xi above the situation with regard to deducing and investigating title if the lease being granted was an underlease rather than a headlease. Similar considerations will apply if the lease being assigned is an underlease rather than a headlease. The open contract rule as to the title to be deduced, mentioned in section ii above, does not entitle the buyer to examine the freehold or superior leasehold title. Therefore if the title is unregistered or if the lease is registered with only good leasehold as opposed to absolute leasehold title, the buyer will want in the contract a condition allowing him to investigate the freehold and superior leasehold titles. This must be a special condition, as there is nothing in Standard Condition 8.1 to cover the point. As on the grant of a lease, the buyer's solicitor will be concerned about the contents of the superior lease and in particular the covenants contained therein. The contract should disclose that the lease being sold is an underlease rather than a headlease.

18 STATUTORY PROVISIONS PROTECTING LONG-TERM RESIDENTIAL TENANCIES

There are a number of statutes which give tenants under long residential leases certain rights both during and at the end of the lease.

1   LANDLORD AND TENANT ACT 1954, PART I

For the Act to be applicable, the tenancy must be a 'long tenancy', that is a tenancy granted for a term exceeding 21 years.[1] The rent must be a 'low rent' which means that it must be less than two-thirds of the rateable value of the property.[2] The appropriate rateable value is the rateable value on 23 March 1965 or when first rated if later. In addition, the tenancy must be a tenancy which would, apart from its low rent, be otherwise a protected tenancy under the Rent Act 1977. This means inter alia that the rateable value of the property must be within certain limits and the tenant must occupy the property as his home.

The effect of the Act is that the tenancy does not expire on its termination date but continues. This continuation can be brought to an end by notice by the tenant or the landlord. If the landlord gives notice he must include either proposals for an assured tenancy under the Housing Act 1988 or state his grounds for wanting possession. The grounds on which he can obtain possession are set out in the Act.

2   LOCAL GOVERNMENT AND HOUSING ACT 1989

Since the Local Government and Housing Act 1989 came into force on 15 January 1989, the majority of long tenancies to which the 1954 Act applied will no longer be protected by that Act but will fall under the similar provisions of the 1989 Act. To qualify under the 1989 Act, the tenancy must be a long tenancy at a low rent and must be one which would qualify as an assured tenancy under the Housing Act 1988, were it not at a low rent.[3] The provisions for security of tenure after the expiration of the contractual term are broadly in line with those in the 1954 Act. The tenant may terminate on or after the expiry of the term by giving one month's notice, whereas the landlord is obliged to serve a notice, in prescribed form, either proposing an

---

1   Landlord and Tenant Act 1954, s 2(1), (4).
2   Ibid, s 2(5).
3   Local Government and Housing Act 1989, Sch 10.

assured tenancy or seeking to resume possession. The landlord will only be granted possession if he can satisfy one of the grounds in the Act.[4]

3 LEASEHOLD REFORM ACT 1967

I *Application of the Act*

The Act applies to a 'long tenancy', that is a tenancy granted for a term exceeding 21 years.[5] A tenancy will qualify if a tenant could at some point have said that he was entitled to remain as tenant for the next 21 years. Thus if there is a tenancy for 14 years renewable at the tenant's option this would qualify, but not a tenancy of 14 years followed by another tenancy of 14 years where the tenant could not insist on renewal, because although the total period of the two tenancies is 28 years, at no point could the tenant have said that he was entitled to a further 21 years.

The tenancy must be at a 'low rent' which, as under the Landlord and Tenant Act 1954, Part I, means a rent less than two-thirds of the rateable value of the property.[6] The appropriate rateable value is the rateable value on 23 March 1965 or when first rated if later, or on the first day of the term of the tenancy if later.[7] (Following the abolition of the domestic rating system, reference is made instead to a hypothetical market rent when appropriate.) This will normally mean that the tenancy is not a protected tenancy under the Rent Act 1977 nor an assured tenancy under the Housing Act 1988. The property comprised in the tenancy must be a 'house'. This includes any building designed or adapted for living in, notwithstanding that it is not structurally detached.[8] If a building is divided horizontally, ie into separate flats, then the separate flats cannot be houses and do not get the benefit of the Act although the whole building could be a house.[9] If a building is divided vertically, the separate units can be houses but the building as a whole cannot. If the property is used partly for residence and partly for business purposes – such as a shop with a flat above – then it could be a house depending on the precise circumstances.[10]

Initially the Act only applied if the rateable value of the property fell within certain limits.[11] The appropriate rateable value is that on 23 March 1965 or when first rated if later, or in certain circumstances on 1 April 1973. In respect of new properties which, following the abolition of the domestic rating system are not rated, reference is made instead to the hypothetical market rent. The rateable value or hypothetical market rent may be notionally reduced to offset the effect of a tenant's

---

4 Ibid., Sch 10 para 5.
5 Leasehold Reform Act 1967, s 3 as amended by s 64 of the Leasehold Reform, Housing and Urban Development Act 1993.
6 Leasehold Reform Act 1967, s 4.
7 There is an exception for properties let between the end of August 1939 and the beginning of April 1963, where the tenancy is not at a low rent if the rent exceeded two-thirds of the *letting* value of the property at the commencement of the tenancy. For the calculation of the letting value, see *Johnston v Duke of Westminster* [1986] AC 839, [1986] 2 All ER 613, HL. A new s 4A, inserted by s 65 of the Leasehold Reform, Housing and Urban Development Act 1993, extends the scope of the Act in relation to enfranchisement by, broadly, applying the low rent list just to the first year of the tenancy.
8 Leasehold Reform Act 1967, s 2.
9 See *Sharpe v Duke Street Securities NV* (1987) 55 P & CR 331, CA; *Malpas v St Comin's Property Co Ltd* [1992] 1 EGLR 109, CA.
10 *Tandon v Trustees of Spurgeon's Homes* [1982] AC 755, [1982] 1 All ER 1086, HL, but also see *Duke of Westminster v Birrane* [1995] QB 262, [1995] 3 All ER 416, where the property included a basement which was partially underneath another property.
11 Leasehold Reform Act 1967, s 1.

improvements.[12] However, a new section 1A of the Act, inserted by section 63 of the Leasehold Reform, Housing and Urban Development Act 1993, removes the rateable value limits in the case of enfranchisement.

A tenant can claim the benefit of the Act if, when he gives notice to the landlord of his claim, he has been the tenant of the house under a long tenancy at a low rent and occupying it as his residence for the last three years or for three out of the last ten years.[13] Thus the qualifying conditions normally have to be fulfilled throughout this three year period. There are provisions whereby certain close relatives of a deceased tenant who have succeeded to the tenancy can add to their own residence as tenant the period of time when they were resident in the property with the deceased tenant.[14] The relatives so entitled include the deceased tenant's spouse, parents and children. There are also provisions covering occupation by beneficiaries under trusts or settlements.[15]

In *Duke of Westminster v Oddy*,[16] the tenant was a bare trustee, holding the leasehold interest in trust for a company and occupying the house under a licence from the company: he was not entitled under the Act, as he was not occupying 'in right of the tenancy'.[17]

2   Effect of the Act

The Act gives a tenant the right either to purchase the freehold of the property (or 'enfranchise' as it is called) or to have an extended lease for a period of 50 years more than the original term. Most tenants in practice will enfranchise rather than claim an extended lease.

3   Enfranchisement

The tenant must first of all give notice to the landlord that he wants to buy the freehold, called a desire notice. This creates a contract between landlord and tenant and if the house is then sold (ie the lease assigned) before the purchase is completed the benefit of the desire notice can be assigned with the tenancy.[18] The contract created by the notice can and should be protected as a Civ land charge if the title to the freehold is unregistered and by notice or caution if it is registered to bind any purchaser of the landlord's interest.[19] If the landlord had entered into a contract to sell the freehold prior to service of the notice, that contract will be discharged by the notice unless it actually provided for the eventuality of the notice.[20] Within two months of the service of the desire notice the landlord must serve a notice on the tenant admitting or denying the tenant's claim.[1]

The price to be paid by the tenant is the open market value of the house and premises on the assumption that the buyer is not the tenant or a member of his family residing with him and that the property is sold subject to the remainder of the tenancy

---

12   See *Mayhew v Free Grammar School of John Lyon* (1991) 63 P & CR 53, 23 HLR 479, CA; the same rule applies in calculating the 'low rent' limit under s 4.
13   Leasehold Reform Act 1967.
14   Ibid, s 7.
15   Leasehold Reform Act 1967, s 6.
16   (1984) 15 HLR 80, CA.
17   Leasehold Reform Act 1967, s 1(2).
18   Ibid, s 5(2).
19   It cannot be an overriding interest; ibid, s 5(5).
20   Ibid, s 5(7).
 1   Ibid, Sch 3, para 7.

including the 50 year extension to which the tenant is entitled under the Act.[2] This means that assuming that the tenancy is not too near the end of its term, the purchase price will be relatively low. It is normally agreed by the parties and is in practice sometimes fixed at a certain number of years' rent, eg ten or fifteen years. However, if the rateable value or hypothetical market rent (reduced if appropriate to offset the effect of a tenant's improvements) is above certain limits, different assumptions apply[3] – for example the 50 year extension is ignored.[4] In default of agreement the price will be fixed by the Leasehold Valuation Tribunal[5] with appeal to the Land Tribunal.[6] If a landlord does not own the freehold but only a superior leasehold interest, the tenant is still entitled to enfranchise but a separate price will be fixed for the superior leasehold interest and the freehold interest *both* of which the tenant will be buying.

In addition to the price the tenant must also pay the landlord's reasonable costs of investigating the tenant's title, of deducing title, of the conveyance and of valuing the property.[7] After the price has been ascertained the tenant can withdraw his claim within one month.[8] If the tenant is able to enfranchise only because of the amendments introduced by the Leasehold Reform, Housing and Urban Development Act 1993, then under section 9(1C) of the 1967 Act, introduced by section 66 of the 1993 Act, the criteria for fixing the price are amended and an additional sum may be payable under section 9A of the 1967 Act.

The procedure for deducing title, raising requisitions, drafting the conveyance and completion is dealt with in regulations made under the Act.[9] The conveyance will be drafted by the tenant's solicitor and the Act makes provision for the contents.[10] Briefly, it will contain such restrictive covenants, easements and other provisions as are necessary to keep the parties in the same position as they were under the lease. The landlord need only give the limited covenant for title which would be implied on a conveyance by a trustee. The landlord must give an acknowledgement for the production of any document of title he retains but need not give an undertaking for safe custody. If the freehold is subject to a mortgage then unless it is discharged before completion in the usual way, the tenant should pay the purchase money to the mortgagee and this will discharge the mortgage so far as the property sold is concerned.[11] From a mortgagee's point of view it is necessary to bear in mind that a tenant does have a right to enfranchise and that therefore the property is only really worth what the tenant would have to pay on enfranchisement.

The landlord as seller has a lien over the property not only for any unpaid purchase money but also for the costs mentioned above and any arrears of rent.[12]

4   Extended lease

The procedure for service of a notice set out in the previous section applies equally to a notice to take an extended lease. A tenant cannot have more than one extension (but can still enfranchise provided the enfranchisement desire notice is served before

2   Ibid, s 9(1).
3   Ibid, s 9(1A).
4   See also Housing and Planning Act 1986, s 23(1), overruling *Mosley v Hickman* (1986) 52 P & CR 248, CA.
5   Leasehold Reform Act 1967, s 21.
6   Housing Act 1980, Sch 22, para 2.
7   Leasehold Reform Act 1967, s 9(4).
8   Ibid, s 9(3).
9   Leasehold Reform (Enfranchisement and Extension) Regulations 1967.
10   Leasehold Reform Act 1967, s 10.
11   Ibid, s 12.
12   Ibid, s 9(5).

the end of the term of the original lease).[13] Again the procedure is laid down in regulations under the Act.[14] The lease – for the remainder of the original term plus 50 years[15] – is drafted by the landlord's solicitor and will contain the same terms as the original lease. The rent will be the same as under the original lease until the end of the term of the original lease and thereafter it will be a ground rent representing the letting value of the site without buildings.[16] The rent can be reviewed halfway through the 50 year extension period. In default of agreement the rent is fixed by the Leasehold Valuation Tribunal.[17] The tenant must also pay the landlord's reasonable costs for investigating the tenant's title, of the lease and of a valuation of the property.[18]

5   Landlord's overriding rights

The landlord can defeat the tenant's claim to an extended lease or to enfranchise in certain circumstances. He can obtain possession, thereby overriding an extension already granted or claimed, if he can show within twelve months before the termination of the original lease, that he wishes to demolish or substantially reconstruct the property for the purposes of redevelopment.[19] He may be able to defeat a claim to an extended lease or enfranchisement if he can show that he wants the property as a residence for himself or an adult member of his family.[20] However, this provision does not apply if the landlord's interest was purchased or created after 18 February 1966. In both cases the tenant is entitled to compensation.[1]

4   LANDLORD AND TENANT ACT 1987, PART I

Broadly, the Landlord and Tenant Act 1987, Part I provides the tenants of flats in a building with a right of pre-emption where the landlord intends to dispose of his interest in the premises. There is an important distinction between the provisions of this Act and those of the Leasehold Reform, Housing and Urban Development Act 1993. The 1987 Act only permits the tenants to collectively buy the landlord's interest where the landlord intends to sell; unlike the 1993 Act, tenants cannot force a sale to them.

Under section 1 of the Act the landlord shall not make a relevant disposal[2] affecting any premises to which Part I of the Act applies unless he has first served a notice under section 5 on the qualifying tenants of the flats contained in the premises, giving them a right of first refusal in respect of the interest of which he wishes to dispose.

Part I applies to premises consisting of the whole or part of a building which contains two or more flats held by qualifying tenants and where the number of flats

---

13   Ibid, s 16(1).
14   See fn 9, p 304, above.
15   Leasehold Reform Act 1967, s 14(1).
16   Ibid, s 15(2).
17   Leasehold Reform Act 1967, s 21.
18   Ibid, s 14(2).
19   Ibid, s 17. This does not affect a tenant who has enfranchised.
20   Ibid, s 18.
 1   Ibid, Sch 2.
 2   Note that a 'relevant disposal' was originally held not to include a contract for sale: *Mainwaring v Trustees of Henry Smith's Charity* [1998] QB 1, [1996] 2 All ER 220: the Housing Act 1996 introduced a new s 4A into the 1987 Act closing this apparent loophole and confirming that the right does apply to contracts, whether conditional or unconditional.

held by the qualifying tenants exceeds 50% of the total number of flats contained in the premises. However, there are a number of exceptions[3] including where part of the premises is occupied or intended to be occupied for non-residential purposes or where there is a residential landlord.

A tenant of a flat will be a qualifying tenant unless the tenancy falls into a number of categories including a business tenancy under the Landlord and Tenant Act 1954, Part II and an assured tenancy under the Housing Act 1988.

The relevant disposal, which brings into play the provisions of the Act, is a disposal by the landlord of any estate or interest (legal or equitable) in the premises, but with a number of exceptions contained in section 4(1) and (2). These excluded disposals include the creation of an estate or interest by way of security for a loan and a disposal in pursuance of an option or right of pre-emption. However, under section 4(3) a disposal does include the grant of an option or right of pre-emption.[4] A disposal by a mortgagee in exercise of a power of sale will be a relevant disposal.

The landlord's notice under section 5 must contain certain prescribed information and must be served on not less than 90% of the qualifying tenants. The notice amounts to an offer by the landlord to dispose of the property on the same terms as the intended disposal which triggers the need for the notice. This offer can be accepted by the requisite majority of qualifying tenants serving an acceptance notice within the period specified in the landlord's notice. The requisite majority of qualifying tenants, defined in section 5(6), is effectively 50%. The Act sets out a detailed procedure to be followed if the tenants do not accept the landlord's offer but one of the most important provisions in practice is section 11 which deals with the effect of a disposal in breach of the Act, where the necessary notice under section 5 is not given. In practice a landlord may be tempted to sell his interest without following the section 5 notice procedure and provide in the sale contract that the risk of enforcement procedure by the tenants is a risk for the purchaser. Section 11 provides that the requisite majority of qualifying tenants can serve a notice on the purchaser from the landlord requiring information about the disposal and can serve a notice under section 12 requiring the new landlord to transfer his interest on the same terms as the original disposal to him. Any dispute as to the terms of the disposal, including the price, is determined in the first instance by a Leasehold Valuation Tribunal with appeal to the Lands Tribunal. The jurisdiction to fix the price to be paid by the tenants is very limited; there is no revaluation of the premises and the Tribunal can fix the price only by reference to the price actually paid by the purchaser from the landlord.[5]

If by the time he receives a notice under section 11 or section 12, the purchaser from the landlord no longer owns the interest in question having himself disposed of it, he must provide details of his disposal and serve a copy of the notice on the purchaser from him. It seems that it is important for the tenants to have served a notice on the first purchaser, as otherwise the price paid by the tenants may be the price paid by the subsequent purchaser, which will presumably be a higher price.[6]

A purchaser from a landlord who is worried that he may be caught by the provisions of the Act, and who may therefore be concerned to establish whether or not the landlord has served the necessary notices under section 5, can himself serve notices

---

3   See further *30 Upperton Gardens Management Ltd v Akano* [1990] 2 EGLR 232; *Denetower v Toop* [1991] 3 All ER 661, [1991] 1 WLR 945; *Kay Green v Twinsectra* [1996] 4 All ER 546, [1996] 1 WLR 1587.
4   See *Wilkins v Horrowitz* [1990] 2 EGLR 217 in relation to a disposal by way of subsale.
5   See *Cousins v Metropolitan Guarantee Ltd* [1989] 2 EGLR 223; *Sullivan v Safeland Investments Ltd* [1990] 33 EG 52; *Venus v Khan* [1990] 2 EGLR 237; and *Gregory v Saddiq* [1991] 2 EGLR 237.
6   *Wilkins v Horrowitz* (above); *Tyson v Carlisle Estates Ltd* [1990] 2 EGLR 229.

on the tenants of the flats contained in the premises, under section 18. Where notices are served on at least 80% of the tenants of the flats and no more than 50% have replied at the end of the period specified in section 18, or more than 50% have replied indicating either that they do not regard themselves as entitled to receive a landlord's section 5 notice or that they would not wish to exercise their right of first refusal if they did receive such a notice, the premises shall be treated as premises to which the Act does not apply.

5   LEASEHOLD REFORM, HOUSING AND URBAN DEVELOPMENT ACT 1993

We have already seen that the Leasehold Reform Act 1967 does not permit tenants of flats to buy their freehold, but that the Landlord and Tenant Act 1987 does provide for the collective purchase of the freehold by the tenants in a block of flats, but only where the landlord is intending to dispose of the freehold and has to offer it to the tenants on the same terms. The Leasehold Reform, Housing and Urban Development Act 1993 combines these two approaches; the tenants have a right to initiate the purchase of the freehold, as under the Leasehold Reform Act, but it is a collective purchase of the freehold through a nominee, which will normally be a company whose shareholders are the tenants. The tenants are therefore not buying the freehold of their individual flats but they become their own landlord through the medium of the nominee or company, and they can, of course, be granted further leases of their flats by the nominee or company. A detailed examination of the provisions of the Act is beyond the scope of this book. What follows is a brief summary of the main provisions in relation to collective enfranchisement.

Section 3 of the part of the Act which deals with collective enfranchisement, as originally enacted, applied to premises which consisted of a self-contained building or part of a building where the freehold was owned by one person; where the premises contained two or more flats held by qualifying tenants; and where the total number of flats held by qualifying tenants was not less than two-thirds of the total number of flats contained in the premises. The requirement that the freehold had to be held by one person created a loophole in the law, as it was possible for a landlord to split his freehold and thus avoid the Act, but this loophole was closed by the Housing Act 1996, so that now it is still possible to enfranchise where there is more than one freeholder. The premises will be excluded under section 4 if a certain part of the premises is occupied or intended to be occupied otherwise than for residential purposes; premises are also excluded where there is a resident landlord and the premises do not contain more than four flats. The tenants have a right to enfranchise in respect of the freehold and any superior leasehold interests and also in respect of other appurtenant property.[7]

A person is a qualifying tenant for these purposes if he is tenant of the flat under a long lease at a low rent, though particularly long leases (broadly, those granted for 35 years or over) do not have to be at a low rent.[8] These expressions are defined in broadly the same way as under the Leasehold Reform Act, as amended by the 1993 Act. A tenancy is excluded where it is a business tenancy.

A qualifying tenant can serve a notice under section 11 to obtain information about the landlord's interest and also has the right to inspect the landlord's title

---

7   Sections 1 and 2.
8   Housing Act 1996.

documents. The purchase of the landlord's interest is initiated by a notice under section 13, which must be given by not less than two-thirds of the qualifying tenants of the flats contained in the premises. At least half the tenants giving the notice must have resided in their flats for the previous year, or three years out of the previous ten years. Before serving this notice the tenants must have obtained a valuation of the landlord's interest and indeed the notice must specify a proposed purchase price. The notice must also name the nominee purchaser of the landlord's interest which will normally be a company owned and created by the tenants who are serving the notice, although it could be an individual tenant. As under the Landlord and Tenant Act 1987 there are then detailed provisions detailing the procedure to be followed following the service of the tenant's notice. Doubtless the most significant provisions are in section 32 and Schedule 6, which deal with the determination of the purchase price. Assuming that the tenants are just purchasing the landlord's freehold interest rather than any intermediate leasehold interests, the purchase price is the aggregate of the value of the freehold interest; a share of the so-called 'marriage value'; and also possibly compensation in respect of any loss suffered by the freeholder which is referable to his ownership of any interest in other property. The marriage value is the increase in the value of the freehold (and every intermediate leasehold interest) in the premises when acquired by the nominee purchaser as compared with the value of those interests when held by the persons from whom they are to be acquired (eg the landlord), being an increase in value which is attributable to the potential ability of the tenants to have new leases granted to them without payment of any premium and within restriction as to the length of the term of the new lease, and which the nominee purchaser would have to agree to share with the seller if the interests were being sold to the nominee purchaser on the open market. The share of the marriage value which goes to make up the purchase price is the proportion which is agreed, or determined by a leasehold valuation tribunal to be the proportion which would have been agreed on a sale on the open market by a willing seller, or 50%, whichever is the greater.

One other significant provision is contained in section 23; where not less than two-thirds of all the leases of the flats contained in the premises are due to terminate within five years and the landlord for the purposes of redevelopment intends to demolish or reconstruct or to carry out substantial works of construction on the whole or a substantial part of the premises, and could not reasonably do so without obtaining possession of the premises, the landlord can successfully oppose the tenant's purchase of his interest. This redevelopment ground is very similarly worded to Ground F of section 30(1) of the Landlord and Tenant Act 1954, Part II, which relates to business tenancies and which is considered in Chapter 20.

The Act contains very little dealing with the position after the purchase of the freehold by the nominee, but presumably the intention is that new long leases can and will be granted to the tenants and indeed this may be necessary in order to raise the mortgage finance to provide the purchase price for the freehold; the completion of the purchase of the freehold and the grant of new long leases to the tenants may be simultaneous. The Act also leaves those tenants who do not participate in the purchase of the freehold at some disadvantage; they clearly have no right to new leases and it does seem possible that in some circumstances relations between the two groups of tenants might become strained.

Finally, under section 36 and Schedule 9, the landlord can require a lease back to him of certain parts of the premises including, for example, any flat not let to a qualifying tenant.

The provisions as to collective enfranchisement are contained in Chapter I of Part I of the Act. Under Chapter II of Part I, an individual tenant, who is a qualifying tenant and who has occupied his flat as his home for the last three years or three out of the last ten years, can serve a notice claiming a new lease of his flat at a nominal 'peppercorn' rent for a new term expiring 90 years after the termination date of his existing lease, in substitution for his existing lease. A premium is payable, calculated under the provisions in Schedule 13 of the Act. The procedural provisions of Chapter II broadly follow those in Chapter I.

Also under the 1993 Act, there is provision in Chapter IV of Part I for estate management schemes to be approved by a leasehold valuation tribunal for an area occupied under leases held from one landlord, being schemes designed to secure that in the event of tenants acquiring the landlord's interest either through collective enfranchisement under Chapter I or by the extension to the Leasehold Reform Act 1967 contained in the Act, the landlord will retain powers of management in respect of the premises. Finally, Chapter V of Part I of the Act gives tenants a right to an audit of the landlord's management.

19 STATUTORY PROTECTION FOR RESIDENTIAL AND OTHER TENANTS

1   GENERAL

A detailed consideration of the various statutory provisions protecting different types of tenant is outside the scope of this book. Nevertheless, quite apart from the matters mentioned in the previous chapter, a solicitor involved in a conveyancing transaction should be aware of the protection which a tenant may have either by way of restrictions on the landlord's right to terminate the tenancy and obtain possession, or of limitations on the rent which can be charged. Thus a seller should not be selling with vacant possession if he will be unable to get the tenant out of the property before completion, and a buyer purchasing a tenanted property will clearly need to be advised of the protection which the tenant may have, any rent limits, and any statutory compensation which may be payable to the tenant on termination of the tenancy.

The following types of tenant may be protected.

i   Business tenants

Business tenants are protected by the Landlord and Tenant Act 1954, Part II, which is dealt with in more detail in the next chapter.

ii   Tenants of agricultural land

The Agricultural Holdings Act 1986 protects tenants of agricultural land, and typically therefore protects tenant farmers. The Act limits the landlord's ability to obtain possession, provides for succession on the death of the tenant and compensation on termination of the tenancy.

iii   Agricultural tied houses

The Rent (Agriculture) Act 1976 provides for security of tenure and rent control in respect of dwellings occupied by agricultural employees, for occupation arising under an agreement entered into before 15 January 1989. After this date, the occupation would be an assured agricultural tenancy under the Housing Act 1988.

iv   Local authority tenants

Under the Housing Act 1985, most local authority tenants will have a 'secure tenancy' which provides some security of tenure by limiting the local authority's right to repossession; a court can only order possession on a number of grounds specified in the Act. The Act also provides for succession on the death of a secure tenant. Similar provision will apply to tenants of other public sector landlords, such as housing action trusts.[1] However, housing associations (now known as registered social landlords[2]) are not in the list in section 80. This has the effect that, even though many local authorities have in recent years increasingly involved registered social landlords in their planning for the provision of affordable housing, tenancies with such bodies are regarded by the law as being in the private sector. Generally speaking, tenancies with registered social landlords created before 15 January 1989 will be secure tenancies under the Housing Act 1985, whilst those created after this date will be assured tenancies under the Housing Act 1988.

v   Private sector residential tenants – tenancy granted before 15 January 1989

The Rent Act 1977 protects most tenants of private sector landlords where the tenancy was granted before 15 January 1989. It covers both periodic and fixed term tenancies. The Act provides comprehensive security of tenure; the landlord can only obtain possession by going to court and showing one of a number of specified grounds. There is also a system of control of rent based on registration of a 'fair rent'.

Tenancies within the scope of the 1977 Act are called 'protected' or 'statutory' tenancies. For a particular type of tenancy called a 'shorthold', the landlord is guaranteed of being able to recover possession at the end of the term of the tenancy.

vi   Private sector residential tenants – tenancy granted on or after 15 January 1989

These tenants are protected by the Housing Act 1988. It covers much the same ground as the Rent Act 1977, but replaces that Act for tenancies granted on or after 15 January 1989. The level of protection of tenants under the 1988 Act is reduced; there are security of tenure provisions which are broadly equivalent to the corresponding provisions under the 1977 Act, but the system of rent control is very much weakened and in many cases virtually non-existent. A tenancy protected under the 1988 Act is called an 'assured tenancy'. There are also assured shorthold tenancies, where again the landlord is guaranteed a possession order at the end of the agreed term of the tenancy.

2   BASIC PROTECTION FOR RESIDENTIAL TENANTS AND LICENSEES

Even if a residential tenancy does not qualify for one of the sophisticated statutory provisions mentioned in the previous section, it may have the benefit of a number of fairly basic provisions under the Protection from Eviction Act 1977 as amended,

1   See the list in s 80(1) of the Housing Act 1985 (as amended).
2   Since the Housing Act 1996.

and other Acts. We are here talking typically about a fairly 'short-term' tenancy; for example, a flat or house or bedsit held on a weekly or monthly tenancy or on a tenancy for a short fixed term such as six months or a year. However, although the term is short in that sense, it may well be that the tenant actually remains in possession for quite a long time, because as we have seen, if the tenancy is protected by one of the statutes referred to in the previous section, the tenant may be able to remain in possession if the landlord cannot show one of the specified grounds for recovery of possession.

Most of the statutes mentioned in the previous section protect only tenants not licensees, whereas some of the provisions providing this basic protection for residential tenants do also apply to licensees. The distinction between a tenancy and a licence can be a difficult one. The leading House of Lords case on the point is *Street v Mountford*.[3] The House of Lords returned to the issue in *A G Securities v Vaughan* and *Antoniades v Villiers*,[4] and there have been a number of subsequent Court of Appeal cases including *Ogwr Borough Council v Dykes*;[5] *Aslan v Murphy*,[6] *Mikover Ltd v Brady*;[7] *Stribling v Wickham*;[8] *Nicolau v Pitt*[9] and *Family Housing Association v Jones*[10] followed by a further House of Lords' decision, in the context of the Housing Act 1985, in *Westminster City Council v Clarke*.[11] The basic test is whether or not the occupier has exclusive possession, but this is judged by the reality of the situation rather than the provisions of the agreement between the parties. There have been a number of cases recently where occupiers of hostels and similar accommodation were held not to be tenants, apparently on public policy grounds.[12] The courts sometimes have difficulty faced with joint occupiers under separate 'licence' agreements, where individuals then move on and are replaced; these may well be held to be valid licences not tenancies.

The following provisions provide a basic level of protection for residential tenants, and in some cases licensees.

i   Termination of tenancy or licence

At common law a fixed term tenancy will expire when the term runs out, or in rare cases there may be surrender or forfeiture of the tenancy. A periodic tenancy will be determined by notice to quit. At common law, in the absence of any express provision to the contrary, the period of notice required to determine a yearly tenancy is at least six months; for a quarterly tenancy it is a quarter; for a monthly tenancy, one month;

---

3   [1985] AC 809, [1985] 2 All ER 289.
4   [1990] 1 AC 417, [1988] 3 All ER 1058.
5   [1989] 2 All ER 880, [1989] 1 WLR 295.
6   [1989] 3 All ER 130, [1990] 1 WLR 766.
7   [1989] 3 All ER 618.
8   (1989) 21 HLR 381.
9   (1989) 21 HLR 487.
10 [1990] 1 All ER 385, [1990] 1 WLR 779.
11 [1992] 2 AC 288, [1992] 1 All ER 695.
12 See *Tower Hamlets Borough Council v Miah* [1992] QB 622, [1992] 2 All ER 667, where an occupier of a local authority hostel was held not to have a tenancy; contrast *Bruton v London and Quadrant Housing Trust* [2000] 1 AC 406, [1999] 3 All ER 481, where it was held that, even where an occupier of accommodation designed as provision for the homeless had agreed that he would not acquire a tenancy, a tenancy might still be created if there was exclusive occupation. In *Gray v Taylor* [1998] 4 All ER 17, [1998] 1 WLR 1093, an occupier of an almshouse was held not to be a tenant even though exclusive possession was not disputed, as the charity did not have the power to grant tenancies.

and for a weekly tenancy, one week. The notice must expire at the end of a period of the tenancy, that is, on the anniversary of the commencement. A notice to quit given by one joint tenant may be effective to terminate the tenancy; *Hammersmith and Fulham London Borough Council v Monk*.[13] We have already mentioned in the previous section that if a residential tenancy is protected by the Rent Act 1977 or the Housing Act 1988, there will be substantial restrictions on the ability of the landlord to terminate the tenancy and obtain possession. However, even if these statutory provisions do not apply, a basic level of protection is provided by section 5 of the Protection from Eviction Act 1977, as amended by the Housing Act 1988. Section 5 provides that no notice to quit in respect of any premises let as a dwelling is valid unless two conditions are satisfied. Firstly, the notice must be given at least four weeks before the date on which it is to take effect, in other words the minimum period of the notice to quit is four weeks. Secondly, the notice must be in writing and contain prescribed information. Under the Notices to Quit (Prescribed Information) Regulations 1988, that information includes a statement that the landlord must get a court order for possession before the tenant can lawfully be evicted, and a suggestion that the tenant could obtain advice from a solicitor, citizens' advice bureau, housing aid centre or a rent officers.

Section 5 also protects a periodic licence to occupy premises as a dwelling, but certain tenancies and licences are excluded. These are set out in section 3A of the 1977 Act, and include tenancies or licences where the occupier shares any accommodation with the landlord or licensor, and certain hostel licences.

ii Unlawful eviction and harassment

The Protection from Eviction Act 1977 and the Housing Act 1988 contain a number of provisions prohibiting eviction and harassment. Under section 1 of the 1977 Act, it is a criminal offence for any person unlawfully to evict a 'residential occupier', that is, unlawfully to deprive him of his occupation or to attempt to do so, unless that person can show that he reasonably believed the residential occupier had ceased to reside in the premises. A 'residential occupier' is a person occupying premises as a residence, including both a tenant and a licensee. We have already seen that when a tenancy is protected by the Rent Act 1977 or the Housing Act 1988, the landlord needs to satisfy a court that one of a number of specified grounds for possession is applicable. Even when a tenancy is not so statutorily protected, section 3 of the 1977 Act provides that where any premises have been let as a dwelling, and the tenancy has come to an end but the occupier continues to reside in the premises, it shall not be lawful for the landlord to recover possession except by court proceedings. Section 3 also applies to licences, but the excluded tenancies and licences set out in section 3A are not so protected. Section 2 of the 1977 Act further provides that where a tenancy of premises let as a dwelling contains a forfeiture provision, forfeiture must be by means of a court order for possession while any person is lawfully residing in the premises.

It is also a criminal offence under section 1 of the 1977 Act for the landlord of a 'residential occupier' or his agent to do acts likely to interfere with the peace or comfort of the residential occupier or members of his household, or persistently to withdraw or withhold services, if in either case the landlord or his agent knows or has reasonable cause to believe that such conduct is likely to cause the residential occupier to give up occupation or to refrain from exercising any right in respect of

---

13   [1992] 1 AC 478, [1992] 1 All ER 1, HL.

the premises. This provision protects both the tenant and a licensee; we have already seen that the definition of 'residential occupier' includes a tenancy and a licence.

The rights of a tenant or licensee in respect of unlawful eviction and harassment can be protected by injunction and an action for damages. However, sections 27 and 28 of the Housing Act 1988 introduce a new statutory tort. A residential occupier will be able to claim damages in a number of situations: firstly where the landlord or his agent unlawfully deprives a residential occupier of occupation; secondly, where the landlord or his agent has attempted unlawfully to deprive the residential occupier of his occupation and as a result the residential occupier does give up occupation; and thirdly (following the wording of the criminal offence of harassment in section 1 of the 1977 Act), where the landlord or his agent, knowing or having reasonable cause to believe that his conduct is likely to cause the residential occupier to give up his occupation or to refrain from exercising any right in respect of the premises, does acts likely to interfere with the peace or comfort of the residential occupier or members of his household or persistently withdraws or withholds services and in either case, as a result, the residential occupier gives up occupation. Under section 28, the measure of damages is punitive rather than compensatory; it is the difference in value of the property with the residential occupier in occupation and with vacant possession.[14] Under section 27 there are a number of defences available to the landlord and also situations in which damages may be reduced.

iii   Supply of information

The Landlord and Tenant Act 1987, sections 47 to 50, set out a number of situations in which the landlord of a dwelling has to supply information to a tenant. Under section 47, any written demand for rent or for any other sums payable under the tenancy, given to a tenant, must contain the name and address of the landlord. If this provision is not complied with in relation to a demand for a service charge, the service charge is treated as not being due from the tenant until the landlord's name and address is provided. Under section 48, a landlord must give notice to a tenant of an address in England and Wales at which notices may be served on him by the tenant. If this provisions is not complied with, any rent or service charge otherwise due from the tenant shall be treated as not being due until the landlord does comply.[15] Section 50, which amends section 3 of the Landlord and Tenant Act 1985, deals with the position where the landlord's interest is assigned. The new landlord must give written notice of the assignment and of his name and address to the tenant within two months of the assignment, or by the next day on which rent is payable if later. The old landlord remains liable under the tenancy until the notice is given, but he can bring this liability to an end by himself giving written notice of the assignment, the new landlord's name and last known address.

iv   Repairing obligations

A tenancy agreement may make provision for liability for repairs, but in certain circumstances the landlord will be under an implied statutory obligation to repair.

---

14   See for example *Tagro v Cafane* [1991] 2 All ER 235, [1991] 1 WLR 378; *Jones v Miah* [1992] NPC 54, [1992] 2 EGLR 50, CA; *Osei-Bonsu v Wandsworth London Borough Council* [1999] 1 All ER 265, [1999] 1 WLR 1011.
15   See *Dallhold Estates (UK) Property Ltd v Lindsay Trading Properties Inc* (1992) 65 P & CR 374; *Hussain v Singh* [1993] 2 EGLR 70, CA.

The Landlord and Tenant Act 1985, sections 11 to 14, applies to leases of dwellings for less than seven years. A lease is treated as a lease of less than seven years if it is determinable by the landlord within seven years. Similarly a lease is not covered by the Act if the tenant has a right to renew it making the total period of the lease seven years or more. In the leases to which the Act does apply, there is an implied covenant by the landlord to repair the structure and exterior of the dwelling, including drains, gutters and external pipes; to repair and keep in working order installations for the supply of water, gas and electricity and for sanitation, including sinks, baths and toilets but not appliances for using gas and electricity, such as cookers; and to repair and keep in working order installations for water heating and space heating (for example, gas fires and central heating). Under the Housing Act 1988, section 116, where the lease is of part only of a building owned by the landlord, the landlord's implied covenant to repair the structure and exterior extends to the whole building, and the landlord's implied covenant to keep in repair the installations for the supply of services and for water heating and space heating extends to any installations serving the tenant's dwelling which are owned by the landlord or under his control.

The landlord is not liable to repair the tenant's fixtures, that is, fixtures which the tenant is entitled to remove when he leaves, nor is he liable for repairs as a result of failure by the tenant to use the property in a tenant-like manner. Neither does the Act make the landlord liable to rebuild after destruction or damage by fire, flood or other inevitable accident. There is an implied covenant by the tenant to allow the landlord to enter on 24 hours' notice to see the state of repair of the property.

With the consent of the County Court, it is possible for the parties to contract out of the provisions of the Act. Otherwise the statutory covenant overrides any express covenants in the tenancy agreement.

v   Service charges

The provisions of sections 18 to 30 of the Landlord and Tenant Act 1985 in relation to service charges have already been considered in Chapter 17, section 2 iii 4.

20 BUSINESS TENANCIES

I   INTRODUCTION

A tenancy of business premises is likely to be for a fixed term, perhaps of 10, 20, 25 or 30 years, rather than periodic as this gives the tenant a time scale against which to plan his future business activities. It is likely that the tenancy, of perhaps a shop or an office, will be of merely part of a building. The lease or tenancy agreement will therefore contain provision for easements for the use of stairs, lifts, corridors etc. There may be a service charge to pay for maintenance of these common parts and possibly also for maintenance of the structure of the building itself. It is very likely that there will be a covenant restricting the use of the property and restricting assignment and sub-letting without the landlord's consent. These are all issues which have been considered in the section on the contents of the lease in Chapter 17.

Before entering into a tenancy of business premises both parties should be advised by their solicitors of the effect of the security of tenure provisions outlined in the rest of this chapter. This is of particular importance to the landlord, who may find it difficult to recover possession of the property.

Generally the grant of a commercial lease will be exempt from Value Added Tax (VAT), but under section 89 of the Value Added Tax Act 1994, if the developer is registered for VAT he has the option to waive his exemption and elect to be rated for VAT liability at the standard rate. This will give him the opportunity to recover his input tax. This election must be made in writing to the Inland Revenue within 30 days of the decision being made. The decision to elect must be made with care as it may put off tenants who are not registered for VAT and are therefore unable to recover their input tax.

The landlord's solicitor must decide which form of contract he is to use. He may decide to use the Standard Conditions of Sale form that is discussed in Chapter 5, with amendments as necessary, or he may decide to use the Standard Commercial Property Conditions of Sale introduced in May 1999. However in most cases the solicitor will use his own version, which incorporates the Standard Conditions and the relevant provisions in the Standard Commercial Property Conditions of Sale.

The tenant's solicitor will be concerned to raise all the normal searches and enquiries before contract, which are discussed in detail in Chapter 12, but in addition will need to make further enquiries relating to the tenancy. Traditionally firms have used their own precedents for the pre-contract enquiries for the commercial property sector. Recently however, a group of city firms have sought to standardise the pre contract enquiries form used in commercial property transactions, with a view to speeding up this part of the transaction. The form will be finalised in summer 2001 and will then be available free of charge.[1]

2   DEFINITION

The Landlord and Tenant Act 1954, Part II covers a number of aspects of business tenancies. The security of tenure provisions apply to 'any tenancy where the property comprised in the tenancy is or includes premises which are occupied by the tenant and are so occupied for the purposes of a business carried on by him or for those and other purposes'.[2] Business 'includes a trade, profession or employment'.[3] As well as the usual forms of commercial activity, business has been held to include the activity of a member's tennis club[4] and the activities of hospital governors in administering the hospital premises.[5] However, the following are excluded:[6]

(a) a tenancy of an agricultural holding;[7]
(b) a mining lease;[8]
(c) a service tenancy;[9]
(d) a tenancy where the business carried on is in breach of a general prohibition under the tenancy against business use (as opposed to a provision for or against particular business use);[10]
(e) a tenancy at will;[11]
(f) a fixed term tenancy where the parties agree to the exclusion of the Act and the court grants its approval before the lease takes effect;[12] apart from this any agreement whereby the parties attempt to exclude the security of tenancy provisions of the Act or impose a penalty on the tenant if he takes advantage of them will be void;[13]
(g) a fixed term tenancy not exceeding six months; the tenancy must not contain any term allowing renewal beyond the six month period, nor must the tenant be in occupation for more than twelve months.[14]

As the Act only protects tenancies, a genuine licence will be outside the scope of the Act. However, the courts will look carefully at the terms of the so-called licence agreement to establish whether it is a genuine licence or whether it is in fact a tenancy.[15]

---

1   [2001] Law Soc Gaz 8 March.
2   Landlord and Tenant Act 1954, s 23(1).
3   Ibid, s 23(2).
4   *Addiscombe Garden Estates Ltd v Crabbe* [1958] 1 QB 513, [1957] 3 All ER 563, CA.
5   *Hills (Patents) Ltd v University College Hospital Board of Governors* [1956] 1 QB 90, [1955] 3 All ER 365, CA.
6   Premises with an on-licence, eg public houses, were also excluded prior to the coming into effect of the Landlord and Tenant (Licensed Premises) Act 1990.
7   Landlord and Tenant Act 1954, s 43(1).
8   Ibid.
9   Ibid, s 43(2).
10 Ibid, s 23(4); see *Methodist Secondary Schools Trustees v O'Leary* (1992) 66 P & CR 364, 25 HLR 364, CA.
11 *Javad v Aqil* [1991] 1 All ER 243, [1991] 1 WLR 1007, CA; *Brent London Borough Council v O'Bryan* (1992) 65 P & CR 258, [1993] 1 EGLR 59, CA.
12 Landlord and Tenant Act 1954, s 38(4); see *Essexcrest Ltd v Evenlex Ltd* (1987) 55 P & CR 279, CA.
13 Ibid, s 38(1).
14 Ibid, s 43(3).
15 The court will probably apply a similar test to that used in relation to residential licences and tenancies under *Street v Mountford* [1985] AC 809, HL. See *Essex Plan Ltd v Broadminster* (1988) 56 P & CR 353, [1988] 2 EGLR 73; *Dresden Estates Ltd v Collinson* (1987) 55 P & CR 47, CA; and *Graysim Holdings Ltd v P & O Property Holdings Ltd* [1992] 1 EGLR 96; revsd [1996] AC 329, [1995] 4 All ER 831, HL.

The tenant is only entitled to protection if he occupies for business purposes or for business and other purposes. In cases of mixed business and residential use, the tenancy will normally be protected by the 1954 Act rather than the appropriate residential tenancy legislation if the business use is of any substance.[16] There may also be marginal cases where it is not entirely clear that the tenant is occupying the premises to a sufficient degree to attract the protection of the Act,[17] or where the tenant has sublet the premises.[18]

To gain the protection of the Act, it must be the tenant who is occupying the premises. In *Nozari-Sadeh v Pearl Assurance*,[19] an assignment of the tenancy had been taken in the name of an individual but it was the company controlled by the individual which was actually running the business from the premises; the tenancy was not protected. There are statutory provisions dealing with the occupation by beneficiaries under a trust and the occupation by members of the same group of companies. Under section 41, where the tenancy is held on trust, occupation by beneficiaries and the carrying on of business by the beneficiaries is treated as being equivalent to occupation by and the carrying on of the business by the tenant. Under section 42, where the tenancy is held by a member of a group of companies, occupation and the carrying on of business by another member of the group is treated as equivalent to occupation and the carrying on of business by the member of the group holding the tenancy.

3   SECURITY OF TENURE

There are two separate aspects to the security of tenure provided by the Act. Firstly, the tenancy will continue, irrespective of effluxion of time of a fixed term tenancy or notice to quit a periodic tenancy, unless and until the tenancy is terminated in one of the ways permitted by the Act.[20] Secondly, even when a tenancy is terminated, the tenant has a prima facie right to apply to the court for the grant of another tenancy.[1] To take the first point, a fixed term tenancy will not terminate at the end of the fixed term. It will continue unless and until it is terminated in a way allowed by the Act. It does not continue as a periodic tenancy, it just continues as an extension of the fixed term on the same terms including payment of rent. Similarly, a periodic tenancy is not terminated by an ordinary common law notice to quit by the landlord, but continues.

i   Termination

The following are the methods by which the tenancy can be terminated under the Act, thus preventing any (further) continuation:

(a) forfeiture, including forfeiture of a superior lease;[2]
(b) surrender;[3]

---

16 *Cheryl Investments Ltd v Saldanha* [1979] 1 All ER 5, [1978] 1 WLR 1329, CA, but see *Gurton v Parrott* (1990) 23 HLR 418, [1991] 1 EGLR 98, CA.
17 *Wandsworth London Borough Council v Singh* (1991) 88 LGR 737, 62 P & CR 219.
18 *Trans-Britannia Property Ltd v Darby Properties Ltd* [1986] 1 EGLR 151, CA, *Latif v Hillside Estates (Swansea) Ltd* [1992] EGCS 75, CA.
19 [1987] 2 EGLR 91, CA.
20 Landlord and Tenant Act 1954, s 24(1).
 1 Unless termination is by forfeiture or surrender or tenant's notice; see below.
 2 Landlord and Tenant Act 1954, s 24(2). A sub-tenant may be able to apply for relief.
 3 Ibid.

(c) renewal of a tenancy by agreement;[4]
(d) tenant's notice;
(e) landlord's notice in statutory form;
(f) tenant's request in statutory form.

Forfeiture and surrender have already been considered in Chapter 17 section iv. When the tenancy is terminated by forfeiture or surrender, the tenant has no opportunity to apply to the court for another tenancy.

Under section 28 of the 1954 Act, where landlord and tenant agree on the grant to the tenant of a future tenancy, the current tenancy is no longer protected by the Act. Thus where landlord and tenant are able to negotiate an agreement to avoid the need for an application to the court by the tenant for another tenancy the old tenancy ceases to be protected by the Act. In order to make sure that the agreement for another tenancy is binding on anyone who may purchase the landlord's interest before the new tenancy is granted, the tenant should ensure that the agreement is protected by registration.[5]

The last three methods of termination – tenant's notice, landlord's notice and tenant's request – will now be considered in more detail.

1   Tenant's notice

If the tenancy is periodic it can be determined by an ordinary common law notice to quit given by the tenant.[6] However, to avoid abuse of this procedure by landlords, the notice cannot be given (and indeed neither can a surrender of a fixed term be agreed) unless the tenant has been in occupation for at least a month. This is to prevent the landlord demanding that the tenant sign a notice to quit (or surrender) as a condition of the tenancy being granted in the first place.

If the tenancy is for a fixed term the tenant can give notice to terminate it, which must be not less than three months' notice to expire either at the end of the term or on any subsequent quarter day.[7] Thus a tenant who wishes to leave the premises, and therefore to prevent his fixed term tenancy continuing, or continuing any further, should serve this section 27 notice. However if the tenant ceases to occupy the premises for business purpose as defined by the Act either on or before the contractual expiry date he need not serve a section 27 notice, as the tenancy has been terminated by effluxion of time.[8]

2   Landlord's notice

Apart from forfeiture or surrender, a landlord must serve a notice under the Landlord and Tenant Act 1954, section 25 to terminate the tenancy. The landlord's notice under section 25 must be in writing and in a prescribed form.[9] It must state the date on which the tenancy is to end. There are two requirements for this date. Firstly, it

---

4 Ibid, s 28.
5 *R J Stratton Ltd v Wallis Tomlin & Co Ltd* [1986] 2 EGLR 104; the agreement would probably be an overriding interest under s 70(1)(g) of the Land Registration Act 1925 if the landlord's title was registered.
6 Landlord and Tenant Act 1954, s 28.
7 Ibid, s 27.
8 *Esselte AB v Pearl Assurance Plc* [1997] 2 All ER 41, [1997] 1 WLR 891. See also *Bacchiocci v Academic Agency Ltd* [1998] 2 All ER 241, [1998] 1 WLR 1313; *Sight and Sound Education Ltd v Books etc Ltd* [1999] 3 EGLR 45 and *Arundel Corpn v Financial Trading Co Ltd* [2000] 3 All ER (D) 456.
9 Or a form substantially to like effect; Landlord and Tenant Act 1954, Part II (Notices) Regulations 1989, see *Bridgers v Stanford* [1991] 2 EGLR 265, CA.

must not be earlier than the date on which the tenancy could otherwise be brought to an end. For a fixed term tenancy it must not be earlier than the end of the term, and for a periodic tenancy it must not be earlier than the earliest date for which a common law notice to quit could be given. It should be noted that it need not be the actual date of the end of the fixed term or the date for which the common law notice to quit could be given; it must just not be earlier than that date. Secondly, the termination date must be not less than six nor more than twelve months after the date of the notice.[10] Thus a landlord, acting promptly, can if he wishes serve a section 25 notice twelve months before the end of a fixed term, to terminate the tenancy at the end of the fixed term.[11]

If the landlord wishes to obtain possession of the property and would oppose an application by the tenant for a new tenancy, he must say so in the notice and state the ground or grounds of opposition on which he relies. There are several statutory grounds of opposition and the landlord cannot later rely on a ground which he has not stated at this stage.[12] The seven grounds will be examined in detail later. The landlord may of course want possession of the property; his objective in serving the notice may merely be to end the old tenancy so that the tenant applies for a new tenancy under which the rent can be brought in line with current market rents.

The notice must also tell the tenant that within two months he must notify the landlord in writing whether or not he is willing to give up possession on the specified termination date. The tenant on receiving the notice must then decide whether he will give up possession or whether he wishes to apply to the court for a new tenancy. The notice will of course tell him whether or not the landlord will oppose such an application and on what grounds. If a tenant is happy to give up possession and does not want a new tenancy he need not do anything. Otherwise he must notify the landlord in writing that he will not give up possession, within two months of the service of the notice.[13] This time limit is strictly enforced and if the tenant fails to give his counter-notice in time he cannot apply to the court for a new tenancy but must give up possession on termination of the current tenancy unless he can negotiate a new tenancy with the landlord. If the tenant's solicitor is responsible for serving the counter-notice he should make a diary note to ensure that it is done in time.

If a counter-notice is served, then unless the landlord and tenant can agree on terms for a new tenancy the tenant must, if he still wants a new tenancy, apply to the court not earlier than two nor later than four months after service of the *landlord's notice*.[14] Again these time limits are strictly enforced and perhaps even greater care should be taken over the timing of the application to the court since it is possible to apply too early as well as too late.[15] The two and four month time limits are calculated by reference to the corresponding days in subsequent months. Thus two months from 30 November is 30 January (and not 31 January being the last day in January on the basis that 30 November is the last day in November). Equally two months from 31 December to 28 February (or in a leap year 29 February) being

10 But see s. 25(3)(b) where a long common law notice to quit is necessary.
11 The landlord should ensure that he knows the precise termination date; if in doubt he should give the later date. See *Whelton Sinclair v Hyland* [1992] 2 EGLR 158, CA.
12 The landlord should have an honest belief in the ground; *Rous v Mitchell* [1991] 1 All ER 676, [1991] 1 WLR 469, CA.
13 Landlord and Tenant Act 1954, s 29(2).
14 Ibid, s 29(3).
15 See *Stevens & Cutting Ltd v Anderson* [1990] 1 EGLR 95, CA in which a tenant who had applied to court too early argued, unsuccessfully on the facts, that the landlord had waived the procedural defect or was estopped from relying on it.

the last available day in February.[16] The best advice, of course, is to serve the counter- notice and apply to court well within the appropriate time limits rather than to leave it until the last moment.

Care should be taken in drafting the landlord's section 25 notice as a notice may be invalid if, for example, it fails to specify the correct landlord or tenant, if it fails to specify all the joint landlords, or if it misdescribes the premises.[17] It seems that if a landlord has served an invalid section 25 notice, he may withdraw it and serve a second valid notice.[18]

If the tenant does apply to court for a new tenancy, it is likely that in practice the old tenancy will not terminate on the date specified in the landlord's notice, simply because the tenant's application for a new tenancy is still pending and has not been heard. Section 64 of the 1954 Act provides that if the termination date in the section 25 notice is earlier than the date three months after the tenant's application is finally disposed of, the old tenancy continues until that date three months after the application is finally disposed of. Thus if the tenant's application for a new tenancy is successful, the old tenancy ends and the new tenancy begins three months after any time for appealing following the court's determination has expired, ie just over three months after the court's determination. Similarly if the tenant's application for a new tenancy is unsuccessful, in which case, of course, the tenant would have to vacate the premises at the end of the old tenancy. This provision also applies where the tenant withdraws his application for a new tenancy in which case the relevant date is three months from the date of withdrawal.

3 Tenant's request

The tenant may be quite happy to allow the current tenancy to continue, particularly as he is paying rent at the amount set under that tenancy. However, he may wish to make long term future plans and establish whether he is going to get a new tenancy on termination of the current tenancy. If he merely waits for the landlord to serve a notice he will not be able to make any such long term plans because it will only be when the landlord does serve a notice that he will be able to apply for a new tenancy. There is therefore a procedure by which the tenant can bring matters to a head; he can bring the current tenancy to an end with the object of applying for a new tenancy. He does this by serving on the landlord a request for a new tenancy.[19] This is analogous to the landlord's notice in that it will specify a termination date for the current tenancy. What was said about the termination date in relation to the landlord's notice applies equally to the tenant's request, in that the date must not be earlier than the end of a fixed term tenancy nor the earliest date for which the tenant could have given a common law notice to quit a periodic tenancy; and it must also be not less than six nor more than twelve months after the date of the request. The request must be in writing and in a prescribed form. It must also propose terms for a new tenancy. The request must be served on the landlord. The landlord must, within two months of the request, serve a counter-notice on the tenant otherwise he loses his right to oppose the tenant's application for a new tenancy.[20] The counter-notice must state

16 See *Dodds v Walker* [1981] 2 All ER 609 [1981] 1 WLR 1027, HL; *EJ Riley Investments Ltd v Eurostile Holdings Ltd* [1985] 3 All ER 181, [1985] 1 WLR 1139, CA.
17 See *Morrow v Nadeem* [1987] 1 All ER 237, [1986] 1 WLR 1381, CA; *Herongrove Ltd v Wates City of London Properties Ltd* [1988] 1 EGLR 82, and *Pearson v Alyo* [1990] 1 EGLR 114, CA.
18 *Smith v Draper* [1990] 27 EG 69, CA.
19 Landlord and Tenant Act 1954, s 26.
20 Ibid, s 26(6).

that the landlord will oppose the application and also state the statutory ground or grounds on which the landlord relies. Thus far, the procedure has been the reverse of the procedure under a landlord's notice; the tenant instead of the landlord initiating the process and the landlord instead of the tenant giving a counter-notice within two months. However, unless agreement can be reached on a new tenancy, it is still the tenant who must apply to the court within two to four months of his request if he wishes to apply for a new tenancy, which presumably he does! This means that it is possible for the tenant to have terminated his tenancy and then have debarred himself from applying for a new tenancy by applying to the court too late (or too early).

Only certain tenants can serve a request, principally tenants whose tenancy is a fixed term of over one year.[1] When the landlord has served a section 25 notice the tenant cannot serve a request and vice versa, the object of both being the same, to terminate the existing tenancy and to allow the tenant to set in motion the procedure for applying for a new tenancy. The effect of the tenant's request is the same as the landlord's notice. It terminates the current tenancy on the termination date subject to the tenant's application to the court for a new tenancy.

A tenant may serve his section 26 request as a tactical ploy to 'beat the landlord to the punch'. If the tenant knows that the landlord will shortly be serving a section 25 notice, he can serve a section 26 request of his own for the maximum period of twelve months. This will keep his rent at the level under his existing tenancy until the end of the twelve month period; an interim rent under section 24A (discussed in section iii, below) cannot take effect before the termination date specified in the request.

ii   The competent landlord

The landlord involved in proceedings under the 1954 Act, Part II that is to say the landlord who can serve a section 25 notice, who should receive a section 26 request, who should receive the tenant's counter-notice to a section 25 notice and who should be made respondent to the tenant's application for a new tenancy, is sometimes called the 'competent' landlord. The competent landlord is not necessarily the tenant's immediate landlord. If the tenant has a head tenancy, held from a freehold landlord, that landlord will always be the competent landlord in respect of that tenancy. However, complications arise where the tenant with the benefit of protection of the 1954 Act, Part II is a sub-tenant. The competent landlord will not necessarily be the sub-tenant's immediate landlord. Assuming a situation of a head tenancy held from a freehold landlord, which is not in itself protected by the 1954 Act, Part II, and a sub-tenancy granted out of the head tenancy which is protected by the 1954 Act, the head tenant (the sub-tenant's immediate landlord) will only be the competent landlord vis-à-vis the sub-tenant whilst there are at least 14 months left to run on the head tenancy; section 44 of the 1954 Act. Thus in relation to 1954 Act procedure on the sub-tenancy, it is important for both parties, but particularly the sub-tenant, to ascertain the length of term left to run on the head tenancy. If there are less than 14 months, the head tenant simply drops out of the picture and the competent landlord vis-à-vis the sub-tenant becomes the head landlord. It is possible for both a landlord and tenant to serve a notice under section 40 of the Act in order that a landlord can discover, for example, whether a tenancy is subject to any sub-tenancies, and in order that a tenant can discover whether his landlord's interest is as freeholder or, if only as tenant, the term of the tenancy.

Matters become further complicated if the head tenancy too is protected by the 1954 Act, Part II which may well be the case if there has only been a sub-letting of part

---

1   Ibid, s 26(1).

of the premises. As we know, the effect of the 1954 Act is that a tenancy continues beyond its contractual termination date unless and until determined in one of the ways envisaged by the Act. In this situation therefore, a sub-tenant is no longer concerned simply with the length of time left to run on his immediate landlord's own tenancy, whether it is more or less than 14 months. The significant factor becomes whether or not 1954 Act procedures have been initiated in relation to the head tenancy in order to bring it to an end, either by a landlord's section 25 notice or tenant's section 26 request or tenant's section 27 notice. All of these will bring the head tenancy to an end within 14 months. Whether or not there are 14 months left to run of the term of the head tenancy, or even whether the head tenancy has already entered the statutory continuation period beyond its contractual termination date is irrelevant; it is only the service of one of these notices which is significant from the point of view of the competence or otherwise of the head tenant, the sub-tenant's immediate landlord. Equally, as soon as one of these notices is served, the head tenant ceases to be competent and the competent landlord vis-à-vis the sub-tenant becomes the head landlord.

Schedule 6 of the 1954 Act contains a number of further provisions relating to a protected sub-tenancy. For example, under paragraph 7 of Schedule 6, if the head tenancy has less than 16 months to run, and the head tenant gives the sub-tenant a section 25 notice or receives a section 26 request from him, the head tenant must send a copy of the notice or request to the head landlord. Further under paragraph 6 of Schedule 6, if the head tenant has given a section 25 notice to the sub-tenant and within two months of the section 25 notice the head landlord has become competent vis-à-vis the sub-tenant (perhaps, for example, because he has served a section 25 notice in relation to the head tenancy) the head landlord can withdraw the section 25 notice served on the sub-tenant but without prejudice to giving a further section 25 notice himself to the sub-tenant; this notice could, of course, state different grounds of opposition to the grant of a new tenancy.

It is clear that the identity of the competent landlord can change during the course of 1954 Act procedure. For example if a head tenant serves a section 25 notice on a sub-tenant, but then immediately serves a section 26 request on his own landlord, at that point the head landlord takes over as competent landlord vis-à-vis the sub-tenant and it is the head landlord on whom the sub-tenant should serve a counter-notice and it is the head landlord who should be made respondent to the application to court for a new tenancy by the sub-tenant. This occurred in *Shelley v United Artists Corpn Ltd*,[2] in which the Court of Appeal decided that in such a situation the head tenant, in serving the section 25 notice on the sub-tenant, was representing that he was the sub-tenant's competent landlord; if the situation changed, there was a duty on the head tenant to inform the sub-tenant of the change in competent landlord. This is a duty over and above the other requirements in Schedule 6 of the Act.

Unfortunately the information which can be requested by a sub-tenant under section 40(2) of the Act does not include information as to the existence of any notices or requests served in relation to the head tenancy.

iii   Interim rent

On the face of it a landlord may be prejudiced by ongoing proceedings under the 1954 Act, because under the old tenancy, which as we have seen will continue until after the date of the court hearing, the tenant will be paying only the rent payable under the terms of the old tenancy. However, it is possible for a landlord to apply for an interim

---

2   (1990) 60 P & CR 241, [1990] 1 EGLR 103, CA.

rent under section 24A of the Act. This interim rent can take effect no earlier than the later of two dates; the date of application for the interim rent or the termination date specified in the section 25 notice or section 26 request. The interim rent is assessed on the basis of a yearly tenancy; this and the 'cushioning' effect which the courts have given section 24A may result in an interim rent which is 10% to 20% less than a market rent would be, fixed under the provisions of the 1954 Act (as to which see later). The yearly tenancy deduction may well be in the region of 12½%; the cushioning deduction will depend on the circumstances and could vary from 50% to no deduction at all.[3]

It should be emphasised that a landlord can only apply for an interim rent once he has served a section 25 notice or the tenant has served a section 26 request.

iv   Application to the court – grounds of opposition

The stage has now been reached either by a landlord's notice or a tenant's request where the tenant has made an application to the court for an order for a new tenancy. This is the tenant's prima facie right but the landlord can successfully oppose the application if he can show one or more of seven statutory grounds. These will have been pleaded by the landlord in his notice, or his counter-notice in reply to the tenant's request. The new Civil Procedure Act 1997 (the Woolf reforms) set out the procedure for applying to the court for a renewal of the tenancy. Practice Direction 8(B), section B contains the procedure that should be adopted. The application for renewal must take the form of a Part 8 application but varied to suit the fact that it is an application for a lease renewal. If the application is to be made in the High Court part 8-claim form should be used, or if made in the County Court form N397. An Answer needs to be filed (incorporating any application for interim rent) and served within 14 days. The court will then issue the claim and fix a date for the hearing. If the landlord is seeking possession, the first stage of the court hearing will involve a decision as to whether or not any ground for possession has been made out. If the court is satisfied that one or more grounds have been proved then the tenant does not get a new tenancy. If the landlord fails to prove one or more grounds to the court's satisfaction or if the landlord is not in fact seeking possession and did not oppose the grant of a new tenancy, the court must, in the absence of agreement by the parties, determine the terms of the new tenancy.

The seven statutory grounds of opposition are set out below.

1   Breach of repairing obligations by tenant

The landlord must show that the tenant ought not to be granted a new tenancy in view of the state of repair of the property.[4] The court will look at the state of repair at the date of the hearing. The ground is discretionary.[5]

2   Persistent delay in paying rent

The landlord has to show that the tenant ought not to be granted a new tenancy in view of his persistent delay in paying his rent.[6] The court will take into account the number of times there has been a delay and the length of the delay.[7] Again, the ground is discretionary.

---

3   See *Charles Follett Ltd v Cabetell Investment Co Ltd* (1987) 55 P & CR 36, [1987] 2 EGLR 88, CA; *Department of the Environment v Allied Freehold Property Trust* [1992] 2 EGLR 100.
4   Landlord and Tenant Act 1954, s 30(1)(a).
5   See eg *Eichner v Midland Bank Ltd* [1970] 2 All ER 597, [1970] 1 WLR 1120, CA.
6   Landlord and Tenant Act 1954, s 30(1)(b).
7   See eg *Rawashdeh v Lane* [1988] 2 EGLR 109, CA; cf *Hurstfell Ltd v Leicester Square Property Co Ltd* [1988] 2 EGLR 105, CA.

3   Substantial breaches of other obligations

The landlord must show that the tenant ought not to be granted a new tenancy in view of other substantial breaches of his obligations under the tenancy or any other reason connected with the tenant's use or management of the premises.[8]

4   Alternative accommodation

The landlord must have offered and be willing to provide or secure alternative accommodation to the tenant on reasonable terms.[9] The accommodation must be suitable for the tenant's requirements, bearing in mind his business and the size and situation of the new accommodation. This ground, unlike the previous three grounds, is not discretionary: if suitable accommodation has been offered on suitable terms, the court must refuse the tenant's application.

5   Possession of whole property required where tenant has a sub-tenancy

If the tenant's tenancy is a sub-tenancy of part only of the property comprised in a superior tenancy, and that superior tenancy is shortly to end, the competent landlord will be the owner of the reversion of the superior tenancy. He may obtain possession from the tenant if he wants to re-let or otherwise dispose of the property as a whole, if the rent available on a letting of the property as a whole would be substantially more than the aggregate rents available on separate lettings of the premises included in the current tenancy and the remainder of the property.[10] and if the court accepts that in view of this, the tenant ought not to be granted a new tenancy.

6   Intention to demolish or reconstruct

The landlord must show that on the termination of the tenancy he intends to demolish or reconstruct the premises, or a substantial part of them, or to carry out substantial work of construction,[11] and that he cannot reasonably do so without obtaining possession.[12] The landlord must have a firm and settled intention to do the work when he obtains possession,[13] but this intention need only be shown at the date of the court hearing, rather than the date of service of his notice.[14] Again, the court has no discretion if the landlord can prove this ground. Evidence of the intention could include the preparation of plans, the granting of planning permission, the obtaining of quotations for the work and the availability of the necessary finance. The landlord will not succeed on this ground if the tenant agrees to the inclusion in his new tenancy of terms giving the landlord access, and the landlord can then carry out the work without obtaining actual possession and without interfering to a substantial extent or for a substantial time with the tenant's use of the property; or if the tenant is willing to accept a tenancy of part only of the property, if necessary with the landlord similarly having access to it.[15]

8   Landlord and Tenant Act 1954, s 30(1)(c).
9   Ibid, s 30(1)(d).
10   Landlord and Tenant Act 1954, s 30(1)(e).
11   See *Barth v Pritchard* [1990] 1 EGLR 109, CA, *Romulus Trading Co Ltd v Henry Smith's Charity Trustees* (1989) 60 P & CR 62, [1990] 2 EGLR 75, CA.
12   Landlord and Tenant Act 1954, s 30(1)(f). If the current lease allows the landlord access, he may have difficulty making out this ground: *Leathwoods Ltd v Total Oil (Great Britain) Ltd* (1985) 51 P & CR 20, CA.
13   See *Edwards v Thompson* (1990) 60 P & CR 222, [1990] 2 EGLR 71.
14   *Betty's Cafés Ltd v Phillips Furnishing Stores Ltd* [1959] AC 20, [1958] 1 All ER 607, HL.
15   Landlord and Tenant Act 1954, s 31A; see *Cerex Jewels Ltd v Peachey Property Corpn plc* (1986) 52 P & CR 127; *Blackburn v Hussain* [1988] 1 EGLR 77, CA; *Romulus Trading Co Ltd v Henry Smith's Charity Trustees (No 2)* [1991] 1 EGLR 95, CA.

7   *Intention to occupy premises*

The landlord must, on the termination of the tenancy, intend to occupy the premises himself either for the purpose or partly for the purpose of a business to be carried on by him at the premises, or as a residence.[16] What was said about intention in the previous paragraph applies equally here. If the landlord is a company then the ground is satisfied if possession is required for a company in the same group.[27] If the landlord is an individual it is sufficient if the premises are required for a company which he controls.[18] A landlord cannot rely on this ground if his interest was purchased by him within the five years preceding the termination date of the tenancy specified in the landlord's notice or the tenant's request.[19] So if the landlord owns the freehold and bought it within the last five years, subject to the tenancy, then he cannot rely on this ground. To take an example, if the landlord bought the freehold in 1998, subject to the tenancy, he cannot rely on this ground until 2003 at the earliest. If the tenancy is renewed under the Act in 2002, perhaps in consequence of the tenant's request, the landlord cannot rely on this ground to oppose the renewal at that time. He can only hope that the new tenancy granted in 2002 is relatively short.[20] Of course, if the landlord *granted* the new tenancy in question he is not a landlord by purchase and there is nothing to prevent him relying on this ground within five years.

v   **Terms of the new tenancy**

If a new tenancy is ordered by the court then the court must, in the absence of agreement between the parties, determine its terms.[1] Even if all the terms of the tenancy have not been agreed, the parties may have reached agreement on some terms, such as the rent or the length of the new tenancy. In the absence of agreement the court has a discretion. The term of the new tenancy must be such as is reasonable in all the circumstances, with a maximum of fourteen years.[2] Obviously the duration of the old tenancy is a relevant factor. The property comprised in the new tenancy will normally be the same as that comprised in the old tenancy but it may exclude a part not occupied by a tenant.[3] The rent must be an open market rent, disregarding any goodwill attached to the premises by reason of the tenant's business, the effect of improvements made by the tenant within the last 21 years so long as they were not made in pursuance of an obligation to the landlord,[4] and the effect on rent of the fact of the tenant's occupation. In practice both the landlord and the tenant will consult a professional surveyor and the figure determined by the court will probably be somewhere between the figures suggested by the two surveyors.

The other terms of the tenancy will also be determined by the court in the absence of agreement and will probably closely follow the terms of the old tenancy;[5] indeed

---

16   Ibid, s 30(1)(g).
17   Ibid, s 42.
18   Landlord and Tenant Act 1954, s 30(3).
19   Ibid, s 30(2).
20   See *Upsons Ltd v E Robins Ltd* [1956] 1 QB 131, [1955] 3 All ER 348, CA.
1   Landlord and Tenant Act 1954, ss 29(1), 32–35.
2   Ibid, s 33.
3   Ibid, ss 23(3), 32. The tenant is only entitled to a new tenancy of the premises occupied by him, but the landlord can insist on including all the premises comprised in the original tenancy, for example where the tenant has sub-let part (which he then does not occupy).
4   Ibid, s 34.
5   Under s 35 the court must have regard to the terms of the current tenancy and to all relevant circumstances.

it will in effect be for a party to persuade the court of the need for change.[6] The terms of the rent review clause will be decided at the discretion of the court.[7] If the lease is an 'old lease' ie granted before the Landlord and Tenant (Covenants) Act 1995 came into force, then it is likely that the landlord will request that the court takes into account the implications the 1995 Act has on alienation and liability for covenants when deciding the terms of the new lease.

If the landlord can show the possibility of redevelopment in the future, then although the landlord is not yet in a position to make out Ground F, the court may take this into account either in granting a shorter lease than might otherwise be the case or by inserting a break clause in the lease.[8] Once the terms of a new tenancy are decided the tenant has an option to withdraw; if for example he cannot afford the new rent, he can apply within fourteen days for the order for a new tenancy to be revoked, although he risks being ordered to pay costs if the court thinks fit.[9] If the tenant does withdraw, the old tenancy terminates on a date to be agreed or determined by the court to allow the landlord a reasonable chance to re-let or otherwise dispose of the premises. In the normal case where the tenant accepts the new tenancy, the old tenancy continues for three months after the date of the determination of the application, ie the end of the time limit for an appeal following the hearing or if an appeal is made and heard, the end of the time limit for any further appeal; the new tenancy then commences.[10] Similarly if the landlord successfully opposes an application to the court by the tenant for a new tenancy, the old tenancy continues for a further three months after the date of determination. The provisions of the Act will apply to the new tenancy and so it also will continue until determined in the appropriate way whereupon the tenant can apply for another new tenancy. And so it goes on.

vi   Contracting out

With the exception already mentioned, where the court gives its prior approval, it is not possible by agreement to exclude the tenant from applying for a new tenancy.

4   COMPENSATION FOR DISTURBANCE

Compensation is payable for disturbance where the tenant fails to obtain a new tenancy. It is payable when the landlord successfully opposes the grant of a new tenancy solely on one or more of the last three statutory grounds, that is where the property is held on a sub-tenancy and the landlord wishes to re-let or dispose of the property as a whole; where the landlord wishes to demolish or reconstruct; or where the landlord intends to occupy the premises himself.[11] If possession is ordered on any other ground then, whether or not it is also ordered on any of the above three grounds, compensation is not payable, The tenant can ask the court to certify whether the landlord successfully opposed the application only on one or more of the above three grounds.[12] Compensation is also payable if the landlord's notice (or counter-

---

6   See *O'May v City of London Real Property Co Ltd* [1983] 2 AC 726, [1982] 1 All ER 660, HL.
7   *Forbouys plc v Newport Borough Council* [1994] 1 EGLR 138.
8   *National Car Parks Ltd v Paternoster Consortium Ltd* [1990] 1 EGLR 99; *Becker v Hill Street Properties Ltd* [1990] 2 EGLR 78, CA.
9   Landlord and Tenant Act 1954, s 36(2), (3).
10 Ibid, s 64.
11 Ibid, s 37(1).
12 Ibid, s 37(4).

notice to the tenant's request) specifies only one or more of the above three grounds of opposition and the tenant then does not apply to the court for a new tenancy.[13] It will be noticed that all the grounds, apart from the three mentioned above, include some aspect of fault on the part of the tenant, except where alternative accommodation is offered in which case although the current tenancy is ending it is being replaced by a tenancy of alternative premises.

Compensation is payable when the tenant leaves the premises. The amount of compensation is the rateable value of the premises.[14] If during the fourteen years preceding the end of the tenancy, the premises have been occupied by the tenant or his predecessors in the same business, the compensation is doubled to twice the rateable value.[15] It is only possible to exclude or restrict the right to compensation where the tenant or his predecessors in the same business have been in occupation for less than five years on the date of termination of the tenancy.[16] Such an exclusion will often be incorporated into the tenancy agreement or lease.

If the tenancy terminates and the tenant leaves the premises, compensation may be payable for improvements which the tenant has made, under the Landlord and Tenant Act 1927.

---

13 Ibid, s 37(1).
14 Because of the re-rating of commercial property from 1 April 1990, the order contains transitional provisions: Landlord and Tenant Act 1954 (Appropriate Multiplier) Order 1990. In particular, until the year 2000 a tenant has an option to elect for compensation to be assessed at eight times (or sixteen times in the case of occupation for over fourteen years) the old rateable value on 31 March 1990 prior to re-rating. This may be beneficial to a tenant depending on the relative old and new rateable values. The option should be exercised by notice on the landlord during the same period as for the application to court for a new tenancy, ie not less than two nor more than four months from the landlord's s 25 notice or the tenant's s 26 request.
15 Ibid, s 37(2), (3).
16 Ibid, s 38(2), (3).

APPENDICES

The National Conveyancing Protocol (Fourth Edition)

ACTING FOR THE SELLER

1. The first step

The seller should inform the solicitor as soon as it is intended to place the property on the market so that delay may be reduced after a prospective purchaser is found.

2. Preparing the package: assembling the information

On receipt of instructions, the solicitor should then immediately take the following steps, at the seller's expense:

2.1 Whenever possible instructions should be obtained from the client in person.

2.2 Check the client's identity if the client is not known to you.

2.3 Give the client information as to costs, information relating to the name and status of the person who will be carrying out the work and, if that person is not a partner, the name of the partner who has overall responsibility for the matter. Give any other information necessary to comply with Rule 15 of the Solicitors' Practice Rules 1990 and Solicitors' Costs Information and Client Care Code 1999. If given orally this information should be confirmed in writing.

2.4 Give the seller details of whom to contact in the event of a complaint about the firm's services (Rule 15).

2.5 Consider with the client whether to make local authority and other searches so that these can be supplied to the buyer's solicitor as soon as an offer is made. If thought appropriate request a payment on account in relation to disbursements.

2.6   Ascertain the whereabouts of the deeds and, if not in the solicitor's custody, obtain them.

2.7   Ask the seller to complete the Seller's Property Information Form.

2.8   Obtain such original guarantees with the accompanying speci-fication, planning decisions, building regulation approvals and certificates of completion as are in the seller's possession and copies of any other planning consents that are with the title deeds or details of any highway and sewerage agreements and bonds or any other relevant certificates relating to the property (e.g. structural engineer's certificate or an indemnity policy).

2.9   Give the seller the Fixtures, Fittings and Contents Form, with a copy to retain, to complete and return prior to the submission of the draft contract.

2.10 If the title is unregistered make an index map search.

2.11 If so instructed requisition a local authority search and enquiries and any other searches (e.g. mining or commons registration searches).

2.12 Obtain details of all mortgages and other financial charges of which the seller's solicitor has notice including, where applicable, improvement grants and discounts repayable to a local authority. Redemption figures should be obtained at this stage in respect of all mortgages on the property so that cases of negative equity or penalty redemption interest can be identified at an early stage.

2.13 Ascertain the identity of all people aged 17 or over living in the dwelling and ask about any financial contribution they or anyone else may have made towards its purchase or subsequent improvement. All persons identified in this way should be asked to confirm their consent to the sale proceeding.

2.14 In leasehold cases, ask the seller to complete the Seller's Leasehold Information Form and to produce, if possible:

      (1) A receipt or evidence from the landlord of the last payment of rent.

(2) The maintenance charge accounts for the last three years, where appropriate, and evidence of payment.

(3) Details of the buildings insurance policy.

If any of these are lacking, and are necessary for the transaction, the solicitor should obtain them from the landlord. At the same time investigate whether a licence to assign is required and, if so, enquire of the landlord what references or deeds of covenant are necessary and, in the case of some retirement schemes, if a charge is payable to the management company on change of ownership.

3. Preparing the package: the draft documents

As soon as the title deeds are available, and the seller has completed the Seller's Property Information Form and, if appropriate, the Seller's Leasehold Information Form, the solicitor shall:

3.1 If the title is unregistered:

(1) Make a land charges search against the seller and any other appropriate names.

(2) Make an index map search in the Land Registry (if not already obtained – see 2.10) in order to verify that the seller's title is unregistered and ensure that there are no interests registered at the Land Registry adverse to the seller's title.

(3) Prepare an epitome of title. Mark copies or abstracts of all deeds which will not be passed to the buyer's solicitor as examined against the original.

(4) Prepare and mark as examined against the originals copies of all deeds, or their abstracts, prior to the root of title containing covenants, easements, etc., affecting the property.

(5) Check that all plans on copied documents are correctly coloured.

3.2 If the title is registered, obtain office copy entries of the register and copy documents incorporated or referred to in the certificate.

3.3 Prepare the draft contract and complete the second section of the Seller's Property Information Form and, if appropriate, the Seller's Leasehold Information Form.

3.4 Check contract package is complete and ready to be sent out to the buyer's solicitor.

3.5 Deal promptly with any queries raised by the estate agent.

4. Buyer's offer accepted

When made aware that a buyer has been found the solicitor shall:

4.1 Check with the seller agreement on the price and, if appropriate, that there has been no change in the information already supplied (Seller's Property Information Form, Seller's Leasehold Information Form and Fixtures, Fittings and Contents Form). Also check the seller's position on any related purchase.

4.2 Inform the buyer's solicitor that the Protocol will be used.

4.3 Ascertain the buyer's position on any related sale and in the light of that reply, ask the seller for a proposed completion date.

4.4 Send to the buyer's solicitor as soon as possible the contract package to include:

(1) Draft contract.

(2) Office copy entries of the registered title (including office copies of all documents mentioned), or the epitome of title (including details of any prior matters referred to but not disclosed by the documents themselves) and the index map search.

(3) The Seller's Property Information Form with copies of all relevant planning decisions, guarantees, etc.

(4) The completed Fixtures, Fittings and Contents Form. Where this is provided it will form part of the contract and should be attached to it.

(5) In leasehold cases:

(i) the Seller's Leasehold Information Form, with all information about maintenance charges and insurance and, if appropriate, the procedure (including references required) for obtaining the landlord's consent to the sale;

(ii) a copy of the lease.

(6) If available, the local authority search and enquiries and any other searches made by the seller's solicitor.

If any of these documents are not available the remaining items should be forwarded to the buyer's solicitor as soon as they are available.

4.5 Inform the estate agent when the draft contract has been submitted to the buyer's solicitor.

4.6 Ask the buyer's solicitor if a 10 per cent deposit will be paid and, if not, what arrangements are proposed.

4.7 If and to the extent that the seller consents to the disclosure, supply information about the position on the seller's own purchase and of any other transactions in the chain above, and thereafter, of any change in circumstances.

4.8 Notify the seller of all information received in response to the above.

4.9 Inform the estate agent of any unexpected delays or difficulties likely to delay exchange of contracts.

ACTING FOR THE BUYER

5. The first step

On notification of the buyer's purchase the solicitor should then immediately take the following steps, at the buyer's expense:

5.1 Wherever possible instructions should be obtained from the client in person.

5.2 Check the client's identity if the client is not known to you.

5.3 Give the client information as to costs, information relating to the name and status of the person who will be carrying out the work and, if that person is not a partner, the name of the partner who has overall responsibility for the matter. Give any other information necessary to comply with Rule 15 of the Solicitors' Practice Rules 1990 and Solicitors' Costs Information and Client Care Code 1999. If given orally this information should be confirmed in writing.

5.4 Give the client details of whom to contact in the event of a complaint about the firm's services (Rule 15).

5.5 Request a payment on account in relation to disbursements.

5.6 Confirm to the seller's solicitor that the Protocol will be used.

5.7 Ascertain the buyer's position on any related sale, mortgage arrangements and whether a 10 per cent deposit will be provided.

5.8 If and to the extent that the buyer consents to the disclosure, inform the seller's solicitor about the position on the buyer's own sale, if any, and of any connected transactions, the general nature of the mortgage application, the amount of deposit available and if the seller's target date for completion can be met, and thereafter, of any change in circumstances.

On receipt of the draft contract and other documents:

5.9 Notify the buyer that these documents have been received, check the price and send the client a copy of the Fixtures, Fittings and Contents Form and, if appropriate, a copy of the filed plan for checking.

5.10 Make a local authority search with the usual part one enquiries and any additional enquiries relevant to the property.

5.11 Make a commons registration search, if appropriate.

5.12 Make mining enquiries and drainage enquiries if appropriate and consider any other relevant searches, e.g. environmental searches.

5.13 Check the buyer's position on any related sale and check that the buyer has a satisfactory mortgage offer and all conditions of the mortgage are or can be satisfied.

5.14 Check the buyer understands the nature and effect of the mortgage offer and duty·to disclose any relevant matters to the lender.

5.15 Advise the buyer of the need for a survey on the property.

5.16 Confirm approval of the draft contract and return it approved as soon as possible, having inserted the buyer's full names and address, subject to any outstanding matters.

5.17 At the same time ask only those specific additional enquiries which are required to clarify some point arising out of the documents submitted or which are relevant to the particular nature or location of the property or which the buyer has expressly requested. Any enquiry, including those about the state and condition of the building, which is capable of being ascertained by the buyer's own enquiries or survey or personal inspection should not be raised. Additional duplicated standard forms should not be submitted; if they are, the seller's solicitor is under no obligation to deal with them nor need answer any enquiry seeking opinions rather than facts.

5.18 If a local authority search has been supplied by the seller's solicitors with the draft contract, consider the need to make a local authority search with the usual part one enquiries and any additional enquiries relevant to the property. (The local authority search should not be more than three months' old at exchange of contracts nor six months' old at completion.)

5.19 Ensure that buildings insurance arrangements are in place.

5.20 Check the position over any life policies referred to in the lender's offer of mortgage.

5.21 Check with the buyer if the property is being purchased in sole name or jointly with another person. If a joint purchase check whether as joint tenants or tenants in common and advise on the difference in writing.

BOTH PARTIES' SOLICITORS

6. Prior to exchange of contracts

If acting for the buyer

When all satisfactory replies received to enquiries and searches:

6.1 Prepare and send to the buyer a contract report and invite the buyer to make an appointment to call to raise any queries on the contract report and to sign the contract ideally in the presence of a solicitor.

6.2 When the buyer signs the contract check:

(1) Completion date.

(2) That the buyer understands and can comply with all the conditions on the mortgage offer if appropriate.

(3) That all the necessary funds will be available to complete the purchase.

If acting for the seller

6.3 Advise the seller on the effect of the contract and ask the seller to sign it, ideally in the presence of the solicitor.

6.4 Check the position on any related purchase so that there can be a simultaneous exchange of contracts on both the sale and purchase.

6.5 Check completion date.

7. Relationship with the buyer's lender

On receipt of instructions from the buyer's lender:

7.1 Check the mortgage offer complies with Practice Rule 6(3)(c) and (e) and is certified to that effect.

7.2 Check any special conditions in the mortgage offer to see if there are additional instructions or conditions not normally required by Practice Rule 6(3)(c).

7.3 Go through any special conditions in the mortgage offer with the buyer.

7.4   Notify the lender if Practice Rule 6(3)(b) or 1.13 or 1.14 of the CML Lenders' Handbook ('Lenders' Handbook') are applicable.

7.5   Consider whether there are any conflicts of interest which prevent you accepting instructions to act for the lender.

7.6   If you do not know the borrower and anyone else required to sign the mortgage, charge or other document, check evidence of identity (Practice Rule 6(3)(c)(*i*)).

7.7   Consider whether there are any circumstances covered by the Law Society's:

(1) Green Card on property fraud.

(2) Blue Card on money laundering.

(3) Pink Card on undertakings.

7.8   If you do not know the seller's solicitor/licensed conveyancer check that they appear in a legal directory or are on the record of their professional body (see Practice Rule 6(3)(c)(*i*) and the Lenders' Handbook).

7.9   Carry out any other checks required by the lender provided they comply with Practice Rule 6(3)(c).

7.10 At all times comply with the requirements of Practice Rule 6(3) and the Lenders' Handbook and ensure if a conflict of interest arises you cease to act for the lender.

8. Exchange of contracts

On exchange, the buyer's solicitor shall send or deliver to the seller's solicitor:

8.1   The signed contract with all names, dates and financial information completed.

8.2   The deposit provided in the manner prescribed in the contract. Under the Law Society's Formula C the deposit may have to be sent to another solicitor nominated by the seller's solicitor.

8.3   If contracts are exchanged by telephone the procedures laid down by the Law Society's Formulae A, B or C must be used and both solicitors must ensure (unless otherwise agreed) that the undertakings to send documents and to pay the deposit on that day are strictly observed.

8.4   The seller's solicitor shall, once the buyer's signed contract and deposit are held unconditionally, having ensured that the details of each contract are fully completed and identical, send the seller's signed contract on the day of exchange to the buyer's solicitor in compliance with the undertaking given on exchange.

8.5   Notify the client that contracts have been exchanged.

8.6   Notify the seller's estate agent or property seller of exchange of contracts and the completion date.

9. Between exchange and the day of completion

As soon as possible after exchange and in any case within the time limits contained in the Standard Conditions of Sale:

9.1   The buyer's solicitor shall send to the seller's solicitor, in duplicate:

(1) Completion Information and Requisitions on Title Form.

(2) Draft conveyance/transfer or assignment incorporating appropriate provisions for joint purchase.

(3) Other documents, e.g. draft receipt for purchase price of fixtures, fittings and contents.

9.2   As soon as possible after receipt of these documents the seller's solicitor shall send to the buyer's solicitor:

(1) Replies to Completion Information and Requisitions on Title Form.

(2) Draft conveyance/transfer or assignment approved.

(3) If appropriate, completion statement supported by photocopy receipts or evidence of payment of apportionments claimed.

(4) Copy of licence to assign from the landlord if appropriate.

9.3   The buyer's solicitor shall then:

(1) Engross the approved draft conveyance/transfer or assignment.

(2) Explain the effect of that document to the buyer and obtain the buyer's signature to it (if necessary).

(3) Send it to the seller's solicitor in time to enable the seller to sign it before completion without suffering inconvenience.

(4) If appropriate prepare any separate declaration of trust, advise the buyer on its effect and obtain the buyer's signature to it.

(5) Advise the buyer on the contents and effect of the mortgage deed and obtain the buyer's signature to that deed. If possible, and in all cases where the lender so requires, a solicitor should witness the buyer's signature to the mortgage deed.

(6) Send the certificate of title (complying with Rule 6(3)(d)) to the lender.

(7) Take any steps necessary to ensure that the amount payable on completion will be available in time for completion including sending to the buyer a completion statement to include legal costs, Land Registry fees and other disbursements and, if appropriate, stamp duty.

(8) Make the Land Registry and land charges searches and, if appropriate, a company search.

9.4   The seller's solicitor shall:

(1) Request redemption figures for all financial charges on the property revealed by the deeds/office copy entries/land charges search against the seller.

(2) On receipt of the engrossment of the conveyance/transfer or assignment, after checking the engrossment to ensure accuracy, obtain the seller's signature to it after ascertaining that the seller understands the nature and contents of the document. If the document is not to be signed in the solicitor's presence the letter sending the document for signature should contain an explanation of the nature and effect of the document and clear instructions relating to the execution of it.

(3) On receipt of the estate agent's or property seller's commission account obtain the seller's instructions to

pay the account on the seller's behalf out of the sale proceeds.

10. Relationship with the seller's estate agent or property seller

Where the seller has instructed estate agents or property seller, the seller's solicitor shall take the following steps:

10.1   Inform them when the draft contracts are submitted (see 4.5).

10.2   Deal promptly with any queries raised by them.

10.3   Inform them of any unexpected delays or difficulties likely to delay exchange of contracts (see 4.9).

10.4   Inform them when exchange has taken place and the date of completion (see 8.6).

10.5   On receipt of their commission account send a copy to the seller and obtain instructions as to arrangements for payment (see 9.4(3)).

10.6   Inform them of completion and, if appropriate, authorise release of any keys held by them (see 11.3(1)).

10.7   If so instructed pay the commission (see 9.4(3) and 11.6(2)).

11. Completion: the day of payment and removals

11.1   If completion is to be by post, the Law Society's Code for Completion shall be used, unless otherwise agreed.

11.2   As soon as practicabie and not later than the morning of completion, the buyer's solicitor shall advise the seller's solicitor of the manner and transmission of the purchase money and of steps taken to despatch it.

11.3   On being satisfied as to the receipt of the balance of the purchase money, the seller's solicitor shall :

(1) Notify the estate agent or property seller that completion has taken place and authorise release of the keys.

(2) Notify the buyer's solicitor that completion has taken place and the keys have been released.

(3) Date and complete the transfer.

(4) Despatch the deeds including the transfer to the buyer's solicitor with any appropriate undertakings.

11.4 The seller's solicitor shall check that the seller is aware of the need to notify the local and water authorities of the change in ownership.

11.5 After completion, where appropriate, the buyer's solicitor shall give notice of assignment to the lessor.

11.6 Immediately after completion, the seller's solicitor shall:

(1) Send to the lender the amount required to release the property sold.

(2) Pay the estate agent's or property seller's commission if so authorised.

(3) Account to the seller for the balance of the sale proceeds.

11.7 Immediately after completion, the buyer's solicitor shall:

(1) Date and complete the mortgage document.

(2) Confirm completion of the purchase and the mortgage to the buyer.

(3) Pay stamp duty on the purchase deed, if appropriate.

(4) Deal with the registration of the transfer document and mortgage with the Land Registry within the priority period of the search.

(5) If appropriate, send a notice of assignment of a life policy to the insurance company.

(6) On receipt of the land or charge certificate from the Land Registry check its contents carefully and supply a copy of the certificate to the buyer.

(7) Send the charge certificate to the lender or deal with the land certificate in accordance with the buyer's instructions.

APPENDIX II

AGREEMENT
(Incorporating the Standard Conditions of Sale (Third Edition))

Agreement date	:
Seller	:
Buyer	:
Property **(freehold/leasehold)**	:
Root of title/Title Number	:
Incumbrances on the Property	:
Title Guarantee **(full/limited)**	:
Completion date	:
Contract rate	:
Purchase price	:
Deposit	:
Amount payable for chattels	:
Balance	:

The Seller will sell and the Buyer will buy the Property for the Purchase price.
The Agreement continues on the back page.

WARNING	Signed
This is a formal document, designed to create legal rights and legal obligations. Take advice before using it.	
	Seller/Buyer

Reproduced for educational purposes only by kind permission of The Solicitors' Law Stationery Society Limited and the Law Society of England and Wales.

STANDARD CONDITIONS OF SALE (THIRD EDITION)

(NATIONAL CONDITIONS OF SALE 23rd EDITION, LAW SOCIETY'S CONDITIONS OF SALE 1995)

1. GENERAL

1.1 Definitions

1.1.1 In these conditions:

(a) "accrued interest" means:

(i) if money has been placed on deposit or in a building society share account, the interest actually earned

(ii) otherwise, the interest which might reasonably have been earned by depositing the money at interest on seven days' notice of withdrawal with a clearing bank

less, in either case, any proper charges for handling the money

(b) "agreement" means the contractual document which incorporates these conditions, with or without amendment

(c) "banker's draft" means a draft drawn by and on a clearing bank

(d) "clearing bank" means a bank which is a member of CHAPS Limited

(e) "completion date", unless defined in the agreement, has the meaning given in condition 6.1.1

(f) "contract" means the bargain between the seller and the buyer of which these conditions, with or without amendment, form part

(g) "contract rate", unless defined in the agreement, is the Law Society's interest rate from time to time in force

(h) "lease" includes sub-lease, tenancy and agreement for a lease or sub-lease

(i) "notice to complete" means a notice requiring completion of the contract in accordance with condition 6

(j) "public requirement" means any notice, order or proposal given or made (whether before or after the date of the contract) by a body acting on statutory authority

(k) "requisition" includes objection

(l) "solicitor" includes barrister, duly certificated notary public, recognised licensed conveyancer and recognised body under sections 9 or 32 of the Administration of Justice Act 1985

(m) "transfer" includes conveyance and assignment

(n) "working day" means any day from Monday to Friday (inclusive) which is not Christmas Day, Good Friday or a statutory Bank Holiday.

1.1.2 When used in these conditions the terms "absolute title" and "office copies" have the special meanings given to them by the Land Registration Act 1925.

1.2 Joint parties

If there is more than one seller or more than one buyer, the obligations which they undertake can be enforced against them all jointly or against each individually.

1.3 Notices and documents

1.3.1 A notice required or authorised by the contract must be in writing.

1.3.2 Giving a notice or delivering a document to a party's solicitor has the same effect as giving or delivering it to that party.

1.3.3 Transmission by fax is a valid means of giving a notice or delivering a document where delivery of the original document is not essential.

1.3.4 Subject to conditions 1.3.5 to 1.3.7, a notice is given and a document delivered when it is received.

1.3.5 If a notice or document is received after 4.00pm on a working day, or on a day which is not a working day, it is to be treated as having been received on the next working day.

1.3.6 Unless the actual time of receipt is proved, a notice or document sent by the following means is to be treated as having been received before 4.00pm on the day shown below:

(a) by first-class post:	two working days after posting
(b) by second-class post:	three working days after posting
(c) through a document exchange:	on the first working day after the day on which it would normally be available for collection by the addressee.

1.3.7 Where a notice or document is sent through a document exchange, then for the purposes of condition 1.3.6 the actual time of receipt is:

(a) the time when the addressee collects it from the document exchange or, if earlier

(b) 8.00am on the first working day on which it is available for collection at that time.

1.4 VAT

1.4.1 An obligation to pay money includes an obligation to pay any value added tax chargeable in respect of that payment.

1.4.2 All sums made payable by the contract are exclusive of value added tax.

2. FORMATION

2.1 Date

2.1.1 If the parties intend to make a contract by exchanging duplicate copies by post or through a document exchange, the contract is made when the last copy is posted or deposited at the document exchange.

2.1.2 If the parties' solicitors agree to treat exchange as taking place before duplicate copies are actually exchanged, the contract is made as so agreed.

2.2 Deposit

2.2.1 The buyer is to pay or send a deposit of 10 per cent of the purchase price no later than the date of the contract. Except on a sale by auction, payment is to be made by banker's draft or by a cheque drawn on a solicitors' clearing bank account.

2.2.2 If before completion date the seller agrees to buy another property in England and Wales for his residence, he may use all or any part of the deposit as a deposit in that transaction to be held on terms to the same effect as this condition and condition 2.2.3.

2.2.3 Any deposit or part of a deposit not being used in accordance with condition 2.2.2 is to be held by the seller's solicitor as stakeholder on terms that on completion it is paid to the seller with accrued interest.

2.2.4 If a cheque tendered in payment of all or part of the deposit is dishonoured when first presented, the seller may, within seven working days of being notified that the cheque has been dishonoured, give notice to the buyer that the contract is discharged by the buyer's breach.

2.3 Auctions

2.3.1 On a sale by auction the following conditions apply to the property and, if it is sold in lots, to each lot.

2.3.2 The sale is subject to a reserve price.

2.3.3 The seller, or a person on his behalf, may bid up to the reserve price.

2.3.4 The auctioneer may refuse any bid.

2.3.5 If there is a dispute about a bid, the auctioneer may resolve the dispute or restart the auction at the last undisputed bid.

3. MATTERS AFFECTING THE PROPERTY

3.1 Freedom from incumbrances

3.1.1 The seller is selling the property free from incumbrances, other than those mentioned in condition 3.1.2.

3.1.2 The incumbrances subject to which the property is sold are:

(a) those mentioned in the agreement

(b) those discoverable by inspection of the property before the contract

(c) those the seller does not and could not know about

(d) entries made before the date of the contract in any public register except those maintained by HM Land Registry or its Land Charges Department or by Companies House

(e) public requirements.

3.1.3 After the contract is made, the seller is to give the buyer written details without delay of any new public requirement and of anything in writing which he learns about concerning any incumbrances subject to which the property is sold.

3.1.4 The buyer is to bear the cost of complying with any outstanding public requirement and is to indemnify the seller against any liability resulting from a public requirement.

3.2 Physical state

3.2.1 The buyer accepts the property in the physical state it is in at the date of the contract unless the seller is building or converting it.

3.2.2 A leasehold property is sold subject to any subsisting breach of a condition or tenant's obligation relating to the physical state of the property which renders the lease liable to forfeiture.

3.2.3 A sub-lease is granted subject to any subsisting breach of a condition or tenant's obligation relating to the physical state of the property which renders the seller's own lease liable to forfeiture.

3.3 Leases affecting the property

3.3.1 The following provisions apply if the agreement states that any part of the property is sold subject to a lease.

3.3.2 (a) The seller having provided the buyer with full details of each lease or copies of the documents embodying the lease terms, the buyer is treated as entering into the contract knowing and fully accepting those terms

(b) The seller is to inform the buyer without delay if the lease ends or if the seller learns of any application by the tenant in connection with the lease; the seller is then to act as the buyer reasonably directs, and the buyer is to indemnify him against all consequent loss and expense

(c) The seller is not to agree to any proposal to change the lease terms without the consent of the buyer and is to inform the buyer without delay of any change which may be proposed or agreed

(d) The buyer is to indemnify the seller against all claims arising from the lease after actual completion; this includes claims which are unenforceable against a buyer for want of registration

(e) The seller takes no responsibility for what rent is lawfully recoverable, nor for whether or how any legislation affects the lease

(f) If the let land is not wholly within the property, the seller may apportion the rent.

3.4 Retained land

3.4.1 The following provisions apply where after the transfer the seller will be retaining land near the property.

3.4.2 The buyer will have no right of light or air over the retained land, but otherwise the seller and the buyer will each have the rights over the land of the other which they would have had if they were two separate buyers to whom the seller had made simultaneous transfers of the property and the retained land.

3.4.3 Either party may require that the transfer contain appropriate express terms.

4. TITLE AND TRANSFER

4.1 Timetable

4.1.1 The following are the steps for deducing and investigating the title to the property to be taken within the following time limits:

Step	Time Limit
1. The seller is to send the buyer evidence of title in accordance with condition 4.2	Immediately after making the contract
2. The buyer may raise written requisitions	Six working days after either the date of the contract or the date of delivery of the seller's evidence of title on which the requisitions are raised whichever is the later
3. The seller is to reply in writing to any requisitions raised	Four working days after receiving the requisitions
4. The buyer may make written observations on the seller's replies	Three working days after receiving the replies

The time limit on the buyer's right to raise requisitions applies even where the seller supplies incomplete evidence of his title, but the buyer may, within six working days from delivery of any further evidence, raise further requisitions resulting from that evidence. On the expiry of the relevant time limit the buyer loses his right to raise requisitions or make observations.

4.1.2 The parties are to take the following steps to prepare and agree the transfer of the property within the following time limits:

Step	Time Limit
A. The buyer is to send the seller a draft transfer	At least twelve working days before completion date
B. The seller is to approve or revise that draft and either return it or retain it for use as the actual transfer	Four working days after delivery of the draft transfer
C. If the draft is returned the buyer is to send an engrossment to the seller	At least five working days before completion date

4.1.3 Periods of time under conditions 4.1.1 and 4.1.2 may run concurrently.

4.1.4 If the period between the date of the contract and completion date is less than 15 working days, the time limits in conditions 4.1.1 and 4.1.2 are to be reduced by the same proportion as that period bears to the period of 15 working days. Fractions of a working day are to be rounded down except that the time limit to perform any step is not to be less than one working day.

4.2 Proof of title

4.2.1 The evidence of registered title is office copies of the items required to be furnished by section 110(1) of the Land Registration Act 1925 and the copies, abstracts and evidence referred to in section 110(2).

4.2.2 The evidence of unregistered title is an abstract of the title, or an epitome of title with photocopies of the relevant documents.

4.2.3 Where the title to the property is unregistered, the seller is to produce to the buyer (without cost to the buyer):

(a) the original of every relevant document, or

(b) an abstract, epitome or copy with an original marking by a solicitor of examination either against the original or against an examined abstract or against an examined copy.

4.3 Defining the property

4.3.1 The seller need not:

(a) prove the exact boundaries of the property

(b) prove who owns fences, ditches, hedges or walls

(c) separately identify parts of the property with different titles

further than he may be able to do from information in his possession.

4.3.2 The buyer may, if it is reasonable, require the seller to make or obtain, pay for and hand over a statutory declaration about facts relevant to the matters mentioned in condition 4.3.1. The form of the declaration is to be agreed by the buyer, who must not unreasonably withhold his agreement.

4.4 Rents and rentcharges

The fact that a rent or rentcharge, whether payable or receivable by the owner of the property, has been or will on completion be, informally apportioned is not to be regarded as a defect in title.

4.5 **Transfer**

4.5.1 The buyer does not prejudice his right to raise requisitions, or to require replies to any raised, by taking any steps in relation to the preparation or agreement of the transfer.

4.5.2 If the agreement makes no provision as to title guarantee, then subject to condition 4.5.3 the seller is to transfer the property with full title guarantee.

4.5.3 The transfer is to have effect as if the disposition is expressly made subject to all matters to which the property is sold subject under the terms of the contract.

4.5.4 If after completion the seller will remain bound by any obligation affecting the property, but the law does not imply any covenant by the buyer to indemnify the seller against liability for future breaches of it:
(a) the buyer is to covenant in the transfer to indemnify the seller against liability for any future breach of the obligation and to perform it from then on, and
(b) if required by the seller, the buyer is to execute and deliver to the seller on completion a duplicate transfer prepared by the buyer.

4.5.5 The seller is to arrange at his expense that, in relation to every document of title which the buyer does not receive on completion, the buyer is to have the benefit of:
(a) a written acknowledgement of his right to its production, and
(b) a written undertaking for its safe custody (except while it is held by a mortgagee or by someone in a fiduciary capacity).

5. PENDING COMPLETION

5.1 **Responsibility for property**

5.1.1 The seller will transfer the property in the same physical state as it was at the date of the contract (except for fair wear and tear), which means that the seller retains the risk until completion.

5.1.2 If at any time before completion the physical state of the property makes it unusable for its purpose at the date of the contract:
(a) the buyer may rescind the contract
(b) the seller may rescind the contract where the property has become unusable for that purpose as a result of damage against which the seller could not reasonably have insured, or which it is not legally possible for the seller to make good.

5.1.3 The seller is under no obligation to the buyer to insure the property.

5.1.4 Section 47 of the Law of Property Act 1925 does not apply.

5.2 **Occupation by buyer**

5.2.1 If the buyer is not already lawfully in the property, and the seller agrees to let him into occupation, the buyer occupies on the following terms.

5.2.2 The buyer is a licensee and not a tenant. The terms of the licence are that the buyer:
(a) cannot transfer it
(b) may permit members of his household to occupy the property
(c) is to pay or indemnify the seller against all outgoings and other expenses in respect of the property
(d) is to pay the seller a fee calculated at the contract rate on the purchase price (less any deposit paid) for the period of the licence
(e) is entitled to any rents and profits from any part of the property which he does not occupy
(f) is to keep the property in as good a state of repair as it was in when he went into occupation (except for fair wear and tear) and is not to alter it
(g) is to insure the property in a sum which is not less than the purchase price against all risks in respect of which comparable premises are normally insured
(h) is to quit the property when the licence ends.

5.2.3 On the creation of the buyer's licence, condition 5.1 ceases to apply, which means that the buyer then assumes the risk until completion.

5.2.4 The buyer is not in occupation for the purposes of this condition if he merely exercises rights of access given solely to do work agreed by the seller.

5.2.5 The buyer's licence ends on the earliest of: completion date, rescission of the contract or when five working days' notice given by one party to the other takes effect.

5.2.6 If the buyer is in occupation of the property after his licence has come to an end and the contract is subsequently completed he is to pay the seller compensation for his continued occupation calculated at the same rate as the fee mentioned in condition 5.2.2(d).

5.2.7 The buyer's right to raise requisitions is unaffected.

6. COMPLETION

6.1 **Date**

6.1.1 Completion date is twenty working days after the date of the contract but time is not of the essence of the contract unless a notice to complete has been served.

6.1.2 If the money due on completion is received after 2.00pm, completion is to be treated, for the purposes only of conditions 6.3 and 7.3, as taking place on the next working day.

6.1.3 Condition 6.1.2 does not apply where the sale is with vacant possession of the property or any part and the seller has not vacated the property or that part by 2.00pm on the date of actual completion.

6.2 **Place**
Completion is to take place in England and Wales, either at the seller's solicitor's office or at some other place which the seller reasonably specifies.

6.3 **Apportionments**

6.3.1 Income and outgoings of the property are to be apportioned between the parties so far as the change of ownership on completion will affect entitlement to receive or liability to pay them.

6.3.2 If the whole property is sold with vacant possession or the seller exercises his option in condition 7.3.4, apportionment is to be made with effect from the date of actual completion; otherwise, it is to be made from completion date.

6.3.3 In apportioning any sum, it is to be assumed that the seller owns the property until the end of the day from which apportionment is made and that the sum accrues from day to day at the rate at which it is payable on that day.

6.3.4 For the purpose of apportioning income and outgoings, it is to be assumed that they accrue at an equal daily rate throughout the year.

6.3.5 When a sum to be apportioned is not known or easily ascertainable at completion, a provisional apportionment is to be made according to the best estimate available. As soon as the amount is known, a final apportionment is to be made and notified to the other party. Any resulting balance is to be paid no more than ten working days later, and if not then paid the balance is to bear interest at the contract rate from then until payment.

6.3.6 Compensation payable under condition 5.2.6 is not to be apportioned.

6.4 **Amount payable**
The amount payable by the buyer on completion is the purchase price (less any deposit already paid to the seller or his agent) adjusted to take account of:
(a) apportionments made under condition 6.3
(b) any compensation to be paid or allowed under condition 7.3.

6.5 **Title deeds**

6.5.1 The seller is not to retain the documents of title after the buyer has tendered the amount payable under condition 6.4.

6.5.2 Condition 6.5.1 does not apply to any documents of title relating to land being retained by the seller after completion.

6.6 **Rent receipts**
The buyer is to assume that whoever gave any receipt for a payment of rent or service charge which the seller produces was the person or the agent of the person then entitled to that rent or service charge.

6.7 **Means of payment**
The buyer is to pay the money due on completion in one or more of the following ways:
(a) legal tender
(b) a banker's draft
(c) a direct credit to a bank account nominated by the seller's solicitor
(d) an unconditional release of a deposit held by a stakeholder.

6.8. **Notice to complete**

6.8.1 At any time on or after completion date, a party who is ready able and willing to complete may give the other a notice to complete.

6.8.2 A party is ready able and willing:
(a) if he could be, but for the default of the other party, and
(b) in the case of the seller, even though a mortgage remains secured on the property, if the amount to be paid on completion enables the property to be transferred freed of all mortgages (except those to which the sale is expressly subject).

6.8.3 The parties are to complete the contract within ten working days of giving a notice to complete, excluding the day on which the notice is given. For this purpose, time is of the essence of the contract.

6.8.4 On receipt of a notice to complete:
(a) if the buyer paid no deposit, he is forthwith to pay a deposit of 10 per cent
(b) if the buyer paid a deposit of less than 10 per cent, he is forthwith to pay a further deposit equal to the balance of that 10 per cent.

7. REMEDIES

7.1 **Errors and omissions**

7.1.1 If any plan or statement in the contract, or in the negotiations leading to it, is or was misleading or inaccurate due to an error or omission, the remedies available are as follows.

7.1.2 When there is a material difference between the description or value of the property as represented and as it is, the injured party is entitled to damages.

7.1.3 An error or omission only entitles the injured party to rescind the contract:
(a) where it results from fraud or recklessness, or
(b) where he would be obliged, to his prejudice, to transfer or accept property differing substantially (in quantity, quality or tenure) from what the error or omission had led him to expect.

7.2 **Rescission**
If either party rescinds the contract:
(a) unless the rescission is a result of the buyer's breach of contract the deposit is to be repaid to the buyer with accrued interest
(b) the buyer is to return any documents he received from the seller and is to cancel any registration of the contract.

7.3 **Late completion**

7.3.1 If there is default by either or both of the parties in performing their obligations under the contract and completion is delayed, the party whose total period of default is the greater is to pay compensation to the other party.

7.3.2 Compensation is calculated at the contract rate on the purchase price, or (where the buyer is the paying party) the purchase price less any deposit paid, for the period by which the paying party's default exceeds that of the receiving party, or, if shorter, the period between completion date and actual completion.

7.3.3 Any claim for loss resulting from delayed completion is to be reduced by any compensation paid under this contract.

7.3.4 Where the buyer holds the property as tenant of the seller and completion is delayed, the seller may give notice to the buyer, before the date of actual completion, that he intends to take the net income from the property until completion. If he does so, he cannot claim compensation under condition 7.3.1 as well.

7.4 **After completion**
Completion does not cancel liability to perform any outstanding obligation under this contract.

7.5 **Buyer's failure to comply with notice to complete**

7.5.1 If the buyer fails to complete in accordance with a notice to complete, the following terms apply.

7.5.2 The seller may rescind the contract, and if he does so:
(a) he may
(i) forfeit and keep any deposit and accrued interest
(ii) resell the property
(iii) claim damages
(b) the buyer is to return any documents he received from the seller and is to cancel any registration of the contract.

7.5.3 The seller retains his other rights and remedies.

7.6 **Seller's failure to comply with notice to complete**

7.6.1 If the seller fails to complete in accordance with a notice to complete, the following terms apply.

7.6.2 The buyer may rescind the contract, and if he does so:
(a) the deposit is to be repaid to the buyer with accrued interest
(b) the buyer is to return any documents he received from the seller and is, at the seller's expense, to cancel any registration of the contract.

7.6.3 The buyer retains his other rights and remedies.

8. LEASEHOLD PROPERTY

8.1 **Existing leases**

8.1.1 The following provisions apply to a sale of leasehold land.

8.1.2 The seller having provided the buyer with copies of the documents embodying the lease terms, the buyer is treated as entering into the contract knowing and fully accepting those terms.

8.1.3 The seller is to comply with any lease obligations requiring the tenant to insure the property.

8.2 **New leases**

8.2.1 The following provisions apply to a grant of a new lease.

8.2.2 The conditions apply so that:
"seller" means the proposed landlord
"buyer" means the proposed tenant
"purchase price" means the premium to be paid on the grant of a lease.

8.2.3 The lease is to be in the form of the draft attached to the agreement.

8.2.4 If the term of the new lease will exceed 21 years, the seller is to deduce a title which will enable the buyer to register the lease at HM Land Registry with an absolute title.

8.2.5 The buyer is not entitled to transfer the benefit of the contract.

8.2.6 The seller is to engross the lease and a counterpart of it and is to send the counterpart to the buyer at least five working days before completion date.

8.2.7 The buyer is to execute the counterpart and deliver it to the seller on completion.

8.3 **Landlord's consent**

8.3.1 The following provisions apply if a consent to assign or sub-let is required to complete the contract.

8.3.2 (a) The seller is to apply for the consent at his expense, and to use all reasonable efforts to obtain it
(b) The buyer is to provide all information and references reasonably required.

8.3.3 The buyer is not entitled to transfer the benefit of the contract.

8.3.4 Unless he is in breach of his obligation under condition 8.3.2, either party may rescind the contract by notice to the other party if three working days before completion date:
(a) the consent has not been given or
(b) the consent has been given subject to a condition to which the buyer reasonably objects.
In that case, neither party is to be treated as in breach of contract and condition 7.2 applies.

9. CHATTELS

9.1 The following provisions apply to any chattels which are to be sold.

9.2 Whether or not a separate price is to be paid for the chattels, the contract takes effect as a contract for sale of goods.

9.3 Ownership of the chattels passes to the buyer on actual completion.

SPECIAL CONDITIONS

1. (a) This Agreement incorporates the Standard Conditions of Sale (Third Edition). Where there is a conflict between those Conditions and this Agreement, this Agreement prevails.

   (b) Terms used or defined in this Agreement have the same meaning when used in the Conditions.

2. The Property is sold subject to the Incumbrances on the Property and the Buyer will raise no requisitions on them.

3. Subject to the terms of this Agreement and to the Standard Conditions of Sale, the Seller is to transfer the property with the title guarantee specified on the front page.

4. The chattels on the Property and set out on any attached list are included in the sale.

5. The Property is sold with vacant possession on completion.

(or) 5. The Property is sold subject to the following leases or tenancies:

Seller's Solicitors   :

Buyer's Solicitors   :

©1995   Oyez   The Solicitors' Law Stationery Society Ltd, Oyez House, 7 Spa Road, London SE16 3QQ

9.2000   F38583
5065046
*
3rd Edition

© 1995 **THE LAW SOCIETY**

Standard Conditions of Sale

Appendix III

SELLER'S PROPERTY INFORMATION FORM (2nd edition)

Address of the Property:

IMPORTANT NOTE TO SELLERS – PLEASE READ THIS FIRST

* Please complete this form carefully. If you are unsure how to answer the questions, ask your solicitor before doing so.

* This form in due course will be sent to the buyer's solicitor and will be seen by the buyer who is entitled to rely on the information.

* For many of the questions you need only tick the correct answer. Where necessary, please give more detailed answers on a separate sheet of paper. Then send all the replies to your solicitor. This form will be passed to the buyer's solicitor.

* The answers should be those of the person whose name is on the deeds. If there is more than one of you, you should prepare the answers together.

* It is very important that your answers are correct because the buyer is entitled to rely on them in deciding whether to go ahead. Incorrect or incomplete information given to the buyer direct through your solicitor or selling agent or even mentioned to the buyer in conversation between you, may mean that the buyer can claim compensation from you or even refuse to complete the purchase.

* If you do not know the answer to any question you must say so.

* The buyer takes the property in its present physical condition and should, if necessary, seek independent advice, e.g. instruct a surveyor. You should not give the buyer your views on the condition of the property.

* If anything changes after you fill in this questionnaire but before the sale is completed, tell your solicitor immediately. THIS IS AS IMPORTANT AS GIVING THE RIGHT ANSWERS IN THE FIRST PLACE.

* Please pass to your solicitor immediately any notices you have received which affect the property, including any notices which arrive at any time before completion of your sale.

* If you have a tenant, tell your solicitor immediately if there is any change in the arrangement but do nothing without asking your solicitor first.

* You should let your solicitor have any letters, agreements or other documents which help answer the questions. If you know of any which you are not supplying with these answers, please tell your solicitor about them.

* Please complete and return the separate Fixtures, Fittings and Contents Form. It is an important document which will form part of the contract between you and the buyer. Unless you mark clearly on it the items which you wish to remove, they will be included in the sale and you will not be able to take them with you when you move.

* You may wish to delay the completion of the Fixtures, Fittings and Contents Form until you have a prospective buyer and have agreed the price.

Prop 1/1

Part I – to be completed by the seller

1 Boundaries

"Boundaries" mean any fence, wall, hedge or ditch which marks the edge of your property.

1.1 Looking towards the house from the road, who either owns or accepts responsibility for the boundary:

(a) on the left?

Please mark the appropriate box

WE DO	NEXT DOOR	SHARED	NOT KNOWN

(b) on the right?

WE DO	NEXT DOOR	SHARED	NOT KNOWN

(c) across the back?

WE DO	NEXT DOOR	SHARED	NOT KNOWN

1.2 If you have answered "not known", which boundaries have you actually repaired or maintained?

(Please give details)

1.3 Do you know of any boundary being moved in the last 20 years?

(Please give details)

2 Disputes and complaints

2.1 Do you know of any disputes or anything which might lead to a dispute about this or any neighbouring property?

NO	YES: (PLEASE GIVE DETAILS)

Please mark the appropriate box

2.2 Have you received any complaints about anything you have, or have not, done as owner?

NO	YES: (PLEASE GIVE DETAILS)

_____

_____

_____

2.3 Have you made any such complaints to any neighbour about what the neighbour has or has not done?

NO	YES: (PLEASE GIVE DETAILS)

_____

_____

_____

3   Notices

3.1 Have you either sent or received any letters or notices which affect your property or the neighbouring property in any way (for example, from or to neighbours, the council or a government department)?

NO	YES:	COPY ENCLOSED	TO FOLLOW	LOST

3.2 Have you had any negotiations or discussions with any neighbour or any local or other authority which affect the property in any way?

NO	YES: (PLEASE GIVE DETAILS)

_____

_____

_____

4   Guarantees

4.1 Are there any guarantees or insurance policies of the following types:

   (a) NHBC Foundation 15 or Newbuild?

NO	YES:	COPIES ENCLOSED	WITH DEEDS	LOST

   (b) Damp course?

NO	YES:	COPIES ENCLOSED	WITH DEEDS	LOST

   (c) Double glazing?

NO	YES:	COPIES ENCLOSED	WITH DEEDS	LOST

   (d) Electrical work?

NO	YES:	COPIES ENCLOSED	WITH DEEDS	LOST

   (e) Roofing?

NO	YES:	COPIES ENCLOSED	WITH DEEDS	LOST

Please mark the appropriate box

(f) Rot or infestation?

NO	YES:	COPIES ENCLOSED	WITH DEEDS	LOST

(g) Central heating?

NO	YES:	COPIES ENCLOSED	WITH DEEDS	LOST

(h) Anything similar? (e.g. cavity wall insulation, underpinning, indemnity policy)?

NO	YES:	COPIES ENCLOSED	WITH DEEDS	LOST

(i) Do you have written details of the work done to obtain any of these guarantees?

NO	YES:	COPIES ENCLOSED	WITH DEEDS	LOST

4.2 Have you made or considered making claims under any of these?

NO	YES: (PLEASE GIVE DETAILS)

4.3 Do you have a maintenance or service agreement for the central heating system?

NO	YES:	COPIES ENCLOSED	WITH DEEDS	LOST

5 | Services

(This section applies to gas, electrical and water supplies, sewerage disposal and telephone cables.)

5.1 Please tick which services are connected to the property

GAS	ELEC.	MAIN WATER	MAIN DRAINS	TEL	CABLE T.V.	SEPTIC TANK/ CESSPIT

5.2 Please supply a copy of the latest water charge account and the sewerage account (if any).

ENCLOSED	TO FOLLOW

5.3 Is the water supply on a meter?

NO	YES

5.4 Do any drains, pipes or wires for these cross any neighbour's property?

NOT KNOWN	YES: (PLEASE GIVE DETAILS)

Please mark the appropriate box

5.5   Do any drains, pipes or wires leading to any neighbour's property cross your property?

NOT KNOWN	YES: (PLEASE GIVE DETAILS)

_____

_____

5.6   Are you aware of any agreement or arrangement about any of these services?

NOT KNOWN	YES: (PLEASE GIVE DETAILS)

_____

_____

6 | Sharing with the neighbours

6.1   Are you aware of any responsibility to contribute to the cost of anything used jointly, such as the repair of a shared drive, boundary or drain?

YES: (PLEASE GIVE DETAILS)	NO

_____

_____

6.2   Do you contribute to the cost of repair of anything used by the neighbourhood, such as the maintenance of a private road?

YES	NO

6.3   If so, who is responsible for organising the work and collecting the contributions?

_____

_____

6.4   Please give details of all such sums paid or owing, and explain if they are paid on a regular basis or only as and when work is required.

_____

_____

6.5   Do you need to go on to any neighbouring property if you have to repair or decorate your building or maintain any of the boundaries or any of the drains, pipes or wires?

YES	NO

Prop 1/5

6.6 If "YES", have you always been able to do so without objection by the neighbours?

Please mark the appropriate box

YES	NO: Please give details of any objection under the answer to question 2 (disputes and complaints)

6.7 Do any of your neighbours need to come onto your land to repair or decorate their building or maintain their boundaries or any drains, pipes or wires?

YES	NO

6.8 If so, have you ever objected?

NO	YES: Please give details of any objection under the answer to question 2 (disputes and complaints)

7	Arrangements and rights

7.1 Is access obtained to any part of the property over private land, common land or a neighbour's land? If so, please specify.

NO	YES: (PLEASE GIVE DETAILS)

7.2 Has anyone taken steps to stop, complain about or demand payment for such access being exercised?

NO	YES

7.3 Are there any other formal or informal arrangements which you have over any of your neighbours' property?

(Examples are for access or shared use)

NO	YES: (PLEASE GIVE DETAILS)

7.4 Are there any other formal or informal arrangements which someone else has over your property?

(Examples are for access or shared use)

NO	YES: (PLEASE GIVE DETAILS)

8	Occupiers

Please mark the appropriate box

8.1   Does anyone other than you live in the property?

NO	YES

If "NO" go to question 9.1.
If "YES" please give their full names and
(if under 18) their ages.

8.2(a)(i) Do any of them have any right to stay
on the property without your permission?

NO	YES: (PLEASE GIVE DETAILS)

(These rights may have arisen without you
realising, e.g. if they have paid towards the cost
of buying the house, paid for improvements or
helped you make your mortgage payments).

8.2(a)(ii) Are any of them tenants or lodgers?

NO	YES: (Please give details and a copy of any Tenancy Agreement)

8.2(b)   Have they all agreed to sign the contract
for sale agreeing to leave with you (or earlier)?

NO	YES: (PLEASE GIVE DETAILS)

9	Changes to the property

9.1   Have any of the following taken place to the
whole or any part of the property (including the
garden) and if so, when?

(a)   Building works (including loft
conversions and conservatories)

YES . . .	NO

(b)   Change of use

YES . . .	NO

(c)   Sub-division

YES . . .	NO

(d)   Conversion

YES . . .	NO

Please mark the appropriate box

(e)   Business activities

YES...	NO

(f)   Window replacement

YES...	NO

If "YES" what consents were obtained under any restrictions in your title deeds?

(*Note*: The title deeds of some properties include clauses which are called "restrictive covenants". These may, for example, forbid the owner of the property from carrying out any building work or from using it for business purposes or from parking a caravan or boat on it unless someone else (often the builder of the house) gives consent.

9.2   Has consent under those restrictions been obtained for anything else done at the property?

YES	NO

9.3   If any consent was needed but not obtained:

    (a)   Please explain why not:

    (b)   From whom should it have been obtained?

(*Note*: Improvements can affect council tax banding following a sale).

---

10   Planning and building control

10.1   Is the property used only as a private home?

YES	NO: (PLEASE GIVE DETAILS)

10.2(a)Has the property been designated as a Listed Building or the area designated as a Conservation Area?
If so, when did this happen?

YES	NO	IN THE YEAR...	NOT KNOWN

10.2(b)Was planning permission, building regulation approval or listed building consent obtained for each of the changes mentioned in 9?

NO	YES	COPY ENCLOSED	TO FOLLOW	LOST

    (*Please list separately and supply copies of the relevant permissions and, where appropriate, certificates of completion.*)

Prop 1/8

11 | Expenses

Please mark the appropriate box

Have you ever had to pay for the use of the property?

NO	YES: (PLEASE GIVE DETAILS)

(Note: Ignore council tax, water rates, and gas, electricity and telephone bills. Disclose anything else: examples are the clearance of cesspool or septic tank, drainage rate, rent charge.)

(If you are selling a leasehold property, details of the lease's expenses should be included on the Seller's Leasehold Information Form and not on this form.)

12 | Mechanics of the Sale

12.1 Is this sale dependent on your buying another property?

YES	NO

12.2 If "YES" what stage have the negotiations reached?

12.3 Do you require a mortgage?

YES	NO

12.4 If "YES", has an offer been received and/or accepted or a mortgage certificate obtained?

YES	NO

13 | Deposit

Do you have the money to pay a 10% deposit on your purchase?

YES	NO

If "NO", are you expecting to use the deposit paid by your buyer to pay the deposit on your purchase?

YES	NO

14	Moving date

Please indicate if you have any special requirement about a moving date.

Please mark the appropriate box

YES	NO

(Note: This will not be fixed until contracts are exchanged i.e. have become binding. Until then you should only make provisional removal arrangements.)

_____

_____

Signature(s): ....

....

Date: ....

Part II – to be completed by the seller's solicitor

Please mark the appropriate box

A. Is the information provided by the seller in this form consistent with the information in your possession?
    If "NO", please specify.

YES	NO

B. Do you have any information in your possession to supplement the information provided by the seller?
    If "YES", please specify.

YES	NO

C. Is there an indemnity policy?

YES	NO

If "YES", please supply a copy.

Reminder to solicitor

1. The Fixtures, Fittings and Contents Form should be supplied in addition to the information above.

2. Copies of all planning permissions, building regulations consents, certificates of completion, engineer's certificates, guarantees, assignments, certificates and notices should be supplied with this form.

3. If the property is leasehold, also supply the Seller's Leasehold Information Form.

Seller's solicitor: ....

Date: ....

SELLER'S LEASEHOLD INFORMATION FORM (2nd edition)

Address of the Property:

If you live in leasehold property, please answer the following questions. Some people live in blocks of flats, others in large houses converted into flats and others in single leasehold houses. These questions cover all types of leasehold property, but some of them may not apply to your property. In that case please answer them N/A.

The instructions set out at the front of the Seller's Property Information Form apply to this form as well. Please read them again before giving your answers to these questions.

If you are unsure how to answer any of the questions, ask your solicitor.

Part I – to be completed by the seller

1 Management Company

1.1 If there is a management company which is run by the tenants please supply any of the following documents which are in your possession:

Please mark the appropriate box

(a) Memorandum and articles of association of the company.

| ENCLOSED | TO FOLLOW | LOST | WITH THE DEEDS | N/A |

(b) Your share or membership certificate.

| ENCLOSED | TO FOLLOW | LOST | WITH THE DEEDS | N/A |

(c) The company's accounts for the last 3 years.

| ENCLOSED | TO FOLLOW | LOST | WITH THE DEEDS | N/A |

(d) Copy of any regulations made by either the landlord or the company additional to the rules contained in the lease.

| ENCLOSED | TO FOLLOW | LOST | WITH THE DEEDS | N/A |

(e) The names and addresses of the secretary and treasurer of the company.

(f) Has the management company been struck off the register at Companies House?

| YES | NO | NOT KNOWN |

Prop 4/1

1.2 If the tenants do not run the Management Company is there a Tenants' Association?

Please mark the appropriate box

YES	NO

If "YES" please supply the contact name and address.

_____

_____

_____

2 | The Landlord

2.1 What is the name and address of your landlord?

_____

_____

_____

2.2 If the landlord employs an agent to collect the rent, what is the name and address of that agent?

_____

_____

_____

2.3 Please supply a receipt from the landlord for the last rent payment.

ENCLOSED	TO FOLLOW

3 | Maintenance Charges

3.1 Are you liable under your lease to pay a share of the maintenance cost of the building?

YES	NO

If "NO", go to question 4.

3.2 Do you know of any expense (e.g. redecoration of outside or communal areas not usually incurred annually) likely to show in the maintenance charge accounts within the next 3 years?

YES	NO

If "YES", please give details.

_____

_____

3.3 Have maintenance charges been demanded for each of the last 3 years?

YES	NO

3.4 If so, please supply the maintenance accounts and receipts for these.

ENCLOSED	TO FOLLOW

3.5 Do you know of any problems in the last 3 years between flat owners and the landlord or management company about maintenance charges, or the method of management?

YES	NO

If "YES", please give details.

_____

_____

Please mark the appropriate box

3.6 Have you challenged the maintenance charge or any expense in the last 3 years?

YES	NO

If "YES", please give details.

_____

_____

3.7 Do you know if the landlord has had any problems in collecting the maintenance charges from other flat owners?

YES	NO

If "YES", please give details.

_____

_____

4   Notices

A notice may be in a printed form or in the form of a letter and your buyer will wish to know if anything of this sort has been received.

4.1 Have you had a notice that the landlord wants to sell the building?

NO	YES	ENCLOSED	TO FOLLOW

4.2 Have you had any other notice about the building, its use, its condition or its repair and maintenance?

NO	YES	ENCLOSED	TO FOLLOW

5   Consents

Are you aware of any changes in the terms of the lease or of the landlord giving any consents under the lease? (This may be in a formal document, a letter or even oral.)
If not in writing, please supply details.

NO	YES	ENCLOSED	TO FOLLOW

_____

_____

6   Complaints

6.1 Have you received any complaints from the landlord, any other landlord, management company or any other occupier about anything you have or have not done?

YES	NO

If "YES", please give details.

_____

_____

Please mark the appropriate box

6.2 Have you complained or had cause for complaint to or about any of them?

YES	NO

If "YES", please give details.

_____

_____

---

7   Buildings Insurance on the Property

7.1 Are you responsible under the lease for arranging the buildings insurance on the property?

YES	NO

7.2 If "YES" please supply a copy of:

(a) the insurance policy and

COPY ENCLOSED	TO FOLLOW

(b) receipt for the last payment of the premium.

COPY ENCLOSED	TO FOLLOW

7.3 If "NO" please supply a copy of the insurance policy arranged by the landlord or the management company and a copy of the schedule for the current year.

COPY ENCLOSED	TO FOLLOW

---

8   Decoration

8.1 When was the outside of the building last decorated?

IN THE YEAR	NOT KNOWN

8.2 When were any internal, communal parts last decorated?

IN THE YEAR	NOT KNOWN

8.3 When was the inside of your property last decorated?

IN THE YEAR	NOT KNOWN

---

9   Alterations

9.1 Are you aware of any alterations having been made to your property since the lease was originally granted?

YES	NO	NOT KNOWN

If "YES", please supply details.

_____

_____

9.2 If "YES", was the landlord's consent obtained?

NO	NOT KNOWN	NOT REQUIRED	YES:	COPIES ENCLOSED	TO FOLLOW

10	Occupation

Please mark the appropriate box

10.1 Are you now occupying the property as your sole or main home?

YES	NO

10.2 Have you occupied the property as your sole or main home (apart from usual holidays and business trips):

(a) continuously throughout the last 12 months?

YES	NO

(b) continuously throughout the last 3 years?

YES	NO

(c) for periods totalling at least 3 years during the last 10 years?

YES	NO

11	Enfranchisement

11.1 Have you served on the landlord or any other landlord a formal notice under the enfranchisement legislation stating your desire to buy the freehold or be granted an extended lease?

NO	YES:	COPY ENCLOSED	COPY TO FOLLOW

If so, please supply a copy.

11.2 If the property is a flat in a block, are you aware of the service of any notice under the enfranchisement legislation relating to the possible collective purchase of the freehold of the block or part of it?

NO	YES:	COPY ENCLOSED	COPY TO FOLLOW

11.3 Have you received any response to that notice?

NO	YES:	COPY ENCLOSED	COPY TO FOLLOW

Reminder

Copies of any relevant documents should be supplied with this form, e.g. memorandum and articles of association of the company, share or membership certificate, management accounts for the last 3 years, copy of any regulations made either by the landlord of the company additional to the rules contained in the lease, name and address of the secretary and treasurer of the company, and copies of any notices served upon the seller under sections 18-30 of the Landlord and Tenant Act 1987, the Leasehold Reform Act 1967 or the Leasehold Reform Housing and Urban Development Act 1993.

Signature(s): ....

....

Date: ....

Part II – to be completed by the seller's solicitor

Please mark the appropriate box

A. Is the information provided by the seller in this Form consistent with the information in your possession?

YES	NO

If "NO", please specify.

B. Do you have any information in your possession to supplement the information provided by the seller?

YES	NO

If "YES", please specify.

C. Please provide the name and address of the recipient of notice of assignment and charge.

D. Do the insurers make a practice of recording the interest of the buyer's mortgage and the buyer on the policy?

YES	NO	NOT KNOWN

E. Please supply a copy of the Fire Certificate.

ENCLOSED	TO FOLLOW	NOT APPLICABLE

F. Are all of the units in the building or development let on identical leases? If not in what respect do they differ?

YES	NO	NOT KNOWN

G. Has the landlord experienced problems with the collection of maintenance charges as they fall due? If so, please supply details.

YES	NO	NOT KNOWN

H. Is the property part of a converted building?

NO	YES

If "YES", please supply a copy of the Planning Permission or an Established Use Certificate, or evidence of permitted use.

ENCLOSED	TO FOLLOW	NOT APPLICABLE

Seller's Solicitor: ....

Date: ....

4/6

This form is part of The Law Society's TransAction scheme © The Law Society 1994. The Law Society is the professional body for solicitors in England and Wales. 7 Spa Road, London SE16 3QQ

 Oyez 5.2001 F39323 5065065 ★★★★

 The Law Society

Prop 4

THE LAW SOCIETY'S FORMULAE FOR EXCHANGING CONTRACTS BY TELEPHONE, FAX OR TELEX

INTRODUCTION

It is essential that an agreed memorandum of the details and of any variations of the formula used should be made at the time and retained in the file. This would be very important if any question on the exchange were raised subsequently. Agreed variations should also be confirmed in writing. The serious risks of exchanging contracts without a deposit, unless the full implications are explained to and accepted by the seller client, are demonstrated in *Morris v Duke-Cohan & Co* [1975] 119 SJ 826.

As those persons involved in the exchange will bind their firms to the undertakings in the formula used, solicitors should carefully consider who is to be authorised to exchange contracts by telephone, fax or telex and should ensure that the use of the procedure is restricted to them. Since professional undertakings form the basis of the formulae, they are only recommended for use between firms of solicitors and licensed conveyancers.

LAW SOCIETY TELEPHONE/TELEX EXCHANGE – FORMULA A (1986)

(For use where one solicitor holds both signed parts of the contract.)

A completion date of   19   is agreed. The solicitor holding both parts of the contract confirms that he or she holds the part signed by his or her client(s), which is identical to the part he or she is also holding signed by the other solicitor's client(s) and will forthwith insert the agreed completion date in each part.

Solicitors mutually agree that exchange shall take place from that moment and the solicitor holding both parts confirms that, as of that moment, he or she holds the part signed by his or her client(s) to the order of the other. He or she undertakes that day by first-class post, or where the other solicitor is a member of a document exchange (as to which the inclusion of a reference thereto in the solicitor's letterhead shall be conclusive evidence) by delivery to that or any other affiliated exchange, or by hand delivery direct to that solicitor's office, to send his or her signed part of the contract to the other solicitor, together, where he or she is the purchaser's solicitor, with a banker's draft or a solicitor's client account cheque for the deposit amounting to £ . . . .

Note

1. A memorandum should be prepared, after use of the formula, recording:

   (a) date and time of exchange;
   (b) the formula used and exact wording of agreed variations;
   (c) the completion date;
   (d) the (balance) deposit to be paid; and
   (e) the identities of those involved in any conversation.

LAW SOCIETY TELEPHONE/TELEX EXCHANGE – FORMULA B (1986)

(For use where each solicitor holds his or her own client's signed part of the contract.)

A completion date of   19   is agreed. Each solicitor confirms to the other that he or she holds a part contract in the agreed form signed by the client(s) and will forthwith insert the agreed completion date.

Each solicitor undertakes to the other thenceforth to hold the signed part of the contract to the other's order, so that contracts are exchanged at that moment. Each solicitor further undertakes that day by first-class post, or, where the other solicitor is a member of a document exchange (as to which the inclusion of a reference thereto in the solicitor's letterhead shall be conclusive evidence) by delivery to that or any other affiliated exchange, or by hand delivery direct to that solicitor's office, to send his or her signed part of the contract to the other together, in the case of a purchaser's solicitor, with a banker's draft or a solicitor's client account cheque for the deposit amounting to £. . . . .

Notes

1. A memorandum should be prepared, after use of the formula, recording:

    (a) date and time of exchange;
    (b) the formula used and exact wording of agreed variations;
    (c) the completion date;
    (d) the (balance) deposit to be paid;
    (e) the identities of those involved in any conversation.

2. Those who are going to effect the exchange must first confirm the details in order to ensure that both parts are identical. This means in particular, that if either part of the contract has been amended since it was originally prepared, the solicitor who holds a part contract with the amendments must disclose them, so that it can be confirmed that the other part is similarly amended.

9 July 1986, revised January 1996

LAW SOCIETY TELEPHONE/FAX/TELEX EXCHANGE – FORMULA C (1989)

Part I

The following is agreed:
Final time for exchange: pm
Completion date: 19
Deposit to be paid to:

Each solicitor confirms that he or she holds a part of the contract in the agreed form signed by his or her client, or, if there is more than one client, by all of them. Each solicitor undertakes to the other that:

(a) he or she will continue to hold that part of the contract until the final time for exchange on the date the formula is used, and

(b) if the vendor's solicitor so notifies the purchaser's solicitor by fax, telephone or telex (whichever was previously agreed) by that time, they will both comply with part II of the formula.

The purchaser's solicitor further undertakes that either he or she or some other named person in his or her office will be available up to the final time for exchange to activate part II of the formula on receipt of the telephone call, fax or telex from the vendor's solicitors.

Part II

Each solicitor undertakes to the other henceforth to hold the part of the contract in his or her possession to the other's order, so that contracts are exchanged at that moment, and to despatch it to the other on that day. The purchaser's solicitor further undertakes to the vendor's solicitor to despatch on that day, or to arrange for the despatch on that day of, a banker's draft or a solicitor's client account cheque for the full deposit specified in the agreed form of contract (divided as the vendor's solicitor may have specified) to the vendor's solicitor and/or to some other solicitor whom the vendor's solicitor nominates, to be held on formula C terms.

'To despatch' means to send by first-class post, or, where the other solicitor is a member of a document exchange (as to which the inclusion of a reference thereto in the solicitor's letterhead is to be conclusive evidence) by delivery to that or any other affiliated exchange, or by hand delivery direct to the recipient solicitor's office. 'Formula C terms' means that the deposit is held as stakeholder, or as agent for the vendor with authority to part with it only for the purpose of passing it to another solicitor as deposit in a related property purchase transaction on these terms.

Notes

1. Two memoranda will be required when using Formula C. One needs to record the use of Part I, and a second needs to record the request of the vendor's solicitor to the purchaser's solicitor to activate Part II.
2. The first memorandum should record:

    (a) the date and time when it was agreed to use Formula C;
    (b) the exact wording of any agreed variations;
    (c) the final time, later that day, for exchange;
    (d) the completion date;
    (e) the name of the solicitor to whom the deposit was to be paid, or details of amounts and names if it was to be split; and
    (f) the identities of those involved in any conversation.

3. Formula C assumes the payment of a full contractual deposit (normally 10%).
4. The contract term relating to the deposit must allow it to be passed on, with payment direct from payer to ultimate recipient, in the way in which the formula contemplates. The deposit must ultimately be held by a solicitor as stakeholder. Whilst some variation in the formula can be agreed this is a term of the formula which must *not* be varied, unless all the solicitors involved in the chain have agreed.
5. If a buyer proposes to use a deposit guarantee policy, Formula C will need substantial adaptation.
6. It is essential prior to agreeing Part I of Formula C that those effecting the exchange ensure that both parts of the contract are identical.
7. Using Formula C involves a solicitor in giving a number of professional undertakings. These must be performed precisely. Any failure will be a serious breach of professional discipline. One of the undertakings may be to arrange that someone over whom the solicitor has no control will do something (ie to arrange for someone else to despatch the cheque or banker's draft in payment

of the deposit). An undertaking is still binding even if it is to do something outside the solicitor's control.

8. Solicitors do not as a matter of law have an automatic authority to exchange contracts on a Formula C basis, and should always ensure that they have the client's express authority to use Formula C. A suggested form of authority is set out below. It should be adapted to cover any special circumstances:

I/We . . . . understand that my/our sale and purchase of . . . . are both part of a chain of linked property transactions, in which all parties want the security of contracts which become binding on the same day.

I/We agree that you should make arrangements with the other solicitors or licensed conveyancers involved to achieve this.

I/We understand that this involves each property-buyer offering, early on one day, to exchange contracts whenever, later that day, the seller so requests, and that the buyer's offer is on the basis that it cannot be withdrawn or varied during that day.

I/We agree that when I/we authorise you to exchange contracts, you may agree to exchange contracts on the above basis and give any necessary undertakings to the other parties involved in the chain and that my/our authority to you cannot be revoked throughout the day on which the offer to exchange contracts is made.

15 March 1989, revised January 1996

THE LAW SOCIETY'S CODE FOR COMPLETION BY POST 1998

PREAMBLE

The Code provides a procedure for postal completion which practising solicitors may adopt by reference. It may also be used by licensed conveyancers.

Before agreeing to adopt this Code, a solicitor must be satisfied that doing so will not be contrary to the interests of the client (including any mortgagee client).

When adopted, the Code applies without variation, unless agreed in writing in advance.

PROCEDURE

General

1. To adopt this Code, all the solicitors must expressly agree, preferably in writing, to use it to complete a specific transaction.
2. On completion, the seller's solicitor acts as the buyer's solicitor's agent without any fee or disbursements.

Before completion

3. The seller's solicitor will specify in writing to the buyer's solicitor before completion the mortgages or charges secured on the property which, on or before completion, will be redeemed or discharged to the extent that they relate to the property.
4. The seller's solicitor undertakes:

   (i) to have the seller's authority to receive the purchase money on completion; and

   (ii) on completion to have the authority of the proprietor of each mortgage or charge specified under paragraph 3 to receive the sum intended to repay it,

BUT

if the seller's solicitor does not have all the necessary authorities then:

   (iii) to advise the buyer's solicitor no later than 4.00pm on the working day before the completion date that they do not have all the authorities or immediately if any is withdrawn later; and

   (iv) not to complete until he has the buyer's solicitor's instructions.

5. Before the completion date, the buyer's solicitor will send the seller's solicitor instructions as to any of the following which apply:

   (i) documents to be examined and marked;

   (ii) memoranda to be endorsed;

   (iii) undertakings to be given;

   (iv) deeds, documents (including any relevant undertakings) and authorities relating to rents, deposits, keys, etc. to be sent to the buyer's solicitors following completion; and

   (v) other relevant matters.

In default of instructions, the seller's solicitor is under no duty to examine, mark or endorse any document.

6. The buyer's solicitor will remit to the seller's solicitor the sum required to complete, as notified in writing on the seller's solicitor's completion statement or otherwise, or in default of notification as shown by the contract. If the funds are remitted by transfer between banks, the seller's solicitor will instruct the receiving bank to telephone to report immediately the funds have been received. Pending completion, the seller's solicitor will hold the funds to the buyer's solicitor's order.

7. If by the agreed date and time for completion the seller's solicitor has not received the authorities specified in paragraph 4, instructions under paragraph 5 and the sum specified in paragraph 6, the seller's solicitor will forthwith notify the buyer's solicitor and request further instructions.

Completion

8. The seller's solicitor will complete forthwith on receiving the sum specified in paragraph 6, or at a later time agreed with the buyer's solicitor.

9. When completing, the seller's solicitor undertakes:

    (i) to comply with the instructions given under paragraph 5; and

    (ii) to redeem or obtain discharges for every mortgage or charge so far as it relates to the property specified under paragraph 3 which has not already been redeemed or discharged.

After completion

10. The seller's solicitor undertakes:

    (i) immediately completion has taken place to hold to the buyer's solicitor's order every item referred to in (iv) of paragraph 5 and not to exercise a lien over any such item;

    (ii) as soon as possible after completion, and in any event on the same day:
       (a) to confirm to the buyer's solicitor by telephone or fax that completion has taken place; and
       (b) to send written confirmation and, at the risk of the buyer's solicitor, the items listed in (iv) of paragraph 5 to the buyer's solicitor by first class post or document exchange.

Supplementary

11. The rights and obligations of the parties, under the contract or otherwise, are not affected by this Code.

12. (i) References to the seller's solicitor and the buyer's solicitor apply as appropriate to solicitors acting for other parties who adopt the Code.
    (ii) When a licensed conveyancer adopts this Code, references to a solicitor include a licensed conveyancer.

13. A dispute or difference arising between solicitors who adopt this Code (whether or not subject to any variation) relating directly to its application is to be referred to a single arbitrator agreed between the solicitors. If they do not agree on the appointment within one month, the President of The Law Society may appoint the arbitrator at the request of one of the solicitors.

Notes to the Code:

1. This Code will apply to transactions when the Code is adopted after 1 July 1998.

2. The object of this Code is to provide solicitors with a convenient means for completion on an agency basis when a representative of the buyer's solicitor is not attending at the office of the seller's solicitor.

3. As with The Law Society's formulae for exchange of contracts by telephone and fax, the guide embodies professional undertakings and is only recommended for adoption between solicitors and licensed conveyancers.

4. Paragraph 2 of the Code provides that the seller's solicitors will act as agents for the buyer's solicitors without fee or disbursements. The convenience of not having to make a specific appointment on the day of completion for the buyer's solicitor to attend to complete will offset the agency work that the seller's solicitor has to do and any postage payable in completing under the Code. Most solicitors will from time to time act for both sellers and buyers. If a seller's solicitor does consider that charges and/or disbursements are necessary in a particular case this would represent a variation in the Code and should be agreed in writing before the completion date.

5. In view of the decision in *Edward Wong Finance Company Limited v Johnson, Stokes & Master* [1984] AC 1296, clause 4(ii) of the Code requires the seller's solicitor to undertake on completion to have authority of the proprietor of every mortgage or charge to be redeemed to receive the sum needed to repay such charge.

6. Paragraph 11 of the Code provides that nothing in the Code shall override any rights and obligations of the parties under contract or otherwise.

7. The buyer's solicitor is to inform the seller's solicitor of the mortgages or charges which will be redeemed or discharged (see paragraph 3 above) and is to specify those for which an undertaking will be required on completion (paragraph 5(iii)). The information may be given in reply to requisitions on title. Such a reply may also amount to an undertaking.

8. Care must be taken if there is a sale and sub-sale. The sub-seller's solicitor may not hold the title deeds nor be in a position to receive the funds required to discharge the seller's mortgage on the property. Enquiries should be made to ascertain if the monies or some part of the monies payable on completion should, with either the authority of the sub-seller or the sub-seller's solicitor, be sent direct to the seller's solicitor and not to the sub-seller's solicitor.

9. Care must also be taken if there is a simultaneous resale and completion and enquiries should be made by the ultimate buyer's solicitor of the intermediate seller's solicitor as to the price being paid on that purchase. Having appointed the intermediate seller's solicitor as agent, the buyer's solicitor is fixed with the knowledge of an agent even without having personal knowledge (see Green Card Warning on Property Fraud).

10. If the seller's solicitor has to withdraw from using the Code, the buyer's solicitor should be notified of this not later than 4.00pm on the working day prior to the completion date. If the seller's solicitor's authority to receive the monies is withdrawn later, the buyer's solicitor must be notified immediately.

These notes refer only to some of the points in the Code that practitioners may wish to consider before agreeing to adopt it. Any variation in the Code must be agreed in writing before the completion date.

FORM OF UNDERTAKING TO DISCHARGE BUILDING SOCIETY MORTGAGES APPROVED BY THE LAW SOCIETY IN CONVEYANCING MATTERS

In consideration of you today completing the purchase of . . . .
WE HEREBY UNDERTAKE forthwith to pay over to the . . . .
Building Society the money required to redeem the mortgage/legal charge dated
. . . . and to forward the receipted mortgage/legal charge to you as
soon as it is received by us from the . . . . Building
Society.

FORMS OF UNDERTAKING AGREED WITH BANKS

FORM NO 1

Undertaking by solicitor – Deeds/Land Certificate loaned to the Solicitor for purpose of inspection only and return.

.... 19 ...

To   BANK LIMITED

I/We hereby acknowledge to have received on loan from you the Title Deeds and/or Land Certificate and documents relating to ....
.... in accordance with the schedule hereto.

I/We undertake to hold them on your behalf and to return them to you on demand in the same condition in which they now are and without the property to which they relate or any interest therein being, to our knowledge, in any way charged, conveyed, assigned, leased, encumbered, disposed of or dealt with.

Signature ....

SCHEDULE

FORM NO 2

Undertaking by Solicitor – Deed/Land Certificate handed to the Solicitor re Sale or Mortgage of property, or part of it, in consideration of promise to account to Bank for net proceeds.

. . . . 19 . . .

To   BANK LIMITED

I/We hereby acknowledge to have received from you the Title Deeds and/or Land Certificate and documents *together with a charge to the Bank relating to . . . .
. . . . in accordance with the schedule hereto for the purpose of the sale/mortgage of this property.

I/We undertake to hold them on your behalf and to return them to you on demand in the same condition in which they now are, pending completion of such transaction. If the transaction is completed I/we undertake

a) to pay to you the amount of the purchase/mortgage money, not being less than £ . . . . gross subject only to the deduction therefrom of the deposit (if held by the estate agent(s)), the estate agent's commission and the legal costs and disbursements relating to the transaction, and

b) if the Title Deeds and/or Land Certificate and documents also relate to other property in addition to that referred to above, to return same to you suitably endorsed or noted.

Signature . . . .

Note: If there are likely to be any deductions from the purchase price other than those shown above, these must be specifically mentioned.

SCHEDULE

* Delete if no charge form has been taken.

FORM NO 3

Undertaking by Solicitor – to send Deeds/Land Certificate to Bank on completion of a purchase, the Bank and/or its customer having provided the purchase monies.

. . . . 19 . . .

To   **BANK LIMITED**

If you provide facilities to my/our client . . . . for the purchase of the Freehold/Leasehold property [Description of Property]

I/We undertake

a)   that any sums received from you or your customer for the purpose of this transaction will be applied solely for acquiring a good marketable title to such property and in paying any necessary deposit legal costs and disbursements in connection with such purchase. The purchase price contemplated is £ . . . . gross and with apportionments and any necessary disbursements is not expected to exceed £ . . . .

and

b)   after the property has been acquired by . . . . and all necessary stamping and registration has been completed to send the Title Deeds and/or Land Certificate and documents to you and in the meantime to hold them to your order.

Signature . . . .

FORM NO 4   (BRIDGING FINANCE)

Undertaking by solicitors (with form of authority from client) to account to the bank for net proceeds of sale of the existing property, the bank having provided funds in connection with the purchase of the new property.

Authority from client(s)

.... 19 ...

To ....

....

(name and address of solicitors)

I/We hereby irrevocably authorise and request you to give an undertaking in the form set out below and accordingly to pay the net proceeds of sale after deduction of your costs to .... Bank Limited
.... Branch.

Signature of client(s) ....

Undertaking ....   19 ...

To .... BANK LIMITED

If you provide facilities to our client ....
....
for the purchase of the Freehold/Leasehold property (the new property) ....
....
(description of property)

pending the sale by our client of the Freehold/Leasehold property (the existing property ....
(description of property)

We undertake

1. That any sums received from you or your customer will be applied solely for the following purposes:

   *a) in discharging the present mortgage(s) on the existing property
   b) in acquiring a good marketable title to the new property *subject to the mortgage mentioned below
   c) in paying any necessary deposit legal fees costs and disbursements in connection with the purchase.

   The purchase price contemplated is £ .... gross.
   *We are informed that a sum of £ .... is being advanced on mortgage by
   .... The amount required from our client for the

transaction including the deposit and together with costs disbursements and apportionments is not expected to exceed £ . . . .

2. To hold to your order when received by us the documents of title of the existing property pending completion of the sale (unless subject to any prior mortgage(s)) and of the new property (unless subject to any prior mortgage(s)).

3. To pay to you the net proceeds of sale of the existing property when received by us. The sale price contemplated is £ . . . . and the only deductions which will have to be made at present known to us are:

   (i) the deposit (if not held by us)
   (ii) the estate agent's commission
   (iii) the amount required to redeem any mortgage and charges which so far as known to us at present do not exceed £ . . . .
   (iv) the legal fees costs and disbursements relating to the transaction.

4. To advise you immediately of any subsequent claim by a third party upon the net proceeds of sale of which we have knowledge.

Note

(1) If any deductions will have to be made from the net proceeds of sale other than those shown above, these must be specifically mentioned.

(2) It would be convenient if this form of undertaking were presented in duplicate so that a carbon copy could be retained by the solicitor.

*Delete if not applicable.

INDEX